THE AUSTRALIAN LANGUAGE

THE
AUSTRALIAN
LANGUAGE

*An examination of the English language
and English speech as used in Australia, from convict days
to the present, with special reference to the growth of
indigenous idiom and its use by Australian writers*

BY

SIDNEY J. BAKER

CURRAWONG PUBLISHING CO.
SYDNEY

TRI-OCEAN BOOKS
SAN FRANCISCO

This Second Edition first published 1966 by

CURRAWONG PUBLISHING CO. PTY. LTD.

129 Pitt Street, Sydney, N.S.W.

(First Edition 1945 Angus & Robertson Ltd.)

DISTRIBUTED IN THE UNITED KINGDOM
BY ANGUS & ROBERTSON LTD.,
54/58 BARTHOLOMEW CLOSE, LONDON, E.C.1

DISTRIBUTED IN THE UNITED STATES OF AMERICA BY
TRI-OCEAN BOOKS, SAN FRANCISCO

Copyright 1966
SIDNEY J. BAKER

LIBRARY OF CONGRESS CATALOGUE CARD NO. 66-23817

Set in Monotype Baskerville
by Craftsmen Type-Setters Pty. Ltd., Sydney.
Printed and bound by Halstead Press,
Kingsgrove, N.S.W.

THIS BOOK
IS DEDICATED TO
ALL THE AUSTRALIANS
WHO HAVE HELPED
TO MAKE IT
A BOOK

Here, surely, is new wealth, expressive of a distinctive and vigorous life, material for an individual literature.

—W. K. Hancock, "Australia", 1930.

Preface

The main aim of this preface is to express my deep gratitude.

Since the time when, as a young man too innocent to realise that I was knotting a noose round my neck, I began to accumulate Australian slang it has been my greatest good fortune to enlist the aid of hundreds of Australians. Their nagging, advice, demands, contributions and criticisms have often been hard to keep pace with, but I wish to make it clear that this job could never have been done without their help. If my correspondence has been enormous, I would doubt whether anyone in the history of Australia has felt a greater sense of purpose in the daily tide of letters that has come his way.

More than anything else, this book is a single voice compounded of all the voices that have spoken to me. I do not intend to name these people, not only because many of them have died since my work on Australian English began, but also because some significant sections of the book come from contributors who fear for their well-being if their names should ever be known. In due course, you will see why. To them and to all the others, I give my deepest thanks.

My gratitude goes also to the Commonwealth Literary Fund for favouring me with yet another grant to make the writing of this book possible.

Errors and omissions inevitably occur in a book of this size. Anyone, anywhere, who can help to track these down will be assured of my thanks. My address is below.

SIDNEY J. BAKER

6 Woods Ave.,
Woollahra, N.S.W.

Contents

THE AUSTRALIAN LANGUAGE

CHAPTER I

The New Language

1. WHAT IS AUSTRALIAN ENGLISH?

THIS IS A BOOK without beginning or end. If it had a beginning it would go back to foggy yesterdays in world history that have never been explored. If it had an end it would pitchfork us down the slippery-dip of time into a world we will never know.

When I wrote those words as the opening paragraph in the first edition of "The Australian Language" in 1945, I certainly never expected (nor had any special wish) to repeat them twenty-odd years later. But since a monograph, however trifling, must begin somewhere even if its subject does not, this is a better place than many to start off.

How does one define Australian English? In the long ago, when I had greater awe of the linguistic novelties of the United States of America and of Britain than I do today, I thought of it mainly in terms of slang – of words and phrases in popular use which were outside "standard" or "approved" English. My measure of what was "standard" or "approved" was mainly the "Oxford Dictionary" in its various forms. But since the passing of time was to make it clear to me that some official edicts on language do not have much more respectability than can be achieved by a retired whore it became obvious that this was not enough. Australian English certainly included a great deal of slang, but this was not all.

In the first place, as I tilled my melancholic furrow in the Fourth Estate, I became aware that the Australian Press continually used words and phrases about which neither the "Oxford" nor any other authority could give me precise guidance.

Terms like *Federation* and *Aboriginal* (not applying to indigenous people generally, but to the *Australian Aboriginal* specifically), and *lay-by* and *home unit*, and the difference between a *prime minister* and a *premier*, and what was a *pastoralist*, and how *finalization* developed, and what's special about a *face-cloth*, and why our use of *primage* deviated from the English use. I shall return to these matters in due course.

Second, although I could conceive that such Australian words as *kelpie*, *shark meshing*, *surf reel*, *billabong*, *Granny Smith apple* and *woolshed* were possibly a little more popular than those given above, I failed to see how they could be classed as slang.

Third, although *dreaming* (its use in relation to the Aborigines), *anting* (its ornithological use), *stump jump plough* (a particular type of plough used in land-clearing), *V.J.* (a small sailing boat) and *monkey muscle* (any small muscle in the human body, especially in the leg or back), were mainly

I

current in specialist groups, they were hardly to be branded as slang either.

Fourth, if terms like *bush, outback, never never, gibber plains, station* and *channel country* had been slang once, they had survived long enough in the Australian community to be accepted as orthodox today.

Quite apart from all this, the Australian had developed a distinctive way of speaking, and this was certainly not an aspect of slang. (See Chapter XXII.)

So there were many reasons why my original idea of equating Australian slang with Australian English had to undergo a drastic revision.

Perhaps the real trouble was that I had paid too enthusiastic attention to J. Stoddart's views in "Glossology" (1858) :

> In order to comprehend any language thoroughly, both in itself and in its relation to other tongues . . . we must carefully examine . . . even the expressions of the vulgar, among which may often be found words and phrases connecting the particular language under discussion with others, by affinities, which, but for such research, might have remained unknown.

But slang was a good starting point. It provided an apprenticeship in distinguishing three things, (a) slang words which Australia had imported from Britain without alteration, like *all Sir Garnet, keep it dark, rattletrap* and *Jesus wept!* (b) slang and dialectal words which Australia had imported from Britain and had given new meanings to, like *cobber, barrack, dinkum* and *smoodge* (c) slang words which Australia had invented, like *Buckley's chance, googly, pozzie* and *whacko!* I could see little reason for including (a) as part of Australian English; I have excluded most such items from consideration here for, quite apart from the fact that these expressions had no indigenous flavour to them, there was a special reason why the large bulk of them should be eliminated.

This was because in 1812 a man named James Hardy Vaux put together a little dictionary which is regarded as one of the important references to English slang of the times. Vaux had an odd status. In 1812, he was a convict in Australia and his work was done during what he described in his "Memoirs" (1819) as his "solitary hours of cessation from hard labour" at Newcastle, New South Wales. There was little in his "Vocabulary of the Flash Language" that was more than remotely Australian, but it gave an extremely good picture of the type of slang our Pilgrim Fathers had imported. However, considerably before this, in fact from the time that white settlement began in Australia, the unique conditions of life here and the special demands which the Australian environment imposed on the newcomers had made the use of new terms imperative.

As Noah Webster was to write a little later in the introduction to his "American Dictionary of the English Language" (1828):

> Language is the expression of ideas, and if the people of one country cannot preserve an identity of ideas [with the people of another country], they cannot retain an identity of language. Now, an identity of ideas depends materially upon the sameness of things or objects with which the people of the two countries are conversant. But in no two portions of the

earth, remote from each other, can such an identity be found. Even physical objects must be different.

A more succinct summary is given by R. C. Trench, in "English Past and Present" (1855): "New words are coined out of the necessity which men feel of filling up gaps in the language."

There was so much difference between the "things or objects" of Britain and those which our oecists found in Australia that familiar words either had to be given new applications or entirely new words had to be used. One source of new words was the Aborigines. Hence such borrowings (no one will ever know now the extent to which poor observation modified their meanings or crude orthography their original sounds) as *kangaroo*, *kookaburra*, *cooee*, *gin*, *lubra*, *budgeree*, *boomerang*, *bunyip*, *gunyah* and *humpy*. Hence also a large number of words which were either new to the English language or had special Australian senses: *bush*, *bushranger*, *stockyard*, *stockman*, *hut-keeper*, *Hawkesbury duck* and *bullock dray*. Through the direct influence of the convicts (see Chapter II) such slang terms as *scrubbing brushes*, *tester*, *bull*, *logs* and *Botany Bay dozen* came into use and a large number of expressions which were "standard" Australianisms almost from the outset: *ticket-of-leave*, *assignment system*, *emancipist*, *currency*, *sterling*, etc.

By 1826, Peter Cunningham could write in "Two Years in New South Wales":

A number of slang phrases current in St. Giles's Greek bid fair to become legitimised in the dictionary of this colony . . . the dross passing here as genuine, even among all ranks.

And in 1829 Edward Gibbon Wakefield wrote in "A Letter from Sydney":

Bearing in mind that our lowest class [i.e. the convicts] brought with it a peculiar language [to Australia] and is constantly supplied with fresh corruption, you will understand why pure English is not, and is not likely to become, the language of the colony.

The fact that Wakefield was, at the time of writing, in Newgate prison for abduction and had never seen Australia does not rob the statement of its pertinency, for Wakefield had closely studied writings on the country and was merely repeating what had been said, perhaps more garrulously, by others. He adds:

Terms of slang and flash are used, as a matter of course, everywhere, from the gaols to the Viceroy's palace, not excepting the Bar and the Bench. No doubt they will be reckoned quite parliamentary, as soon as we obtain a parliament.

Little wonder then that by 1840 A. Russell could declare in "A Tour through the Australian Colonies" that "slang terms [were] in use for everyday occurrences in sermons in Presbyterian and Episcopal churches."

But Australian English was more than this. Remembering Webster's words, we are aware that language thrives best against its native background. Transplant it and you begin to remould the language.

There were some features of Australian life concerning which scientific observers of the time saw fancied resemblances in non-English sources and burdened us with strange words. There are simple Australian examples in *opossum* and *iguana*. *Opossum* comes from North American Indians (from about 1610, says H. L. Mencken) and in the U.S. is applied to the marsupial family Didelphyidae. In Australia we have applied it to an entirely different group of marsupials, the Phalangeridae. The term *iguana* was applied in the West Indies and South America to a large arboreal lizard. In Australia we have applied it to our Varanidae or monitor lizards, which are a different group altogether. Over the years we have been able to exert correctives by changing the words to *possum* and *goanna*.[1]

There is also a question of dates. Now, it is a basic assumption of lexicography that whatever country can produce the earliest printed record of a word can claim to have originated it. In consequence, although the general public has heard little about the matter, some arduous three-cornered tussling has gone on between Australia, England and the United States of America. Since I deal with the matter in some detail in Chapter XX, I will confine myself here to a few simple examples. *Down Under* is an often-used expression to describe Australia and/or New Zealand. Which country recorded its first use – England or Australia? The answer is Australia in 1900; it was not recorded in England until eight years later. The U.S. has claimed to have originated *Chink*, for a Chinaman, in 1901. Is that correct? No, it was used in Australia at least twenty-two years earlier in 1879. The U.S. used the word *bush* to denote forest-covered land in 1827. The same word was in Australian use in 1803.

A little earlier I listed a few words with special Australian uses – *premier* among them. In the English of England no distinction is made between *premier* and *prime minister*, although the latter is more common. They both denote a country's political leader and principal minister. But we are aware that from the time of Federation at the beginning of the century, Australia not only had a national government, but a government for each of the six States. So the principal minister of the national government was given the title of *prime minister*, which is its orthodox use, while the principal minister of a State was called a *premier*, which is not orthodox. Recent editions of oversea dictionaries have allowed the verb *finalize*, meaning to complete, to creep into their pages, and in due course I suppose we can expect to find *finalization*, an act of completion, there also. But there is a good deal of evidence to suggest that *finalize*, like *removalist* (a person or firm engaged in moving furniture, etc.), *lay-by*, *home unit* and *pastoralist*, which are all dealt with later, is an Australian original or a word to which we have given new meaning.

---

[1] Some interesting points were raised by J. R. Bernard in an article "The Need for a Dictionary of Australian English" in "Southerly", Sydney, No. 2, 1962. He wrote: ". . . I compared the descriptions of some common fish in the 'Shorter Oxford' with those they have in 'Fish and Fisheries of Australia' by T. C. Roughley (Angus & Robertson, 1951). Apparently the Australian *bass, catfish, cod, garfish, mackerel, mullet, perch, sole, tailor* and *whiting* do not even belong to the genus described in the 'Oxford'. *Sprat* and *anchovy* do but are different species, while local *whitebait* is not the same as English whitebait and our *tuna* is not the kind referred to in the dictionary."

Of course, there is always the danger of pushing these distinctions to a degree where they almost disappear. Take the apparently simple case of *face-cloth*, which many Australians use to denote a small square of fairly absorbent cloth used in personal ablutions. Now, it is not that this expression has failed to earn recognition by the "Oxford". Far from it. But the "Oxford's" definition of *face-cloth* is "a cloth laid over the face of a corpse". In English company it would perhaps be better to use *washer*, which is indubitably Australian, but we often employ this term to denote a cloth or mop or some other instrument for washing dishes as well as an equivalent for *face-cloth*. Then, take the case of *primage*. According to the "Oxford", the word *primage* means "a customary allowance formerly made by the shipper to the master and crew of a vessel for the loading and care of the cargo; now, a percentage addition to the freight, paid to the owners or freighters of the vessel." Australia has also given a special use to this word. In 1893, the Victorian Parliament imposed a 1 per cent *primage duty* on what is known to Customs law as the *prime*, which is the first entry of goods In 1930, the Commonwealth Parliament inflicted a $2\frac{1}{2}$ per cent ad valorem duty on all imported goods, whether dutiable or not dutiable. This was also called *primage duty*, or, more tersely, *primage*.

⸫ One has to take only a small step further to get into a lexicographical ‑ swamp. When Professor E. E. Morris was compiling his extremely valuable "Austral English Dictionary" (1898), he took the step and look where it got him. Here are some of his entries:

> *Christmas*, n. and adj. As Christmas falls in Australia at Midsummer, it has different characteristics from those in England and the word has therefore a different connotation.
> *December*, n. A summer month in Australia. See Christmas.
> *July*, n. A winter month in Australia. See Christmas.
> *Midwinter*, n. The seasons being reversed in Australia, Christmas occurs in the middle of summer. The English word *Midsummer* has thus dropped out of use, and "Christmas" or "Christmastide" is its Australian substitute, whilst *Midwinter* is the word used to denote the Australian winter-time of late June and early July. See Christmas.

If these entries were justified, then Morris should have included other terms such as Christmas Eve, New Year's Eve, January, February, March and all the rest, because our seasons are different from those of England. And he might have been justified in including a note about north and south, because an Englishman looks to the south-east to see the sun rise and we look to the north-east. More to the point, he could have said something about the east, if only to diminish the long-standing mental blindness in which we indulge by trying to use terms *Far East*, *Near East* and *Middle East* as the English use them. When an Australian speaks of the Far East he is speaking in terms of an idea divorced from the sense of the words themselves, for the English Far East is our *Due North*. In the same way England's Near East is our *Far West*, her Middle East our *Middle West*. Quite apart from any other reason, domestic geography makes *Far West* difficult for us to use with clarity – it may denote Western Australia; it may also (especially in N.S.W. where we have a Far West Children's Health Scheme) denote no more than the far western parts of New South Wales, so this conspiracy is particularly confusing.

What emerges from all this is that, however you look at it, Australian English consists of a great deal more than slang, although we are going to encounter more than enough slang before we come to the end of this book. And on the way we are going to find that, quite unpredictably, a lot of slang changes its nature and, at least within our linguistic community, becomes orthodox. The imported word *squatter* is a good example of this. Chapter III shows how unsavoury were its Australian beginnings, how it became respectable, and then how it was largely pushed out of use by another word altogether.

Since it has become clear that an expression such as "the Australian language" can be interpreted in many ways, it becomes necessary to define the scope of our inquiry. Strictly speaking, the Australian language should be interpreted as including every word or phrase that has originated in Australia, every new meaning Australia has given to expressions originally used in England or other parts of the world, and the origins and characteristics of our accent. Yet even as we reach this conclusion, we can sense a trap of our own devising. Morris's "Austral English Dictionary" fell into it with a soggy thud. Among the many expressions that have originated in Australia are thousands of common names given to our flora and fauna. I deal with many of these in Chapter XIV, but except where there are special reasons have made no effort to provide the comprehensive cover that should (and no doubt will in due course) be given by a botanical and zoological dictionary.

In any case, the Australian language we want to examine is something closer to the blood-beat of everyday life than such a dictionary can achieve. It is something that will help us see the Australian in the round, as a person living and talking in his own way and not much more concerned with English traditions, customs and clichés than the average American. We want to hear him talk as we will hear him in Subiaco and Footscray and Surry Hills and Oodnadatta and from the back benches of Federal Parliament; as he has spoken since our earliest days at work and at play; as he has spoken in the outback, in mining towns, in jails and at war.

For the purposes of this book, therefore, we will forget about most of our flora and fauna and we will avoid hair-splitting of the Morris type. We will try to make a simple examination of Australian history in terms of the dialect we have developed as incidental to our cultural growth. These things become necessary because out of them springs the picture we seek.

"Language most shows a man: speak that I may see thee!" quoth Ben Jonson. "It springs out of the most retired and inmost parts of us, and is the image of the parent of it, the mind. No glass renders a man's form and likeness so true as his speech."

2. GOOD ENGLISH AND ALL THAT

IN THE Second Part of King Henry IV (act ii, scene iv) one of Shakespeare's characters exclaims: "A captain! God's light, these villains will make the word as odious as the word occupy, which was an excellent good word before it was ill-sorted." On only one other occasion in all his writings did Shakespeare use the word *occupy*. The reason was that, about the end of the sixteenth century, *occupy* had come to be regarded as one of the most unseemly words in the language. It had acquired the meaning "to cohabit, to have sexual intercourse with" and as a result a ban had settled on it which was not to be lifted for nearly two centuries. The "Oxford Dictionary" tells us that, against a total of 194 quotations of the word found in sixteenth century writings, only eighteen were recorded in the next two centuries. Not until the beginning of the nineteenth century did the word drift back into approved use again.

How did *occupy* survive its long twilight? By being absorbed into slang.

Words like *jabber* and *hoax* were slang in Swift's time; so were *mob* and *sham*. Even as late as 1860 *to send a man to Coventry* was classed as slang by J. C. Hotten. In "The Pains of Opium" Thomas de Quincey refers to "the slang use of the word *accomplishment* as a superficial and ornamental attainment." And in his "Glossology", Stoddart protests against "such barbarous terms as *snobbishness* and *flunkeyism*".

Language is never static; it is being continually moulded and modified. Fan the pages of Murray's "New English Dictionary"[2] and pause at the simple word "in". There are more than nineteen columns of closely packed type on that one word alone. If one fragment of the English language requires so much to be written about it in order that its every shade of meaning and use may be understood, we should not be amazed to learn that 50,000,000 words are within the covers of Murray's gigantic work, and that all these are necessary to explain the uses and applications of the 400,000-odd words defined.

Work finished in 1943 on a "Dictionary of American English on Historical Principles", edited by Sir William A. Craigie, who was co-editor of the "New English Dictionary", and Dr James R. Hulbert, Professor of English at the University of Chicago. Millions more words were harnessed to the job of defining new U.S. terms and new meanings that America has given to English terms. And now a "Dictionary of Australian English" (or some such title) is in process of compilation by the Australian Language Research Centre at Sydney University.[3]

---

[2] Now generally known as the "Oxford Dictionary" and so referred to in this book.

[3] "Dictionaries beget dictionaries as nations beget or extend languages, and while English has flourished longer in America than anywhere else, there are other lands awaiting the same historical lexicography [as the new "Dictionary of American English"]. It will soon be the turn of Australia and New Zealand, and of South Africa." – "Times Literary Supplement", April 26, 1941.

Long before Murray's "Dictionary" was completed research workers were compiling a supplement to it. It will be the same with the "American English Dictionary" and with the "Australian English Dictionary". To the making of new words there is no end.

It is somewhere just a little below the borderline of current respectability that slang appears. For instance, in 1899 when Sydney "Truth" and its tub-thumping chief John Norton were putting *wowser* into circulation in Australia, you might have heard it used in Redfern and Woolloomooloo, but it would not have been current in Elizabeth Bay or Darling Point, because respectable people did not read "Truth" in those days (or were supposed not to) and they could not be expected to know what went on in the columns of that now defunct journal. But a couple of generations have changed *wowser* from low journalistic slang to a well-established Australianism.

The Sydney "Telegraph" in a leading article on July 31, 1937, said:

> If Australia had given nothing more to civilization than that magnificent label for one of its most melancholy products – the word *wowser* – it would not have been discovered in vain.

Or we could take an older example, *larrikin*, which came into currency in Melbourne a little before 1870. There are good reasons to suspect that *wowser* has English dialectal antecedents,[4] but of *larrikin* we can say that the case is watertight.[5] Australia lifted this word out of obscure English dialect into popular use, and from popular use in this country it was passed back to the country of its origin without the English being aware of what had taken place. Thus the "Encyclopaedia Britannica" in its 1911 edition:

> Australia . . . as may be seen from the novels of Rolf Boldrewood and other writers, possesses an ample store of slang peculiar to itself, but of this *larrikin* is the only word that had found its way into general use in the mother country.

Murray's "Oxford Dictionary" throws no more light on its history than to remark that the term is "Of uncertain origin; possibly from *Larry* (a nickname for Lawrence, common in Ireland) + *kin.*"

The problem was thrashed out, however, early this century and the history of the word has been told many times since. Here is a version of the case as published in "The Lone Hand" in 1908:[6]

---

[4] For instance, *wusser*, "a bad person, a ne'er-do-well", *wissere*, "a teacher", *whizz*, "fussy, troublesome person", *waw*, "to whine, grumble or complain".

[5] Due largely to E. E. Morris, who gave the story number one position in his theories concerning the origin of *larrikin*, the Australian has held to the apocryphal legend that an Irish policeman's broad pronounciation of *larking* gave us the term as we know it today. Skeat's warning that "as a rule, derivations which require a story to be told turn out to be false", was repeated by Morris, but footnotes to satisfying stories are rarely read and the legend still thrives. However, see what I have to say in Chapter VI.

[6] December 2, 1908, p. 115. The story was also told by A. G. Stephens and S. O'Brien in their "Material for a Dictionary of Australian Slang", 1900-10 (MS. in Mitchell Library, Sydney) and by E. J. Forbes in an article entitled "On the Larrikin's Trail", published in the Sydney "Telegraph" of June 18, 1908. A sound hint on the origin of the term was also given in the supplement in "Webster's International Dictionary" of 1908, wherein the origin was suggested as being related to the provincial English *larrick*, lively, careless, and *larack*, to frolic or romp.

Of all Australian words perhaps none has been the subject of so much discussion as *larrikin*. The most generally accepted explanation of its origin is the Irish policeman's pronounciation of *"larking"*, and doubtless, this indicates the true affinities of the word. But whatever its ultimate origin, *larrikin* has come to us, not from the tongue of the Irishman, but from the Englishman of the provinces. The Yorkshireman uses *larrack* for careless, and says of a giddy, frolic-loving person that he "goas *larracking* about". These words come close enough; but in Dr Jago's "Glossary of the Cornish Dialect" (1882), we find the very term itself: *"Larrikins:* Mischievous young fellows, larkers", together with a quotation from a Penzance newspaper, which speaks of "mischievious *larrikins* who pull the young trees down". After this it is rather amusing to read the declaration of Messrs Barrère and Leland [in "A Dictionary of Slang, Jargon and Cant", 1897] that "larrikin", as used in colloquial English, is "imported from Australia".

Here, then, is the crux of the problem. If *wowser* and *larrikin* came to us from English dialects and there are many other words we acquired in the same way:[7] *cobber, dinkum, fossick, barrack* and *swagman* to name but a few – what right have we to regard them as Australianisms? And, quite apart from that question, can we class them as slang since they obviously have dialectal histories?

In so far as they touch Australia these questions represent what is, in fact, a single problem.

Dialect is essentially a localized form of language, with local peculiarities of vocabulary and diction. It is the possession of a few, but it is none the less part of the vast body of language, and as such is subject to modifications no less than that part of English we are pleased to regard as "standard". If, therefore, we take a term out of this localized dialect and toss it into what Mencken described as "the gaping maw of the proletariat", we place it in possession of a vast concourse of people who will have small, if any, knowledge of its original application. Its meaning and uses inevitably tend to change, and since the broadening process consequent upon its absorption into popular speech will produce new non-standardized connotations, that word will, for the time being at least, be classed as unorthodox and its absorption into literary and social language will be resisted. If its usefulness grows – if, for instance, it describes something more pungently than any other term we have at our disposal – it will graduate swiftly from unorthodox speech to approved speech. It will no longer be presented in print with the taint of quotation marks upon it.

Wowser, larrikin, cobber, dinkum, to barrack – these are in the "Oxford Dictionary" and classed as Australian along with many scores of terms that are either indigenous or have found a new lease of life through Australia.

"Nearly all slang," observes Eric Partridge,[8] "consists of old words changed in form or, far more often, old words with new meanings or new shades of meaning." This should give us an answer to our question about

---

7 See Chapter XX.

8 "Slang Today and Yesterday" (1935). Partridge was born in New Zealand and lived in Australia for many years. His best-known work is "A Dictionary of Slang and Unconventional English", originally published in 1937 and later extended to two volumes.

dialectal importations. We can be justified in accepting as an Australianism any term original to this country or any term out of the English or American languages to which we have given a fresh shade of meaning. Whether we regard such terms as slang, however, depends on our opinion as to their orthodoxy or unorthodoxy.

If we require as an imprimatur of approval the admission of a term to the "Oxford Dictionary", we will face some knotty problems.

For example, the Oxford "Supplement" gives *chink*, a Chinaman, as "originally U.S. slang" and the first textual quotation offered is dated 1901. But as I pointed out in the previous Section, *chink* was used in Australia many years before America got hold of it.[9] We may not like the sound of *chink*, but if the Oxford authorities pass it, does that make everything all right? If they also list *chow* for a Chinaman and the first use was also in Australia[10] is that all right, too? And *John Chinaman*, if that is on Oxford record and also has an earlier Australian reference than any found elsewhere[11] are we to accept it as orthodox speech? And if they include such Australianisms as *forty*, a sharper, *duck-shoving*, unfair methods of business adopted by cabmen, and *bonzer*, good, excellent, are we to feel complacent about these terms and to dismiss with contempt *nineteener*, *touching off* and *bosker* (which have the same respective uses as the three previous words), because they are not in the "Oxford Dictionary"?

It is clear that the Oxford yardstick is not entirely satisfactory, magnificent though that work is. The question is not that words like *nineteener*, *touching off* and *bosker* have never been in print in Australia, whereas the other three have. *Nineteener* was recorded by Cornelius Crowe in his "Australian Slang Dictionary" of 1895, *touching off* by a writer in 1898, *bosker* in the "Bulletin" in 1906.

We are right in saying that *nineteener* and *touching off* are rare terms (indeed, we have now forgotten them completely), but so are *forty* and *duck-shoving;* and we would be right in saying that *bonzer* has been used more frequently than *bosker* in the past generation, but this was not always the case. At the beginning of this century *bosker* and its variant *boshter* were a good deal more popular.

It becomes clear that we need some better starting point than Murray's "Dictionary". We have to work out the problem from the viewpoint of Australia, not from the viewpoint of England and of the judgments she passed upon our language because she did not know it as well as we do. The Oxford authorities are not altogether to blame for their cross-eyed view of our language. They looked through the spectacles of Morris,[12] who

---

[9] By W. J. Barry in "Up and Down" (1879), p. 51.

[10] The "Supplement's" first textual reference for *chow* is from C. J. Dennis's "Ginger Mick" (1916). It was used nearly thirty years earlier in Australia: cf. "Bulletin", April 14, 1888, p. 8, col. 2. The form *chow-chow* was used similarly by E. Howe, "Boy in the Bush" (1869), p. 215.

[11] "Sydney Revels of Bacchus, Cupid and Momus", by C. A. Corbyn (1854), p. 125. He also uses the form *John*. The first Oxford texts for these expressions are 1872 and 1873 respectively.

[12] Here in part is what the "Bulletin" had to say (December 18, 1897) about Morris's "Austral English": "The Dictionary is misleading. Even an Australian is liable to be put wrong: a

saw only a fragment of the picture, and of a few who no more than scratched the surface of the subject. If they had had the requisite help, the Oxford authorities would have done a great deal better by Australian English than they did.

In the introduction to his dictionary, Morris records that Dr Murray "several years ago invited assistance from this end of the world for words and uses of words peculiar to Australasia, or to parts of it". This was a genuine plea for help and the Oxford lexicographers – working, it must be remembered, 12,000 miles from Australasian speech – did their best to treat our language fairly.

If we class as slang every Australian term that sounds strange to English ears, much of our language will certainly fall into that category. If we are going to set a time limit on the subject and declare that all Australian terms without a history of, say, at least twenty-five years are slang – irrespective of whether they have been in print or not – the result will be hopeless confusion, since obviously a good deal of the language tossed up by our social growth last century was ephemeral, while many expressions that have become established in the past quarter-century are here to stay.

Nor can we rely solely on instinct to tell us what is slang and what is not.

Only a few years ago, following the Intermediate Certificate Examination in New South Wales, the examiners reported[13] that essays written by the children were "often marred by colloquialisms, and even slang". Among the lapses from grace noted by officials were: *eats*[14] for eatables; *windy* for winding; *chap*[15]; *bloke; have a go; lend*[16] for a loan; *care a hoot; sling off at; roared him up.*

There was clearly a difference of opinion between the teachers and the children (and you could probably count a good many parents on the children's side) as to what constituted good English. The examiners declared:

foreigner can hardly go right. This is because Mr. Morris, with a stupidity certainly unexpected in a man of his attainment, has included (a) obsolete or obsolescent words without the least hint to show that they are not in daily use like their next-column neighbours; but included (b) words of limited use in a particular Australian district without the least hint to show that they are not used like their next-column neighbours throughout Australia; (c) has curiously failed, in some important instances, to supply adequate definitions and (d) has supplied some definitions altogether erroneous . . . As a guide to Australian language, the Dictionary is worthless except to an Australian expert who can supplement with local knowledge the makers' numerous errors and omissions."

From the "Sydney Morning Herald", January 1, 1898: ". . . It is evident that the editor [i.e. Morris] has tried to make the most of his subject and has included a vast number of words that hardly strike one as being distinctive enough to be entitled to a place in these pages."

13 "The Education Gazette", N.S.W., July 1, 1939, p. 188.
14 Henry Sweet, in his "Anglo-Saxon Reader", gives the *circa* 1000 A.D. use by Ælfric of this plural form: "Moyses . . . *ætes* ne gimde on eallum ðam fyrste" – which should provide a reasonably satisfactory precedent for its revival, with the U.S. first in the field, during the past seventy-odd years.
15 Used for "fellow or person" since the early eighteenth century.
16 A use anticipated in Scottish and north English dialect. In Sir James Balfour's "Practicks; or a System of the More Ancient Law of Scotland", *circa* 1575 (published in 1754), the following use appears: "Quhat is ane *lenne*, and of the restitution thairof."

Candidates should understand that when they are asked to express their thoughts on a given subject, they are expected to write the best English of which they are capable. Essays are a test, not merely of the construction and development of a theme, but also of the adequacy and appositeness of the vocabulary used.

On this basis men like Shakespeare and Ben Jonson would be well marked down in the Intermediate. Here is a little of the slang used by Shakespeare: *dry*, dull; *tester*, sixpence; *clay-brained*, stupid; *lob*, a country bumpkin; *geck*, a fool; *fap*, drunk; *lifter*, a thief; *nut-hook*, a constable. And some of Jonson's uses: *smelt*, a simpleton; *clap*, noise or clatter; *circling boy*, a crook or sharper; *puckfist*, a braggart; *hit*, a fiddle.

The odd idea that there is a definable something called Good English which is pure and beautiful and eternal, and that everything else is Bad English – and accordingly trivial, ugly and ephemeral – seems to have grown out of man's puny illusion that he can stop evolution in its tracks.

Good English is a fiction beloved of littérateurs, smatterers and pundits. It is a clumsy misshapen monster patched up by all the petty Frankensteins who infest classrooms and pulpits and editorial chairs and rostrums and who think that because they open their mouths and words come out they are thereby authorities on speech.

This question of Good English I am talking about is not one of grammar or syntax; it is a matter of words. And it is not simply a matter of words, but of certain fashions in words. What one person or group of persons regard as objectionable, others accept without question.[17] Horace and Martial and Aristophanes used the slang of their day without hesitation; so did Chaucer and the Elizabethans; so did Congreve and Smollett; so did James Joyce; so too with those vivid Americans, Hemingway, Dos Passos, Faulkner, Saroyan. There are, of course, other writers like Swift, Addison, Goldsmith and Johnson who avoid all forms of colloquial speech.

Are we to say that Swift is right and Shakespeare is wrong? Can we say that only "Good English" – that is, a form of language sterilized against colloquialisms and slang – makes good literature?

Surely, remembering what happened with *occupy*, *hoax*, *sham*, etc., even Pure-Well-of-English addicts will guard their replies. Incidentally, Australian Pure-Wellers may be delighted to include as one of their pioneering visionaries a Chinese of Maryborough, Queensland, who (according to the "Bulletin" of August 9, 1890, p. 15) refused "to send his children to the State School on the grounds that there they learn too much slang".

3. EARLY STUDENTS OF OUR SLANG

IT WAS NO LESS a literary figure than Dickens who, when writing of Australian additions to the English language in 1853, remarked: "What are they, till they are marshalled in a dictionary, but slang?" As in quite

---

[17] "Slang always horrifies a few sensitive spirits, yet it ends by being respectable." – G. Sampson in his introduction to R. C. Trench's "On the Study of Words."

a number of other things, Dickens was wrong. The appearance of a word in a dictionary or even in a series of dictionaries is no guarantee that it has become respectable. Australia's brief literary history provides a quite astonishing number of examples to prove the point, as we will see in a minute.

Due to a prolonged love affair with her own past, Australia's interest in her slang has always been considerable, but it was not until H. L. Mencken, one of America's greatest linguistic authorities, pointed out several important facts to me that I realised the special value of that interest. In a personal letter to me, dated June 19, 1942, Mencken wrote: "The Australian record [of her slang and colloquial speech] is immensely superior to the American record. Until 1925 or thereabouts only a handful of competent philologians ever showed any interest in the subject. There is a better spirit now, but so far it has not produced a slang dictionary of scientific merit."

Although I would not care to claim much scientific merit for our own slang dictionaries, the fact that they were compiled and (in most cases) published gives us an extremely intimate view of the Australian language in the making. Not only are we made aware of the fact that, in proportion to the size of her population, Australia has done as much as – perhaps even more than – the United States in rearranging and adding to the splendours of English, but we can also follow what happened and approximately when, how words or phrases changed their forms and sense applications over the years, how some expressions suddenly became important while others died.

It is easy to see these things now, but it was not always so. Just as once there were many contradictory opinions as to whether or not we had produced an Australian accent (see Chapter XXII), observers of our linguistic habits were sharply divided on the issue of whether we had any slang at all. On one hand, R. E. N. Twopeny commented in "Town Life in Australia" (1883) on "the bent of colonial genius in the manufacture of a new dialect", an author in "All the Year Round" (July 30, 1887) said "the popular vocabulary of the antipodes . . . is both large and varied", Karl Lentzner wrote in 1891 of the "rich and racy slang of the fifth continent – the mighty Australian commonwealth of the future", and the London "Daily Chronicle" of November 22, 1905, declared: "There are *Australianisms* enough to make a dictionary an essential for the proper understanding of an antipodean journal." On the other hand, J. A. Froude remarked in "Oceania" (1873): "The first thing that struck me – and the impression that remained during all my stay in Australia – was the pure English that was spoken there"; the Sydney "Evening News" of July 11, 1908, said: "Contrary to common opinion, Australia possesses a very limited slang vocabulary"; and "The Lone Hand" of November 2, 1908, said: "The discovery and colonization of this country has added remarkably few words to the English language." This conflict has survived even to the present day. Yet anyone who has paid attention to the subject will know that from about 1880 there has hardly been a year without practical evidence of the growth of Australian idiom. In its earliest form, this was due largely to the influence of the old "Bulletin", which virtually from the outset of its career became a focal point for all manifestations of Australian culture.

These manifestations hardly represented the orthodox idea of culture, but they encompassed most of the special experiences, tasks and enthusiasms which had grown out of the whiteman's contact with the unique Australian environment. Among the products of that contact were slang and colloquial speech. Since almost from the beginning, this country had been a country of the common man, slang was a linguistic common denominator, and what the Australian did not use he wanted to learn about.

I have already referred to the "Vocabulary of the Flash Language" which James Hardy Vaux compiled when he was a convict here in 1812. True, there is not much in it that could be described as Australian, but there are sundry pointers as to the way our language was to go.

For instance, Vaux gives *awake*, "to see through or comprehend", which we still commonly use in the expression "*I'm a wake-up* to you!" – I'm up to your tricks; I can see through you! In the senses "vigilant, alert", *awake* is standard English, so the Australian use has some solid backing. Vaux lists *bush'd* to denote a state of pennilessness; this could quite well be a term he picked up in Australia. Of the word *chum* Vaux provides a note: "A fellow prisoner in a jail, hulk, etc. So there are *new chums* and *old chums* as they happen to have been a short or a long time in confinement." From this use was developed our application of *new chum* to a new immigrant (1839) and to an inexperienced worker in the outback (1848), together with such derivatives as *new chumism* (1854) and *new chumhood* (1882).

He defined *down* as "suspicion, alarm, discovery" and noted *put a down upon*, which is rather similar to our current use *have a down on*, to dislike. As a result of American propaganda, we may imagine that *pal*, a friend, hails from the U.S. It does not; Vaux reminds us that it comes from *pall*. He defined *gray* as a halfpenny or any other coin having two heads or tails. We use the term in two-up slang today, but solely for a double-tailed penny. He listed *hog*, a shilling, which we clipped to *og* or *ogg; push* a non-specific use for "a concourse of people, a crowd", which graduated to a notable position in larrikin slang later; and *leary* for "fly", cunning or alert, which we converted into *lairy* with a different meaning.

After Vaux there was a gap of nearly seventy years until the next dictionary of slang was put together in Australia.[18] As to the person responsible for it no clue can be given; we are even uncertain when it was published, although it was probably published in Sydney. The little book is entitled "The Australian Slang Dictionary". A copy in my possession has the following words on its cover: "The Detectives' Handbook. Slang Phrases comprising all the Quaint Slang Words and Flash Dialogues in use in the Australian shadows of Life. Sporting, Stage and Gambling Slang, Low Life Glimpses, etc. The Most Curious Work ever issued in Australia." The

---

[18] The first English dictionary to include Australian expressions was J. C. Hotten's "Slang Dictionary", 1873 edition, which listed *bale up* (for bail up), *blackbirding, cooey* (for cooee), *currency* (as opposed to *sterling*, as Australian-born and English-born inhabitants were known respectively), *gully-rakers, swag* ("luggage carried by diggers") and *wallabee track*.

publisher was H. J. Franklin, Sydney. A copy of the dictionary is in the Mitchell Library, Sydney, lacking covers and bearing on its front page the date in ink "2/3/82". Beyond the evidence in the book itself that it was compiled in the early 1880s there is no information.

Much of its contents is English slang – perhaps not more than one-fifth is Australian. But once again we are given valuable information on the way our language was going.

Here we find *Johnny Warder*, "an idle drunkard who hangs about pub corners looking for a drink – called after a publican named John Ward who formerly kept a low house in Sydney noted for that species", who was probably the father, or at any rate a cousin, of our *Jimmy Woodser* (who now seems to have retired to the bush). We find *bart* for a girl, which was later displaced by *cliner* and *donah*, and later still by *sheila*. We find the English cant term *moskeneer*, to pawn, which survives in Australia today in the phrase *gone to Moscow*, which has nothing to do with the Soviet capital, but which simply means "pawned". We find *on the wallaby* for "on a drinking bout in town", which gives us a new angle on the phrase; we find *ponce*, "a degraded man who lives on a woman", which we have converted into *punce* (or *poonce*), a male homosexual; we find *rest*, a year's jail, *snooze*, three months' jail, and *dream*, six months' jail; we find *sheen*, *shug*, *sug* and *spons* for money.

In short we are given enough evidence to show that our slang and colloquial speech were widening. That in this and succeeding dictionaries a good deal of slang was included that was not and never has been Australian must be regarded not only as bad workmanship, but doubly unfortunate in that it encouraged unbelievers to persist in their conviction that our slang had little originality in it.

Enthusiasts though they undoubtedly were for the cause of local slang, both Lentzner[19] and Crowe[20], who were next in the slang field, did us considerable damage in the eyes both of Australians and the English.

Lentzner had an intelligent enough approach to his subject, but his execution was bad. Of Australian slang (and what he thought was Australian slang) he wrote:

> These eccentric forms of expression are for the most part of modern origin, invented because they were absolutely needed, or because they expressed some idea more ingeniously, sententiously and amusingly than others had done.

The "Bulletin"[21] comment on Lentzner's work provides a fair statement:

> The illustrations given of Australian slang are very funny for the most part, and where they are exact and authentic, the source, in nine cases out of ten, is inaccurately stated.

---

[19] "Wörterbuch der englischen Volkssprache Australiens", Leipzig (1891). An English edition was also published, but was withdrawn almost immediately because it infringed sundry copyrights. Lentzner described himself as "formerly examiner in modern languages at the Sydney Grammar School and at the King's School, Parramatta."

[20] "The Australian Slang Dictionary" (1895).

[21] January 30, 1892.

About Crowe's "Slang Dictionary" of 1895 the "Bulletin"[22] was even more severe – and not without reason, for Crowe was a Melbourne police officer who should have been able to do a much better job, while Lentzner was a foreigner who had lived only a few years in this country:

"The Australian Slang Dictionary" is an amazingly ignorant production. The author has mixed up an olla podrida of linguistic scraps picked up everywhere – most of which are either not Australian or not slang – and enriched it with little bits of his own. The spelling is atrocious and the definitions are worse.

Again the criticism was justified, although Crowe had admitted that "very few of the terms it [i.e. the dictionary] contains have been invented by Australians". To the good Australian word *barracker* he gave the definition: "One using low language to aid his party", and of *barrikin* he wrote: "Coarse language used by roughs in applauding their party in a contest". He made no mention of *bingy*, or *binjey*, from the Aboriginal, meaning stomach, but gave it instead as "a term used in the butter trade, meaning bad butter", which is straight out of English dialect. He tells us that *bloody* is "a word used very often inadvertently by the uneducated"; that *shaler* (instead of *sheila*) means a girl; that a *squirt* is a revolver; that *Yarra bankers* are "vagrants living on the banks of the Yarra"; that *Tom Collins* is "a fellow about town whom many sought to kill for touching them on sore points: he always managed to vanish before his destroyers as he was imaginary".

In short, the dictionary is pretty much of a mixture, valuable in parts, trivial in others. It might have been expected that a man with the enthusiastic approach to language that Professor E. E. Morris, of Melbourne, possessed, would have found some usefulness in the dictionaries mentioned above – not much, perhaps, but enough to give him a guide in putting Australia's lexicographical house in order. But Morris was either ignorant of them, or did not care to check them over to see what was indigenous and what was not. He dismisses Crowe in a couple of lines, and does not mention the other works. Yet in his presidential address before the fourth meeting of the Australasian Association for the Advancement of Science (Literature and Fine Arts Section) held in Hobart in January, 1892, when he urged that a body of investigators should compile a dictionary of Austral English, he admitted that " . . . even slang, being the speech of the people, is not undeserving of some scientific study".

Morris's suggestion for organized research appears to have been made hastily. He made no concrete proposals as to how the work might be accomplished apart from noting that "twenty or thirty men and women, each undertaking to read certain books with the new dictionary in mind, and to note in a prescribed fashion what is peculiar [to Australasia], could accomplish all that is needed". He concluded his address with the lame comment, "Of course, we are all horribly busy . . .", which was probably

---

[22] August 17, 1895.

as good a reason as any why Morris's "Austral English Dictionary" was an incomplete, out-of-balance work.

Through the reverse telescope of time we have tended to see his dictionary a little distortedly. In the first place it was more a catalogue of flora and fauna[23] than a dictionary. What little there is of "standard" Australianisms, colloquialisms and slang is often overloaded with unnecessary textual quotations. Moreover, he included a good deal of the trivial,[24] while omitting much that was important, largely, it must be imagined, because he did not familiarize himself with the speech of the people.[25] In principal, however, Morris was correct. He set out to record Australianisms, give definitions, origins, dates and textual quotations along the lines laid down by the "Oxford Dictionary" authorities. As a source of reference his work is one of the best of its kind that Australia possesses, but that does not mean it is either complete or adequate. It is a valuable addition to Australiana, but no more complete than, say, J. H. Heaton's "Australian Dictionary of Dates" (1879) or D. Blair's "Cyclopaedia of Australasia" (1881) in their respective fields.

Morris tells us that in the early 1890s the New York publishers, Funk and Wagnalls, included numerous Australasian terms in their "Standard Dictionary". Among their lapses were: *beauregarde* for *budgerigar; swagman,* with a definition "a dealer in cheap trinkets"; *taihoa,* wait! quoted from Tasmania instead of from New Zealand. Since it fell to my lot to attempt to reduce the mountain of preposterous errors about Australia which this dictionary managed to accumulate in the succeeding seventy years, a few samples may help to explain why Americans have an extremely hazy knowledge of this country; Tasmanian Sea instead of Tasman Sea; *billy* from the given name Billy; *cooeey* for cooee; Paramatta for Parramatta.

A much better job was done by "Webster's International Dictionary" in 1898, when a special supplement devoted to Australasian expressions

---

23 His listing of flora and fauna is both out-of-date and inadequate in many instances. In reviewing Morris's book, the "Australasian" of January 22, 1898 (p. 217), wrote: "We should say that fully half of the book is more of the nature of a cyclopaedia of natural history than a dictionary proper. As a compendious account of the fauna and flora of Australia, it will be found useful, but it rather overloads the more strictly philological portion of the book."

24 He includes such terms, for instance, as *fist it,* to eat with the hands; *tannergrams,* sixpenny telegrams; *to run round rings* instead of *to run rings round; patriot* "humorously applied to convicts"; *mihanere,* "a Maori variant of the English word missionary" – a lone and irrelevant example of Maori pidgin; *wakiki,* "the shell money of the South Sea Islands" – another irrelevant term far beyond the intended scope of the work; *government,* "a not unusual contraction of 'Government service', used by contractors and working men".

25 Evidence that Morris felt some need to recognise Australian popular language is shown by his inclusion of a number of slang terms – *without* dates or textual quotations – but his selection of these terms is so haphazard that it represents anything but an adequate cross-section of Australian slang in the 1890s. It is the old-time academician's cross-section of our life – illbalanced, incomplete and unrepresentative: *butcher,* "South Australian slang for a long drink of beer"; *Cobb,* "sometimes used as equivalent to a coach"; *cronk,* "used of a horse run crookedly"; *dead bird,* "a certainty"; *to be* (or *come*) *down,* "to fail in a University examination"; *nut,* "a dare-devil"; *Jo-Jo,* "a name used by Melbourne larrikins for a man with a good deal of hair on his face". It is clear from an examination of his material, that Morris dismissed Australian slang and colloquialism – "the element is comparatively small" in Austral English, he wrote – because he was ignorant of its scope and made no more than a halfhearted attempt to acquaint himself with it.

was added to the work. This supplement, compiled by Joshua Lake, of Cambridge, ranks as one of the best of its kind yet published. It gives a representative cross-section of Australasian speech, avoids overloading with flora and fauna, and – although it is not always correct — gives us a much better taste of indigenous slang and colloquialism than Morris does. The editor says:

> The vocabulary might easily have been doubled in size, but only such words, phrases and usages have been admitted as are already well settled or seem likely to persist. Local words and usages are specially designated. Many of these, however, will unquestionably extend their boundaries in the immediate future.

In subsequent editions of "Webster's Dictionary" this supplement lost its identity, such words as the lexicographers chose to include from Australasia being merged with the main body of the work. Lake was the first to suggest the English dialectal origins of *barrack*, *larrikin* and *fossick;* he noted *spieler*, *penner* and *tarboy* (woolshed terms), *coppertail* and *bushy* (the noun), which, among others, Morris had ignored. In short, he took the study of our language a step further. The "Bulletin" of May 27, 1899, commented as follows:

> An extra-special merit of the new Webster is its Australian supplement. There is a list of local words and phrases – not complete by any means and open to many cavils – but very helpful . . .

About this time Australian slang was finding its way into English slang dictionaries on a substantial scale. In 1873 a few Australianisms had crept into J. C. Hotten's "Slang Dictionary". There were still more in the "Dictionary of Slang, Jargon and Cant" (1897). Barrère and Leland and Farmer and Henley followed these leads with dictionaries peppered with Australian terms. Unfortunately these works are full of errors.

Of the "Dictionary of Slang, Jargon and Cant" the "Bulletin" complained (after quoting a few examples):

> Isn't it awful! And so it goes on throughout the dictionary – ignorant or misleading explanations of actual slang; disquisitions on imaginary ditto; attributions to all Australia of expressions which, a dozen years ago, had temporary vogue in a limited district – backed up and enforced by scores of references to D. B. W. Sladen's reminiscences, or quotations from his unspeakable verse! . . . One can only hope that the historian of the period will be able to refer to this notice (it is written to that end) and authoritatively contradict the philologist [responsible for this dictionary].

There is a good case in point in the alleged indigenous expression *Australian grip,* "a hearty handshake". It was recorded originally by Lentzner, repeated in the dictionary just mentioned, included by Farmer and Henley in their "Dictionary of Slang" (1905) and by Partridge in his "Slang Dictionary", yet I have never seen it in print outside a dictionary, nor have I heard it used.

It was the feeling that Australasia had been given a raw deal by the lexicographers that prompted A. G. Stephens and S. O'Brien to start compiling an authentic dictionary of our slang and colloquialisms. Stephens was at the time book-critic of the "Bulletin" and he realized, perhaps better than any other man of his period that there was a good deal more to the subject than Morris, Lake, Crowe and their kind were disposed to believe. What originally inspired him to take up the cause of Australianisms was almost certainly his disappointment with Morris's "Austral English".[26] Almost immediately after the book was published, the "Bulletin" embarked on a campaign to collect items of indigenous slang and idiom, and throughout 1899 the *Red Page*[27] was liberally sprinkled with contributions sent in from all parts of Australasia.

In Chapter XXI detailed comment is made on the "Bulletin's" influence on the evolution of our slang and to the encouragement it gave Australian writers to use our idiom. At its peak it was perhaps the most influential single factor that has been brought to bear on colloquial speech in the history of the English language. Between 1885 and 1900 it represented more power, in terms of national culture, than any journal in England and America.

Stephens and O'Brien made an intimate study of Australian idiom. It was unfortunate that their researches remained in typescript,[28] for they would have served (though they suffered from the inclusion of certain non-Australian elements) as a counter to allegations that Australian idiom was thin and meagre, tottering paltrily to extinction beneath an avalanche of Americanisms.

In the 1904 edition of "Webster's International Dictionary" – although, as already stated, the supplement was by then not exclusively Australasian – allusion is made to "the rich contribution of words and meanings peculiar to Australasia" and to the fact that "the wonderful development of this branch of the English-speaking race has had its natural accompaniment in the growth of a new vocabulary".

This fact has been recognised in other oversea dictionaries, and in several cases[29] special supplements have been devoted to Australasianisms.

C. J. Dennis tossed in a vocabulary of alleged Australian expressions with his New York edition of "Doreen" and "The Sentimental Bloke";

---

[26] Stephens wrote the critique of "Austral English" from which quotations have already been made.

[27] *Red Page* was the name given to the inside front cover of the "Bulletin" so named from the colour of the covers. It acquired its nature in 1895 when critical notices displaced book advertisements. The first use of the title was "For the Red Page" on August 22, 1896. This became "The Red Page" in the succeeding issue and, except for a few issues when the title was changed to "Under the Gumtree", remained so throughout the life of the old "Bulletin".

[28] A copy is in the Mitchell Library, Sydney, entitled "Material for a Dictionary of Australian Slang", by S. E. O'Brien and A. G. Stephens, 1900-10. Another copy with the note, "Material for an Austrazealand Slang Dictionary", by A. G. Stephens and S. J. O'Brien, is in the Turnbull Library, Wellington, New Zealand. This work contains some 650 entries, many of which have no further elaboration than "See Morris", but the great bulk of it represents a sincerer attempt to study the subject than any work up to that time.

[29] Especially "A Modern Dictionary of the English Language", published in 1912, by Macmillan and Co., London, more or less a brief repetition of Morris – I have also seen a 1916 edition of this dictionary with an Australasian supplement – and "The Modern Standard English Dictionary" (1939). Some other dictionaries have followed suit since World War II.

Jice Doone[30] gave a list of Australian slang in his "Timely Tips to New Australians", published in London in 1926; selections have also been given in the "Encyclopaedia Britannica" since its 1929 edition; and Partridge gave us a list (probably the first authentic one, but not by any means complete) in his "Slang Today and Yesterday" with its elaborations appearing in his "Dictionary of Slang and Unconventional English".

These, with the exception of "Digger Dialects" (1919), by W. H. Downing – the first dictionary of war slang published after World War I and devoted almost exclusively to Diggerisms – and L. G. D. Acland's "Sheep-Station Glossary",[31] represent most of the important research done on our language until the 1940s.

Since 1940 the most detailed surveys have been my own and a valuable undertaking at the University of Sydney, the Australian Language Research Centre, which was formed in 1962. A report by Professor G. H. Russell describes this Centre as "a group of academics who meet regularly to exchange information upon work which its members have in hand, to stimulate and co-ordinate efforts to further the study of the English language in Australia, and to provide a central repository in which archives may be properly maintained and organized". He adds that the Centre may later "be in a position to play a more positive role in the attack upon the problems of the English language in Australia and may gradually become the sponsor of large projects". Among the Centre's preliminary activities is the compilation of "a massive but orderly record of the Australian vocabulary", historical documentation of that vocabulary and the publication of a series of Occasional Papers on various aspects of Australian English. In due course, it is hoped that these undertakings will develop into a "Dictionary of Australian English" or some similar title on principles adopted by the "Oxford" authorities.

4. WHAT WE HAVE SACRIFICED

IT IS CLEAR that we could not have acquired an Australian language without losing something of the language of our English forefathers. We have already seen how *bush* displaced "forest" and "woods" and how other words also fell by the wayside. But this was only the beginning.

Here is part of the case put by the eminent Australian, Professor W. K. Hancock, in his "Australia" (1930):

[The Australian] has rejected almost at a blow the beautiful names of an intimate countryside – fields and meadows, woods, copse, spinney and thicket, dale, glen, vale and coomb, brook, stream and rivulet, inn and village. But in their place is a new vocabulary of the Bush – *billabong, dingo, damper, bushwacker, billy, cooee, swag, swaggie, humpy, stockman, jackeroo,*

---

[30] Nom-de-plume of James Vance Marshall, author of "Jail from Within" (1918) and "World of the Living Dead" (1919).

[31] Published in "The Press", Christchurch, New Zealand, at weekly intervals, September-December, 1933, with revisions and additions in January, 1934.

squatter, bushranger, sundowner, brumby, drover, never-never, outback, backblocks.
One is *on the track, on the wallaby.* Many words have come from the aborigines, some have worked upwards from "St. Giles' Greek", others (*digger, fossick, pan-out*) derive from the gold rushes, and others still are originals coined offhand out of experience and a matter-of-fact humour.

This type of loss was noted in New Zealand last century by W. Pember Reeves[32] when he lamented that New Zealanders no longer used such terms as brook, moor, heath, dale, copse, meadow and glade, and it has been reiterated in many forms since.[33]

Jice Doone makes an interesting comment on the matter in the introduction to his "Timely Tips to New Australians":

> A remarkable feature of the Australian's manner of expression . . . is the frequent evidences of his absolute rejection of accepted English words. For instance, such standard English words as fields, woods, meadow, inn, tavern, brook, hatchet, jacket and village find no place in the Australian vocabulary and their use to the Australian sounds foreign. A brook is known as a *creek.* Such a term as "in the woods" conveys no meaning, the woods, like a forest, being classified under the all-embracing heading of *bush.* Paraffin is known as *kerosene.* A hooligan is known as a *larrikin* and the word *corn* is only ascribed to maize. A *coat* is never referred to as a jacket; the word *scone* is pronounced "skon" in place of "skoan"; hatchets are *tomahawks;* pails are known as *buckets.*

Dr Thomas Wood, in "Cobbers" (1934), echoed the complaint: "The whole rich treasury of words from the [English] countryside and words from the dialects has been thrown away and has died. A heavy loss."

This tendency to reject English environmental terms was not an accident. It sprang quite logically from the fact that our outback was not, and never will be, "intimate". Our environmental concepts were different and the terms we developed to describe those concepts were a measure of the difference between England and Australia.

Not only have we tossed aside many words from the northern hemisphere, but we have also given new applications to many English terms. Our *borough,* for instance, differs from its standard English connotation of "a town possessing a municipal corporation and special privileges conferred by royal charter; a town which sends representatives to Parliament". In Australia the word is applied generally to "a district of not less than nine miles square, of which no part is more than six miles from any other part, and having a specified number of inhabitants as required by Statute".

Our *township* is not the same as the English *township.* The "Oxford Dictionary" defines the Australian use as "a site laid out prospectively for a town, meanwhile often consisting of a few shanties grouped around a railway station, store, hotel, post office or the like; a village or hamlet". Though wide, this definition is scarcely satisfying so far as Australia is concerned; the "Modern Standard English Dictionary" (1939) does better

---

[32] "The Long White Cloud" (1898).
[33] Commenting on those losses in New Zealand in the "Review of Reviews", January, 1901, the Rev. Joseph Barry said: "These changes . . . are not improvements. The schoolmasters would do well to bring back sweeter English words to their true use."

with the simple meaning "any collection of residences". The following distinctions are made on a map of Australia issued by the Government Printer, Canberra, 1938: Capital cities; *towns*, ranging in population from "above 20,000" to "below 1,000"; and *townships*, minor settlements, homesteads, etc." which leaves the term undefined, but reduces it to the level of being much "below 1,000".

The problem of trying to fix the numerical distinction between a town and a township in Australia has been with us for generations and has never been properly solved. It probably never will be solved.

The official report on the Census in 1961, "Part III – Population and Dwellings in Localities", sidesteps the issue partly by ignoring *township* altogether, but aggravates it by imposing a numerical distinction on the size of a *town* on the mainland and in Tasmania. It bases its findings on the view that a mainland *town* consists of 1,000 persons or more, but fixes a figure of 750 for Tasmania. It then plunges deeper into the morass by referring to cases in which "details are shown for both *town*" and "*near*" where either had twenty or more dwellings or a population of fifty or more persons – which implies that, in certain instances, an Australian *town* can have as few as fifty inhabitants.

Many deviations from accepted English use have occurred in Australia. *Pastoralist, premier* and *primage* are a few of them. Even our use of *bishop's court* differs from the English; in Australia (as was first noted by Lentzner in 1891) we use it for a bishop's palace, but in standard English it is an "ecclesiastical court held in the cathedral of a diocese".

It was with reason, therefore, that I. L. Bird, in her "Australia Felix: Impressions of Victoria" (1877), pointed out that anyone coming to Australia would require "to learn something of a new vocabulary and in some cases unlearn the familiar meaning of words or limit it locally".

This subject will be discussed in greater detail in Chapter XIX.

Ours is not an isolated instance where this rejection and modification of old terms has taken place; it was the same in America and South Africa. If it is axiomatic that all language tends to become universal in relation to its publicizing agents, it is equally axiomatic that any language can remain alive only in so far as environment sustains it. Environment is something more than hills and trees and plainlands; it is the people and the things that fill their lives, because people put down their roots and merge with their conditions of life just as a tree does.

As I point out in Chapter X, much of the traditional nature of Australian life began to change in the early 1940s. Many interlocking influences – the growth of an affluent society, absorption of a vast tide of immigrants, development of new secondary industries, commercial discovery of our teenagers, the onslaught of television, etc. – were to bring about major linguistic alterations in Australia. We will see how, although the demands of the Australian environment and the tasks and enthusiasms of our people originally involved the loss of many English words, the new life upon which we entered after World War II was to involve the loss of many words which the Australian had counted as his own.

CHAPTER II

Beginnings

1. CONVICTS

LIFE RAN THINLY in the new world of the south in the years between 1788[1] and the end of the eighteenth century. A few thousand people had been thrown together on the edge of a vast wilderness, before them the Pacific, behind them the grey, bleak unknown. They had scratched a toehold for themselves in a new land – a few huts, barracks for the convicts, the beginnings of cultivation and little else amid forbidding bush that pressed around them and made their attempt at settlement no larger than a grain of sand on the rim of a plate. Yet out of that small fragment of a colony emerged the first glimpses of a new language.

It is important in studying this remote part of our history to look not only at the physical environment, but at the people themselves, for these were no ordinary colonists. They did not come with good intentions and high hopes. They were pitchforked into a new life and for most of them there was to be no going back. The original idea was that, after working out their sentences, they were to be permitted the privilege of becoming peasants. There was nothing else to look forward to.

Many of the convicts represented the worst types that the English prison system could throw together. No matter how trivial the offences which sent them into exile on the other side of the world, if they were not brutal and animal-like by nature, the system made them so. It was impossible for refinement in any form to survive.

However, our interest is not concerned so much with the nature of these reluctant oecists as with the language they spoke. They were proficient in the use of prison cant and vulgarism, the former because it was the *lingua franca* of their type, the latter because it was the natural concomitant of raw living and brutal discipline.

Peter Cunningham in his "Two Years in New South Wales", gives us a glimpse of the picture as he saw it in 1826:

> All the natives round Sydney understand English well and speak it, too, so as to be understood by residents. The Billingsgate slang they certainly have acquired in perfection, and no white would think of competing with them in abuse or hard swearing, a constant torrent of which flows from their mouths as long as their antagonist remains before them.[2]

---

[1] The First Fleet arrived in Port Jackson on January 26, 1788, the colony being formally proclaimed on February 7.

[2] An earlier comment on the facility with which Aborigines picked up vulgar speech was made by Samuel Kittle, "Concise History of the Colony and Natives of New South Wales" (Edin-

A number of slang phrases current in St. Giles' Creek bid fair to become legitimized in the dictionary of this colony: *plant, swag, pulling up* and other epithets of the Tom and Jerry school are established – the dross passing here as genuine, even among all ranks. In our police offices, the slang words are taken regularly down in examinations and I once saw a little urchin not exceeding ten years *patter it* in evidence to the Bench with perfect fluency. Among the lower classes these terms form a part of every common conversation, and the children consequently catch them.[3]

The "proverbial cant" of the convicts, of which J. O. Tucker makes mention in his "Australian Story"[4] was certain to influence the subsequent story of the Australian language. Through the literature of the times, or what passed for literature – books, pamphlets, journals and newspapers – we are able to reconstruct part of the picture.

In collecting material for his novel, "For the Term of His Natural Life",[5] Marcus Clarke was at pains to recreate the atmosphere of the time. Much of his story represents the adaptation of material from reports on convict life in both Van Diemen's Land and Norfolk Island. Accordingly, we find Clarke referring to "the horrible slang of the prison ship" on which his hero, Rufus Dawes, was transported, and later to the "hideous jargon of the chain gangs". Speaking of Norfolk Island convicts in 1846, he alludes also to "language . . . such as was never before heard out of Bedlam".

A point that visitors to Australia note is that a criminal or jail-bird is rarely referred to as a *convict* by Australians. For us the word *convict* has acquired a specified historical meaning. This avoidance of its use is not new. If we are to believe early writers, the Australian public was once extremely sensitive about the word.[6] In 1826 Cunningham spoke of "the term *convict* being erased by a sort of general tacit compact from our Botany dictionary as a word too ticklish to be pronounced in these sensitive latitudes". Still later, William Shaw tells us in "The Land of Promise": "The asperity of the word *convict* shocks their ears, so the more mollifying term of *Government man* has been substituted." Comments on the same subject are given by F. Fowler, "Southern Lights and Shadows" (1859) who says that the word convict "is always spoken sotto voce"; and by A Clergyman

---

burgh: *circa* 1815). He wrote: "They are . . . great proficients in the language and Newgate slang of the convicts; and in case of any quarrel are by no means unequal to them in the exchange of abuse."

[3] The similarity of this quotation with the following from W. Shaw's book, "The Land of Promise" (1854), should be noted: "The expressions *lifting, swag, planting*, etc., from frequent application, seem likely to become legitimate figures of speech . . . This thieves' slang children, of course, readily adopt and use them as household words." Shaw adds that "even ladies sometimes inadvertently let slip barbarisms" in Australia.

[4] Published in 1865. A. Russell, "A Tour Through the Australian Colonies" (1840) provides the note: "Slang terms and a little *bouncing* are the order of the day with the convicts."

[5] Originally published in Melbourne in 1874 under the title, "His Natural Life".

[6] A total of about 157,000 convicts was transported to Australia: to N.S.W., some 80,000; to Tasmania, 67,500; to W.A., 9,721. Transportation ceased at the following dates: to N.S.W. in 1840; to Tasmania in 1852; to W.A. in 1868. Some 2,000 "exiles" were also sent to Victoria and N.S.W. in 1849-50, under Grey's scheme for reviving transportation there.

("Australia in 1866") who declares: "There is no word in the English language of which one requires to make a more studied use in Australia than *convict*." Only since the mid-twentieth century has a major change been evident. Today, many residents of N.S.W. and Queensland (*not* the other States, however) would be gratified to list one of the original convicts among their forebears.

It was probably because of early sensitivity that a large number of synonyms for convict became current, among them *canary*,[7] *transport*, *old hand*,[8] *crossbred*, *legitimate* (i.e. a person with a legitimate or legal reason for coming to Australia), *demon* (a Van Diemen's Land convict), *cockatoo*, *Cockatoo hand*, *Cockatoo bird*, *Cockatoo islander* (for a Sydney convict),[9] *Hawkesbury duck* (a convict assigned for work in the Hawkesbury area) and *Derwent duck* (a Hobart convict)[10] – terms which, in subsequent years, were to be edged out of use by euphemisms such as *exiles*, *absentees*, *empire builders*, *patriots* and *pioneers*, for the sensitivity of the convicts was nothing compared with the sensitivity of many of their descendants who were to find in an expression such as *First Families* a decided sneer.

Our early history is strewn with examples of contests between the socially eligible and the socially ineligible – of *ticket-of-leavers* (a *ticket of leave* was a document issued to a convict, enabling him to work for wages and choose his own employer), *expirees* (convicts whose sentences had expired) and *emancipists* (former convicts; technically, convicts who had received pardons)[11] who struggled to gain niches in the small Australian world of their day, and the bitter opposition they encountered from the *exclusionists* or *exclusives* (free settlers who opposed the admittance of the *emancipists* to full civic rights).

From the outset, considerable stress was laid on the gulf separating those who *came out* and those who were *sent out* (*under hatches*) and, as early comments on Australia show, the word *free* acquired an exaggerated importance. In 1809 we find some Hawkesbury settlers, who sent an address to Governor Bligh, emphasizing that they *came free into the colony*. These were the type of people who styled themselves the *aristocracy*, *sterling* (as opposed to *currency* which was applied to convicts and Australian-born

---

[7] Both *canary* and *canary bird* were in old English slang for a jail-bird, but the application to a transported convict was peculiarly Australian.

[8] Although *lag*, a convict under sentence of transportation, was originally in English cant, the use of *old lag* seems to have been an Australian development to describe an ex-convict or ticket-of-leave man. However, W. W. Dobie, "Recollections of a Visit to Port Phillip" (1856), refers to convicts (not, be it noted, ex-convicts) "known in the colony by the aristocratic cognomen of *Old Legs*". He uses this version *old legs* several times, possibly because he confused the terms *lag* and *old hand*.

[9] Cockatoo Island, Sydney, was first established as a place for convicts in February, 1839, and was constituted the penal establishment of N.S.W. in 1841.

[10] *Ex* the Derwent River. The *Sydney ducks* who came into prominence half a century later were Australians who swarmed to California in the 1849 gold rush. A different type of *Hawkesbury duck* earned mention in "Ralph Rashleigh" (1845); this denoted a cob of parched maize presumably from the Hawkesbury River area in N.S.W.

[11] In 1825 Governor Darling described *emancipists* as "the *old settlers*", and in 1833 Governor Bourke called them "emigrants", although it is difficult to interpret the meaning of the latter.

whites) and *pure merinos* and, since they had no "legal" reasons for coming to Australia, who also bore the title *illegitimates*. Cunningham uses all these terms in his "Two Years in New South Wales" and so does James Mudie in his "Felonry of New South Wales" (1837).

Although it is almost forgotten today, the term *currency* bulked largely in the early years of last century. Joshua Lake gives us the following note about it in his "Webster's Dictionary" supplement of 1898:

> In the early days a great variety of specie was in circulation. English silver, American and Spanish dollars, johannes, ducats, mohurs, pagodas, rupees, guilders, as well as paper money of different kinds and notes of hand issued by established tradesmen. Such notes and other paper were called *currency notes* and the various coins were called collectively *currency*. English gold pieces were called *sterling*, as opposed to the mixed colonial currency.

Cunningham gives some varied uses of the term, including *currency lad, currency lass, currency belles, currency females, currency criminals, currency sprouts, currency urchins* and *currency youths*. In 1852 we find G. C. Mundy ("Our Antipodes") using *un-currency* as the equivalent of "un-Australian".

If the way of most of the convicts was hard, there were some who had easy lives and were favoured by the authorities. These were the *legitimate exquisites, felon swells* and *gentlemen convicts* whose wealth or aristocratic ties in Britain gained them preferment. A. L. Haydon, in his "Trooper Police of Australia" (1911), notes that under a loose system of classification in the early days convicts were divided into "town thieves, rural labourers and gentlemen". T. H. Braim tells us in his "History of New South Wales" (1845) that these *gentlemen convicts* were "considered the prizes in the assignment scheme" because of their education. William Hay refers to a "gentleman convict" as a *long-coater* in "The Escape of the Notorious Sir William Heans (and the Mystery of Mr Daunt)" (1919), but his style is so peculiar that it is impossible to judge whether he has bothered to check either historical facts or contemporary terms in this Tasmanian novel. (I can find only four other expressions in the book of possible validity: *second-sentencer*, a convict re-sentenced in Tasmania and sent to Port Arthur; *five pounds catcher*, a man who caught Aborigines at £5 a head then offered by the authorities; *crows*, Aborigines; *geers*, triangles for flogging.)

The story of convict slang began almost as soon as the *First Fleet*[12] dropped its anchors off Sydney Cove. The Sydney settlement became known almost immediately as *the Camp;*[13] later the term was transferred to the Hobart convict settlement. In subsequent years the Hobart Town Penitentiary became known as *the Tench*. In Western Australia the prison at Fremantle was *the establishment*, a term which is fit to rank with *the System* – as transportation in general and the maltreatment of prisoners in particular

---

[12] Although there is no record of the term *First Fleet* in the dictionaries of Morris, Webster (1898) and Lentzner, *Second Fleet*, for the contingent of convicts that arrived in 1790, is found in literary use in 1845 and *first fleeter*, a convict who arrived in 1788, is found in 1848. These expressions were doubtless used long before the *Third Fleet* reached Sydney in 1791.

[13] J. West, "History of Tasmania", vol. ii (1852), says the convicts "gave and long preserved to the site of the city [Sydney] the name of Camp".

became known – as notable examples of understatement. There was not much understatement, however, about *the Ocean Hell*, the title given to the Norfolk Island convict settlement whither the worst offenders were sent. Nor did the convicts err on the side of politeness when they tacked the name *Pinchgut* on to the little island in Sydney Harbour officially known as Fort Denison.

Perhaps the first authentic example of convict slang in Australia was the use of *scrubbing brushes* for bread containing more chaff and bran than flour – noted by D. Collins in his "Account of N.S.W." (1802). It is not recorded in oversea slang dictionaries. Nor is *red shirt* for a back scarified by flogging. Nor, though they are formed on English slang terms for coins, are *tester*, a flogging of twenty-five lashes (also known as a *Botany Bay dozen*); *bob*, fifty lashes; *bull*, seventy-five lashes; and *canary*, one hundred lashes.[14] Nor are *old fake*, a convict on his second probation; *logs*, a prison (Collins refers to "log prisons" at Sydney and Parramatta); *clean potato*, a free man; *wheelbarrow*, a bullock waggon taking supplies to men in an iron gang; and *domino*, the last lash in a flogging.

Simply because many new words came to be used with great frequency, they underwent changes – always in the direction of shortening. Thus, *ticket-of-leave* became simply *ticket* and *ticket-of-leave man* became *leaver* (there was also *ticket of occupation*, Government permission for a farmer to occupy land); *assigned servant* became *assignee;* the society of felons became *felonry;* an institution at Parramatta called "the house of correction for females" became known as *The Factory*. We should pause here for a moment to consider this *female factory*, for this was probably the site of Australia's first secondary industry. The product was known as *Parramatta cloth*. A booklet entitled "Concerning Wool", issued in 1946 by The Australian Wool Board and The Associated Woollen and Worsted Textile Manufacturers of Australia is worth quoting on the matter:

> The first woollen products manufactured in Australia, 306 yards of woollen blankets, were produced in 1801 under the supervision of an Irish convict in the New South Wales settlement of Parramatta on two or three primitive looms established in the prison . . . Operations were extended and in August, 1803, the extensive room over the new gaol was set aside for the manufacture of wool and flax products . . . known as *Parramatta cloth;* this was well spoken of in the wool trade for many years . . . in 1852 the output had reached 235,000 yards a year, and *Parramatta tweed* exported to England gained such a favourable reputation that Bradford manufacturers began production of a tweed which they called *Parramatta cloth*.

---

14 Although sundry historical sciolists would have it that Australia's early convicts lived easy-going lives, here are a few quotations from early documents (see Sidney J. Baker, "The Drum", 1959, pp. 5-6) which reveal a different story: " . . . tho' I was two perches from them [i.e. the floggers] the flesh and skin blew in my face as they shooke the cats"; "He got one hundred on the back and you cud see his back bone between his shoulder blades"; "The inquisitions of Spain and Portugal in their worst days were nothing in atrocity and diabolical sacrifice as those earthly hells"; "The Governor would order the lash at the rate of 500, 600 and 800: and if the men could have stood it they would have had more". It was apparently judged that some men *could* stand more: the upper limit of floggings was some-times 1,000 lashes. In 1835, an official return shows that 7,103 sentences were imposed on Australian convicts – an average of 46 lashes each, totalling 332,810 strokes.

Its colour was apparently white or off-white. In 1826 Cunningham refers to "the Government gangs of convicts with their white woollen Parramatta frocks or trowsers".

Although it came considerably after *Parramatta cloth, Tasmanian bluey* is also worthy of special mention because it is still widely sold in Australia. This heavy (dark) woollen cloth was originally woven in Tasmania and is not only warm but waterproof. Bush dwellers, gold prospectors, orchardists and others whose daily toil takes them outdoor in rainy and bleak weather speak highly of it. It is currently manufactured in Victoria. (Further details are given in Chapter V.)

While we are listing orthodox terms, several other expressions merit attention, perhaps none more than *Botany Bay* itself. This natural harbour just south of Sydney (first called Stingray Harbour, then Botanist Bay) was never the site of a convict settlement, yet for many years it was identified as the destination of all convicts sent to New South Wales. Indeed, wool exported from N.S.W. was later known for generations in England as *Botany Bay wool, Botany Bay tops*, etc. Residents of Sydney town were partly responsible for this inaccuracy. If freed convicts were called *Botany Bay swells* as we are told in "Fell Tyrant" (1836), and black eyes were known as *a Botany Bay coat of arms* (or *colonial livery*), we glimpse through these expressions – minor though they undoubtedly are – some part of the picture that was our early Australia.

So, too, with *Straitsmen*, a name given to sealers, runaway convicts and others ("a complete set of pirates", according to a comment in 1827) who settled on islands in Bass Strait from about 1800 onward. These settlers became *Eastern Straitsmen* and *Western Straitsmen*. They should not be confused with the *Overstraiters*, who in the 1830s and later took stock and possessions from Van Diemen's Land (known from January 1, 1856, as Tasmania) across Bass Strait to the new settlement opened up in southern Victoria. They were the V.D.L. equivalent of the *overlanders* from N.S.W. about whom we will hear more in due course.

Far less conventional were *old dogs*, "as the experienced convicts were called", according to Marcus Clarke; the *Norfolk Dumpling*, "that's what we call sending 'em to Norfolk Island, the most out-and-out cruel punishment that they can give"[15]; *Little Go Court*, the Commissioners' Court of Requests; *Pittites*,[16] a name given by convicts to mutton-birds on Mount Pitt, Norfolk Island; and *to oval*, "a term in use among the convicts which means to bend the round ring of the ankle fetter so that the heel can be drawn through it".

No review of Norfolk Island convict cant could omit reference to *the Ring*. According to R. P. Stewart, "A Report on Norfolk Island" (1846), this *Ring* was a part of the island where the worst criminals collected. These convicts terrorized their more timid fellows, exacting tribute from

---

[15] J.W., "Perils, Pleasures and Pastimes" (1849). The term is probably derived from a much earlier English use for an inhabitant of Norfolk, England, in this case being associated with dumpling (the food).

[16] Ernestine Hill, "My Love Must Wait" (1941), refers twice to mutton-birds as *Mr Pitt birds*.

them. Marcus Clarke describes *the Ring* as "some forty of the oldest and worst prisoners" on the island. The term is of particular interest, since it preceded the U.S. underworld use of *ring* for a criminal clique (a sense which emerged about 1872). Although it is uncertain whether there is any direct connection between the organizations, D. Collins refers in his "Account of N.S.W."[17] to "The Fraternal Society of Norfolk Island", an anti-government body which the convicts formed among themselves. From this *the Ring* may have developed.

Norfolk convicts also gave us *slant*, a deliberate offence committed by a convict in order to obtain a trial in Hobart or Sydney. It may have come from the English dialectal *slant*, a lie, and probably influenced our later use of *slinter* and *slanter*, a trick or ruse.

Another term we may have inherited from the convicts is *cockatoo* for a person who stands guard as lookout. These days, we also call him a *nitkeeper* and say he is *on the blink* and *keeping yow*. Cunningham records that it was "a common trick [of certain gangs] to station a sentinel on a commanding eminence to give the alarm, while all the others divert themselves or go to sleep. Such are known here by the name of *cockatoo gangs* from following the example of that wary bird."

Worthy of note also were *bolter* for a runaway convict or an absconding assigned servant; *Government stroke*, defined as "a lazy method of working" adopted by the convicts, which has now become a well-accredited term in Australia, especially when applied to Civil Servants; *clearing gang*, a group of assigned convicts engaged in clearing land; *hut-keeper*, an assigned man who occupied and cared for a hut on cleared land (whence *to hut keep* and *hut-keeping*); and *crawler*, which first came into use as a pejorative in convict days, considerably before it was used in English slang for a sycophant or toady.

In "Ralph Rashleigh" (1845) we are told that a *crawler* was a convict who escaped from his gang in collusion with the overseer and, after a period of freedom, allowed himself to be recaptured by the overseer, so that, in exchange for his brief liberty the latter would receive a reward. Rashleigh also uses the expression to describe a malingering convict.[18]

No review of the period would be complete without an allusion to those scurrilous papers, lampooning high officials and other prominent figures in the early settlement, known as *pipes*. These papers (of which the Mitchell Library, Sydney, has a collection of manuscript and printed copies) were left in places where they would fall into public hands as well

---

[17] An entry under the date July, 1798.

[18] Subsequent Australian uses of the term have been varied. Briefly they are: (a) A term of contempt for a person: 1847, A. Harris, "Settlers and Convicts". (b) A shepherd (many of these were ex-convicts): 1852, "Emigrant in Australia". The writer adds that the term was "one of the most opprobrious in the colonial vocabulary". (c) A sheep: 1847, J. Sidney, "A Voice from the Far Interior". (d) Slow cattle or cows of peaceable habits: 1853, "Letters from Victoria Pioneers". (e) Slow or timid horses: 1863, E. M. Curr, "Pure Saddle Horses". (f) A lazy cattle dog or sheep dog: April 1, 1899, "The Bulletin". (g) A sheep farmer or squatter: 1896, H. Lawson, "While the Billy Boils".

In his "Voyage of the Beagle" (1845), Charles Darwin gives the definition: "A *crawler* is an assigned convict who runs away and lives how he can, by labour and by petty theft."

as into the hands of those they criticized. It was symptomatic of the times that the first *pipe* was circulated in 1803 against Governor King whose efforts to prevent the sale of rum had met with general hostility. Those were the days when liquor was dear to almost every man's heart – rip-roaring brutal days when almost the only escape from the monotony and crudity of colonial life lay in a few simple directions of which alcohol was the most available. "The whole study of both sexes is drinking, gambling and whoring", declared a writer in 1836. (See Chapter XI.)

Strong drink gave Australia such notable expressions as *rum currency* (see the earlier comments on *currency*); *rum traffic*, trade in spirits in Australia's early years; *rum rebellion*, January 26, 1808, when Governor Bligh was deposed; and *rum hospital*, a hospital built in Macquarie Street, Sydney, by Riley, Blaxcell and Wentworth in exchange for the right to import 45,000 gallons of rum and dispose of it in three years. However, authorities say that the New South Wales Corps was never known as the *Rum Corps* or the *Rum Puncheon Corps*.

Several convict groups have earned names which are still remembered:
Scottish Martyrs, five men sentenced to transportation to Australia at sedition trials in Scotland in 1793-4.

Tolpuddle Martyrs, six men from the village of Tolpuddle, Dorsetshire, transported in 1834 for having administered "unlawful oaths" to members of a newly formed agricultural workers' union.

Canadian Exiles, 149 political prisoners from Canada, deported to N.S.W. and Tasmania in 1839.

Irish Exiles, name given to three groups of Irish political prisoners sent to Australia – in 1800-6 (to N.S.W.), in 1848-50 (to Tasmania) and in 1867 (to W.A.).

2. BUSHRANGERS

ALTHOUGH MUCH of his history relates to post-convict days, the *bushranger* and his profession grew out of our formative period and his story is best told here. To those who see bushrangers as a succession of Ned Kellys wearing cast-iron headgear, it will be well to add a reminder that our original bushrangers did not choose their way of life because they were lured by adventure. They were convicts who had escaped from their prisons or gangs. The sole avenue of freedom open to them was the Australian bush in which only an Aboriginal could maintain life. Robbery from outlying settlements and homesteads was a result. That they added murder, rape and arson to their catalogue of crimes was almost inevitable once they had become outlaws.

The first use in print of the word *bushranger* occurs in the "Sydney Gazette" of February 17, 1805, but the term had been adumbrated in a letter by George Suttor to Sir Joseph Banks[19] in which he remarked:

---

[19] Dated March 10, 1804, in Bladen's "Historical Records of New South Wales".

"Surely it cannot be said that the country is in safety while the most abandoned [convicts] have permission *to range* the country at large."

The Tasmanian bandit, Mike Howe, who was killed in October, 1818, styled himself "Governor of the *Rangers*". Like *rangers*, other synonyms emerged – *croppies* (1845)[20], *white Indians* (1878)[21] and *stickers-up* (1879). *Demon* was once used for an old hand at the game.

As we will see in the next chapter, *squatter* has undergone a notable transformation over the years. So, too, apparently with *bushranger*, for after Hume and Hovell's journey to Port Phillip in 1824, the "Australian" was moved to comment that "Mr Hovell lacks all the qualities befitting a bushranger". Presumably, this was equivalent to the modern use of *bushman* as one skilled in *bushcraft*.

From its use to describe a renegade convict, *bushranger* soon acquired the specified meaning by which it became known. But that has not been all. For many generations, it has been applied opprobriously to anyone who takes advantage of others (e.g. *political bushrangery*) or robs them cold-bloodedly in business deals. In "New Zealand Slang" (1940) I pointed out that *beachcomber* was recorded in N.Z. in 1844, but that there had been a still earlier form of the word, *beach ranger* (1827), which was almost certainly formed on the Australian use of *bushranger*. The derivative *bushranging* (1823) is, of course, worthy of special note.

Although the most colourful days in bushranging history were those which followed the discovery of gold in 1851, numerous terms connected with highway robbery came into use considerably earlier. *Bail up*, meaning to hold up and rob a traveller or party of travellers on the road, was current in the early 1840s, and by 1850 had acquired extended colloquial uses. In "Melbourne as I Saw It"[22] we find a person being *bailed up* by thieves and prostitutes in the city streets, and in Henry Kingsley's "Geoffrey Hamlyn" (1859) an allusion is made to Thermopylae where the Greeks "got *bailed up* among the rocks".[23]

There has been some dispute, notably by the "Oxford Dictionary", as to whether the bushranging use of *bail up* is connected in any way with its application to the *bailing up* of cows. "Webster's Dictionary" of 1898 notes, however: "In some English dialects *bail up!* in the sense of *stand still!* is used as a command to cows at milking time. It was adopted by Australian bushrangers as a command to travellers whom they wished to detain on the highway for the purpose of robbing them . . . From this use the more general senses are easily derived."

---

20 Noted in "Ralph Rashleigh". It doubtlessly came from the English slang *croppie*, "one who had his hair cropped in prison" and the earlier use for an Irish rebel of 1798 when "sympathy with the Irish revolutionaries was shown by close-cut hair".

21 This appears to be a Boldrewood invention. He uses it in his "Ups and Downs" (1878). He also describes tracks left by Aborigines as *Indian sign*. It may be noted that our earliest records of Australia and New Zealand contain many references to the natives of both countries as *Indians*.

22 By A Minister, *circa* 1850.

23 J. C. Hotten's "Slang Dictionary", 1873 edition, listed as Australian the use of *bale up*, "equivalent to our 'shell out'. A demand for instantaneous payment".

An interesting comment on the term appears in Boldrewood's "Robbery Under Arms"[24] when a character says:

> The same talk for cows and Christians! That's how things get stuck into the talk in a new country. Some old hand like father, as had spent all his mornings in the cowyard, had taken to the bush and tried his hand at sticking up people. When they came near enough, of course, he'd pop out from behind a tree or a rock with his old musket or a pair of pistols, and when he wanted them to stop, "Bail up, d—— yer!" would come a deal quicker and more natural-like to his tongue than "Stand!" So "Bail up!" it was from that day to this and there'll have to be a deal of change in the ways of the colonies and them as come from 'em before anything else takes its place between the man that's got the arms and the man that's got the money.

This quotation introduces us to *sticking up*, which was derived from an earlier verbal use of *stick up*, to hold up and rob a person, also current in the early 1840s, and first brought into popular use by bushrangers.

In many ways Boldrewood's "Robbery Under Arms" serves as our first handbook of bushranging. It is something more, too. It uses our idiom. We have no feeling that the characters are exiled Englishmen pining for the northern hemisphere. In the adaptation of the Australian scene for the purposes of fiction and in the use of Australian expressions, Boldrewood set the cornerstone of what has since become an indigenous literature.

Here are some of the bushranging and stock-stealing terms Boldrewood employs: *bush telegraphs*, confederates of bushrangers who warned them of police movements; *traps*, mounted police; *stuck up*, held up and robbed; *to take to the bush* and *to turn out*, to become a bushranger; *cattle duffing* and *horse duffing*, the stealing of cattle and horses; *clearskin*, an unbranded animal; *cross beasts*, stolen stock; *duffing yard*, a corral in the bush where stolen stock were yarded and their brands altered; *dart*, a plan, scheme or dodge; *cattle duffer*, a cattle thief; a *plant*,[25] a place where stolen stock is hidden, and *to spring a plant*, to reveal the hiding place of stolen stock; *derry*,[26] the hue and cry of police pursuit; *cattle racket*,[27] the public outcry

---

[24] First published as a serial in the Sydney "Mail" in 1881; issued in book form in 1888.

[25] *To plant*, to conceal, hide, was in old English cant. Both it and *spring a plant* were listed by Vaux. In 1845 ("Chambers' Miscellany", Part I) a writer alludes to *planting* as "the colonial expression", and it is safe to say that – as a result of stock-stealing activities in Australia – all these terms have been more used in this country than elsewhere. W. Kelly, "Life in Victoria" (1859), notes: "*Planting* is a branch of colonial horse-traffic, which consists in first stealing a horse, and, as soon as the reward for his recovery is offered, planting or placing him in a place where the thief pretends to have found him."

[26] Boldrewood uses the term in the following contexts: "When the derry was off", "till the derry's off" and "when all the derry was over". The term possibly comes from English dialect *deraye*, confusion, noise, through its link with hue and cry. Subsequently *derry* became synonymous with "a *down on* or dislike for a person" (it is used in that sense in the "Bulletin" 1902) and its earlier connotation was lost.

[27] A. Harris, "Settlers and Convicts" (1847), defines the expression as "the agitation of society which took place when some wholesale system of plunder in cattle was brought to light". The same author in "The Emigrant Family" (1849) notes that the origin was "generally the discovery of some wholesale aggression on cattle . . . [and] as an immediate consequence a universal suspicion of all parties who seem to have acquired large herds, or the reputation of possessing large herds, in a short period".

raised as the result of the large-scale stealing of stock; and *logs*, a jail.[28]

The *bush telegraphs* noted a little earlier had a special reason for earning a fixed place in Australian speech. More accurately, there were two reasons. One was the encouragement given to bushranging by the large-scale discoveries of gold in the early 1850s. The other was the coincidental development of telegraph services; the first telegraph line in Australia was established in 1854. Hence the rapid spread of such terms as *bush telegrams*, *bush wires* and *mulga wires* as figurative sources of information received by bushrangers. Much later, we were to hear of the *bush wireless* and *bush radio* or *bush mail*.

One important old term which Boldrewood does not use in "Robbery Under Arms" is *gully-raker*, a cattle thief, especially a thief who combs wild country and steals unbranded stock. It was current before 1847. In his English "Slang Dictionary" of 1873, Hotten gives it the following definition: "Cattle thieves in Australia, the cattle being stolen out of almost inaccessible valleys, there termed gulleys." The expression has also had wide use for a stockwhip; in 1848 one writer on Australia gives *gully-raking* for the wielding of a stockwhip.

Other terms employed by stock-stealers during various phases of Australian history have been: *fryingpan brand*, a large brand used by cattle thieves to cover the rightful owner's brand (1857); *dunneker*, a cattle thief (from English cant, *dunnock*, a cow); *nuggeting* and *poddy dodging*, the stealing of unbranded calves; *scrub-running*, the combing of wild country for stock to steal; and *to pluck a brand*, to fake a new brand on stolen cattle or horses by pulling out the hairs round the existing brand.

It was to describe the altering of stock-brands that the old English slang word *duff*, to fake old clothes as new, was introduced into Australia. Its wide use in this country has served to change the meaning considerably, so that when we speak of a *cattle duffer* today we generally mean a cattle-thief, rather than a person who merely fakes brands.

---

[28] The convict use has been noted.

C

CHAPTER III

The Soil

1. SQUATTING: OLD AND NEW

ALTHOUGH THE WORD *squatter* arrived in this country via America, it is one of the many imported terms to which Australia has given a strongly individual meaning. It is doubtful whether it ever had the strict U.S. sense in this country. In America its sole use was for a settler having no legal right to the land he occupied. In Australia our original *squatters* not only took possession of land to which they had no title, but indulged in a number of other illegal activities. Charles Darwin in his "Voyage of the Beagle" (1845) gives the definition:

A squatter is a freed or ticket-of-leave man, who builds a hut with bark on unoccupied ground, buys or steals a few animals, sells spirits without a licence, receives stolen goods – and so at last becomes rich and turns farmer; he is the horror of all his honest neighbours.

A similar description was given in 1835 by a witness before the Legislative Council Committee on Police. He said that *squatters* were "almost invariably the instigators and promoters of crime, receivers of stolen property, illegal vendors of spirits and harbourers of runaway bushrangers and vagrants." Two years later, we find James Macarthur saying that *squatters* were responsible for "an extensive system of depredation upon the flocks, herds and property of established settlers."

We can measure the disapproval with which the *squatter* was once regarded by the fact that until well into the 1840s the term was accepted as one of considerable disrespect.[1] In 1840, for instance, the Governor of New South Wales (Sir George Gipps) is found protesting that *squatter* is "hardly a proper word" by which to describe the occupier of 10,000 acres.

The definition given by T. H. Braim in his "History of New South Wales" (1846) lends colour to the story. Squatters, he said, were "ticket-of-leave holders or freed men who erected a hut on waste land . . . or on the outskirts of an estate . . . and immediately became a nuisance to the district".

Perhaps the most forceful description of all is given in a pamphlet issued by the South Australian Company about 1839 in which reference is made to "the mere squatter . . . content to lead a savage life in the wilds,

---

[1] Apparently, our original *squatters* were not always regarded with contempt, however. The "Australian Encyclopaedia" (1958) records a lone case in which authority was given for a *squatter* to settle on public land. However, S. H. Roberts reports in "The Squatting Age in Australia" (1935) that, by the mid-1830s, "the term was universally used as one of opprobrium".

remote from the decencies of society, with no company but his felon dependents".

Even in 1851, J. F. L. Foster ("New Colony of Victoria") is calling the word "a barbarous appellation" and in 1852 S. Mossman ("Gold Regions of Australia") declares that, "Stockholders, *erroneously named squatters*, are in this district [i.e. Queensland] a very superior class of men and are considered the aristocracy of the colony."

Some substantial changes have been wrought in the use of the word since those days. In 1903, Tom Collins wrote in "Such Is Life": "We use the term squatter indifferently to denote a station owner, a managing partner or a salaried manager." Today, its use for a large landowner is well established.

There have been numerous derivatives, some ephemeral, others enduring. In common Australian use have been *squatterdom*, descriptive of the squatter class in general; *squattocracy* (1846),[2] *squattocratic* and *squatterarchy*. The verbal noun *squatting*, pertaining originally to the activities of a squatter in the derogatory sense of that word, dates from 1826, and *squattage* the holding occupied by a squatter, from 1852.

By the end of the 1940s, *squatter* was being edged out of use by *pastoralist* and *grazier*. Although these uses were adumbrated in orthodox English, their Australian senses were new. In English usage, the "Oxford Dictionary" tells us, *pastoral* applies to shepherds and to the use of land for pasture, while a *grazier* is one who feeds cattle for market. By contrast, Australia's *pastoral industry* or *pastoral production* not only covers sheep, but horses, beef and dairy cattle, pigs, meat of all descriptions, tallow, furred skins, etc. (cf. Commonwealth "Year Book"), while a *grazier* not only feeds and breeds cattle for market, but raises sheep for their wool and/or meat. Our uses of *pastoral lease*, *pastoral tenure*, *pastoral permit*, *pastoral worker*, *pastoralism*, etc. are also Australian originals.

Squatter is by no means the only well-entrenched Australian word to decline in use. In much the same way, we are (temporarily, at least) dispensing with *run*, while firmly retaining *station* for a large holding and using *property* for a small holding. These terms are given detailed attention in the next Section.

At a quite early stage in our history, the squatter's anxiety to accumulate vast holdings of land gave currency in Australia to a special adjective of disapproval – *hungry*. At a later stage in this book, for example, mention will be made of a man called *Hungry Tyson*. The hunger was primarily for land.

Until the 1840s, as their areas of activity became ever wider, the squatters fought (against each other and against the virtually defenceless Aborigines) to possess land. They succeeded so well in eliminating small landholders that the cry *Unlock the lands!* became the tag for one of

---

[2] I. L. Bird, "Australia Felix" (1877) alludes to the *squatter aristocracy*, which was possibly the origin of this portmanteau word. Doubtless it was the "aristocratic" theme which was behind the use of *Government house* for the homestead of a head station. The spoiled sons of these "aristocrats" were called *greenhides*.

Australia's first major movements. In due course, great stretches of land were *unlocked*, but by then many of the squatters had enough wealth to suborn almost any opposition.

The opening up of land brought in its train a peculiar vocabulary of terms, practically all of which are now obsolete. Most of them arose from the activities of big landowners and practices known as *gridironing, peacocking, land dummying* and *dummyism*.

The *gridironer* earned his name because he bought good farming land in strips – after the fashion of a gridiron – so that intervening land was rendered worthless and might be bought at the gridironer's pleasure.[3] The *peacocker* was a man of the same breed: he selected the best portions of a district and left the worthless sections for people with smaller means. The practice was known as *eye-picking;* thus we often find in old books references to farmers *picking the eyes out of the country*, and even today we use the expression *pick the eyes out of* (something) to mean to pick the best. In the Ararat (Victoria) "Advertiser" of June 13, 1865, for instance, it is reported that "sections were taken up and the 'eye picked from the area'." These expressions are apparently derived from reference to the ocelliform markings on a peacock's tail.

Spotting was another synonym for *peacocking*, and the same idea was behind it – that of seizing the best parts of a district.[4] The word *eye* itself became the epitome of all that was choice in the land. In the "Australasian" of June 23, 1865, we find reference to "the great prizes – the allotments which were the *eyes* of the runs."

In their land-hungry operations, the squatters dodged the law by fair means or foul. To which end the *medium* or *dummy* came into existence. Under the law a buyer of land at Crown land auctions (the *free selector;* hence to *free select* and *free selection*) was required to attend in person and to swear that he was selecting land for his own use and benefit. It was here that the *dummy* stepped in, took up – under his own name – land for the unscrupulous person who was paying him, committed perjury and edged the small landseeker out. In the Ararat "Advertiser" we find several classes of *dummy* described, notably the *substantial dummy*, the *hired dummy*, the *speculative dummy* and the *stringing* (probably this means hoaxing) *dummy*.

The *medium* was usually a person who acted on behalf of a squatter, part of whose land had been offered for sale by the Government at a land lottery. The *medium* took lot-tickets, attended the drawing, and, if his ticket were drawn before his principal's land was gone, selected it and then

---

[3] In their typescript notes (Mitchell Library, Sydney), Stephens and O'Brien note the Australian use of *gridiron railways*: "Those built by private capitalists under a land grant concession; they work on the gridiron principle in taking up their grants so as to gain additional advantage."

[4] In their "State Socialism in New Zealand", Le Rossignol and Stewart say that "*Spotting* consisted in buying small sections of from 20 to 100 acres so as to include all the available creeks, rendering the adjoining ridges secure from purchase owing to lack of water." The authors add that, "*Gridironing* consisted in buying a series of 20-acre sections so surveyed as to leave 19 acres unbought between each two sections bought; and as no one could buy less than 20 acres without going to auction, the alternating 19-acre sections were left to be occupied by the runholder,"

handed it back to the squatter on the payment of an attendance fee. Thus *medium* was more or less a synonym for *dummy*, and the terms *mediumism* and *dummyism* were used to describe the practice. Between 1865 and 1896 many derivatives of *dummy* came into currency, among them *dummy bummer* (1882), *sub-dummies* (1890), *dummy-proof* (1891), *dummy-swindler* (1896) and *dummydom* (1882).

Gradually, however, the small landowner found a place in Australia and this by-no-means trivial achievement led to the development of many new terms. In 1836, the author of "The Fell Tyrant" split up the Australian farming community into four classes, the *swell settler* (also called the *gentleman settler*), the *souge settler* (probably from *soojee*, a Hindustani word used to denote coarse sacking), the *dungaree settler* (sometimes called the *moleskin squatter*) and, poorest of all, the *stringybark settler*. *Dungaree settlers* had apparently been around quite a while; an 1826 author said they were minor farmers who wore dungarees as "their usual clothing". The expression *gebung settler* denoted an old settler; geebungs are partly edible fruits of certain species of Parsoonia. These terms have been forgotten long ago. Not so *cocky*, which we apply to farmers and landowners of all classes today; for example, *cow cocky*, *cherry cocky*, *fruit cocky*, *cane cocky*, *scrub cocky*, depending on their type of production and where they operate.

This word *cocky* originated in an old use of *cockatoo* and *cockatooer* for a small farmer who, according to legend, was "just picking up the grains of a livelihood like cockatoos do maize". *Cockatoo*[5] came into use about 1850 and remained current until the end of the century when *cocky*, which had made its appearance in 1884, took over the running. The form *cockatoo* is not dead yet, however. As recently as 1941 Oliver Duff used it in his "New Zealand Now".

Related terms which are encountered frequently in Australian writings at the latter end of last century are *cockatoo settler* (1869), *cockatoo farmer* and *cockatoo squatter* (1873) and *cockatoo selector* (1893). A. J. Vogan in "Black Police" (1890) even introduces us to *Mrs Cockatoo* and *Mrs Cockatoo Squatter*. The verbal noun *cockatooing* also occurs frequently in old commentaries on our rural life.

Cockatoo's weather,[6] i.e. "fine by day and rain by night, or sometimes fine all the week and wet on Sunday", and *cockatoo fence*, for a crude boundary fence of a small farm made of axed branches resting on uprights, can also be noted. A writer in the "Bulletin" of September 3, 1903, says that he heard *cockatoo fence* in Australian use in 1858 and adds: "The cockatoo fence came first, then the cockatoo – named after his fence." This may be correct, but evidence is to the contrary.

Derivatives of *cocky* include *cockydom*, small farmers collectively (1906); *cockying*, farming (1907); *cocky's clip*, "in rural slang a cocky's clip is given to a sheep when practically every vestige of wool is removed by a shearer"; *cocky chaff*, particles of straw thrown out by a mechanical winnower or

---

[5] Tradition says that an alternative form was *ground parrot*, also used for a small farmer.

[6] Listed by Acland in his "Sheep Station Glossary".

harvester; *cocky's coal*, corncobs used as fuel for a fire; *cocky's crow*, dawn or before dawn (a play on "cock crow"); *cocky's joy*, treacle (later, especially in Queensland, rum); *cocky's string*, fencing wire; and *boss cocky*, which is used almost as often in the city today for a leader or industrial organizer as for a farmer or major landowner.

Since they have a great deal to do with our pastoral industries, mention should be made here of the *broad-brimmer* as city folk often call a *pastoralist* or *cocky* these days because of the broad-brimmed hat he wears as protection against the sun; *tank*, a water-storage dam on a station (the first was reputedly dug for Thomas Rose, N.S.W., in 1825); *turkey's nest tank*, a circular retaining wall raised to impound water; *cess*, earth removed from a sunken tank and placed in a wall round the excavation (also known by the more orthodox word *berm*); *receiving tank*, a large iron tank, with a capacity of up to 25,000 gallons, into which water is pumped for subsequent drawing off into a stock-watering trough; *tank-sinker*, a worker who excavates a tank; *bore*, a pipe driven to tap artesian water (such water was first discovered in Australia in 1878 at Kallara station, N.S.W.; the biggest of our artesian *basins*, known as the *Great Australian Basin*, is the largest in the world – which is perhaps just as well since this is the world's driest continent), and such derivatives as *bore-channel, bore-drain, bore-sinker, bore-water; super*, a shortening of "superphosphate", an artificial manure widely used for pasture improvement; and *waterbag*, a canvas container for water (in its original form a *waterbag* was "a bag of skin or leather used for holding or carrying water, especially one used in Eastern countries for transporting and distributing water" – the quotation is from the "Oxford Dictionary"), the Australian contribution being the use of canvas in the waterbag's manufacture.

2. THE BACKBLOCKS

COLOURFUL though it may sound, *Great Outback* leaves too much to be taken for granted. We have many synonyms to give us richer pictures of our vast inland country. At the end of last century when the "Bulletin" was at the peak of its influence, the violently pro-Australian writers who filled its pages with bush and outback lore strove to outdo each other in the propagation of terms for the inland.

Here are some of their best offerings: *back-o'-beyond* (the form *back-of-beyond* is in orthodox English for "any very out of the way place", but the Australian use is much more general than that), *outback, wayback, rightback, back-o'-Bourke* (N.S.W.), *back-o'-outback, beyond outback, behind outback, set-o'-sun, back of sunset, sunset country, death-o'-day, past-west, westest-west,[7] beyond set-o'-sun, right behind death-o'-day, beyond the beyond, right at the rear of back-of-outback*.

These were, in the main, variations on the theme of *backblocks*. The use of *block* for an area of land was applied originally in the 1850s to districts

---

[7] For reasons explored in Chapter I, the allusions in *past-west* and *westest-west* were to remote areas in Central Australia, not to W.A.

which the Government had split up for settlement, when lands were *unlocked*. Today, we have blocks varying in size from a few acres to 1,000 square miles or more, but they are still known as *blocks*.

A *backblock* was originally more or less what it purported to be – a block or section of land in a remote part of a sheep or cattle station. But as these *backblocks* were populated the term came to denote inland country in general. By 1878 Boldrewood was using it in "Ups and Downs", and derivatives such as *backblocker* and *backblockser*, for a person who hailed from the wayback country, were putting down their roots. In 1879 the Sydney "Telegraph" gave us "drawing-room *backblockers*" and in 1963 the same paper referred to the people of Alice Springs, N.T., as *outbackers*. Today, the occupier of an irrigation block on the Murray River is quite naturally called a *blocker*.

These by no means exhaust the terms for our country or parts of it. The *mallee*, the *mulga*, the *big scrub*, the *brigalow* and the *Channel country* contain stories in themselves; so do the *Overland*, the *black north*, the *back door*,[8] the *Top End* and those long-established expressions, *never never, never land, never country, the Centre, Red Centre, Dead Heart*. Henry Lawson[9] weighs in with such additional terms for our remote inland as *No Man's Land*, the *No More* and *Nevermore*. Even the roundabout description *Land of Sin, Sweat and Sorrow*[10] is extremely old. *Land of Wait*[11] is a reference to inland Queensland. These, however, are mainly blanket terms that are colourful rather than specific, although we will see later that some have reasonably precise uses. During a visit to Australia, Mark Twain was taken by the expression *never never country*, and recorded that the comment "She lives in the Never Never Country" meant that "the lady alluded to is an Old Maid".

Something more detailed is apparent in the following: *Bay of Biscay* or *Bay o' Biscay country*, country with a surface of alternate hillocks and hollows, also called *dead men's graves* (all these expressions are apparently mainly used in S.A.); *debil debil* or *devil devil country*, pitted country, especially land pocked by bilbies, which are rabbit-bandicoots, long-eared burrowing marsupials, hence *bilby country* (expressions mainly used in Queensland and the N.T.); *crabhole country*, country hazardous to horsemen because it has been undermined by the digging activities of several members of the freshwater crayfish family Parastacidae (mainly used in Victoria and northern Tasmania); *gilgai country*, a name used by soil specialists to cover all of the foregoing; *melon hole*, a shallow hole in open country which the paddymelon wallaby is alleged to make; *bunyip hole*, any muddy depression in the outback; *mickery country*, country which holds moisture after rain (*mickeries* are specifically soakages in the sandy beds of inland rivers; they

---

8 "The forgotten lands that border the state [inland border] corners." – I. L. Idriess, "The Great Boomerang" (1941).

9 "In the Days When the World Was Wide" (1896).

10 Kenneth Mackay, "Out Back" (1893).

11 "Current Affairs Bulletin", vol. 34, no. 6, 1964, comments: " . . . minority whites, seeing themselves as neglected dwellers in a 'Land of Wait', despair of even the simplest provisions of the distant city-civilisation . . ."

are often shallow, but carry good water for stock); *soak country*, as for *mickery country*; *drummy country*, rough limestone country which sounds hollow when ridden across; *red country*, country with reddish soil and/or enclosed by red-coloured cliffs (the *Red Centre* was noted earlier); *gibber country*, country covered with stones or *gibbers* (the "g" is hard); *black soil plains*, country with black soil; *black spring*, "a narrow hill, rising out of some rich, dark soil"[12]; *blind country*, closed-in country of colourless type and of little worth; *buck-shot country*, "soil, generally poor in phosphates, containing sperules of pisolitic ironstone"; *burnt grass country*, areas where there is a rich growth of grass after the district has been burnt off; *fly country* and *sticky fly country*, sections of the inland where the fly pest is particularly bad[13]; *skeleton flats*, flat areas of land where the trees have been ringbarked and are dead; *pindan*, light bush in waterless sand country; *quartz downs*, country in which the topsoil has been blown away from an underlying quartz base; *basins*, open valleys near the tops of hills[14]; *rangy*, mountainous; *jump-up*, a sudden rise in country; *go-down*, a sharp declivity; *jumping sandhills*, sand-dunes that are blown about by the wind in inland deserts; *knife edges*, razor-backed sandhills; *cowal*, a swamp left in a depression of low undulating red country; and *bulldust*, finely powdered dust, often encountered in deep pockets and almost blinding when disturbed.

Although given contradictory definitions, *blows* can be noted here. In an article in the "Victorian Naturalist" for May, 1961, *blows* are reputed to be large sandy spots used for Aboriginal camps. In J. A. Porter's "Roll the Summers Back" (also 1961) they are defined as large granite watersheds at the edge of which Aboriginal *soaks* can be found.

A peculiar use reported from outback Queensland is worth mention. This is the use of *desert* to describe timbered country, in contrast to treeless areas, which are called *downs*. The latter usage is more or less in accord with standard English, but the former is in direct conflict with orthodox use overseas.

Although neither *gully* nor *creek* is Australian in origin, both have been given meanings and applications in this country so wide that it would be almost impossible for us to part with them. As a broad definition, a *gully* from the Australian point of view is "any geographical indentation from a fair-sized drain to a Grand Canyon". In the Kimberleys, gullies formed

---

[12] Recorded in 1848 by H. W. Haygarth, "Bush Life in Australia", but apparently long-since obsolete.

[13] "It seems an unfortunate habit of Australians," remarked Judge Sheridan in Sydney in 1937, "to speak through their teeth as if they came from the *fly country*, afraid to open their mouths for fear of flies." See Chapter XXII.

[14] "All the highest tops of a run are sometimes called the *basins*." – Acland, "Sheep Station Glossary". The word *run* provides a particularly good example of Acland's linguistic labours, based on his experience as a sheep farmer in New Zealand. Here are some of the many senses he records for the word: Country held under a particular lease or pastoral licence; a group of *runs* held by one owner or in one station, the whole area being described as a *run*; leasehold as opposed to freehold farmland; open as opposed to fenced country – "out on the *run*", i.e., not in an enclosed paddock; a division of a *run*, e.g., *ewe run, upper run*; as an adjective, *run sheep, run cattle* as opposed to paddock-sheep or milking cows and hand-reared calves; as a verb, to send (a dog), and to work (used of a young dog: "That dog is just beginning to *run*").

by erosion are called *breakaways*. *Gut, guts* or *shoot (chute?)* denotes a narrow, newly formed watercourse or gully with steep sides. Our use of *creek* is just as wide. Both terms have been in Australian use since the 1790s and are commemorated in scores of place-names. J. S. Farmer states in his "Dictionary of Americanisms" (1889) that the U.S. use of *creek* was – until that time anyway – confined to a small stream or brook. The Australian application has always been broader than this. In the outback the word is often rendered *crick* – a dialectal development which we share with the U.S.

The original forms of both *soak* and *waterhole*, which have been current in Australia for many generations, are to be found in English dialect and represent a small part of the great debt we owe to provincial forms of the language. Since water (or the lack of it) is one of Australia's enduring problems, we should pause a moment to examine several indigenous terms: *anabranch*, a branch of a river which flows round an island before rejoining the main river, *billabong*, a waterhole in the bed of a river or creek which flows only after heavy rain (I will examine its derivation later), *pool*, a reach of a river or any waterhole.

Now we come to some problems upon which the modern reader would possibly welcome enlightenment. "How is it," asked a correspondent in a Sydney journal in 1906, "if a person leaves the coast to go *in*land, they say he is going *out*back, and when he reaches the very *in*terior, he's right *outside*?" That question has probably puzzled many people, but it is worked out like this: If you are far inland you are on the outer rim of civilization, you are *outback, outbush*[15] – you are, in short, right outside, and the farther inland you go the more *outside* your surroundings become. When a man from the far interior comes to the city he says that he is coming *inside*. From the bushman's point of view an *inside* area is one that is well populated and long settled, but as far as he is concerned the real *inside* is the city. Thus an *inside squatter* is a large landowner nearer to a large centre of population than an *outside squatter*, and there is similar distinction between *inside country* and *outside country*. The city man is inclined to forget that these were originally bush terms and that they represent the bushman's attitude. When we come across the use of *outsider* for a squatter living in far inland areas, in E. B. Kennedy's "Four Years in Queensland" (1870), it is not meant slightingly, but as a statement of fact from a bushman's viewpoint.

Our uses of *up* and *down* also need explanation. One always goes *up the bush* when one goes inland; and one goes *down to the city* when the journey is in the other direction. Indeed, *up the bush* has become synonymous with outback or inland. Thus the Sydney "Telegraph" of February 1, 1940, asked in a leader: "Canberra – a small town up the bush, or the National Capital?" The clue to this is to remember that, since these terms were originally used by bush dwellers, they regarded *up* as going towards home and *down* as going away from it. When Australian settlers crossed the Tasman to Canterbury, N.Z., they spoke of going *down* (not "over") to

---

[15] This term is not heard often, in spite of the fact that Mrs Aeneas Gunn uses it nearly fifty times in "We of the Never Never" (1907).

New Zealand. Lawson gives "*down* in Maoriland" and "*down* on Auckland gum-fields" in "While the Billy Boils".

Both *station* and *run* have acquired highly important indigenous meanings in Australia. The former is distinctively our own and came into currency in the early 1820s. In Hovell and Hume's "Journey of Discovery to Port Phillip" under the date October 13, 1824, the entry reads: "Arrive at Mr. Hume's *station* about one in the afternoon". *Stock station* emerged in 1826 and thereafter came a flood of derivatives: *heifer station* (1845), *head station* (1848), *home station* (1853), *out-station* (1846) and *outstationed* (1853), *outside station* (1878), *back station* (1890), *station black*, an Aboriginal, *station super*, a manager, *station mark*, a brand, *station-bred* (*stock*), stock bred on a station, and *station jack*, the name given to a kind of meat pudding made by mixing a pastry and then adding chopped beef, after which it is boiled.

Run, which was anticipated in orthodox English, but has always been chiefly Australian, made its first appearance here in 1804 and soon developed the forms *stockrun* (1825), *back-run* (1826) and *sheep-run* (1826). For a brief period in the 1820s the terms *location*, a land grant, and *to locate*, to make a farmer a grant of land, had some currency, but they were soon forgotten.

In numerous cases we have seen how Australia took old English words and remodelled their meanings to suit her own requirements. One of them is *property*, used in Australia to denote a farm holding; its area is certainly smaller than a *station*, but just at exactly what point a *property* can be classed as a *station* is obscure. Another good example is *paddock* which was in use in sixteenth century England for a small field or meadow. In Australia there is no limit to the size of a *paddock*: it may be one acre or 60,000 acres, but it is a paddock as long as it is enclosed by a fence. We have also made a useful verb out of it: *to paddock land*, to fence it; *to paddock sheep*, to place them in a fenced pasture. Combined forms worth noting are: *accommodation paddock*, a field near a rural hotel where stock may be pastured overnight; *bush paddock*, an area of bush-covered land used as a source of firewood by a farmer; *cultivation paddock*, a field used for raising grain and vegetables (1853); *wheat paddock*, often a vast field in which wheat is grown, *branding paddock*, a slang term used by soldiers for a parade ground (1919); *heifer paddock*, a school for girls (1885); *saddling paddock*, a suitable alfresco site for amorous dalliance (1898).

Although England was using the word *homestead* long before Australia was colonised, and although America went so far as to have a Homestead Act in 1862, this was another term that Australia shaped to her own needs. Its original connotations were a dwelling place on a farm or a small farm itself. But if, once again, we turn to the Australian "Year Book" we will find a distinction made between *grazing farms* and *grazing homesteads*, between *agricultural farms* and *agricultural homesteads;* in addition, we will find used such distinct terms as *homestead farms*, *homestead selections* and *homestead grants*, all of which apply to areas taken up and occupied under lease or licence under various Land Acts.

Perhaps this is as good a place as any to note that Australia has developed such indigenous combinations as *scrub lease, snow lease, prickly pear lease* and *prickly pear selection, closer settlement* and *soldier settlement*, the last two referring to farm grants for the benefit of men discharged from the Services.

On the subject of fences, the Australian contributions are well worth listing. Here are some of the more notable, most of which are self-explanatory: *deadwood fence* (1844), *dog-leg* or *dog-legged fence* (1854), *kangaroo fence* (1854), *chock-and-log fence* (1872), *rough-and-tumble fence* (1875) and *cockatoo fence* (1884), the last – as already noted – being used for a fence on a small farmer's property, and (at least in the past) often of makeshift construction. A worker is said to *dummy* a fence when he puts in new posts alongside the old ones; hence *dummies* or *dummy posts* for such new posts. A *dropper* is a batten stapled to fence wires to keep them apart.

The *sliprail* should not be forgotten. This term has well over a century of applied history in Australia. *Drop rails*, rails used in making a wooden gate which has no hinges, and *hurdle gate*, a five-barred gate made of split wood, were both recorded in 1826. *Rider* is a synonym for *sliprail*.

The *swing-gate* is more important than these, for, like the *stump-jump plough* (or *stump-jumping plough*), it is an Australian invention of inestimable worth to the farmer. The *swing-gate* was invented by Lockhart Morton to facilitate sheep-drafting in yards, and has been described as "the most important pastoral invention except the shearing machine". The *stump-jump plough* is used for ploughing rough partly-timbered land; it was invented by R. B. and C. H. Smith, of Ardrossan, S.A., registered in 1877, but not patented; it served a crucial part in cultivating the mallee lands of Victoria and S.A.

Although the name *Mallee gate* sounds important it denotes just about the meanest gate of all – a short, loose panel in a fence consisting of little more than droppers and wires. It probably has countless names, e.g. *Mullengudgery gate* and *Bogan gate*. (*Bogan Gate* is a place name in N.S.W. and Mullengudgery is in the district.)

3. WORKERS

IN THE LATE 1840s when *colonial experience* meant finding one's feet in the new land of the south, many names were developed to describe rural workers of all types.

One of the first was *jackeroo*, used originally to describe a young Englishman learning sheep or cattle farming; he was a *colonial experiencer*, a *new chum*, a *cadet* and, later, an *archie*, who usually bought his knowledge with a premium. Sometimes he was employed on the basis of *even terms*, which meant working for his keep.

As the London "Times" once suggested, *jackeroo* was practically the equivalent of tenderfoot, but it is more generally applied to a youth who gains experience on an outback *property*, usually to prepare for taking up *property* of his own. One theory says that it is derived from a Queensland Aboriginal term *tchaceroo*, used to denote a bird, the shrike, because of its garrulous nature. Other suggestions have been made that it is from *Jack Carew*, the name of a person, *Jacky Raw*, a combination of *Jack* and *kangaroo*, and the Spanish *vaquero*, a herdsman or cowboy. We have made a verb out of jackeroo, and now speak of *jackerooing* (just as we speak of *rouseabouting*), for work as a station-hand. In "Bail Up!" (1908) H. Nisbet uses the unusual form *jackeries* for "favoured station-hands". Although this did not have wide use it is interesting to note that, much earlier—in 1853—a writer had referred to a squatter as a *Jacky Rue*, "as they are called by the Sydneyites".

Much later we were to have the variant *jillaroo*, a female station-hand (the play is on Jack and Jill), especially used during World War II for a Land Girl, but surviving long after the war was over.

Other novelties were *ringneck*, originally applied to new immigrants because of their collar-wearing habits; there was a fancied resemblance to the light-coloured band round the neck of the Ringneck Parakeet; *leatherneck*, a handyman on a station, otherwise called *rouseabout*, *roustabout* (this was the U.S. use for a ship's deckhand), *rouser*, *rousie*, *knockabout*, *blue-tongue* (after the lizard of that name), *spoonbill*, *jack*, *loppy*, *wop wop* and *wood-and-water joey* (sometimes abbreviated to the simple *joey*).

A station manager was formerly known as a *super* or *cove* – both date from before 1850 – or, if in a small way of business, a *pannikin boss*. (Oddly enough, the last expression has survived in Australia and has found a firm niche among city workers.) An overseer is a *packsaddle*. An analogous term is found in old woolshed slang. When shearers work in two rows the outside row is referred to as the *packhorse* side, possibly because it is under closer observation and has to work harder.

Another interesting old term, similarly derived from horses, was *hobbling out*. This was used before World War I in western Queensland to mean being paid off from a station job.

In the Sections which follow, on sheep, cattle, etc., we will encounter many other toilers.

Outback workers were once subject to a number of maladies which acquired localized names. Among them were: *Barcoo rot*, *Kennedy rot* or *Queensland sore*, a festering sore difficult to cure under inland conditions – it rapidly disappeared when the sufferer ate plenty of fruit or green vegetables;[16] *Barcoo spew*, *Barcoo vomit* or *Belyando spew*,[17] a sickness characterized by vomiting after food was taken especially suffered by shearers because of heat, sweating and prolonged bending; *blight* (1826), *sand blight* (1846) and *sandy blight* (1859), a form of ophthalmia in which the eye feels full of sand; *fly blight* (1848), *swelling blight* (1867), *fly-bung* and *bung-eye* (1898), an

---

[16] In South Africa it was called *Veldt sore* and was probably similar to the *Delhi sore* and *Baghdad date*. The sores occurred most frequently on the bridlehand, on which the skin was sometimes broken when a horse, worried by flies, continually jerked at the reins.

[17] The Barcoo, Kennedy and Belyando are outback Queensland districts. *Barcoo challenge*, a shearing expression, also hailed from the first-named district. It was a challenge for the day's best tally among shearers, made (i) by scraping the points of a pair of handshears on the woolshed floor or wall, or (ii) by throwing the belly of a fleece over another shearer's head. *Barcoo buster* is the name given to a westerly gale in outback Queensland – a local variation of *southerly buster*.

eye ailment caused by fly attacks; *Darling Pea,* upon which Stephens and O'Brien offer this comment: "One of Australia's poisonous plants; cattle eating it become afflicted with staggers and die: so a man wandering in gait or dazed in appearance is said to be suffering from Darling Pea"; *Cumberland disease,* name originally given in N.S.W. to anthrax which, beginning about 1859, killed many tens of thousands of sheep as well as cattle and horses; *Yalgogrin disease,* name given to a disease among rabbits caused by inoculations with chicken and cholera virus, applied first on Yalgogrin station, north-west of Wagga, about 1890; *myxomatosis,* a virus disease spread among rabbits in the 1950s.

4. SHEEP

AUSTRALIA is the world's chief wool-growing country. We have a saying about it. Australia, we have said for many generations, is *on the sheep's back.* Even in these days, when our primary and secondary products have become widely diversified, a large part of our social well-being depends on sheep. From about one-sixth of the world's woolled sheep, Australia produces about a third of the world's apparel wool (30 per cent in 1963) and about 55 per cent of the total fine quality Merino wool.

In due course, synthetic fibres will make a dent in our earnings from wool, but we should not forget that our highest earnings ever from wool production were reaped as recently as 1950-1951 – nearly $1,304,000,000. That was less than 150 years since Australia's first commercial export of wool (245 lb.) to England in 1807.

There should be no astonishment if sheep-raising and shearing are found to have been prolific sources of word-making in Australia. Let us begin on the orthodox level by looking at our sheep population. (There was a record of 164,763,000 sheep and lambs in Australia in 1964.) A large percentage of them is *Merino,* but these sheep are so different from the Merinos first introduced into Australia in 1797 that they are virtually a new type of sheep. There are others, the *Polwarth* for instance, which is a fixed breed of *comeback* type (i.e. the progeny of a Merino ram and a cross-bred ewe); it originated in southern Victoria in the 1880s and was officially recognised as a breed in 1919. Another is the *Zenith,* a Merino-Lincoln cross dating from 1947. More important is the *Corriedale,* first evolved in Otago, N.Z., in the 1860s. There are also various hornless breeds: *Poll Merino, Poll Polwarth* and *Poll Dorset.*

In his valuable "Sheep-Station Glossary", L. G. D. Acland offers useful notes on breeding. The expression *halfbred sheep,* he says, was originally applied only to a sheep by a longwool ram from a Merino ewe, but is now loosely applied to the type. He adds that Corriedale sheep were originally called *in-bred half-breeds* and that "now *in-bred halfbred* flocks are those which reintroduce Merino or longwool blood, while the Corriedale flocks can only introduce Corriedale blood".

One of the first things we observe when we look at a sheep station is that the terms *to shear* and *to run* can be equivalents for the verb "to own". "How many sheep have you?" – "I generally *shear* about 10,000" or "The station *runs* about 10,000". The word *shear* can be used in other ways. A prospective buyer of sheep or sheepskins asks "How old are they?" The reply is "so many weeks or months *off-shears*", meaning it is so many weeks or months since they were shorn, which gives the purchaser an idea of the amount of wool carried on the animals or skins. Sheep are *off the shears* when they have just been shorn; they are *shears* or *in the wool* when they are ready for shearing. (The odd expression *lambing off shears* denotes pregnant ewes which are shorn six to two weeks before lambing begins.)

However, before we proceed too far with this examination, we should pause a moment to consider the word *jumbuck*, which Australians widely use to denote a sheep. Writing in 1896, A. Meston, of Brisbane, stated:

> The word *jumbuck* for sheep appears [in Aboriginal speech] as jimba, jombock, dombock and dumbog. In each case it meant the white mist preceding a shower, to which a flock of sheep bore a strong resemblance. It seemed the only thing to which the aboriginal imagination could compare it.

I was prepared to accept this imaginative theory until I noted that Charles Harpur had recorded the Aboriginal use of *junbuc* – or it could be *jimbuc*, for his handwriting is not as good as it might be – in a footnote to his papers in the Mitchell Library. He says that this is:

> An Aboriginal name of a little shag-haired species of Kangaroo peculiar to mountain copses. It may be called the mountain wallaby, being in relation to the wallaroo what the common wallaby is to the Kangaroo proper. The *junbuc* [or *jimbuc*] is the least elegant in its form, and the dullest in its nature, of all the Kangaroo kinds – of all such at least as I happen to be acquainted with. The Blacks of the Hunter call the sheep *junbuc* [or *jimbuc*] no doubt from a resemblance, however remote, arising out of the hairy shagginess of the one and the woolliness of the other . . .

Sundry terms used to denote the ages of sheep merit attention. It hardly needs to be explained that a sheep is a *lamb* until it is weaned, that a male is a *ram lamb* until it is castrated and then becomes a *wether lamb*, and that a female is a *ewe lamb*. However, the picture becomes more complex from this stage on. After weaning, a lamb becomes a *hogget* (*weaner* is used in preference in some Australian States) until it is shorn; thereafter it is known as a *shorn hogget* until the next *drop* (i.e. birth) of lambs have passed through their weaning stage. By this time, the hogget is getting its first two teeth and it is called a *two-tooth*. However, it can be noted that some sheepmen call a hogget a *two-tooth* as soon as it is shorn; this eliminates the use of *shorn hogget* as a description. A year after cutting its first two teeth, a sheep acquires another pair and is then called a *four-tooth*. The following year a third pair of teeth is cut and the sheep becomes a *six-tooth;* a year later, with the advent of its final issue of teeth, the sheep becomes an *eight-tooth* or *full-mouth*. A sheep remains *full-mouthed* so long as its teeth are in good condition, but as they decline it becomes *failing-mouthed*, *broken-mouthed* and, finally, a *gummy*. Acland says:

> Dealers and stock-agents use various terms, such as *chisel-mouthed*, to make failing-mouthed sheep sound younger; but these terms are not in common use by sheepfarmers and shepherds.

When a sheep is considered of poor value because of its advancing years, it is described as *age-cast*. A *cast-for-age* ewe is a ewe about seven years old which is not regarded as satisfactory for good breeding. (*Age-cast* is also applied to a cow which has passed its usefulness for breeding – at about the age of nine years.)

We use the term *join* to mean mate. The sheepman speaks of *joining rams* when rams are run in with ewes; rams are *rung in* when they are separated from ewes at the end of the mating season.

In many parts of Australia, especially in what is known as *fly country*, serious losses are caused by *crutch strike* and *body strike*. The former denotes blowfly maggot infestation in folds of the skin in the breech of ewes. This has been countered by what is known as the *Mules operation*, a technique, originally developed by J. H. W. Mules, for the surgical removal of the skin folds. Maggot infestation also occurs around the anus and is prevalent when tails are docked very short; for this reason, tails are now left about 4 in. long. *Body strike* occurs in wool along the back. Common native blow-flies are responsible for *fly-strike*. Sheep attacked in this way are said to be *fly-struck*. A remedial oil applied to some stricken sheep is called *fly-oil*. Although it is by no means the only blowfly attacking sheep, the insect *Chrysomyia ruffaces* has been responsible for putting the terms *hairy maggot* and *woolly boy* into common use among sheepmen. These terms are applied to the larva of the fly and, in turn, have resulted in the entomologist giving the vernacular name, *hairy maggot blowfly*, to this pest.

Sheep are subject to other ailments. Among them is *loco disease* – a listless, delirious state suffered by sheep which have eaten any of several toxic species of Swainsona, called Darling Pea and found in western N.S.W. Such sheep are said to be *pea-struck*. *Coast disease* and *steely wool* both occur in S.A. and are due to pasture deficiency; the former is due to deficiency of both copper and cobalt, the latter is due to copper deficiency and is marked by lack of lustre and crimp in the fleece. Pasture temporarily unsuitable for carrying sheep is called *sheep sick*. *Pinkeye* is an infectious eye disease (it occurs also in cattle). A sheep is called a *dopey* when it becomes disoriented because of some illness; if it prefers to live alone, it is a *hermit* or *hatter;* if it remains in one place, it is a *placer*, but a sheep which is put on its own because of illness is a *hospital sheep*. Sheep are susceptible to various types of *shock*, especially *shearing shock*, which sometimes occurs when cold nights and heavy rain follow shearing (hence *cold shock* and *rain shock*), and *lambing shock*, when pregnant ewes are shorn just before a drop.

Woolmen use the term *wool-blind* to refer to sheep whose eyes have become covered with long wool (Merinos are common sufferers). In the case of *wool-blindness* the remedy is *to wig, wink* or *eyeclip* the sufferer by cutting wool away from round the sheep's eyes, and these clippings are known as *wiggings*.

Of *smother*, Acland has this to say:

Run sheep, especially Merinos, are very easy to *smother* on broken hill ground. An injudicious turn with a dog in an abrupt gully may stop the lead and cause some sheep to be knocked over. Other sheep make a rush and are brought down, too, so that in a second or two there is a struggling heap; and before the shepherds can pull them off one another the bottom ones are smothered. They smothered 1,200 once on the Stew Point country at Mount Peel [N.Z.] and I believe there was a still worse smother on a station called Roxburgh in Otago. People who fill their woolsheds too tight often smother sheep on a smaller scale, perhaps half a dozen or so in a night.

The word *shepherd*, just used by Acland, was imported from England, but, like many similar borrowings, has not remained unaffected by a change of linguistic climate. In Australia today, *shepherd* (also called a *lizard, crawler, snail, motherer* or *monkey dodger*) is rarely applied to any person other than the employee of a sheep drover; its orthodox use for a man who tends sheep has largely vanished.

However, a little booklet entitled "Our Shepherds", by W. R. Glasson,[18] suggests that all is not yet lost. Here is a group of expressions which Glasson lists – the definitions are also his – in a glossary:

shepherd's broom – A bunch of boxtree or pine twigs, their tips being cut level and all bound tightly around a long handle.

shepherd's call – "Cooee", the call or cry used as a signal by the Australian Aborigines and adopted by the colonists in the bush.

shepherd's harp – A musical instrument, usually played solo and in solitude. The concertina was first favourite; alternatives, mouth-organ, jew's harp, tin whistle.

shepherd's hat – Generally a cabbage-tree, made from the *Livostina australis* palm . . . Some shepherds made a less durable hat from long kangaroo grass. Only a few eccentrics, as a protection against flies, hung corks to the brim of their hats.

shepherd's lamp – Within his hut, at day's close, the slush lamp or the glow of his fire; without, at day's beginning, the morning star.

shepherd's lantern – To make this, a clear glass bottle was turned over a candle flame till hot all round in a straight line near its base. The bottom would crack off when dipped into cold water. A piece of tallow candle would be dropped into the bottle's contracting neck, which served as both socket and handle.

shepherd's mill – Some shepherds . . . were supplied with wheat instead of flour, and this they ground for themselves. The mill was roughly cast and small. The hopper held only about two pounds of grain, and the handle was like that of a grindstone.

shepherd's sundial – A piece of circular bare ground, so marked that a tree or stake in the centre indicated by its shadow the hour of noon.

shepherd's whistle – A signal to the dog. Some could never whistle well; good teeth were helpful. To whistle effectively one shepherd needed only to twist his tongue and adjust his lips; another inserted in his mouth the

---

[18] Published originally in the early 1940s. My copy of the second edition, for which I am indebted to Mr Glasson, is dated 1945.

tips of his little fingers, his bent index finger or even the leaf of a tree, while still another used a little piece of tin folded flat with a small nail hole through the centre.

Although *shepherd*, in its orthodox sense, is now vanishing from the Australian linguistic scene, Glasson is perhaps not altogether astray when he declares: "Surely the best and fullest meaning of the beautiful word *shepherd* is to be found in its Australian use." At least from the historical viewpoint we have put it to good use, and if, in the process, it has acquired some applications it never possessed in Britain, we should regard these rather as testimonials to its service than as evidence of our disdain for it.

Glasson's little book contains some other sheepmen's terms which, although he does not define them separately, are worthy of attention. Among these are: *watch box*, a movable sleeping compartment used by shepherds – "its length was about six feet six inches, width two feet six inches, height four feet"; *fencer's tea*,[19] a weekly ration of ¼ lb. of tea given to shepherds, "because of its absence of leaf and preponderance of *posts and rails*"; *killers*, unwanted sheep that the shepherd could kill for eating – "these were very old ewes, lean and tough"; *runner*, a rail placed on each side of the roof of a bush dwelling to hold it down; *wash pen*, a pool or *hole* in a creek in which sheep were sometimes washed before shearing in old days; *shepherd's cabbage*, stinging nettles, used for cooking and eating.

Also to be noted here is *crow's nest*, an elevated platform usually built in a tree, from which a shepherd could keep an eye on his charges.

A sheep musterer is called a *dog driver; calico* are strips of calico or other cloth used to keep sheep from wandering when they are held in a place during droving – a *Paroo dog*, a rattle made of tins, can perform much the same service; *come off* means to come down from a hill – "At the end of the day musterers *come off* the hill; they do not say they 'descend' or even 'come down' " (Acland); *dozie* is a loose term suggesting poor quality, applied to country where sheep do not thrive or to sheep from such country.

Box, for a mixing of sheep, is well-rooted in our language. It came into use about 1870, but ten years later Boldrewood was using it in "Robbery Under Arms" as equivalent to "confused" or "muddled". Today a person who is in a quandary or confusion is said to be *boxed up;* to confuse or muddle something is *to make a box of it* or even *to box it*, which, of course, goes right back to the original.

In an attempt to relieve the congestion here, I will reserve comments on sheepdogs until Section 7 in which dogs are given the separate attention they merit.

Before we look at the *woolshed*, a few moments should be spent examining some essential pens, yards and chores of a sheep property: *holding pen*, a pen in which sheep are held for various purposes; *crush pen* or

---

[19] In addition to ¼ lb. of tea, the weekly rations, according to Glasson, were: "1½ lb. dark treacly sugar, which the merchants then supplied in cane mats; 1 lb. of coarse salt; 10 lb. of flour – no baking powder; 12 lb. of meat. This was all!" Compare this with the *ten, twelve, two and a quarter* mentioned in Chapter V. There is an 1826 reference to *property* for "provisions and other necessaries" supplied to farm employees.

forcing pen, a small pen close to the narrow, enclosed lane or *race* in a *drafting yard* or *dip yard; dip pen* or *bath pen*, a pen in which sheep are held before dipping – since *sheep showers* are now replacing the dip, the *shower pen* is more likely to be heard of these days, together with its attendant *shower gate, draining pen* and *draining gate; double gate*, two gates from the race in a sheep yard, which allow sheep to be let into any of three pens, so that a mob can be drafted into three lots at once (note the expression, *take the gate*, to draft sheep); *holding paddock* or *camping paddock*, a small paddock close to the yards, woolshed or mustering hut on a sheep station for holding (not feeding) sheep; *shearing paddock*, a paddock near a woolshed in which sheep are held before shearing; *receiving yard*, a large yard into which sheep are driven when they first enter the assorted sheep yards of a station.

Dip yard and *drafting yard* were mentioned above; to them should be added the *cutting and tailing yard* or *marking yard*, both euphemistic allusions to the yard in which lambs are castrated. *To cut*, meaning to castrate, is taken from standard English, and although it is widely used in this sense in Australia, there has been an increasing tendency for it to be replaced by the verb *to mark*, meaning the same thing but apparently more agreeable to the ears of woolmen. A similar motive seems to be behind the use of the verb *to class*. This, of course, appears in the expressions *woolclasser, wool-classing* and *to class wool*, but less well-known is its use, in relation to ewes and rams, to denote a sorting of sheep for mating. In much the same way, *to crutch* and *crutching*, both referring to the chore of cutting away wool round a sheep's tail and hind legs, have acquired other uses. The long, forked pole used for forcing sheep under water in a *dip* is often called a *crutch* and the process is known as *crutching*, although as I noted earlier the *sheepdip* is being displaced by the *sheep shower*, so the days of these uses are numbered.

Here, as reminders (if such reminders are still necessary) that our sheep language covers an extremely wide field, are some general terms:

> *apron*, the neck fold of a Merino ram.
> *barebelly*, a sheep that has lost the wool on its belly or the inner portions of the hind legs. (I also have a Queensland report of *bluebelly*, denoting a sheep whose belly wool has become laden with dust by being driven along a road or stock route.)
> *black wool*, any wool that is not white, but not necessarily black.
> *bull*, a ram.
> *canary stain*, a light yellow stain which cannot be scoured white, found in wools from some States, mainly Queensland and W.A.
> *cocky*, often used by irreverant employees to denote the farm-owner, however mighty.
> *dog tucker*, an old sheep kept as food for dogs.
> *double fleece*, a name given to the fleece of a sheep that has missed one shearing and comes in for the next clip. Whence *double-fleecer*, such a sheep. These uses should not be confused with *doubler*, a ram; because of difficulty in shearing them, rams over six months old are counted as two sheep in a shearer's tally.
> *eaglehawk*, to pluck wool from a dead sheep.

freezer, a sheep or lamb bred for export as frozen meat.

frosty face, a defect sometimes occurring in Merinos, characterised by chalky, harsh white hairs covering the face.

gamble, a length of wood or iron placed through a sheep's hocks after killing so that it can be hung up.

longtail, a sheep that has not been castrated and still has an undocked tail.

monkey, a sheep. Whence, *monkey dodger*, a shepherd.

moph, or *morph*, a hermaphroditic sheep.

pie pieces, pieces of skin with wool adhering which have been cut from skins in the course of fellmongering.

shirt, the cloth covering in which a carcase of mutton or lamb is enclosed for export.

stag, an imperfectly castrated ram. Whence the adj. *staggy*.

stranger, a stray sheep.

suint, dried sweat of the sheep in the wool.

teaser, a castrated or partly-castrated ram placed in a ewe flock to pick out the ewes on heat.

tick stain, discolouration of wool caused by excreta of the sheep tick or *ked*.

trotter, "the part of the leg left on sheep skins, up to the knee, not the foot alone" (Acland).

wet, a pregnant ewe.

Now for the *woolshed* (often called *the shed*), which in many respects is the axis round which a sheep station revolves. It has three parts, the *pens* where the sheep are held, the *board* where they are shorn, and the *woolroom* (often an area rather than an enclosed room) where the wool is classed, pressed and stored. Some sheds have a loft above the pens to give extra storage space. In old-fashioned sheds, the board was usually in the middle, the pens (they were often called *skillions*, which is an English word) at each side and the woolroom at one end. A *depot shed* is a type of woolshed found "in many districts . . . where small graziers, who have no woolshed of their own, may send their sheep for contract shearing."

Although strictly speaking the *board* is that part of a woolshed where the sheep are shorn, its application is often wider. For instance, Boldrewood refers in "Ups and Downs" (1878) to "100,000 sheep on the board". He does not, of course, imply that all these sheep will be on the board at the same time, but that they are due to be shorn during one season. The term is also applied to "the whole number of shearers employed in a single woolshed" – thus we have *boss-over-the-board* and *man-over-the-board* for the woolshed overseer. *To clear the board* is to complete shearing (or to *cut out a shed*) and *to ring the board* is to become the most expert shearer in a shed.

The *board* has a number of *stands* for shearers. In the days of blade shears, it could be said that a *stand* (really no more than a place of work on a floor) was localised close to an opening in the side of the shed known as the *porthole* or *chute* (spelling variations include *shoot* and *shute*). After a sheep is shorn it is pushed through the *porthole* – not necessarily with any great tenderness – and down a ramp into a small *counting out pen*, where each shearer's shorn sheep are held for tallying. In these days of machines, a stand is not only localised by the *porthole*, but also by the *tube* which leads from the shed's *driving gear* to the shearer's *handpiece*. Close nearby is the shearer's *catching pen* from which he takes (or *catches*[20]) his victims. When two shearers use the same *catching pen*, they are known as *pen mates*.

Before we get down to the business of shearing, it is important to dress the shearer for his task. At this point I take pleasure in drawing attention to a valuable survey conducted by the Australian Language Research Centre at Sydney University into "The Terminology of the Sheep Industry" (Occasional Papers, Nos. 5 and 6, 1965). The Centre records an interesting observation by one of its informants:

> It's droll hearing the young learner of today (sweat shirt instead of Jacky Howe, modern "dungas" instead of shearing pants, bodgie boots instead of shearing moccasins) using the century-old terms the bearded boys used, like *cobbler* and *bell sheep*.

This is not only an assurance that a good deal of Australian sheep jargon survives with little change from the past, but it tells us something about the shearer's dress. A *Jacky Howe* is a short-sleeved shirt favoured by older shearers (commemorating the name of a blade champion); *dungas* are dungarees (I have already noted that we were using the expression *dungaree settler* as long ago as 1826); *shearing moccasins* are soft shoes, which are sometimes replaced by *bag boots* (made from bagging, as were the older *Prince Alberts* and *toerags*) as well as by *bodgie boots* (I will come to the *bodgie* in due course). Since these clothes become saturated with lanolin, the fat which permeates raw wool, they are collectively known as *greasies*. The Language Centre notes the use of *breast plate* for a section on the front of a shearer's shirt reinforced by cloth or leather to prevent sheep-borne burrs penetrating the skin.

Much woolshed lore is preserved in the pages of the "Bulletin", especially during the closing years of last century. A fine collection of shearing terms is given, for instance, in the December 17, 1898, issue of the journal. Here is a selection: *cobbler*, a dirty, sticky, matted and wrinkly sheep (not always the last, but often left to the last in shearing); *to battle for a cut*, to look for a job as a shearer; *fine cut*, a particular boss; *rough cut*, an easy-going boss who does not mind rough shearing; *to pink 'em*, to shear a sheep closely so that the pink flesh shows[21]; *to tomahawk*, to shear roughly and gash a sheep; a *chip* or *wire*, a reprimand; *to shot* or *spear* a man, to fire him; *to wait for a death*, to hang around a woolshed waiting until someone is sacked in order to secure a job; a *gun*, an expert shearer, "generally speaking, a man who can shear over 200 a day"; *snagger*, a shearer who

---

[20] Acland notes of the use of the word *catch*: "Just before stopping time in a woolshed, a shearer tries to finish the sheep he is on and catch another which he can finish at ease after knock-off. This is called *getting a catch*, e.g. 'How many more can you do this run?' – 'Two and a catch'."

[21] The traditional expression *to show the pink but not the red* was a warning given to shearers that care should be taken to give sheep a *tight cut* or *fine cut*, but not to wound them in the process.

is learning the trade and handling fewer than fifty sheep a day[22]; *drummer*, the slowest and sometimes the laziest shearer in a shed; *rosellas*, sheep that are shedding their wool; *stragglers*, sheep missed in the general shearing which are mustered later and shorn at the *straggler-shearing; raddled*, robbed – "Before the Union was established squatters used to raddle, i.e. mark with red or blue raddle, any sheep they didn't deem satisfactorily shorn. Whole pensful were often thus turned out and not paid for." (Somewhat later, a shearer would be said to be *raddle-marked* when he was due for early dismissal.)

The *gun* shearer just mentioned (he is also called a *deucer* or a *gun deuce man*) is not the only expert. Better still is the *dreadnought*, a shearer who can handle more than 300 sheep a day. There were never many of these. Even the most notable Australian *blade-shearer* of them all, Jack Howe, could *turn off* no more than 321 Merinos in a standard working day (at Alice Downs in 1892), although it was not until 58 years later that this feat was bettered – by a machine shearer! The best shearer in a shed was known as the *ringer* or the man who *rung the shed*, but no specific total was involved, only that he should perform better than his fellows at *undressing sheep*.

This word *ringer* came into use towards the end of last century, and described a shearer who could *run rings around* other shearers in a shed. Attempts have been made to link these expressions with the game of quoits or with a game in which horseshoes are thrown at a stick in the ground. A writer in the "Bulletin" of April 22, 1899, declared: "*Ringer* and *good iron* are both derived from the game of quoits; a *ringer* being a quoit which rings the peg, while *good iron* corresponds to *good ball* at cricket." Our phrase *to run rings around* has now gone out into the world. In a London "Times" leader of January 3, 1940, the version *make rings around* was used. Lawson used the version *write rings round* in "Over the Sliprails" (1900).

Somewhat less skilful than the *gun* is the man who can shear a *ton* or *century*, i.e. 100 sheep, in a working day. A *learner* is a shearer who has not yet shorn 5,000 sheep; one stand in five in a woolshed is held for a learner.

Worthy of special notice are the uses of *cut in* and *cut out* when applied to shearing. During the 1840s *cut out* was given its original currency to describe the separating of a selected animal or group of animals from a herd of cattle. Soon after, it was being applied to sheep. By the 1880s its application had been extended and a woolshed was said to have *cut out* when the season's shearing was completed. By analogy, a shed *cuts in* when shearing commences. These shearing uses hailed from the actual cutting of wool; we find, for instance, that a shearer gets a *cut* (it is also called a *stand* or *pen*) when he is employed. He *cuts out* a cheque at shearing, and he *cuts out* a fellow shearer of, say, twenty sheep a day when he shears twenty more than his companion. An important general use is derived from the verb: when any job is completed it is said *to cut out* or *to be cut out*.

Shearers have been called *woolhawks* (especially if expert), *studs* (shearers regularly employed by a contractor), *brutes*, *greasies*, *stoopers* and

---

[22] The most common use of *snagger* these days is to denote a man who was once a good shearer, but is now old and content to jog along with 100 or so sheep a day.

bladesmen, although little is heard of the last term these days because most shearing is done with machines. However, short-bladed handshears are often still used by *daggers*, *wiggers* and *crutchers* in their work. To *chip* or *chop* a sheep is to gash it or to remove *skin pieces* or *bootlaces* from its hide. To *barrow* is to shear or partly shear a sheep for a shearer; this is usually how beginners get their first practical experience. Acland notes: " 'No *barrowing* allowed on the board' was at one time a rule when the Shearers' Union got into the award. Boys often finish or begin a sheep for a shearer who, of course, is responsible for its being properly shorn."

Along with *skin pieces*, noted above, *second cuts* or *double cuts* are among major problems of the Australian wool industry. Hence the expressions *rough a sheep*, to shear it badly, *run a sheep*, to shear off only the top wool, and *run out*, to shear beyond the intended length of a *blow*, which means that a shearer fails to shear all the staple at its base and has to make another stroke to clean the wool left.

Let us go back a little, however, to see how the shearer's working day is organised. Its basis is the *run* or two-hour spell. The ordinary day for a shearer is divided into four runs of two hours each, as follows: 7.30 to 9.30 a.m., 10 a.m. to noon, 1 to 3 p.m., 3.30 to 5.30 p.m. The periods between the first and second runs and between the third and fourth runs are called *smoke-ohs* (or *blows*).

This comment by Henry Lawson ("In the Days When the World Was Wide and Other Verses") on the use of *bell-sheep* is worth repetition:

> Shearers are not supposed to take another sheep out of the pen when *smoke-ho*, breakfast or dinner bell goes, but some time themselves to get so many sheep out, and *one as the bell goes*, which makes more work for the rouser, and entrenches on his smoke-ho, as he must leave his board clean.

The morning or afternoon tea brought to shearers and woolshed hands at *smoke-os* (this spelling is more generally used these days) is called *lunch* and the midday meal is always *dinner*.

Dry in the hide means out of practice; *to carry the drum* means to work slowly or lazily; so do the expressions *to camp* and *to drag the chain*. The last metaphor appears to have come originally from ploughing or work in which bullocks were used; a horse or bullock that is not pulling its weight will allow its chains to drag on the ground. *To swing the gate* is used of a fast and expert shearer, the gate swung being that of the catching pen, *to do a Jimmy Gibbs* means to rush the shearing of a sheep (Jimmy Gibbs was another notable old-time shearer), and *yabber* was once used to mean to put on speed.

Whereas a good shearer can *swing the gate*, there are many hurdles for the learner to clear before he becomes a *ringer*, let alone a *gun* or *dreadnought*. For example, *concertina*, a sheep hard to shear because of wrinkles in its skin, *devil's grip*, a depression between the shoulder blades, indicating bad conformation (an old hand at shearing can spot such a defect in a moment by what is known as *playing the piano*, running his fingers over the backs of sheep in a *catching pen*, and leaving *nowlers*, sheep hard to shear, to the ministrations of his *pen mate*), *sweat locks*, wool from the belly of a sheep, often matted with dirt and sweat, *cocky* or *parrot*, a sheep which has lost some of its wool (also called a *rosella*, although this is more properly a sheep which has been so badly *fly-struck* that, when being treated or shorn the whole of the fleece may be lifted off from the shoulders to the rump, leaving a raw, red surface pitted with maggots), *wet sheep*, a sheep with a fleece wet from rain (such wetness is often sufficient to cause shearing to cease altogether until the fleeces are dry, during which period the sheep are officially *declared wet* by the workers), and, of course, the *snob* or *cobbler*.

The sheepman's use of the term *snob* is worth close attention, if only because it illustrates the tortuous way in which some slang develops. A *snob* is the last sheep shorn in a day's work in a shearing shed; almost inevitably it is a dirty, wrinkled sheep which bears little personal appeal for the shearer. *Cobbler* is used similarly. Since, according to historical report, a cobbler "sticks to his last", the last sheep in a shearing pen came to be known as a *cobbler;* and since, in slang, a cobbler is called a *snob*, it was only a matter of time before the sheep that had been left to stand round in a catching pen for many hours acquired the name also. Long before the word *snob* was used in standard English to describe a person "whose ideas and conduct are prompted by a vulgar admiration for wealth or social position", as the "Oxford Dictionary" puts it, it denoted a person with "no pretensions to rank or gentility". The Australian use of *snob* to describe a disreputable and rejected sheep is, therefore, an interesting reversion.

It is not generally realised how early in our history machines began to displace blades. The first patent for a sheep-shearing machine was granted in 1868 to J. A. B. Higham, of Melbourne, and the first man to take all the wool off a sheep by machine was Jack Grey, a successful blade-shearer and blacksmith, in the early 1880s. After those beginnings, it was not long before the more advanced sheds took over machines in a big way. In 1888, the world's first complete shearing by machines occurred at Dunlop station, Louth, N.S.W.

However, in some parts of Australia many years were to pass before blades were hung up for the last time except for such basic tasks as *crutching, wigging, shanking* and *dagging*. (When a machine is used for the task, *dags, wigs, topknots*, etc., are said to be *poked off*.) For this reason, there are still many old-timers who can remember such terms for handshears as *daggers, jingling johnnies, tongs* and *bright and shiny swords* (actually, for all its seeming imaginativeness, *knight of the bright sword* was a fairly reasonable description, for constant use of handshears gave the metal almost a mirror finish); who can remember, too, what was meant by the *sardine blow, Moran's great shoulder cut* and *Pierce's rangtang block*. The *sardine blow* is made on the second or *whipping* side – also called the *money side* or *money-maker* – when the fleece of a sheep seems to peel away like the lid of a sardine tin when it is opened. The original meanings of the other expressions have been lost.

These men and their predecessors gave many names to various parts of handshears – *cockspur* or *knocker*, a stop fastened to the heel of one blade to prevent its crossing the other blade; *driver*, a strap through which the hand is passed to hold the shears; *bows*, the curved portions of the shears above the grip; *yakka*, the pull-back of a pair of shears; *stopper*, a guard placed over the closed points of shears when not in use to prevent their springing open. Some seventy years ago, *to put Kinchela on shears* meant to sharpen them; the "Bulletin" of September 25, 1897, says that Kinchela was the author of a pamphlet on the care and sharpening of shears.

Machines inevitably brought new terms, among them *hotbox*, an early model handpiece, *plate*, a thin and worn comb, *merry widows*, broad combs and cutters (not now used), *boggi* (pronounced bog-eye) for the handpiece, allegedly because an early model was mottled and shaped like the stump-tailed boggi lizard[23]; *outrig*, a shearing handpiece and equipment; *giggling pin* or *giggler*, the tension pin in a handpiece; *tube*, the flexible casing linking the main driving gear and handpiece; *guts*, the flexible driving shaft in the *tube*. When combs and cutters are put in place in a handpiece, it is said to be *loaded*. The man who cares for shearing machinery and sharpens cutters is called the *expert* or (by rhyme) *squirt*.

Then round about 1963, we heard of a completely new style of shearing called *tally-hi*, invented by the first world champion shearer, Kevin Sarre, of Victoria, and another Australian champion Vin Parkes.

Whether the shearer has used blades or machines, he has had many workers behind him – the *carrier-away* or *pony*, the *fleece-picker* or *fleecy* or *picker*, the *penner-up*, the *broomie* or *sweeper*, the *skirter*, the *dagger* or *dag-picker* or *dagboy*, the *tarboy*, the *piece picker*, the *pearl diver*, the *wool-roller*, the *classer*, and the *presser* or *screw-spinner* or *tickjammer*.

However, it should be pointed out that many of these tasks require minimal skill – with the notable exceptions of *classers* and *pressers*, of course – so that shedhands often fill several roles. I am told that the *carrier-away*, a man or boy who carries fleeces from the *wool table* (i.e. the bench on which fleeces receive their preliminary classing) to their bins after classing has been done, is employed only in large sheds.

Some generations ago, the *tarboy* did in fact apply tar to any wound in a sheep's flesh caused by shears. Later substitutes included carbolic dip fluid, kerosene and Condy's fluid, but the name *tarboy* remains. One of his jobs is to apply the *vulcaniser* which is the name given to the needle and thread used for sewing severe cuts.

The wool-baling terms to *dump*, *double dump* (now obsolete), *monkey*, *woolcap*, *spade press*, a makeshift wool press, are also Australian. So are *woolscour*, a shed usually near a river bank for scouring greasy wool (also called a *woolwash*) and *topping-up*, an expression used by waterside workers when loading ships to denote the stacking of the top tiers of bales in a hold – usually with light bales.

Many terms used on the modern sheep station come from English, especially from dialectal origins. Earlier, it was noted that in old-fashioned shearing sheds the *catching pens* were often called *skillions*. This is directly from the dialectal word *skillion* or *skilling*, used to describe a shed, outhouse or lean-to. It is apparently obsolescent in the land of its origin, but it is

---

[23] However, there is another possible derivation. Early shearing machines were so crude that shearers said they were useless for shearing little else than around a sheep's *bog-eye*, anus.

still current in Australia; our architects use it to describe a roof that is pitched only one way.

Other English terms which outback Australia has adapted to its own needs include: *clip*, the season's clipping of wool, either on the basis of the individual sheep or all Australian sheep collectively[24]; *to cull*, to draft out inferior stock, and the noun, *cull*, an animal so drafted out; *dag*, a faeces-clotted lock of wool about the hind parts of a sheep, and the verb, *to dag*, to cut away such clotted locks of wool; *parly*, a small, weak lamb (from Scottish dialect); *teg*, a sheep in its second year; and *tally*, both as a noun and a verb, used in relation to the counting of sheep. *Tally* is often used to denote the fixed number of one hundred sheep; when a large mob of sheep is counted each *tally* is marked with a notch on a stick, the combined total (also rather confusingly called a *tally*) being so many hundreds plus any odd number that may not make a full *tally*. The term *call* is applied to the call of tallies in counting both sheep and cattle.

Another interesting old word we hear occasionally is *yo* for ewe. People hearing this doubtless consider it a neologism or a mispronunciation. Actually, it represents a perpetuation of what was probably the original pronunciation given to the name for a female sheep; compare the Scottish *yowe*.

There are 13 wool-selling centres in Australia (largest is Sydney, with an annual offering of more than 1,000,000 bales) and more than 90 per cent of our annual clip is sold at auction. Auctioneers and buyers have a language of their own; some 300 samples of it were listed in "Concerning Wool" (1951) which was published by the Australian Wool Board. Since many of these terms are not originally Australian, I will content myself with a few examples:

belly, wool shorn from the belly of a sheep; belly wool is packed separately from fleece wool.

binders, fibres that grow from one staple to another and hold the fleece together.

broad, a term applied to wool to signify that it is coarser or stronger in quality than is usual for that particular type of wool.

crimp, the "wave" in wool fibre, a visible indication of its character and quality: the smaller and more even the crimp usually the finer the wool.

dingy, (of wool) thin, discoloured and wasty wool that may not scour white.

doggy, (of wool) straight in fibre, lacking what wool-classers call "breeding", with little felting property.

fadge, a butt of a bale or two bags sewn together, usual weight 60 lb. to 150 lb.[25]

---

[24] Acland notes an important intransitive use of *clip*: "My ewes *clipped* seven lbs. all round", i.e. an average of 7 lb. of wool was shorn from each ewe. Actually, the average weight of fleeces obtained by shearing is 10.41 lb. for a sheep and 3.25 lb. for a lamb.

[25] *Fadge* is an old English word, dating from 1588. The "Oxford Dictionary" defines it as "a bundle of leather, sticks, wool, etc.; a bale of goods". I listed it in the first edition of "The Australian Language" for "an irregular package of wool, less than $11\frac{1}{2}$ lb.", but this is

fribby, (of wool) containing an excessive amount of what are called *second cuts* and *sweat points*, i.e., inferior wool.

gummy, (of scoured wool) containing a large quantity of yolk or lanolin.

hungerfine (also called *hungry*), an ultrafine type of wool caused by starvation.

moity, (of wool) carrying vegetable matter other than burr.

shivy, (of wool) carrying small, fine particles of vegetable matter.

The Australian public became aware in 1958 that wool-buying was not always a straightforward operation. The reason was the revelation that some buyers were combining into *pies* (also called *rings*) to bid and then share purchases, so that competition was reduced. Such *pies* were alleged to have operated in Australia since 1945.[26] A derivative was *pie system*.

On a lighter note, the *wool saw* deserves mention. This is a stock joke in wool stores; when a bale is too big to fit into a space in a stack or truck-load, storemen call for the *wool saw*. Another example (this time from woolsheds) is the *wrinkle stretcher*, an imaginary piece of equipment to remove folds from a sheep's fleece.

5. CATTLE

IN THE LONG and complicated story of the Australian soil and of the people who have tamed it (perhaps it would be better to say "come to terms with it" for the Australian soil is not easily tamed), few words bulk more significantly than *stock*. Practically the first indigenous term supplied by Australia to the English language was *stockyard*, which was in use before 1797.

As the horizons of Australian life were pushed inland, a crop of allied expressions sprang into being, each of them falling into the niche where necessity thrust it: *stock-keeper* (1800), *stockman* (1803), *stockfarm* (1806), *stockhouse* (1808), *stockholder* (1819), *stockrun* (1825), *stockhut* (1826), *stock-station* (1833), *stockwhip* (1845), *stockhorse* (1847), *stockbook* (1847), *stockfarming* (1849), *stockrider* (1859), *to stock up* (1878), *stockroute* (1886), *stocksick*, used of land upon which animals have been pastured too long (1890), *to stock-keep* (1890), *stock-agent* (1897), and *stockist*, a grazier, which came into use this century.

As used collectively for farm animals the word *stock* dates from the sixteenth century. Until about 1850 it retained this application in its Australian derivatives. Since 1850, however, there has been an increasing tendency for it to become synonymous with cattle. Thus a *stockman* is now a cattle man; *stockrider*, one who looks after cattle; *stockwhip*, a whip used in driving bullocks or yarding cattle (a stockman rarely strikes his mob apart

---

inadequate. Acland says that a *woolpack* "becomes a *bale of wool* when filled and pressed and a *fadge* when loosely filled". A full bale of greasy wool usually weighs around 300 lb.; a full bale of fleece wool may weigh up to 400 lb. and other wools 450-495 lb.

[26] "He said he had known since 1945 that 'pies' were operating". – "Sydney Morning Herald", March 25, 1960, p. 7.

from flicks round the feet of stock, control being exerted by cracking the whip); *stockyard*, a place where cattle are yarded as distinct from *sheep-yards* or *sheep-pens*.

Stock-keeper is not only a person who looks after stock, but also the name given to the loop on a stockwhip which unites the thong with the handle. The use of *stock* for the handle of a whip dates from the seventeenth century. Incidentally, the stockwhip is mainly an Australian invention; usually (but not always) it is made of kangaroo hide, the length of the normal thong is 7-8 ft. with a *cracker* of cord or horsehair. By contrast, the *bullock whip* had a thong 8-10 ft. long and a handle about 4 ft. 6 in. long.

I write about the bullock whip in the past tense because few *bullock teams* are now left in Australia. As early as 1795, such teams were in use round Sydney and most of our first roads were *bullock tracks*. For much more than 100 years, these teams carted supplies to outlying areas and brought back wool (the large tarpaulin used to cover a wool dray was called a *wool-rag*), and legends grew round the *bullocky* and his flair for colourful profanity. Indeed, he was such a well-known figure in outback places that many synonyms came into use: *bull puncher, bullocker, buffalo navigator, bovine puncher, ox-persuader, steer pilot, horny steerer* and *cow conductor*. As recently as June, 1942, a Sydney daily used *oxen-conductor* for a bullock driver.

Many terms used in the Australian outback apply equally as well to life on cattle stations as to the less boisterous activity of sheep runs. Here are examples: *book-keeper*, the accountant of a station who also serves as the store-keeper; *boy*, any of several station employees not necessarily under the age of consent, e.g. *horse-and-buggy boy*, who is the owner's or manager's personal attendant although buggies do not figure largely in station life these days, and *spare boy*, the assistant to a team driver (in Australia, *cowboy* is a youth or man who milks cows – not the romantic figure of U.S. prairies); *manager*, the man who directs the running of a station, but who, as the attendant terms indicate, does not always possess the managerial qualities associated with the standard English word: *real manager*, a man who is permitted by the station owner to act entirely as he thinks best; *parcel post manager* or *head office manager*, a man who acts on orders received from the individual or firm owning the property who may live at a great distance; *working manager*, a man who works about the station as well as directing the labours of others; *office manager*, a man skilled in the financial aspects of running a station, but who has little practical knowledge of handling stock; *verandah manager*, a man who idles away his time and directs operations with little practical understanding of what they involve.

To these can be added: *hut*, quarters where station hands sleep and eat, as distinct from *quarters*, accommodation for the élite such as overseers and jackeroos; *missus*, the inevitable name given to the wife of a manager; *lane*, a stock route which has fences on both sides; *frontage*, any land, which may be a mile or more deep, fronting on to a creek, anabranch or billabong; *cattle tight*, (of a fence) one that will hold cattle.

The spread of the cattle tick, *Boophilus microplus*, in Australia since it was introduced to this country in 1872 on Zebu cattle from Java, has led to the development of many terms. Among them are: *seed tick*, the larval stage of the cattle tick; *tick worry*, a condition in cattle caused by the cattle tick, when the irritation of many thousands of attached ticks and loss of blood cause emaciation and may lead to death; *redwater*, blood-coloured urine of cattle severely affected by ticks; *redwater country*, areas in northern Queensland and the Northern Territory where tick fever is prevalent; *bleeder*, a beast which, having been immunised against *tick fever*, is used as a blood reservoir for innoculating other cattle in tick-infested areas; *buffer country*, any property or district dividing tick-infested areas from areas where ticks do not occur; *clean country*, country free from infestation by cattle ticks; *tick-dip*, a dip in which cattle are immersed to kill ticks; *tick-free*, *tick-infested*, *tick infestation* and finally *tick dodger*, an inspector engaged in preventing the spread of ticks.

Cattle suffer from misfortunes other than those brought by ticks. *Pleuro* (or *ploorer*) is an abbreviation of pleuro-pneumonia; *cuckoo scab* is a skin disease at the back of the head and ears; *pink-eye* is a form of ophthalmia caused by dust; a head of cattle suffering from "rickets" caused by eating Zania leaves is a *rickety* – "an insidious and incurable disease which is very prevalent over much of the Queensland cattle country" (F. Ratcliffe, "Flying Fox and Drifting Sand", 1938, said: "It has actually been known for a pen of *ricketies* to take first prize in a fat stock show"); like sheep, cattle also suffer from *fly-strike*, maggot infestation caused by native blow-flies, but the special victims are beasts which have just been dehorned, flies striking at the polled stumps; *bush sickness* is a loose term to denote stock sickness caused by lack of minerals in pastures.

In standard English, *herd* has been applied for many centuries to a company of animals, especially cattle. Its use in this sense has been largely superseded in Australia by *mob* (also applied to a flock of sheep). On the other hand, *herd* has come to be an overall term applied to the sum total of cattle that a cattleman owns, even though he may not know their exact number. *Herd cattle* can thus be distinguished from *stud cattle* and *dairy cattle*.

Another English term to which we have given a special meaning is *notice*. Drovers who are travelling stock – incidentally, this use of *travel* is an Australian revival of an English application some three and a half centuries old – are required to give *notice* not less than 24 hours and not more than 48 hours before crossing the boundaries of others' land. An employee of the station through which the stock is travelled usually accompanies the drover to protect his station's interests, a chore that is known as *seeing through*.

According to the "Oxford Dictionary", the nounal use of *drove* to describe the action of droving is "only Old English", but it has both a long and current use in Australia. A recent newspaper report commented on "a long *drove* down the Darling to Adelaide" which a man had made with stock.

We have also added something to the verb *to tail*. In the language of our cattle country, *to tail* means something more than merely following (i.e. the tails of) stock; it means to look after a travelling mob. When a man or group of men is detailed to water and hold a mob during the day while more cattle are mustered, they are said *to tail the mob*. The word also means to ride behind a mob, to stop break-aways and urge on poor or weak beasts; a task entrusted to men who are called *tailers* (a *tailer* is also a man who looks after horses in a drover's camp). It may be of some interest to record the set positions taken up by stockmen (or *ringers*, as they are commonly called) when travelling a mob of cattle. The usual layout is somewhat as follows:

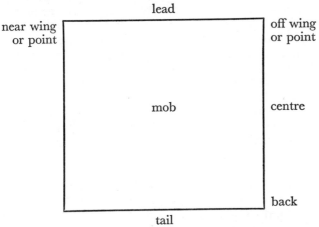

Two or more men may be placed in each position, depending on the size and tractability of the mob. Their primary job, of course, is to keep the mob moving in a compact unit. To this end, certain strict rules of droving etiquette are observed. For example, a man riding at the side of a mob always tries to turn a recalcitrant beast back into the head end. It is regarded as bad form for him to go after a beast that breaks behind him. If two stockmen change places while travelling stock they are said *to cross*. Once again, strict etiquette must be observed – the man initiating the *cross* must not ride in front of the other stockman.

In the previous Section, I recorded how the verb *to cut*, meaning to castrate, was being replaced by the euphemistic use of *mark* among sheepmen. Similar refinement is creeping in among the cattle fraternity. In Queensland particularly, *to brand* not only means to sear a brand on the hide of a beast, but also embraces castration and, sometimes, dehorning.

While on this delicate subject it can be noted that the Middle English word *spay*, meaning to operate upon (especially upon the female of certain animals) to remove the ovaries and destroy reproductive capacity, is widely used among cattlemen, although it is not infrequently corrupted to *splay*. However, *splay* in this sense has been recorded in English dialect, so the time may yet come when Australia will accord it a national, and hence orthodox, use. Another English dialectal word with an established place in Australia is *slink*, which abbatoirs workers apply to the foetus of a calf, and which cattlemen use to describe a full-time unborn calf. In its dialectal use, *slink* is applied to an aborted or premature calf.

We use the standard English *springer* for a heifer or cow in calf, but have added some indigenous colour with *backward springer*, a cow or heifer early in calf, and *forward springer*, a cow or heifer late in calf. Standard English also are the verbs *to drop*, to give birth to, and *to slip*, to miscarry, applied to cows and sheep, but the nounal use of *drop*, for a birth and, more particularly, as a collective term for all calves or lambs born in a season seems to be Australian.

Here are a few more old English words that have acquired new life through outback Australian usage: *to spring*, to draw a mob of stock out in a long line, especially when bringing them to water with a narrow *frontage;* *to dewlap*, to cut a triangular flap in the dewlap of a head of cattle so that it can be identified easily; *store*, a head of stock in fair condition before being fattened for market; *fat*, a head of stock ready for market; *bumble*, a bullock (also a cow or a horse) with a deformed hoof; *bobtail* (also called a *bangtail*), a head of cattle that lacks the "brush" on the end of its tail – such a beast will have been included in a *bangtail muster*, during which every beast rounded up has the tuft of its tail docked to prevent its being counted twice. *Muster* and *musterer* are both Australian terms, in relation to sheep or cattle.

For a country as deeply experienced in frontier life as Australia, we have absorbed remarkably few words from the prairies and ranges of America's cattle lands. This is, perhaps, the best evidence possible of vigour and independence of our own cattle-raising industry. If we have never embraced some of the tiresome bric-à-brac dear to Hollywood and the American Dream, in the form of lariats, six-shooters, chaps, high-heeled boots and sombreros, we have pursued an unreluctant linguistic career of our own. Apart from our common interest in the verb *to buck* and its derivatives and in the verb *to bulldog*, meaning to tackle and throw a beast from horseback, the languages of Australian and U.S. cattlemen have little in common. Where the American speaks of *broncos* we have *brumbies;* his *dogies* are our *poddies;* his *coyotes* are our *dingos;* his *cowboys* are our *ringers;* his *rustlers* and *rustling* are our *duffers* and *duffing;* his *prairies* are our *outback;* his *ranches* are our *stations* and *properties;* and so on down a long line of terms too numerous to mention. Perhaps I should record here that the U.S. cowboy has an animal in his mythology called the *wouser* (a word closely approximating the Australian *wowser*, although the meaning is different). A reference in "A Treasury of American Folklore", edited by B. A. Botkin, discloses that the U.S. *wouser* has a good deal in common with our bunyip.

Australian cattlemen have put into currency dozens of terms of their own to describe cattle of various kinds: *clearskin* and *cleanskin*, unbranded animals; *table-tops*, well-built and well-fed cattle; *scrubbers, bush scrubbers, mulga scrubbers, mallee pikers, kangaroos, myalls, scrub danglers, runabouts, brumby cattle*, stock that have run wild and deteriorated in condition; *wind splitters, hatracks, pigmeaters, razorbacks* and beasts whose *hides are holding them together*, scraggy, lean animals; *coachers*, tame cattle used as decoys; *dummy mob*, used similarly; *frames*, draught cattle; *stags*, half-grown bulls; *poley*, a dehorned or hornless animal; *snailey*, a cow or bullock with a curled horn; *snagger*, a cow difficult to milk; *beefer*, an animal bred for meat; and *micky* or *mick*, an unbranded steer, perhaps from the Aboriginal *micky*, quick.

For calves we have the expressions *poddy*, *poddy-calf*, *bobby calf* and *staggering bob*. The last is not often heard, but is found several times in Australian writings; J. Williams uses it for "meat from newly-born calves" in his "Experiences of a Colonist" (1880), and in "We of the Never Never" Mrs Aeneas Gunn refers to "staggering bob tack" (i.e. food). It apparently had some currency in the outback for blancmange. It is sometimes used also to denote any beast in poor condition. Our use of *poddy* is probably from the English dialectal *poddy*, fat. How we acquired *bobby calf* is more problematical, but it perhaps came also from English dialect in which *bob* and *bobby* are used for small, common things, as in bobby wren, the common wren. The use of *poddy* for a handfed calf is well known; its use for a handfed foal (1898) and a handfed lamb (1908) were extensions. So is the verb *to poddy*, to hand-feed, and *poddy-dodging*, the stealing of unbranded calves (more or less the equivalent of *duffing* in the Kimberleys and Northern Territory).

An old term worth noting, since it has been obsolete for seventy years or more, is *Russians* for wild stock, dating from 1847. The version *Rooshians* appears in 1869. An interesting revival, under a disguise difficult to penetrate, occurs in S. H. Roberts's "Squatting Age" (1935) in which he refers to "the wild *Bushians*".

The continuous lowing of a herd of cattle is termed *roaring;* if they *ring* or show other signs of restlessness they are described as being *rowdy* or *ropeable*. This last term has long since ceased to apply solely to stock. Indeed, it is now rarely used in its original connotation: any person who is angry or infuriated may be said in these days to be *ropeable*[27]. Few Australians realize that its first application was to cattle so wild that they could be controlled only by roping.

Cattleman's kid describes methods adopted by ringers and stockmen to calm a restless mob of stock – usually by singing or what passes for singing to the average overlander. From the cattle man we have also inherited *moonlighting*, a method of mustering scrubbers by night when they come out on to open country to feed and mix with quiet cattle (however, there is nothing especially connected with cattle about this word for it is used in other ways, e.g. the *moonlighting* of possums, the shooting of possums seen in tree branches against the light of the moon); *to cut out stock* and its derivative, *cutter-out; crush*, for a funnel-shaped runway used in branding cattle, which dates from the 1870s; *catching pole* (1849) and *roping pole* (1878), a long pole used in a stockyard to drop a noosed rope over the horns or heads of cattle; *breakaway*, a panic rush of stock; *stick to it!* a routine cry during a muster when a stockman is trying to run down a scrubber; *fizz*, to move rapidly and erratically, originally applied to a lively bull in a yard; *to scuffle*, also *to scruff*, to throw a calf by hand for branding; *to box* (cattle), to hold a mob in temporary yards (on the other hand, *to box* sheep means to mix mobs or types, and *to box* a creek means to

---

[27] In outback N.S.W. a casual acquaintance was describing to me how angry another person had been. "He was *rapeable*," he said.

dig for water in a dry creek bed and line the sides of the hole with wood); *camp*, a highly-flexible word that can be used to denote, (a) a rest or sleep, (b) a place where rest is taken, (c) a group of men, (d) a place where stock gather, (e) a place where stock are handled, e.g. where they are drafted, (f) a place where stock are kept under guard. *Dinner camp* is an example of (a), except that it should be noted that *dinner* means *lunch; to draft on the camp*, is an example of (e).

The *Illawarra Shorthorn* is an Australian breed of cattle, but it originated so long ago (before 1850) and its beginnings are so clouded that even cattle experts – who are no slouches at laying down the law – hesitate to arbitrate on details.

In many respects, the Australian cattle industry remains one of those far-off activities of which the public knows little. But there have been big changes since World War II. One of them is *air-beef*, a term applied to the movement by air of frozen carcases from cattle stations to markets or export ports. Another is the *road train*, the *beef train*, and the all-weather *beef road*, which are collectively ending the *overlanding* of cattle in the old sense of weeks or months of cattle on the track. The *road train* is a series of two or three large trucks or vans, equipped to travel on outback roads, drawn by a prime mover, and used to move stock (sometimes merchandise) in remote areas.

Among old-time activities which these things have eliminated are the *cueing* or *kewing* of cattle – the shoeing of beasts so that they could cross hard terrain which would otherwise damage their hoofs. An old-timer in the Kimberleys tells me: "On the Ord River Station in East Kimberley in the early days we had two or three *kewing pens*. *Kews* were made by the black-smith out of old *slippers* – two for each foot and a No. 4 nail used. The *slipper* (or worn-out horse-shoe) was cut in the middle, flattened at the back, and always cut short for the front feet and four nails for each *kew*. The *kewing pen* was V-shaped with three rails, the bottom one approximately 18 in. off the ground. The leg was lifted and bound to the rail with a rope while the operation was being done. As the hoof of a bullock is very thin, all care has to be taken not to prick the foot when *kewing*."

From the dairy farm have come: *cow spanker, cow banger, cattle banger,* a cowboy or milker; *galloper*, a zealous worker; *sookie*, a hand-reared calf (better known as *poddy*), which is apparently derived from "suck" and which has almost certainly given rise to the use of *sook* for a coward or timid person; *office*, cow bails; *buller*, a cow on heat; *bulling*, (of a cow) to be on heat; *to look away*, (of a cow) to be on heat; *elder*, a cow's udder; *to hold, to click* or *to take*, (of a cow) to become pregnant after service by a bull; *drier*, a non-lactating cow; *cracker*, a worn-out cow.

6. HORSES

AUSTRALIA'S PEAK YEAR for horses was nearly half a century ago – in 1918, when our horse population was more than 2,500,000. Little wonder, therefore, that the language of horses had a big place in our past, even if that language means little today.

Perhaps the best place to start is with *buck* and *buckjumper*. Since, as Morris suggested, "all early quotations of *buck* and cognate words are connected with Australia", we are immediately entitled to claim ownership of some highly interesting terms. The verb *to buck*, used to describe the wild jumping and shying of an unbroken horse when saddled or ridden, has been current for much more than a century.

It occurs in 1848 in the "Statement by Jackey Jackey", an Aboriginal, on the death of the explorer, E. B. Kennedy. The native speaks of horses which "*bucked* all about". The verbal noun, *bucking*, was also current in 1848. It is to be found in H. W. Haygarth's "Bush Life in Australia".

Related examples are to be found before this, however. Letters written from Sydney and Adelaide in 1837 and 1838 by Stephen Black say: (a) "I am now [November, 1837] in possession of a splendid, powerful bay horse, 15 hands 3 inches high, four years old, and one that springs under you like a *buck*". (This is not, of course, a direct use of the term, but it is interesting in view of what follows.) (b) June 17, 1838: "I bought a colt, that had only been mounted a week, to help my poor old horse on the remaining journey. I was vain enough to think I could ride him, but in a week he convinced me of the fallacy of this idea by sending me up in the air like a sky-rocket by *buck-jumping*." (c) September 1, 1838: "I have bought the horse today for 65 guineas. His name is Bucksfoot and he is rightly named, for it's my belief he is the worst *buck-jumper* in South Australia."

From these beginnings, we have developed many variations on the theme – *bucker*, the nouns *buck* and *buckjump* as distinct from the verbs; *to have a buck in at*, to attempt something; *to buck at*, to resent. In addition we have put into currency the descriptive phrases *to buck a hurricane*, *to buck a town down* and *a horse that can buck its brand off*.

During the 1890s another set of terms became popular with the introduction of *pigjump*, *pigjumper* and *pigjumping*. It should be noted that *buckjump* and *pigjump* are not synonymous; the *pigjumper* does not bring its feet together in its leaping, but holds its legs stiff, whereas the *buckjumper* arches its back and gathers its feet.

The horseman also points to the *cow kicker*, a horse that kicks forward with a hind leg, the *striker*, a horse that kicks with one of its forelegs, the *bit bucker*, the horse that bucks only spasmodically and for no perceivable reason, the *lunger*, a horse that bucks or tries to bite when it is being mounted.

Horses are said *to have a busy foot*, *to scratch*, *to split* or *to speel* when they travel fast. The last two expressions are revivals of English dialect, of which the noun *speeler*, a speedy horse, is an Australian extension. *To prop*, to come to a sudden stop when travelling at a fast pace, and *to plant*, to stand perfectly still, both used of horses, date from 1870 or before. The former is well established in Australia and its application has been extended considerably. Thus, a newspaper in 1942 told us: "Big British interests in Thailand *propped* at the last moment and Japan got their holdings intact." Here we find the verb acquiring the meaning "to jib at a command, to refuse to co-operate". Another extension is the adjectival use of *proppy* for

D

a horse that jibs and plays up when ridden or driven. In his "Man-shy" (1931) Frank Dalby Davison writes of a cow that *propped*, and today we find that even a human can *prop* when he comes to a sudden halt or stubbornly holds to a decision. An unusual use occurred in newspapers of February 13, 1965, when certain preference shares on the Melbourne Stock Exchange were described as *propping*.

Horses have almost as many recognisable qualities (or lack of them) as humans. Here are some samples: *bad doer*, a horse that never puts on condition; *blower*, a broken-winded horse; *brusher*, a horse that strikes its near foreleg with its off forefoot (whence *brushing*, which is almost synonymous with the English *over-reaching*, also used in Australia); *chewer*, a horse that relentlessly mouths its bit; *pigrooter*, a horse that *pigjumps* or bucks with stiff legs; *reefer*, a horse that continually throws up its head; *side-stepper*, a horse that tends to move sideways during the early stages of being ridden; *stumbler*, a horse that repeatedly stumbles without apparent reason when it walks; *nut*, a vicious horse; *scrubber*, a poor-looking, ill-bred horse; *weaver*, a horse that is restless when placed in its loose box. Some of these terms are international, and it would be unwise to claim them as exclusively Australian.

Not so for *brumby*, the name given to our wild or outlaw horse, which goes back a century or more. The origin is obscure. It may come from the surname of Major James Brumby, who arrived in Australia in 1795-6 and reputedly left a number of horses in N.S.W. which ran wild and became known as Brumby's horses; from the surname of Major William Brumby, a once noted Australian horsebreeder (at least, legend says he was); or from the Queensland Aboriginal *booramby*, wild. A writer in the "Bulletin", of March 21, 1896, suggested a derivation from *Baramba*, the name of a creek and station in the Burnett district, Queensland, and another writer in the same journal of September 17, 1898, noted:

> I have heard *brumby* used by blacks on the Balonne, Paroo and Bulloo rivers [Queensland] sounded *baroombie* and on one station in particular to distinguish the unbroken from the broken horse.

This term has not been left in its classic form. In "Brindle Royalist" (1956), Henry G. Lamond refers to wild cattle as *brumbies* and as *brumby cattle*.

The old Scottish use of *crock* for a broken-down horse has probably influenced the evolution of the Australian outback slang *crocodile* for a horse. Both *croc* and *crocky* have been employed similarly, the latter dating from 1893. The process seems to have been something like this: from the Scottish *crock*, by extension to *crocodile*, by clipping to *croc*; so that *crock* and *croc* (although they could be spelt the same way) are, in reality, different terms. By transference, a *crocodile* is also called an *alligator*.

Moke is another dialectal term we have put to our own uses. In England it denoted an ass. Here we have applied it to a horse, especially one of inferior type. A similar process has been gone through with *cuddy*, used in North English dialect for a donkey. In Australia we use it for a small, solidly built horse, although a more popular term for an animal of this type is *nugget* (whence the widely-current adjective *nuggety*, sturdy, compactly-built, used of both animals and humans – an equivalent is *blocky*, e.g. "a blocky little bloke").

Taffy horse, a chestnut with a lighter – often silver – mane and tail (from a fancied resemblance to the coarse sweetmeat known as *taffy*); *creamy*, a white or cream-coloured horse; *tuppy*, a worthless horse (English dialect had *tup*, a ram); *nut*, a difficult horse to break, i.e. a hard nut to crack; and *waler*, originally a horse exported from New South Wales to India for army use (in modern times, a light type of army horse used in Australia) – these are also worth noting.

To be thrown from a horse is to *get slung* or *shanghaied;* to break and train a horse is *to rough it off;* a harness cask is a *round yard*.

A correspondent tells me that an *Empress* was "a much thought-of and especially elegant side-saddle supposed to be a model of that used by the Empress of Austria". The term was apparently current in the 1890s. *Dee* or *D* is the name given to a D-shaped loop or clip on a saddle; a *monkey* or *monkey-strap*, a looped strap on the offside of a saddle pommel, used by inferior "rough-riders" (this is an English term, although the verb *to rough ride* is apparently Australian) in mounting and during the bucking of a horse; a *cradle* is a wooden frame that fits on a pack-saddle for use when posts or logs are carried.

Another type of saddle is the *poley*. This is a saddle without kneepads – "like a poley bull without horns, but generally considered to be derived from polo saddle". Such a saddle is more likely to aid a buckjumper than a buckjumpee. The so-called *English saddle* possesses even more of the same disadvantages. It is a saddle with a flat seat and lacking knee and thigh pads. Its alternative slang names, *automatic emptier* and *sliding seat*, are probably sufficient commentaries on its value to outback horsemen. A good deal more popular is the *stock saddle*, which has a dip in the seat and is equipped with both knee and thigh pads. The term *gin* for a saddle is an allusion to an Aboriginal female.

Another word with a "horsy" flavour is *flash*, as used to describe the skittishness of a highly strung or unruly horse. Here is an observation on the Australian uses of the word by J. Kirby, "Old Times in the Bush of Australia" (1895):

> I think it conveys more meaning than any of the other slang words we have in this colony. *Flash* is applied to anyone who is proud and has nothing to be proud of. It also applies to the manner in which a kerchief is worn round the neck; to bell-bottomed trousers; the way in which a hat is worn; to conversation in which every second word is an oath; or to a shearer . . . In those days [i.e., the middle of the century] *flash* and *shearer* were such as linked together and seemed inseparable in our minds.

Kirby is somewhat astray in the senses he gives to the word as Australian. Its connotation of ostentatious, boastful, etc., had been anticipated in English slang, but we have probably put *flash* to better use in the antipodes than England ever did.

The *overlander* and *boundary-rider* are closely linked in their destinies with the horse. The original *overlanders* were travellers who made long expeditions with stock from one colony to another – the first of them took a herd of cattle from the Murray River to the Port Phillip district in 1837. Settlers who arrived by *the overland* came to be known as *overlanders* during the middle of last century. Later, *sundowners, walers, coasters* and other tramps were sometimes called *overland men* because of the distances they travelled.

The *boundary rider* is a station employee who patrols the boundaries of a property to prevent stock straying and to mend fences. In the "Australasian" of July 14, 1865, reference is made to "the shepherds and *boundary riders* of the past and present", which perhaps shows that the word was originally used on sheep stations. In New Zealand a shepherd who prevents sheep passing an unfenced boundary is called a *boundary-keeper*. A sheep dog chained to a kennel at a gateway on a road to prevent sheep passing through is called a *boundary-dog*. Boundary riders were once known as *topwire lizards*, and this supports the idea that the former term was originally used on sheep stations, since it was noted in Section 4 that shepherds were sometimes called *lizards*.

It was possibly through the agency of the horse that Australia acquired those useful expressions, *double-bank, double-dink* and *double-donk*, employed mainly today when a cyclist gives another person a ride on the bar of his bicycle. *Doubler, dink, dinkie* and *donkey* are interchangeable variations. We will take a closer look at these terms later.

"Rose and I *double-bank* on a fat round pony named Sulky", writes Bernard O'Reilly in "Green Mountains" (1940). "Kelly came down from Black Mountain every Sunday after that, and we went *double dinking* on his white mare", says Eve Langley in "The Pea Pickers" (1942).

Many horses have defects of various types. To which end I draw attention to comments by Michael Sawtell on "those monstrosities of bronze figures that are supposed to represent horses" outside the National Art Gallery, Sydney ("Sydney Morning Herald", April 3, 1950, p. 2). He describes them as "*chuckle-headed, thick-gulleted, lop-eared, ewe-necked, bullock-shouldered, straight-backed, goose-rumped, cat-hammed* and *splay-footed* Suffolk Punch cuddies". To this critical list can be added *gig-headed, roach-backed, sway-backed, three-cornered, cow-hocked* and *sow-lugged*. Of horses in poor condition, you say that you could *hang your hat on their hips*.

Now for some of the many general slang terms used by horsemen:

> *cold shoeing*, fitting a stock-sized shoe without moulding it with heat.
> *concertinas*, a type of leggings with wrinkles in them.
> *cross brander*, a horse that has changed hands several times, mostly by dishonest means.
> *dog poisoners*, new leggings.
> *fall on one's crupper bone*, to fall off a horse.
> *fessilo* or *festlo*, a fistulous wither. Also called *setfast*.
> *flood marks*, leggings.
> *go up a tree*, to fall off a horse.
> *grease one's saddle straps*, to prepare to leave a job.

hang the Condamine on, to put a bell on a horse. "It comes from the fact that bells for stock used in Queensland were first made in Condamine". Tom Collins gives us *Wagga pot* for a bullock bell.

hang up a horse, to dismount and drop the bridle of a horse over a hitching post.

hooks, spurs.

laughing sides, elastic-sided riding boots.

Major Mitchell, to zigzag or follow an indirect course when riding over country. (Commemorating Sir Thomas Mitchell, 1792-1855, and his method of exploration in our early days.)

night mare, a horse kept in a home paddock overnight for morning work.

pinhorses, the nearside and offside horses of three (sometimes two) in front of the shafters and behind the leaders.

remover, an old horse-shoe used again. Also *slipper.*

ride up a gumtree, to fall off a horse.

run up a horse, to fetch a horse from pasture.

sanded, allusion to a horse that has swallowed large quantities of sand in drought country.

setfast, a fistulous wither. See *fessilo.*

slipper, an old horse shoe used again. Also *remover.* See note on the *kewing* or *cueing* of cattle at the end of Section 5.

slug, a horse lacking vitality.

smash, the panic flight of horses (or camels) during an outback journey, with resultant loss of loads, stores and water supplies; leading to a *scramble out,* the ensuing grim retreat.

snake charmers, leggings.

spider, a type of leading harness.

split bag, a partly split chaffbag used for carrying goods on a saddle.

squabbles and hell, horse hobbles and bell (a sample of rhyming slang).

submarining, riding through long grass.

Sunday rider, an inexperienced horse rider.

take up a selection, to fall off a horse.

toey (of a horse), speedy, nervously ready to go.

turn on a cabbage leaf, used of a spirited horse that can wheel smartly.

twist a plate, (of a horse) to shed a shoe.

twitch a tail, said of a horse that is becoming tired, from the tail movements a tired horse usually makes.

wad tucker, said of a horse that cannot grind its food properly because of bad teeth.

well-sprung, (of a horse) having a good rib formation.

To these should be added an interesting group of terms given in "Australia Astride" (1959), by Desmond Martin: *aged,* (of a horse) more than seven years old; *bat, mop* or *stick,* a whip carried by a rider; *lepper,* (of a horse) a jumper; *Wagga grip,* a leather strap or binding through the pommel Ds of a saddle – also called a *jug handle* or *monkey; ratbag,* an over-excitable horse; *roarer,* a horse that makes a loud roaring sound when breathing; *shake hands,* (of a horse) to kick; *warrigal,* an outlaw horse or wildly behaved station hack – also called a *yarraman.*

Horses suffer from various diseases; one of the few distinctively Australian is known as *walkabout disease* and occurs especially in the Kimberley area of north-western Australia. This disease is attributed to eating *rattle pod* or pea bush; in the final stages, the victims plod in circles until they die of starvation or exhaustion (cf. sheep diseases, Section 4).

A note should be added here on *bushmen's carnivals*. These are Australian equivalents of the U.S. *rodeo*, but the latter term is tending to take over in much of the Australian Press, which does not seem to know what a *bushmen's carnival* is. At the same time, although the word *rodeo* was filched from the U.S., we have given it a pronunciation of our own. The Americans say RODeo (with the stress on the first syllable, like "radio"); we say roDAYo, with the stress on the second syllable.

· 7. HARVEST

MUCH OF AUSTRALIA's good earth has been plundered ruthlessly for the sake of animals – or more accurately in the cause of the bank balances of animal-raisers. There is another area of outback activity that demands attention. This is the vast collection of things that grow out of the soil, e.g. wheat and barley, rice and hops, sugar cane and fruit, tobacco and timber and canary seed. We will see later, when we examine some of the jargon of the canefields, that much of the specialised language of these fragmented activities is too localised to be dealt with here. This Section will, therefore, deal mainly with some of the many orthodox expressions – i.e. "orthodox" so far as Australia is concerned – which have come to us from the earth as a producer of harvests.

At the outset, it should be noted that wheat (which was first grown in Australia in 1789) is our main source of national income after wool. While most of its language is understood by all wheatgrowers, the layman will soon lose his way as he battles through the intricacies of the *long fallow, normal fallow, short fallow, bare fallow* and *sheeped fallow*, of *dry farming* and *land-spelling* and *supering*. He will be more at home with terms used to denote various types of land-clearing: *ringing, ring-barking, frilling, bush bashing, sucker bashing, brushing, scrub rolling, double logging, smoodging, cabling* and, of course, *burning off* (incidentally, 1964 statistics showed that burning off caused about 30 per cent of all Australian bushfires). Rather than go into these activities in detail, perhaps it would be wiser to content ourselves with remembering that the *stump-jump plough* and the *stripper* were Australian inventions and that they were mainly responsible for the opening up of the *mallee lands* of Victoria and South Australia.

Among words of general application in Australian rural speech few are more worthy of admission to our "approved" list than *chip*, meaning to harrow. The fact that the word in this sense is credited to Australia by the "Oxford Dictionary" should serve as an indication that its credentials are extremely good. But Australians have not been content to use the term in this limited sense alone. *Chipping* is often more than the harrowing of ground; it is commonly applied to the removal of weeds from cultivation areas, usually with a hoe, and the breaking up of surface soil. A *chipper* is one who engages in such labours.

' Australia has made contributions to primary production in many ways. For example, the *Granny Smith apple* (originally cultivated by Maria Ann Smith, at Eastwood, N.S.W., in the 1880s) is ours; so is the *Winter Cole pear* and the *Packham's Triumph pear*. So is the *Australorp*, the Australian utility Orpington hen, which was officially recognised as a breed in 1930. So is the *Bunyip level*, a type of water level used in farm surveying, invented by P. A. Yeomans. "It consists of two aluminium staffs, each 5 ft. long, graduated in feet and inches; these are connected by 60 ft. of tubing with 'atmosphere' press buttons at the ends to let in air before a reading is made and closing down again to prevent excess leakage during movement from point to point when not in use. A sliding pointer on the face of the scale and a slope-meter at the back are additional features." Mr Yeomans also gave us the equally simple *Keyline Plan*, which is designed to show how contour farming and water conservation can increase pastoral production.

• One of our oldest indigenous inventions was *eucalyptus oil*, an antiseptic and disinfectant. The first still for its production was set up by Joseph Bosisto in Victoria in 1854, but it had been extracted long before – Governor Phillip sent a sample to Sir Joseph Banks in 1788.

‘ As for scourges, we have had a full share of these. Prickly pear, for instance, which was brought to Australia by the First Fleet in 1788 and, at its peak in 1925, had covered some 65,000,000 acres; it was eventually largely eliminated by the insect *Cactoblastis*, introduced from South America. *Cacto* we called that insect and in its name erected the world's only public memorial to an insect at Boonarga, Queensland – Cactoblastis Memorial Hall. *Myxo* was a popular abbreviation of the rabbit-killing disease myxomatosis which was introduced in 1951 when Australia's rabbit population was estimated at not less than 100,000,000,000. We have vast locust plagues, too – the insects are variously called *grasshoppers, hoppers, grassies* and *locos* and originate in what are called *outbreak areas*. We call the Giant Toad a *bufo*, but that is really part of his zoological name, *Bufo marinus;* these creatures were introduced into Australia from Central South America in 1935 to control the grey-back beetle, which in the larval stage damages sugar cane; results have been disappointing and *bufo* is now often classed as a pest in its own right. *Bufo* should not be confused with *buff*, an abbreviation of the word "buffalo". Buffaloes were introduced into Australia from Timor in 1825, and have since run wild in our far north; now they are being killed as pests.

۰ Just as we have seen how various soil deficiencies have led to such stock ailments as *coast disease*, so we find that the lack of boron in soil produces *corky core* (apples), *brown heart* (swedes) and *hollow stem* (cauliflowers). I have noted various forms of *pasture sickness* in Sections 4 and 5.

‹ Now some promised examples of canefields jargon:

arrow, the top of the growing cane.
bagpipes, an armful of cut cane carried on the shoulder.
barrow, a cane truck.
benzine rat, fire used to burn off trash before cane is cut. Also *red steer*.

borer, a cane cutter who gets ahead of other members of his cutting gang.

crow's nest, to cut out a section of cane. The term is also used as a noun to denote a badly-loaded truck.

cut, the amount of cane to be cut.

floater, a piece of burning trash carried into the air when cane is being burnt off.

hairy mary, hairs on the cabbage of the cane leaf.

headland, a fallow strip dividing growing cane into sections.

jockey, a last tier of cane on a truck.

line lizard, a man employed by a sugar mill to lay or shift the narrow gauge railway lines used in transporting cut cane to the mill.

money box, a cane truck.

plucking, the pulling of stray pieces of trash from a truck loaded with cane.

red steer, as for *benzine rat*.

sleeper, a length of cane dropped by a *borer* across the path of his mate, implying a demand for increased speed by the latter.

tail chain, to, to haul out full cane trucks with horses over portable rails.

tram, a section of cane burnt before cutting.

trash, the leaves of cane and weeds growing in cane, which are burnt off before cutting (only enough cane for two days' cutting is burnt at a time, otherwise it loses sugar content).

These expressions provide a fair example of what we find in almost every branch of crop-gathering: while some of them are Australian originals, many have been imported. In any case, they are highly specialised in use and rarely find places outside specific areas.

8. DOGS

AUSTRALIA'S DEBT to working dogs, especially the *Kelpie* and the *Australian Heeler*, can never be repaid. Those who think of such dogs only in terms of an aberrant animal which sat on a tuckerbox near Gundagai, have little idea of how much our well-being has depended on them.

We have developed five types of dogs, but only four have been recognised as Australian breeds. These are:

• The *Australian Cattle Dog*, also called the *Australian Heeler*, the *Queensland Heeler*, the *Blue Speckle Cattle Dog* and the *Bluey*. It was originally a cross of the smooth-haired Scotch sheepdog and Australia's native dog, the dingo. The first dogs of the type were produced in the 1840s and were known as *Hall's heelers*, after a N.S.W. squatter named Hall. Later, Dalmatian and Kelpie blood was fused with the cross. The breed was officially recognised in 1890.

• The *Kelpie* is a tireless worker with sheep – indeed, it is so tireless that it has to be chained each night or it will go out and work sheep on its own. There is some possibility that the dingo was among its ancestors, but this is uncertain. The name reputedly originated with a Fox Collie bitch from Scotland named Kelp, on Hanging Rock station, Wagga. One of Kelp's successors was a bitch named Kelpie, which won the world's first sheepdog trials – held at Forbes, N.S.W., about 1871-2.

• The *Australian Terrier* (also called the *Aussie Terrier*) was bred from Scotch Skye and Irish terriers and the Dandie Dinmont.

• The *Australian Silky Terrier* (originally known as the *Sydney Silky*) derived from a mating of a Yorkshire Terrier and an Australian Terrier. The breed first made a bid for public favour about 1909.

• To these should be added what is known as the *Kangaroo Dog*, originally developed for hunting kangaroos (also dingos). Because of greyhound blood in it, the *Kangaroo Dog* was also known at one time as the *Bush Greyhound*.

• Of these dogs, the *Kelpie* is the most widely known. Acland offers some valuable comments on how they are used:

> Sheep dogs run naturally either to bring sheep towards you or to drive them away; and when a puppy shows a preference he is broken in for that work. The dogs that bring sheep are called *heading dogs* and most of these can be taught to *lead* if desired. Dogs which take to driving sheep away are broken in *to huntaway* and are called *huntaways*. Some dogs will both *head* and *huntaway* and are called *handy dogs*. They are not generally high-class *heading dogs*, but very useful *about hand* and sometimes very useful mustering dogs. Some men have a special *slewing dog*; but a well-trained heading dog or huntaway will usually *slew*.

An explanation of some of the words used in this quotation will be in order. A *heading dog* is one that will go round to the far side of a mob of sheep and stop them. If he does it well he is said to *make a good head. Stopping dog* is sometimes used synonymously. A dog that drives a mob towards a shepherd is said to *hoozle* them. A *leading dog* is one trained to run ahead of a mob of sheep to keep them steady; a *huntaway* is a dog that drives sheep forward when mustering; a dog working close to a shepherd or drover is said to be *about hand*; a *slewing dog* is one trained to head a mob or *turn* them. A *huntaway* is sometimes known as a *forcing dog*, this being a particular application of the term *force*, which is used to describe the capacity of a dog to control a mob of sheep. A good dog will be said to have *a lot of force*, because of its ability to move sheep without *legging* (i.e. leg-biting) or barking. Some dogs have what is known as *eye*, or, in other words, an ability to control sheep merely by looking at them.

A dog trained to run across the backs of sheep when they are yarded is a *backing dog*; a *topsider* is a dog which prefers to work from high ground; a *worrier* is a dog that worries sheep – sometimes it is called a *woolclasser*; a sheepdog that capers round in front of sheep is said *to skite*; a lazy dog is a *sundowner*, a *sooner* (i.e. a dog that would sooner rest than work) or a *Sunday dog*. *To sool on* is to incite a dog to attack, whence to encourage anyone in an activity; a separate use of *sool* means to travel fast.

The phrase *tinning the chicken* is worth explanation here. Two brothers named King and another dog breeder named McLeod, who dominated Australian sheepdog trials between 1900 and 1920, used to show the excellent working abilities of Kelpies by having one of these dogs drive a chicken into a jam tin.

To these words can be added *nester*, a rabbit dog that is especially good at ferreting out rabbit warrens; *dogger*, a dingo-trapper – bonus money, averaging £1, is paid for a dingo scalp, which is required to have a strip of skin attached, running from nose to tail-tip, including the ears; *kangarooer*, which originally denoted a kangaroo-hunter who operated with a Kangaroo Dog, but today the kangarooer does his "hunting" at night with a blinding beam of light and a high-powered rifle – his main aim is to secure *butts*, hindquarters shorn of the lower parts of the legs, for the pet-food trade; and *dog fence*, a fence built around pastoral country to exclude dingos (world's longest is in Queensland, some 3,500 miles long; S.A. has a dog fence which runs 1,350 miles).

General slang terms for sheep or cattle dogs are *pancleaners* and *tripe-hounds*. Assorted expressions on the "dog" theme: *dog's disease*, influenza or dengue fever; *dog's breakfast*, a turmoil; *dog's dinner*, a shilling (an approximate rhyme on *deaner*); *dog's vomit*, inferior food (close to English nautical slang, for a moist mash of meat and biscuits); *under the dog act*, forbidden to drink in hotels. *Poor man's racehorse* for a greyhound is worth a terse notice.

CHAPTER IV

The Bush

1. BUSH, BRUSH AND SCRUB

ALTHOUGH in the early 1890s Henry Lawson was moved to write:

> Don't you fancy that the poets better give the bush a rest,
> Ere they raise a just rebellion in the over-written west?

it was during that period, when bush lyricists could be found along almost every outback track and when the original "Bulletin" was thumping away on its nationalist drum, that bush slang and idiom became widely popular. They had been on their way up for a long time. Their influence had spread so greatly that it is difficult in many cases to decide where the story of the bush ends and that of the city begins.

Writing of ordinary Australian conversation as heard by a visitor in 1879, J. Inglis noted in "Our Australian Cousins" that "the speech of the shebeen, the stockyard and the bush shanty will often be ostentatiously obtruded". Here was a mixture. There was no watertight compartment between outback slang and city slang; they had broken their banks and had begun to merge into the vast sea of words which is our language today. If, therefore, the chapters of this book are entitled "The Soil", "The Bush" and so on, they should not be regarded as self-contained. These headings are used largely for convenience.

The first term of significance in bush vernacular was, of course, the word *bush* itself. Derived from the Dutch *bosch* it arrived in Australia at the beginning of last century via the Cape of Good Hope – not as Mencken suggests via America. The first evidence I have found of it is in 1801 in the form *bush native*. In 1803 it occurs as a noun in the "Sydney Gazette" of April 17. By 1820, after a rather severe tussle, it had more or less ousted the English "woods" and "forest". By 1826 it was being used to describe the country in general outside a capital ("the interior, or bush, as it is termed") and had already begun to acquire important variations. There are a multitude of these, among which the following are important: *to go bush, take to the bush, up the* (or *out*) *bush, bush apes* (rural or bush workers; fruit-pickers in South Australia), *bush baptist* (a person of doubtful religious persuasion), *bush boy, bush bread, bush brother* and *bush brotherhood* (one of several religious organizations), *bush carpenter, bush craft, bushed, bushfire, bush house, to bush it, bush lawyer* ("everyone is a lawyer in the bush", an old saying goes), *bushman, bushmanship, bushman's clock* (the kookaburra), *bush miles* (miles reckoned in winding through the bush, "longer than road or regulation miles"), *bushranger, bushranging, bush scrubber, bush telegram, bush telegraph* (means whereby rumours and reports are circulated) with its modern variants *bush wireless* and *bush radio, to bushwhack, bushwhacker,*[1] *bushwoman, bushy* (a person who lives in the bush), *bushwalker* (one who hikes in the bush), *bush walk, bushwalking, bushytail* (crafty) and *bush tucker,* food found and consumed by one who lives on the country.

Bushed, meaning lost in the bush, has been used since the 1850s, but its meaning has now been extended. In 1885 Mrs R. C. Praed ("Australian Life: Black and White") described a person lost in the confusion of London's streets as *bushed.* We can even – by a strange stroke of literary imagery – be *bushed* at sea. Charles Barrett shows how this can be done in his "Coast of Adventure" (1941). He asks:

> Had we [i.e. a small ship] gone wide of the light; become *bushed* in the great Van Diemen Gulf [in the Northern Territory] where a small craft could easily be wrecked in half a gale?

In addition, a man who is in a quandary or confusion is said to be *bushed;* and *to bush up* a person is to confuse him.

As pointed out in Chapter II, the original *bush telegraph* was a confederate of bushrangers who warned them of police movements. Gradually the expression became synonymous with any rumour or false report, and several other terms with similar connotations sprang into use. Among these are *bush wire, mulga, mulga mail, mulga wire, spinifex wire, gidyea, sugarcane, Tom Collins* and, probably best known of all, *furphy.* At the end of last century, *Tom Collins* was a mythical being to whom rumours and reports of doubtful authenticity were attributed in the Riverina and other parts of the south-eastern States. Tom Collins was the nom-de-plume chosen by the Australian writer, Joseph Furphy, best known for "Such Is Life" (1903). By a strange stroke of destiny it was Joseph's brother John, through another agency altogether, who gave the word *furphy* to our language.

At the outbreak of World War I the metal-bodied carts used in Victorian military camps for water and sanitary purposes were supplied from the foundry established by Furphy at Shepparton, Victoria, in 1874. The name of Furphy appeared on each vehicle, and camp rumours or latrine rumours came to be known as *furphies.* From its original military use it spread into popular speech. *Furphy king* and *furphy merchant,* for retailers of rumour, are derivatives.

Although a utility term of long standing, *bush dray* is also Australian (so is *bullock dray*). The original English use of *dray* was for a brewer's delivery cart. In 1848 H. W. Haygarth noted that it was "the only vehicle used in New South Wales for the conveyance of wool and other produce". *Dray-track* is a derivative.

Bushfire blonde, a red-haired girl or woman; *full of bushfire,* full of vim and spirit; *Sydney or the bush,* a phrase indicating the choice of distant alternatives; and the time-honoured chant of derision, *What's this, bush*

---

[1] Used originally in the American Civil War for a deserter who raided defenceless towns and homes for food and valuables; also for a guerilla; in Australia a person who lives in the bush. The derogative city use of *w(h)acker* for a person is possibly inherited from it.

week? are a few more expressions we have wrung out of that Dutch word *bosch* in a little over a century and a half.[2]

Although neither *brush* nor *scrub* was originally Australian, both have been given particular uses in this part of the world. *Brush* (1799) preceded *bush* in Australia and kept pace with it for several generations. As a result a section of our flora and fauna bears its imprint, e.g. *brush apple, brush cherry, brush turkey.* The "Oxford Dictionary's" definition (quoted as used especially in the United States, Canada and Australia), "the small growing trees or shrubs of a wood; a thicket of small trees or underwood", is scarcely applicable to Australia where we know nothing of woods and thickets. In Queensland there is a particularized use of *brush* for jungle vegetation, especially a jungle-filled valley or a densely-covered stretch of bushland; much earlier (1828) it would seem that the word *brushland* had brief currency to denote rich land with a water frontage.

Both America and Australia borrowed *scrub* from the English (it came originally from Danish dialect, *skrub*, brushwood, and the Norwegian *skrubba*, the dwarf cornel-tree) and put it to extensive uses. It probably features more in Australian speech than in American. We have extended it a good deal past the standard English status of "stunted trees or shrubs, brushwood; also a tract of country overgrown with 'scrub'." The Pilliga Scrub of New South Wales is a forest covering 625,000 acres, with trees up to a hundred feet tall. The Mallee Scrub (also called *the Mallee* and *Mallee Country*) of northern Victoria and south-eastern S.A. is an immense area of *Eucalyptus dumosa* which is something more than a shrub or brushwood. There is also a good deal of Mallee in N.S.W. and W.A. and the derivatives *Mallee land, Mallee region, Mallee root, Mallee sandhills* and *Mallee soil* have developed.

Here is a group of Australian derivatives on the *scrub* theme: *scrub cattle, scrub danglers* and *scrubbers,*[3] cattle that have run wild and deteriorated in condition; *scrub cocky,* a small farmer working rough scrubland; *scrub dashing,* riding through bush or scrub, especially after strayed cattle; *scrubdom,* land covered by scrub or the back country in general; *scrub falling* and *scrub bashing,* the clearing of scrub-covered land; *scrub-itch,* a skin disease found in New Guinea jungles; *scrub-rider,* a horseman who rides through scrub.

As with Mallee, we have used *mulga,* Aboriginal name for the *Acacia aneura,* to good effect. In colloquial speech *the mulga* denotes the remote bush or outback; as already pointed out, along with the variations *mulga mail* (or *wire*), it can mean a source of rumour; *in the mulga* means lost or in trouble.

---

[2] *Absentees,* or well-to-do Australians, who prefer life in the West End of London, are known as *Piccadilly bushmen.*

[3] It should be noted that both *schrubbes* and *scrubs* were used in sixteenth-century England to denote a weedy type of cattle. A mean or insignificant fellow was called a *scrub* in English dialect.

3. DWELLINGS

IT WAS an accident of environment that gave Australia the name *wattle* to describe the genus of plants (some 600 varieties of them) known as *acacia*. Early settlers found it necessary to build shelters against the weather. They had learned how to build *wattle-and-daub huts* in the English provinces with long pliant twigs plastered over with mud. There were plenty such twigs in Australia. So, from the wattle-and-daub method, the twig or *wattle* gave its name to the plant. *Wattle Day* is a national festival held on August 1 or September 1 each year, according to the wattle-flowering peak in each State.

Just as the New Zealanders took *whare* from the Maoris and put it into colloquial speech to describe a small hut or cottage, so we have taken the words *wurley, gunyah, goondie* or *gundie, mia mia* and *humpy* from the Aborigines and used them to denote huts or shelters. Best known is *humpy*, which has been in popular speech for well over a century. Morris says that the native word is *oompi* and that "the initial *h* is a Cockney addition"; he also points out that the old convict settlement in Moreton Bay (Queensland) was called Humpy Bong, i.e. *Oompi Bong*, a dead or deserted settlement.

The *bush house, bush hut, breakwind, breakweather, badger box, watch box, V hut* and *skillion* are additional terms for various kinds of shelters. Comments have already been made on the *watch box* and *skillion*. The *bush house*, given without definition in the previous Section, deserves attention. This is a shed built near a station homestead for coolness (e.g. for keeping meat) or for growing flowers or vegetables; these days, city gardeners sometimes have *bush houses*. The *bush hut* is any rough dwelling, made of slabs, packed earth and corrugated iron (because of its relative cheapness, corrugated iron has been one of the foundations of outback Australian architecture).

The use of *slab* for a hewn plank is an Australian application of an old English word; however, its use to denote an undressed log (1829) is indigenous. So are *jockeys, jockey sticks* and *riders* for a framework used to hold the roof of a bush hut in place. Strictly speaking, *riders* are slabs or logs running from the ridge of the roof to the eaves, and *jockeys* are logs laid horizontally across the riders at their lower ends.

From the employment of shingles or wooden tiles in hut-building, the Australian developed several useful expressions, among them *to have a shingle short* (1847), *short of a sheet of bark* (1885) and *short of a sheet* (1891), all implying that a person has "a tile loose" or is silly. The simple word *short* is sometimes used without elaboration. "That fellow's a bit *short*", we say, meaning he's stupid or out of his mind.

In due course, we will encounter some other Australian dwellings – *doover, leafy, donga, weekender, home unit*, etc. – but this is not the place to go into details about them.

4. OUTBACK FOODS

DUE LARGELY to the influence of the bushdweller and the swagman, a considerable vocabulary has grown around Australian food, especially around those staples of outback diet, mutton and damper.

As a generic title for food of any description *tucker* has been in Australian use since 1852 – it comes from the English dialectal *tuck*, food or appetite – and we have put it to sundry uses in *tuckerbag, tuckerbasket, tucker bill, tuckerbox, tucker-time, tuckertin, tuckerless, to tucker* (to feed), *tuckering day, bush tucker* and *gin tucker*. Most of these terms are readily understandable, but several need explanation. For example, *bush tucker* denotes game, fish and other food gathered by one who is living off the country; *gin tucker* consists of snakes, goannas and other food eaten by wild Aborigines. *Tuckerbox* also needs some comment; as probably every Australian knows it occurs in Jack Moses's poem, "Nine Miles from Gundagai" – "And the dog sits on the tuckerbox / Nine miles from Gundagai"; hence the use of the word *dog* for food.

Outback cooks have been known by many names (since most outback cooks are men, these names have had revivals in time of war), the most common of which are: *bab, babbler, babbler's offsider, babblins, baitlayer, doctor, gut starver, dough puncher, grub pusher, belly punisher, water burner, blacksmith, poisoner* and *crippen*. Partridge claims *babbler* (a clipped form taken from the rhyming slang, *babbling brook*, a cook) as English military slang, but it was in Australian currency in 1906 before the English got hold of it. *Greasy* is also clipped from a rhyme, *greasy look*, cook. Crippen, of course, was an English murderer. A term of somewhat doubtful origin is *Sally Thompson* as applied to a shearer's cook. A correspondent says that this was once "a common appellation". It may be noted that Thompsons have frequently been nicknamed *Sally* in the British Army, in the way that Clarks are nicknamed *Nobby*.

Most of these expressions for cooks are particularly used by shearers (who, of course, have their own cooks). An old term worth recalling is *standing out*, which was intended to denote how, if two or more cooks applied for a job with a shearing team, the vote would take place in some open area with each shearer casting his vote by standing behind the cook he preferred.

The *damper* is a foundation of bush eating in more ways than one. The word was first recorded here in 1827. Strictly speaking it is bread baked in the ashes of a campfire or a camp oven; it is usually in the form of a flat cake two or three inches thick and up to 2 ft. in diameter, and is generally eaten in wedges like a cake. The mistake (repeated in the 1958 edition of the "Australian Encyclopaedia") has often been made of calling it always "unleavened". Although yeast could not usually be used under bush conditions, the flour was often made to rise with baking powder, or with a mixture of bicarbonate of soda and cream of tartar or tartaric acid, which was easily obtainable. Eno's Fruit Salts gives better results as baking powder than soda and cream of tartar, because its proportions are correct, but it was too expensive for use in the great damper-cooking days. The first Australian record of the term is in 1826, and once again it proves to be an adaptation of an older English use. In English the word *damper* is given as a snack between meals or a wet blanket – which might be applied to the products of some damper-cookers! In "Our Antipodes", Mundy observes that they are "a damper sure enough to the stoutest appetite". The term *sod damper* is sometimes used to denote the unleavened damper. *Mud spring* denotes a doughy damper.

The damper has many culinary offspring. Small dampers or scones cooked on the ashes (instead of in them) variously rejoice in the names *beggars-on-the-coals, buggers-on-the-coals, devils-on-the-coals* and *buck-jumpers* ("eat one of these and a horse will never throw you"). The *johnny cake* is somewhat similar, but those who link this with the American *journey cake* are astray, for the ingredients are widely different: my informants suggest that it can either be cooked on the coals of a fire or in a dry pan.

Then there is the *brownie, fattie* and *tommy*, all mixed in the same way as the damper with the addition of sugar, currants and fat; I have one recipe for a *brownie*, which says that cocoa should be added to colour it, and still another which says that it is cooked in exactly the way of a damper. The *whitey* is a brownie cooked without fat; the *baking powder brownie* is a brownie made with baking powder; and a *blade brownie* is one made with yeast instead of baking powder. A *fat cake* is a piece of fried dough (1865); a *flooper in the pan*, "that bush luxury . . . which is a sort of greasy pudding" (1840); *dips* were knobs of dough dropped into boiling water (1859); *leatherjacket* was the name given to a mixture of flour and water that was either fried or cooked on red-hot embers (1846); and *pufftaloonas* or *puftaloons* are hot fried cakes, spread with jam, sugar or honey – one of my informants says that they should be cooked in "an abundance of fat". There is some lack of agreement on how the last item should be spelt, e.g. Mrs Aeneas Gunn, "We of the Never Never" (1907) uses *puff de looneys* and Eve Langley, "The Pea Pickers" (1942), renders it *puftaloonies*.

Here are some additional slang terms for damper and similar foods: *dorkum, bunghole, nightmare* and *woppidown*, all used for dampers; *dog's jew's harps* and *floaters*, dumplings; and *death adders*, johnny cakes, which a writer in the "Bulletin" of July 7, 1897, said was a term that had been "introduced by city bushmen". This observation may be wrong for Mrs Hill lists the Northern Territory use of *death adders* for "old cynics, gossips", and Jock Marshall and Russell Drysdale, "Journey Among Men", 1962, report its use in the Kimberleys to mean *hatters*, i.e. men who live alone – "it is reckoned they will bite your head off if spoken to before noon". Another synonym for *hatter* is *scrub bull*.

Because they were natural developments, *kangaroo steak, kangaroo tail soup, cockatoo pie* and *cockatoo soup* need no comment, except to point out that the only Australian dish which has earned international recognition is *kangaroo tail soup* (first mentioned by that name in 1830, but adumbrated ten years earlier: "the tail of the forest kangaroo in particular makes a soup"). However, some explanation is obviously needed when we are confronted with *Gundaroo bullock* and *Grabben Gullen pie*, since only old bushmen could clear the fog of time away from these expressions. They were mainly localized in use, both Gundaroo and Grabben Gullen being N.S.W. townships. The term *Gundaroo bullock* was used in the 1890s to describe a dish of native bear or koala meat; *Grabben Gullen pie* was a pumpkin scooped out and stuffed with possum meat and then baked. *Dunlop*, mutton, also needs elucidation. It commemorates the name of one of the largest stations on the Darling River where, according to the "Bulletin" of August 7, 1897, "the owners gave liberal quantities of mutton to travellers". *Burdekin duck* is a North Queensland name for a dish of sliced beef fried in batter; the *Diamantina cocktail* (the Diamantina is a river which runs occasionally in south-western Queensland) is a drink consisting of condensed milk, Bundaberg rum and a well-beaten emu egg; and the *Murrumbidgee oyster* (from southern N.S.W.) is a raw egg taken with vinegar, pepper and salt.

Steamer was a dish of stewed kangaroo flavoured with pork (1820). *Stick-up meat* was meat roasted over a bush fire on a spit of wood that rested on two pronged sticks (1830), and *station jack* was a meat pudding made with flour, water and chopped beef (1853). P. Cunningham reported in 1827 that a *steamer* also included chopped kangaroo tail and was "stewed with a very small quantity of water for a couple of hours in a close vessel".

Colonial goose and *colonial duck* have been established Australian dishes for more than seventy years. The former is a boned leg of mutton stuffed with sage, onions and breadcrumbs; the latter is a boned shoulder of mutton treated in the same fashion. Both are baked.

It was what W. W. Dobie in 1856 called the *muttonous* diet of the outback that produced the expression *the Old Thing* for a meal of mutton and damper. It dates from 1848. *Ram-struck mutton*, tough meat; *concertina*, a side of mutton; *banjo*, a shoulder of mutton (also used for a frying pan); *killer*, a sheep to be killed for meat; *stag and brownie*, a meal of mutton and brownie – these are poured from the same linguistic vat. Perhaps we could also add *underground mutton* for rabbit flesh. And perhaps we could pause to consider *lambs' fry*, as a euphemism for testicles from *marked* or castrated lambs. An old-timer writes: "In the old days, when all hands and the cook went out on horseback to mark a paddock, the wives of station hands and others along the track used to come out to us with pillow-slips, calico bags or billy-cans with the request that we bring them back *a feed of lambs' fry*. In the evening, every saddle would have gory bundles dangling from the *D*s which were eagerly and thankfully received by the populace. On the job, or towards tuckertime, when men were beginning to feel hungry many cods were swallowed raw like oysters to stay the pangs temporarily." That use is actually standard English, but Australia has probably added considerable weight to its currency. Our later use of *lamb's fry* for lamb liver is one of our most "refined" additions to the English language.

One of the few indigenous desserts is *quandong pie*, made from the fruits of a small tree once found widely throughout Australia, but now rare. The fruits can be preserved by extracting the nut and sun-drying the fruit.

The *Coolgardie safe* deserves special mention, since it was widely used in the outback to keep food fresh. This is a wooden frame cupboard with the sides sloping slightly outwards and covered with hessian. A dish of water was placed on top with four strips of cloth leading from the water to the top of each hessian wall; water seeped down the wicks and wet the walls. A breeze cooled the structure on the same principle as the *waterbag*. The name *Coolgardie safe* seems to have been influenced mainly by the first syllable.

While the *bushman's hot dinner*, a meal of damper and mustard (tramps' slang), the *bush dinner*, "mutton, damper and tea" (from 1852), the *duck's dinner*, water alone, the *stockman's dinner*, a spit and a smoke, and the *bullocky's breakfast*, a hitch in the belt and an attention to natural requirements, seem to have featured so often in outback life that they required comment, there is indeed little variety in outback diet, which is probably why we have inherited so many terms for what, after all, are practically the same things. Consider, for example, these slang names for treacle and golden syrup: *long-tail*, *spare boy*, *Kidman's blood mixture*, *Kidman's joy*, *donkey lick*, *beetle bait*, *black jack*, *blackstrap*, *bullocky's joy*, *cocky's joy*, *cocky's delight*[5] and *tear-arse*.[6] We are left to mourn that the bushman and his fellows did not have many more items of food to work on with their imaginations.

There were, of course, a few such items. Stews were called *hash-me-gandy*, *mulliga stew* and *flyswisher stew*. The first may be a play on *hash* (there is a version, *hash magandy*, in 1905), and the second is probably a corruption of U.S. tramps' slang *mulligan*, a stew, influenced by the Australian *mulga*. *Flyswisher stew* was oxtail stew. *Dust* was flour; *dynamite*, baking powder; *leprosy* or *chow*, cabbage; *bee-jam*, honey; *flybog*, jam; *goog*, an egg (a word perhaps formed on the sense of *gog*, as in *goosgog*, a gooseberry); *bull's eyes*, fried eggs; *mutt eyes*, corn; *frog's eyes*, boiled sago; *cowyard cakes* and *bush cakes*, cakes and buns containing a few sultanas; *burgoo*, oatmeal and water taken to a woolshed or harvest field to be drunk during work (from the English nautical *burgoo*, porridge or oatmeal gruel); *dover*, provisions, food in general, also a clasp knife,[7] whence *flash the dover*, eat with a clasp knife; *ointment*, custard; *slosh*, coffee; *goldfish*, tinned fish or smoked herrings; *speedball*, a rolled ball of mincemeat; *dodger*, bread (which dates from before 1897 in Australia, but was anticipated by the U.S. use of the term for a hard-baked cake or biscuit, usually called a *corn-dodger*); *Massey Harris* or *free-cut*, cheese (the former because of its reputation as "the greatest binder

---

[5] To this "joy" and "delight" series might be added *waler's delight* – also known as *Murrumbidgee jam* – which is used to describe brown sugar moistened with cold tea and spread on damper. The references in these terms are, of course, to the *Murrumbidgee waler*. On a different tack, we find *digger's delight*, but the subject was not food; recorded in 1891, this expression was used for a large felt hat worn by New Zealand gum diggers.

[6] Used in English slang for cheese.

[7] "Every man carried his own knife, usually a strong, single-bladed one, branded *Dover*, and this was fastened to the waist by a lanyard, passed through a hole in the handle." – Edmund Morey, "Reminiscences of a Pioneer Squatter", "Sydney Mail", November, 1907.

in the world"); *to bite someone's name, to sign one's hand, to make food laugh,* to eat; and *banyan day,* the name by which Friday was known in the bush a couple of generations ago.

In their typescript of Australian slang, Stephens and O'Brien note: "Any day of starvation or short diet is also called a *banyan day* [in the outback]. With boundary riders or out-station dwellers the last day of their weekly rations is so known." Hence its application to Fridays, which were the end of the ration week. This expression also had English nautical origins. It meant a day on which sailors ate no flesh. Australia has had a long association with it. For instance, the note "No banyan days", meaning that meat would be supplied every day, is used twice in a Certificate of Victualling, dated March 10, 1796.

As might be expected in an enthusiastic tea-drinking country such as ours (only after World War II did coffee-drinking become popular), we have developed a useful vocabulary around this beverage. Three old expressions are *ration tea,* poor quality tea included in station rations, *post-and-rails* (also called *post-and-rail tea*) and *jack the painter;* the second is derived from the pieces of stalk and leaf floating on top, and the last from the stain left round the drinker's mouth or in the billy (at least, that is the approved explanation).

The *billy* is the focal point round which all good tea-drinking should gyrate. It is as intimately Australian as the *sundowners, walers, overlanders* and *bushmen* who walked it millions of miles. The *billy* is something more than a tin in which water is boiled; it is used extensively for cooking in the bush, especially for boiling vegetables and for stewing. Owing, perhaps, to the influence of tea-packers who named their product *Billy Tea* this fact is often forgotten, but, even so, it can scarcely excuse the "Oxford Dictionary" for defining *billy* as "the Australian bushman's teapot".

The origin of *billy* is by no means as obscure as Morris and others would make it. It is academic nonsense to seek an origin in the French *bouilli.* The source is the Aboriginal word *billa,* a creek or river, by transference to water. *Billa* makes its appearance in another well-known Australian term, *billabong,* which, as its origins – *billa,* creek, and *bong,* dead – show, is a portion of a river that is no longer running.

Billycan and *billypot* are self-explanatory derivatives.

The *black jack*[8] is also a billy, often used as a synonym for *quart pot.* The history of *quart pot* dates from 1844; *billy* was not used in print until 1850. *Jackshea* or *Jack Shay* are other nicknames for a quart pot; to these, *pint pot* may be added without explanation.

There has probably always (or nearly always) been a close link between *billy* and *smoke-oh.* We saw in Chapter III that *smoke-ohs* are recognised breaks in woolshed operations. Away from woolsheds, they are breaks for morning or afternoon tea, but in the bush they are any time at all deemed suitable for boiling the billy.

---

[8] *Blackjack* was noted earlier as a slang term for treacle, by transference from the billy of that name (treacle tins were ideal for the purpose). The term was used in English for a leather drinking vessel.

Tea is said to be *bulled* when soda is added to make it stronger. This use of the verb is closely allied to *bull*, meaning to add to the strength of a mining blast by packing more dynamite at the base of a bore than along the bore itself. From the 1890s came another use of *bull*, to add cold water to tea or spirits to dilute it; by contrast to the above, this theme of dilution was noted in Australia as far back as 1827 when we find it applied to the washings of a sugar bag.

Cuppa is a national expression for a cup of tea which we have used since early this century; *to take tea with a person*, to associate with someone, dates from 1881; *easy as tea drinking*, extremely simple, was used by an Australian writer in 1893.

Three expressions related to the Aborigines are *lazybed cooking*, the native method of cooking in the hot ashes of campfires, *jump-up*, a mixture of "flour and water boiled into a paste with sugar" and *sugar bag*, the honey of native bees. In the case of *jump-up* the bubbles which rose to the surface during boiling were described by the Aborigines as *jump-up*. After 1859 several references are found to the dish.

Among Aboriginal delicacies are birds known as galahs. There is a saying in the bush: "Put a stone in the pot and when it's soft the galahs are ready". But this is an exaggeration. Young galahs make as rich a dish as wild pigeons.

The station hand of our now remote yesterdays knew little of sausages, for which reason the following words are almost certainly of city origin: *snags, snaggles, snorks, snorkers* and *bangers* – and for saveloys one simple expressive word, *starvers*. And the station hand probably never heard of the *Lamington*, a square-cut piece of sponge, chocolate coated and sprinkled with coconut, but I know of many Australians who, having been in foreign fields, identify it as a luxurious symbol of Australia. I fail to understand why.

5. BUSH IDIOM

IN THIS SECTION we come to one of the most colourful parts of the Australian language – the multitude of phrases and idiomatic expressions that grew up in the outback. Once again we cannot say that all these phrases are purely bush idiom. They have extended far beyond the boundaries of the bush, no matter how wide a meaning we give to that term. Some of them will still be heard as often as in a capital as in the outback and we will encounter some of them in disguises in Chapter XXI. But there is a tang about them, an atmosphere to make you feel that their true background was never anonymous city streets, but the individual worlds which men carved for themselves out of the bush and backblocks.

This Section should be of interest to writers, for it shows that even this part of our idiom extends far beyond the limitations of *stone the crows!* and *strike me up a gumtree!* which are regarded by many people as our main contributions to colourful speech.

Although it is a lengthy quotation, it is impossible to pass by this commentary on bush lingo by John Drayman, published in the "Bulletin" of November 11, 1899:

Some of our bush phrases were transplanted from America, probably per the California digger and Yankee whaler of half a century ago; but in transplantation have become so Australianised that their own coiners would not recognise them.

Among others, our *hills too steep for a crow to fly down without breeching* is akin to the Yankee *hills so steep that chain lightning couldn't go down 'em 'thout putting the shoe* (brake) *on*.

J. R. Lowell claims old-world origins for nearly all Yankee words, but holds that most of his countrymen's quaint phrases are native. Some day, soon, we will be in a position to make the same claim to originality.

Of course, the Australian's quickness to adapt old similes to local requirements will always make it difficult satisfactorily to draft our *quandongs*[9] from Yankee nutmegs. Also, the similarity of our surroundings with those of early American folk – big distances, big trees, lack of history, log huts, bullock teams, the solemn stern fight with unkindly Nature, the common language – will certainly produce a similarity of phrase and (barring that tired feeling) even character, which will be scarcely distinguishable from plagiarism.

However, surely the bulk of the following – many of them in common use and all heard in the bush – are genuine *kangaroos* :[10]

A man so short that to mount his horse he had to stand on his head to get his foot in the stirrup.

A sheep described by a shearer as having *enough leather* (loose skin) *about his neck to make*, say, *dewlaps for a team of bullocks*.

Another sheep described by a shearer as having *as many wrinkles in his hide as a concertina*, or *wrinkled from breech to breakfast time*, or *from afternoon to appetite*, meaning in sailor's parlance from stem to stern; but the Australian bushman generally put his saying stern first . . .

A snake *longer than anyone can remember*.

A long journey to an indefinite goal – *a thousand miles the other side of sundown*.

An aperture so small and tight that *you couldn't drive a tin tack in with a ton monkey*.

Blankets so worn and devoid of nap that *they wouldn't catch a burr if you dragged them from Bendigo to Bourke*. Anyone *too slow to catch worms* or *to catch a cold*, or *to go to his own funeral*, or *to get out of his own road*.

. . . The average Australian has no better standard of speed than *he's pretty sudden* or *swift* or *he can run* (or *jump*) *like a blanky kangaroo with a pot of horse blister stuck to his tail*.

From jackass to jackass is sometimes varied with *from jackass to mopoke* – from dawn to dark.[11]

There are thousands of mere exaggerations used:

Hands like feet and feet like No. 4 shovels; head like a woolshed; mouth like a horse-collar, etc., but the comparisons are seldom incongruous or quaint enough to raise a smile.

Poverty of simile accounts for a lot of blanky [i.e. *bloody*] in the bush.

---

[9] The fleshy fruit of the quandong-tree here used as a synecdoche.
[10] This is another good example of localized synecdoche.
[11] The version *from magpie to mopoke* has also been recorded.

The hottest day is only spoken of as *hotter than blanky hell with the blanky lid off* or *as hot as the blanky hobs of hell*.

Next to *blanky, hell* is the word most used by our natives. They run, jump, swear, ride, fight, shear, skite and lie *like hell*, and the cook can even cook like hell . . . .

A round-barrelled horse is often *ribbed up like a mosquito;* a round-barrelled man is generally *ribbed up to the neck like a mosquito*.

A horse with good staying power has *a bottom like a camp oven*. So has a good fighting man; but the latter is generally *overloaded with science* as an additional reason for *taking to water* or fighting shy of a *go* with him.

[A sundowner's] tucker bags not seldom have *necks on 'em like blanky emus*. A dirty careless mate is slyly referred to as *a real clean bloke; he washes himself every six weeks whether he wants it or not*, or *he gets up at nine o'clock every morning, daylight or starlight*.

The wittiest bush similes are unprintable in a polite paper, but, my colonial! aren't they expressive and original!

Drayman's summary gives us a fair picture of bush idiom seventy years ago, but it omits a great deal, doubtless because the writer was not sure how far he could go without encroaching on Americanisms. Moreover, he made little call on flora and fauna which, in every country, fall early victims to simile and metaphor.

Consider these modern city newspaper quotations: "He need be no more filled with a passion for active soldiering *than a peeved paddymelon*." "This is an open season for the racketeer. He's *as safe as a koala in a reserve*." "Grey was *as aggressive as a bull ant*" and "Cast Well hadn't *as much whiz in him as a sick sheep*."

These are continuing proofs that the idiomatic enthusiasms of our bush yesterdays can still light fires in the imagination. At a later stage in the book, when we come to examine city idiom, we will see that its coverage extends far beyond this.

There are many comparable strokes of simile tucked away in odd corners of our language. Take, for example, the bandicoot,[12] and see what we have done to it; *balmy* (or *barmey*) *as a bandicoot, lousy as a bandicoot, miserable as a bandicoot, poor as a bandicoot, not the brains of a bandicoot, bald as a bandicoot, bandy as a bandicoot*. In his "Capricornia" (1938), Xavier Herbert treats us to *fleeing like bandicoots before a bush fire*. Sir Henry Parkes once found apt simile when he described a lonely and forlorn opponent as being *like a bandicoot on a burnt ridge*.[13]

Many of these phrases are, of course, gross libels on a sagacious little marsupial, but they are none the less effective for that. They are sufficient to show that we have come a long way since days when the only Australian contribution to the world of fun and laughter was the riddle[14]: Why is a

---

[12] J. I. Hunt ("Hunt's Book of Bonanzas", 1889) refers to "This ole pumpkin-headed *bandicoot* ov a pos'man". *To bandicoot* is to take tuberous vegetables, especially potatoes, out of soil, but to leave the tops standing. This is done by burrowing under the plant. Whence, *bandicooter*, one who steals vegetables in such a way, and *bandicooting*, the practice.

[13] Rendered *miserable as an orphan bandicoot on a burnt ridge* in the "Bulletin" of March 24, 1904.

[14] Noted by William Shaw, "The Land of Promise" (1854).

dun like a platypus? – Because he is a beast with a bill! This trite pun found its way into Farmer and Henley's "Dictionary of Slang" (1905) under the entry: "*Ornithorhynchus*. A creditor, a beast with a bill." It is repeated by Partridge who plunges deeper into the swamp by saying it was current in Australia between *circa* 1895 and 1915, but produces no evidence to support his contention.

When we discover such glimpses of colourful speech as "I've tasted better stuff in *a billabong full of dead wallaroos*", "A Labor College has been founded in Sydney to remove the *bowyangs* from the minds of the workers" and "The bright river of reminiscence *ran a banker*" we begin to feel that our slang and our environment have been put to good uses. In terms of fact, this form of colour can be traced back a long way.

Contrary to popular belief, Henry Lawson made few original contributions to Australian idiom, although he used Australian slang liberally. In nine books of short stories published between 1896 and 1910, Lawson used only a dozen Australian similes, and some of these were not original. His own inventions were colourless and were, like much of his work, the product of a reporter rather than of an interpretative writer. The best of Lawson's similes (and some of these may not be his own) are: *a thirst like a sunstruck bone*, (a person) *squinting round like a great goanna, cold and dark as a bushman's grave*, (a horse) *came curvin' up like a boomerang* and *meaner than a goldfield Chinaman*.

At one time we had a big Chinese population (they were largely responsible for the establishment of that legal fiction, the *White Australia Policy* – first printed use of *White Australia* occurred in the "Boomerang", Queensland, on June 2, 1888) and they have left their mark in such old metaphors as *awkward as a Chow on a bike, mad as a Chinaman, fat as a Chinky's horse* and *not for all the tea in China*.

Naturally enough, the gumtree found its way into Australian popular speech at an early stage. In 1859, Oline Keese ("The Broad Arrow") referred to an Australian-born boy who used the synecdoche: "I'm a *gumtree!*" meaning that he was a native of this country. *Gumsucker* was a nickname by which Victorians were once known (it was used a quarter of a century before Victoria became a State); later it was applied to Tasmanians and Queenslanders, thence to Australians as a whole. *To fix the old gumtree*, to settle down; *to have gumleaves growing out of one's ears*, to be a country bumpkin; *up a gumtree*, in a quandary (a variant is *up a wattle*); *to have seen one's last gumtree*, to be on the verge of death; and the exclamation *by gums!* (a simple extension of the mild English oath *by gum!*) – all these came into our speech from the same source.

Here, as evidence that people who lived in the outback generations ago were able to wrest some effective similes from their environment, is a selection covering a wide field:

ANIMALS, ETC.

mournful as a scrub dingo, i.e. mournful in sound.
sick as a blackfellow's dog, extremely sick. (Compare *thin as a swaggie's dog* and *fat as a larrikin's dog*.)

rough as a pig's breakfast, crude, rough and ready.

touchy as a scrub bull in a bog, dangerously irritable.

touchy as a taipan, dangerously irritable. (The taipan is a snake.)

touchy as a Queensland buffalo, dangerously irritable.

flat out like a lizard drinking (or *like a lizard on a log*), lying prone or, figuratively, working at great speed.

fat as a poddy (calf), plump.

leap like a lizard, to dart forward.

climb like a possum, to climb rapidly.

happy as a possum up a gumtree, extremely happy. (The gumtree is the only Australian part of this phrase.)

mad as a cut snake, mad as a frilled lizard, mad as a goanna, mad as a gumtree full of galahs, mad as a beetle, mainly to be interpreted as descriptions of silliness.

wriggle like a cut snake, to wriggle dementedly.

game as a pissant, extremely courageous.

drunk as a pissant, extremely drunk. (We have also extracted a verb from *pissant*: someone is said to be *pissanting around* when he shows no purpose in his activities.)

happy as a boxing kangaroo in fogtime, a meiotic phrase which is intended to denote considerable unhappiness.

as free from sense as a frog from feathers, silly, stupid.

BIRDS

silly as a curlew, extremely silly. (This is another zoological libel; it is perhaps based on the weird nocturnal cries of the stone curlew.)

mournful as a curlew's cry, mournful in sound. (See comments above.)

dry as a bird's arse, extremely dry.

wary as a mallee hen guarding her eggs, extremely wary.

rare (or *scarce*) *as hen's teeth*, non-existent.

poor as a fowl, of extremely poor quality. (Still another libel!)

GENERAL

tough as fencing wire, long-lasting, durable.

thin as a fence rail, extremely thin.

teeth like a dogleg fence, with irregular teeth.

black as a burnt log, black, extremely dark.

solid as an ironbark stump, firm, unshakeable.

like the heatwave from a bushfire, exceedingly hot.

rough as bags, rough as a bag, rough as a sandbag, crude, rough and ready.

dry as a sunstruck bone, utterly parched.

useless as a dry thunderstorm, without value.

like a Ballarat jewshop, in a confusion.

beards like frayed out Millaquin ports, long and untidy beards. (This Queensland simile needs explaining. Millaquin is the name of an independent sugar refinery established at Bundaberg in 1882. *Port* was a slang term for a sugar bag.)

tea as weak as gin's piss, extremely weak tea. *Maidswater* is used similarly.

to sit up like Jackey, to sit up straight. (This is presumably a reference to an Aboriginal male, but it is worth recalling that English nautical slang once used *jackey* or *jacky* for gin, in which case the original reference was possibly to an Aboriginal female.)

This, of course, is only the beginning for simile is but part of metaphor. Here are some of the other colourful turns of speech bequeathed to us from the bush:

ANIMALS, ETC.

country too thick for a black snake to wriggle through, country covered with dense scrub.

to keep a dog and bark oneself, said as an indication of futility.

to ring one's tail, to be cowardly. (The terms *ringtail* and *possum-guts* for a coward show that the origin is the possum.)

not to care if the cow calves or breaks her neck, to be indifferent to events.

out where the bull feeds, in the outback.

kneehigh to a grasshopper, extremely small. (Usually said of a child.)

no flies about, alert, wide awake.

to dingo on, to betray, to act as a coward.

to white ant, to undermine, sabotage. (Taken into industrial and political jargon. Also as noun, *white ant* or *white anter,* a saboteur, with *termite* as an occasional equivalent.)

home on the pig's back, said when a task is properly and easily completed. Equivalents of later vintage are *home and dried* and *home and hosed.*

to have more points than a porcupine, to be alert to the advantages one can take in a situation. (See *pointer,* Chapter VI, Section 4.)

to feel as though one might give birth to bullants, said usually when one is in a state of stupefied confusion.

to have kangaroos in one's top paddock, to have the white ants, to have white ants in the billy, to be silly or stupid.

to go and kill a snake, to go and catch a horse, to leave company in order to urinate.

to take the edge off a horse, to break a horse.

to hang up a horse, to tether a horse after dismounting.

all behind like Barney's bull, exhausted; also said of someone with large buttocks. (An Australian adaptation of an English slang phrase.)

BIRDS

a bit of a lyrebird, a minor liar.

to be a bower bird, to accumulate trivia.

to have a crow's eye, to be cunning, alert.

out where the pelican builds her nest, in the remote outback.

reared with the brolgas and born in a drought, said of a toughened outback man.

GENERAL

over the fence or *over the edge,* unreasonable, unfair.

full of bushfire, full of energy or vim.

to go up a hollow log, to hide.

to have the wood on, to have an advantage over (an opponent).

dry old stick, an old and ironic man. (The use of *stick* for person is in standard English.)

to get hold of the wrong end of the stick, to misunderstand, misinterpret an idea or situation.

to find one's home paddock, to settle down after much wandering.

to put the legrope on (someone), to discipline a person, to control him.
to bet your best Sunday bowyangs, to bet enthusiastically.
to pull the wrong rein, to make an error.
to give (something) *a buck*, to attempt. (Later, the word *buck* was replaced with *burl, belt* or *bash*.)
to carry the mail, to stand treat in a hotel bar.

In addition, many more involved expressions took shape in the outback. For instance, these descriptions of hunger, *a hole in my belly a man could drive a team of bullocks in and lose 'em* and *my belly thinks my throat's cut;* this avowal of worldly wisdom, *to have crossed* (or *been up*) *too many dry gullies to be fooled* or *to have been up too many hard stumps to be taken in;* this description of a person who is not to be trusted, *he's the sort of bloke who'd kid you up a tree and then chop it down;* this advice to someone who has "got on" to return to being a member of the proletariat, *take off your boots and become respectable again!* And, of course, there is a large selection of comments in which *this side of the Black Stump* is used as a loose standard of comparison, as in *the best feed you'll get this side of the Black Stump* and *the crookest deal this side of the Black Stump*. Over the years, spasmodic argument has occurred over whether the phrase applied to a specific *Black Stump* in the outback or was just a generalization for the *bush*. H. P. ("Duke") Tritton says firmly in "Time Means Tucker" (1959): "The Black Stump was real. About nine or ten miles from Coolah, on the Gunnedah road, it had been a wine-shanty. When I saw it in 1905 it had been closed down for many years, and was a ruin .... the property on which it stood is still known as The Black Stump today." Among other claimants for the *Black Stump* title is a place called The Black Stump one mile from Munduberra, in Queensland's Central Burnett district: the stump was officially unveiled on May 5, 1958.

Even these do not exhaust the rich vein of bush idiom. Consider *the Tantanoola tiger*, which the "Australian Encyclopaedia" defines as "in some degree an Australian catch-phrase as indicative of something mythical or at least almost incredible" (it came from a report in 1889 that a "tiger" had been sighted at Tantanoola, S.A.); *Hell, Hay and Booligal*, allegedly the hottest places imaginable (Hay and Booligal are in southern N.S.W.); *Woop Woop*, a fictional outback place, supposedly the most primitive of all outback settlements; *Mulga Bill*, reputedly the most simple of all bush simpletons; the exclamation *well, I'm willy-willied!;* and a host of impossibilities among the least-trite of which are *to see a bunyip chase an Abo, to watch a sheep climb a tree* and *to hear a bull oyster roar*.

Probably through the influence of the shearer we have inherited *dag*, a "hard case", a character (doubtless from the *dags* cut off a sheep), *dip*, a swim, a bathe (from the *sheepdip*), *merino*, a Don Juan, i.e. a ram, *to swing the gate*, to work at great speed, *to look for one's swag straps* and *to roll one's pannikin to another shed*, to leave a job, *the July fog*, the dead season when no shearing is done, and *run rings around*, to out-do. From the bushman, living in continual dread of summer bushfires, have come *the red mare* and *the red steer* for such fires. From the tramp, *there's a bug in the billy*, there's still something left, we're not hard up yet. And from countrymen in general, *ironbark*, unyielding; *the old square days* and *the earlies*, old times; *before the yeast bread* and *before the walnut*, used of early times; *joey*, a young child, a minor lie or evasion, something worthless (from the young of a kangaroo or other marsupial); *maggoty*, angry, peevish, irritable (which is close to standard English); *settler's matches*, long, pendulous strips of bark hanging from some eucalypts which are readily ignited and used as kindling; a person's *muttons*, the thing that is desired[15]; *blow-in*, a newcomer, a person of brief residence in a locality; *bushman's squat*, a method of balancing on the balls of the feet with the knees under the arms; *bushman's cocktail*, a dry gin.[16]

The phrase *send her down, Hughie!* is worth close attention. This is an appeal to the authorities in heaven either to begin or to continue a fall of rain. It has been in Australian use since the beginning of this century, and holds a special poignancy for people living in outback areas where rainfall is often problematical. It has been responsible for the word *Hughie* coming to serve as a jocular, and irreverent, form of reference to the deity, e.g. "Blame it on Hughie", "Hughie did it" ("The Australian", August 6, 1964, p. 18, printed: "And who was to blame – mainly *Huey!*"). W. H. Downing recorded in his "Digger Dialects" (1919) the phrase *send her down, Steve!* with the note: "Compare the French soldiers' phrase, 'Envoyez, Dieu, la pluie en bas'." An old British army use was *send it down, David* (or *Davy*). The following extract from a "sonnet" on March by L. J. Villiers reveals that *Hughie* also serves as a term for rain:

That's March's way: it gets the break uv 'eat,
Like kliner's kisses w'en y're 'oldin' on
Erbout the finish uv a smoodgin'-meet;
Then, fore it's over, w'ere the sunblaze shone
Down Hughie pours, en Summer's limp en beat,
En takes the offis straight it mus' be gone.

An old-timer, who worked in the outback, tells me that when the weather broke another cant-phrase was used: "*Good-oh! Fat horses and silver cheques!*" He adds: "Why silver in days when sovereigns were common I could never fathom". The invocation *send her down, Hughie!* is one of those rural offerings that, long since, have become imbedded in city jargon. It has even got into *surfie* talk: *whip 'em up, Hughie!* is an appeal for a lively surf.

Before we continue, let us summon our cliché expert to answer a simple question.

Q. When needed rain falls in a pastoral area, what do farmers become?
A. They don't "become" anything. They "are" it.
Q. Well then, what "are" they?
A. They are *jubilant*.

---

[15] Almost certainly, although remotely, from the French, *revenons à nos moutons*, let us return to our subject. In "National Education" (N.Z.) February 1, 1940, an example appears: "Milk is small Charlie's muttons".

[16] This, of course, is a play on *gin*, an Aboriginal female, and the liquor.

Q. Anything else?

A. No, the Australian Press declines to recognise that they are anything other than *jubilant*.

From the outback came, too, a couple more phrases worth attention. *There's more than what you're welcome to* almost has the savour of an Australian proverb. Francis Ratcliffe notes it in "Flying Fox and Drifting Sand" (1938) as used among men living in northern mountains. He says: "I had it thrown at me half a dozen times when I was with them". It denotes a giver's modest generosity: "Don't you worry; there's more than what you're welcome to". Another such saying was addressed to someone with old and thin blankets; he was advised to drag them through clover-burrs *to put a bit of nap on 'em*. This is obviously not far removed from a saying, noted by Drayman in 1899, that blankets could be so worn that they *wouldn't take a burr if you dragged them from Bendigo to Bourke*.

Apart from a mistaken regard for Ned Kelly and his gang (after examining all the relevant evidence, I have little doubt that they were a group of homosexuals), there are few Australians who are even remotely to be classed as folk-heroes. There is much the same deficiency in our list of folk-places; the *Speewaa* (the official spelling is *Speewa*) is probably the nearest we have come to one. This was a legendary station of notable (and improbable) deeds. Ernestine Hill says that "the original Speewaa station is near Swan Hill on the Murray River, home of great men and tall tales in the very earlies." I am advised that there is a Speewah station in the north Kimberleys, W.A.

At one stage in our yesterdays, the outback began on the fringes of Sydney, Melbourne and the other State capitals. Over the generations, it has been slowly pushed back, so that these days one has to go to the far north of Queensland, the Centre, the Top End and the Kimberleys to find something that approaches the traditional idea of what the outback was. For this reason we owe some debt to Mrs Hill for the glossary she appends to "The Territory" (1951), which shows that we have by no means come to the end of outback idiom. Here are some samples gathered by Mrs Hill during her northern journeys: *blind tiger*, a store in the faraway bush that sells liquor without a licence; *boomerang cheques*, cheques that are returned unhonoured; *brands and descriptions*, identifications, characteristics; *carry the stockwhip*, to be boss, often applied to dominating wives; *chuck* (or *throw*) *on the packs*, to leave; *"It's a fine day for travellin'*," notice to go; *go up a gully*, to make oneself scarce; *hide cracking*, time to go in for drinks or on a bender; *on the Lochinvar*, an old term for catching lubras to work cattle, etc.; *piccaninny daylight*, false dawn; *playing ping-pong*, travelling backwards and forwards across a border; *roly-poly*, rumours that gather as they go, from roly-poly grass; *write account with a fork*, to charge three times too much.

Mrs Hill also has an interesting footnote on *Malley's Cow*. She says that this is "the Australian equivalent of Alfred and the Cakes. Back in Monaro folklore one Malley in a mustering camp was told to hold a particular cow. When the boss came back and asked for it, Malley grinned. 'She's a goner!' he said. Hence the proverbial *Malley's Cow*."

An expression originally used in north Australia and borrowed in all English-speaking countries during World War II is *had it*. Anything can be said to have *had it*: food after it has been eaten has *had it;* a dead sheep has *had it;* a book that has been read has *had it*. It is one of those expressions almost defying definition, but of great utility.

By now it should have become obvious that Australian idiom is far above the *stone the crows!* class of phrase; but to underline the fact, here are some variations on the theme to show that we have not been idle even in such a simple matter: *starve the lizards! starve the mopokes! starve the wombats! starve the bardies!* (a Westralian version), *starve the ninnies!* (from South Australia), *starve the sparrows!* and even *starve the rats!* (recorded in the "Bulletin", January 9, 1908), *speed the wombats! stiffen the lizards! stiffen the snakes!* and *stiffen the wombats!*

CHAPTER V

The Road

1. GOLD

EVEN TODAY, the road is often more a symbol than an exact term in Australia. The word "road" gives you some impression of a highway or a well-beaten thoroughfare leading definitely from one place to another. But the road countless Australians travelled was anything but well-beaten; at the best it was often only a track leading vaguely from some place over the horizon into the wilderness, and it has sometimes been simpler to strike off on your own than to follow the footsteps of others.

Of wanderers there were plenty in the first sixty years of Australian history: these were the men who pushed back the boundaries of settlement into the ranges along the eastern seaboard, then into the plainlands and Mallee, into the wild bush and the sandy desert, men who, by the turn of 1850, had either begun to dig down their roots in far outback stations with the feeling that their journeyings were over and that they could reap some rewards for perilous adventure, or were nomadic workers who were forced to move relentlessly from one place to another in search of jobs. Since there were far more would-be workers than station-owners, the Australian nomad was to become almost the greatest symbol of all of those days.

But the turn of the mid-century was to bring a new spirit of wanderlust to Australia, was to set moving the feet of countless thousands. With 1851 came the commercial discovery of gold.

It has for long been a cliché that this country achieved nationhood during World War I, but in many respects she achieved that nationhood in the 1850s. Linguistically, at any rate, she acquired an identity in gold-rush days from which she has never looked back.

No longer was it necessary for men to toil wearily against nature, against heat and drought and flies and loneliness, against the stupidity of cattle and sheep, in order to make livelihoods. Here, on the goldfields, was wealth: great chunks of raw gold, gold that you could kick out of the surface with the toe of your boot, gold that you could take out of a creek-bed in handfuls, gold that you could find in dusty town streets.

So the trek began and the tracks were beaten with the passing of many feet.

From all parts of the world people poured into the country, hungry for easy money. Population jumped from 400,000 in 1850 to nearly 1,200,000 ten years later. Most of this increase was due to gold.

But gold brought poverty as well as prosperity, and with that poverty came the language of wanderers and deadbeats; it widened the criminal cant that had been brought to Australia by the convicts and reinforced by *The System;* it spread the argot of sly-grog joints and pubs and our early larrikins; it meant – and this is the great importance of that symbol, The Road – the establishment of a kinship between city dwellers and people of the backblocks.

In 1853 a writer named C. R. Read urged that Englishmen going to the Australian diggings should search their souls and ask themselves "if they can stand a little colonial slang". It should be obvious by now that the adjective "little" was conservative. Records of Australian life after 1851 are fertile in slang.

No term bulks more significantly in this period than *digger*, with its many derivatives, *diggerman* (1854), *diggeress*, the wife of a miner (1855), *diggerdom* (1855) and *diggerism* (1857). *Digger* had been recorded in Australia before 1850, but it was not until 1851 that it came into prominence as gold *broke out* first in New South Wales and then in the newly created State of Victoria, bringing in its train scores of expressions concocted to meet the needs of the times. *Diggings* had been in English use in 1769 and it came to this country via America. An old and now obsolete Australian version (which is found in many old books) was *diggins;* a rare singular form *diggin* was sometimes used.

Scarcely less important than the digger was the *fossicker* (1853), derived from the old English dialectal verb, *to fossick*, which found an easy place in our gold-seeking vocabulary. *Night-fossicking* referred to the theft of gold at night from others' claims. The verb has now a wide colloquial use: we *fossick* for something when we search for it, we *fossick it up* or we *fossick around*.

Here are a few more names for those who *chased the nimble pennyweight* in one way or another: *reefer,*[1] *cradler, dryblower* or *blower, specker, sand-scratcher, nuggeter* and *dodger.* The *dodger* did his gold-chasing in a rather peculiar way. Apparently, he idled away his time until more energetic diggers proved that ground next to his claim was auriferous – then he went to work. If you can imagine a *dodgers' rush* (one is recorded in the "Armidale Express" of February 20, 1860), you become aware that *dodging*, rather like *shepherding*, which denoted "keeping passive possession of a hole and keeping watch around for the run of the *gutter* (i.e. the lead of gold)" was a popular non-industry on the goldfields. *To shepherd,* to retain legal right to a claim by doing a minimum of work on it with the aim of making a profit by sale, is recorded in 1856. The main difference between the *shepherd* and the *dodger* seems to have been that the former made a considerable excavation on his claim while the latter's excavations were never more than six inches deep – up to 300 of them – to conform with minimum official requirements.

᾿ *Nugget* is an Austral-American term for a piece of gold (the early textual quotations in the "Oxford Dictionary" are Australian), and *plug, specimen, slug, cake, fly-spot* and *fly-sh*t* also seem to be indigenous. *Colour* for

---

[1] *Quartz-reefer* is also Australian. So is *quartz boil*, an outcrop of a quartz reef on the surface (R. B. Smyth, "The Gold Fields and Mineral Districts of Victoria", 1869).

E

gold or specks of gold is recorded in this country in 1857 and in America slightly earlier. We shall have to class it – with many other gold-mining expressions – as a common possession. Of 1857 vintage also we find *raise the colour* and *get the colour*, to strike gold.

The uses of the verb, *to bottom*, to reach solid rock or clay in a gold-mine (1852), or to reach earth which contains gold in a mine (1857), are particularized Australian versions of standard English; *to bottom on to* (or *on the*) *gold*, to strike luck, to succeed, is indigenous.

The use of *show* for a mine (later to become the equivalent of a chance or opportunity, as in *give him a show*, let him have a chance to do his best) is another expression of our own; but *to prospect, pan out* and *pan off* seem to be American originals. According to the "Oxford Dictionary" we are entitled to claim as our own *prospect*, for "an examination or test of mineral richness in a locality or of material from which ore, etc., is to be extracted", but *prospector, prospecting* and kindred terms were used earlier in the U.S. However, the expression *woolly-nosed prospectors*, for old prospectors whose noses were alleged to be woolly from blowing the dust in their pans, is possibly Australian. If there is any cause for wonder at the number of terms in this category which were anticipated in the U.S. it should not be forgotten that the California gold-rush broke out at the end of the 1840s, was patronised by many Australians (especially the *Sydney Ducks* or *Sydney Coves*) and, through the agency of E. H. Hargraves, partly spurred our commercial gold discoveries.

Leader or *lead*, an alluvial gold claim or a vein of gold; *deep leader*, a man who works a deep alluvial claim; *Gympie*[2] *work*, single-handed hammer and drill work (a Queensland use); *wash* and *washing stuff*, alluvial soil from which gold is extracted by washing; *reef*, a lode of auriferous quartz; *blow* or *floater*, a mineral outcrop; *monkey shaft*, a trial shaft in a mine; *leg*, a nearly vertical prolongation of the saddle of a quartz reef; *standing ground*, untimbered ground at the bottom of a shaft; *loom*, to follow grains of gold in the hope of finding the leader; *pennyweighting*, prospecting for minor discoveries in poor ground; *Jenny Lind*, a miner's cradle; *burnt stuff*, a stratum of iron-hard rock or compacted clay and rock encountered during digging; and *hungry quartz*, an unpromising quartz reef – these are all terms of long history belonging to the Australian miner's vocabulary.

Dart, earth or deposits "worth washing for gold as distinguished from that considered worthless" (1859), *fine carrots*, a miner's solecism for "carats fine" (1857), *mullock*, unwanted spoil or rock from a mine[3] (1864), and *miner's right*, a licence to dig for gold, are a few more of the long-established terms to which we may make claim. The *miner's right* needs some additional explanation. Miners were issued with monthly or fortnightly *licences* from 1851 to 1857 and with annual *miner's rights* after 1857.

The *gold-licence* led to considerable unpleasantness in Victoria. In 1852 a local act was passed in Victoria imposing payment of a licence fee on all

---

[2] "The single-hand or *Gympie hammer* was also called a *Massey* hammer," states a correspondent.

[3] Whence, *to mullock over*, to work shoddily; *to poke mullock* (also *muck*) *at*, a variation of *poke borak at*, to make fun of a person.

diggers (originally $36 a year, later $24 a year). This licence fee and the manner in which it was officially enforced led to the stand by the miners at Eureka Stockade in 1854. As was to be expected, events which moved close to the miners' lives erupted in numerous expressions which, although obsolete now, are worthy of a place in our memory.

In 1851 C. J. Latrobe, an ardent champion of law and order who between 1839 and 1851 had been Superintendent of the Port Phillip District, was appointed Governor of Victoria. His administration bred riots at Beechworth and Castlemaine, for it was under his guidance that *licence-hunting* or *digger-hunting*,[4] as the practice was called, was instituted to see that every miner had his licence.

Latrobe bequeathed to the miners' language the simple word *Joe!* (his Christian name was Joseph) which often makes its appearance in records of gold-mining days. *Joe!* and the additional forms *Joe-Joe!* or *Joey!* were cries of warning used by diggers at the approach of police. T. McCombie writes in his "Australian Sketches" (1861): "To *joey* or *joe* a person on the diggings, or anywhere in Australia, is grossly to insult and ridicule him". In "The Eureka Stockade", an extremely odd report on the Eureka affair, Carboni Raffaello notes the use of *joeing*. In 1863 B. A. Heywood said that the term was becoming "the chaff for new chums", and was being hurled at new arrivals on the goldfields. By the 1860s it had found its way to New Zealand and, even as late as 1871, C. L. Money reports in "Knocking about New Zealand": "The word *joe* expresses the derision usually bestowed on new chums on the diggings".[5]

It was a natural development that police troopers should come to be called *joes* (incidentally, *trooper*, for a mounted man, and *black-trooper*, are both Australianisms), although this use is not found often, *demons* and *traps* (1853) being more widely used.

The Camp, which according to McCombie "used to be the terror of all", was a digger nickname for the section of a diggings which contained the police courts, the residence of the gold commissioners and the escort office. A *warden* was a government official, holding magisterial powers, in charge of a goldfield.

The police were not without their uses, however. Lack of tact in the way the miner's licence was supervised certainly caused conflict, but there were many illegal practices to be checked among the miners.

The *salting* and *peppering* of claims was widely prevalent. To *salt a claim* (1853) described the practice of "doping" or faking a worn-out or useless claim with gold dust to make it appear productive. One writer describes it as "the practice of burying gold in localities whither prospectors are

---

4 The police ("largely recruited from Tasmania . . . many were ex-convicts who had risen to be gaol-warders") were called *digger-hunters* and, in the parade of their authority, they were said to hold *licence hunts* or *licence meets*. A writer of 1857 informs us that *digger-hunting* in the days of Latrobe was "a fortnightly proceeding and never . . . at less than weekly intervals".

5 Lyricist Charles R. Thatcher, "Colonial Ministrel" (1864), takes the term into verse: "We nail the ringleaders and though they shout Joe! / Straight off to the lock-up right onward they go". From "The Song of the Trap".

attracted by rumours of ore having been found". *Planting* was a synonym.

Shicer (1857) and *duffer* (1861) are two of our oldest terms for an un-productive gold-mine, sometimes for an unproductive shaft, although the principal use for the former today is for a swindler, crook or racecourse welsher. *Shyster*[6] and *schiser*, spellings which were recorded before 1890, support the contention that the word is derived from the German vulgarism *Scheisser*.[7]

Yellow fever, the equivalent of the U.S. gold fever; *weight*, an abbrevia-tion of pennyweight; *poor man's diggings*, easily-reached alluvial gold deposits (i.e. gold which a poor man can work, contrasting with reef gold which requires capital to develop); *to make a rise*, to find gold; *specking* and *nuggeting*, which describe the practice of searching for surface gold especially after heavy rain (*surfacing* dates from 1858 or earlier) – all are expressions of a colloquial nature which the digger and his kind put into currency.

To duffer out, said of a mine which fails; *tucker field*, an area yielding a gold-seeker only enough for subsistence; *salt bush claim*, a worthless claim; *new chum gold*, iron pyrites, which is likely to mislead the uninitiated; *hatter*, a lonely miner, and *hatting*, his way of life (later, the use of *hatter* was extended to anyone who lives alone by choice in the bush or outback); and *centrepede*, a ladder made of a single upright with cross-pieces nailed on at intervals, are also worthy of inclusion.

It should be noted that in mining parlance one is always "*on*" a field, not "*at*"; thus a digger spoke of being *on Ballarat*, *on diggings* and *on the gold*.

In Chapter III reference was made to new uses to which Australia has put the word *paddock*. There was also a development in the mining sphere, a *paddock* being "an excavation made for procuring wash-dirt in shallow ground, or a place built near the mouth of a shaft where quartz or wash-dirt is stored". This use dates from 1863. It appears, after 1873, as a verb, *to paddock*, to store ore in a paddock and to excavate for the purpose of procuring wash-dirt in shallow alluvium.

In the 1890s Western Australian mining shares and their dealers on the Stock Exchange earned the name *kangaroos;* penny stocks were termed *shypoo shares*, and the mines themselves *shypoo shows*. *Shypoo*, for cheap or unstable, seems to be of Westralian origin; it has also been used in that State for colonial beer and, as *shypoo joint*, for a beer house.

According to Anthony Trollope, the use of *verandah* for "a kind of open exchange . . . on the street pavement, apparently selected by chance, on which the dealers in mining shares congregate", was popular before 1873 in Melbourne, Sandhurst and Ballarat.

Some names worth remembering:

Kerr Hundredweight, first big mass of gold found in Australia; 1,272 oz., N.S.W., 1851.

Welcome Stranger, largest nugget of its kind ever found; 2,520 oz., Victoria, 1869.

---

[6] Used in U.S. slang for an unprincipled lawyer.

[7] The English dialectal form *shice*, no good, worthless, should be noted.

Holtermann nugget, largest mass of gold ever found; about 3,000 oz. of gold, N.S.W., 1872.

Southern Cross, most unusual pearl-compound formation ever found; originally of eight pearls (a ninth was added later) in the form of a cross; Broome, W.A., 1883.

Star of the West, most notable single pearl found in Australian waters (it was about the size of a sparrow's egg); Broome, W.A., 1917.

Star of Queensland, world's largest cut black sapphire.

Queen of the Earth, world's most famous opal; found at Lightning Ridge, N.S.W.

The Cornishman has been known in English slang as *Cousin Jan* or *Cousin Jacky* for nearly a century. In Australia (tin was first found here in 1851, the same year as the commercial beginnings of gold), we have called Cornish miners *Cousin Jacks* since the 1880s. They have proved themselves expert tin miners.

Here is a brief glossary of tin miner's terms supplied by a correspondent:

banjo, a device in which tin is cleaned. It was originally a hole scooped out in the shape of a banjo and lined with bag. The dirt was placed in the large round portion of the banjo and water baled on to it by means of a *banjo scoop.* The modern *banjo* is usually a V-shaped box made of wood (see *V-box*).

banjoing, a method of cleaning tin as described above.

banjo scoop, a kerosene tin with one side cut out, attached to a handle by means of wire, used in baling water into a banjo.

bung, an obstruction in a reef.

cut, ground worked by a dredge at one site.

duffer, a shaft containing no payable dirt.

face, the depth of wash or dirt which bears tin.

feed-water, clean water needed for the feed tank of a boiler.

fossicker, a tin miner who works alone.

grizzly, as for *hopper-plate.*

hide bucket, a bucket made of greenhide and used in shafts.

hopper-plate, a sieve arrangement at the head of the boxes for passing large stones through (whence, *hopperings,* the stones therefrom).

horse, as for *bung.*

metal, used colloquially for tin.

muck-shoveller, a tin miner.

overburden, dirt stripped from top of the *wash.*

slide, a stout fork with uprights for holding a cask and with a swingle bar attached, used for carting water by horse power.

slurry, soupy water from boxes which settles into boggy clay.

tail-dump, a place where tailings are tipped from a sluice-box.

tom, timber used in a shaft.

V-box, a box V-shaped at the head of a sluice-box where wash-dirt is first dumped.

wash stones, water-worn stones present in dirt which bears tin.

whip, a method of drawing water or mullock, by hand or horse power.

willoughby, a machine for removing black sand (similar in appearance to tin) from tin. Said to be from the name of its original maker.

Opal-mining has also been developed extensively in Australia and we now produce 95 per cent of the world's output. Here is a number of expressions from the opal miner's vocabulary also sent to me by correspondents:

> *amber potch*, yellow Mexican Fire Opal.
> *boulder opal*, valuable opal found in cracks of Queensland ironstone boulders.
> *colour*, the flash of opal in *potch*.
> *floaters*, raddled opal found on the surface.
> *nobbies*, matrix opal. *Nobby opal* is a recognised variety.
> *noodling*, prospecting old opal dumps for what is left.
> *nut*, see *yowah nut*.
> *opal matrix*, as for *boulder opal*.
> *opaline*, old name for Australian opal.
> *parcel*, a find of opal. "Any fair haul of opal is always a 'parcel'."
> *pineapple*, a bunch of crystal found with seam opal.
> *potch*, opal silica, resembling delft.
> *Queensland opal*, as for *boulder opal*.
> *skin-cracker*, a subsoil of close-grained, brittle sandstone where the *potch* or silica runs.
> *tucker field*, an area which yields only enough opal for subsistence.
> *yowah nut*, a minute boulder containing a *boulder opal*, found west of Cunnamulla.

"The Opal Book", by Frank Leechman (1961), includes a long and interesting glossary. Among the items listed is *sea opal*, "not opal, but pieces of a brilliant New Zealand shell, the paua, used in jewellery." This univalve is called a *mutton-fish* or *abalone* in Australia.

A couple of other types of precious stones have been given Australian names: *Australian jade*, described as "high-quality crysoprase", which can be distinguished from genuine Chinese jade only by experts, found near Rockhampton, Queensland, in 1963; *Australian ruby*, "throughout this part of the Harts Range [Central Australia] great quantities of garnets, more commonly called Australian rubies, are found."

Several terms from the jargon of pearlers:

> *barrack*, mutilation of the word "baroque", describing an irregular pearly formation on a pearl-shell.
> *lay*, a bonus paid for each ton of pearl-shell raised.
> *setting*, a small pearl.
> *stone*, a pearl of quality.

2. WANDERERS AND DEADBEATS

WORLD WAR II served to bring home to Englishmen and Americans the fact that Australia had something of a national song in "Waltzing Matilda". This discovery in its turn raised questions as to the origin of *waltzing matilda* for humping a swag. As was to be expected, Australians had not worried their heads on the matter. If they had worried, they might have turned to Partridge's "Dictionary of Slang" and contented themselves with the erroneous explanation that it originated with the poem that Banjo Paterson wrote in the first decade of this century,[8] to which music was subsequently composed.

The exact origin of the expression is difficult to establish, but at least we know that the first recorded version in Australia was not *waltzing matilda*, but *walking matilda*, and it was in popular use long before Paterson heard it.

In "Cobbers" (1934), Thomas Wood tells a story worth repeating:

> Banjo Paterson used to come and stay with old Robert McPherson (*sic*), out at Dagworth Station [Queensland], years ago. They were driving into Winton one day, in a buggy, along with McPherson's sister and Jack Lawton, the drover. He's told me the tale many a time. On the way they passed a man carrying his swag. "That's what we call *waltzing matilda* in these parts", said McPherson; and Banjo Paterson was so struck with the phrase that he got a piece of paper and wrote the verses there and then. When they got to Winton, his sister, who was a bit of a musician, wrote the tune; and they all sang it that night.

The first printed reference to the expression seems to be an 1893 commentary by Henry Lawson on "Some Popular Australian Mistakes".[9] In this he records both *matilda* as a slang term for a swag and *walking matilda*. The next reference is a brief lament by the "Bulletin" of December 12, 1897, in its criticism of Morris's "Austral English", that the word *matilda* was not included in the dictionary. Shortly after this, on August 20, 1898, we find another writer in the "Bulletin" voicing regret that *waltzing matilda* was "now rarely heard".

The general impression one gets from these notes is that the expression was not widely known at the tail-end of last century, although it had probably been in use for ten years or so. Subsequent printed examples almost invariably avoid the *waltzing*. Thus, in 1898, we find reference to a man "travelling" *with matilda;* in 1909, an example of *humped matilda* and the sentence, "Jim . . . dropped along and let *matilda* down at the door"; in Jack Moses's book of poems "Nine Miles from Gundagai" (1938), occurs the example "where *matilda* roams the West".

Now we come to an interesting matter which may go some way towards explaining how *matilda* came to be waltzed. Several Germans have written to me on the theme and they all say (more or less) the same – that among other things the German verb *walzen* means to roam, to hike, to tramp. And it apparently acquired these senses from a special application. To quote:

> "When an apprentice was finished with his learning years and solemnly pronounced a journeyman, he was expected to go 'auf die Walz(e)' for some years, in order to see something of the world and of other craftsmen's

---

[8] The exact date when Paterson wrote the poem is unknown. It was published with his third collection, "Salt-bush Bill, J.P.", in 1917, and was probably written before 1895.

[9] In the "Bulletin", November 18, 1893.

work in his own line. He used to wander by foot, carrying a bundle with his belongings and begging at doors for money. The tramping journeyman was called a Kunde. My father was a Kunde, but he has been dead for a long time and so far I have not found anyone old enough to have 'walzed' who could tell me whether they ever called their bundle Matilde".

The fact that the earliest known record in Australia was *walking matilda* and that this became *waltzing matilda* suggests German influence. Were this an isolated sample of such influence we could reasonably regard the suggestion as far-fetched, but quite a number of other terms in Australian slang are to be traced from German origins, e.g. *spieler*, *spruiker* and *spruik* (from *sprechen*), *cronk* (from *krank*), *schicer* and *shyster* (from *Scheisser*), *sane* (from *zehn*), *drack* (from *Dreck*), *swy* (from *zwei*).

The fact is, however, that *matilda* never had much importance among Australia's nomads. Of far greater use (and antiquity) is *swag*, which dates from the beginning of last century. From its original English use to describe stolen booty, it had, by 1812 (the record is Vaux's), been extended to include "a bundle, parcel or package."

A writer in 1857 gave it the vague definition: "Portable luggage that can be carried on the person".

Henry Lawson's detailed description – in "The Romance of the Swag" (1907) – both of the contents of a swag and how it should be rolled is probably the best of its kind. He says:

> The swag is usually composed of a tent "fly" or strip of calico (a cover for the swag and a shelter in bad weather . . .), a couple of blankets, blue by custom and preference . . . and the core is composed of spare clothing and small personal effects.

As the great swag-rolling days are past, Lawson's careful analysis of the correct professional method is of historical value.

Derived forms include *swagman* and the clippings, *swagger* and *swaggie*. The form *swagsman* was current for a period, but is now obsolete. *To swag it* and *swagging* date from 1861.

Since most of our original swagmen were work-seekers, their wandering took them on some perilous journeys. Hence such expressions as *to do a perish*, almost to die for want of a drink and sometimes for lack of food (whence *perishing track*, a journey where no water is to be found); *blind stabbing over a dry stretch*, said of uncertain efforts to cross a waterless stretch of country; *to go through without the waterbag*, to be in a great hurry.

At this stage, as we stand on the edge of the pool of slang left by *swagmen* and their kind, several points must be made. The Australian nomad was mainly a work-hunter – shearers, fruit-pickers, seasonal workers of all kinds – but increasing jobs in the cities made a good deal of wandering unnecessary. Except for the Depression days, which set thousands of unemployed wandering again, the *swag-humping* era came to a virtual end around 1910; under conditions of social affluence since the end of World War II, that era is decisively over. The few swagmen you will find now on Australian outback roads are more likely to be dedicated tramps than honest work-seekers. Certainly, "tramp" was far too loose an expression to apply to all the species in Australia, for there were many differences in degree. Generalized Americanisms like *hobo* and *bum* are inadequate to suggest the shades of meaning between a *bagman* and a *waler*, between *travelling labour* and the *sundowner* or *battler*, between *coaster* and *coiler*, between the *swamper* and *drummer*, although all were used for wanderers and itinerants of various types.

The English use of *bagman* for a commercial traveller anticipated our application of the word to a swagman (1907; this was probably due to rhyme) and later to a tramp who travels the country with his possessions in a suitcase (1918).

The *battler* was one of our poorest wanderers. Stephens and O'Brien defined him as "a hard-up traveller or swagman, who is battling for a crust". An 1898 use of the word for a prostitute and another quotation in 1909 for any person who has to struggle for a means of existence underline its *deadbeat* origins.

Falling into almost the same class is the *toe-ragger*. *Toe-rags*, otherwise known as *Prince Alberts* or *Prince Alfreds*, were worn by tramps of low degree in place of socks to prevent blistering. *Toe-ragger* is doubtless derived from this. In Sydney "Truth" of January 12, 1896, a writer suggested that it came from the Maori *tau rika rika*, a slave, used as a term of contempt. This far-fetched theory has little to sustain it. The term is also used as a general pejorative and in prison argot is applied to a man serving a short sentence.

Karl Lentzner, who compiled a small dictionary of Australianisms in 1891, wrote that "in Australia, ne'er-do-wells are termed *sundowners*, *dry hash* or a *stringybark*". This generalization dismisses some important points. In 1881, for instance, A. C. Grant defined a *dry hash* as a man who would not shout drinks, but drank alone. Six years later the meaning was extended to "a miser, a bad egg; also, by implication, a loafer". *Stringybark* had uses before the middle of last century to describe crudity, lack of polish and "of the bush". *Tough as stringybark* and *a stringybark person* have early textual records, and the use of the noun for a ne'er-do-well was an extension of these.

The original *sundowners* were not quite as Lentzner defined them. They were certainly of ne'er-do-well type, since they dodged work by arriving at outback stations at sunset with requests for rations. Bush romanticism has turned the sundowner into the typical Australian nomad, and the original sense has become obscured. *Sundowning*, for instance, serves now as a description of the life of any outback vagabond, but it applied originally to the work-evading activities of *sundowners*. They were well aware that if they arrived at a station before sundown they would be *woodheaped*, set to work cutting wood, or some such task; they also had to be careful about their time of arrival for, if there was any light for travelling, they would be *creeked* as well, which meant being sent to camp on a nearby creek infested with mosquitoes. If they did not invent it, sundowners did their share in pioneering the *hollow woodheap*, which for all its apparent simplicity takes some expertize to erect. A *hollow woodheap* is a shell of split firewood, carefully built up to appear solid.

Bender (1885) and *drummer* (*circa* 1890) were once popular terms for wanderers of slightly better class than the sundowner. A *drum*, of course, is the equivalent of *swag, bundle, curse, matilda, shiralee* (the origin of this is unknown), *parcel, turkey, donkey, national debt* or *bluey* as the tramp's rolled blanket is variously called.

The *scowbanker* or *skullbanker* (1866), *coaster* (1878), *sundodger, overlander* and *overland man, tussocker* (a New Zealand equivalent of *sundowner*), *never-sweat, sooner, river-banker, barber* (apparently from the Latin *barbarus*, a stranger) and *coiler* were other vagabonds who loafed in the outback or who drifted from station to station with little other object in life than to satisfy food requirements.

The *Murrumbidgee waler* was a tramp of especially indolent type. He often camped for long periods where fish could be caught, especially along big rivers like the Darling, Murrumbidgee and Murray. The original, or perhaps the best-known *Murrumbidgee walers* were probably New South Wales tramps, as distinct from vagabonds who came from other States,[10] especially when we find J. Inglis describing a resident of New South Wales as a *waler* in his "Our Australian Cousins" (1879).

There is another theory that *Murrumbidgee waler* should be spelt *whaler*. The late A. S. Kenyon, historian, wrote to me: "The original *Murrumbidgee whaler* was the possessor of a boat; he worked up to the sources, Albury, Wagga, for the summer and the lower river for the winter. He caught fish and sold or bartered them for tucker. Latterly the term has been used loosely for any swaggie, infesting or frequenting the rivers, but *whaler* is the correct version."

The phrase *herring-boning the Darling on Jackie Dow's mutton* is possibly relevant here.

Blood brethren of the *waler* (or *whaler*), to be found in Sydney and Melbourne respectively, are the *Domain dosser* (1894) or *Domain squatter* (*circa* 1900) and the *Yarra banker* (1908), specialists in the art of loafing. The true *Yarra banker*, however, is a soapbox orator who frequents the banks of the Yarra River in Melbourne. Thus we have *Yarra bank* for soapbox oratory, illuminated by the following newspaper report in 1942:

> "Mr Curtin's attack on members of the Opposition was pure *Yarra bank* in the manner of thirty years ago," said Mr Menzies, a former Prime Minister, to-day.
>
> To which Mr Curtin replied: "The Yarra Bank was my university."

Traveller and *commercial traveller*, together with *food inspector, bird of passage, wallaby tracker, tourist, footman* and *professional pedestrian*, were sometimes applied to itinerants. The expression *travelling labour* is noted in New Zealand by Edward Wakefield in 1889, this being used for nomads in general. E. S. Sorenson, in "Life in the Australian Backblocks" (1911),

---

[10] A map of Australia in G. C. Mundy's "Our Antipodes" (1852) shows the N.S.W.-Victoria boundary as the river Murrumbidgee, not the Murray as it is in fact.

adds illumination with the comment: "Nearly everywhere in country parts *traveller* is more often heard than swagman." (Eighteenth century English slang had *traveller* for a tramp.)

Bicycle bum is an Australian adaptation of the U.S. *bum* (synonyms are *flying bum* and *tin horse jockey*), but we were using *bummer* for a swagman long before bicycles came on the scene; a *dole chaser* was a tramp who wandered the country living on food obtained by orders issued from *dole stations* by the police[11]; a *steel jockey* is a tramp who *scales* a train or rides without paying; a *bowerbird* is a tramp of low degree who lives on scraps of food picked up anywhere (after the collecting habits of the bird); a *swamper* is an itinerant who entrusts his swag to an obliging teamster to carry on his waggon (Stephens and O'Brien say he was also a traveller on foot to the Westralian goldfields.)

Expressions to describe being on the tramp are varied and colourful. Here are some of the best of them: *on the wallaby, on the track, on the wallaby track, on the sunshine track, to swag it, to chase the sun, to coast about, to packsling, to wear the Jubilee robe* (a rare use from Queen Victoria's days), *to waltz matilda* (already noted at length), *to push the knot* or *be on the knot, to sundown, to live off the land, to lead the bundle, hump one's swag* or *bluey, carry the curse* (also *carry* or *hump a drum, parcel, shiralee,* etc.), *coil one's turkey* (strictly speaking this applies to the rolling of a swag), *to sleep with Mrs Green* and *to doss in the Star Hotel* (the last two reported from New Zealand).[12]

Bluey, for a swag, deserves particular mention, since there have been arguments as to its origin. It was derived from the use of *bluey* for a blue-coloured blanket. For instance, in "The Days When the World Was Wide" (1896), Henry Lawson alludes to "*blueys* which were rotting in their swags".[13] A character in "A Bush Tanqueray" (1900) by A. Dorrington says "I'm gone in the 'igh notes through sleepin' in the wet without a *bluey*". Mrs Aeneas Gunn, "We of the Never Never" (1907), says that she "was sound asleep, rolled up in a *bluey*".

It is worth noting that *bluey* was rarely used for a swag in Tasmania.[14] This was because a type of blue-coloured rough smock or jumper, apparently worn originally by convicts, had come to be known as a *bluey*. A corres-

---

11 Station rations handed out to itinerants were usually referred to as *the dole*. Boldrewood, "Ups and Downs" (1878), defines it as "a pound of meat and a pannikin of flour, which is now found to be the reasonable minimum, given to every wayfarer by the dwellers in Riverina, wholly irrespective of caste, colour, indisposition to work or otherwise".

Periodical rations handed out to back-station workers were known as *the ten, twelve, two and a quarter*, i.e. ten pounds of flour, twelve pounds of meat, two pounds of sugar, a quarter pound of tea. The sugar, generally termed *ration sugar*, was of the commonest type. E. B. Kennedy, "Four Years in Queensland" (1870), says it was "a horrible sticky black mess", and another writer in 1886 says that it was "brown sugar of coarse type". Tea of extremely poor quality was called *ration tea*.

12 *Jabbing trotters* and *tea and sugar burglaring* are a couple of doubtful synonyms listed by Lawson in "The Romance of the Swag".

13 In "While the Billy Boils" (1896) Lawson refers to a *bluey* and describes it as "a stout, dumpy swag, with a *red* blanket outside . . ." which indicates that by the mid-1890s blue blankets were no longer regarded as inevitable features of tramps' possessions.

14 *Derwent drum*, a swag, is a particularized Tasmanian use.

pondent in the Melbourne "Argus" of January 3, 1896, refers to "the *blue-shirt* race", meaning convicts. Added light is thrown on the term by a writer in the "Bulletin" of February 11, 1899, when he says:

> The term bluey is never applied to a swag in Tasmania. The Tasmanian bluey is a rough overcoat of blue-grey, woollen, and never seen by the writer in any other part of Australasia.

This *bluey* was originally made in Hobart. Its reputed uses for convict dress cannot at the moment be traced; we first hear of it as a knee-length overcoat, "guaranteed all wool and waterproof", known as the *miner's bluey* and especially used on Tasmania's wet West Coast. Its colour was practically black. Manufacturing rights for it were purchased in 1938 by the North-Western Woollen Mills Pty. Ltd. at Stawell, Victoria, which marketed it (and continues to do so) as *Tasmanian bluey*, although that name has never been registered.

To push the knot is another phrase the "Bulletin" is able to elucidate to good effect. Here is a comment on bush lore by a writer in that journal of October 8, 1898:

> [The swagman's] swag consisted of blanket, spare singlet, pair of moles, towel, couple of coloured handkerchiefs for binders, and woollen muffler for sling (wool being springy and easy on the shoulder). Swag was fastened near the ends with binders, through which was passed the sling, so arranged that the knot came just below the breast and gave a rest for the hand, which thus acquired a habit of pushing the sling outwards from the body as the man neared the end of his tramp.

A basic point to be noted was that the genuine swagman used only *two* straps round his *bluey* (near the ends). On the other hand, a tramp often advertised his non-genuineness by using three straps. The expression *to put* (or *tie*) *a knot in* (a swag strap) means to quit a job. *To roll it* or *to roll one's swag* (or *pannikin*) *to another shed* was used by shearers to mean the same thing.

Among items in the swagman's equipment were the *camp sheet*, "the canvas wrapping of a swag, used as a shelter and waterproof bed in sun and rain", the *Wagga*[15] *blanket* or *rug*, a covering made from two chaff or corn sacks, carefully cut open and stitched together (also called a *bagman's two-up* and *Sydney blankets*); *early risers*, thin blankets which, because of their poor protection, induced a nomad to rise early; *port*, a sugar bag used to carry possessions, mainly in Queensland, whence *C.S.R. port* and *Millaquin port; hipper*, something soft – such as a piece of possum fur or a stuffed strip of bagging – to put under the hip when lying on hard ground; *bobbers*, *corks* or *flyjerks*, quandong seeds or small pieces of wood or cork, fastened by string to the brim of a hat to ward off flies[16]; and, of

---

[15] Wagga Wagga is a town in New South Wales.

[16] According to bush humour, the wearing of *corks* is one of the stages of *mulga madness*, as the queerness of *hatters* or lone outback dwellers is called. Other stages are reputed to be the carving of quandongs and the carrying of puppies in a billy ("Bulletin", February 25, 1909). Lawson says in "The Romance of the Swag", "the corks would madden a sane man sooner than the flies could". *Troppo, tropical madness, tropical neurasthenia* and *bloody-mindedness* were

course, the *billy*. Among oddities bequeathed to us by our early itinerants were an old bush saying, *swim out, your swag's wet!* that rather tired joke about a swagman carrying a knife to defend himself against a possible sheep attack at night, and the expressions *bagman's gazette* and *drover's guide* as names for fictitious publications which were alleged sources of rumour.

It is, perhaps, a source of astonishment that largely from the men who used the assorted expressions listed in this Section came what amounted to a basic article of Australian faith – that of *mateship*. Many people would deny that there is anything special about our uses of *mate* and *mateship* except that they are heard too often. In some ways they are right. Both *mate* and *mateship* are extremely old English words. The Australian contribution was to add something to the dimensions of both, and the new dimensions have remarkably little to do either with those who sentimentalize over the words or those who reject them angrily.

Basic to the concept of *mateship* in Australia is the principle that, when confronted with similar unpleasant circumstances, many different people, especially men, will react separately to these circumstances in much the same way. In short, *mateship* is more of a state of mind than of the emotions. Since circumstances calling forth such manifestations must be "unpleasant", it follows that they will be particularly apparent in times of crisis and only minor in favourable times. That is, in periods of social affluence, high employment and collective well-being (as at present) there will be little accent on *mateship*, but in periods of social crisis – war, wide unemployment, economic depression, social injustice – *mateship* will become increasingly apparent.

Australia's history has provided plenty of crises for such developments – repeated depressions, wars, strikes which failed, generations of nomadic work-chasing. They gave many opportunities for the special Australian concept of *mateship* to be tested and refined. We will have occasion to return to this matter in later chapters.

Just as the *swagman* and *sundowner* came to be classed as typical outback nomads, so the *deadbeat*, a man down on his luck or penniless, long ago came to be regarded as the city equivalent. How long ago can be gauged from the fact that *deadbeat* was in Australian use before 1882. Here was the real tramp and he rarely showed much enthusiasm for the bush; his travels were almost always limited to what he called *rounds*[17] unless he could *scale* his way to new territory. To *scale a rattler* is our version of the U.S. *jump a rattler;* but *scale* has wider uses than this. It means (a) to ride on a train, tram or bus without paying a fare, (b) to steal, or to rob a person, (c) to

terms concocted in World War II to describe the good-natured tomfoolery in which bored soldiers indulged while waiting for action at tropical bases. This tomfoolery erupted in strange ways, such as in the milking of non-existent cows, in holding greyhound races without dogs, in insistence that everyone salute a mythical girl-friend supposedly clinging to one's arm. There seems a substantial link between the original *mulga madness* and these forms of pleasant insanity.

17 In the "Bulletin" of June 14, 1902, a writer described two Sydney *rounds*. One was known as *the single triangle*, "along Lane Cove Road to Hornsby, thence to Parramatta and back to his base by way of Sydney". The other was *the double triangle*, "from Parramatta to Penrith, thence to Windsor and back to Parramatta".

swindle. One can *get scaled*, in the sense of being done down, when over-charged for goods, and also when an assignation is not kept. A George Street corner, near Central Station, Sydney, was known as *Scale 'em Corner*, "where appointments are made when one has no intention of keeping them". *To scale*, *scale off* and *do a scale* all mean to depart hurriedly. A *scaler* is a person who rides in a vehicle without paying, or one who decamps with money with which he has been entrusted.

To ride plush also means to ride on a train without paying. In tramp slang a *sweeper* is a train that stops at all stations; this is probably from the "sweeping up" of all *steel jockeys* who decline to take the train "on the fly".

Other items worth mention are: *bottle green* and *greasy as a pork chop*, descriptive of a derelict; *pitch*, a camp (e.g. *to have a pitch with someone*, to share a camp); *the long paddock*, the open road; *Struggle Valley*, nickname for any collection of rough humpies, usually beside a river, where down-and-outs live; *cigarette swag*, a small swag carried by a tramp within city limits; *to battle the subs*, to hawk goods from door to door in suburban areas; *susso*, unemployment sustenance; *durry*, a cigarette; *bumper* or *dumper*, a cigarette butt, and *bumper-sniping* or *dumper-dashing*, the picking up of cigarette butts; and *inspectors of city-buildings*, as city tramps have been called (a rural tramp was once called an *inspector of roads*). *Bumper* and *susso* are the only words here which have survived the passage of time, and we don't hear too much of *susso* these days. However, a term related to the latter, *compo* for workers' compensation (and its related expressions *on the compo*, in receipt of workers' compensation, and *compo king*, a man who exploits the benefits of workers' compensation) will probably endure for many years.

3. RIVER WORDS

JUST AS the road was often no more than a track, so it was sometimes a river. Indeed, for many years the river was a much better way of travelling in parts of outback N.S.W. and Victoria than any road or track. The first steam vessels on the Murray River began running in 1853 and soon most of the Darling was carrying traffic (at one stage, about 200 steamers ran on the Murray, the Darling and associated rivers and more than 4,000 miles of waterways were navigated) – wool to be carried away, supplies for inland centres and, of course, the nomads in search of work.

I am greatly indebted to a South Australian author, Mr Ian Mudie, for the river terms appearing in the following glossary. He spent many months ferreting them out, both by searching through old records and by rubbing conversational shoulders with the folk who still remember the boats on the Murray, in the course of collecting material for a story of the Commonwealth's most important river system. Some of the expressions in the list are not Australian originals, but have been borrowed from overseas, especially from the language of American river boatmen. How-ever, historians should find them all of interest:

Anderson barge, a logging barge in which logs were put lengthwise, but in disorder. See *inside barge*.

baby on the river, an employee on a river boat who has not had more than fifteen years' experience.

big ditch, the Darling River.

blow one's boiler, to become excited or enraged.

bottom end, the mouth of the Murray or that part of the river flowing through South Australia. See *top end*.

bottom ender, any river boat or worker operating from South Australian river ports, such as Milang and Goolwa. See *top ender*.

brandy box model, a roughly-constructed river boat or one with unattractive lines, and length about thirty feet. See *model*.

clear as gin, (applied to water in the Murray or one of its main tributaries) extremely clear.

coldwater man, a teetotaller.

Darling pea, have the, to be cranky, irritable, moody; an allusion to the river Darling and to the poisonous plant popularly called the *Darling pea*, which causes animals eating it to stagger about and die.

dust, a Customs officer inspecting a steamer was said to *dust* it.

driver, the engineer of a river boat.

farmer, an unskilled deckhand.

Father Millawah, an old name for the Murray river; from an Aboriginal name for part of the river.

fly light, to travel with little cargo on a falling river.

Goolwa scrub, from the, a river boat employee newly recruited from the bush – Goolwa is a river port near the mouth of the Murray; up to 1863 most of the boats on the river came from Goolwa and even after that time its fleet was second only in numbers to the fleet at Echuca.

gutter, the Darling River.

heave your guts out, to warp a river boat over shallows during low water.

hobnail express, the unloading of cargo from a river boat by manpower, not derricks.

inside barge, a log-carrying barge on which logs were laid neatly lengthwise.

inside man, a river sailor.

inside ticket, the certificate for a river skipper or mate.

jerk, to search a ship for illegal cargo; an old term used by Customs officers. (There is an 1875 example.)

long-haired mate, the wife of a river boat captain who is travelling with him.

low water boat, a river boat with a shallow draught.

model, a general name for any river boat, e.g. *brandy box model* (q.v.).

mud pirate, a riverhand.

Murrumbidgee knot, a granny's knot.

Murrumbidgee seaman, an unskilled deckhand.

Norwegian praam, see *praam*.

nose the bottom, a reference to the swinging motion of a flat-bottomed steamer in shallow water.

outrigger barge, a barge used in carrying logs with outriggers laid across from which red-gum logs (which will not float) are suspended on the surface of the water.

outside, on the sea, in contrast to the rivers. Whence, *outside man*, a salt-water sailor. A river boat that makes a sea journey is said *to go outside*.

outside boat, any seagoing boat.

outside skipper, any captain who had gained his ticket in sea-going ships; especially such a captain who has taken command of a river boat.

paddleboat, although this is a long-established English word for any boat driven by paddlewheels, it seems to have acquired at least one specialized meaning on the Murray, i.e. it is equivalent to *sidewheeler*, a boat which has a paddlewheel on each side, but is distinct from *stern-wheeler*, a boat with a single paddlewheel at the stern. Mudie quotes the example: "The Kookaburra is being converted from a stern-wheeler to a paddle-boat", and he adds "*sidewheeler* is not common on the Murray".

plant, a river boat, including any barges it is towing, under the command of any skipper; also the engine and boiler of a river boat.

praam, *praam boat* or *Norwegian praam*, a small rowing boat; a Murray adaptation of the Dutch word *praam*, applied to a flat-bottomed boat or lighter. Overseas pronunciation is with a long "a", the Australian with a short "a" as in *pram*.

puffing billy, an old term applied to a river boat; borrowed, of course, from the application of this expression to early locomotives.

pulling boat, a small rowing boat, usually flat-bottomed, often used for transporting cargo.

real farmer, a poor steamer hand.

real mud pirate, a riverhand who indulged in any rascality.

sag, an old term meaning "to drift" – e.g. "We had a barge with us and we had to keep well up to the points to keep the barge from sagging into the bends" ("Riverine Herald", October 16, 1883, p. 3).

shallow up, (applied to a river boat) to be held up in a river owing to the lowness of water or by falling water, e.g. "The Victoria, badly snagged, landed her cargo well short of Albury, had the two snag holes stuffed with blankets, and ran for Echuca to avoid being shallowed up" ("Southern Argus", December 1, 1866).

shoot the mouth, to go out the mouth of the Murray River, usually a rough passage.

sidewheel, a river boat driven by a paddlewheel on each side – e.g. "altered into a sidewheel instead of a sternwheel as before" ("Southern Argus", May 17, 1872, p. 2). Also used attributively – e.g. "this iron side-wheel steamer Moolgewanke" ("Adelaide Observer", September 28, 1872, p. 3). See also under *paddleboat*.

smell the bottom, (of a river boat) to become difficult to handle because of shallow water.

snagger, a steamer that clears away snags.

snag pole, either of two poles attached to each paddlewheel of a river boat to fend snags off the paddles.

steamboatie, any man who earns his livelihood by working on river boats.

steering pole, a pole rising vertically from the bow of a river boat, used for taking sights for steering – e.g. "He was over fifty yards away when he first saw his steering pole" ("Riverine Herald", October 19, 1886).

sternwheel, see under *sidewheel*.

stick, the arm of a derrick on a river boat.

suburban skipper, the captain of a river boat that operates only on a regular short run.

talk river, to talk about the Murray River.

tender, liable to get out of control – e.g. "He noticed that the barge was tender coming up the river" ("Riverine Herald", November 5, 1889, p. 2).

tom, a length of board nailed or screwed over a bag or some other material that has been used to plug a hole in a river boat's side.

top end, the upper reaches of the Murray; a river boat or man from Echuca was called a *top ender*.

unship, an old term meaning to discharge a river boat employee. (Actually, an orthodox English word.)

wheel, to steer a boat.

wood, to supply a river boat with wood for fuel. (Another word from orthodox English, but in constant use on the Murray after river boats began to run.) Whence, *wood up*, to load with wood fuel at a *woodheap*.

Mr Mudie has also unearthed the interesting point that, at least in the early days, river boat men did not use the terms "port" and "starboard", but clung in landlubberly fashion to "left" and "right". In the "Riverine Herald", of November 5, 1889, William Glew, mate of a river boat called the Waradgery, declared that he did not know the meaning of the words "port" and "starboard".

• 4. MONEY

PART OF THIS SECTION became virtually redundant while being written. I refer to the many slang words developed over the years for various items of Australian £.s.d. currency. By the time this book appears these words will be mainly of historical interest, since we have now changed to a decimal currency. As yet it is too early to be sure what words Australians will use for the new coins and notes.

I will give a formal list of Australian slang terms for the old currency later. In the meantime it will be obvious that many expressions relating to money or the lack of it will remain in use. For example, *on the strap, strapped, on the outer, stiff* (which has inspired that colourful Australian comment, *you don't have to be dead to be stiff*), *stiffened, stumped up, broke to the wide, stumered, in the blue, to have taken a thrashing* (or *beating*), and *flyblown* describe pennilessness in various shades. On the other hand a man well supplied with cash is said to be *holding, financial, standing, in the note* and to have *what it takes*. He may even be fortunate enough to have *a roll Jack Rice couldn't jump over* (Jack Rice was a racehorse noted for his performances over hurdles) or his roll may be *big enough to choke an anteater* or *a bullock*. If he is lucky he is *tinny, arsy* (both of them from *tin-arse*, a lucky person, which has a respectable synonym in *tin-back*), *protected, touched* and, oddly enough, *hurt*.

To flyblow a person, to relieve him of his money by trickery or robbery, was used in Australia more than a century ago.

Since the condition of penury and that of being a borrower are closely allied, it is worth while to recite some of our numerous indigenous expressions for what the English call "scrounging" and we once called *scunging* (with *scunger* for a borrower; but see Chapter X for modern uses).

Here are some pleasant euphemisms: *to put the acid on someone, to put the hard word on* (this phrase is more commonly used with amorous implications), *to put the drags on, put the nips in, put the fangs in, put the cleaners through, put the weights on* (with the concomitant phrase, *to pull the weight*, meaning to pay up), *to stick it into someone* or *to sting, tickle* or *nip a person*, and rather an unusual selection of phrases on the subject of ears – *to chew, lug* or *nibble someone's ear* (or *lug*), together with *lug-biting* and *ear-chewing*, borrowing, and *ear-lugger*, a borrower.

The "ear" phrases are Australian variations on the earlier English slang, *to bite someone's ear, ear-biter* and *ear-biting. To hum*, another term meaning to scrounge or borrow, also has English antecedents, although it is now mainly our own. In eighteenth century England it meant to cheat or deceive.

To pole and *to bot* are strictly indigenous. *Poling*, imposing on, found its way into a Parliamentary Report by the N.S.W. Libraries Advisory Committee (1939). The Committee said that inter-library loans had been summed up as "*poling* instead of pooling". *To bot* is apparently related to *bots*, larvae of insects of the family *Oestridae* or bot-flies, which infest the stomachs and internal organs of several types of animals. Any parasite came to be known as a *bot* and the term fell into a natural niche to describe a cadger. *How are the bots biting?* as a greeting, and *to have the bot*,[18] to feel out of sorts, irritable, are popular in New Zealand.

A refinement of the term occurs in deadbeat slang in which *cold botting* is used for a straight-out request by a down-and-out for food at doors while *cold biting* indicates a bald request at doors for money. On the other hand, *cold pigging* describes the hawking of goods from door to door without strategical trappings, nothing more than the simple hawking of cheap articles. However, it should be said that these are relics of Depression days; we hear little of them now.

Hummer, poler and *bot-fly* are additional synonyms for a cadger.

To dip south is to search in one's pocket for money; *to have death adders* (or *fishhooks*) *in one's pocket* or *to have short arms and long pockets* is to be mean; *to be broke for* something is to be short of it (e.g. *broke for a feed*, to be hungry); *to break* is an Australianism meaning to cost (e.g. *how much did that hat break you for?* How much did that hat cost?); and *stumer*, a penniless person, a failure, appears in such variations as *to be in a stumer*, to be worried, to be "in a stew", *to come a stumer*, to crash financially, *stoomey* and *stumered*, broke.

Just as penury has led us to borrowing, so does borrowing lead us to many slang names Australians have invented for money. As general terms for money we have *celluloid, chaff, bran, mustard, gons, hoot* (from New Zealand, *ex* the Maori *utu*), *oodle, oscar* (from *Oscar Asche*, noted Australian

---

[18] In obsolete Scottish dialect *botts* or *batts* was used for a bowel complaint or the colic. The "Oxford Dictionary" quotes a lone example from 1816. The antipodean uses are completely independent.

actor, as a rhyme on "cash"), *sheen* (in English cant it was used earlier for counterfeit coin), *shug* and *sug* (clippings of the word *sugar*), *spon* and *spons* (clippings of the U.S. *spondulics*).

And now, money in its various denominations:

½d. – *mock* or *oddie*.

1d. – *bronze*, *brum*, *cobar* (from the name of a N.S.W. mining town), *sunburnt two bob* and *sliver*.

3d. – *tray*, *Alma Gray*, *Bobby Gray*, *Dora Gray*, *Dollie Gray* (all rhyming slang), *joe* or *joey*,[19] *pen*, *scrum* (perhaps a rhyme on the English *thrum*), *trezzie*, *trizzie*,[20] *trut* and *tridley*.

6d. – *zack* and many samples of rhyming slang: *Andy Mac*, *hammer* (*and tack*), *I'll be back*, *Jill and Jack*, *Jack* and *Melbourne* (see Section on rhyming slang).

1s. – *deaner* (originally English, but more used in this country than abroad) and several rhyming slang versions, *Riverina* and *Murrumbeena* (a Melbourne suburb); *og* and *rogan* (a clipping of the English rhyming slang *rogue and villain*, a shilling); *colonial robert* (a play on the word *bob*); *joe dillon* and *john dillon* (other rhymes on shilling); and – during the 1890s in Sydney – a *Bishop Smith*.[21]

2s. – *sway* and *swy*[22] (from the German *zwei*, two), *two-peg* (from the Scottish *peg*, a shilling), *deuce*, *two holes* and *twob* (an elided form of *two bob*).

10s. – *sane* (from the German *zehn*, ten); *half a flag*, *half a toad*, *reddie*, *ten holes* and *half a yid* (the last is a rhyme on *quid*).

£1 – *carpet*, *rug*, *cracker*, *oner* or *oncer*, *fiddley* and *fiddley-did* (the last two from a rhyme on *quid*), *flag*, *toad*, *toadskin*, *frog* and *frogskin*, *jim* (from the old English slang *jimmy o'goblin*, a sovereign), *John Dunn*[23], *tiddley*, *toe-rag*, *smacker*, *yid* (a rhyme on *quid*) and *slice*.

£5 – *spin*, *spinner*, *spinnaker*, *five-o*, *bluey* and *blueback*.

£10 – *brick*, *salmon*, *red 'arry*.

£25 – *pony*, *lifer*.

£50 – *monkey*[24] (the English use of this word is for £500, which is also current in Australia), *two ponies* and *half a spot*.

£100 – *spot* and *four ponies*.

£250 – *half an ape*.

£500 – *ape* (an Australian version of the English *monkey*).

£1,000 – *winky* and *grand*.

Wink, used for sixpence, was an equivalent of the English *kick*. Thus,

---

[19] Former English slang had *joe* for a fourpenny piece, which Partridge says was *ex* the name of *Joseph* Hume, politician and financier. The Australian use is probably independent and comes from our use of *joey* for a baby kangaroo, possum, etc. – the smallness being emphasized.

[20] English slang has *tizzy*, sixpence.

[21] From the name of a former primate of Sydney who once paid off a cab with a shilling and thereby earned publicity. The "Bulletin" of January 9, 1892, noted: "Primate Smith thinks that 1/– is a legal cab fare, just as 3d. is legal church tender". The same journal of November 26, 1892, said that the primate's nickname was *Bishop Bob-cab Smith*. By 1899 Sydney "Truth" had developed the nickname to *Shillingy-Smith* and *Bob Smith*.

[22] *Swy-up* is used as a synonym for *two-up*; also *swy-deaner* for 2s.

[23] A writer in the "Bulletin" of September 25, 1897, said that this was taken from the name of the founder of an Australian bank.

[24] Strangely enough this is a reversion to an old English use. Partridge notes that "the 'Oxford Dictionary' cites an 1832 text in which, probably erroneously, the term means £50."

one and a wink meant 1s. 6d. A *grinder* is a small coin; a *Broken Hill* is a silver coin; *docker* and *motser* or *motza* are used to describe large sums of money. The last two may be of Jewish origin, from the name of the Pascal bread.

With the replacement of our old coinage by a decimal currency, an important question will have to be solved. By tradition, influenced by the solidity of the coins, Edward VII pennies are used in authentic two-up schools. When existing Edward VII pennies are lost or stolen by two-up addicts, what coins are going to be used as substitutes? Can our so-called national game survive?

Whatever happens to two-up, we will certainly say goodbye to *pig* for a counterfeit florin, although it may well be transferred to other counterfeit coins.

Two Australian uses of particular interest are *razoo* and *skerrick*. Like those two hard-worked Australianisms, *haven't a bolter's* and *haven't Buckley's*, these words are employed mainly in negative texts. For instance, one says one *hasn't a brass razoo*, but one rarely says that one actually possesses a razoo; in much the same way we can say that there *isn't a skerrick of anything left*, but a remnant itself is only rarely described as a skerrick. Loosely, *skerrick* may be defined as "a small amount of anything, a small amount of money", but it nearly always indicates the lack of rather than the possession of anything. The origin is to be found in Yorkshire dialect[25] in which it is defined as "the smallest thing or fraction". English dialect has *scuddick*, anything of small value. *Razoo* presents a more difficult problem. It may, as Partridge hazards, be derived from the Maori *raho*, but this is extremely doubtful, especially since *razoo* has never been in wide currency in New Zealand.[26]

In Chapter II reference was made to *rum currency* as used at the beginning of last century. From the same period in our history came *dump* and *holey dollar*. The former was a small silver coin, worth 1s. 3d., in Australian circulation after 1813. It had been punched out of the centre of a silver dollar which, valued at 5s., became known variously as a *holey* (or *holy*) *dollar*, *colonial dollar*, *government dollar*, *pierced dollar* and *ring dollar*.

The 1898 edition of "Webster's Dictionary" gives an additional Australian meaning for *dump*, "a small piece of gold formerly current in Australia at the value of a sovereign", but this lacks verification. No mention of such a gold coin is made by C. P. Hyman in his "Account of the Coins, Coinages and Currency of Australasia" (1893).

A *calibash* was an order for payment in money or in kind, used by New South Wales farmers in the 1890s and later. *Joey* and *joey-cheque* are applied

---

[25] I quote from R. W. Hamilton's "Nugae Literariae" (1841).

[26] A list of slang terms for coins as used in New Zealand was given by a writer from that country in the "Bulletin" of January 14, 1899: *zweideener*, *brace of pegs*, *twopence*, used for a florin; *flimsy*,* *rag*,* *carpet*, £1 note; *thickun*,* *goldie*, a sovereign; *half thickun*, *little goldie*, a half sovereign; *caser*,* *K*, and *bull*,* a five-shilling piece; *half bull*,* *half caser*,* *two and a buck*,* 2s. 6d.; *colonial robert*, *deener*,* *bob*,* 1s.; *tizzie*,* *sprat*,* *tanner*,* 6d.; *thrum*, *half-tiz*, *tray* and *tray-piece*, 3d.; *brownie*,* *copper*,* and *Maori half-crown*, 1d. Terms marked with an asterisk are listed by Partridge in English slang.

to worthless cheques. *Shinplaster*, a correspondent states, is still current for "a paper token issued by storekeepers in remote districts, and used as small change. Some storekeepers bake the notes to make them brittle and more liable to fall to pieces in someone's pocket; thus an illegal profit is made." The original users of *shinplasters* in Australia appear to have been station hands and drovers, who were *cheque-proud*, i.e. had just received payment by cheque. The term was used originally in America for a banknote.

An expression popular in Australia eighty years ago was *brusher*. Departure without paying one's debts was described as *giving someone brusher* or *entering for the brusher stakes*. An old English slang verb *brush*, to run away, is probably the origin, although Morris suggests that it comes from an Australian use of *brusher* for a small wallaby. In Dyson's "Fact'ry 'Ands", we find the meaning extended: *giving someone brusher* meant leaving one's employment or walking out of a job.

Blue, a bill (also used widely for a summons); *money-spinner*, a good financial investment; *to blister*, to charge exorbitantly for goods (as well as to borrow a substantial amount from someone); *poultice*, a mortgage; *alley up*, to pay one's share; and *Jewish pianola*, a cash register, are also worth noting as established Australianisms.

The original names suggested in June, 1963, for the major units in Australia's decimal currency were *royal* and *crown*. These were the subjects of so much derision that they were replaced three months later by dollars and cents. One reason was that the *royal* had been promptly nicknamed *castor*, a truncation of the rhyming slang *castor oil*. According to the earthy proletariat from which the term sprang, both the name *royal* and *castor oil* "gave you the sh*ts".

Some mention of lotteries and art unions should be made here. At the time of writing, all Australian States except South Australia and Tasmania have lotteries. However, it should be noted that the best-known Australian lottery, Tattersalls, which gave us the expressions *Tatts*, *a ticket in Tatts* and *safe as Tatts*, was based in Tasmania for many years before it was shifted to Victoria; Tattersalls originated in Sydney in 1881 and moved to Queensland for a period before going to Tasmania.

The expression *art union* has considerable interest for us. In its original form, as developed first on the Continent of Europe and then in Britain, the *art union* was much as its name implied – it was a form of lottery in which paintings were offered as prizes for purchasers of "shares". Over the years, almost anything except art prizes came to be offered in Australian *art unions*: cars, houses, TV sets, refrigerators, etc.; New Zealand took the matter further by offering large money prizes in *art unions*, so that the word came to be synonymous with lottery.

Interestingly enough, there was a period in Australia – at the end of the 1840s – when money prizes were offered here in *art unions*. For example, in the "Sydney Morning Herald" of November 27, 1849, we find James T. Grocott advertising an art union in Sydney, guaranteeing "the respective sums of £50 and £40 to the drawers of the first and second prizes".

It is not without historical interest that in 1848-49 a form of property lottery called a *bank lottery* was in vogue in New South Wales and that, at the same time, W. C. Wentworth launched a lottery of 12,000 tickets at £5 each for sundry properties. Following the drawing of the "Bank of Australia lottery" early in 1849, the "Sydney Morning Herald" commented:[27]

> We were and still are at a loss to discover why a whole community are to be stimulated into a spirit of gambling because a Banking Proprietary have not otherwise a good market for their properties. Lotteries cannot but demoralise the people engaged in them. Should it even be granted that they somewhat benefit one or two, it is certain that they injure thousands.

Perhaps it is not without interest that, more than a century later,[28] the same journal presented the world with the expression *art unionism*, although in this case it was used to denote trades union interests among artists.

Owing to various State Statutes which, in the case of States conducting official lotteries, are aimed at eliminating inter-State competition, there have come into usage the euphemisms *consultation* or *investment* as references to any lottery organised by another State. *Consultation* is applied particularly to Tattersall's lottery, but is also applied to other lotteries. Whereas in New South Wales, for instance, it is quite improper for a State inhabitant to win a prize in, say, the Golden Casket lottery in Queensland, it appears that everything is satisfactory if he or she wins a prize in an *inter-State consultation*.

[27] January 22, 1849, p. 2.
[28] January 26, 1950, p. 2.

CHAPTER VI

The City Yesterday

1. LARRIKINS

IN THE FIRST EDITION of this book, I said that if an Australian boy or youth did not have a little of the larrikin in him, he was scarcely worthy of his inheritance. That is all very well provided one knows what a larrikin is, but here we are only twenty years later and the word has been almost lost or at any rate considerably softened, displaced by *bodgie* (for a period after World War II) and then by various imported terms such as *rocker*, *surfie*, *jazzer* and *mod*.

Yet when we look into the history of the larrikin we find that he was by no means a static figure even in his own beginnings. He dates back to the *cabbageites* and *cabbage-tree mobs* of the early nineteenth century. He was the original *currency lad*, tough, defiant, reckless. He might even have been one of the *larky boys* who were mentioned in the "Sydney Gazette" of July 21, 1825. Certainly, by the time he earned the name *larrikin* in the 1860s and began to gather in *pushes*, there were few to deny that he had become an Australian figure, even though there was lack of agreement on his characteristics.

He had a number of recognizable features, however. Generally, he was young, between the ages of 15 and 25, he was a city dweller, he dressed with exaggerated precision, he extracted comfort from being a member of a gang, he was alleged to have too much money and to lack parental control, he looked upon refinement in social conduct as a form of weakness, he spoke a weird jargon which it seemed only his own kind could understand, he was given to spasms of violence. In short, he was exceedingly like modern Australian louts.

But there is this to be said about the larrikin – he has left a greater mark on Australia's social conscience than any of the modern substitutes shows signs of doing. If we are to believe Ambrose Pratt ("Blackwood's Magazine", July, 1901), Australia had far more amateur than professional larrikins; Pratt places the number of push members at between 6,000 and 10,000 at the time of writing. He says that in some pushes would-be members had to apply in writing and pay a 10/- entry fee; after six months' probation they were allowed to sign *the push* (or *crime*) *book*. Thereafter, they paid 6d. a week each to remain members. The leader of a push was its *king*. A form of internal discipline was the *sock;* the victim was stripped, bound face down, beaten raw with stockings filled with wet sand, had salt rubbed into his wounds and was kept in custody until those wounds had healed.

If the larrikin could be said to have had a birthplace, it was in the Sydney *Rocks*, at Dawes Point. As many observers delighted in pointing out, this was "the St Giles of Sydney" in its earliest days, where slang and vulgarity were mixed in lavish quantities, where harlots and riff-raff, ex-convicts and the scum of all the oceans collected. Here in the Rocks was born the Australian hoodlum, as tough and vicious and as well-versed in unconventional ways of speech as any person in the world.

Oddly enough, we have a better documentation of larrikin speech in Melbourne than in Sydney, due especially to the work of Edward Dyson and C. J. Dennis (sometimes called "the laureate of the larrikin"). When Dyson's "Fact'ry 'Ands" was published in 1906, the "Bulletin" wrote: "The Australian slang that the Beauties [i.e. Melbourne factory girls] speak causes us some speculation as to how the book will be received in England, where possibly the language will prove as difficult to penetrate as a Somerset dialect is to us."

Dennis made a collection of various words and phrases which he claimed were used by larrikins, but, like the text of "The Sentimental Bloke" and other poems, much of it was a libel on larrikin imagination and belonged to the East End of London rather than to the pushes.

The larrikin was a vigorous linguistic innovator, but then many other Australians who had preceded him had been equally inventive. As for the larrikin's desire to gather in mobs, there was nothing new about this either. Indeed, as far back as 1826 we find P. Cunningham commenting: "Our currency lads are noted for spirit and courage as well as for great clannishness."

Then there was the larrikin's attitude to dress, something of which he was self-conscious while maintaining the pose that such self-consciousness was ridiculous. "The larrikin taste in dress runs to a surprising neatness", notes Louis Stone in "Jonah" (1911). The bell-bottomed trouser, the *nan-nan* (straw hat, probably in its original form *nanny-goat's breakfast*) or the *monty* (a soft, shining black felt hat), the wasp waist, the high-heeled fancy boots (sometimes called *Romeos*) with decoration which even ran to inlaid cameos of the reigning *clinah* on the toes[1] – these were symbols of the larrikin a few generations ago.

There was a hard, sleek finish to the larrikin's Sunday-off dress, not given to colour, severe, almost uncomfortable yet perhaps just a shade overdone, just sufficient to bring those words *flash* and *lairy* to your thoughts, just a little too burnished for a walk in the park with a girl, or for a two-up school, or for holding up a dance-hall wall. Perhaps it was because the contrast with the workaday larrikin, who seemed to care little for his appearance, was so great. Perhaps it was because the larrikin's contempt for anything effeminate – in speech, in thought, in manners – erupted in a

---

[1] Stone says " . . . their boots were remarkable, fitting like a glove, with high heels and a wonderful ornament of perforated toe-caps and brass eyelet-holes on the uppers." Stone also notes that "the height of larrikin fashion" in Sydney was "tight-fitting suits of dark cloth, soft black felt hats, and soft white shirts with new black mufflers round their necks in place of collars."

way that took him perilously close to effeminacy where dress was concerned. We certainly see the same thing among his modern successors.

To understand the larrikin's intimate link with Australia it is necessary to step back a little in our history. For more than half a century Australia was almost entirely a masculine country. As late as 1840 the proportion of males to females was two to one. Not until 1880 was a reasonable balance struck between the sexes. In consequence, it was inevitable that men should be thrown together, that they should rely on one another, that a strong accent should be placed on the very thing we have discussed earlier, only now we see it taken over by the city from the outback – *mateship*. This was the heritage passed on to men and youths long after the population balance between the sexes had been adjusted.

The larrikin's heydey, during the 1880s and a little later, was a period of tremendous urban growth when, within a decade, the populations of Melbourne and Sydney jumped by nearly 75 per cent, and when the drift of people from country to capital was already under way.

H. H. Hayter, former Government statistician of Victoria, declared in 1892, in an address before the Australasian Association for the Advancement of Science:

> The increases which have occurred [in urban populations] point to the probability that when the census of 2001 is taken, half the population of Victoria and perhaps also half that of South Australia and 40 per cent of that of New South Wales will be found to be living within the metropolitan limits.

Hayter's expectations were more than fulfilled in less than a third of the time he suggested. At the 1933 census it was revealed that of New South Wales's population of 2,600,000 more than 1,235,000 lived in Sydney, or 46 per cent; of Victoria's population of 1,820,000 more than 990,000 lived in Melbourne, or 54 per cent; of South Australia's 580,000 more than 310,000 lived in Adelaide, or 53 per cent. Collectively, nearly 44 per cent of Australia's population was living in the principal cities in 1933 and today that figure is well over 50 per cent.

It is clear from these figures that, no matter how great the word-making enthusiasm of our original rural inhabitants, their efforts could no longer outweigh those of the city, and since the larrikin and his kind were the most likely individuals to prove expert in creating new forms of expression it is to them that we must now look for material. It may be, as the "Bulletin" observed in 1881, that larrikins were "as much the outcome of the prosperity of the labouring classes as of anything else" and that they "do not as a rule belong to well-to-do classes",[2] but the fact remains that the larrikin speaks with a representative voice and a good deal of what he has said has sunk its roots so deeply into our language that it will never be torn out. No watertight walls can be erected around this larrikin speech; it is not a

---

[2] P. Clarke, "The New Chum in Australia" (1886), says, however, that "the colonial larrikin is often of respectable parentage and well-dressed". This point is well worth remembering in considering *surfies*, *rockers* and other modern successors of the larrikin.

self-contained argot, although, at its best, it is often too obscure for the uninitiated to understand.

One of the features of the Australian language is its persistent "low-browism". There is a deliberate speaking down, an avoidance of anything suspected of being highbrow in thought or word, a straining after the simplest and lowest common denominator of speech. The effect of this tendency towards lowbrowism is to make larrikin slang far more typical of Australia than we might anticipate.

As will be seen in subsequent pages a good deal of the larrikin slang current at the end of last century is now obsolete. Here is a segment of a jingle published in the "Bulletin" of February 9, 1895, which stresses the point:

> Lord strike me fat! what yer givin' us?
> Don't you poke borak at me, you old jay!
> *You* didn't 'ave to pay for *my* clobber;
> I'm ryebuck and the girl's okay.
> Oh she's a good iron, is my little clinah;
> She's my cobber an' I'm 'er bloke.
> Got a cigar in yer old clothes, matey?
> Lor' blue me if I'm not dead for a smoke.

This limping lyric is notable mainly for providing us with the first-known printed use of *cobber* – another adaptation of English dialect.[3] *Strike me fat! poke borak at, ryebuck, clinah, good iron, Lor' blue me!* (a version of *blimey*) and *dead for* (i.e. in need of) appear to be Australian originals.

A much more competent poem – perhaps one of the most successful "slang" poems ever produced – is "The Great Australian Slanguage",[4] written by W. T. Goodge in 1897.[5] It is long, but worth reproducing in full to give some evidence of Australia's slang vocabulary half a century ago:

> 'Tis the everyday Australian
> Has a language of his own,
> Has a language, or a slanguage,
> Which can simply stand alone.
> And *a dickon pitch to kid us*
> Is a synonym for lie,
> And *to nark it* means to stop it,
> And *to nit it* means to fly!
>
> And a bosom friend's a *cobber*,
> And a horse a *prad* or *moke*,

---

[3] From the Suffolk verb *to cob*, to form a friendship for, or from the Cornish *cobba*, or from other dialectal uses of *cob* and *cobbis*, a person. Attempts have been made to link the term with the Yiddish *chaber*, a companion, and the Aboriginal *cobbra*, the head. There is no support for the latter theory, but the independent growth of Budapest slang *haver* (pronounced *hovver*) for a friend or mate, can be noted as support for the former theory.

[4] The U.S. journal "American Speech" (February, 1930) said that the word *slanguage* was invented in 1925 or thereabout. This is hopelessly astray. It was in English use in 1892 according to the "Oxford Dictionary" and, as shown above, was in Australian use in 1897.

[5] First published in the "Bulletin", reprinted without acknowledgment to the author in M. Davitt's "Life and Progress in Australia" (1897), subsequently included by Goodge in his "Hits, Skits and Jingles" (1899).

While a casual acquaintance
Is a *joker* or a *bloke,*
And his ladylove's his *donah,*
Or his *clinah* or his *tart,*
Or his *little bit o' muslin,*
As it used to be his *bart.*

And his naming of the coinage
Is a mystery to some,
With his *quid* and *half-a-caser*
And his *deener* and his *scrum.*
And a *tin-back* is a party
Who's remarkable for luck,
And his food is called his *tucker*
Or his *panem* or his *chuck.*

A policeman is a *johnny*
Or a *copman* or a *trap,*
And a thing obtained on credit
Is invariably *strap.*
A conviction's known as *trouble,*
And a gaol is called a *jug,*
And a sharper is a *spieler,*
And a simpleton's a *tug.*

If he hits a man in fighting
That is what he calls a *plug,*
If he borrows money from you
He will say he *bit your lug.*
And to *shake it* is to steal it,
And to *strike it* is to beg;
And a jest is *poking borak,*
And the jester *pulls your leg.*

Things are *cronk* when they go wrongly
In the language of the *push,*
But when things go as he wants 'em
He declares it is *all cush.*
When he's bright he's got a *napper,*
But he's *ratty* when he's daft,
And when looking for employment
He is *out o' blooming graft.*

And his clothes he calls his *clobber*
Or his *togs,* but what of that
When a *castor* or a *kady*
Is the name he gives his hat!
And our undiluted English
Is a fad to which we cling,
But the great Australian slanguage
Is a truly awful thing!

Here is a lyric worthy to rank alongside W. E. Henley's translation of Villon's "Straight Tip to All Cross Coves", each stanza of which ends with the line "boose and the blowens cop the lot". It includes many expressions, however, which are not Australian, such as *prad, joker, bloke, quid, panem, chuck, pull your leg, ratty* and *togs*, but there is a sufficient sifting of indigenous material to make the poem notable. Moreover it can be accepted as an authentic record of the type of slang once used by larrikins and their kind.

Sydney and Melbourne have always been the natural homes of *the Talent*, as *half-axes, nuts, rats, lurchers, pebs, pebbles, pebblers, picklers, perishers, pushites, horribles, bashers, booveroos* and other members of *pushdom* have been known at various stages of our history.

Here is a brief list of some Sydney pushes[6] active in the early 1890s: "*the Rocks*, descendants of the first families of old Sydney; *the Livers*, composed mostly of butcher-boys and gentlemen engaged in kindred occupations; the *Burley Boys*, bullies from the classic purlieus of Woolloomooloo; and the *Gipps Street*, a mixed and motley crew." The last were also called the *Gibbies*. Other Sydney pushes were the *Golden Dragons, Gore Hill Tigers, Stars, Bantry Bay Devils* and *Blue's Point Mob*.

And here is a list of Melbourne pushes as recorded by a writer in the "Bulletin" of July 14, 1900: *the Ivanhoes, the Red Roses, the Flying Angels, the Eastern Road push, the Montague Dingoes, the Montague Flying Squadron, the City Road Flying Squadron, the City Road Bug Hunters, the Bouveroo push,* of Carlton, *the Fitzroy Murderers* and *the Richmond Dirty Dozen*. I also have references to *the Heart and Arrow push* (Footscray) and *the Fitzroy Forties*.

During the past half-century in Australia we have used *forty* to describe a crook or sharper. It possibly has Adelaide as well as Melbourne antecedents. Stephens and O'Brien declare:[7]

> In Hindmarsh, Adelaide, in the late '70s and '80s there was a particular crowd of roughs known to all and sundry as *the Forty Thieves* and the particular aversion of magistrates and police . . . *Forties* in Sydney preceded larrikins as a name for street prowlers, gamblers, thieves, etc.

I have a reference which says there was a push in Adelaide in 1888 called *the Swifties*.

Stephens and O'Brien offer some important notes on the word *push*, which, they declare, was "first heard in Sydney by the writer about 1885 or 1886. Originally, crowds of toughs or larrikins; later, any coterie, clique or class". (As already pointed out, the word was used long before this in these senses.) The *bell-bottomed push*, they say, was "a section of the Mel-

---

[6] R. H. Thornton, "American Glossary" (1912), notes the U.S. use of *push*, for "a combination of low politicians". He adds that "the term is derived from Australia where it is applied to gangs of rowdies and young criminals". However, it can be noted that – as J. H. Vaux observed in his "Vocabulary of the Flash Language" (1812) – *push* was old English cant for "a concourse of people, a crowd", and it probably arrived in America direct from England, not via Australia.

[7] Some support is given to this story by W. J. Barry, author of "Up and Down" (1879), who relates the tale of an Australian bank robbery for which forty men were, at one time and another, charged and discharged. He says that these men came to be known as "the forty thieves".

bourne public who mostly affected bell-bottomed trousers", and the *nan-nan* push was a gang of Sydney youths who affected the *nan-nan* or straw hat "either from cheapness or showiness".

Most of the history of the word *larrikin* has been given earlier. Australian variations on this theme include *larrikinism* (1870), *larrikiness* (1871), *larrikinalian* (1893) and *larrikinish*. We have also made considerable alterations to the English cant *leary* or *leery*, wide-awake, knowing, cunning (uses surviving in America), which now appear in the forms *lairy*, overdressed, *to lair-up*, to get dressed, especially in a flashy style, *lair*, a person who overdoes his dressing[8] and behaves crudely or ostentatiously, whence *lairiness*, and *lairize* or *lairize around*, to act as a lair or to show off. An unusual meaning for *leery*, "a common person", was given in Sydney "Truth" of April 27, 1924. Crowe reported in 1895 that *larry* was an Australianism meaning idleness. He is not supported by textual evidence, but this expression may be another elaboration of those given above.

Terms like *frill, boiled dog, jam* and *guiver*, connoting "side" or affectation, together with the phrases *to cut the flash* (1853) and *do the posh*, underline larrikin sensitivity towards social posturing. *Tollolish*, overbearing and foppish, *toey*, a swell, and *silvertail*, a social climber or society figure, have been current since the 1880s. (Contrasting with *silvertail*, we have *coppertail* and *bronzewing* which denote a proletarian; *bronzewing* refers to the flock pigeon or harlequin bronzewing, which was formerly found in vast numbers in Australia).

The larrikin has a strong desire to be regarded as a *hard doer* or *good doer* or just a *doer*, a *hard case*, a *hard thing*, a *finger* or a *dag*, all of which serve to show that he is appreciated by his fellows – tough, maybe, but sometimes with the saving graces of sharp humour and bravado.

2. FIGHTING TALK

ONE OF THE RESULTS of the larrikin's wish to earn approval from his fellows and to assert his masculinity was the growth of an extensive vocabulary of fighting terms.

Here are some of them: *to bump, comb down, dish, dong, job, pass a jolt, lift, hoist, spike, sort out, stonker, rip into, top off, do* (someone) *smartly, go the knuckle on, towel up, weigh into, roll into, wipe* and *quilt* a person. And these are not all. A man who attacks another successfully is said *to come all over him, knock saucepans* (or *smoke*) *out of him, knock him rotten, to give him curry* or *curried hell, to make a job of him, to wipe* (or *rip*) *hell out of him, do him in, to knock into* and *take a piece out of him*. A man who provokes a fight is said *to tie one on, to mix it, to hop into* (someone), *take a poke at* (someone), *to have* (someone) *on, to take* (someone) *on* and *get stuck into* (someone). If he fights with energy he is *willing* or *a tiger for punishment* (later absorbed into general

---

[8] *Mug lair* and *bush lair*, used offensively, *teddy bear* (rhyming slang), *all laired up* and its synonym *all mockered up* may also be noted. *To quean up*, which, strictly speaking, means to dress like an effeminate, is used similarly, although usually more contemptuously. A generation ago *lair* was often used to denote a "flash" and/or "fast" girl.

use to denote anyone who works or acts with unreserved enthusiasm), *game as a pebble, game as a piss ant, game as Ned Kelly, fond of the knuckle;* he fights *like a threshing machine*, he is *a ball of muscle*. If he is inefficient at fighting he *can't fight his way out of a paper bag* or is *blinded with science*. If he shows signs of cowardice he is a *gutless wonder* or *squib*, hence *to squib on*, to let down (an older version was *fizz out on*), and that chant of defiance *my* (or *his*) *mother never raised a squib!*

As a consequence of larrikin enthusiasm for fisticuffs, he and his predecessors found many heroes among professional pugilists – for instance, "Young" Kable, of Windsor, N.S.W., who in 1824 was the first *currency lad* to beat a visiting English pugilist; Larry Foley, who came into prominence in the 1870s and who is still (partly) remembered in the expression *give some Larry Dooley to*, to chastise or bestir someone into action, and is just possibly behind that long-used simile *happy as larry;* Albert Griffiths, "Griffo", a remarkable fighter born about 1871, recalled in the simile *fight like Griffo;* and someone (perhaps a wrestler) called McGinnis, who got into the phrase *put the (crooked) McGinnis on*, meaning to make an opponent's defeat inevitable.

Special mention should be made of *king hit* and *blue*. The true *king hit* is a sudden, cowardly blow designed to end a fight before the opponent can prepare to defend himself, and a *king hit merchant* (or *artist*) is one who specializes in such a method of fighting. However, in its more general application a *king hit* is a fair blow which knocks out an opponent; thus *to king* him.

Blue is one of those Australian terms which over the years have gathered an extremely wide range of meanings. It denotes a summons, an error of judgment, a mistake; it is an abbreviation of *bluey*, a swagman's bundle; it is an inevitable nickname for any red-haired person; it is used as a reference to a blue-speckle cattle dog; but perhaps more than anything it denotes a row, an argument, a fight, especially in the forms *bung* (or *stack* or *put*) *on a blue;* indeed, a *blue* is not only a fight between individuals, but a brawl between groups and in this sense is the equivalent of a *stoush-up, rough-up, smack-up, yike, bowl-over, hop-out, fair go* or *take-on*.

There is a distinct likelihood that *blue* originated in Australian shearing sheds in the 1890s when shearing machines were beginning to displace hand shears. This is the way an old-timer put it in a letter to me: "It was necessary to keep sharpening the cutters on a fast-spinning wheel. This was done by the *expert*. In the early days of handpieces, no one was very skilled in the sharpening business. If a cutter was held against the wheel too long it would turn blue and lose its temper. Nothing enraged a fast shearer (always looking for an excuse to cover any drop in his tally) more than if the expert *made a blue* of one of his cutters. If you *made a blue* you most likely had a fight on your hands."

The Australian use of *fair go* is also worth a comment. In some respects, we have seen great merit in providing *fair gos* for people both in fights and other activities. These *fair gos* mean that the participants are given unhindered opportunity to act as they wish to act so long as they do so without resort to underhand methods and aid from others. To breach the concept of fairness is to outrage the right of anyone to make a fool of himself if he chooses – or to prove himself in his chosen field.

To be beaten in a fight is to *get stoushed* or *stonked*, to be *strapped*, *stitched*, *tonked*, *stiffened*, *flattened* and to *kiss the cross*. *Stoush* is a well-established word, almost certainly derived from English. *To stash*, to stop or relinquish, was recorded by Vaux in Australia in 1812. Boldrewood uses it in 1881 in the phrase "we *stashed* the camp", we broke camp. The form *stoush* came into prominence in the 1890s for a blow or brawl and was spread across the world by the diggers of World War I. For a considerable period that war was known as *the Big Stoush*, until a bigger Stoush came along in 1939 to force it out of currency. In English dialect there was the expression *stashie*, an up-roar, commotion or quarrel, to which the Australian use is probably related.

Stousher and *stoush-merchant*, a fighter or bully, and the phrase to *put in the stoush*, equivalent to *putting in the dirt*, are Australian elaborations. While we are at it, we should spend a moment for *put in the boot* or *sink the boot*, to kick a prostrate foe, if only because the old-time larrikin seems to have been somewhat partial to the practice. *Boots and all* denotes "all-in" fighting – also called an *all-out go*.

An old larrikin expression that apparently once had a vogue in Sydney was *to give someone Bondi*, implying that a person was severely manhandled. The phrase probably had some link with the Sydney suburb of Bondi or with the Aboriginal *bondi*, the heavy nulla. Sydney "Truth" of October 19, 1890, employs it in the sentence: "A live policeman is on the ground while members of a push are '*giving him Bondi*'." In another issue the same journal refers to "two or three others who looked fully competent and perfectly willing *to give him Bondi*". *To give Bondi* clearly meant much the same as putting in the boot.

Since the early 1860s we have used *barney* for a row, argument or serious debate. C. R. Thatcher employs it in his "Colonial Minstrel" (1864) and Boldrewood in his "Ups and Downs" (1878). The first English use given by the "Oxford Dictionary" is for a prize-fight in 1882.

Anger and dislike are described in a variety of ways. A man in a temper is said *to be brushing*,[9] *to have the dingbats* or *the pricker* or *the stirks;* he is said *to be ropeable*, *snaky*, *maggoty* or *pippy; to go crook*,[10] *to do his block* or *pegs* or *nut*, *to get off his bike*, *to get wet*, *to go hostile*, *to go to market*, *to go lemony* or *woolly-headed* at a person, *to be snake-headed* and *to rouse on* (someone).

A man who has acquired a strong dislike of another person is said to have *a down on* (1849), *a derry on* (1892), *a snout on* or *be dead nuts on* him. He *gets someone set* and *words him*, rebukes him, *hits* or *knocks* him, criticizes him. Someone or something disagreeable is said *to get on one's works*, *quince*, *quoit* or *tit*, *to make one's nipples ache* or *to give one the worms*, most of these phrases falling into the category of low colloquialism.

To throw a fit is *to chuck a six, sixer, seven* or *charley* or *to throw a sixer, willy* or *seven* (the phrases in which numbers appear are related to dicing).

---

[9] A writer in the "Bulletin" of June 4, 1898, says that this term was used "between the lower waters of the Namoi and the Castlereagh" (N.S.W. rivers).

[10] *To go* (or *be*) *butchers* and *to go butcher's hook* at someone are formed by rhyme on *go crook*.

3. THE LARRIKIN'S GIRL

IF THE AUSTRALIAN MALE puts stress on his masculinity, it is not because he disowns all contact with the feminine world. It may be, as Marcus Clarke once suggested,[11] that the Australian wife of 1977 or thereabouts "will be a thin, narrow woman, very fond of dress and idleness, caring little for her children, and without sufficient brain power to sin with zest", but the larrikin and his kind have always chosen to see the female more as a background for the parade of masculinity than as a frail creature demanding suave manners and discreet wooing. The special reason why he was not expert in suavity or discretion was his inability to maintain the flow of small talk necessary to sustain either.

As C. J. Dennis showed in "Doreen" and "The Sentimental Bloke" our larrikin can become maudlin with the best of them, but he is unlikely to reveal his state of mind by much more than a glazed eye and paltering platitudes. He is more inclined to go out and have a fight with someone to prove his worthiness. His code of conduct in his relations with the female seems to serve mainly as a protection for himself against her. He likes to keep his masculine world self-contained, to insulate himself from softening feminine influences, to retain a solid hard core in his soul against the fripperies and fancies of womanhood. Hence, doubtless that aspect of male-female relations in Australia upon which so many visitors have commented – the tendency at almost any social gathering for men to congregate separately from the women.

It is significant that the first indigenous slang term for a girl or woman did not make its appearance until the 1870s when, for the first time in our history, some sort of balance was being reached by males and females in the population. This word was *bart*, which, an old Australian slang dictionary of about 1882 tells us, was used for a girl and "generally applied to those of loose character". An apocryphal story alleges that it is derived from Ho*bart* Town Polly,[12] a nickname applied to a harlot in the early days of Hobart Town, Tasmania. Confirmation is lacking. The origin is more probably in a rhyme on *tart*, which came into use in English slang in the 1860s. Modern English slang uses *tart* for prostitute, but we generally retain it to describe – with the variants *tom-tart* and *tom* – any girl or young woman.

Donah and *clinah* were also in wide currency for a girl or sweetheart before the close of last century. The former was originally Cockney,[13] and the latter apparently came to us from the German *Kleine*.

Most popular of modern expressions is *sheila*, which came to us out of

---

[11] "The Future Australian Race" (1877).

[12] English nautical use of *poll*, a harlot, and the still earlier *moll*, may have influenced the origin of this expression.

[13] "Never introduce your donah to a pal" is an old Australian cant phrase, apparently taken from a once-popular music hall song.

the English dialectal *shaler*, although it is commonly (and erroneously) regarded as pure Irish. This supposition has been due to a marriage of *shaler* with the Irish girl's name *Sheila* – a form of Cecilia or Celia – and has produced such bastardizations as *shielah* and *shielagh* by writers who have confused its origins.

Other Australianisms for girls or young women include: *charlie* (from *Charlie Wheeler*, a rhyme on *sheila*), *bush, brush, whisker, rabbit, skinny* (apparently a Westralian term of the 1920s when short skirts revealed feminine legs), *slimdilly, chookie* and *chicky, sninny, snickle, tab, square girl* or *square jane* (this is from the U.S. use of *jane* for a girl), *clue* (i.e. something to be followed), *bushfire blonde* (a redhead), *a bit of heifer dust* and *sort* or *good sort*. The last expression, *good sort*, is used in colloquial English, but has acquired a peculiarly Australian tang. An amiable girl, especially one likely to respond to amorous approach, is *a good sort*, but it also appears in such sentences as "girls going out with their *sorts*", i.e. boy-friends, and "fellows taking their *sorts* to the pictures", where the sex of the term is changeable. In the late 1950s, young Australians became tired of *sheila*, etc., and began to use *bird*, which is out of old English slang.

Virtue is not questioned in most of the above Australianisms. We have another vocabulary altogether for the harlot and her kind: *chromo, half-squarie, half-and-halfer, chippy, lowheel, rattlesnake, princess of the pavement*,[14] *shingler, turtle, toby, fork, bike* (a willing girl is sometimes described as *an office bike*, etc.), *belt, wheat belt* and *endless belt* (these appear to be Australian variants of the U.S. *band*, a woman), *barrenjoey* (a play on the Sydney place-name: *barren* + the slang use of *joey* for a child), and *tarry rope* (an old term for a waterfront prostitute who consorts with sailors).

A lesbian is known mainly as a *charlie* (from its earlier use for any girl), *lezo* and *lover under the lap*.

A brothel is a *bang, jacksie* (Brisbane) and *shop* (Perth).

An effeminate male is a *homo, queen* or *quean* (from an old English use which now seems to be obsolete), *hock, poof*, and various rhymes such as *cow's hoof* and *horse's hoof, poofter, punce* (the vowel is sounded as the "oo" in *foot*: the English slang *ponce*,[15] a harlot's bully, is the original), *pood, quince, gussie, spurge, sonk* and *wonk*. Queens were once called *royalies*. A procurer for homosexuals is known as a *poofter rorter*.

One of the most popular Australian pejoratives came to us from the seamy side of the street. This is *bludger*, originally a man who lived on the earnings of a harlot (there is an 1882 record of this), later any indolent person who imposes on others or whose "scrounging" habits make him objectionable. Stephens and O'Brien note:

> The word has come to be applied to any person who takes profit without risk or liability, or without effort or work. Practically any cadger, loafer, bummer or beggar, who has not the excuse of inability to work or thieve.

[14] *Nymph of the pave* is recorded in Australia in 1854.

[15] *Poncess*, a harlot who keeps a man, is listed as Australian by Crowe (1895) and does not appear to have been in English use.

F

To bludge, therefore, means to impose on. The phrase *to bludge on the flag*, to fail to justify one's existence as a soldier, is recorded in W. H. Downing's excellent dictionary of war slang, "Digger Dialects" (1919). The participle *bludging* is also widely used. Time has softened the original nature of these terms; *bludging* or *having a bludge* often mean no more than having a rest or working slowly.

Bludget, "a female thief who decoys her victims", was included by Crowe in his slang dictionary, but it is open to suspicion.

The Australian has devised numerous expressions for love-making, but many come too close to outright vulgarity to be included here. Here are a few of the terms: *shook on*, infatuated with; *to pirate* or *to be on the pirate*, to be on the lookout for casual feminine acquaintance; *to do a knock* (or *a line*) *with* a girl, to take her courting (this is a softening of the English vulgarism *knock*); *to track with* a girl, to court her; *to drag on* or *pull on* a girl, to marry her; *to put the hard word* (or *acid*) *on* a girl, to make a request to her for her favours, also *to go for the drag off; to give* (a woman) *a length* or *to crack it*, to record a success in an amorous affair (this is solely a masculine term, but it is also used in other senses, meaning to succeed); and the jocular greeting between man and man, *gettin' any?* which draws such set replies as *climbing trees to get away from it! got to swim under water to dodge it! knocking it back with a stick!* and *so busy I've had to put a man* (or *a boy*) *on!*

Smoodging for love-making – also used to describe toadying – and the forms *to smoodge* and *smoodger* are Australian adaptations of English dialect in which both *smudge* and *smouch* mean to kiss.

Saddling paddock, a popular site for alfresco amours, and *butcher's shop*, a wedding, mainly used in the phrase *to open a butcher's shop*, are two obsolescent expressions.

A woman who has infatuated a man is said *to have him by the wool;* and a popular cant phrase among women who admire a man is *he can put his shoes under my bed* (*any time he likes*), which should require no elaboration. A variation of the last phrase, *I'd put my shoes in his wardrobe any day*, is used by Sumner Locke-Elliott in his play "Interval" (1939).

Since we have wandered rather far from the original intention in this Section, to look at the larrikin's girl, we can at least return to the theme by examining what larrikins knew as *cass dancing*. Louis Stone gives us details in "Jonah". The partners "revolved slowly on a space the size of a dinner-plate" with the girl's head on the man's breast, "their bodies pressed together, rigid as the pasteboard figures in a peep-show". After more than half a century of oblivion, this reads like the sort of dance that would appeal to modern teenagers as a change from twists, jerks and shakes.

4. GOOD AND BAD

IN ALL SLANGS the good, the bad and the stupid always secure wide mention, because these are some of the simplest and most persistent things upon which we are inspired to comment. The Australian's collection of terms for that which is excellent or notable need yield nothing to overseas offerings.

Inevitably associated with this country, although it has faded considerably in recent years, is *bonzer*, an expression that developed so many variants that it almost merits a chapter to itself. It came to us by syncope from the American *bonanza*, used to describe (1847) a rich mine, (1875) "a valuable thing, a source of wealth or profit", and (1882) anything large. The origin is in the Spanish *bonanza*, fair weather, prosperity, with its roots the Latin *bonus*, good.

In the "Bulletin" of November 22, 1906, a writer notes:

> I have noticed repeatedly in the "Bulletin" that what is known here [in Victoria] as *boshter* is called *bosker* in Sydney. We never hear of *bosker* here. There is a *bonza*, a sort of improvement on the *boshter*, and *bonzarina*, feminine of *bonza*. Occasionally one hears of a *dabster*[16] (a variety of *boshter*) and *bontosher* which denotes something abnormal in the *boshter* line.

This comment drew a reply from a Sydney correspondent in the "Bulletin" of December 20, 1906:

> *Boshter* is as common as *bosker* – perhaps even more so – in Sydney, and, at least five years ago [i.e. in 1901] a barber in Paddington proclaimed himself, in drunken and disorderly capitals which wandered all over his shop front, "The Boshter Barber".

The writer added that *boshter* had been current for ten years or so.

Since the first printed example of *bonzer* is not to be found until 1904 we are left to surmise that this term was either a good deal less popular than *boshter* and *bosker* at the beginning of this century, or that it arrived subsequent to them. If the latter is correct, then *boshter* and *bosker* are not variants of *bonzer* but independent terms, which merely have similarity in use and sound.

Whatever is the case, these words have left a deep imprint on our language. Here is a list of elaborations on the theme, with the dates when they came into printed use: *bon*, which approximates the French adjective and noun (1906: "Ain't it a *bon*?" asks a writer); *bons* (1904: probably a clipping of *bonzer*); *bonster* (1904: a writer describes it as "that bulwark of the Austral slanguage"); *bonsterina* (1904); *bontoger* (1904: the writer suggests an origin in the French *bon toujours*, always good, and uses the spellings *bontodger* and *bontojer*); *bontogerino* (1908: an elaboration of the above); *bontosher* (1904: also rendered *bontoshter*); *bonus* (1904: "A fair *bonus* is a real trier, a fair goer, or a bit of a don" – an interesting reversion to the Latin original); *bonzerosity*, something with notable or excellent features (1906); *bonzerina* (1906: with the subsequent version *bonzerino*); and two variations that came into use much later, *bonziorie* and *bonzo*.

Here are some of the many synonyms for *bonzer*: *all gee, all cush* (from the Hebrew *kosher*, lawful, especially as applied to meat), *blitherer, bottler* and *bottling, rubydazzler, rube* and *dazzler, grouse, curl-the-mo, dodger, just the shinin', pearl* and *pearler, peg, purt* and *purter, rip-snorter, rorter, scutcher, snitch*

---

16 This is old English slang.

and *snitcher, snodger, snozzler, sollicker, swinjer, swiz, toby (roacher), trimmer, trouncer, whopcacker, pewster* and *rumptydooler.* Many of these terms are now obsolete. They provide a comprehensive example of the wear and tear which slang undergoes. All of them were in fairly constant use when I put this Section together originally; today, only *bottler, grouse* and *curl-the-mo* have much signs of life in them.

Curl-the-mo was apparently first used to denote the self-satisfaction of a man who twirled the ends of his flowing moustache. It was then applied to anything meriting approval, was shortened to *curl* and then transferred to *twist.* A *twist* is accordingly something especially good, and a *big twist* is the superlative of excellence. A popular song "Curl-the-Mo, Uncle Joe" – written in praise of Joseph Stalin, who had a large moustache – by Australian journalist Jack Hatch, ended with the words *"Big Twist!"*

We also describe something especially good as a *gig,* a *snack* or *snackeroo,* as *good iron, ribuck* or *ryebuck* (now obsolete) and as *ridge* or *ridgey-didge.* It is *right* (or *fair*) *into one's barrow* (or *barrel* or *tomahawk*). You are willing to admit that *you can't complain* (or *growl*)*!*

Dinkum also has the senses of notability and excellence attached to it on occasions, although it is used mainly to describe that which is honest or genuine. Here again we can look to English dialect to supply an origin, which appears in the form *fair dinkum,* fair play. Boldrewood first introduced us to the term in 1881 when he wrote of *"an hour's hard dinkum",* meaning hard work, in his "Robbery Under Arms". *Fair dinkum,* meaning genuine, occurs in the "Bulletin" of May 5, 1894. *Square dinkum, straight dinkum* and *honest to dinkum* may also be noted.

The variants *dink, dinky* and *dinky-die* (the form *dinky-di* seems to be preferred in printed versions we see these days) have followed as a matter of course and, since the diggers of World War I made great use of the word, we find Anzac soldiers described as *Dinks* and *Dinkums.*[17] A native-born Australian is called a *dinkum* (or *dinky-di*) *Aussie.* News or information that can be relied on is called *the dinkum article* and *dinkum oil* (synonyms are *good oil, right oil, straight oil*). We have even made a superlative out of the term, which already implies superlative characteristics, and have developed *dinkumest*[18] just as we have taken *bonzer* into the forms *bonzerer* and *bonzerest*[19] in our desire to lay stress on what we say.

Synonyms for *dinkum oil* are *the office, the drum, the good guts, the (good) griff, the straight wire, the strong of* or *strength of* (something) and *the fair doose* (or *does*).

Perhaps for the reason that Australians are usually tempted to find refuge in expletives and "bad" language to describe disagreeable things, our vocabulary of terms for that which is disliked is not large.

Sope is an old larrikin word in this category. A writer in 1907 described

---

[17] Details of these uses are given in the chapter on War Slang.

[18] For example, "the *dinkumest* looking devil-dodger". – "Aussie", October, 1918.

[19] For example, "Trix is the *bonzerest* absolutely girl that ever was". – N. Lindsay, "Saturdee" (1933) – and "You'll make the *bonzerest* couple ever seen this side the Tropic". – X. Herbert, "Capricornia" (1938).

it as "the direct antithesis of *bonzer* . . . It expresses all that is condemnable in anybody or anything". It is now obsolete. *Drack* and *bodger* are modern equivalents. The former has developed into *drack sort,* an ugly woman or girl (and, by a weird form of antithesis, into a reference to an exceedingly beautiful woman or girl), into a reference to a police officer or detective (as seen by a criminal), probably by rhyme on *jack,* a version of *john* as occurring in *johnhop,* which is itself a rhyme on *cop,* and as a reference to anything unpleasant. *Bodger,* originally meaning counterfeit, worthless, second-rate, was converted into *bodgie,* which had a vogue after World War II to denote the modern Australian larrikin and bred such derivatives as *bodgiedom* and *bodgie-type.*

Perhaps the best terms we have to replace *sope* are *cow*[20] and *fair cow,* both of which can be used with great flexibility. Their modern use was foreshadowed in 1864 by C. R. Thatcher who, in his "Colonial Songs", applied *cow* to a bullock, but since *cow* did not appear in Australian use until the beginning of World War I we are faced with an extremely interesting problem. Many Australian diggers served in France. Now, in French slang the word *vache* (cow) denotes a policeman or a "nasty fellow" and is used as an adjective meaning "nasty, wicked" (I quote from "A Dictionary of French Slang" by Oliver Leroy, 1935). We must consider it a distinct possibility that the French use helped to shape our own, although the Australian experience of cows meant that we were probably quite as disposed to use *cow* as a derogatory term for a person as we were to use *larrikin,* having (as I pointed out in Section 1) used the expression *larky boy* as early as 1825. With a solitary exception, not until 1916 and after did *cow* and *fair cow* appear in print in Australia, and then in senses which paralleled the French use.

The exception? It is dated not much more than a month before World War I began – "Bulletin", July 2, 1914, p. 47. To quote:

> "The old cow," he grunted.
> Then he jerked his head back at the weather outside. " 'S goin' ter be a cow of a day . . ."

So there it is! By the narrowest of margins *cow* is established as an Australianism. In which case, did the French use of *vache* derive from some influence imparted by our cultural ambassadors in World War I, was it independent and/or did it merely confirm our use? Interesting questions, all of them.

The *pointer* also deserves attention. He takes unfair advantage of a person, situation, undertaking. He *points* or *works a point* or *works points.* His activities are called *pointing.* He is said to have *more points than a porcupine.*

Up to putty, up to mud, up to tripe, up the pole, up the chute, onkus (or *honkus*) and *tatty* describe things that are bad, disliked or out or order. An unreasonable demand – such as an excessive price for goods – is called

---

[20] In outback use, only after a heifer has borne a calf is she classed as a *cow.* This is an extension of the standard English use of the word for the female of any bovine animal.

a bit rough or a *roughie, a bit hot*[21] and *a bit solid.*

We have elaborated few U.S. expressions more than the vulgarism *bullsh*t* for nonsense or humbug. At least, it is to be presumed that this is an Americanism, although the vast number of variants we have evolved shows that we have made it almost a native. Best known of the Australian versions is *bullsh*, but some of the following run it close: *bull dust* (not to be confused with *bulldust*, the finely powdered and often deep dust found in remote areas of Australia, although each term may have reinforced the other), *bull fodder, bullock waggon, bull's wool, buffalo chips, cowsh, cowflop, cowyard confetti, Flemington confetti,*[22] *heifer dust, meadow mayonnaise, bumfluff, bovril* and *alligator bull.*[23] *Bovril* is now almost obsolete, but *bovrilize*, to confuse, render stupid, has developed from it and is still current.

A person given to bragging or empty chatter is known as a *bull artist* or *bilge artist,* a *blow-bag, blower* and *blowhole.*[24]

Berley denotes ground bait used by fishermen. It has been current in that sense for more than eighty years. In the past generations, however, we have applied it to humbug or nonsense, e.g. *a bit of berley*, leg-pulling or something to induce others to show interest, and in this way have started it off on a new career.

Guiver or *guyver* (I have an S.A. report "about 1895" stating that the term once denoted self-assurance), *kidney-pie, kidstakes, macaroni, mash, bilge-water* and *borak* cover the same meaning of misleading chatter. Best established of these is *borak*, which appears in the phrase *to poke borak at* a person, to tease, chaff or jeer at him, although like so many old-time phrases it is now falling out of use.

Much academic argument has surrounded the origin of *borak.* Morris, for instance, says that it is an Aboriginal word, and the "Oxford Dictionary" goes to the length of suggesting – quite erroneously – that our verb *to barrack* is derived from it. The truth of the matter is that there was probably no such word as *borak* in Aboriginal dialects. In any case, *to barrack* comes from English dialect. As all early textual quotations of *borak* are found in Aboriginal pidgin,[25] we must regard it as highly probable that the English *barrack* was taken over by the Aborigines in their efforts to talk English.

Writing on Aboriginal pidgin in 1904, Ernest Favenc declared:

> There are two words which go back, at any rate, more than fifty years, which sound aboriginal, but I cannot trace them – *chyack* and *borak*, both meaning much the same.

---

[21] This sense is also found in the French *ç'a m'a coûté chaud* (literally, that cost me hot), I paid through the nose for it.

[22] Derived from the Flemington stockyards, Sydney. This expression was used over the Bathurst (N.S.W.) radio station 2BS in 1937 and caused a local stir.

[23] Alligators are not found in Australia. The creatures so referred to are crocodiles. However, there are three Northern Territory streams called Alligator Rivers.

[24] *To blow*, used in Australia since 1864 or earlier, is a revival of fifteenth century English dialect; *blowing*, boasting, is recorded in Australia in 1858. America has also used these expressions extensively.

[25] An 1845 quotation: "You pilmillally jumbuck, plenty sulky me, plenty boom, *borack* gammon," meaning "If you steal my sheep I'll be angry and shoot you, no fooling!" An 1856 quotation: "*Borak* you ever see black fellow with waddie (wooden) leg".

Chyack is probably a corruption of "cheek", influenced by an earlier English use of the same word meaning "to hail, to praise noisily" and "to chaff ruthlessly". There is no reason why we should go past the English language in our search for the origin of *borak*.

To poke borak came into popular Australian use in 1882 or slightly earlier. Morris says that *to barrack* – which was at one time ruled un-parliamentary by the Speaker of the Victorian Legislative Assembly – also made its appearance about 1880. It was used originally in sporting parlance, meaning to shout or jeer at opponents with particular application to the football or cricket field. Derivatives include *barracking* (1885), *barracker* (1892) and *barrackese*, language used by barrackers (1894). Since about 1940, *to barrack* has acquired almost directly converse meanings. Thus, *barrack for* means to support, especially in a vocal sense, and a *barracker* is often a supporter or partisan.

Since the middle of last century, Cockney slang had contained the term *barrikin*, for jargon or speech, borrowed from the French *baragouin*, gibberish. This use of *barrikin* comes close to the original Australian *barracking*, and probably influenced it. Joshua Lake points out that provincial English contains the terms *barrack*, to brag, and *barracker*, a braggart.

Mishearing has probably been the cause of *poke borak at* being converted to *poke borax at*, an interesting example of the Law of Hobson-Jobson or the displacing of unfamiliar by familiar words owing to similarity in sound. *Poke borax at* was used in 1890. Another variation was *poke mullock* (worthless spoil or debris is called *mullock*), which subsequently developed into *poke muck* and then into *poke mud*, all meaning to tease or chaff. So well-established are these expressions that Henry Lawson dismisses *borak* or *mullock* altogether in "While the Billy Boils" (1896) when he speaks of "*poking it* at him".

Fools of one kind and another have carved a considerable niche for themselves in Australian speech: *lardhead, loop, nit, no-hoper, nong* (also *nong-nong* and *ning-nong*), *plat* (a clipping from *platypus*), *quoit, hoon, tonk, twit, Billy Muggins, blob, boofhead, bunny, lolly, dill, dilpot, dillypot, gaylo, drip, flathead, possum, gammy, gazob, gimp, gup, drube, galah* and *drongo*. A couple of comments are necessary on the last two. The *galah* is a rose-breasted, grey-backed Australian cockatoo, given to much chatter (it is favoured as a cage-bird); hence the colourful simile *mad as a gumtree full of galahs*. The *drongo* is a small migratory bird with bluish and green plumage, and its popular zoological name has only the remotest link with the use of *drongo* to denote a slow-witted or stupid person. That application seems to have come from the use of Drongo as the name of a horse. To quote: "In Melbourne, in the early 'twenties, a Victorian horse by the name of Drongo won a certain claim to fame by consistently finishing last or near last. Black-and-white artist Sammy Wells, then of the Melbourne 'Herald', adopted Drongo as a character in his political and sporting cartoons. Drongo was the no-hoper in every situation . . ."

A correspondent who devoted much time to studying the origin of *drongo*, says that the horse with that name raced five times in 1923 and sixth was his best placing. In 1924, he had fifteen starts, running two seconds, three thirds, one fifth and one sixth (one of the seconds was in the V.R.C. Victoria Derby; the other was in the St Leger Stakes). In 1925, Drongo earned three seconds and four thirds. Which makes one wonder whether Sammy Wells was fair in nominating the horse as an all-round no-hoper. My correspondent adds: "It occurs to me that, as the glossy black plumage of the Australian bird called the Drongo is sometimes described as dark blue, this may have been the actual start of the slang usage of the word, and the association with the horse-that-never-won-a-race merely an afterthought. All new service recruits are traditionally regarded as no-hopers by the old hands – which may explain why raw recruits to the R.A.A.F. got the name about 1940."

I will have something to say later about *nong;* the only thing to be noted in the meantime is that it appears to be the sole word from pidgin English in New Guinea to have achieved general use in Australia.

Guppy, soapy, dilly (the forms *dilpot* and *dillypot* come from this rhyme on "silly") and *sonky* mean foolish. The negative form *don't be auntie!* also comes from a rhyme *don't be uncle Willy!* In earlier times, the state of being stupid was described variously as being *off one's kadoova, pan, pannikin, tile, top* or *saucer,* as being *dingbats,* and as having any one or more of the following: *the coconuts* (a Queensland term), *the cogwheels, the white ants, the Darling Pea, the quandongs* (the last two were mainly bush terms), *a shingle short, a sheet short* or *a shingle off the roof.* Modern examples on the theme are to be found in Chapter X.

5. WOWSERS AND THEIR KIND

PERHAPS because of his great capacity for tolerance (which even extends to being tolerant of intolerance), the Australian seems doomed to fill the role of a cockshy for all the petty moralists, religious fanatics and other humbugs who infest the average social group. Until only the most recent times he has been a prey to all purveyors of prejudice and misinformation.

It was no accident that skyrocketed the word *wowser* to a position of enduring importance in our language. Moral and social philistinism, which run hand in hand with ignorance and a low standard of education,[26] had endowed us with the brand of clerical mind that battens on mild and normal pleasures and exaggerates them into orgiastic lusts. It is the mind typical of ill-educated communities, where vision is clouded by prejudice, where commonsense is interpreted by a succession of clichés and slogans, and where the mills of god pulverise joy and wisdom out of everything.

In more ways than one the *wowser* is a typical Australian. The word denotes a puritan of advanced prejudices, a killjoy, a "blue-stocking". The first use of the term I have discovered is in an alliterative "Truth" heading of October 8, 1899 – "Willoughby Wowsers Worried".

---

[26] I have drawn detailed attention to the long educational twilight through which we passed in "The Drum" (1959).

Legend has it that John Norton, politician and owner of the journal, invented *wowser* from the slogan "*W*e *O*nly *W*ant *S*ocial *E*vils *R*emedied (or *R*ighted or *R*ectified)", but this amiable theory lacks confirmation.

All the important variations of *wowser* were first used by "Truth". When on May 3, 1942, the Sydney "Sunday Telegraph" used the phrase "they raised a *wowsing* quibble", the paper published a special note on the front page, claiming that at last the verb *to wowse* had been invented. The statement was incorrect. In the first place, the verb *to wowse* had not been invented, but only a theoretical participle used adjectivally. In the second place, "Truth" had done a much better job thirty-five years earlier, when it referred to "the vinegary and pessimistic *wowsings* of the oratorical picture painters of Hell".

Also invented by "Truth" were *wowserism* (1906), *wowserites* and *wowserdom* (1907). *Wowserish, wowseristic, wowserised* and *wowsery* have followed by natural development. *Wowser belt* (modelled apparently on the U.S. *Bible belt*) embraces the States of Victoria, South Australia and Tasmania, wherein wowsers flourish like Paterson's Curse. I even have a 1965 record of *Wowserville* for a mythical place supposedly infested with wowsers.

Our concept of the wowser has always been closely linked with clerics, and it is to be expected that such people should have left other imprints on our speech. Here are some self-explanatory Australianisms: *bible banger, bible basher, bible hawker, devil dodger, amen snorter, grasseater* (a Seventh Day Adventist) and *hallelujah hawking*.

While on the subject of religion we can note that Australia was partly responsible for encouraging the *Christian Israelite* sect, a group of South-cottians, followers of John Wroe, who came to be known as *beardies* in Australia about the middle of last century – so-called from their long beards.

Two indisputably Australian sects are the *Victorian Church*, the Presbyterian Church of Victoria, constituted in 1859, as severed from the Established Church of Scotland, and the *Australian Church*, a breakaway movement from the Victorian Church, founded in Melbourne in 1885 under Dr Charles Strong.[27]

The slang use of *tike* or *tyke* (perhaps, as Partridge suggests, a pun or rhyme on "*Mike*", an abbreviation of Michael) and *mick* (from the same source) for a Roman Catholic are other Australianisms. There is also a comprehensive list of words ending in *-o*: *Bappo*, Baptist; *Congo*, Congregational; *Metho*, Methodist; *Presbo*, Presbyterian; *Protto*, Protestant; *Salvo*, Salvation Army.

Nark was originally used in English cant for a police spy or stool pigeon, but in Australia it comes close to being a synonym for *wowser*. *To nark*, to annoy or infuriate, was originally dialectal; from this verb we obtained the common nounal version. *Holy Joe* was another English term, used in sea slang for a parson; but once again we have changed its meaning until its wowser characteristics are undeniable. *Lemon avenue*, used especially

---

[27] 1845-1942. A church flourished in Flinders Street, Melbourne, for some years, but subsequently support was lost and a transfer was made to a smaller building in Russell Street.

for a female wowser, was apparently first given currency in the "Woman's Mirror". Another Australian synonym for a wowser is *a grape on the business*. So is *waterbag*, but this word specifically denotes a teetotaller or temperance fanatic.

6. MINOR PEOPLE

WE HAVE NUMEROUS utility expressions for people, such as *king dick* and *say-so*, for a boss or leader, *pannikin boss* or *panno*, for a foreman or boss of minor importance, *sparrow, slab, squib, nugget* and *streak*, for men of varying sizes, *fang carpenter, gum digger* and *gum puncher* for a dentist, *greasy*, a butcher, *rabbit snatcher*, a midwife, *bottle-oh* and *bottle shepherd*, for a bottle collector, *bottle-oh's rouseabout*, a nobody, and quite a number of others whom we will meet in due course.

None of them has quite the stature of the *ratbag*, for in some ways he is as much a distinguishable figure in Australia as the *wowser*. Unlike Britain, Australia has no great enthusiasm for eccentrics. Hence, the use of *ratbag* for eccentric carries a certain disapproval and *ratbaggery* some suggestion that such conduct is un-Australian, or at any rate not quite acceptable in this environment. *Ratbagging it* denotes acting in an eccentric way. *Ratbag* has been in use since the 1930s.

An older term, meaning much the same, but now obsolete was *wad* or *wod*.

Stephens and O'Brien tell us about another old expression, *brewer's jockey*, "a man who rides about with the driver of a brewer's waggon, helping him load and unload on the off-chance of a share of the drinks which fall to the lot of a brewer's man".

A schoolteacher is called variously a *chalk-and-talker*, *guzinter* (i.e. one "guzinter" two, two "guzinter" four, etc.), a *bid* or *biddy*.

An eavesdropper is an *earwig*; an inquisitive person, a *stick* or *stickybeak*. To *stick* or *stickybeak* mean to be inquisitive, and *stickybeaking* is the practice. An interesting nursery cant phrase that has developed round this word is the set answer to a child's question, "What's that?" – "*Flypaper for a stickybeak!*"

Skiter and *skite* (used both as a verb and a noun) are Australian clippings of the original Scottish *bletherskite* which was taken into U.S. slang as *blatherskite* and, way back in 1885, was recorded as *bladderskite* in Australia. We put the verb into use in 1864 and have good reason to regard it as our own.

Pitcher and *bugler* for chatterboxes (we say a man is *bugling* when he is boasting or bragging); *grizzleguts* or *whinger* (it is important to note that the original verb *whinge* is pronounced "whinje", as in "ginger", and that the derivatives *whinger* and *whingeing* should never be spelt "winger" and "winging" because they lead to absurd mutilations of pronunciation) or *mizzler*, a person given to complaining; and *offsider*, an assistant or intimate, are also to be noted. Tradition says that the last is derived from *bullocky's offsider,* an assistant in yoking up, etc., whose main job was to urge beasts on the off-side of a team into action, while the bullocky attended to the near-side.

We are probably entitled to lay claim to *flatite,* a person who lives in a city flat (*flatette,* a small flat, also appears to be indigenous), *lounge lice,* a local adaptation of "lounge lizards", and *vip,* a miserly person – not to be confused with a V.I.P. or Very Important Person.

7. POPULAR JARGON

ANY ATTEMPT to split up the Australian language into divisions so that various terms may be grouped together obviously leaves many loose ends, especially in such a chapter as this. The fact is that, although The City Yesterday seems an easy enough field to define it inevitably leads to an examination of The City Today and, for reasons which will become apparent in Chapter X, I see the break between the two as occurring round about 1940. In short, The City Yesterday covers a large section of our history, while The City Today covers only a brief period. If some simple test is wanted, I would suggest that any person born around 1940 could supply an answer. Up to that time, there had been a strong continuity in our linguistic development. Thereafter a great change occurred. For which reason, although many older Australians will recognise the terms which follow, the new generation will look at most of them with an uncomprehending stare.

A few minor groups:

To accost or approach a person: *to barge up to, float up to, blow up to, line up to, bang up to* (someone); *to breast, to bridge, to front, to sprag* and *to bump* (someone). *To front* has acquired wider applications; one *fronts* a court, inquiry, etc., when one appears before it.

To interfere: *to prat one's frame in, put the mocks* (or *moz*) *on.*

To depart, especially in a hurry: *to smoke, smoke off, sling off, hive off, go for one's quoits.*

To arrive at a place: *to lob* somewhere. To return: *to lob back.*

To make an attempt at something: *to have a stab* (or *fly* or *belt*) *at, give* something *a burl* (or *pop*).

To stink: *to hoot, to honk* and *to ponk* (by rhyming slang, the South Australian place-name *Onkaparinga* is also used for a stench).

And a brief glossary of tailings:

apples, right, satisfactory – e.g. "How are things?" – "She's apples".
chuck up, to vomit. Also *go for the big chuck* (or *spit*).
crack on, to discover.
crockery, false teeth.
crople on, to take.
dip one's lid, to raise one's hat.
dwell on, to follow a person; to wait for an event.
fed with, "fed up with", of which it is an abbreviation.

full jerry, to understand; also *jerry* alone.

full up of, as for *fed with*.

go a raker, to fall heavily, "come a gutzer".

guiver, flashy talk calculated to impress a listener. Also *to guiver*, talk in such a fashion, and *sling the guiver*.

hooroo! goodbye! Also *ooroo!* and *hooray!*

juicy about, be, to understand, to be wise to something.

laughing gear, (false) teeth.

light on, in short supply.

mote, to travel or move quickly.

nadget, the head.

not a bar of, non-acceptance of any part of a person, thing, idea. *Can't stand a bar of, won't have a bar of*.

on the tooth, hungry, eager to eat. Also, tasty.

over the edge (or *fence*), unreasonable, beyond the pale of fairness or decency.

pass in one's marble, to die.

square off, to apologize, to produce a glib explanation for some lapse or misdemeanour.

sweet, ready, prepared, satisfied, e.g. "Have you enough money?" – "Yes, I'm sweet." As in the use of *apples*, a persistent feminine use has developed in Australia. Answers to almost any relevant question can be *she's apples, she's jake, she's goodoh* or *she's sweet* depending on the linguistic preferences of the speaker.

throw a map, to be sick.

toey, worried or anxious; nervously alert.

trizzer, lavatory.

tryanthewontigong, a thingumebob.

warb, a worker, a member of the proletariat, a nobody.

whingy, querulous. (See previous Section.)

whips of, much, an abundance of, e.g. *whips of time*, with plenty of time to spare.

CHAPTER VII

The Underworld

1. CRIMINALS

JUST AS THERE IS a close link between the ordinary Australian and the larrikin as we studied him in the last chapter, so there is an intimate link between the larrikin and the underworld. The push and its members constitute the great levelling influence in Australian speech, the common ground on which cant, slang and colloquialisms have met and fused.

In the survey of early convict slang, relatively little attention was paid to cant in the strict sense of that term. What we were concerned with was a record of convict life, rather than of linguistic relationships between members of convict society.

This advertisement from the "Sydney Gazette" of September 9, 1804, hardly needs comment:

CANT DICTIONARY

Some time ago a fmall Publication, entitled a SLANG DICTIONARY, was borrowed from a Gentleman, but neglected to be returned.

Whoever may have the faid Book in their poffeffion is requefted to fend it to the Printer of this Paper, in Back Row, Eaft, and as it is valuable to the owner from reafons not neceffary to be explained, it is hoped no perfon will withhold its furrender after this Notice.

The "reafons" behind this appeal mainly concerned the plenitude of slang used by the convicts.

We are fortunate that Vaux compiled a vocabulary of underworld cant while he was a convict in Australia in 1812, for, although the bulk of that cant hailed from London and English prisons, it provides us with an intimate glimpse of what were probably the speech habits of Australia's first white inhabitants.

Here is a brief selection from his observations:

bash, to beat.
blow the gaff, to reveal a secret.
bounce, to bully, talk loudly, affect importance.
chats, lice.
cheese it! stop it!
dollop, a large quantity of anything.
fence, a receiver of stolen goods.
frisk, to search.
gray, a coin with two heads or tails.
grub, food.
kid, to deceive.
mizzle, to run away, decamp.

nuts on, infatuated with.
office, a hint or signal – e.g. *give the office*.
put up affair, a preconceived plan.
ramp, a trick, offence.
ring in, to defraud.
school, a number of persons met together to gamble.
shake, to steal.
sharp, a gambler, swindler.
snitch, to betray.
stink, an uproar.
turn (it) up, to cease, stop.
up the spout, in pawn.

If these old English words with lowly beginnings have become acclimatized in Australia we can see that this is with excellent reason. That the Australian is content to use them today is not due to any perverse desire to "talk American", but to the fact that generation after generation of Antipodeans has found these expressions in the national vocabulary and put them to continuing use.

Among the terms quoted above from Vaux was *traps* for police. During the gold rush days Australia modified the word to describe *mounted* police, just as we took *trooper*, which described a soldier in English slang, and applied it also to mounted men. England was originally responsible for the word *cop*, which Australia elaborated into the now-obsolete *copman* and *copperman* and which, by a process of rhyme, gave us the popular Australianisms *john hop*, *jonnop* and *hop*. England also seems to have used *jack*, *john* and *johnny* for a policeman before we did, but these words now have their main currency in Australia. England took the French *gendarme* and turned it into *Johnny Darby*; we have altered it to *John Darm* and *John Dunn*.

We also call a policeman or detective a *rat*, *mug copper* or *mug john* (these two last terms are regarded as especially objectionable by the police), *drack* (probably by rhyme on *jack*, but with offensive connotations of its own), *demon*, *dog*, *body snatcher*, *hostile*, *slop* (possibly another rhyme on "cop", but there are English antecedents), *vulture*, *paddler* and *walloper*.

The inhabitants of Australian crookdom fall into two reasonably well-defined groups – the artisans or "working class" of thieves, murderers, etc., and the parasitic "intelligentsia" who live by trickery and swindling.

Crooks in general are known as *hard heads*, *takes*, *twicers*, *forties* or *artists*. Australians also employ *artist* in much the same way as Americans use *fiend*, to describe someone who is enthusiastic and expert in some vocation or other, although we do not always imply admiration for the accomplishment. Thus we have *bilge artist*, *big-note artist* and *bull artist*, persons given to bragging or talking nonsense, *booze artist*, a drunkard, *pigskin artist*, a jockey, *gyp artist*, a swindler, and *leg-shake artist*, a pickpocket. Most of these "artist" elaborations will be generally understood, but when we reach the last we begin to feel that we are in an alien world.

There are sound reasons, for even such a lowly operator as the Australian pickpocket has a vocabulary that is well-nigh stupefying. He is a *knockabout man*, a *leg-shake man*, a *leg-shaker*, a *shake man*, a *take*, a *hoister*, a *lift* and, of all things, a *good thief*, which a retired pickpocket admits to me is "a strange use, but it's in name only, not by nature". The *leg-shaker* usually works with a partner, who is called a *lumber man*, *approach man* or *contact man* (on the rare occasions he operates alone he is called a *wizzer* or *ripperty man* and is said to be *one out* or *working hot*, i.e. increasing his chances of being caught). The *lumber man's* job is to *position* the victim and distract his attention by *slewing the nut*, turning his head, shake his hand or otherwise hold the victim's interest, while the *leg-shaker* goes to work. My informant gives this advice: "A *knockabout man* should never tackle more than one client at a time."

A generation ago, when masculine dress was somewhat different from today, the various pockets were known as *left outer* and *right outer* (outside coat pockets), the *inner* (the inside pocket of a coat), *left bin* and *right bin* (top pockets of a waistcoat), *left lower bin* and *right lower bin* (lower pockets of a waistcoat), *the safe* (inside pocket of a waistcoat), *left kick* or *pit* and *right kick* or *pit* (trouser pockets), the *seat* (hip pocket) and *obfar* (fob pocket). Some remarks will be made later on the use of "pig Latin" in the Australian underworld. The *shake man*, i.e. the pickpocket, always takes charge of the *willy*, wallet, *pap*, banknotes, or *smash*, coins, stolen from the victim. Both *pap* and *smash* are originally English.

To return for a moment to the *wizzer* or *ripperty man*, i.e. the pickpocket who works alone on crowded buses, trams or trains. His method of work, because he has not been able to learn many particulars, is called the *donkey* or *blind stab*. He is a *donkey dipper*, *donkey diver* or *blind stabber*.

I have records of *break man* and *bumper up* as synonyms for *lumber man*, but they are used only rarely these days. However, there are other spheres of activity which require the work of an assistant. For example, in sideshow parlance a *gee man* or *amster* (sometimes wrongly rendered as *ampster*) is a decoy who works with a sideshow operator to induce the public to spend its money. *Amster* is an abbreviation of *amsterdam*, which is a rhyme on *ram*, used similarly, and *amrar* is a variant. Any person who uses a set routine of talk (a *come-on*) to secure victims is a *spieler*, *eeler-spee*, *eeler-whack* and *illy-whacker* (the last three are formed by mutilation from the first: a trickster of this kind is said to *whack the illy*), *nineteener*, *piker*, *rorter*, *scaler* and *lurkman*.

The word *lurk*, although imported from England up to a century ago, has been given many applications in Australia. Its older uses were largely of a criminal nature; there is, for example, an 1882 reference to *dead lurk*, "entering a dwelling house during divine service". In some cases we still use *lurk* to denote a dodge, racket or scheme, but its outlines have been softened in recent years so that it sometimes does not mean much more than a line of highly-competitive business, with competitive ruses being the lurks. Hence, *lurkaday world*, *lurkmanship*, *lurkola* (our version of the U.S. *payola*), *out-lurked*, out-manoeuvred, etc. Lurks can take many forms; for instance, some metropolitan taxis were reported in 1953 to be sporting a *lurk light* over their rear windows, about the same shape and size as a vacant sign. To quote: "When a taxi approaches at night with the *lurk light* on, it looks as if the cab is advertising itself for hire, even though it is already engaged. The driver takes it from there".[1] To push the matter a little further, we find that the *lurkman*, *lurker* or *lurko* can vary from the largely honest operator who *works a few points* to the petty racketeer, who extracts money from innocents by unloading *drack* (worthless) goods on them, *twining* (ringing the changes), *glimfaking* (selling spectacles and other articles in country areas at 500 per cent profit or so), and otherwise taking the public down in bars, on racecourses or at shows.

A correspondent has given this picture of an unusual lurk: "The man I'm talking about had a real *money spinner* in the form of a spinning top. It was numbered one to nine on its sides, was about the size of dice and had a peg through the centre, pointed both ends, with about ¾″ at each end of the top. To set it in motion, one end was flicked with the forefinger and thumb. (It's necessary to go into details.) The peg was very securely fixed in the top, but when pressed down by only a fraction, the top, when spun, would never show a number above five. That was for the *mug's* spin. When the *shrewdie* was spinning, he just pressed the peg the other way and also spun it the reverse way. When he spun, the top would never show less than six to nine. It was so made that the top could not *blue* and the *gaylo* was never in the race. He usually operated in a pub bar or bar parlour and after a bit he'd suggest spinning the top for drinks; after a few drinks, then for money, and a *brick* would change hands in a few minutes. He'd let the *mug* double up as often as he liked. No one ever seemed to wake up that they were being gypped. However, this *lurko* was *buckled* once – for being drunk! The cops noticed the top among his possessions, but when he had sobered up he told them he only used it at parties to have a bit of fun. They returned it to him without question. No one had ever complained about him using it."

A *hold-out man* is a criminal who withholds part of the proceeds of a crime from his partner. He *weeds off* some items for himself. He is also called a *lasher*, a term which is extracted from an odd underworld saying, "*Lash yer, lag yer!*" – meaning, more or less, "May you get jailed if you don't divide the plunder fairly."

Since many criminal activities depend on the generous co-operation of assorted *mugs*, the following terms for the latter can be noted: *possum*, *poss*, *possodeluxe*, *gay*, *gaylo*, *galah*, *imbo*, *thirty-first of May* (a rhyme on *gay*), *milkjug* (a rhyme on *mug*), *milkie*, *Beecham's pill* (a rhyme on *dill*), *bunny*, *bush bunny*, *lolly*, *alec*, *sim*, *log*, *mahogany*, *cedar*, (someone) *carved out of wood*, *soap*, *gig*, *touch* and *bite*.

Thieves are described variously as *bust men*, *bursters*, *night hawks* or *night hunters* (these expressions also denote prostitutes), *barbers*, *dwelling dancers*,

---

[1] *Jockeys* and *snipers* are associated with taxi rackets that grew up in World War II, but disappeared at its end. A *jockey* was a taxi-driver's accomplice who pretended to be a passenger in order to encourage legitimate travellers to pay extortionate fares to secure the taxi. A *sniper* was a private motorist, who did not pay taxi-licence fees, but who *sniped* fares from legitimate taxi-men.

stoops and *possums*. A *bust man* in one of our capital cities has complained to me (and sent documentary evidence to support his claim) that certain police are lowering the tone of his profession. He says: "A *bust man* is approached by a *drack* who suggests to him, if he will *carry the bucket* for about 30 or 40 burglaries in the suburb where he was caught, they will *break it down* for him and get him off with a lighter sentence than expected. The idea is that he might be guilty of only seven or eight of them, but it wraps it up, making believe the whole lot was cleaned up as the result of good work by the *dracks*". The bust man's part in such an arrangement is called *copping a plea, nodding the nut, bobbing the skull* and *taking a dive*. Or that is what my *bust* friend says. The police version is somewhat different. A little later, I will give a detective's round-up of criminal slang, in which it will be seen that such expressions as *nod the nut, bow the crumpet* and *duck the scone* mean no more than to plead guilty to an offence.

There are, of course, many ill-doers in our midst apart from pickpockets and burglars.

A *necklace* or *choke* is a garotter; a *stick slinger* is a thief who works in company with a prostitute; a prostitute (i.e. one who *hawks the fork*) who robs a man by taking money from his clothes is a *gingerer;* the *ginger girl* usually works with an accomplice, and *to ginger* and *gingering* are associated terms. However, of recent years *ginger joint* has been used with another application altogether, as a place where, if the customer's perverted tastes run in such a direction, both the prostitute and her *hoon* (*silver spoon* is a rhyme on it) or *bludger* join with the client in a complex sexual act.

A *fence* is a person who can show a customer how to obtain such esoteric pleasures. This use has no relation to the English use of *fence* for a receiver of stolen goods.

Harlots whose activities are not organised by *hoons*, and who, accordingly, work lone-handed or in pairs, are called *battlers*. Many of them conduct their affairs by what is known as *working a door*. That is, they do not walk the streets or *swing a bag* in search of clients, but sit or stand in the doorways of their business premises. Clients come to them and they cannot, therefore, be charged with soliciting. Often they pay agents or *touts* to bring customers to their *door* (as a brothel is sometimes loosely known), and they also employ lookout men, called *gigs* or *cockatoos*, to warn them of the approach of police. *Bag-swingers* who solicit custom from sailors are said to *cover the waterfront*.

The accomplice of a woman who *works a ginger* on a client – i.e. robs him – is also a *backer-up*, and the practice is called *backing up*. A harlot's handyman, who does *gigging* and other necessary jobs in or near the place of business, is sometimes called a *bumper-up*, a *bumper-upper* or a *candy boy*. An amateur harlot or one who undercuts regular professional prices, with little thought for the consequences of this deflationary activity, is called a *charity dame* or a *for-free*. An occasionally used term for a prostitute, which dates back many years, is *wop*, and *wopshop* denotes a brothel. Similarly *cake* and *cakeshop*. A harlot who consorts with Negroes or other dark-skinned men is called a *boong moll; boong*, of course, is an Australian term for an

Aboriginal or a native of New Guinea. Other terms generally applied to harlots include *charley* or *charlie*, *chippy*, *K.P.* (a common prostitute) and *lowy*, a familiar form of *lowheel*, *band*, *belt*, *endless belt*, *ferry*, *half-squarie*, *prosso* and *prossie*.

To steal or to rob a person is to *frazzle*, *oozle*, *muzzle*, *razz*, *razzle*, *rogue*, *rat*, *scale*, *stiffen* or *touch* someone. *To scale* and *to touch* also mean to cheat; *to stiffen* is related to the Australianism *stiff as a crutch*, completely broke, penniless. A sneak thief is a *sleepwalker* or *porch climber*. To swindle is described as *to work a ready* or *to ready up* and *to rib* (a person), and a dodge or scheme to cheat someone is known as a *dart*, *lurk* (we have already seen some of the many uses of the term) or *rort*. *To brass a mug* means to trick a victim into parting with his money, *the brass* being a form of betting trick mainly worked on racecourses. A *bridge* is a fake bet laid with the same object.

This brings us to the *con man*. Although this seems to have been originally a U.S. term, in more ways than one it describes the typical Australian crook. Here is an uninvited tribute from a detective in the Tower Police Court, London, in 1938:

> I have been in this kind of work for years, and I think that 95 per cent of the confidence tricksters in this country either come from or have lived a long time in Australia.

If, however, we are reluctantly obliged to abandon claim to *con man* out of deference to earlier American exponents of the craft, we can at least claim *con girl*, and such synonyms as *take*, *brass man*, *strong man* and *prospector*.

The *standover*, *standover man* or *standover artist* is also an Australian native. To *work the standover*, to demand money in exchange for "protection", is a line of criminal business that developed particularly around the *S.P. shop* and *S.P. operators*. These latter terms refer, of course, to starting price betting and book-making which is illegal in most States. However, now that *T.A.B.* (Totalisator Agency Board) *shops* have begun operating in all States except South Australia (Tasmania has legalized off-course betting shops), *S.P.* is being squeezed out in many parts of Australia.

Here are other underworld terms worth noting:

ace, to cease. *ace it!* or *ace it up!* stop it!
aste it, see *edge it*.
barrow, a police van or Black Maria.
Bengal lancer, a razor slasher (from the Bengal make of cut-throat razor).
birdlimed, this term is used to describe a person who has been convicted for another's crime.
blow a tank, to break open a safe with gelignite.
blow down (someone's) *ear*, to give a tip or information to someone.
bodger (or *bodgie*), anything worthless, such as a fake receipt.
braille or *bit of braille*, a tip or piece of information.
bridgewater, any fake article, such as a letter or jewellery.
chop-up, a division of spoils.
chuck a dummy (or *scranny*), to sham a fit in a crowd so that pickpockets can work easily.

clout on, to steal or take without permission.
copshop, a police station.
crumb act, put on the, to impose or *bludge* on another person.
crust, a vagrancy charge.
dog-cart, a police van. See *trawler*.
draw the crabs, to attract attention, especially from the police.
dud up, to arrange wares for sale so that goods of poor quality are hidden.
edge it, to keep quiet, concentrate on the job. Also, *aste it*.
face, as for *dud up*.
fit, a case that can be proved against a criminal.
fly canaries, to pass off used bus, tram or train tickets as new ones.
foreigners, trinkets.
fugleman, a petty gangster or strongarm man used to protect a racket.
   gig, (1) someone who stares inquisitively, (2) a private detective, (3) a fool. Also verb (1) to stare *at*, (2) to tease.
   gobble up, to arrest.
   guts, the bowels as a symbol of knowledge – *hold one's guts*, stay silent; *spill one's guts*, talk, confess.
   hoist, to arrest.
   lounge, the prisoner's box in a police court.
   marjie, marihuana.
   mount the box, to give evidence in a court case.
   push up for, to approach a victim.
   reef off, to steal (from someone). Whence, *reefing*, the practice.
   rock spider, a petty thief in a park, who robs the handbags or other possessions of couples otherwise engaged.
   shaving money, a negligible sum of money, especially heard in such a statement as "Ar, that no-hoper! He couldn't get shaving money".
   skull dragging, pulling a victim downstairs by his feet so that his head is painfully battered.
   slug up, equivalent of the U.S. *frame-up*.
   slanter (or *slinter*), a trick.
   squarehead (or *squarie*), a criminal who is currently at liberty.
   squeeze, an impression made of a key.
   tickle the peter, to rob a till.
   timothy, a brothel.
   trawler, a police van in which arrested persons are taken to a police station.

Stool pigeons have a significant variety of names in Australia. Here is a list of well-established expressions worthy of a notable place in any underworld cant: *spur, crab, copper-nark* (this is an extension of the original English *nark*, an informer), *dead-copper, fizz, fizgig, shelf, shelfer, top-off, dropper man* and *stinker*. To act as a stool pigeon is *to spur, crab, fizz on, top off, shop, dob in, shelf, copper on* and *put* (someone) *in*.

A bribe accepted by a police officer is a *lolly* or *sugar bag*.

Future students of criminal jargon in Australia will owe a considerable debt to Detective Sergeant Brian K. Doyle, of the Sydney C.I.B. In 1950 he published a long list of current underworld argot in "The Australian Police Journal". Among the many terms he notes are:

   big note man, a wealthy person. There is also a verbal sense of *big note*, meaning to exaggerate one's wealth.

bow the crumpet, to plead guilty to an offence. See also *nod the nut* and *duck the scone*.

bung a game on, see *set up a joint*.

burn, a safety match.

corner, a share; especially a share of plunder.

down the chute, found guilty or convicted of an offence.

droob, a minute portion of anything, especially used in the negative phrase, "*He didn't get a droob*", meaning "He got nothing".

drop the bucket, to throw responsibility (e.g. for an offence) suddenly on to someone else.

duck the scone, to plead guilty.

foreign smoke, opium.

front, to appear before, especially in the phrase *front a court*, to appear on a charge.

jack up, to plead not guilty; to protest; to offer resistance.

joey, something worthless; a fraud. Applied to a faked receipt (known as a *bodger*) and to a false report (called a *furphy*) among other things.

lie down, to withdraw a statement; to back pedal; "if a witness *lies down* he will not swear to what he has previously said".

lolly, one who is timid or half-hearted; "usually one who commits a crime in company, yet does not want to be 'in it' so far as the risks are concerned".

long-stopper, a nitkeeper or look-out man; "a more superior type of *cockatoo*, one who has graduated from a two-up school to a pub corner". The expression *long nit*, for a guard stationed at a distance from the scene of illegal activities, is perhaps more common.

nod the nut, to plead guilty.

paddles, feet; whence, *paddler*, a policeman.

position, in, "to put someone in position usually means to put them in the 'firing line' or in a position to achieve some particular purpose".

pound note man, a wealthy person.

set up a joint, to commence an illegal game of chance, such as two-up; "in New South Wales it is *bung a game on*".

sing, to pay blackmail; "if it is said that a particular mug *sings* well, then it means that he pays well without *bunging on a blue*".

sit in, "to place someone in position to effect a certain purpose".

slew your brew, to confess; "*Don't slew your brew* is to say 'Keep your mouth shut and don't do your head'."

snodger, "if something is a *snodger* it is *mighty* in Queensland, it is *colossal* in New South Wales, and just 'very nice' everywhere else".

split, a safety match.

spur, to spoil, ruin the chances of (someone).

straw bail, worthless bail, where the surety is without assets to cover the amount of the bail.

tank, a safe.

tank car, a motor car used for the purpose of safe-breaking.

throw, to outwit, to dodge trouble; "to beat anything, particularly used to refer to charges at Court".

treacle, opium.

trilbys, female legs.

It should not be assumed that all the words in Detective Sergeant

Doyle's list are Australian originals. Far from it. Here are some of the American terms he includes: *blow*, to depart, go away; *boob* and *can*, jail; *black stuff*, opium; *broads*, playing cards; *gat*, revolver; *gimmick*, a house-breaking instrument; *hophead*, a drug addict; *reet*, right or O.K.; *stiff*, a corpse; *spring*, to bail out; *snow*, cocaine; *sticks*, country districts. There are also many terms borrowed from England in the collection, e.g. *brass*, money, which dates from the sixteenth century; *pinch*, to arrest, *plant*, to hide, and *quid*, £1, dating from the seventeenth century; and *beak*, a magistrate, which has been current for about two centuries. Other English incorporations are: *do a bust*, to break out of jail; *cat*, a sneak burglar; *caser*, five shillings; *doll*, a female; *drum*, a brothel; *darbies*, handcuffs; *fan*, to search; *hoist*, to steal; *knock off*, to steal or rob; *lagging*, a term of imprisonment; *mitts*, hands; *moll*, a prostitute; *packet*, a large sum of money; *scarper*, to run away; and *stir*, jail. In spite of these twin sources of inspiration, there is also a good deal in the list which is clearly Australian.

It is now necessary to spend a few moments considering how small-time criminals act when police gaze is on them. This is best told by the criminals themselves. I am informed that one of the greatest difficulties a criminal faces is the avoidance of looking guilty. Hence a peculiar expression, *the hunters*, to describe "the hunted look or exaggeratedly innocent actions which give many *crims* away".

An ex-practitioner writes: "If surprised, criminals such as a *leg-shaker* have a method of warning their partner – a noise is made at the back of the throat. It sounds like a guttural 'huck' and means shoot through quickly."

Now for another peculiar expression, *ripe*, meaning subject to immediate arrest under the Consorting Act. Here is part of a letter from a different source: "This act made it very hard for the *hard heads*. It put the kybosh on two or three gathering together. If two were in company they were *booked*; after ten or twelve bookings, you were *ripe*, could be *buckled* on sight. If you were an *old hand*, anything up to a *sixer*. Even a *squarie* or *cleanskin* would be booked if in company with a reputed *crim* if you had been noticed by the *demons* several times with the same bloke. After a *cleanskin* had got the required number of bookings, he went up. First he got a couple of bonds, then he went to jail. If you escaped being booked for three months, then the slate was wiped clean. One of the ways to dodge a booking was by *long stalling*, keeping fifty or sixty yards behind your mate or walking on the other side of the street. You had to keep your eyes open for signs from your mate as well as look out for the *jacks*. The usual signs are, if he rubs his nose with forefinger and thumb, that means 'look out, drop back'. Rubbing finger and thumb up and down the lapel of the coat has the same meaning. One means *on the nose*, the other means *on the coat*. If your mate puts finger and thumb to the brim of his hat it's O.K. 'It's sweet, join me, it's *castor*'. *Castor* is an old word for hat."

To conclude this section, a note on the use of 'pig Latin' by Australian criminals is worth making. To quote an informant: "In Australia, this argot differs from what the Americans use. For instance, the Yanks use

-*ay* at the end of a word, but the Aussies use -*ar*. The Yanks would say *ixnay* for *nix*, but we say *ixnar*. Say you have a sentence like 'Talk to the mug, Joe' this is how we'd say it 'Alkta oota the ugmar ojar'." Additional details are given in Chapter XVII, Section 4.

2. JAIL

ONE OF THE most colourful glimpses of Australian prison life in our literature is Vance Marshall's little book "The World of the Living Dead" (1919). Although not of outstanding literary merit, it is an important record of Australian underworld idiom.

   Marshall[2] introduces us to the *donkey-dipper*, a lone pickpocket who works on the principle of "grip, rip and run", the *dead rough-up*, which apparently describes a robbery of this nature, the *push-up men* and *break men* who work as confederates of pickpockets, the *tipslinger* and *magsman*, as racecourse "urgers" are known, the *household barber* and the *dwelling dancer*, transient lodgers who steal from boarding houses. Many of these expressions are no longer in use, but we have encountered some of them in the previous Section. Marshall also tells us that a *toe-ragger* is a prisoner on short sentence, that *ragtimers* and *sixers* are men with six months' sentences, that a *hum* is a "scrounger" or persistent borrower in jail, that *footballers* are warders who kick prisoners, that *the Bay* is a nickname for Long Bay jail, Sydney.

   Long before Marshall went to jail, various terms for jail sentences were listed in "The Detectives' Handbook" published about 1882. These included *drag*, three months, *dream* and *half a stretch*, six months, *stretch* or *rest*, a year.

   Some of these expressions have fallen out of use. Indeed, jailbirds are apparently so subject to linguistic fashion that it is difficult to be sure that the terms listed below as currently used are not in the process of being rejected or modified:

> *deuce*, two months.
> *lag*, three months.[3]
> *snooze*, three months. Also *snore*.
> *sleep*, three months or any short sentence.
> *six doss (in the steel)*, six months.
> *dream*, six months.
> *zack* (or *zeck*), six months.
> *sprat*, six months.
> *sane*, ten months.
> *rest*, twelve months.
> *clock*, twelve months.
> *round the clock*, twelve months.
> *all the year round*, twelve months.
> *swy*, two years.

---

[2]   Under the pen-name of Jice Doone he compiled and published a brief dictionary of Australian slang in his "Timely Tips to New Australians" (1926).

[3]   The original use of *lag*, a transported convict, and *to lag*, to transport a convict, were recorded by Vaux and were certainly associated with Australia, although it is presumed that they were first in English cant.

lagging, more than two years.[4]
tray (or *trey*), three years.
spin, five years.
full hand, five years.
brick, ten years.
jade, an indefinite term.
kath (or *kitty* or *kathleen maroon* or *kathleen mavourneen*), an indefinite term.
(These are related to the refrain of the song: "It may be for years and it may be for ever".)
key, an indefinite term.
twist, an indefinite term.
the lot, life imprisonment.

At this stage it gives me pleasure to draw attention to a remarkable study undertaken by a life-sentence prisoner in one of New South Wales' jails. This man spent more than a decade behind bars and a sizeable part of that time he devoted to recording and annotating the slang in use among jail inmates. The result is an extraordinarily interesting glossary of terms, which he has called "The Argot".

Such notice as I have space to give here cannot do full justice to the patience and instinct for philological enterprise which the author of "The Argot" – who calls himself "Thirty-five" – gave to his task. In my view, "The Argot" is one of the finest pieces of linguistic research to have come out of any jail in any part of the world, including America, where sundry enterprises of this nature have been encouraged by jail authorities.

Apart from Vaux, who as I have already pointed out compiled a slang dictionary while working as a convict at Newcastle early last century, "Thirty-five" is, to the best of my knowledge, the only Australian criminal to produce a first-hand commentary on prison argot in this country. Vaux's work naturally has historical interest, but I believe that "Thirty-five's" effort can be regarded as much more important.

The well-balanced and understanding attitude he took to his task is shown in the following extract from a long introduction to "The Argot":

Because society imposes sanctions for violations of its rules, criminals, to protect whatever vestiges of self-respect remain to them, must perforce hold civilised standards up to ridicule, and postulate, by implication, the moral superiority of their own immorality . . . The thorough-paced criminal is half-aware, at any rate, that society holds him in contempt, a contempt he heartily reciprocates. He is convinced that society has conspired to put him behind bars, and that, to this end, police, magistrates, judges, juries and even solicitors have combined to convict him, innocent or guilty, and to give him the harshest possible sentence. The question of why he should be singled out for this persecution he answers to himself by aligning himself with the martyrs of the ages. The way in which he thinks of authority is shown by his use of the words: *cold, demon, dock defence, gig, give up, shrewdy, smarty, mug* and *use*.

The criminal thinks that he has a moral right to plunder society ("*No one is exempt*") and that people who assist in his detection and arrest are

---

[4] *Lagging*, a term of penal servitude, was also recorded by Vaux.

morally depraved. Those who work for a living are *mugs* and *squareheads*, whilst those who live by robbing the mugs are *smarties* and *shrewdies*. The victim who complains *bellers* (bellows) *like a bad mug*, and any witness who lays any information is a *gig*.

In line with his assumed right to live by his wits is his assessment of every woman according to her eligibility as a mistress, and in the [i.e. "Thirty-five's"] list there are given no fewer than twelve words which are deprecatory terms for women. Since the criminal spends a good part of his life in jail, normal relations are the exception rather than the rule, so it is not surprising to find sixteen terms referring to homosexuality among males. (Only three referring to lesbianism are recorded, but perhaps women prisoners could provide additions.) That the inversion has reached its natural conclusion is shown by the fact that eighteen terms are in common use for the male genitals, not counting those found in schoolboy slang.

Like members of other anti-social groups, criminals fail to agree among themselves, and have, indeed, no very high opinion of each other. "All professions berogue one another", and murderers despise burglars, sneak thieves sneer at perverts, and embezzlers deride the lot. Another prisoner may be variously described as a *Beecham's pill, bunny, rabbit, chat, crawler, crayfish, pie eater, dill, dog, drip, drongo, zombie, falser, twicer, galah, gay, imbo, lair, melon, mug, possum, possodeluxe, rat* or *teddy bear*.

Consulting the following words (all of them in everyday use in the argot) will give some idea of the life in jail and of prisoners' chief interests: *boob, boss, brew, buy, grouse, haste, hot, jigger, pound, ridge, screw, bodger, tinder box, twist, weed* . . .

"Thirty-five" obviously possesses a rare talent for understanding the linguistic habits of his fellow men, and an even rarer ear for catching the nuances of meaning they give to words. Such defects as his work suffers from are the inevitable limitations imposed on him by his loss of freedom, chiefly in his lack of adequate reference works for comparative notes.

Here is about 10 per cent of the examples from his glossary. They should do much to convince readers that "Thirty-five" is a lexicographer of great sensitivity and skill (the definitions are as given by him):

ace, on one's, on one's own.
bludger, the criminal's commonest term for a policeman.
brat, a seventh-class prisoner, i.e. one under 24-26 years.
bridge, a plausible tale or excuse.
brokie, a person completely out of funds. See *pursie.*
buckle, to arrest.
build on, to add to, especially tobacco, when the beggar has insufficient to make a cigarette – "Build on this".
bull ring, the, the old punishment section at Parramatta Jail.
buy (up), the amount a prisoner may spend from weekly earnings on groceries; what he actually purchases. Prisoners who have served a specified term may spend up to a fixed amount from bonus earnings on butter, jam, cheese, etc. The scale is: over one year's servitude, 2/6; over three years' servitude, 3/–; over five years' servitude, 4/–; over seven years' servitude, 5/–.
Christmas hold, a hold applied by grabbing an opponent's testicles (a "handful of nuts").

cold, not guilty of an offence – "I'm cold" or "I'm doing it cold".

corn growing for someone, there's, said of a prisoner who is bound to be a recidivist. (Corn meal was the pièce de résistance at Long Bay breakfast.)

crust, doing the, said of prisoners convicted under the Vagrancy Act.

cunning up on oneself, to be too smart, to be hoist on one's own petard.

cut out, to serve a term of imprisonment instead of paying a fine.

dock defence, the legal aid provided by the Crown for a destitute prisoner. (The term is always one of opprobrium; criminals believe the solicitor provided acts in conjunction with the prosecution to secure a conviction.)

drop, to execute by hanging.

drunk act, the Inebriates Act, 1912.

dud up, to (mis-)inform a person from ulterior motives. Whence, *dudder* or *dudder-upper*.

falser, a shammer, a false pretence "artist"; also *false pretencer*.

full quid, in full possession of one's faculties; a person who is said to be *ten bob* or *ten deaners* or even *tuppence in the quid* is held to be a few shingles short.

gigglesuit, prison garb.

grapes, haemorrhoids.

grouter, an unfair advantage; possibly because criminals expect to enjoy unfair advantages as a matter of course, this original meaning is disappearing, and the word is commonly used to mean simply something extra, beyond what has been bargained for.

haste! (Imperative only) desist! Originally it was probably an injunction by a *cockatoo* to hasten away at the approach of the law; now it corresponds to the public schoolboy's "cave!".

head, a high prison official; hence, a privileged prisoner . . . Few heads are short-timers. To become and to remain a head, a prisoner is always: (1) "institutionalised" either in jail or before he arrives (e.g. in the Services), (2) a tradesman or professional man whose skill makes him useful to the administration, (3) sufficiently discreet to keep off others' toes. *Heads* are usually long-timers, I suspect, because murder is not an occupation, whereas theft often is. Occasionally, a sedate citizen runs off the rail to commit a serious or even capital crime, but to commit a petty theft, never.

heads on 'em like mice (or *boar pigs* or *bastard pigs*), used in the argot to express awe at any strong combination, e.g. a group of officials inspecting a prison.

hominy gazette, jail rumour; it goes round when the cells are opened to distribute the morning hominy (meal-porridge).

Hoyts, the man outside, a mythical person who starts all false rumours; the source of stolen property which an innocent (!) receiver is found to have in his possession.

joe gardiners, boots (from the name of Joe Gardiner, Ltd., of Sydney, boot and shoe makers).

joe jorgensen, a person who kicks in a fight (from the name of a once-noted Sydney footballer).

kangaroo, a warder, by rhyme on "screw"; also used in the abbreviated form *kanga*.

key, the Habitual Criminals Act, 1905, or detention under this Act –

"He's doing a swy and the key", "He's done his spin and he's into his key now". Whence, *keyman*, a prisoner detained under the Act.

kick along, to get along nicely, especially under discouraging circumstances – "You're doing it tough, aren't you?"; "I can kick along".

knock, to rape.

kway, a thief who does not specialize in any one line of activity.

lounge, the dock in court.

lugger, a shameless beggar; also an *earbasher*.

maverick, a piece of property of uncertain ownership, which may hence be taken with an easy conscience; also, a "strayed" prisoner, e.g. one who is in a workshop or other place where he has no right to be. (A local adaptation of a U.S. term.)

Moreton Bay (*fig*), any witness who lays an information, anyone who unwarrantably attends to or meddles in the affairs of others; by rhyme on *gig*, which is used similarly, and which may be a contraction of *fizgig*, an informer.

mug, a criminal's term of contempt for a respectable person who is, by virtue of his very respectability, a proper victim for every lurk; anyone who is not on the wrong side of the law.

muldoon, a glutton.

on the grass, free, out of prison.

oz. (pronounced to rhyme with "was"), an ounce of tobacco; the weight is printed on the packets issued to prisoners: 1 oz., 1½ oz., 2 oz.

perve, a pervert; *perve on*, to contemplate with erotic interest.

pie eater (or *cruncher*), a small-time crook.

pursie, a person who is in funds.

reef, to take, usually dishonestly.

Rhodes scholar, an expression of derision addressed to a prisoner who thinks he is above the common herd; however, it is not always derisive as it may be used to express gratitude for a favour done – "Good on you, sport; you're a Rhodes scholar".

roast, a calumny; an ill-report.

rort, a trick, a cunningly devised plan; rarely used as an intransitive verb, when it means to live by *rorting;* whence, *rorter*, one who so lives.

sane, ten, ten months, ten ounces of tobacco; but note that ten years or £10 is always a *brick*.

Sargent's pie, an eye, by rhyme.

screaming on, strongly biased against.

secko, perverted; also, *sexo*.

sh*tcan, to report unfavourably on; hence, to prevent from obtaining a good post.

sh*tkicker, a short-sentence prisoner, often employed on sanitary work.

short story writer, a forger.

shovel, a house or flat; a corruption of "hovel"?

slime, flattery; as a verb, to flatter.

square, not addicted to homosexuality in any way; hence, the litotes: "square as a billiard (golf, tennis) ball", i.e. irredeemably perverted.

strong of, the meaning, the object of; corruption of "strength of".

teddy bear, a flashily-dressed, exhibitionistic person; by rhyme on *lair*.

throw, to cajole (someone) into granting or parting with (something).

toe, take to the, to run away.

toe-ragger, a short-sentence prisoner.

toey, anxious to be gone, restless, especially of a prisoner who anticipates early release or transfer to a prison camp.

tootsie, a lesbian.

track, a warder who will carry contraband messages or goods out of or into jail for a prisoner.

trey bits, breasts; by rhyme on "tits".

trump, the senior official at any location who may be: (1) the overseer of a workshop, (2) the Governor – now Superintendent – of a prison, (3) the Comptroller-General of Prisons.

tub, the sanitary bucket used in jails; whence, *tubman*, a prisoner employed on sanitary work; *do it on one's tub*, to serve a jail sentence with light heart.

turn over, to search (a cell).

use, to exploit – "Always use a mug".

warb, a dirty or untidy person; also (by rhyme) *wattle and daub*; whence, *warby*, dirty or untidy.

water, go to, to betray one's fellows.

weakie, an unreliable confederate.

weed, tobacco. (This is an old English slang use, but "Thirty-five's" notes on it are especially interesting): Half a pound of butter is worth a *swy* (2 oz. of tobacco); a tube of toothpaste or shaving cream, about the same; a tin of syrup or plum jam, one ounce; more expensive jam, two ounces. In jail, every service, favour and commodity is as readily reducible to value in tobacco as it is to money in civil life.

whitewash someone's kidneys, to commit pederasty on; prisoners entertain the most eccentric notions about anatomy.

wifestarver, a prisoner confined under the provisions of the Deserted Wives and Childrens Act, 1901-6.

yarra, mad – "He's stone yarra".

In the course of his annotations, "Thirty-five" makes a note, which is worth quoting here, because it underlines an important point in language – the fact that most linguistic changes originate among the proletariat and are not imposed from above. The author says:

> Slang "ex alto" rarely catches (among jailbirds) because it fails to harmonise with the spirit of the users of the Argot. For example, a prison official, now retired, who had an extremely tenuous grip on reality, was something of a dandy. The acme of his sartorial splendour was achieved when he appeared on duty one Sunday resplendent in wing collar and lavender gloves, and swinging a gold-knobbed cane. I attempted to dub him "The Immaculate Misconception". I failed lamentably because some wag who read the Sunday comics named him for all time, and for all men, "The Little King".

In spite of the excellence of his work, "Thirty-five" has missed a few items – or my criminal correspondents say he has. Here are some of the terms they list: *on the corn*, in jail or, perhaps more accurately, on a diet of hominy which is served in jails; *polisher*, a jailbird; *upper ten push*, head prisoners in a jail; *pebbles*, incorrigible prisoners; *dodger*, jail bread; *flat*, tobacco other than that issued by the Prisons' Department; *snore weed* or *hammer and tack*, jail issue tobacco (the latter probably a rhyme on "black"); *milk cans*, jail sanitary tubs; *pound*, the solitary confinement section of a jail; *ramp*, to search a prisoner in jail; *boss*, a common term of address to a warder or jail overseer; *crim*, the criminal ward in a lunatic asylum, also known as *the flat; flea*, a prisoner who curries favour with warders and at the same time seeks to remain on good terms with his fellow inmates, i.e. he "hops" from one to another; *gig*, a visitor to a jail, i.e. one who is regarded as an inquisitive interloper; *chromo*, any girl or woman, taken from the more general use of the word for a harlot; *clock the mug* and *get the mug clocked*, expressions related to the photographing of prisoners when they enter jail; *moosh*, porridge; *hominy pimples*, an itchy rash which many prisoners suffer in hot weather, due, according to general jail opinion, to the wheatmeal, oatmeal and cornmeal porridge called *hominy*, which forms part of their diet (the jail tram that ran between Darlinghurst Police Station and Long Bay Jail was called the *hominy bus*); *hook job*, a prisoner serving a sentence of two years or more (from the letter C, or *hook*, which is stamped above the prison number on the coats of such prisoners); *white it out*, to serve a prison sentence in preference to paying a fine; *diamond cracking*, hard labour at stone breaking; *slot* or *peter*, a prison cell; *stiff*, a letter written by a prisoner and smuggled out of jail; *pie eater*, a term of abuse; *animal*, another term of abuse, especially describing a person lacking in human feelings, applied to certain types of warders.

The verb "to do" is given a good deal of hard work by jail inmates. For example, a prisoner does not serve a sentence – not, at least, in prison vernacular – he *does* a sentence. An accepted courtesy greeting in jail is, *"How are you doing it?"* To this the required answers are *"Doing it easy"* or *"Doing it tough* (or *hard*)"*, depending on the prisoner's view of how he is making out. *Doing it cold* means serving a sentence for a crime of which the prisoner is innocent – or claims he is innocent. To *do polly* is to pick oakum.

The verb *see* is also given a specialized meaning among jailbirds. It circulates through the grapevine when an escape has been made. *To see Tommy* means to break out of jail; on a more general basis it means to leave in a hurry.

Also worth noting are *jigger*, a name given to a minute radio set made by prisoners; *stick of weed*, an ounce of tobacco, which is commonly used as a medium for gambling transactions; *shanghai*, to send (a prisoner) back from a prison camp, where certain privileges are available, to a main prison, where privileges are hard to come by; *first-timer*, a prisoner who is in jail for the first time; and *silvertail*, a prisoner who, because of his personal qualifications or outside influence, is able to secure privileges which other prisoners do not enjoy.

3. GENERAL CANT

AMONG THE WORDS of our underworld and of those who hover near its edges few are more typically Australian than *cockatoo*, *nitkeeper* and *long-*

stopper, used to describe persons who stand guard while some illegal activity is afoot. *Cocky, cockatooer, nitkeep* and *nit* are variants of the above, and *to keep nit, to keep nicko, to keep tab* and *to keep yow* describe their activities; a *long nit* is a guard stationed at a considerable distance from the site of illegal activities. Hotel licensees who indulge in after-hours trading often pay a *cockatoo* to warn them of the approach of police, the role these cockatoos play being somewhat similar to that of the *bush telegraphs* who used to pass on news of police movements to bushrangers.[5]

To screw or *spark* means to watch closely; to be *on the grass* or *to reign* means to be at liberty; a *jacky* or *stew* is anything underhand that has been deliberately arranged, such as a boxing contest in which one of the contestants allows himself to be beaten. Cocaine is called *angie* or *angel*, apparently as a comment on the effects of that drug, *marjie* is marihuana, and opium was once known as *twang* in bush slang (the later use of *treacle* was noted earlier).

Additional items in underworld vernacular worth mention are: *please take me!* a roll of banknotes which has been exposed by a drunk; *put a knife through it!* said of a share-out of plunder; *to drum, drum up* and *give someone a drum*, to warn or tip off; *to smoke*, to decamp, and *in smoke*, in hiding; *leather* and *poque*, a purse (the latter is from the English *poke*, a bag or pocket); *seventeener*, a corpse; *nose*, a magistrate (a variant of the English slang *beak*); *fruit for the sideboard*, easy money; *sweet as a lolly*, a snack or *the grouse*, a very easy job; *in the biscus*, in trouble; *send off*, to steal, purloin (an object); *work back*, to return (an object); *dusters*, testicles; *shot of*, rid of; *go for the doctor, see Tommy* and *go on the toe*, to run away; *top off*, to reprove, put someone in his place (this is a sense additional to that given earlier for a stool pigeon).

As far as possible, I have weeded out English and U.S. expressions so that an unmarred picture may be gained of the indigenous material, although it will be clear that in ordinary speech both Australian and imported expressions are mixed. To show the extent of this mixing, I append a vocabulary supplied to me by an ex-con man. He had operated extensively in Australia, but had also been in business both in England and in America, so that the jargon he spoke represented an interesting mélange of underworld cant as used in the three countries.

Here is his glossary with the Australianisms italicized and some notes on the non-Australian elements:

> *alec, dill, gay, sim, lolly, bunny* and mug, a trickster's victim. (*Mug* is English slang.)
> *strong man*, a confidence man.
> *mulligans*, broads, playing cards. (*Broads* is old English slang.)
> *tale, pitch, rort*, spiel, patter used by a showman to draw the public. (*Spiel* is in American slang.)
> *ampster, ram*, shill, *urger*, a trickster's confederate. (*Shill* is U.S. slang.)

---

[5] In October, 1954, a boy soprano on a radio amateur hour in Sydney was asked by the compère what his father did. The boy, obviously nervous, replied: "He's a cockatoo at Clarke Island."

layout, setup, a trickster's plan of action.

flash, front, a trickster's dress or appearance. (*Front* may be originally U.S. slang.)

marching money, money for travelling.

still time, the period of the year when there are no shows. Con men often work from town to town in the country, following the annual agricultural and stock shows where good pickings are to be had among gullible patrons.

(*to be*) *resting,* (to have taken) *a trip to the country,* to be in jail. (The latter may be originally English, although the form has perhaps been modified.)

bite, lug, nip, touch, to borrow money from a person. (*To nip* may be English; *touch* certainly is.)

kick, a pocket (old English slang).

dip, a pickpocket (English slang).

reefer, accomplice of a pickpocket.

sleepwalker, porchclimber, a sneak thief.

shelf, topoff, stool pigeon, copper's nark, a police informer. (*Stool pigeon* is U.S.; *copper's nark* is presumably English.)

paperhanger, a man who passes worthless cheques (U.S. slang).

shoddy dropper, a hawker.

kite, a worthless cheque (probably English slang).

hay, money (probably U.S.).

smash, loose change (English).

pap, paper money (English).

the come on, an inducement held out to a victim.

ice, diamonds (U.S. slang).

pewter, bad silver coins (probably English).

standover, shake down, strong arm, to handle roughly, to bully or intimidate a victim. (*Strong arm* is U.S. slang.)

sandman, a footpad.

square off, an apology.

heat, pressure, police investigation. (*Heat* is probably U.S. slang.)

to smice, tommy, go through, to decamp, abscond.

fly gay, an intelligent victim. (*Fly,* artful, cunning, is old English slang.)

cop, profit, a job or trick from which a large return is gained.

blue, a loss.

In several cases above the notes "probably English" or "may be U.S. slang" are appended. This is because, although English and American slang dictionaries do not show the exact shade of meaning given here, they closely approach it. There is, however, enough material left to show that the Australian element is strong.

CHAPTER VIII

Australia at War

1. WORLD WAR I

FEW VULGATES have left a more emphatic impression upon our language than the Australian soldier. We are too remote from Boer War days to know if our soldiers of those times – they were called *Bushmen, Cockyolly Birds, Contingenters* and *Tommy Cornstalks*[1] – were as inventive as their successors of World Wars I and II, but we may feel reasonably sure that they were not idle in this matter.

At the outset, we should note that the *A.I.F.* (*Australian Imperial Force*) was founded in August, 1914, and named by Sir William Throsby Bridges, who was Inspector-General of the Commonwealth Military Forces at the time.

The war of 1914-18 affected our language in many ways. It not only produced hundreds of new expressions and revitalized old ones, but it sent our men overseas to take that slang to many parts of the world and allowed them to draw fresh colour from new surroundings.

Much of their war slang was, of course, dated or localized; except in the memories of old diggers it was bound to die, because the conditions and circumstances that gave rise to it had ceased to exist. The corrupted snippets of French which our soldiers picked up on the European battlefront, the scraps of Hindustani they learned in Mesopotamia, the odds and ends of Italian, Russian, Arabic, German and pidgin English they acquired in scattered sections of the globe were not, in the main, destined to have a lasting effect upon the Australian language. They might have been forgotten altogether had not fate brought us another war in which, once again, our soldiers were to roam the world and pick up or re-use a multitude of expressions their fathers had employed in World War I.

As a result, scores of old digger words which, before 1939, had been relegated to the lingual dustheap, suddenly became useful again. We did not have much opportunity of mutilating the French language once more, except for a brief time in Syria and New Caledonia, but there were ample opportunities for picking up oddments of pidgin English and Arabic. Arabic like *cha* or *char*, tea; *saida*, good day; *quas kateer* or *quies kiteer*, very good; *maleesh*, it doesn't matter, came back into digger slang as though they had never been out of it.

We are fortunate in having had an observer of the acumen and

---

[1] This was a concession to *Tommy Atkins*, an English soldier. The "Anzac Book" (1916) referred to an Australian soldier as a *Tommy Kangaroo*. Subsequently *digger* displaced these expressions completely.

enthusiasm of W. H. Downing to keep a close check on the development of slang in World War I. Downing's "Digger Dialects", published in Melbourne in 1919, was not only an excellent study of Australian war slang, but was the first dictionary of soldier speech published after the war. That it has been neglected by oversea commentators on slanguage is a misfortune not so much for Australia as for the commentators themselves, for "Digger Dialects" contains so much valuable material that it ranks as one of the best studies of its kind ever done. Six years after it had been published Fraser and Gibbons produced a dictionary of "Soldier and Sailor Words and Phrases". Another five years later Brophy and Partridge compiled "Songs and Slang of the British Soldier, 1914-18". Both these works contained a smattering of diggerisms, a poor and incomplete selection that did anything but justice to the lively imagery of the Australian soldier. Had they but known it,[2] the picture they presented could have been greatly improved; it would not only have given them a better appreciation of the digger as an inventor of colourful idiom, but would have discouraged the writing of such nonsense as the following extract from G. Irwin's "American Tramp and Underworld Slang" (1931):

> *Australian* – The underworld cant and slang from Australia, composed largely of rhythmic and colourful couplets, and often spoken with an affected "English" accent. Much of this cant was undoubtedly derived from the Cockney rhyming slang taken to Australia by English emigrants at any time after 1850. Largely used and improved upon (?) by the Anzacs in the World War, this slang lost much of its appeal merely because it was so much used that it became wearisome, while a fair amount of it was in poor taste, even for the trenches. It is but little used in America today and may be regarded as a schoolboy's "hog Latin" rather than as a true slang.

No one would suggest that Australian soldiers are models of restraint or social polish in their speech,[3] but they are clearly worthy of something better than dismissal in the manner of Irwin. If they were capable exponents of vulgarism – and why shouldn't they be, as inheritors of the bullocky's traditional flair for colourful language?[4] – they were capable of a good deal more than vulgarism; they could fight and they had as much wit and imagination as they had courage.

Here is a note added by Downing to his "Digger Dialects":

---

[2] Correspondence I have had with the Imperial War Museum, London, shows that they, too, were formerly ignorant of Downing's work.

[3] "We've forgotten all our manners/And our talk is full of slang," wrote Tom Skeyhill, "Soldier Songs from Anzac" (1915).

[4] In an article on war words in the "Bulletin" of June 8, 1922, Padre Green held that the Australian soldier was not the swearer he was represented to be, and that the Australian's slang phrases excelled those of the British. In the "Bulletin" of June 29, 1922, Will Vernon commented: "A careful observation led me to the conclusion that 75 per cent of the most filthy-minded diggers were Australian only by adoption, while most of the remaining 25 per cent had the 'Loo or Fitzroy or some similar neighbourhood on their personal records. Naturally, their influence was felt, but it was only a trickling tributary that was quickly swallowed by the broad river representing the Australian's own standard of ethics as regards blasphemy."

By the conditions of their service, and by the howling desolation of the battle-zones, our men were isolated, during nearly the whole of the time they spent in theatres of war, from the ways, the thoughts and the speech of the world behind them.

It followed that the members of their little communities – batteries, squadrons, battalions – unique not only in the unanimity of their aspirations, but also in their keen and vigorous mentality, were thrown inevitably upon their own intellectual resources. This Glossary represents the sweat of those strivings; it is a by-product of the collective imagination of the A.I.F.

Australian slang is not a new thing; but in those iron years it was modified beyond recognition by the assimilation of foreign words, and the formulae of novel or exotic ideas. This process of enrichment is common to every living language in all the ages.

Neither is it definite, for there are divergencies within every division; even within every brigade. In the Flying Corps it is different from the speech of the Infantry. In France, in Egypt, in Palestine, Mesopotamia, Salonika, the Caucasus, Russia, the Pacific Islands, it is nowhere the same. But it savours of a new national type, and its characteristics are the same.

Downing's glossary is by no means all Australian; it contains scores of expressions which were originally English, but which were more or less common possessions of all English-speaking armies in World War I. But almost 60 per cent of the glossary is authentically Australian.

A good deal of the material it contains was, of course, bound to become obsolete. Here are some obviously dated examples: *Abdul*, a Turk; *Annie*, a big German howitzer, which fired on Bailleul during March and April, 1918; *Belgium*, a fatal wound; *Bernhardi's Botts*, a regimental band (so-called from General Bernhardi, the apostle of German frightfulness); *The Boil*, the Australian corps in the line (i.e. impossible to take the "core" out); *to come a Cadorna* or *Kerensky*, to come a gutzer; *Corpse Factory*, the Western Front; *Fanny Durack*, the hanging Virgin of Albert Basilica (named after a noted Australian swimmer); *Foch's Reserves*, the Chinese Labour Corps.

It would be unfair to Downing to reprint here a complete list of all the authentic diggerisms in his dictionary, but it will perhaps serve as some tribute to his labours if we take a representative selection of his material. That a good deal of this material has passed into popular Australian speech will be clear to any student of our language. Some of these expressions may have been current before World War I, but Downing's little book is the first record of them in print and we will have to accept them as primarily fostered or invented by our soldiers.

Since there is humour in some of the definitions given by Downing, these are for the most part left unchanged:

> *Anzac button*, a nail used in place of a trouser button.
>
> *Anzac soup*, shell-hole water polluted by a corpse.
>
> *Anzac stew*, the food upon which Birdwood's army made a world-wide reputation. It consists of an urn of hot water and one bacon rind. Much appreciated in the Suez Canal Zone.

G

Anzac wafer, a hard biscuit, which was supplied to the A.I.F. in place of bread. One of the most durable materials used in the war.

arsapeek, upside down.

Aussie, (1) Australia; (2) an Australian soldier; (3) a wound of sufficient severity to cause its recipient to be invalided to Australia.

bass attack, a drinking bout. (A humorous perversion of "Gas Attack". *Bass* is a brand of English beer.)

beer-swiper, a drunkard.

bird, a military prisoner.

blowhole, a garrulous person.

blow to fook, shatter to fragments.

bludge[5] *on the flag*, to fail to justify one's existence as a soldier.

bollocks, absurd; an absurdity.

bounce the ball, to assert oneself.

branding paddock, parade-ground.

brasso king, an officer who insists that his men should polish the brasswork on their equipment and uniforms.

broken-doll, an inefficient staff-officer returned to his unit.

buckshee, an acting n.c.o. drawing the pay of a private; a lance-corporal.

bumbrusher, an officer's servant.

camel dung, an Egyptian cigarette.

camouflaged Aussie, an Englishman serving with the A.I.F.

choom, an English soldier.

consumption stick, a cigarette.

concrete macaroon, an army biscuit.

cream puff, a shell-burst.

disaster, a piastre (Egyptian coin).

down south, hidden, buried.

eat-up, a meal.

F.I.A., converse of A.I.F. "*Forced Into Action*".

freeze-a! a popularity-hunter (corruption of "for he's a jolly good fellow!").

frogsh, nonsense, humbug. (A version of *bullsh*.)

furph, abbreviation of *furphy*, a rumour.

gezumpher, a big shell.

grouter, an unfair advantage. "Come in on the grouter" – gain an unfair advantage.

hairy-belly, a sycophant.

hashmagandy, an insipid and monotonous army dish.

hummer, a cadger.

iodine king, a regimental medical officer.

joey, a military policeman. (Also *pretty joey*.)

junker, a superior staff-officer.

kangaroo feathers, (1) a tall tale; (2) an impossible thing; (3) spring millinery of the Light Horse.

kennel-up, stop talking.

king o' the nits, provost sergeant.

lance-corporal bacon, bacon consisting of fat through which runs a thin streak of lean.

maggoty, angry.

---

[5] This adumbrates the current use of *bludge*, to loaf.

mug gunner, a Lewis machine-gunner.
nose-bleeds, red tabs worn by staff officers.
on one's pink ear, down and out.
pig's ear! a contemptuous ejaculation. (This is a euphemism.)
pom, pommy, an English soldier.
pongo, a soldier; one of the rank and file.
possie, position; place; dugout; home.
pot-hole, a short trench, capable of holding one or two men.
pull on, to, to undertake.
rammies, breeches.
reinstoushments, reinforcements.
ring it, to, to play the coward.
rissole king, an army cook.
rough-up, a brawl; horseplay. Also, an unmannerly, violent or ir-
responsible person.
shining stars, an officer commissioned in Australia.
shrewdy, a cunning person.
sin-shifter, an army chaplain.
slanter, schlanter, a trick.
smudged, killed by being blown to pieces by a shell.
snaky, angry, irritable.
snottered, killed.
souvy, to steal, find, "souvenir".
steady lapper, an inveterate drunkard.
stoush merchant, a fighter.
stoush-up, a fight.
tailie, a man who backs tails in the game of two-up.
tarp, a tarpaulin.
throw a seven, to die.
throw six and a half, almost to die.
tinkle-tinkle, an effeminate man.
treacle miner, a man who boasts of his wealth in Australia or his position
in private life.
upter, bad, useless; a corruption of "up to putty".
woodbine, an English soldier.
work a passage, to scheme with the object of being sent back to Australia.
would-to-godder, a civilian who "would to God that he could go to the
war".
ziff, a beard.

Being general in application and not confined solely to the activities or
life of soldiers, many of these expressions have become popular Australianisms, such as *beer-swiper, blowhole, choom, eat-up, furph, maggoty, possie, shrewdy,
snaky, stoush-up, upter* and *ziff.*

Others laid in abeyance for a quarter of a century to be dragged into
use again in World War II. Among revivals were: *Anzac wafer, pongo,
disaster, reinstoushments* (given above); *flybog,* jam; *dingbat,* a batman; *dodger,*
bread; *Ack-i-Foof,* an A.I.F. man; *bab* and *babbler,* an army cook.

There are several sound reasons – apart from the fact that many
diggers of the 1914-18 war fought again in World War II – why army slang
has had a strong influence on Australian popular speech. One important

reason is that there has probably been a stronger Returned Soldier movement in Australia than anywhere else in the world. In the second place one of the Commonwealth's best-known journals, "Smith's Weekly",[6] fostered the digger spirit until its demise. Under the heading "Unofficial History of the A.I.F.", "Smith's" devoted space to digger memories and humour, with black and white illustrations. This resulted in an astonishingly faithful preservation of soldier slang, humour and traditions.

It is to be noted that "Digger Dialects" was not the only glossary of soldier speech published in Australia after World War I. An extensive list of war expressions – containing, it should be added, more of the English element that Downing admitted – was included in the 1920 edition of "Aussie", the diggers' magazine during the war, which was specially reprinted for the Australian War Museum. By one of the quirks of unjust fate this glossary is probably better known than "Digger Dialects" and, because of its extensive English incorporations, has mis-represented the digger's word-making abilities.

2. ANZAC AND DIGGER

FEW EXPRESSIONS belong more undeniably to this part of the world than *Anzac* and *digger*, and a brief pause is warranted to trace their history.

The eminent Australian historian C. E. W. Bean suggests[7] that the originator of *Anzac*, as a code name for the Australian and New Zealand Army Corps, was Lieutenant A. T. White; but claims have also been made on behalf of Sir Ian Hamilton, General Birdwood, Major C. M. Wagstaff and two Australian sergeants, Little and Millington. The word first came into use in January, 1915, and almost immediately began to extend its meaning. Here are some of its many subsequent applications:

(a) The area on Gallipoli Peninsula occupied by the A.I.F. and N.Z.E.F.

(b) Official name of the two Australian and New Zealand Army Corps in France (1st Anzac Corps, 2nd Anzac Corps).

(c) "Universally applied by British troops in France to the Australians and New Zealanders of the two Anzac Corps" – C. E. W. Bean.

(d) "In Palestine, often used to denote men of the Anzac Mounted Division, as distinguished from those of the Australian Mounted Division" – C. E. W. Bean.

(e) In Australia, and eventually in the A.I.F., used to denote Australians and New Zealanders who served on Gallipoli; later, any soldier from Australasia who fought in the 1914-18 war, no matter where he fought.

(f) Revived in 1939 for any Australian or New Zealand soldier, although he had not then been in action and there was no common

---

[6] Sometimes referred to as *the Diggers' Bible* in the way the old "Bulletin" was sometimes called *the Bushman's Bible*.

[7] In the "Official History of Australia in the War of 1914-18", vol. i (1921), pp. 124-5.

command. For a period the expressions *New Anzac* and *New Digger* were used, but after the Libyan campaign in 1941 the *New* was dropped.

Here are some important combinations in which the word is used adjectivally: *Anzac area*, a blanket term for the south-western Pacific war zone in World War II; *Anzac Day*, the date April 25 each year, commemorated as the day in 1915 when Australian and New Zealand troops landed on Gallipoli; *Anzac memorial*, a war memorial raised to honour men of World War I; *Anzac Pact*, an agreement between Australia and New Zealand signed in 1944 (displaced by, and not to be confused with the *ANZUS Treaty*, a security pact between Australia, New Zealand and the United States, signed in 1951).[8]

More important than any of these is the expression *Anzac* (or *Gallipoli*) *legend*. A combination of One-Day-of-the-Year sentiment and the haze that settles over any event with the passage of time has led to what seems to me to be a great deal of misunderstanding about this legend. A tendency has developed for it to be seen in isolation, as THE Australian legend, which has a uniqueness without any relation to our history in general. My own feeling is that such a view not only reduces the magnificence of the effort which the legend involves, but sets it apart as a sort of aberration which no one can hope to explain. As I see it, the Anzac episode should no more be regarded in isolation than Eureka.[9] They were aspects of a theme which can be traced back to our early days; certainly, it had begun to take shape by the mid-1820s. In its simplest form, you could say that this theme was one of *mateship*, but has remarkably little to do with simple ideas of friends, companions, comrades, buddies and pals.

Australia has added a new dimension to the concept of mateship. To repeat my earlier definition: Basic to the concept of mateship in Australia is the principle that, when confronted with unpleasant circumstances, many different men will react separately to those circumstances in much the same way. We see the outlines of the new dimension among the convicts; it was strengthened in nomadic work-hunting days before the middle of last century when men came to rely on each other in countless trials; it was strengthened again among the gold-diggers – and by Eureka; strengthened still more by a new generation of work-seekers in the outback; by bush-dwellers in general; by the larrikins and the people behind The Faces in the Street; by the 1890s depression; by the outback misery of the great drought in 1902; by war in 1914-18 and Gallipoli and the ghastly years in France; by the Great Depression of the 1930s; by World War II and the Kokoda Trail and Changi and the Burma Railway. And, in the 1960s, by

---

[8] It is worth noting that, when during the early 1960s increasingly strong moves were made towards economic co-operation between Australia and New Zealand, the term *Anzac* was often used to mean "Australia and New Zealand". Thus, "The Australian" of January 29, 1965, p. 8, refers to "some sort of Anzac marriage" and "the long-term essentials of Anzac co-operation". Here, it is forgotten that the suffix -*ac* originally stood for Army Corps.

[9] In his book, "The Digger" (1945), Colonel A. G. Butler expresses the view that the future of Australia lies largely in the hands of the *diggers*, "using the term in its wider reference as the 'commonours' of Australia". He also alludes (p. 45) to "that highly *diggerish* episode – the affair of the Eureka Stockade".

what I suspect is the weirdest manifestation of all, although a good deal of linguistic debris will have to be cleared away before we can come to it.

Few would deny that there have been plenty of "unpleasant circumstances" in Australia to serve as testing grounds. Of course, there *is* a special feature about Anzac. It was a small and incredibly difficult piece of terrain held for eight months by many Australian and New Zealand soldiers who fought with great skill and tenacity. It represented a concentration of all the crises of our past. At the same time, in essence it was not different from those other crises.

Dr Bean gives an interesting note on the use of *digger*, which, he says, "became common among New Zealand and Australian soldiers in 1917. It displaced *cobber* (comrade) and *mate* as a form of address. During the third battle of Ypres it came to denote an Australian private, much as Tommy denoted a British soldier." Bean adds that the term was "said to have been used originally among gumdiggers, especially in New Zealand". This theory is generally accepted, although it cannot be stated definitely that New Zealanders used the word before Australians did. It was current on the goldfields from the early 1850s.

Often abbreviated to *dig*, the expression is used widely as an affectionate form of address. In May, 1937, the Sydney "Telegraph" described the phrase *good old dig* as "the high Australian accolade".

In May, 1949, a member of the Commonwealth House of Representatives suggested that Australian soldiers should be called *"digger so-and-so"* instead of "private so-and-so", but the idea had no supporters.

World War II wrought changes in the use of *digger*, most important of which was its extension from a soldier on active service to a militiaman in training. The old *dinkum diggers* might have regretted this loss of their identity, but it was one of the incidentals of lingual growth. It is also worth noting that, from 1943 to the end of the war, *digger* was often used derisively or cynically for a soldier; as a form of address, it was largely ousted by *sport*, and at the same time the expression *a good soldier* (occasionally, *a soldier and a half*) came to be regarded as the highest tribute that could be paid to a member of the second A.I.F. Just as *digger* acquired ironical tones, so did *Anzac*. Perhaps some well-meaning sentimentalist or maybe a journalist in search of something to fill space had given heroic dimensions to *bronzed Anzacs* (and called them *bronzed gods*, too), but the soldiers themselves wanted no part of such romantic nonsense. Their own version was *bronzies*, and they didn't use that too often either. They were not alone. Nurses in army hospitals made an interesting contribution, and there is some likelihood that this went back to World War I days. It was certainly used in World War II. Walking wounded soldiers had to make their own hospital beds. A sister would accuse a soldier of *anzacking his bed* if he had just pulled up the blankets etc. and smoothed them out, instead of removing them all and making the bed properly.

Although it was current in Australia considerably before 1914, *dinkum* was pressed into hard service during the war. *The Dinkums*, for instance, were the second shipment of Anzacs sent abroad (the first shipment were known as *Tourists* or *Six-Bob-a-Day Tourists* because some had joined up mainly in a spirit of adventure); the *Super-Dinkums* were the third shipment; and later groups that went abroad were called *War Babies, Chocolate Soldiers, Hard Thinkers* and *Neutrals.*

3. WORLD WAR II

IN BOTH WORLD WARS, a good deal of sensitivity surrounded the use of *chocolate soldier* or, in its more customary forms, *chocko* and *choc.* Downing said that the *chocs* of the first war were the 8th Brigade –"Tivey's Chocolate Soldiers. Originally an abusive name; now an honourable appellation." In World War II, militiamen and conscripts generally were called *chocos,* the main difference between these men and the voluntary A.I.F. being that the former could not, until 1943, be sent to fight in non-Australian territories. Their fighting qualities were amply displayed in New Guinea, however, and in a tribute to them the Sydney "Sun" headed a leading article on September 2, 1942: "Chocos with Hard Centres".

Other nicknames for conscripts were *sugar babies, dingos* and *wheelbarrows* (because they had to be pushed).[10]

That Australian soldiers of World War II were quite as prolific as their fathers in inventing new slang is shown by the following extract from the Sydney "Telegraph" in January, 1940 – at a time, be it noted, when the war had scarcely begun:

> Soldiers' slang often shows a rich inventiveness. In the 2nd A.I.F. a Lewis gun is called a *chatterbox* and a man on a kitchen fatigue is a *spud barber.* Favourite expression of the troops, of course, is *Wouldn't it?* – short for "Wouldn't it make you sick?"[11]
> Popular phrase to deflate anyone who is talking too big is to tell him, "You'll be a character when you're seventeen."
> *I. D. Herb* is sometimes a Digger way of saying "How d'ye do?"
> Members of the 2nd A.I.F. have the same word as the old A.I.F. for porridge. It's *burgoo* to them. Sausages are *snorkers.* A slice of bread is called a *yunk of dodger.*
> When a new Digger puts on his bandolier he refers to it as *corsets.* A chin-strap is *free chewing-gum,* a rifle is a *smoke-stick,* a machine-gun is a *death-adder.*
> When a sergeant is promoted to lieutenant the men speak of him as a *newly-wed.* A soldier toadying for stripes becomes a *wobbler.* A malingerer is a *swinger* and a compulsory trainee in the Militia is called (good-naturedly) a *dingo.*
> The new Diggers have various names for members of the different forces. Some of these names were used in the last war. The Army Medical Corps is referred to as the *Iodines,* and the Tank Corps as *Farmers* (because they go over the land). The Light Horse are *Kookaburras,* the Engineers are

---

[10] An attempt was made in October, 1942, to pin the name *koala bears* on the militia, "because you can't shoot at 'em and you can't export 'em", but the term had small currency.

[11] *Wouldn't it?* dates back to the mid-1920s in Australia, according to Partridge.

Gingerbeers, and the Provost Corps are *Squealers.* Men of the Army Service Corps are known as the Army *Slop-carriers,* and of the Air Force as *the Gentlemen.* A militiaman is a *sugar baby,* a member of the Signal Corps is an *S.O.S.* and an anti-aircraft man is a *Bring-me-back-alive.*

In an article on army slang in the Melbourne "Argus" of November 15, 1941, G. Johnston wrote:

Darwin appears to have the copyright of an interesting use of slang. The captain in charge of the Base Post Office, official Deputy Assistant Director of Posts, is given the Army abbreviation of DAD Posts. He is known everywhere simply as *Dad,* and his assistant, a lieutenant, is *Mum.* They are referred to everywhere by everybody as *Dad* and *Mum.*

Johnston also gave a brief glossary of army slang in his article, among which the following appear to be Australian inventions:

doleys, soldiers in employment platoons.
February, the Brigadier (seeing him always means 28 days).
fronting the bull, facing a charge.
glamour gowns, khaki dress uniforms.
goon stick, a swagger cane carried by officers.
goong session, a yarn after lights out.
hooks, chevrons.
Mabel, the girl-friend.
nerve war, grousing or complaining to get things done.
panic hat, a steel helmet.
paper war, Army red tape; departmental files, etc.
promote, to borrow or scrounge something.
skitterbugs, Bren-gun carriers.
snatch your time, to resign from the army or threaten to leave.
snake pit, the sergeants' mess.
spine bashing, having a rest; loafing.
stewkeeper, an army cook.
tee up, to make arrangements.

Still more items of digger slang were listed by John Quinn in the Sydney "Sun" on August 26, 1942, some of his additions to the terms already given being: *to fly for the bombo* or *raise steam,* to engage in a drinking bout; *to go down the track,* a Darwin expression for going on leave in the south; *panic party,* any rush move; *reos,* reinforcements; *a stab,* a medical inoculation; *the mad minute,* bayonet drill; *Tojo,* a Japanese soldier or airman; and *to treat with ignore,* to overrule.

The use of *track* above has special interest for us; it was a name given to the newly-built north-south transcontinental road and appeared in such forms as *track driver,* the driver of a military truck carrying goods north, and *track happy,* a form of nervous exhaustion often suffered by convoy drivers. Today, that track is known as *the bitumen.* During the war, the Kokoda trail, New Guinea, was also called *the track.*

Before we proceed too far with examining what World War II diggers did with these beginnings, some attention should be given to a loose-leaf notebook sent to me by Gavin Long, editor of the history of Australia's part in the war. He wrote: "In the middle 1940s some of us who were working on the war history jotted down some A.I.F. slang. It is a long time ago, but I think the rhyming slang is nearly all from the 16 Brigade war diary of 1940.[12] This was then kept by Roly Hoffman, a Sydney newspaperman who died a few years later. The principal handwritten notes are by David Dexter, who served in commandos and wrote a volume of the history. Major Hill's contribution resulted from discussions in Borneo in 1945. He had served in the 9th Division throughout."

In short, this collection has some excellent credentials. I have cut it a little to eliminate obvious borrowings from the Forces of other nations, but the definitions are virtually untouched:

Ack-I-Foof, A.I.F.

ack-willie, A.W.L.

acre, the anus.

act the fit, to play the fool.

air, any air force, e.g. "his *air*".

all over the place like a mad woman's sh*t, complete chaos, or a great litter of something.

ankle banger, an overcoat.

back, on the, on the bed.

back up, to ask for a second helping at the cookhouse.

ball, on the, keen, enthusiastic.

balls up, to make a muddle of. A *balls-up*, a mess.

barge, widely and incorrectly used for landing craft such as LCM and LCVP.

barrel, to shoot and kill.

bash down, to reprimand. *Ear bash*, to talk without moderation. Sometimes, to reprimand. Also, *lugbashing* (a synonym was *lugwalloping*). A variant is *mastoid bashing*. *Spine bashing*, lying down to rest, generally used of resting in the daytime.

battle bowler, steel helmet.

battle buggy, used for a variety of vehicles in the desert. The station-waggon, a Chev with squat, roomy, wooden body, was variously referred to as a *passion-waggon*, *shaggin'-waggon* and *gin-palace*.

be in on it, to join in an enterprise or a fight.

blot, the anus. *On the blot*, seated.

bludge, to loaf. A *bludge* is the act of loafing; an *organized bludge* is a bludge engineered by a group or unit in a semi-official way. Also, *bludger*. "Come out, you *bludgers!*" a phrase used by Australians when routing Italians out of dugouts at Bardia and Tobruk.

blue, a fight, a show.

boomerang, it's a (or *make it a*), make sure that you give it back to me.

boong, v., to carry a load along a track in New Guinea like a native bearer, e.g. "We'll have to *boong* our rations forward."

boong, n., an Aboriginal. Used in the N.T. in 1937. *Yank boong*, an American Negro.

bore it up them, to shoot at the enemy rapidly and effectively.

---

[12] The rhyming slang mentioned is included in Chapter XVII of this book.

bowler hat, discharged S.N.L.R. (A neat but uncommon variant for "to get a bowler" was *to take felt*, refers to officers only.)

break it down! don't be so severe! make less noise! don't exaggerate so much!

brew, to make a, to make tea, cocoa; later, almost any drink.

brew up, our army adopted *brew up* to mean that a tank burst into flames on being hit.

bronze, the anus.

brothel, a mess.

browned off, bored stiff, fed up. Also *bronzed off*.

bugle, nose.

bull, bullo, bulldust, bullsh*t, nonsense.

bumph, written or printed matter.

cocky's joy, honey.

comedian, a commando, a disparaging name.

cop this! take this! have a look at this!

crash, a concentration of artillery fire.

cruet, head. Whence, *silly in the cruet*.

c**t cap, forrage cap issued to A.I.F. till about 1942.

dice, to throw away, to jettison. Said especially of equipment.

do, to kill (enemy troops); to denounce. As a noun, a party, a dance, parade or attack.

Don R, a despatch rider. Old soldiers still say "Don Company".

doover, this general utility term can mean a manoeuvre, exercise, thing, gunyah, dugout, box, soldier, clothing, wood. (*Doover-joey*, a male hospital nurse; here, *doover* denotes a hospital bottle for urination.)

drack, bad.

drongo, a fool, idiot.

drop, a girl or woman, especially *a tasty drop*.

drunk as a skunk, drunk.

dry rots, the sh*ts, e.g. "He gives me the *dry rots*".

dry your eyes (Alfie)! stop complaining!

fair crack of the whip! don't be too severe!

flake out, to pass out, to go to sleep.

Foo, a mischief-making and legendary person, probably originated by the R.A.N. In character, Foo resembles an Air Force gremlin.

Foof-I-Ackers, militia (Forced Into Action), as opposed to *Ack-I-Foof* (A.I.F.).

galah, stupid person.

George, the Government, e.g. "*George*'ll pay for it!"

get a knock-down to, to be introduced to.

get on, an invitation to look with derision or wonder at something.

gigglesuit, fatigue dress. Also *gigglehat, gigglepants*.

give it away, to abandon, desist from. Also *give the game away*.

go for, to be keen on.

go off, to be stolen.

goldfish, tinned herrings.

good horse, originally a good informant. Later, 1943-5, a man of outstanding courage and fortitude.

go like a bomb, to go very fast.

go pokering on, to play poker, based on "soldiering on".

go through, to go away, to go A.W.L.

griff, good griff or *GG*, information, the news.

grog on, to continue drinking.

grouse, exceptionally good.

half colonel, a Lieutenant-Colonel.

hammer into the floor like a tack, reprove, punish; a development of *bash down*.

happy, used in conjunction with almost any noun indicating that something is straining someone's nerves or endurance, e.g. *bomb-happy, pack-happy, grog-happy*.

harch, to go. From a Sergeant Major at Cairo who shouted "Quick harch!" *To harch into some work*, to buck into it.

hasn't got a clue, said of someone who knows nothing or is hopelessly stupid.

have had it, to, to have one's efficiency lowered, to be fed up.

have someone on, to mislead, to pull someone's leg.

have the game sewn up (or *by the throat*), to be master of, to know how.

hit yourself, to have a drink.

hock flogger, an overcoat. See *ankle banger*.

homer, a wound serious enough to send a soldier home.

ho-ho-ho, call of the 9th Australian Division, used to express joy or discontent and as a battle cry.

how'd he be! he's exceptionally lucky; also, he's a miserable opportunist (at the expense of his mates).

how's his DRF, how's his dirty rotten form!

I'm going home to Mum, I'm going back to camp. Sometimes it actually means *I'm going home to Mum*.

it's no good farting against thunder, you're powerless against circumstances (or the authorities).

it's on, something has begun. Often refers to a military attack.

I've been through the green hell of it! an expression used to debunk hardship or danger, as presented in American films or magazines.

jungle grasshopper, the Auster, the smallest operational aircraft in the R.A.A.F.

jungle juice, any alcoholic beverage brewed by an amateur, especially in the tropics.

Jack system, the, a "system" whereby one looks after one's own comfort and interests, disregarding those of others. A leading exponent is called *president of the Jack Club*.

Lady Blamey, a beer bottle with the neck cut off, used as a drinking vessel.

lair, a show-off. Often, a *two-bob lair*.

Little Brown Man, a Japanese. Used at least three years before the war.

lolly-water, soft drink.

Mandrake, a waterproof cape.

mate, me dumb, a term of endearment.

mug gunner, a machine gunner.

mungaree or *munga*, food or a meal. A *good munga man* or a *munga merchant*, a large eater.

Namfu, a non-self-adjusting military f**k-up.

Nip, a Japanese.

no-hoper, an inefficient soldier who is unlikely to improve. Particularly of an officer. (An officer, before leading his Company out on an exercise in which n.c.o.'s took the place of officers, said: "If you don't make a —— good job of it you'll show you're no better than these —— no-'opers you've been running down for the last four years.") Also used in reference to a likeably lazy person.

nose, on the, objectionable. Sometimes *nasal*.

on for young and old, lively (of an occasion, battle, party or argument).

on one's back, over-working one, never leaving one in peace, e.g. "X is always on me back", is always worrying me.

pale view, a dim view.

peanut, a stupid person.

pig's arse! Nonsense!

play silly buggers, to act the fool.

poor as piss, said of a very poor effort.

pull your neck in! don't talk so much!

root, to exhaust. Whence, *rooted*, exhausted.

rotten drunk, very drunk.

scone, head.

sewn up, arranged.

shagged, exhausted. See *root*.

shaggy, bad, unattractive, usually a *shaggy bitch* or *drop*, referring to an unattractive girl or woman.

shooftee, have a look, make a recce. (*Shooftee-scope*, a telescope or binoculars.)

shoot one's head off, to talk loudly and out of place, and nonsense at that.

shoot through, to depart, to go A.W.L. Variant of *go through* and *blow through*.

Skipper or *Skip*, used when addressing a captain by some other captains or subalterns, generally strangers; also by old hands (first A.I.F.) junior in rank, who did not like using "sir".

snarler, one whose services no longer were required by the Army, a SNLR. Only used to refer to soldiers returned from the Middle East on these grounds.

stiff, you can be, one certainly can be unlucky!

swish, A.W.L.

troppo, mad, referring (generally) to a person on whose nerves the tropics, the heat or the war (or a combination of these) are having an effect.

Uncle Tom, Field-Marshal Sir Thomas Blamey.

up the camel's arse looking for an oasis! ironical reply to a question regarding someone's whereabouts.

up the pole (or *up the sh*t* or *up to sh*t*), all wrong; sometimes contracted to *upter*, e.g. "How do you feel?" "*Upter.*"

wet, silly. Sometimes *damp*.

what's it to you? mind your own business! (emphasis, strangely, on the word "to").

who's up who (and who's paying the rent)? Just what is happening? Who's in Control? e.g. "Nobody knows who's up who" etc., said of a complete mess-up.

whinge, to complain (bitterly or through boredom).

whizz in, to come into an enterprise briskly, effectively.

wipe, to ignore, fail to perform. Also to throw away, jettison.

Wo (pronounced "woe"), a warrant officer.

wog, an Arab. Later extended to include any inhabitant of Libya, Egypt, Palestine or Syria. Later still, Ceylon. Used as an adjective, e.g. *wog beer*, *wog truck*. *To wog*, to sell army property to a *wog*. Some say the origin of *wog* is "western oriental gentleman" or "worthy oriental gentleman".

yackai, a shout, e.g. "He let out a *yackai*." *To yackai*, to shout.

yacker, work. *Hard yacker*, hard work.

Although this list may appear comprehensive, we will soon see that it does not do much more than shift the overburden of wartime slang. Here are some other samples:

Officers and ranks: *adj.* or *adjie*, adjutant; *batty*, batman; *cock orange*, commanding officer; *dingbat*, batman; *dinger* or *dingo*, batman; *gok*, G.O.C. of a division; *jeep*, gun position officer; *newly-wed*, a newly-promoted n.c.o.; *Q bastard*, quartermaster; *rosella*, any high-ranking officer; *squeak*, sergeant; *trump*, commanding officer; *pannikin soldier*, a soldier who seeks a job remote from the war zone; *base bludger* or *fountain pen fusillier*, a soldier serving in a home base unit; *retread*, a soldier of World War I who joined up again. (The term *rosellas* was also applied to a base Provost unit with a red and green colour patch, which earned displeasure at Tel Aviv in 1941; they were also called *Jerusalem screws*.)

Food: *afterbirth*, rhubarb; *bullamakau*, bully beef (in New Guinea); *camel*, bully beef (in North Africa); *dorothy*, any plate or container from which food was eaten (ex rhyming slang *Dorothy Gish*, dish); *elephant's dandruff*, breakfast cereals; *kai*, food (in New Guinea); *munga*, food (in North Africa), whence *hard munga*, iron rations, *soft munga*, normal rations or civilian food.

Girl or sweetheart: *sheila*, *sort*, *chickie*, *charlie*, *squaw*, *sack*, *line*, *bit*, *bint*, *popsie*, *floosie*, *frail*, *grail*, *drop*, *bag*, *baggage*, *fairy*, *crow*.

Mental disturbance (especially in tropical areas): *troppo*, *tropical neur-asthenia*, *Malayan madness* (a relic of the ill-fated Malaya campaign), *bloody-mindedness*, *scrub happiness*, *camp happiness*.

Exclamations: *bash* (or *belt*) *it up you!* go to blazes! take it away!; *get off yourself!* stop fooling yourself!; *how'd ya be!* really! for crying out loud!; *how's your rotten form!* addressed to a person who, by some shrewd or lucky maneouvre, brings off a personal success; *I'll say no more!* another mild exclamation, with much the same senses as *how'd ya be!*; *pull your head* (or *skull*) *in!* shut up!; *stop laughing!* stop complaining!; *whacko!* an exclamation of approval; *wipe your boots!* a sarcastic exclamation commonly addressed to a fellow soldier or an n.c.o. making an excessive demand – associated with the expression *on one's back* – the general idea being "Wipe your boots or they will dirty the back of my shirt!"; *wouldn't it!* an exclamation of disgust; *you'll be sorry!* a warning chanted by old-timers to new recruits. Several of these demand additional attention. *Wouldn't it!* had many variations. The authentic digger form was *wouldn't it root you!* A regimental paper "Wiry" (1941) took its name from the first letters of the words in this phrase. Other versions were *wouldn't it rotate you! wouldn't it drive you mad! wouldn't it rock you! wouldn't it rip you* (The last two were given in the Melbourne "Argus" on November 15, 1941.) There has been some debate concerning *pull your head in!* It was certainly used widely during the war, but I have record precisely dated "12.40 a.m. January 1, 1930, Moseley Square, Glenelg, S.A." when my informant noticed its use on a tram, the full sentence being "Pull your head in, you make it look like a cattle truck". A war variant was *suck your scone in!*

Phrases: Many cant phrases, some of a baffling nature and requiring explanation, were used by our Servicemen, e.g. *how are those peanuts?* a phrase usually employed in exasperation (a *peanut* is a stupid person); *dig out for a new Rexona town*, to move quarters (referring to signs along many Australian railways, advertising Rexona soap – "ten miles to Woop Woop, a good Rexona town"); *hold a pissing-off parade*, to retire from an untenable position in the field; *how are you? how is it? how are the galahs?* and *how is the galah?* all mild forms of reproach or protest (a *galah* is a stupid person); *heard the bugles late*, said of someone who delayed joining up until late in the war; *go* (or *shoot*) *through like a Bondi tram* (or *bus*), to go A.W.L. or depart hurriedly (in commemoration of an express tram between Sydney city and the suburb of Bondi, which went out of business in 1960). *Shoot through on the padre's bike* was used similarly.

Many of the expressions listed above have long since ceased to be remembered. One of the terms, only briefly mentioned, which has had a quite extraordinary history is *wog*. Long before Australian soldiers took it to North Africa and called an Arab a *wog*, it was used in a different context in this country.

We first began to employ it extensively in the early 1930s (perhaps the 1920s, but certainly not as far back as World War I) to denote a germ or parasite, a speck of dirt, any small insect or grub. Possibly a *wog* was even smaller than this originally, and no larger than a virus. *To get the wog* meant to become ill, especially to contract influenza or a cold. The term, also used in nursery parlance for a child, was probably shaped in these applications by the English dialectal *polliwag* or *polliwig*, a tadpole. In his "Dictionary of Americanisms" (1889) Farmer lists the U.S. use of *polliwog* similarly. Australian nursery elaborations of *wog* include *woggy*, *poggy* (by rhyme), *pog-wog*, *poggy-woggy*, *poggy-wog*, *poglet*, *poggles*, *poggle-pie* and *poggle-top*, all used as endearments. These introduce an interesting reversion, for *pug* as applied to a child or person was used as an endearment and diminutive in sixteenth-century English. (The word survives in *pug-dog*.)

The elaborations *pog-wog*, *poggy*, etc. apparently emerged independently, in spite of the fact that Boldrewood, "Ups and Downs" (1878), p. 94, refers to "the *pug-wuggies*, or little people", which would indicate a lengthy Australian association with the expression.

Jack Moses, "Nine Miles from Gundagai" (1938), refers to "boot the *woggles* out", meaning "blues" or sad thoughts. C. Barrett, "Coast to Adventure" (1941), gives *wogs* as "a miscellany . . . from bullants to scorpions and centipedes" – a use that is reflected in the "West Australian"

(Perth) of May 23, 1942, in which reference is made to "perennial hordes of *wogs*, comprising everything that crawls, hops or flies".

In short, it can be reasonably claimed that Australia has had long acquaintance with the term. According to my informants, when the diggers first went to Egypt in World War II, they speedily picked up infection from water and other sources. In short, they *got the wog* or *wog gut*.

Now, quite independently of this, the English had been calling the Indians *wogs* for many years. Whether there was a simple geographical transplantation of this use or whether it developed from Australian awareness of *wogs* of another type, the fact remains that the word *wog* came to denote an Arab. Gavin Long's glossary lists some good examples. New applications developed among Australian troops captured in Malaya and held as prisoners-of-war by the Japanese. In that context, we find *wog* applied to any coloured person and anything native, such as native tobacco; *to wog it* meant to live like an Asiatic coolie.

In due course, when Australian troops were included among the occupation forces in Japan, the Japanese became *wogs*. Thus, in T. A. G. Hungerford's "Sowers of the Wind" (1958) we read of *bloody wogs*, Japanese, foreigners (i.e. not Australians), *to wog*, to engage in black-marketing activities with Japanese, *wogging*, mixing with Japanese women. Derivatives include *woggery* and *woggishness*.

After the war, Australia had a large intake of foreign migrants. Towards the end of the 1950s, we began to hear them described as *wogs;* then apparently to differentiate between one type of *wog* and another, since the term was originally applied only to migrants from Europe, we began to hear of *pom wogs*, British immigrants, *yank wogs*, immigrants from the U.S., and (as a crowning absurdity) *wog wogs*, all immigrants other than those from Britain and the U.S. About the same time, both Britain and the U.S. began to use the term *wog* for any alien using a language other than English. Somewhere along the line, Australia had some part in the development, but it is impossible to decide the extent.

Here, now, is a list of expressions which had widespread currency among Australian troops both in forward areas and on the Australian mainland:

    adjitate, to be or act as an adjutant (formed on "agitate").

    angry man, a soldier in a forward battle area; *up with the angry men, where the angry men are*, in a battle area (used especially by the 6th Division); *see an angry bullet*, serve in a forward area, especially applied to a man who should be sent to see an angry bullet.

    animal, a term of contempt for a person. See *insect*.

    arse and pocket pants, loose-fitting trousers.

    arty, the artillery.

    Aussie wuzzies, an Australian carrying party in New Guinea; formed on *fuzzy wuzzies*, as New Guinea natives became known. The latter was imported from Africa, and led to the form *fuzzy wuzzy angel*, a native medical helper in New Guinea – which Judge David Selby described in "Itambu!" (1963) as a "revolting phrase".

    baggy-arsed, used in various ways, e.g. "How are you for a *baggy-arsed* mate!" a form of reproach; "how is my *baggy-arsed* mate?" a greeting; "a *baggy-arsed* job", a rough piece of work.

bagoes, fine, excellent, good; pronounced *baa-goose*, this word first came into use in Dutch New Guinea in 1943, and was later used in Borneo and Morotai.

balalaika, a balaclava.

bash, a drinking spree; *to give it a bash*, to go on a spree.

bash it! a contemptuous ejaculation. Also, *belt it! cob it! stick it!*

bastardry, ill-treatment, injustice, anything unpleasant, especially when done at the whim of a superior officer.

bat the breeze, to gossip or talk.

Bight job, an unpleasant officer aboard a troop transport which crossed the Great Australian Bight.

bingle, a battle, skirmish, brawl or drinking party.

bodger, worthless, second-rate; a person who makes a mess of something. (This term is apparently related to English dialect in which *bodge* means to botch or work clumsily.)

boong basher, not as the expression might suggest one who brutalised New Guinea natives (*boongs*), but a Serviceman who worked with natives in getting (i.e. *bashing*) through a convoy of food and ammunition in spite of any difficulty. Whence *boong bashing* and *on a boong bash*.

boots and all, an expression applied to a person who is thought to be currying favour with a superior rank, i.e. one who is figuratively said to be *up someone's arse;* hence *in boots and all* and *only his boots showing*.

box, in the, in the front line, in a forward area.

brooms bass, a big moustache.

bugle, on the, said of some object or experience that is unpleasant or greatly disliked; also *on the nose, on the trumpet*.

bullet proof colour patch, a colour patch worn by a soldier who has a base job far from any risk of war danger.

bushrangers, guerilla fighters in the New Guinea jungle and hills.

castor, good, excellent.

canyon, a field gun. (A play on "cannon".)

Charley the bastard, the Boys tank attack rifle.

chuck it and chance it experts, members of the artillery.

chuff, the backside or anus.

chunder, to vomit; whence, *chundering*, vomiting; also *chunder*, a noun, vomit.

clanger, a coward.

coit, as for *chuff*.

Curtin's chosen children, members of the civilian organisation known as the C.C.C. (John Curtin was Australian Prime Minister at the time this expression came into use).

cut lunch commandos, soldiers serving with a home base unit.

de facto, a common law wife.

desert rose, a urinal (an expression apparently localised in the Townsville and Atherton Tableland area, Queensland, but see also *rosebowl*).

dill, an officer. (From the common use of *dill* for a simpleton or fool.)

dinger, the anus.

done over, wounded, injured.

donga, "a ravine or watercourse with steep sides", a term from South

Africa which had a vogue among 8th Division men stationed at Bathurst, New South Wales: *donga*, any gully or depression in which men could settle themselves in order to loaf; *dongarer*, a loafer; *to donga*, to loaf or *bludge;* and *dongaring*, loafing or *bludging*. Also used both in Tobruk and New Guinea for a makeshift shelter – anything from a hole in the ground to a *leafy* (q.v.). As late as 1965, *donga* was being used similarly by Australian army personnel (a member of Melbourne University Regiment wrote that a *donga* was "anywhere one sleeps – a tent, hut, etc."). Not long after the end of World War II, the word acquired use among New Guinea's white population for a house.

doover, a battle exercise; a specific use of the term which had earlier been used as an equivalent for "thingumebob". Another specific use of *doover* was for a rough shelter, often called a *doover bug*.

drop short merchants, members of the artillery. See *chuck it and chance it experts*.

dolacky, a thingumebob; apparently formed in imitation of the U.S. *dohicky, dofunny, dojigger*, etc.

drube, a term of contempt for a person.

emu bobbing, the task of picking up cigarette butts and other refuse round a camp. Also, *emuing, bumper sniping*. See *panic*.

fanny, a combination dagger and knuckle duster.

fighting, working.

flipper, an incompetent.

fust, an anal escape of wind.

G., see *glider*.

G.G., the facts, the truth; short for *good guts*. A notice board at a staging camp at Oonoomba, near Townsville, Queensland, used for indicating the times of meals, parades, etc., was at one time headed *The G.G.*

gas producer, a respirator.

gay, an officer. See *dill*.

geek, to look. Also, *gink*.

get it easy, to have a job that demands little work.

give the game to the blacks, to become disgusted with Service life.

glider, a Dutch guilder (used by Australians in the Indonesian area); often shortened to *G* or *gee*.

good soldier, an expression that came to be the highest tribute that could be paid to a soldier in the second A.I.F.; it was perhaps slightly surpassed by *soldier and a half*, which was the ultimate in praise.

gorgonzola, something notable or unusually good.

hairpin, derogatory reference to a male.

half-bulled, drunk.

head them, to get a wound sufficiently serious to be sent home, i.e. to be lucky (a term from two-up).

hock, a male homosexual.

insect, a term of contempt for a man, with much the same emotional intensity as was given to *animal*, applied similarly.

jack of, tired of (something).

jack up, to arrange, organise.

Japan man, a Japanese (taken from pidgin English in New Guinea).

jeep number, any Army number of six figures. See *late thinker*.

joey, a fake.

jungle cream, an Army biscuit (recorded from Salamaua in 1943).

kipper, a Serviceman from Britain, allegedly "two-faced and gutless".

Kiwi up, to dress with care; from the name of a well-known boot-polish.

know someone's form, to know all about a person; note also the exclamatory statement, *how's your rotten form!* usually employed in an approving or envious sense for some successful action or achievement.

late thinker, a soldier who did not enlist until relatively late in the war; sometimes used in a snobbish fashion for anyone whose service number was above 30,000 in N.S.W. and Victoria.

laugh, to complain. Especially used in the form *stop laughing!* stop complaining!

leafy, a lean-to of palm thatch (New Guinea). See *donga*.

left for dead, a man who was ignored or sent to Coventry by his fellows was *left for dead;* also applied to a person whose companion failed to keep an appointment.

lemon squeezer, the peaked hat worn by New Zealand troops.

lizard pit, a corporals' mess; formed in imitation of the earlier *snake pit*, which was used to denote a sergeants' mess.

lurk men, loafers, dodgers.

mary, mosquito repellant, used by troops in tropical areas.

Middle Easter, a soldier who served in the Mediterranean War Zone.

No. 7 seat, a source of rumour, referring to a seat in a latrine.

no-mater, a term of contempt for a person; a toady, one unfit for friendship.

nong, a simpleton or fool (from New Guinea).

not seen, not present at a crucial moment in a clash or skirmish.

nudge, used in reference to drinking, e.g. *give it a nudge, nudge it*, to drink alcoholic liquor.

occ. r., release from the Army for occupational reasons; ex "occupational release".

panic, to pick up cigarette butts and debris round a camp (from 1942); whence, *panic nights*, nights set aside for camp clean-ups, *panicking*, the performance of clean-up duties. This use is distinct from *panic man* (or *merchant*), an excitable soldier.

parson's pox, non-specific eurythritis, a false venereal disease.

pay, to agree to or with; as in the sentences, "I won't pay that" and "I'll pay that".

pelican, a contemptuous term for a person.

picture, a plan, programme of action; *paint the picture*, to describe a plan; *put someone in the picture*, to explain details of a proposal to a person; *to be in the picture*, to understand a plan of action.

pissaphone, an open air latrine. A correspondent writes: "I saw this term used in an Australian Army Engineer works report from Merauke in Dutch New Guinea in 1943, stating, 'Eight pissaphones were constructed during the week ending so-and-so'." Whence, *pissaphone joe*, a latrine orderly.

priority one job, anything important.

punish, to reprove, tell off, overwork. Whence, *punisher*, an officer who makes excessive demands on his men.

rabbit, an article souvenired from the Japanese; this term, used by

Australian occupation troops in Japan, was apparently a revival of English naval slang for "property stolen from the Royal Dockyards".

rail, over the, to vomit, but not necessarily at sea.

rap on an act, to create a fuss.

re-bored, a solecism for "re-boarded" or examined by a Medical Board for a second time, and its associated expression *boarded out,* discharged on medical grounds after examination by a Medical Board.

rosebowl, an open air latrine.

sharkbait, an unpleasant officer, especially aboard a transport taking Australian troops overseas.

shiny arse, a man who has a job in a base unit, especially a job that ties him to a desk.

sh*tkicker, a ranker; "one of the boys".

skull, a simpleton or fool; a general term of contempt for a person. As verb, to strike (someone).

spine-drill, loafing, resting.

splat, the backside or anus.

stew, a "framed" misdemeanour charge against a soldier.

strategic fever, a fictitious disease, which allegedly prompted some men to seek medical attention and sick leave when a major action was pending; a simulated attack of malaria was a common form of this "fever".

stuffed off, prevented from finishing a job in hand.

susso, the subsistence allowance paid to troops living out of barracks.

tax evasion unit, an abusive appellation given to staff officers posted at headquarters in Melbourne, who allegedly sought to spend three months outside Australia each year in forward areas, under the guise of duty, in order to reduce their taxable income. Often abbreviated to *T.E.U.*

three P. boats, the three Ps were Pox, Prisoners and Provosts. These boats were mainly Liberty ships or old freighters, which returned A.I.F. personnel to Australia from the Middle East most of whom had contracted syphilis or were under sentence for various misdemeanours. The Provosts were in charge.

throw (someone), to talk one's way out of trouble, especially in dealing with a superior officer.

torpedo, to steal.

uphill, a difficult job or situation; *to be uphill,* to be facing such a job or situation.

white boong, a man on service in New Guinea or the neighbouring islands who did work of a kind usually or often performed by natives.

woodpecker, a Japanese .77 machine-gun.

yabberer, a tiresome talker.

zebra, an n.c.o. (From the arm chevrons.)

zoombie, a soldier who acts as though he is half dead. (From *zombie,* a name given to "the walking dead".)

Many other expressions were, of course, used by Australian soldiers in World War II. These embraced not only wartime inventions, but a vast range of terms they brought into the Army from civilian life. Lawson Glassop gave a representative round-up of examples in "We Were the Rats" (1944), a novel about the *Rats of Tobruk.* Here are some of his choices: *reos,* reinforcements; *wouldn't it rip you!* an exclamation of disgust or disapproval; *wog*, a native, an Arab, an Egyptian; *no-hoper*, a contemptuous term for a person; *get off your bike*, to become angry; *grouse*, good, excellent; *scrub*, to reject, abandon; *on the nose*, objectionable; *grape on the business*, a misanthrope, a person without any sense of adventure; *bullo*, nonsense; *crack a lay*, to tell; *a wake-up*, an alert or intelligent person; *like steam*, easily; *touch of 'em*, nervousness, more precisely, "a touch of the sh*ts"; *pirating*, the accosting of girls; *crooked on*, ill-disposed towards; *south it*, to put (an object) in one's pocket; *easy*, indifferent towards, as in the common statement "I'm easy"; *feller*, a form of "fellow" used mainly as a method of address, comparable to the use of *digger* and *sport; stink*, the world war; *stickybeak*, to display inquisitiveness towards something; *pool*, to betray, give away (someone); *standover merchant*, a person who adopts a bullying attitude; *pull your head in!* mind your own business! keep quiet!; *spinebashing*, loafing or wasting time; *gigglesuit*, an Army working dress, with *giggle jacket*, *giggle trousers* and *giggle hat* as parts of the *gigglesuit; oot, smash*, money; *dogs tied up*, debts; *latrine wireless*, a source of rumour; *crook*, unpleasant; *blue*, the war; *five bob a day tourists*, Army privates; *waddy* and *nulla nulla*, a club; *wog gut*, dysentery; *Palestine ache*, a painful stomach ailment, probably allied with dysentery; *speed the crows!* an exclamation; *long thinkers*, men who did not arrive in a battle area until late in the war (*late thinkers* was noted earlier); *not worth a c**tful of cold water*, worthless; *reef*, to take, especially *reef from* and *reef off*, to take away from (someone); *top-off merchant*, an informer; *furphy*, a rumour; *sweet*, satisfactory; *two bob lair* or *mug lair*, a flashy, exhibitionistic type of person; *dirty big*, anything at all to which it is desired to draw attention; *hollow log out Alice Springs way*, a fictitious place of safety; *murder suit*, overalls worn by a man detailed to carry munitions or other lethal supplies; *doover*, a dug-out or hut; *wipe*, to reject, abandon; *two chances, mine and Buckley's*, practically no chance at all; *whacko!* an exclamation of approval or joy; *drop one's bundle*, to panic, give up hope; *base walloper*, a man who has a job in a base unit.

While we are on this theme, it might not be out of place to pay a small tribute to J. H. Henderson's excellent little war book, "Gunner Inglorious" (1945). This is primarily concerned with the experiences of New Zealand soldiers in the Mediterranean, but it contains many Australianisms. Among Henderson's uses worthy of record are: *cock*, nonsense, balderdash, especially in the phrase *lot of cock; blitz*, to reprove or reprimand (an application that does not commonly occur in uses of this word); *she's right!* everything is satisfactory!; *pongo*, an Englishman; *Pig Island*, New Zealand (the plural form *Pig Islands* is more common); *wouldn't it rock you!* and *wouldn't it rotate you!* exclamations of disgust; *shite-hawks*, scavengers; *doggins*, cigarette butts.

Here, as some sort of a closing tribute to the men who fought so gallantly in New Guinea and the islands, is a brief poem written by a serviceman in that area (Mr J. H. Taylor) and sent to me as an example of how Australian slang was being kept alive at the time:

THE DIGGER'S LETTER TO HIS WIFE

Dear Liz – Last night I was *shickered;*
   To-day I'm as *crook* as can be.
I've finished with pots – I'll have no more spots,
   No *plonk* and no *grog* – just tea.

You know my old *cobber*, Curley.
   We've quarrelled, I'm sorry to say.
I *shouted* last night at the canteen
   And found that I hadn't a *trey*.

I think, as I gaze at your photo,
   There's no other *sheila* so cute,
You're *Phar Lap* and *Bradman* all wrapped up in one,
   You *trimmer*, you're *bonzer*, you're *beaut*.

I'm coming on leave in a fortnight;
   I can't wait till I'll be on my way.
With the *game by the throat* I'll leap in the boat.
   My oath! Will that be the day?

My love to the sheep in the *paddock*.
   My love to your old mother, too.
Your uncle – *poor cow* – is he better?
   Good on you! Yours ever, Blue.

4. AIR FORCE AND NAVY

MEMBERS OF the Royal Australian Air Force made much less of an impression on our slang than our soldiers. One of the main reasons was that a great deal of R.A.A.F. jargon was taken from England where the R.A.F. proved extraordinarily fertile – as well as fickle – in its concoction of new terms.

Here is a brief list of indigenous Air Force slanguage:

   beef it, to turn tail, make off.
   bird, an aeroplane. See *nest*.
   biscuit bombers, planes which dropped supplies and mail in remote areas of New Guinea.
   blear, to fly about when lost, seeking a landmark.
   blind stabbing, blind flying.
   bosey, a single bomb dropped from a plane. (In cricket parlance a *bosey* is a googly ball.)
   Bourke Street bombers, Air Force personnel stationed in Melbourne. (Bourke Street is one of Melbourne's main thoroughfares.) See *George Street zoomers*.
   bully beef bomber, a transport or supply plane (in N.G.).
   capstan, a plane on the secret list; used originally to denote Spitfires, which were brought secretly to Australia at the end of 1942.

chop rate, the current situation, especially of casualties in a squadron.

chopper, a Tomahawk aeroplane.

do a penang, to turn tail, run away.

drongo, a raw recruit.

emus, ground staff.

flaming a***hole, the large red circle painted on the side of a Japanese plane.

flying a***hole, an observer.

Foo, a fictitious person to whom all lapses and bungling were attributed. (The term became general slang in 1942.) A derivative is *Fooism*, an exploit or saying attributed to *Foo*.

George Street zoomers, Air Force personnel in Sydney. (George Street is one of Sydney's main thoroughfares.) See *Bourke Street bombers*.

googly, as for *bosey*.

go through, to desert (from a northern base to the south).

grasshopping, flying low to beat anti-aircraft fire.

Great Brown Bomber, a Lockheed Hudson plane.

grid, a flight of planes in formation.

in the cactus, in trouble.

jockey, a pilot.

lift your undercarriage! Get out! Go away!

Little Brown Man, a Japanese (not, be it noted, Little *Yellow* Man!).

milk run, a lone raid or a reconnaissance run by an enemy plane.

moth balls, tracer bullets.

nest, an aerodrome (where *birds* congregate).

peasant, an ordinary rank.

photo Joe, a single enemy reconnaissance plane or raider.

pig, an officer.

pongo, an Englishman.

pot, a cylinder.

put the cleaners through, to take down (a person).

rouseabouts, ground staff.

sewing machine Charlie, a single enemy reconnaissance plane or raider.

snakes, a sergeant.

snarler, a man sent back from overseas for some misdemeanour. (From SNLR, Services No Longer Required. Also used by the A.I.F.)

sprog, an ordinary rank. Whence: *chief sprog*, the Warrant Officer Engineering; *chief sproggery*, the place where n.c.o.'s in charge of flights met to discuss general plans. (Probably from dialectal *sprug*, a sparrow, via the Australian version *sprog* or *sproggy*.)

wags, signallers.

Whirling Spray, a Wirraway plane.

Woe, Warrant Officer Engineering.

Wog, Warrant Officer Gunnery.

yow, to keep, to act as an observer.

yike, a dogfight.

zoomer, any member of an air crew.

It will be seen that some of these are adaptations of terms used in other Australian fields, but that fact does not rob them of their interest. When R. G. (later, Sir Robert) Menzies was Prime Minister members of the R.A.A.F. were known to some sections of the public as *Menzies' mannequins* or *Menzies' emus;* later, when J. Curtin became Prime Minister they were called *Curtin's cowboys.* The use of *Daffodils* for R.A.A.F. men – a variation on the English theme of *Blue Orchid* for an airman – appears to be indigenous. It was also applied for a period to members of the A.I.F. Armoured Division at Puckapunyal camp, Victoria.

Few jargons are more world-wide in their use than the slang of naval men. It has penetrated to all corners of the globe and, as a result, we would not expect a particularly large selection of new terms from the Australian sailor. It is not that navy slang is meagre – rather the reverse – but Australian and English naval traditions are closely akin, and few English traditions are kept more rigidly than those of her navy.

As a result, the Australian sailor used a good deal of the slang originated by the English sailor. He was not, however, overwhelmed by it, for new experiences inevitably bred new expressions.

Matapan stew was one of these expressions. It described a stew made of a multiplicity of odds and ends in the way of meat and vegetables, and commemorates the Battle of Matapan. Working under fire, the cooks of H.M.A.S. *Perth* first made *Matapan stew* on March 28, 1941.

Tobruk ferry is another historical expression belonging to World War II. It was applied to Australian destroyers running from Alexandria, Egypt, to Tobruk during the historic Tobruk siege.

Additional references to events and places in which the Australian navy had special interest will be found in the following glossary:

> *alberts,* sea boots (from *Prince Alberts* or *toe-rags* worn by tramps).
> *bang bag,* a cordite case.
> *bang box,* a six-inch gun-turret.
> *barking belly,* a four-inch anti-aircraft gun.
> *Battleship Corner,* in Melbourne, Princes Bridge and Flinders Street stations; in Sydney, a George Street corner opposite the Town Hall.
> *beagle,* an officers' steward.
> *bish,* a ship's chaplain.
> *body snatcher,* an R.A.N. surgeon keen on performing operations on seamen.
> *boy scout's leave,* shore leave requiring return on shipboard before 10 p.m.
> *bumped* (of a ship), torpedoed; hit by a shell or bomb.
> *burn,* a cigarette. *Twist a burn,* to roll a cigarette.
> *button tosser,* a radio telegraphist (formed on the English slang *bunting tosser,* a signalman).
> *buzz merchant,* a rumour spreader. (*Buzz* is a rumour in English service slang.)
> *C.G.I.* (also *Corticene Grabber's Itch*), a desire to throw oneself on the deck during a dive-bombing attack.
> *casa,* a masher (from *casanova*).
> *Charley raft,* a Carley float.
> *Charley's coat,* a Carley float.
> *charlies,* sailors in general.

chickie, chook or *chookie,* a girl or sweetheart.

Chicken Run, the main path in Hyde Park, Sydney, where sailors met girl friends or picked up casual acquaintances.

chippie, a shipwright.

chook, a defaulter or prisoner.

chute, to throw away.

cobbseybash, a friend or mate (apparently a play on *cobber*).

coiler or *curler,* a cigarette.

cook's lost hope, a heavy steamed duff.

Corner, the, Garden Island naval prison, Sydney.

crash, to sleep.

depot stanchion, a draft dodger at a naval depot.

didah, a radio telegraphist.

dig out! (As an order) Help yourself!

dimple, a hole in a ship's hull caused by a torpedo.

dit, a yarn, story (from *ditty*).

Domain dawdler, a sailor who frequented the Sydney Domain with the object of picking up casual feminine acquaintance.

doss bag, a hammock.

double, the, sentences of second class for conduct and second class for leave meted out as punishment to a sailor.

drain the bilge, to be badly seasick.

dufer, a cigarette end (i.e. "do for after").

eagle, a Stuka dive-bomber.

eats bosun, chief cook.

flatterback, the wearing of one's cap on the back of one's head.

frog's eyes, tapioca.

gash, a second helping of food.

George Street sack, a girl who met her sailor friend, or who made a casual acquaintance with a sailor, in George Street, Sydney.

G.I., Garden Island.

gip (or *G.I.P.*), Garden Island naval prison.

goffer, a drink of beer. (In English naval slang it is used for mineral water or for a seller of mineral water or lemonade aboard ship.)

gumleaf sailor, a rating on shore duty.

gut spiller, a Gurkha soldier.

hammer, the penis.

have a run, to get drunk, go on a spree.

howling box, a gas chamber (from the effects of tear gas).

Hyde Parker, a sailor who frequented Hyde Park, Sydney, in search of feminine company.

Ities' guts, to have, to be cowardly.

Jacka, H.M.A.S. Ajax.

Jack Strop, a new recruit who tried to pass himself off as an old hand.

Johnny's, any doss-house for servicemen.

joss man, a master-at-arms or jonty.

kellick, a leading hand. (Among fishermen *kellick* is used for a weight, often a stone, tied to a rope for mooring a boat; whence, *kellick,* v., to moor a boat with a *kellick.*)

macaroon, a new rating (also *maca* or *macker*).

Maltese holiday, a heavy air raid.

mine-swept area, the main city area of a port. Here the word *mine* indicates girls in general.

molly, a malingerer.

mucko, a sailor.

napper, a member of the Naval Auxiliary Patrol.

nudged, (of a ship) slightly damaged by bomb, shell or torpedo.

off-cap, to be a defaulter.

on the patch, in trouble, on the carpet.

oony, seasick.

perm, a permanent member of the navy.

pigs, officers.

plonker, a bad mood.

projie, a projectile.

pump packing, tough steak.

pusser, that which conforms to naval regulations, e.g. *pusser's waggon*, a warship; *pusser's duck*, a seaplane; *pusser's cow*, tinned milk; *pusser's rig*, naval clothes.

rabbit, an article made by a sailor at sea as a gift to a friend or girl. As verb, to scrounge.

ringer, an officer.

sack, a casual feminine acquaintance.

Saturday afternoon sailor, a naval reservist.

slug, the penis.

snake-pit, the bar in Royal Naval House, Sydney.

sprog, a youngster; hence a young recruit. The Air Force use of this term has already been noted.

squarie, a girl friend.

star, a friend, companion. (This extremely interesting term is formed on *sport*, but influenced by the nautical use of port and starboard.)

straight striper, a permanent member of the navy.

stray, a sausage.

tank, a hammock.

Taswegian, a Tasmanian sailor.

tiddley, not according to naval regulations; the opposite of *pusser* (q.v.).

twirly, a cigarette.

uppers, loafers (i.e. on the upper deck).

wet (as a scrubber), extremely stupid.

winger, a comrade, cobber.

woof run, a restaurant.

wrannery, an establishment operated by the Women's Royal Australian Naval Service.

On the home front the Australian urge to sprinkle new terms over our speech was also active. It produced *blacketeers*,[13] for people who dealt in black markets, *white market* for legitimate trade, *black market betting* for off-course betting on horseraces, with its derivatives *black marketeers*, *ebony*

---

[13] Australian terms with similar suffixes were: *budgeteers*, people who handle a domestic budget, *munitioneers*, munition workers, *brown muscateers*, drinkers of muscat, *divoteers*, golfers, *infanteers*, foot soldiers.

marketeers, *black boys* and *boongs*, off-course bookmakers; *brownout romeos*,[14] men who molested women and girls in darkened streets; *jungle juice*, poor quality petrol; *jillaroo*, a land girl[15]; *Waussie*,[16] a female member of the Services; and a string of expressions to describe a type of throat complaint current among soldiers in camp – *Brighton throat* (Tasmania), *Ingleburn throat* (New South Wales), *Puckapunyal* and *Pucka throat* (Victoria), *Woodside throat* (South Australia) and *Redbank throat* (Queensland). These were names of various military camps. In New Zealand the same infection was known as the *Burnham bug*.

The arrival of American servicemen in Australia produced *Yankee cream*, taxi-driver's slang for highly lucrative returns from U.S. fares, *Yank happy*, a reaction from the first enthusiasm with which U.S. troops were welcomed, *unit girl*, a girl of loose morals who was passed on from one member of a Service unit to another as they went on leave, *Yank boong*, an American Negro.

We acquired a new term in *Brisbane Line*, allegedly a strategic line of defence, running from slightly north of Brisbane to north of Adelaide, to which it was intended to retire if the Japanese had forced an invasion of Australia early in 1942.

The children began playing new games – *Hess and Hitler, Commandos* and *Japanese Round Up*. Of the last-named game, a newspaper noted:

> Apparently the Aussies and Yanks (boys) can claim "barley" if they can get to a certain place. But the Japs (girls) have no "barley". All they get is cuts and bruises. The rules don't allow them to hit back.

Journalists invented *Umbrella Regulations* for the National Security Regulations, "which cover everything", *penemy*, a person who betrayed military secrets in a letter, *zoot suit* (which came originally from U.S. jive slang) for the crude civilian clothes given to discharged servicemen, *latch-key kids* for children left at home on their own by mothers engaged in war industry, *Corset Commandos* and *Corset Quota Catchers* for women who rushed to buy declining stocks of corsets.

Preparations for air raids produced a rash of "alphabeticisms" – *N.E.S.*, National Emergency Services, *C.D.F.*, Civil Defence Force, *C.D.C.*, Civil Defence Council, *C.D.L.*, Civil Defence Legion, *S.E.S.*, State Emergency Services.

Other Australian alphabeticisms linked with war were: *A.C.F.*, Australian Comforts Fund, *A.M.F.*, Australian Military Forces, *A.A.M.W.S.*, Australian Army Medical Women's Service, *A.W.A.S.*, Australian Women's Army Service (called the *Ar-wars*), *A.W.C.*, Allied Works Council, *C.C.C.*, Civil Constructional Corps, *C.M.F.*, Citizens' Military Forces (the Militia),

---

[14] The use of *brownout* both as a noun and a verb seems to have been originally Australian, current from 1941. Derivative forms were *browned out* and *browning out*. As late as June 1, 1961, the "Sydney Morning Herald" had a heading "Victoria Faces *Brownout*" with reference to electricity restrictions.

[15] The word is created from association with *jackeroo*.

[16] An extension of *Aussie*.

R.A.A.F., Royal Australian Air Force, *R.A.A.F.N.S.*, Royal Australian Air Force Nursing Service, *R.A.N.*, Royal Australian Navy, *R.A.N.N.S.*, Royal Australian Navy Nursing Service, *V.D.C.*, Volunteer Defence Corps, *W.A.A.A.F.*, Women's Auxiliary Australian Air Force (called *Waafs* or *Woffs*),[17] *W.A.F.S.*, Women's Air Force Services, *W.A.S.P.S.*, Women's Agricultural Security Production Service, *W.R.A.N.S.*, Women's Royal Australian Naval Service (called *Wrans* or *Rons*).

5. PRISON CAMP LANGUAGE

THE JOCULAR EXCLAMATION *you'll be sorry!* which older troops had aimed at new recruits, as a warning of unenviable experiences to come, became bitter truth when the Japanese captured Singapore and many thousands of Australian troops in their swift advances of 1942. For three and a half years a wall of silence surrounded the fate of these men at the hands of their enemies. Scattered in prison camps throughout south-east Asia, starved, beaten and tortured, dispossessed of almost everything except the spark of life that somehow kept them going, they were forced to accommodate themselves to a destiny in which one of their main sources of consolation was mateship. It was inevitable that the communities in which they lived for seemingly interminable years should become closely knit. It was equally inevitable that they should build up linguistic groups of their own. Not until towards the end of 1945 was the rest of the world given a glimpse of the nature of these linguistic groups.

Here is what one observer wrote:[18]

> The men use a mixture of Malay, English, Japanese and Cockney rhyming slang. Troops had to learn a smattering of Japanese and Malay to understand the orders of the Japanese, and thus save themselves bashings. Prisoners were required to number and give commands in Japanese. They think the Japs are *dummy dummy* (no good). *Piggy la cass* is go away, quick. *Doovers* are cakes or pasties made from rice, while *Java* is not coffee, but tobacco. Diggers never talk food, but use instead the Malay word *makan*. When an Australian asks for *leggi char*, he is requesting more tea. An *oodie scrounger* is a man who steals tapioca. Japs, of course, are *mutton flaps*. Diggers always regretted that their rations were *ketchil* (Malay for small). What they wanted was *tuc saan*, Jap for plenty. When a man was sick he was *beokee*, but when well he might use the hoe in the *enoch arden*, garden. *Snow white* is not the girl of the Seven Dwarfs fame, but the white-coated Jap who beat up the *dromies*, as the Diggers who built the Changi aerodrome were known. When a prisoner was *knighted* he did not get a medal; the term meant a blow on the head with a stick. The English were the *to and froms*, while *army tanks* did for Yanks.

Here is another commentary, by an Australian war prisoner, Rohan Rivett, in some introductory remarks to a glossary of prison camp slang

---

[17] A barracks or centre where these women lived was a *Waafery* or *Woffery*.

[18] "Sun", Sydney, September 22, 1945.

included in his outstanding war book, "Behind Bamboo" (1946):

> In every camp throughout the world, slang and service jargon played a big part in nearly all conversations. But in the P.O.W. camps we had a fusion of army, navy and air force slang from representatives of Australia, Britain, the United States and the N.E.I. Superimposed on this were all the words we acquired from the local vernaculars of Java, Malaya, India, the Middle East, Burma and Siam. Then we had to learn certain words in Japanese, and we adopted a number of pidgin English or dog-English expressions used by our guards. In one sentence it was not uncommon to hear a man use a Hindu word acquired on service in India, a Malay word picked up in Singapore, a Jap P.O.W. term and some service slang. Many of the terms will perish with the ending of our captivity; others will produce only an uncomprehending stare when we come out with them at home. But for three and a half years they were in our ears daily.[19]

Here are some of the expressions which the Australians concocted as a result of their experiences, or which they drew from the established body of Australianisms to apply to the circumstances and events of their prison lives (again acknowledging a debt to Mr Rivett):

> *agent*, a person who wields influence, as in the statement, *"I have my agents"*, there are ways of getting things.
>
> *backup*, a second helping of food; and its associated expression *backup king*, a man who is always seeking additional food.
>
> *bad house*, a cell or prison.
>
> *bamboo-and-attap*, a Japanese aircraft.
>
> *bamboo rattler*, a man who disturbed his sleeping neighbours by his movements on the *bali* or bamboo sleeping platform.
>
> *banga*, a bag and poles for carrying dirt.
>
> *banjo bottle*, name given to a Dutch toilet necessity. (Partridge notes the old English slang use of *banjo* for a bedpan.)
>
> *bash artist*, a Japanese guard who frequently beat prisoners.
>
> *beat it up*, to celebrate, "make whoopee".
>
> *beokee house*, a hospital; from the Japanese *beokee*, a sick man.
>
> *big fellows*, Liberators or other four-engined Allied bombers.
>
> *bimbo*, a batman.
>
> *birdie*, a secret radio.
>
> *blue danube*, prison camp "stew" (by rhyme on *blue*).
>
> *boong*, any Asiatic or coloured person (originally applied to a native of New Guinea or Papua); whence, *boong brandy*, native spirits, *boongs with boots on*, Japanese.
>
> *braid, pull the*, to invoke the rights due to superior rank.
>
> *bronzie*, a member of the 8th Division, "used by officers to indicate other ranks, by British to indicate Australians"; from the description

---

[19] An interesting example was the Japanese word *butai*, battalion, which was corrupted by war prisoners into *beauty*, as in the name *U Beauties*, taken by "U" battalion who were among the slave labourers used by the Japanese on the Burma-Thailand railway. The following is a quotation from the "Sydney Morning Herald", April 23, 1949: "On parade in the prison camps, the battalion commander, Major R. Newton, would address the troops as *'U Beauties'*. 'The Japs sometimes caught on,' he said at last night's reunion, 'but they never could do anything. It was just my bad Japanese. Calling ourselves "U Beauties" instead of "U Butai" was a great morale builder'."

bronze gods applied by a romantic female journalist to the Australians and later used derisively. (See my earlier note in Section 2.)

brothel of a place, an unpleasant place to be or live in.

bug, the, fever.

bullshartist, a garrulous person; also a *bullsh*t artist,* of which it is a contracted form.

Burma apple, a vegetable, "somewhere between a potato and an apple".

Burma bowler, a bowler-shaped hat made of bamboo.

Burma spinach, a native vegetable.

burnt off, fed up, furious; a variation of *browned off.*

Changi major, a man promoted to field rank on or after February 15, 1942.

chat happy, weary of delousing clothes, etc.

cheese eater, a Dutchman.

chicken feed, weed served in "stew".

clomper, a wooden clog, "typical P.O.W. footwear".

coconut oiler, a Japanese aircraft.

coffee king, "a man with a large business, probably employing other P.O.W.s. making and selling hot coffee – often 'ersatz'."

college of colonels, a gathering of senior officers.

death house, a hospital hut containing dysentery and other serious cases with high mortality.

deknackered, emasculated.

dicky bird, a secret radio; also called a *birdie.*

dog's disease, malaria.

doings, news, secret radio bulletins.

doover, a rice cake or anything "extra", also radio news.

extra, "a rissole or other addition to a meal apart from rice and soup".

fly spot, an officer's pip.

form, news, the situation or position.

go bush, to take to the jungle; to run away.

good guts, news, information, secret radio news.

go through, to leave.

go through on, to take something away from, steal.

grass, jungle leaves put into soup.

greveller, a try-on.

grouter, on the, descriptive of a sly attempt to gain an advantage, "putting something over".

hag's bush, tobacco.

hank, a quantity of native tobacco.

hot cock, nonsense, boasting, empty talk.

how is it possible? a Dutchman; from the extensive use which the Dutch gave to this rhetorical question.

imperial war museum, Hut 4, Kanburi camp, occupied by senior British officers.

impi house, a tool house; from the Japanese *impi,* a tool.

Jap happy, "anyone unduly afraid of or subservient to the Japanese". Abbreviated to *Jappy.*

jeep, a Japanese.

jungle leaves, any herb or leaf added to stew.

jungle spinach, a type of jungle leaf.

kipper, an Englishman.

lats, latrines.

little yellow bastards, an everyday expression used to describe the Japanese.

mad as a maggot, particularly crazy.

means, the, tobacco and cigarette papers necessary for making a cigarette.

mind your backs, please! get out of the way! clear a path!

monty, a certainty, a safe thing.

mulga, the surrounding jungle.

mutta mutta birds, aircraft; Allied bombers.

nightingale, radio news; a secret radio. See *birdie* and *dicky bird*.

no good house, a cell or prison.

no second prizes! "You are only copying!"

offal eater, a Dutchman.

ooloo, jungle, scrub.

orderly dog, an orderly officer.

organize, to steal or scrounge.

over the fence (or *wire*), outside the camp – used particularly to describe trading activities.

peanut basher, a man who ground peanuts in a mortar to make "peanut butter" for the prison canteen.

peanut coffee, a drink made with burnt peanut kernels.

peanut star, peanuts set in congealed sugar.

peter, a cell or prison.

pips, pull the, as for *braid, pull the*.

pissaphone, a bamboo urinal.

radish water, "stew" made of hot water, white radish and, if available, pepper.

raw prawn, something far-fetched, absurd.

rice coffee, "cooked or uncooked rice burnt on a dry pan produced a drink when hot water was poured over it; but it was very 'ersatz' coffee."

rice happy, descriptive of the attitude of a person who has lived too long on a diet of rice.

rotate, to surprise or amaze.

shove it! take it away! I don't want it!

skip, a wicker basket used for carrying vegetables and fruit.

squeeze, "Japanese graft, commission, a racket."

steamtug, a bug (rhyming slang).

Thai wine, an alcoholic drink with a fruit flavour secured in Siam.

to-and-from, an Englishman (a rhyme on *pom*, short for *pommy*).

tong, a bath, wash.

trader, anyone going out of camp to buy or sell goods.

troppo, "mad, sunstruck, weak-minded, affected by captivity."

tunga, a carrying litter for earth, wood, etc., "usually a rice bag stretched over two bamboo poles".

up the ladder, an expression applied to someone who was clearly thinking only of his own interests.

white death, melon used in "stew".

white Jap, a war prisoner acting like a Japanese or in Japanese interests. Also called a *white Nip*.

wog, any coloured person; anything native; native tobacco.
wog it, to act or live like an Asiatic coolie.

A study of these terms will tell a great deal about how prisoners-of-war lived. Although many of them have now certainly been forgotten, the future historian who wishes to explore the ways in which Australians faced their bondage at the hands of the Japanese will have many of his questions answered by these expressions.

6. WORLD WAR III

WITH THE WORLD apparently determined to indulge in another major war, Australia has lined up for a place on the international slippery dip. In the next generation or less she will doubtless reap the reward that comes to those who mind other people's business in foreign fields.

Since the end of World War II, Australian Forces have served in Korea (against North Korea, Communist), in Malaya (against Communist rebels), in Malaysia, including Borneo (against Indonesian guerillas) and in South Vietnam (against Communists and nationalist rebels). However, the linguistic returns from these ventures have been small; the most prolific was Korea, but it was largely swamped by U.S. and Japanese terms.

Here is a Korean selection:

'Arry's gaiters, thank you! (a corruption of Japanese).
baggie, a subaltern (derived from *baggie-arsed*).
bushfire, an English-issue cigarette.
Charlie, the enemy; a member of the Chinese or North Korean troops.
choofer, an oil-burning stove.
cobberdobber, one who betrays a friend.
cock oboe, a commanding officer.
homer, any wound requiring evacuation from Korea, and rest and recuperation.
hutchi, a bunker or dugout (from the Japanese *uchi*, house).
mumma-san, an elderly female (ex Japanese).
munga, food. (Revival of a hard-worked term.)
nog, a Korean. As verb, to become friendly with a Korean; to steal. Also, *noggie*, a Korean. (Perhaps influenced by *wog*.)
number one, excellent; *number ten*, extremely bad.
poppa-san, an elderly male (ex Japanese).
skipper, a platoon commander.
sundah, dead (ex Japanese).

At home, the introduction of National Service Training produced (in the early 1950s) *nasho*, such training, also a trainee, and *the compulse*.

Australia's revived interest in military affairs focused attention on the activities of the Royal Military College at Duntroon, whence come Australia's permanent army officers. A newspaper account of the college's activities recorded the following slang terms in use among the college cadets:

backta, illegal sleep after reveille.

bashings, cigarette tobacco and papers, "the makings".

father and son, cadets whose regimental numbers vary by 100, i.e. Cadet No. 101 is the "son" of Cadet No. 1.

leap, to dress quickly for a parade.

lord and master, a senior cadet.

mash, to study excessively.

rusticate, (said of the Commandant) to send a cadet away from the college for a period because of a grave offence.

slime, melon and lemon jam.

staffka, a staff cadet.

stook, a cigarette.

surl, to show bad temper.

toc, morning or afternoon tea or supper (however, *having toc with the Commandant* means to be paraded before the C.O.).

Within a short time of their arrival in South Vietnam in 1965, Australian troops had revived *hutchi*, which had been used earlier in Korea, and modified both its spelling and meaning. A *hutchie* was a shelter, mainly against rain, made by a small sloping patch of dull green nylon, and therefore somewhat akin to the *leafy*, which was used by Australian troops in New Guinea in World War II. Also current among the Australians in South Vietnam were *bush bashing*, searching in a jungle-covered area for the enemy, whence *go on a bush bash*, and a synonym, *emu bob*, such a search.

CHAPTER IX

The Vulgarism[1]

1. STRONG WORDS

IF THE AUSTRALIAN SERVICEMAN has proved an important contributor to colourful speech, and even excelled himself now and then with some witty terms, he has also been a dedicated vulgarian. His language has always been liberally sprinkled with what Thomas Wood described in "Cobbers" (1934) as ". . . words you must not print. The words that won the War. The Big Five. Australian stories need them all and use them lavishly. The effect is stunning."

I don't altogether agree with Wood's estimate of five, but he had the right idea. There was certainly nothing new about it. Here is a quotation from the "Bulletin" of July 7, 1900, which comments on our representatives in the Boer War:

> Correspondents in South Africa pay a unanimous tribute to the great Australian Blanky, and state that, in curse-language, the man from this great blank continent is laps ahead of Tommy Atkins. When an occasion arrives for extra-special profanity, the Cornstalk or Gumsucker is deputed to meet the case, and he never fails. Even mules and bullocks which have become absolutely impervious to the indigenous curse, wake up suddenly when the Australian attacks with his exotic objurgation.[2]

In World War I profanity was reputedly so current among the troops that a Clean Lip Brigade was established by a Church of England padre, every member of the brigade pledging himself to count ten when he felt like swearing. Some agitation was raised in World War II to have this Clean Lip Brigade revived. In the "Sunday Sun" of May 3, 1942, comment was made on the "increasing bad language among Australian men and women" and a correspondent declared, "swearing seems to be the rule in ordinary conversation in this country".

In the Sydney "Mirror" of October 9, 1941, a military spokesman at Victoria Barracks was interviewed on the use of profanity in the army.

---

[1] "Our dictionaries, while they tell us much, yet will not tell us all. How shamefully rich is the language of the vulgar everywhere in words which are not allowed to find their way into books." – R. C. Trench, "On the Study of Words" (1851).

[2] A similar view was expressed by Bennett Burleigh, London "Daily Telegraph" war correspondent, in 1900: "When we look for variety, vigour and vilification, we call upon the colonies to give due lurid expression to exacerbated feelings. There is no monotonous re-iteration about their extensive diction . . . The very dumb brutes acknowledge their giftedness, for oxen and mules, which would not strain a pound or budge an inch for native or British objugation, the instant a Colonial takes up his parable, hasten to break thews, muscle and bones, rather than stand stuck in a drift and have such abuse showered upon them."

The "Mirror" reported: "He said that the use of bad language in the A.I.F. was always deprecated, but as it was part of the common colloquial speech no special action had been taken and it was not usually made the basis of an offence unless of a nature likely seriously to prejudice good order and discipline."

Such a comment would tend to distract us from the fact that Australia's contact with profanity goes back to our beginnings, and that wartime use of it was no more than one of those safety valves for the release of pent-up feelings of protest against Australia's lavish supply of "unpleasant circumstances".

In "The Fell Tyrant" (1836), the author, commenting on Sydney life, declares: "The whole study of both sexes is drinking, gambling and whoring. Their language is the most profane." In 1850, a visitor to Melbourne said that in that southern city, "Oaths, execrations and obscenity grate upon your ear." C. R. Read wrote in "What I Heard, Saw and Did at the Australian Goldfields" (1853): "Such dreadful and horribly disgusting language may be heard expressed by children on the diggings that I do not imagine could be surpassed by the most hardened adults on Norfolk Island, and this does not rest with boys alone, but little girls from eight to ten years of age."

Other visitors to Australia vowed disturbance at the constant shocks they experienced on the goldfields. In "A Lady's Visit to the Gold Diggings of Australia in 1852-53" (1853), Mrs Charles Clacy says this of a woman: "In a loud masculine voice she uttered the most awful words that ever disgraced the mouth of man – ten thousand times more awful when proceeding from a woman's lips."

In short, there was good reason why the Australian's reputation for strong language went abroad at an early stage in our history. Immigrants were given repeated warnings. Francis H. Nixon, in "Population: A Plea for Victoria" (1862), says: "According to a portion of the British Press we are all more or less . . . given to interlacing our everyday conversation with slang and blasphemy." And the Reverend A. Polehampton, whose "Kangaroo Land" was published in the same year, showed that new chums were put on their mettle by the local vulgates:

> As swearing is an unusually common habit among the colonists new arrivals often endeavour, and most successfully, too, to become proficient in this easily acquired art, and soon add the stock of oaths peculiar to the colony (and very peculiar some of them are) to the "home" vocabulary.

One of the few good words spoken on Australia's account – at least, it asserted that our use of "undesirable epithets" was not so extensive as it might be – was uttered by G. J. James in "Shall I Try Australia?" (1892). He pointed out that the average Australian was "capable of improvement" in the matter of vulgar speech, but added:

> Not that one meets with the cold-blooded profanity which is so commonly used in certain parts of America; but many expressions of a more than questionable nature are somewhat generally used, and boys

and even young children have very often a stock of bad language in active service, by far too plentiful, which I suppose did not originate with them.

In the "Bulletin" of October 20, 1900, it was recorded that at Bala-clutha, New Zealand,[3] a man named W. Evans – to whom a suitable monument is surely due – was sentenced to four days' jail "for using obscene language to his team of bullocks". To a country such as Australia, which has developed a deep appreciation for the *bullocky*[4] and his speech, this sentence handed out by the New Zealand Bench will probably seem a little unjust.

In 1848 H. W. Haygarth, in his "Bush Life in Australia", felt obliged to note: "Profane swearing prevails throughout the interior of New South Wales to an extent hardly conceivable, but by those who have not actually witnessed [*sic*] it."

A little later – in 1857 – Charles R. Thatcher, in "The Colonial Songster", put the *bullocky* in his rightful niche when he wrote the jingle:

> If nice expressions you would learn
> Colonial and new,
> Some bullock driver who is bogged
> Is just the man for you!

A sentiment of similar type was expressed in the "Australasian Printers' Keepsake" (1885) by a jongleur who sang of:

> Those brawny owners of fat sheep and lambs
> Whose creeks and language are both full of dams.

The *bullocky* and his kind have proved so expert, indeed, in adding new splendours to profanity that few of their inheritors have been deemed worthy of being grouped in the same class. We have already read how useful were his talents in the Boer War. There is some likelihood that he has been a source of inspiration to later *diggers*. Here is what Will Vernon had to say in the "Bulletin" of June 29, 1922:

> The true Australian oath was a thing of beauty, providing a speedy means of relief for depression, exasperation, hard luck . . . It was descriptive, vigorous and decisive . . . It was seldom used in idle or casual conversation. Because of that it failed to stick as a habit with many of those boys and men who were jettisoned temporarily on the ash-heap of war.

Tom Collins (pen-name of Joseph Furphy) was the first Australian writer to discover the full richness of Australian profanity, but either from personal squeamishness or as a concession to the moral myopia of his times he shrank from unseemly displays of virtuosity. He adopted his own form of

---

[3] Profanity is also widely current in New Zealand, although perhaps to less degree than in Australia. In "New Zealand after Fifty Years" (1889), Edward Wakefield noted that shearers and swagmen in the Dominion "use shocking language and seem to take a pride in rivalling one another in the ingenuity and elaborateness of their oaths and epithets".

[4] Barrère and Leland, "Dictionary of Slang" (1897), note: "Bullockirs in Australia are as proverbial as bargees or Billingsgate fishwives in England for the forcibleness of their language."

censorship in which brackets played a large part. Thus, he wrote (ensanguined) or (adj.) for *bloody*, d—— for *damn*, (sheol) for hell, (go and get verbed) for *go and get rooted*, and so on. Here is an example:

> O, go to (sheol). You're no (adj.) good. You ain't fit to (purvey offal to Bruin). An' here's them (adj.) sneaks gone; an' Martin he'll be on top o' me in about two (adj.) twos; an' me left by my own (adj.) self, like a (adj.) natey cat in a (adj.) trap.

Fill in the gaps and you get the brand of lyricism for which the Australian *bullocky* became famous. But, of course, the linguistic deceits of Tom Collins were not basically different from those practised by earlier writers. They represented, at best, only a slight lifting of the curtain. Consider this example from Henry Kingsley's novel "Geoffry Hamlyn" (1859): "You d——d humbug!" And this quotation from Rolf Boldrewood's "Robbery Under Arms" (1881): " 'It's a d—— shame', we heard Starlight say as he turned and walked off." And this from Fergus Hume's "The Mystery of a Hansom Cab" (1887): "I wish to G— I had never seen or heard of Whyte."

In spite of Furphy's good-natured pretences, although the *Great Australian Adjective* acquired that name during the 1890s, it had been in use many years before. For instance, F. Eldershaw commented in "Australia As It Really Is" (1854) that, "When irate, the old hand appears to be violently addicted to adjectives, and *blood* is invariably his most convenient circulating medium."

William Kelly, author of "Life in Victoria" (1859), felt constrained to offer this apology for using *bloody* in his book:

> I must be excused for the frequent use of this odious word in giving colonial dialogues, because general conversations amongst the middle and lower classes at the antipodes is always highly seasoned with it.

Here is another comment, given by F. Fowler, "Southern Lights and Shadows" (1859):

> Your thoroughbred gumsucker never speaks without apostrophising his oath and interlarding his diction with the crimsonest of adjectives.

In a leading article on "those beautiful and expressive words, Damn, Blast and Bloody", Sydney "Truth" of May 15, 1898, declared: "*Bloody* has been so completely vulgarised and has descended so low, that it can never be picked up again." A bad guess it has turned out to be.

How *bloody* came to be called *THE Great Australian Adjective* is uncertain, but it was probably through the agency of the "Bulletin".[5] For instance, in the August 18, 1894, issue of that journal it was stated:

---

[5] The "Bulletin" of February 11, 1893, noted: "A certain 'slang' dictionary published in England discourses on the word *bloody*. This is described as an adjective of common use in Australia, where it is employed to express various shades of meaning, i.e. 'It is a *very* hot day' becomes, when Australised, 'It is a —— ' and so on."

The "Bulletin" calls it the *Australian adjective* simply because it is more used and used more exclusively by Australians than by any other allegedly civilised nation.

Cornelius Crowe, who compiled a dictionary of Australian slang in 1895, dismisses the expletive with the comment, "a word used very often inadvertently by the uneducated". More than thirty years later, the critic A. G. Stephens became so wrath over the currency of *bloody* in this country that he penned the following to the "Sydney Morning Herald" of March 28, 1927:

> There is a common word often heard in Sydney streets on the lips of men in common talk, and shocking and disgraceful talk it is . . . This vileness exists in other Australian cities, and in some British and foreign cities, but really we have never heard it as bad as we hear it in Sydney...Thoughtlessness, carelessness and horrible custom allow it to go without interference and without reproach . . . The literary jesting with the word by such Australian writers as Goodge and Dennis, however excusable, is not the most creditable feature of their writings . . . The constant use of the word by thousands of Sydney residents is vile . . . We do trust that this public protest will help to remove a public blot on the life of Sydney.[6]

However earnest, Stephens was fighting an uphill battle against a habit long ingrained in Australian speech. By 1941, Dr George Mackaness could do little more than proffer this resigned comment:

> In my boyhood days [in Australia] it had undoubtedly become a wicked swear word. Now we are witnessing the process of "elevation", operating to place it amongst the nobler words of the language. I mean the Australian Language.

In his "public blot" comments on *bloody*, A. G. Stephens mentions the "literary jesting" of W. T. Goodge and C. J. Dennis. Since Dennis addressed his message to Australian soldiers in 1915, in a poem called "The Austral——aise", he found a ready audience. Here is the first verse and chorus of his epic:

> Fellers of Australier
> Blokes an' coves an' coots,
> Shift yer —— carcasses,
> Move yer —— boots.
> Gird yer —— loins up,
> Git yer —— gun,
> Set the —— enemy
> An' watch the —— run.

---

[6] A correspondent in the "Herald" of March 31, 1927, replying to Stephens, noted that, "There is an even worse word, a low disgusting word, which has come into common use of late". In the same paper, on April 2, 1927, "Disgusted Aussie" wrote: "Twenty years ago foul mouths were something to note, but now the everyday conversation of the bulk of the toilers is an endless hellsbroth of blasphemy, blood and sewage." Another correspondent on April 4 suggested that a "No-swearing Week" should be held, but his suggestion gained no support.

[7] In the "Herald" of March 1, 1941.

(Chorus)
Get a —— move on,
Have some —— sense,
Learn the —— art of
Self-de——fence.

Goodge's poem, published in 1899 in his "Hits, Skits and Jingles", is entitled "The Great Australian Adjective" and is worth being quoted in full if only because it was plagiarised by U.S. troops during World War II. Here is Goodge's original:

The sunburnt —— stockman stood,
And, in a dismal —— mood,
  Apostrophised his —— cuddy:
"The —— nag's no —— good.
He couldn't earn his —— food,
  A regular —— brumby."

He jumped across the —— horse,
And cantered off, of —— course!
  The roads were bad and —— muddy,
Said he: "Well, spare me —— days,
The —— Government's —— ways
  Are screamin' —— funny."

He rode up hill, down —— dale,
The wind it blew a —— gale,
  The creek was high and —— floody.
Said he: "The —— horse must swim,
The same for —— me and him,
  Is somethin' —— sickenin'."

He plunged into the —— creek,
The —— horse was —— weak,
  The stockman's face a —— study,
And though the —— horse was drowned,
The —— rider reached the ground,
  Ejaculating "——!"

This was stolen, changed and published in a U.S. collection of war verses, "G.I. Songs" under the title of "The Cowboy". Here is the American version:

The —— sunburnt cowboy sat
Beneath his —— Stetson hat,
  An inde——pendent guy
Who watched the —— sunset sky,
His —— daydreams only of
His —— half-breed greaser love.

He vaulted on his —— horse
And galloped off, of —— course,

The —— roads were full of mud,
And thick as —— spit and blood.
Said he: "Well, damn my —— eyes,
Ain't this a —— fine surprise?"

He rode up hill, down —— dale,
The wind it blew a —— gale;
The —— creek was running high,
A —— cloudburst ripped the sky.
Said he: "We'll swim this —— swill,
We abso——lutely will!"

He plunged into the —— creek,
The horse was pretty —— weak;
But though the —— nag was drowned,
The cowboy reached dry —— ground,
And staggered down the —— road,
His —— love a —— goad.

He reached the dusty —— town
And bought his —— wench a gown,
With every —— kind of frill
To please a —— greaser jill.
He found his —— sweetheart there
And kissed her greasy —— hair.

The editor of "G.I. Songs" adds this comment to "The Cowboy" version of Goodge's poem:

> The Australian soldiers, who may or may not have learned this heart-rending ballad from our own, insert the beloved British expletive *bloody* for the dashes. The version given here is slightly expurgated and lacks the final verse which no amount of cleaning could make printable.

From this quotation it becomes clear that Americans use another word to fill in the blanks. However, this can scarcely be offered in extenuation of America's plagiarism.

"G.I. Songs" also includes the following (wartime) Australian tribute to the Northern Territory town of Darwin, where many Americans served for a period:

This —— town's a —— cuss,
No —— tram, no —— bus;
Nobody cares for —— us!

(Chorus) ——! ——! ——!

All —— clouds, no —— rains,
All —— stones, no —— drains;
The —— dust gets in your brains!

(Chorus) ——! ——! ——!

In spite of such evidence, we should not be misled. Neither war nor bullock-driving was the original forcing ground of strong language in Australia. The convicts, both *sentencers* and *emancipists*, were skilled in the use of vulgarisms and the conditions of life in Australia's early days encouraged the preservation of forthright terms. Hence doubtless this report in the "Sydney Gazette" of December 30, 1804:

> Paffing through an alley the other day, our ears were harfhly affailed by the vociferation of a *lady mother*, who paffionately exclaimed, "You Julia-Maria-Matilda Sophonisba, come out of the kennel you dirty little b——h!!"

One cannot avoid feeling slightly dumbfounded that many of our Law Courts act as though vulgar speech was a novelty in these parts. Samples:

In January, 1939, a magistrate at Newtown Court, Sydney, held that the word *bloody* might be sometimes offensive, but not indecent, and fined a man £1 for the use of offensive language. In December, 1944, a magistrate at Lismore, N.S.W., fined a Hindu for having used the word *bloody* in addressing an impounding officer. The magistrate declared that the word was "indecent". On the other hand, in 1948 Judge Stacy ruled in the Sydney Quarter Sessions Appeals Court that the word, *plus* an upward gesture of the thumb, was neither offensive nor indecent. His view was that neither the word nor the action could be construed as "offensive to public taste or decency". The Judge added: "While his (the defendant's) conduct might be considered rude, it was not offensive behaviour according to an objective standard." This benevolence did not last long. In 1964, a magistrate at Coffs Harbour, N.S.W., found the word "indecent" again. And so we travel the wearisome circle.

Australians have been using the word *bloody* so long and so repetitively that it is no longer a "great" adjective. Indeed, in these days, the avowals of agreement *bloody oath!* and *my bloody oath!* are often converted into *blood oath!* and *my blood oath!* Perhaps in the years to come we may reach a stage where members of the constabulary and similar sages will cease to feel horror at the sound of the word. However, that will probably not curb official meddling with words entirely. Since 1947, I have records of policemen bringing charges against people for calling them *dear* and *nong* (as noted earlier, this word was taken from New Guinea pidgin during World War II. "The Book of Pidgin English", by John J. Murphy, defines it as "having nothing to say; stupidly silent."). I also have a record from 1882 when a policeman charged a man with having used profane language, to wit: "My God, you are a *Parramatta native*." (Parramatta is a N.S.W. city.) In short, our police seem to have done their best to keep the long-standing proletarian resentment against them in Australia seething at a steady white heat.

In spite of many criticisms Australians do not use more vulgarisms than the English and Americans. They merely use some of those vulgarisms more often. The vocabulary of vulgar speech used throughout the English-speaking world is much smaller than generally thought. At one stage, Partridge estimated that only about 0.5 per cent of the expressions in his "Dictionary of Slang" were vulgarisms. Less than 1 per cent of Australia's slang inventions are vulgarisms or near-vulgarisms. Admittedly we have produced some colourful and effective phrases of a profane nature, but it is not against these that the critic usually rails when he talks of the popularity of vulgar speech in this country. His main complaint is against a group of (sometimes) unprintable words.

If we include *damn, hell* and *devil*, we find that there are sixteen main vulgarisms. These include the four Indispensable Bs – *bastard, bitch, bloody* and *bugger*. The subject matter of the remainder is almost exclusively biological.

The repetitive nature of Australian vulgarism has had the important effect of robbing many allegedly objectionable words – especially the Bs – of their taint of indecency. Offensive they may still be at times, but much depends on the tone of voice in which they are spoken. *Bastard*[8] and *bugger* are frequently used as terms of genial or even affectionate address between men. The fact that Australian women also use the four Bs widely is additional evidence that they are becoming innocuous.

This lack of insult in Australian profanity[9] is a point that should be noted, not as an excuse for the continued use of certain words, but as evidence that even in his employment of vulgar terms imported from the Old World the Australian has managed to express something of his own personality.

The development of *bludger* as a pejorative exclusive to this country owes a great deal to the currency of *bugger*. The latter is generally less offensive in Australia than the former, although *bludger* was used originally to describe a harlot's bully, and could not in fact be labelled indecent.[10]

---

[8] During World War II *bastard* was used increasingly in print in Australia. In the army journal "Salt", in May, 1943, a soldier wrote asking for "a chance to get stuck into these Jap bastards". The appeal was republished in numerous newspapers. *The bastard from the bush*, an extremely old (and always humorous) reference to a bushdwelling male, and *not a bad poor bastard*, a moderate Australian accolade, are to be noted. It can also be observed that whereas *crazy bastard* or *dopey bastard* or *funny bastard* are generally accepted in Australia as beningly approving, *dirty bastard* is not, nor is *rotten bastard*, nor (if emphasis is deemed necessary) is *dirty rotten bastard*.

[9] Extract from a story in the Perth "Sunday Times" of December 7, 1941: "Two unhurried eyes regarding them in turn and a slow deliberate voice: 'You're two of the —— wretches looking for bushrangers, aren't you?' 'Now, now . . . ,' began McGinnerty, *who knew the lack of insult in Australian profanity*."

[10] An indication of the current tendency to regard *bludger* as indecent may be seen in the following quotation from the Sydney "Sunday Telegraph" of September 13, 1942: "Said elderly Mr White, swallowing a piece of noodle: 'Don't take any notice of that uncouth animal. He is only a ——' (Mr White used a word which indicates that a man is living on the immoral earnings of a woman)." Yet on the same page the "Sunday Telegraph" used "dirty little bitch", and, slightly earlier in the year – May 17, 1942 – had put the following into print: "Renowned for many years as a Redbaiter of dictatorial aptitudes, Thorby yet amazed even his own colleagues when, in December, 1938, he said he wouldn't 'spit' on John Curtin (*spit* is a euphemism)."

The evolution of *bludger* into *bludgasite* (a combination of *bludger* and *parasite*) is perhaps also symptomatic of popular disapproval of the original term. *Bludgasite* was first used in the Australian army journal "Salt" in March, 1943.

It is worth noting that in 1948 a Sydneysider sued a woman (unsuccessfully) for having addressed the word to him; on the other hand, a man who sued an acquaintance for having called him a *ratbag* was awarded the verdict.

A well-known Australian writer tells me that one of his publisher's compositors refused to set in type the word *arse*, but he agreed to set the word *backside* in its place. Another compositor who had a different "take" of copy before him set the word *arse* without any hint of protest. Since the word is recognised by the "Oxford Dictionary" and other authorities, the issue was clearly one of emotional prejudice.

The pressure exerted in this way against the direct use of certain emotionally-coloured words has forced authors to adopt many euphemistic ruses, although it is exceedingly difficult to imagine who would be deceived by them. Thus, we find Sarah Campion using *blunny* for *bloody*, *barstid* for *bastard* and *bukka* for *bugger* in her novel "Bonanza". Jean Devanny uses *sterky*, frightened, in "By Tropic Sea and Jungle"; it might appear innocuous enough, but it is derived from "stercoraceous" and a number of associated words, all of which relate to excreta. A newspaper reported a boxer as saying: "As I sat on the floor I thought of all them *flogging* people who came to see me", where *flogging* is clearly a euphemism for a stronger word. Another newspaper published an Australian cartoon strip with a character saying: "Aw, can it boss! You're gettin' on me *quince*", where *quince* is an allusion to the male genital. In "The Fiddlers of Drummond", Arthur Davies uses the term *bitch* to refer to a male, but it is apparently acceptable because a change of sex is implied. It thus seems that it is regarded as socially permissible to use thinly-disguised words, but intolerable to be straightforward, which is not a particularly flattering commentary on either our honesty or our collective mental level.

Interpolation, which Partridge describes as "a minor characteristic of unconventional speech" in England, has been well-developed in Australia. Principal interpolations used are *bloody*, *f**king*, and their euphemisms – e.g. *transconti-bloody-nental*, *abso-f**king-lutely*. The chorus of the C. J. Dennis poem quoted earlier gives a good example: *self-de——fence*. These efforts represent attempts to intensify and to colour, but they tend to become wearisome and have little to recommend them.

2. EXCLAMATIONS

THOUGH THE AUSTRALIAN often resorts to strong language in order to express his emotions and enthusiasms, he has a store of mild, or reasonably mild, ejaculations that can be called upon in polite society and cause little offence.

However, even this was not always so. I am reminded of a view expressed in "Australian Etiquette" (1885):

> All slang is vulgar. It lowers the tone of society and the standard of thought. It is a great mistake to suppose that slang is in any manner witty. Only the very young or the uncultivated so consider it . . . The woman who

exclaims, "The Dickens!" or "Mercy!" or "Goodness!" when she is annoyed or astonished is as vulgar in spirit, though perhaps not quite so regarded by society, as though she had used expressions which it would require but little stretch of the imagination to be regarded as profane.

Naturally enough, many Australian exclamations have changed over the years. Some have vanished from use altogether – like *my cabbage tree!* which dates back to days when cabbage-tree hats were in favour, *joe!* and *joey!* and *joe! joe!* which were cries of warning against the approach of troopers used by miners on the goldfields, and *bovril!* which had a brief vogue in the 1930s as a synonym for *bullsh!* On the other hand, *my colonial!* and *my colonial oath!* are still with us after more than a century of use; I have two records of the former in 1965 and they were not used in historical texts.

Other exclamations are virtually obsolete, like *my word!* I have a printed record of this in 1852, whereas the "Oxford Dictionary's" first English quote is dated 1857. We are, therefore, entitled (if we want to make an issue of such a minor matter) to claim it as an Australian original; certainly, we put the expression to constant use some generations ago. For example, in "Robbery Under Arms" (1881) Boldrewood employs it more than thirty times.

Other exclamations which at one time were more or less common property throughout Australia have been largely rejected by our cities and now persist mainly in the outback. For example, those variants on the *stone-the-crows!* theme, involving the stiffening, starving and speeding of such fauna as lizards, snakes, wombats and bardies. (See Chapter IV.)

Other terms have tended to become localized. Whereas *dickin!* meaning cut it out! be reasonable! is still known in most parts of Australia, it flourishes quite remarkably in South Australia. Here, depending on the intonation, it can mean "Yes, of course!" "Certainly not!" "Do you really think so?" and "You don't say!" Thus, we have such versions as "*Dickin* he'll go!" meaning "Of course he won't go!"; "*Dick-on!*" meaning "You bet your life!"; "Mother's won Tatts – *Dickin!*" meaning "That's excellent". The N.S.W. uses of *righto!* are also varied, but less comprehensive. Once more depending on intonation, *righto!* can mean Yes! Perhaps! and Stop it! *By hang!* an exclamatory intensive, seems to be localized to Queensland.

By contrast *up there Cazaly!* a cry of encouragement which not only originated in Melbourne, but among Australian Rules football fans in that city, has become a national possession. It commemorates a noted South Melbourne footballer, Roy Cazaly, 1893-1963. And the expression *send her down, Hughie!* which originated in the outback as an appeal to the heavens for rain or for a continuance of rain, is firmly entrenched in our cities.

In short, it is extremely difficult to predict how long an exclamation will survive and in what form. Here is a selection current in 1965:

Approval: *beauty!* (often pronounced *byoody!* with the suffix lengthened for special emphasis), *fair enough! goodoh! more hair on your chest! only a rumour! there's no doubt about you! whacko! what do you know! you beaut! how's your rotten form! good on you!* (often elided to *goodonyer!* as though it was one word), and *not bad!* which can mean anything from passable to excellent.

Agreement: *blood oath! kern oath! myking oath! too right! no risk!*

Slight surprise: *blimey Teddy! holy farmer! spare me days! strike me handsome!*

Exasperation: *chop it out! crack it for a dill!* (preceded with the words "So I've got to," the general meaning is "the person I'm dealing with is a fool"), *for crying out loud! go and have a roll! in your dipper! pig's! pig's arse! wouldn't it! myst all critey! ace it up! bust! bust it! bast!*

Moderate protest: *be your age! break it down! cut the rough stuff (out!) cut the kidstakes! don't be auntie! wake up to yourself! get off yourself! stop having yourself on! that'll be the day! thanks for nothing!*

Strong protest: *bash it! belt it! fluck off! get rooted! get stuffed! shove it! stick it!* (whence, *stick it up your guernsey* or *jumper!*) *stuff it! upya! upya for the rent! bore it up you!*

Assorted: *aroo!* goodbye; *bet you what you like!* expression of special emphasis; *don't do anything I wouldn't do!* have a good time, but don't overdo it; *don't wake it up!* don't talk about it; *half your luck!* an expression of envy; *hooray* or *hooroo*, goodbye; *just quietly!* between you and me; *pinch it off!* hurry up; *pull your head* (or *skull* or *scone*) *in*, mind your own business; *see you!* goodbye; *sh*t eh!* expression of moderate astonishment or irony; *wake it up!* hurry up; *who's robbing this coach!* mind your own business. Early this century an exclamatory formula of triumph was *How do you like your eggs done!* The approved answer of the times was *Scrambled, like your brains!*

Also worth noting is a number of phrases of greeting, all put in the form of queries, but not necessarily requiring answers: *how would you be? how'd you be? how is it? howzit? how yer doin'? how yer doin', mate, all right?*

CHAPTER X

The City Today

1. THE BIG CHANGE

A DATE has been arbitrarily set for the beginning of this Chapter – 1940. It is only an approximation, yet several things of great importance to Australia took shape round that time.

In the first place, of course, Australia was at war. Second, for the first time in our history, the population of our capital cities was almost as large as the population of the rest of the country, and was soon to excel it. Third, due mainly to the war, our secondary industry was in the process of such vast expansion that it would not be long before the leading sources of employment for both sexes would be manufacturing and commerce. Fourth, Australia's intake of a greater tide of aliens than ever before had begun – "refugees" (called *reffos*) at first, then "displaced persons" from Europe, then *New Australians* from Britain and the Continent and many other countries: 1,000,000 by 1955, 2,000,000 by 1964.

By the end of World War II, although few people would have had the courage to predict it, Australia was headed in the direction of becoming an affluent society. One of the consequences was the rejection of many slang expressions which had been used in this country for generations. Oddly enough, by the mid-1960s we were to find that this rejection was not final; that, far from the onset of television (which began in 1956, using about 80 per cent of film footage from the U.S.) and the intake of migrants obliterating Australianism, there was to be a resurgence of nationalistic feeling. For reasons which I will examine later, Australia was "in" again. And many of the expressions – such as *bonzer*, *cobber* and *larrikin* – which seemed to have lost favour, were restored to use.

In the interval, i.e., largely between the publication of the first edition of this book (1945) and now, we were to sense a good deal of confusion. Some of that confusion still remains, but due mainly to factors which have been observable for several generations, the outcome is more predictable. Since late last century, Britain (traditionally) and the U.S. (geographically) have had considerable influence on Australia – the former generally, the latter particularly along the eastern seaboard. The influence of U.S. films, the wartime U.S. "invasion" of this country, the so-called entertainment emanating from the U.S. seen on television, have had considerable propagandic effect on Australians. This has been largely countered by traditional influences from Britain, which have drawn strong backing since the end of World War II from the fact that more than half our migrants have come from Britain. Since the war's end, tens of thousands of New Australians have migrated here from the mainland of Europe, but their influence has been fragmented. As a result, Australianism has been under some severe pressures and only since 1960 has it begun to reassert itself. The main reason would seem to be that non-Australian elements are tending to cancel each other out, and the voice of Australia (which is no more the voice of Britain than it is of America) is being heard again.

However, in choosing 1940 as the date for this Chapter to begin, many difficulties emerge. Australia was then climbing into uniform and, as we have seen in Chapter VIII, a formidable Service slang developed. We will naturally be interested in examining what part of that slang survived and what changes it underwent after the war was over. There were also many expressions – among them such standard terms as *lay-by*, *anting* and *home unit* – which had begun to take shape in the 1930s. We will have to see what became of those. And, as noted earlier, there were a host of ancient words (*bonzer,. cobber, larrikin* and so on) which almost died and were disinterred again. And then there were new words (*scungey, gas lash, to rubbish, Faceless Men, norks*, etc.) which edged their way into popular use. And a gathering torrent of idiomatic turns of speech (*in the tub, drag at the lights, not worth a mintie*, etc.) which certainly need attention, if only to relieve curiosity.

This, then, will be the main task of the present Chapter. Among the things we will find is that the Australian's flair for linguistic invention is far from dead, in spite of the many factors which could have been expected to erase that flair almost entirely.

⟍ 2. MODERN IDIOM

SINCE *lay-by* was mentioned a little earlier as one of the words which began to edge their way into popular attention in Australia in the 1930s, let us begin with it. In terms of fact, both England and the U.S. had used the term for a long time, but the senses they gave to it were vastly different from Australia's. In England, a *lay-by* was "a portion of road widened to permit a vehicle to stop there without interfering with traffic" (I quote from the "Oxford Dictionary"); in the U.S. *to lay by* meant "to store up, save" (the quote is from Funk and Wagnalls "Standard Dictionary"). The latter could well have had some influence in shaping the Australian use, but here the meaning was more specific. It came about in this way.

During the Depression in Australia, few people had money to spend on clothes and even those with money were chary of making purchases. As a result, business in our department stores was virtually at a standstill, and the stores tried various ruses to tempt customers. For example, on October 10, 1930, the Sydney firm of Anthony Hordern's advertised what they called the *D.P.S.* Six days later, Hordern Brothers, also of Sydney, addressed customers with the lure "Avail yourself of our Lay-By Service". There is some doubt as to the exact nature of the now-forgotten *D.P.S.*, but in January, 1931, Anthony Hordern's elucidated a little in another advertisement; this system, they said, "enables you to secure Sale Bargains without the necessity of paying in full at once. Leave a deposit, pay the balance as it suits you, and on the completion of payments the goods will be delivered in the usual way. No interest is charged." In essence, this was the idea behind the *lay-by*. The latter term was slowly taken up and in December, 1932, Farmers (still another Sydney firm) also advertised what they called a "*Lay-By* service". Subsequently, any non-perishable goods – not merely sale bargains – could be bought on *lay-by*, and during the war years this form of purchase was greatly favoured by women.

Australia's rag-trade was by no means the only type of business which found difficulty in shifting its goods during the Depression. Many people could not afford more basic essentials – such as milk. The resulting surplus led to the establishment (apparently first in 1930) of what became known as the *milk bar*, a type of business originally devoted to the sale of milk drinks. The first of these establishments was reputedly introduced in Pitt Street, Sydney, by Messrs Clarence and Norman Burt. Previously, milk drinks had been sold in confectioners' shops, but this was the first time a separate shop was given over to that purpose. The *milk bar* was so successful that, in the mid-1930s, Hugh D. McIntosh took the idea to England with somewhat indifferent results. A decade or so later, Australia's economists began using the expression *milk-bar economy* to denote "the tendency for non-essential consumer goods industries to expand beyond the capacity of basic industry to supply them with raw material." Milk bars have now spread to many parts of the world. I have reports of them under that name in Paris, South Africa and Santiago, Chile (three instances), of *Milch Bars* in Germany, Austria and Switzerland, of a *Bar Leitaria* in Rio de Janeiro and of some three dozen establishments called *Bar Lácteo* in Buenos Aires.

The building trade was also almost at a standstill during the Depression. When a contractor conceived the idea of building the "Astor" flats in Macquarie Street, Sydney, in the late 1930s, he covered himself by inducing a number of people to pay for the flats in the building and thereby to become the owners of those flats when the building was completed. The idea had been tried overseas with some success, but it was not until after the end of World War II that builders in our main cities took it a step further – they would build a block of flats first, then sell those flats to various purchasers. But what were you going to call the idea? In May, 1949, came the answer: they would be called *home units*.

While we are on this architectural theme, it is worth noting that we have apparently added something to traditional concepts of *cantilever verandah*, an unsupported extension in front of a shop, *cottage*, any detached house in which all the rooms are on the ground floor (often a good deal larger than the English cottage, which is always small and often of two storeys). *Semi*, a semi-detached house which may have two or even three storeys, *weekender*, a cottage or shack at some beach or bush resort where week-ends and holidays are spent, and *Macquarie style*, a late-Georgian type of building erected between 1817 and 1821 by Governor Macquarie and a group of architects led by Macquarie's protégé, Francis Greenway, are also Australian. It might not be out of place to take this opportunity of referring to the word *square*, used in relation to building space. It often baffles folk and I have heard it claimed as an Australian innovation. Actually, it is a standard English word, dating from the seventeenth century, used to describe an area of 100 square feet, and is usually applied to floor space in a house in Australia. Thus, a house is said to have so many *squares*. The Japanese have a somewhat similar term. The standard-size Japanese floor mat is about 3 ft. by 6 ft. in area and a "mat" is a unit of measurement of floor space. As a result, the Japanese speak of a "seven mat room" or a "ten mat room" although it may not have a single mat in it.

We became concerned in many specialist fields other than architecture. For example:

Anthropology: After World War II, anthropologists hastened their attempts to make up for generations of virtual neglect and the public heard increasing references to *the old people, dream time, dreaming, mimi art, property, message stick, flesh, old men old men*, etc., all related to Australia's Aborigines. These and associated terms are examined in Chapter XV.

Art: The Archibald Prize (worth about £500 annually) was established in 1921. After the *Dobell case*, which developed when the painter William Dobell was awarded the prize in 1943, it became known generally as *The Archibald*. In 1961, artist John Olsen began a series of (mainly) non-figurative paintings which he called *You Beaut Country*. (Whence doubtless "*a touch of You Beautery*", enthusiasm for Australia – "Nation", July 24, 1965, p. 16.)

Children: During World War II, we heard a lot of the *cuddle-seat*, a lightweight harness in which mothers carried their children, invented here about 1941 (a refinement is the *cradleseat*)*; from 1957, youngsters were caught up in the Australian craze of the *hula hoop* (which spread throughout the world), when bamboo hoops were introduced "in moving formation into the massed display by 2,000 schoolgirls at the Royal Sydney Show in the 'Carousel Dance'."

Drama: Ray Lawler's play "The Summer of the Seventeenth Doll" (1955) was so successful that soon it became known generally as *The Doll*.

Engineering: Many new names began to edge their way into popular attention after the end of World War II – *the Snowy*, where one of the world's greatest engineering projects, the Snowy River Hydro-Electric Scheme, began in 1949; *Rum Jungle* (N.T.), where our first major discovery of uranium was made in 1949; *Weipa* (Queensland), where one of the biggest deposits of bauxite in the world was found in 1956; *Moonie* (Queensland), where oil was first found in Australia in commercial quantities in 1961. In 1948, we were first introduced to the *Holden*, a completely Australian-made car. And at long last, we actually began to do something about the *single gauge*, which wouldn't have much meaning in other parts of the world, but which means a lot to us; it refers to the unifying of the width of tracks on which trains run (we have five gauges).

Literature: A literary movement called the *Jindyworobaks* (abbreviated to *Jindies* and developed into *Jindyworobakism*) was established in the late 1930s "to free Australian art from whatever alien influences trammel it, that is, to bring it into proper contact with its material". Twenty years later, an opposing school had developed which used *outbackery*, *bushbashing* and *eucalyptusy* as terms of contempt. In 1944, we were introduced to the mythical figure of *Ern Malley* in our best-known literary hoax. After 1957, benevolent Australians came to refer to themselves as a *weird mob* – taken from the title of a book "They're a Weird Mob", by Nino Culotta. About 1960, actor-playwright Patrick White introduced *Sarsaparilla*, the name of a fictitious suburb near Sydney about which he has written extensively.

Popular music: Crude musical instruments called the *bush bass* or *wonk* and the *lagerphone* became known. A *bush bass* is a crude rhythm instrument made from a tea chest, a length of broom handle and a piece of sturdy cord. A *lagerphone* is a home-made percussion instrument (sounding something like a tambourine) made from a broomhandle on which are loosely nailed some 40 or 50 beer bottle tops. This instrument is bounced on the floor in rhythm with whatever music is being played and struck at the same time with a short piece of 2 in. x 1 in. hardwood. It is sometimes called a *Jingling Johnny*. In 1960 Rolf Harris invented the *wobble board* to provide accompaniment to his songs – a piece of Masonite, 2 ft. x 3 ft.

Zoology: In 1935, bird expert A. H. Chisholm invented the words *anting* and *to ant*, to denote a practice followed by many birds of rubbing ants or other acidulous substances, ranging from vinegar to aromatic leaves, beneath their wings and tails, or sitting on ant beds.

In short, many things in many different directions began moving for us. As we shall see soon, our language kept pace with the big change that was upon us almost before we knew it.

First of all, however, we should pause to consider what became of the vast tide of linguistic inventions by our Servicemen. In Chapter VIII, I listed some 600 expressions (mainly Australian in origin) used in the Forces. Many of them were, of course, by no means new. Some had been used by diggers in World War I; others were current before World War II began. It may cause some surprise to realise that today, not much more than twenty years after the war's end, probably fewer than fifty of them survive in general use. However, war veterans keep many more alive in specialized groups (e.g. *R.S.L.* clubs) and recent Australian military operations at home and abroad are reviving others.

By 1965, these were the main survivors (in quite a number of cases the wartime meanings changed considerably when the words went into civilian use and these changes are noted here): *animal*, a term of contempt for a man; *back, on one's*, descriptive of harassing or bullying activities by a superior, *get off my back!* a demand for relief from such activities; *back up*, to seek a second helping of food; *bastardry*, unjust or unscrupulous actions; *bludge*, an instance of loafing or taking it easy (*bludger*, *to bludge* and *bludging* were, of course, in use long before the war); *bombo*, cheap wine; *boomerang*, that which is expected to be returned by a borrower, also a verb (this is as good a place as any to note that only one of three types of boomerang made by the Aborigines has the property of returning to the thrower); *boong*, an Aboriginal; *break it down!* be fair or reasonable!; *brothel*, a confusion or mess, e.g. *a brothel of a place; dice*, to throw away; *dob in*, to betray; *drack*, ugly, dirty; *drongo*, a stupid or slow-witted person; *drube*, ditto; *flake out*, to rest especially from exhaustion, to sleep; *get off yourself!* stop fooling yourself!; *give the game away*, to abandon a task or obligation; *go off*, said of a thing which is stolen; *go like a bomb*, to travel fast, to succeed well; *grouse*, excellent, with its elaboration *extra grouse; how'd ya be!* a greeting; *jack of*, tired of, disinterested in; *know someone's form*, to know how a person will behave; *leave for dead*, to surpass, outdo; *lollywater*, a (sweet) soft drink; *no-hoper*, a stupid person, one who has no chances of success; *nong*, a stupid person (also *nong-nong* and *ning-nong*); *on the nose*, unwanted, high-smelling, also *on the bugle* and *on the trumpet; perve*, to watch a male or female undressing or in an undressed condition, a genial term which may mean no more than inspecting bikini-clad girls on a beach; *promote*, to obtain illicitly; *pull your head in!* mind your own business!; *rap on an act*, to give way to temper, to complain at great length, also *bung* (or *stack*) *on an act; shoot through*, to leave; *snatch your time*, to leave a job, especially at brief notice, also *snatch it; spine-bashing*, loafing, resting supinely, and the rest of the *bash* derivatives (*ear-bashing, give it a bash, bash it!*)*; sport*, a genial form of address; *whacko!* an exclamation of approval; *wog*, any migrant to Australia (especially of non-English speaking origin) after the war.

I have included *whacko!* here as one of the terms brought back into civilian life by our Servicemen after the war's end, but it was not long before it fell into disuse. However, I would offer a warning here to those who might think that when an expression disappears it is unlikely to be revived. In the course of making the survey necessary for this book, I came across two expressions which originated in Sydney and a third which had its main currency in Melbourne preserved elsewhere. The Sydney originals were *go through like a Bondi tram* and *brickfielder*. The former was repeatedly reported from Adelaide, the latter from Kalgoorlie, W.A. The original *brickfielder* was the first name given to the *southerly buster* in Sydney; it denoted a heavy southerly gale which blew dust and dirt into the main Sydney settlement from brickfields where Anthony Hordern's department store now stands. Later, the term moved to Victoria and denoted a hot, dusty wind blowing from the interior. Now it has moved across the continent to Kalgoorlie, to describe heavy dust-storms whipped up there. As for *go through like a Bondi tram*, it is perhaps enough to note that Bondi is a Sydney suburb; the expression was discussed earlier. The Melbourne term (although it was anticipated in Sydney in 1825 and certainly had considerable currency in Sydney) is *larrikin*. It is strongly preserved in South Australia and now, after being temporarily obliterated by the U.S. *hoodlum* and *hooligan*, is being revived in the Eastern States.

The fact of the matter is that one can never be too sure that a word which has been out of use for decades will not return. Many years ago, and then not too often, Australia was called *Kangaroo Land*. On the day I am writing this in 1965, the term has been printed in one of our leading newspapers. If, then, we suspect that *Billjim*, an Australian, *cabbage-tree mobs*, gangs of youths wearing cabbage-tree hats, *scrubbing brush*, a loaf of bread containing more chaff and bran than flour, and similar terms of ancient vintage will never return to use again, we may well be right, but we cannot be sure. Consider the case of *cocky's joy*. Towards the end of last century it denoted treacle and then golden syrup in the outback. In World War II, it came to denote honey. It is still current to denote rum.

One of our casualties during and soon after the war was *bonzer*, good, excellent. It made a tentative comeback about 1960, but its many derivatives (*boshter, bonziorie*, etc.) seem to have been lost entirely. *Cobber*, a friend, companion, also virtually disappeared, and the English terms *pal* and *mate* and the U.S. *buddy* took over; once more, it has shown modest signs of revival in recent years. Much the same can be said of *sheila* and *good sort*, a girl or young woman, *dinkum Aussie*, a true or native-born Australian, *fair cow*, an unpleasant person or event, *push*, a group of people, a gang, and *squatter*, a large landowner and sheepraiser.

As our society moves into a new and more affluent shape, many of these changes are inevitable. *The sundowner*, the *swagman*, the nomad who *humps a drum* or *waltzes Matilda* from one shearing shed to another, are almost all gone. The nomads travel by car or plane these days, they wear bodgie boots and jeans and sweat shirts, they carry transistors and use electric razors. Yet, rather astonishingly, it is these young people who are doing the linguistic preserving and who, long after the old-timers who know nothing else are gone, will be adding new dimensions to well-used Australian terms. Probably in only a few parts of our vast land are changes not in progress. True, the overlapping jargons of woolshed, droving camps and harvesting are fairly intact, but horses have been displaced by bulldozers and axes by mechanical saws and gold-digging by rutile and tantalite and uranium and bauxite. These are times of great development and the old days are going.

At this stage, another point should be made. Traditionalism is far better preserved in the outback than it is in our cities. Canberra and the six State capitals occupy an area of some 3,000 square miles – about one-thousandth of the total area of Australia – yet they hold more than half Australia's population (over 56 per cent at the 1961 census). It is only to be expected that large aggregations of people will slough off proportionately more new terms than small communities. With that fact well in mind, let us now look at some (not all, for we will discover more of them in Chapters to come) of the words which grew in our modern cities:

> *alf*, a heterosexual male. See *daphne*.
> *back-up*, a heterosexual act.
> *balloon*, to leave immediately. (Probably ex rhyming slang on "soon".)
> *barney*, a row or argument. Also verb.
> *beach-bash*, to recline on a beach, especially at night and for amorous purposes.
> *big curl*, an easily accomplished task.

big note, to laud, give exaggerated praise to. Especially *big note oneself*, to exaggerate one's importance. Whence *big noting*.

bike, a girl or woman who is indiscriminate in granting her favours. Especially, *office bike, town bike*.

bingle, a crash.

black, to declare (a job) "black".

blinder, a dazzling display of skill, especially in sport.

bodgie, an adolescent pseudo-tough, the post-war larrikin. (Ex earlier use of *bodger* for anything fake or counterfeit.) This term had a big vogue in the 1950s, was then swamped by *rocker* and returned to us about 1964. See *widgie*.

bodgie up, to attend to exterior appearance, e.g. of a car, to impress an inexpert purchaser.

bomb, an old mass-produced car or motor cycle.

bomb on, extremely good. Also *bommo* (as distinct from *bombo*, cheap wine). *go like a bomb*, proceed rapidly, succeed well.

boofhead, a simpleton or fool.

bore into, work hard at; attack violently.

bottler, something extremely good.

bowser, a petrol pump. (This term seems to have been first used in Australia about 1920.)

brasker, a lavatory.

broke for, short of, in need of (e.g. *broke for a feed*, in need of a meal) because of lack of money.

brown bomber, a parking policeman.

bug, offensive term for a person.

bunk off, to leave. *Do a bunk*, to leave.

bulldoze around, to wander aimlessly, be on the prowl.

bunce, something for nothing.

bushfire blonde, a red-haired woman.

carry-on, an act of misconduct, bad behaviour. Also in the phrase *a bit of carry-on*.

cat, a male homosexual.

charlie, a lesbian.

choof, to go away. Especially in the form *choof off*.

chop rate, a situation and its prospects.

chromo, a lesbian. (The term was formerly used for a prostitute.)

chuck-in, a voluntary subscription made by a number of persons, sometimes for the benefit of another, but more often to defray the costs of a celebration.

chunder, to vomit. *chunderous*, in reference to vomit or a disposition to vomit.

clapped, worthless. Also *clapped out*.

clever, in good health, in good order, proficient, used mainly in negative sense, *not too clever*, which often means extremely bad.

clout (on), to steal (something).

clunk, a simpleton or fool.

conniver about, to fuss or potter about aimlessly.

corner, one's due share, especially of plunder; due punishment.

crack it, (of a male) to record success in an amorous exploit.

custards, pimples.

daphne, a heterosexual female.

dead duck, someone who fails badly.

dead loss, a person, event or thing without merit.

dead sweet, extremely good. See *sweet*.

death knock, the end or climax of an event.

dice, to reject.

did, a lavatory. Also *diddy*.

dillybags of, much of.

dip out, withdraw from an undertaking.

donk, the engine of a car. Also *donkey*.

drip drama, a radio serial, mainly with a domestic theme. Such serials, which began in Australia in the late 1920s, virtually ceased in 1964.

drum up, to invite, promote, e.g. *drum up business*.

duck in, to enter a place, especially hurriedly.

dwell on, to follow or watch (a person); eagerly to await another's decision or action.

easy, moderately disposed towards (e.g. towards some proposal by another person); indifferent whether a decision is made for or against.

eggshell blonde, a bald person.

false gigging, the exaggeration of one's importance. See *big note*.

fang, the act of eating; *big* (or *good*) *on the fang*, hungry. Also *fang a bottle*, to open a bottle of beer with the teeth.

fed with, tired of, bored with (someone or something).

fem, a male transvestite. (Ex French *femme*.)

financial, in funds, with ready money available.

fizz-out, an unreliable person. *fizz out on*, to let down, fail in a promise.

flea-rake, a hair comb.

flib, contemptuous term for a person.

fluff, to break wind anally.

fly, an attempt at, especially *give it a fly*, *have a fly at*. An alternative to *bash*, *belt*, *burl*, *lash* and *whirl*.

gabbleguts, a loquacious person. Whence, *gabblegutser*, *gabblegutsery*.

gang splash, a heterosexual orgy. Also *gang bang*.

garbo, a garbage collector; a garbage tin.

gas lash, copulation, especially that which the participants deem highly satisfactory. (*Gas*, the best, is ex U.S.)

geek, an act of looking; to look at. Probably from next.

gig, one who stares inquisitively, a prying inquirer, a private detective. Also a fool or simpleton, as in *big* (or *prize*) *gig*. As verb, to stare inquisitively, to tease.

give away, to reject or abandon; *give the game away*, used similarly.

gloik, a simpleton or fool.

go-fasters, "pep" pills. Also *go-fast pills*.

gollion, a gob of phlegm. Whence, *gooey*. *Goo* or *goob*, to spit.

go on, to like (someone), to approve (an idea, an undertaking).

greta, a garbage collector (ex Greta Garbo).

gripper, a member of a Masonic lodge.

hack pusher, a taxi driver. Synonymous is *hack pilot*.

hell off, go away, decamp. Often as an order, *hell off!*

herbs, the power of a car, the rate at which it can travel.

hive off, to leave.

holding, in funds, with ready money available.

hoon, a stupid or silly person.

hoot, to stink. As noun, that which is absurd or ridiculous; a source of astonishment.

hostile, angry, annoyed; *be* (or *go*) *hostile* (*at*), become angry (at).

hot, well (in health), good, proficient at; often used negatively *not so hot*, not feeling well or not achieving much; excessive; stinking, as for *hoot*, v. Whence, *hot cack*, excellent, *hot cock*, nonsense.

hoy, to call, as in *give a hoy;* to lift, to haul, to move.

humpback, a supposed deformity caused to a man by someone (employer, wife, etc.) being continually *on his back*.

issue, the, everything, the lot.

jack up on (someone), to resist another's suggestion or order.

jellyfish, to act spinelessly.

keep down, to retain (especially a job), to hold against any competition.

killer, the final action or argument which means the end to whatever hopes have been held; "the straw that breaks the camel's back".

knock, to criticize unfairly. Whence, *knocker*, an unfair critic, *knocking*, the practice. (Originally ex U.S.)

knock back, to consume, especially to consume an alcoholic drink. As noun, a rebuff.

knock out, to earn (a sum of money).

knock up! stop it! be reasonable! (A version of the U.S. *knock off*.)

light on, a shortage of, a deficiency in, e.g. "the tucker was *light on*", in short supply.

lair, a flashily dressed and uncouth mannered young man; *dead lair*, *mug lair*, intensives; *teddy bear*, rhyming slang; *lair up*, to dress up, especially to don one's best clothes; *lairy*, vulgar in manners, flashily dressed.

lairize, to dress or act as a *lair*.

liquid cops, water police.

lob, to throw upon, e.g. "I *lobbed* it with a gooley" – I threw a stone on it.

louse-bound, mean, "stingy".

mad, often used as an adjective of approval, e.g. "You're a *mad bastard!*" (this is a case in which *bastard* is also used approvingly), "How's your *mad mate?*"

merchant, a synonym for the earlier use of *artist*, an excessive practitioner of some form of (usually antisocial) conduct, e.g. *bite merchant*, a persistent borrower, *panic merchant*, one who gives way to panic in any situation of alarm, *touch merchant*, a swindler, a shopkeeper who overcharges.

mike, an excessive talker. (Probably ex "microgroove".)

mizzle, to complain.

monty, a lie.

mott, to look at, stare at.

mouthy, an excessive talker.

mud, often used to mean fat, e.g. *fat as mud, mud-guts, muddy-guts.*

naughty, used (mainly by females) as a mild-sounding reproach, when in fact sharp criticism is often intended.

Naussie, a New Australian.

New, a New Australian.

nork, a female breast, usually in plural. (Ex Norco Co-operative Ltd., a butter manufacturer in N.S.W.) The form *norg* is reported from Melbourne; also *to norg*, to caress the breasts of a female partner.

nut, a male homosexual.

on at, be, to scold, nag.

onkey, stinking. (Ex *honk*.)

oodle, money.

oozle, a "turn", as in "It's your *oozle*, mate".

pack 'em, to be frightened.

perform, to swear luridly, to give way to temper.

perk, to vomit.

picnic, any unpleasant experience; a disagreeable and complex task; *no picnic*, an intensive.

pie at (or *on*), expert at.

pink-eye, a sycophant.

plonk, cheap (sweet) wine; sometimes wine in general. *plonk-dot, plonko,* a wine addict.

ponk, a stench. Also *pong*. Both used as verbs.

poof(ter), a male homosexual. Pronounced to rhyme with *hoof*, which is used as a rhyming equivalent.

poucher, a child. Equivalent to the earlier *joey* so-used.

prawnhead, a simpleton or fool, a pejorative.

protected, (of a person) phenomenally lucky.

proverbial, the, a bad mistake. *come the proverbial,* to meet one's Waterloo.

pull on, to undertake, to test, to eat.

punisher, a person who talks at great length.

quick smart, rapidly.

quince, an effeminate male.

rare, a drinking bout, a celebration. (Probably ex *r(e)aring to go*.)

ratbagging, eccentric activities. Derived, of course, from *ratbag*, an eccentric, and synonymous with *ratbaggery*.

reffo, a refugee, who migrated to Australia before or during World War II.

ridge, honest, genuine.

rock-hopper, a person who fishes from rocks on a sea coast.

rock-spider, a person who climbs cliffs or rocky places.

root, (of a male) to copulate. *be rooted*, to be exhausted; *get rooted!* exclamation of dismissal; *rooted for* (something), short of, lacking in.

rort, a lively, especially a drunken party; an orgy. Earlier uses for a dodge, racket or scheme have been retained. Whence, *rorter, rorting.*

rubbish, to reject, treat as worthless.

sangoes, sandwiches.

sanno, a sanitary carter or inspector.

say-so, a leader, boss.

scrag, a woman.

scrub, to reject, disown. *get scrubbed*, to be rejected.

scungey, dirty, untidy, disreputable. Whence, *scungies*, old clothes; a *scunge*, a dirty, untidy person; a serious confusion or mess; *the scunge*, utter disorder and dirtiness; *scungerous*, as for *scungey*.[1]

scone, to hit (someone) on the head.

set someone, to oblige someone, especially in negative form, *I can't set you*. Usually refers to a loan of money.

shemale, a lesbian.

shirt lifter, a sodomite.

shook on, (of a person) keenly interested in or infatuated with.

shove off, to depart.

sidekick, a friend, companion.

skate, something easily accomplished.

sling, a tip (money).

slug, to charge exorbitantly. As noun, a heavy charge, especially if unexpected. *get slugged*, to be charged exorbitantly.

slunge, to wash oneself.

snack, a certainty.

snaps, moving pictures, a cinema.

snoozer, a child.

soda, a certainty.

solid, unfair, unreasonable.

sonk, a timid or cowardly person. *sonky*, timid.

square off, to apologize, set matters right in a misunderstanding, "cover up" for someone. *square-off*, an apology; *to square off for* (something), *to square off with* (someone).

start, a job.

stickybeak, an inquisitive person. Whence, *stick*, *sticky*, both nouns; the latter is also used as an adjective.

sting, to charge. *get stung*, to be overcharged.

stitch, to overcome, to beat in any contest.

sub, an advance on wages.

sudden, speedy, drastic, e.g. *sudden service*.

surface, to waken, rise from bed, appear in public after sleep.

sweat on, to wait, usually to wait anxiously (for some event).

sweet, excellent, satisfactory, beyond complaint. The popular form, *she's sweet*, everything is all right, has many equivalents, e.g. *she's apples, she's jake, she's ridge, she's right, she's chooks*.

swillery, a hotel. (Influenced by, and doubtless derived from what is remembered as the *six o'clock swill*.)

sword swallower, one who eats from the blade of a knife.

take-down, a deception or fraud.

thrash, to consume, use competely, e.g. *thrash food*, eat heartily; *thrash money*, spend it all. Also to complain to (someone), apparently by rhyme on *earbash*.

tin-ear, an eavesdropper.

ton, a figurative measure of large quantity, e.g. *ton of guts*, great energy or courage, *ton of bull*, a great deal of nonsense, *ton of money*, much money.

These terms began to emerge (from Sydney University) about 1960 and soon spread widely. They appeared to be new, but had been anticipated in the 1920s by *scun(d)ge* and *scun(d)ging*. Xavier Herbert recalls their use in W.A. The verb *scun(d)ge* then denoted begging, getting something for nothing, "scrounging" (which is English slang). In "Larger Than Life", p. 243, Herbert refers to a character "coveting and scundging and bickering".

tonk, a simpleton or fool; a homosexual male.

toot, a lavatory.

top, a boss, leader. A genial form of address, as in "How'd ya be, top?"

toss, to better, especially in an argument.

trot, a sequence. *good trot*, a sequence of successes; *bad trot*, a sequence of failures.

turf out, to reject.

turps, any form of alcohol. *on the turps*, to be drinking.

twicer, a double crosser.

warb, a low-paid manual worker; a dirty or untidy person.

warby, unattractive, second-rate.

wax borer, a person who talks at great length.

wet (season), *the*, menstruation.

whip-round, a collection of money for the benefit of another or for some celebration.

whirling spray, a person who talks at great length.

whittled, drunk. Whence, *whittled as a penguin*.

wipe, to dispense with; to have nothing to do with. Whence, *wiped like a dirty nose*.

wombat, derogatory reference to a person.

This is by no means all. Before we turn attention to the many idiomatic phrases which flourished in our cities after the war, there are several matters to be noted. During the war, our Servicemen used a large amount of rhyming slang, much of which was not notable – as is the way with most rhyming slang – for anything more than that the words used rhymed (more or less) with what was intended. After the war, rhyming slang persisted and will be examined in Chapter XVII. We also added considerably to various groups of words with set suffixes, e.g. the *-o* suffix (*garbo*, a garbage collector, *info*, information, *oppo*, opportunity, *sanno*, a sanitary carter or inspector), the *-ie* suffix (*goodie, hottie, roughie, tallie, shrewdie, swiftie*, descriptive of assorted tales or acts) and the *-up* suffix. While the last is often encountered in orthodox English (*dress up, shut up*, etc.) the Australian offerings are extensive enough to be worth consideration. Here are a few of them: *beer-up, booze-up, drunk-up, grog-up*, a drinking party, *flossy up, lair up, mocker up, poon up, queen up, tiz up*, to dress, *bunk-up*, an act of assistance, *chop-up*, a division of spoils, *jack-up*, a labour dispute, *back up*, to seek another helping or share, *boil-up*, a row, *first up*, for the first time, *frig up*, to mar, *word up*, to advise, and such phrases as *have the brits up*, to be frightened, *up to mud* (or *putty*), worthless, and *who's up who and who's paying the rent!*

Now for a list of popular phrases. It should be understood that quite a number of these were current before World War II, but they became particularly evident during and after the war. Since at a later stage in this book, detailed attention will be given to the development of Australian idiom (Chapter XXI), many metaphors otherwise worthy of places in this list have been withheld:

argue the toss, to dispute an issue.

ball of muscle, well, in good health.

bib in, push (or *put* or *stick*) *one's*, to intervene.

big chuck (or *spit*), *go for the*, to vomit.

bike, get off one's, to become angry.

bit hot, a, unreasonable, extreme.

bit of hurry up, give (someone) *a*, to demand or encourage prompt action.

bit rough, a, unreasonable, unfair.

blue, in the, in error.

book, in the, used especially in the sentence, "He's in the book, but he doesn't know what page he's on!" – He's all right, but he's not very smart.

boots and all, completely, utterly. Originally from no-punches barred fighting.

break it down! be reasonable!

breast stroke, do the, (of a male) to caress a woman companion's breasts.

bull warrant, a warrant against a male for maintenance.

bung on side, to act affectedly.

chuck off at, jeer at, tease.

close to the knuckle, vulgar, indecent.

clue (someone) *up*, to advise (someone) in detail. Whence, (*get*) *clued up*.

come good, to perform well after setbacks, especially in sport.

couldn't do it in the time! you (*he*), you (he) have no chance of success, especially in a fight.

crack down on, to exert authority (over).

crack hardy, to put on a brave face against misfortune.

crow, cop (or *draw*) *the*, to have the hardest job in a group activity.

crutch merchant, a male who boasts of his conquests of women.

die on it, to abandon trying, give up easily.

do the dirty on, to let down; see *put in the dirt*.

do your lolly, become angry.

don't do anything you couldn't eat! watch your step! don't bite off more than you can chew!

down on, get, to seize, steal.

drop one's bundle, to go to pieces, give up.

ear, on one's, said of an easily accomplished task or undertaking; drunk.

edge on (or *against*), *have an*, to have an advantage over (another).

eyes out, go, to work hard; travel fast.

fair shake of the dice! be fair! City version of the old bush phrase, *fair crack of the whip!*

flue, up the, (of a woman) pregnant. Equivalents are *in the tub, up the* (*well-known*) *creek, up the pole* (or *stick*).

freeze, do a, to be ignored, to be left out of consideration.

get on (someone's) *works*, to anger or irritate someone. Also, *get on* (someone's) *tit* (or *quince*).

get stuck into, to work hard at a task; to fight (someone).

get the spear (or *run*), to be dismissed from a job.

get under (someone's) *neck*, to anticipate another's act; to forestall.

gink at, have a, to look at. Ex *gig*, to stare at inquisitively. See *geek*.

go and have a roll! go to the devil! go away!

go for one's quoits, to hurry, travel rapidly.

go the knuckle on, to cheat, defraud, take down.

go to water, to display cowardice.

good for yourself, do some, (especially of a male) to succeed in an amorous exploit.

good on you! a general term of approval, but sometimes used ironically.

hang (something) on (someone), to ask (someone something).

have one's chips (or *oppo*), to have a chance. Especially used in passive sense, *to have had one's chips* (or *oppo*), to have lost one's last opportunity.

hit the anchor, (of a car driver) to put on the brakes suddenly.

hit the bitumen, to leave.

improve, on the, improving in health or proficiency.

keep out of the rain, to avoid trouble.

leave for dead, to surpass, outdo by a wide margin.

main event, the, sexual activity as the culmination of any courtship, however brief.

make a sale, to vomit.

more than you could shake (or *poke*) *a stick at,* more than you could imagine; liberally endowed (i.e. with money).

nasty piece of work, an unpleasant person.

nick, do a, to leave hurriedly. Also *nick off.*

not nominated, with no chance of success.

not worth a bumper (or *cracker* or *crumpet*), worthless.

not worth a mintie, worthless. *without a mintie,* penniless.

only a rumour! not half! of course!

on the halves, a 50-50 contract between, say, the landlord and tenant of a property, whereby one supplies the land, implements and seed, and the other the labour, and they share the profits equally.

on the patch, in trouble with an employer; "on the carpet".

pack, go to the, to collapse (in figurative sense); to lose one's morale; to go to pieces.

pot on, put (someone's), to betray.

pull the weight, to find the necessary finance for an undertaking, e.g. for a drinking party.

pull your finger out! hurry up!

put in the dirt, to treat badly, especially (in a fight) to resort to unfair tactics. Also *do the dirty on.*

put the hard word on, to make a pertinent demand (e.g. of a woman for her favours or of an employer for increased wages).

raw prawn, come the, to attempt to deceive or hoodwink (someone).

scratching, to be, to be in difficulty.

shagger's back, a painful ache in the back.

silly as a stunned mullet, extremely silly or stupid.

smack on a blue, to be responsible for a fight or dispute.

snout on, have a, to dislike, to maltreat.

sort (someone) out, to reprove a person, to put him in his place, sometimes by fisticuffs.

strife, be in, to be in trouble, "in the doghouse".

surl, in a, to be angry, ill-humoured.

take a piece out of, to reprove, "tell off" (someone).

take the knock on, to avoid or reject responsibility, e.g. for a debt.

tie one on, to provoke a fight.

tiger, on the, (of a man) in pursuit of feminine companionship; on a drinking bout. In fighting parlance a man is sometimes said to be *a tiger for punishment;* a task or undertaking which makes heavy demands is said to appeal to someone who is a *tiger for punishment.*

tin, bash (or *beat* or *belt*) *a,* to boast.

weight's right! all arrangements have been made!

work (something) *back,* to return something to its rightful place, either overtly or furtively.

you reckon? Is that what you think?

you're too right! you're quite right! usually used ironically. An elaboration of the Australian *too right!* yes, of course, certainly.

A fairly recent development has been the emergence of what is called *Strine,* a name given to verbal distortions recorded in Australia. In essence, it concerns variant forms of Australian pronunciation, less as scientific records than as occasions for highbrow "send-ups". I will examine its nature and peculiar import in Chapter XXII.

3. MEN AT WORK

ONE OF THE DIFFICULTIES one faces when offering a survey of craft slang is how far to go. There is probably not a single craft in Australia that has not developed some jargon of its own. We saw some part of this much earlier when looking into the slang of sheepmen, cattlemen, horsemen and so on. There is this difference: Whereas Australia as a whole had had long acquaintance of our main primary industries, craft jargons (basically city products) are so specialized that they have little meaning to outsiders.

If this generalization should be doubted I recommend for inspection the Commonwealth Census bulletins devoted to analysing the occupational groups in Australia. Here are some of the occupations we pursue: *bottle sighter, bar charger, swager, whizzerman, backer-up, breaker-off, can reclaimer, cracker, doffer, gut runner, hat bumper, heaver-over, junction slicker, taker-off* and *throwster.*

When a census was held in Britain in 1931, about 35,000 different types of jobs were listed. By eliminating complexities in classification, Australia's census officials have reduced the Australian total to about 3,000 different jobs. One of the classifications is "Hands", e.g. *backwash hand, jolly hand, pot hand, slag hand, Willey room hand.* "Labouring Occupations" include the *ice cart offsider, motor boy, rock chopper, tipman* and *water bailer.* "Farm Workers" include the *banana chipper, bunchy top detector, carrot digger* and *property conductor.* Clerical workers include the *time study man, estimator* and *progressman.* Men who work in Australia's mines include the *boodler, bratticer, braceman's offsider, flatter, onsetter, platman* and *stoper.* General workers include the *scutcher, rumbler, banksman* and *digester.*

To elucidate a few samples: the *scutcher* is a textile worker, whose job is to operate a machine that dresses wool and other fibres by beating; the *rumbler* helps in making nails; a *banksman* works in the mining industry; a *digester* works in a paper mill. If we are familiar with bulldozers we might expect that a *bulldozerman* would be a man who drives one of these machines.

But he is not. He works in the blacksmith's trade. A *planker* is not a carpenter's assistant, but a millinery worker. So are the *bodymaker* and the *hatformer*. *Screeners* and *viewers* have nothing to do with the film industry. A *screener* works in a mine; a *viewer* is an aircraft inspector. An *earbasher* is not necessarily a tiresome talker; this is a craft name given to a man who knocks out the *ears* on overhead wires.

A little earlier I recorded the word *bratticer*. This is a mining term. A *brattice* is hessian used in a mine to divert air for ventilation. A *bratticer* or *bratticeman* is a worker who erects or looks after this means of ventilation. Another highly important word for coalminers is *darg*, a fixed or limited quantity of output or labour (a term which has well-established English antecedents). Miners also give a specialized sense to the word *back* – meaning alternate, as in the phrase "working back Saturdays". They also have a craft meaning for the word *stump;* it is the place, perhaps a cabin, shed or room, where all union dues are paid – a name allegedly dating from days when a mining lodge secretary took up his position at a tree stump to collect dues.

Long existence of a craft does not necessarily result in its jargon becoming known to the general public. Here, for example, are some expressions used by tailors, all apparently, but by no means certainly, indigenous; *to do a bake*, to do work at home; *cat's face*, a small business opened by a journeyman tailor; *to chance one's wing*, to speak uncertainly, to make a shot in the dark; *jack the ripper*, a worthless type of person; *to have one's sleeveline twisted*, to be in difficulties; *can you spare the boot?* will you lend me some money?; *someone's staytape is uneven*, a person is dishonest or underhand in his activities; *tiger*, an apprentice; *wrong way of the charley*, (used of tweed cloth) on the bias.

Probably few people have heard these terms before. In the same way we find newspaper workers using expressions that are unknown to the public at large; *grass*, a temporary hand on a printing staff; *dinkus*, a small drawn illustration to break up an article; *tibby*, a paper of magazine size (probably from the dialectal *tibby*, a term of endearment or diminutive); *bullring*, *cage*, *stonehand*, *slugger* and *bulk*, all of which have specialized industrial meanings; *snuff box* and *stiff box*, a newspaper morgue; *Canberra Circus*, reporters who cover the Federal Parliament; *Hansard hangover*, exhaustion suffered by Hansard reporters.

A waterfront term of fairly recent origin is *sniper*, a non-union labourer. *Pirate* is used similarly. Other terms from the waterfront: *panno* (short for *pannikin boss*), a foreman; *delo*, a union delegate; *midnighter*, a wharflabourer on double time; *disso*, a wharfie suffering from disability or advanced age, who is fit only for wharf not ship work; *vet*, a man over 65 who works irregularly; *floater* or *blood donor*, workers who supplement gangs as needed; *bull*, a company man who gave a bribe (or *sling*) to a foreman to secure work; *bull system*, a system whereby company men secured work by bribery (displaced by a rotary gang system); *scramble*, to battle for a job under the *bull system;* *Long Servile Leave*, the wharflabourer's ironical reference to his long service leave; *dark 'uns*, 24-hour stints which wharfies once had to face;

louse house, the union rooms of the Waterside Workers' Federation in Sydney.

In Trades Hall jargon a *bell-wether* is a unionist who leads a return to work when men are resisting union instructions to end a strike. A *tombstone* is a union vote recorded in the name of a dead man. *To get a bung* means to lose pay for being late. A job is a *start;* to find work is *to spear* or *harpoon a job; to get the hunt, spear, run, push, shunt, jerk, hunt* or *wallop* is to be dismissed from a job; *to jack the contract, to snatch it, to snatch one's time* is to leave a job voluntarily.

From dockyard workers: *bilge-diving*, cleaning a ship's bilges in dock; *tail-end job*, any work on propellors, stern tubes and tailshafts; *back-end job*, work on the back tube plate in a marine boiler; *cooking*, the heating of rivets in portable forges for use in ship construction and repair; *seagull*, a man who does the finer interior painting in a ship (perhaps from the white boiler suit worn, but influenced by the white paint used).

From taxi drivers: *high flagging*, picking up a customer and leaving the taxi "flag" up, thereby not starting the meter; *flea* or *hot plater*, the driver of a car – sometimes fitted with a meter – who illegally plies for hire without official registration, whence *hotplate* or *hotplate car*, such a vehicle; *koala*, a motorist immune from being booked for a parking offence, a "protected creature" such as a diplomat; *jockey*, a person who travels in a taxi with the driver so that unwanted customers can be rejected if they do not look like good prospects, on the fictitious grounds that the taxi is already booked, whence *jockeying*, the practice; *jitneying*, the multiple hiring of a taxi, the carrying of different clients at one time (an Australian adaptation of a U.S. term); *shepherd* or *convoy car*, a vehicle which sometimes accompanies illegal taxi operators to block pursuers. I also have a report from Melbourne of *bottle-oh*, especially used in the phrase *take a bottle-oh*, to denote a break from duties by a taxi driver for his own purposes.

Here, now, is an assortment: *spiff*, a bonus paid to shop assistants in a department store for the sale of slow-moving articles, whence such derivatives as *spiff-suit*, a suit on which a selling bonus will be paid, *spiff-hat*, etc.; *buttinski*, a term used among telephone mechanics for the hand telephone used for cutting in on private phone calls; *boodle*, to clean out train or tram rails, whence *boodler*, a man who does this work, and *boodling*, the task itself; *preparator*, a worker in a museum who makes plaster, latex or plastic models of fish, animals, etc., for exhibition; *prem, premmie* or *premmo*, hospital terms for a premature baby; *slunge*, a hospital room where bed pans are washed; *slit*, (an inventor's term) to beat a competitor in placing an invention on the market, especially used intransitively, i.e. *slitted*, beaten; *kelly*, a tram or omnibus inspector; *troub*, a member of a tram crew (*trammie*, used similarly, *bussie*, a member of a bus crew, and *connie*, a conductor, are also used); *retread*, a schoolteachers' word for a teacher who has been recalled to duty from retirement; *whizzbang* or *switchpull*, an application of electric shock in the treatment of certain mental disorders, whence *switchpuller*, a doctor who officiates in such treatment, to which can be added *hoon*, an assistant to a doctor in such treatment, usually a wardsman; *his hand was trembling*, said of someone who is overpaid for his work; *you should have been here this morning!* said to someone who is late for work; *did you stay in for a second?* said to someone who is late for work, the implication being that he was delayed by an amatory matter; *get-ups* and *twirlies*, the number of mornings ahead before annual holidays, i.e. the number of times one will have to "get up" or arise "too early"; *to sweat off*, to go slow or mark time in one's work; *bogger* or *nipper-bogger*, a man who catches so-called *nippers* or snapping prawns, which grow to more than 2 in. long and are prized for bait by fishermen; whence *nipper-bogging*, such work, also known as *splodging*, and *to bog nippers; guttersnap*, a street photographer; *warb*, a circus labourer; *snake-charmers*, *snakes* or *lizards*, railway platelayers; *dog-spike*, a heavy nail which spikes a rail to a sleeper; *pigs'-feet*, a heavy claw-hammer used to pull out dog-spikes; *black coat*, a hotel waiter, and *to flog a floor*, to be a floor steward in any hotel, club or restaurant; *tuberculars*, men who construct tube-steel scaffolding; *chin* or *bluechin*, an actor; *lightning jerker* or *lightning squirter*, a telegraph operator; *scooter*, wool storemen's name for a hand truck.

Practically all these terms are ancillary to true craft slang, though by no means divorced from it. They give some idea of the vastness of this linguistic field.

Although the days of hansom cabs and cabmen are far behind us, several Australianisms that developed round that profession are still current. *Duck-shoving*, used in modern times to describe political wire-pulling and unscrupulousness in general, had its origin in Melbourne cabmen's slang in the late 1860s. *To duck-shove* (in these times we often abbreviate the verb to *shove*) meant to gain an unfair advantage over a fellow workman by breaking into a cab rank ahead of him. Anyone who pushes in ahead of others or usurps their rights is said to *duck-shove;* it has also been used to describe petty thievery and cheating. *Touching off*, *gagging* and *plumming* were other old terms. *Touching off* was once the Sydney equivalent of *duck-shoving; gagging* meant touting for fares in the city streets by cabmen (a forbidden practice); and *plumming* was the practice adopted by *plummers* – i.e. men who possessed cabmen's licences but no vehicles – who *did a mind* for a regular driver.

Another old survival is *robbo*, which was used in Sydney seventy years ago to denote a sulky. It was derived from a man named Robinson, who hired out horses and traps for 4s. a half-day. He acquired the nickname *Four Bob Robbo*, which was eventually transferred to the vehicle. A writer in the "Bulletin" of January 23, 1897, also declared: "*Robbo* has, in an extensive Sydney circle, come to mean anything unsatisfactory."

It might be thought that an expression of this nature would be doomed to an early death, if only for the reason that sulkies are now rarely seen. But it appears again in Kylie Tennant's "Foveaux" (1939) in which she provides the story:

> There was old Bert Robinson – God-rest-his-soul – 'e's gorn now, poor fellow. Ever heard of Bert Robinson? No, I don't suppose you would. 'E kept a livery stable down at the Foot. I s'pose you've 'eard of the Four-bob Robbos, then? The chaps used to go an' hire a cart for four bob and take

it round loaded with vegetables. The kids used to call after 'em, "Four Bob Robbo, Four Bob Robbo!" Old Bob Noblett, 'e's an old man now, but I can remember when Bob Noblett was a four-bob robbo.

Although scarcely entitled to be called craft slang the following terms used by consumptives are worth noting as jargon from a highly specialized group; *mike* or *wog*, a consumptive; *mikes*, T.B. microbes; *mikehouse*, a T.B. sanatorium; *blow* or *squirt*, a haemorrhage; *fill*, artificial pneumo-thorax, i.e. the injection of air into a lung; *poso*, sputum which still has positive T.B. infection, e.g. *to spit poso*, *to be poso*, to be consumptive.

CHAPTER XI

Pastimes and Pleasures

1. DRINKING

AUSTRALIANS have always been enthusiastic if not particularly intelligent drinkers. Admittedly, there have been some good reasons. History has told us so much about the old rum days, about vast thirsts acquired by diggers during the gold rushes,[1] about wild life in outback shanties and about the enthusiasm with which the average Australian regards a pot of beer that the picture has been clouded by a good deal of half-truth. Instead of looking back on our past as a continual riot of drinking, we should see it rather as a series of alcoholic spasms. Actually none of them has been as collectively dedicated to strong waters as the period of affluence which followed World War II. In the brief passage of time between mid-1939 and now, our population has grown by about 63 per cent.; in the same period, our consumption of beer and wines has jumped 200 per cent. and our consumption of spirits only slightly less. A report from the Brewers' Society of Britain in 1964 said that we had become the world's third largest beer drinkers (after Belgium and West Germany).

Of course, at various times, we had a good deal of practice in preparing ourselves for such distinction. In 1819, for instance, G. W. Evans wrote in "A Description of Van Diemen's Land" that *grog fever* was "the only prevailing disease in the colony". Nearly seventy years later R. E. N. Twopeny ("Town Life in Australia", 1883) gave this grim picture:

> The quantity of spirits drunk in Australia is appalling . . . And what about drunkenness? Statistically it is not very much worse than England, but the difference lies in the class who get drunk. Here it is not merely the lower classes, but everybody that drinks. Not a few of the wealthiest and most leading citizens are well-known to be frequently drunk, though their names do not, of course, appear in the papers or in the police reports. The state of public feeling on the subject, though improving, is much as it was in England twenty or thirty years ago. Society says, "Capital fellow, Jones; pity he drinks!" but no social reprobation attaches to Jones.

The public attitude may not have changed greatly in the past eighty years, but the point to be stressed is this: If drunkenness appears to have been prevalent in Australia, it is less because of excessive drinking than because of insane licensing laws which, until the most recent times, have made people drink hurriedly and in discomfort; which have made hotel bars places for guzzling liquor in haste and not places where men could

---

[1] Of those days a writer in 1857 used the expression *colonial disease* to describe "the human rot arising from the excessive use of ardent spirits".

sit and drink leisurely; which gave men half an hour or an hour at the most between the time they ceased their day's work and the time hotels were closed (known as the *six o'clock swill*); which sent them out into the streets clutching a quart of fortified wine so that a bad job could be finished off quickly with even worse results.

I mention these points because they are reflected in some measure in our drinking vocabulary. There is a heavy accent on expressions for types of liquor which no educated drinker, in reasonable possession of his faculties, would think of consuming. It is some relief to note that, since the first edition of this book was published, drinking hours have been extended in New South Wales and Victoria from 6 p.m. to 10 p.m. and many licenced clubs have been established – without increased drunkenness. (In all other parts of the Commonwealth except South Australia the closing hour is also 10 p.m.)

Australia is capable of producing excellent wines, yet of these the average member of the public knows little. Often his acquaintance extends no further than port, sherry and muscat – heavy drinks, often fortified, sold cheaply, an easy means of getting drunk quickly and at a minimum of expense – and, as some indication of our oenological barbarity, various fizzy drinks including a concoction called sparkling sweet sherry.

Here is a group of indigenous terms used to describe cheap wines: *Africa speaks, bombo,*[2] *Clever Mary,*[3] *corroboree water, ink, lunatic soup, bagman's blood, nelly, nelly's death, paint, plonk,*[4] *madman's broth, plink* (described as cheap plonk), *red, red Ned,*[5] *scarlet runner, steam, hen wine* (one "lays" where one drinks it), *sneaky pete* – and *fourpenny dark*, although inflation has long since eliminated it from the lures offered by wine saloons. The original *fourpenny dark* was served in a miniature mug with a handle and a saying went: *Around the world for fourpence!*

Addicts of cheap wine are known variously as *winedots* (a play on Wyandottes, domestic fowls of a U.S. breed), *plonkdots, plonkos, plonkies, plonk fiends* (or *artists* or *merchants*), *bombos, bombo-bashers, darkies* (addicts of *fourpenny darks*, but surviving its eclipse), *bunches of grapes* and *muscateers*. It is symptomatic of our lack of knowledge of the subject that almost the only Australian expression that can be used to refer to good wine is the familiarism *clarrie wine* for claret, which appeared in the 1950s. *Pig* is used for a demijohn containing bulk wine.

The difference between methylated spirits and some cheap wine is (or was) not great. To which end it is worth quoting this comment by a writer in the "Bulletin" of January 21, 1882, when dealing with "the Sydney

---

2   Perhaps related to the Aboriginal *bombo*, thunder, but more likely from the eighteenth-century *bumbo* or *bombo*, a drink made of rum, sugar and water.

3   From the name of a well-known household cleanser, "because after drinking it a man goes home and cleans up the house"!

4   Apparently originally a digger corruption of *vin blanc* from World War I. Another corruption of similar type, noted by Downing in "Digger Dialects", was *mazonk*, for mademoiselle. There was a time in South Australia when *plonk* was used to denote "any strong drink"; this was doubtless in deference to the fact that S.A. is the main Australian State for wine-growing.

5   English slang has *red biddy* for cheap red wine.

acceptation of the term *sherry*" : "The greater part of the sherry out here [i.e. in Australia] is composed of methylated spirits, furniture polish and rosin." Fortunately, sherry these days is a great deal better than this.

However, methylated spirits have featured rather extensively in the habits of certain drinkers. Here are some drinks in which methylated spirits feature: *bidgee, pinky, Fitzroy cocktail, Domain cocktail, Domain special* and *white lady*. There are other methylated spirits concoctions which do not seem to have well-defined names. Here is a group of recipes as published by an outback newspaper in 1936:

(a) Methylated spirits, cloves and a little camphor.
(b) Methylated spirits, ginger beer and a teaspoon of bootpolish. (This is the *Fitzroy* or *Domain cocktail*. In Queensland a mixture of methylated spirits, tan bootpolish and Condy's crystals or bluestone is called *Banyan rum*.)
(c) Methylated spirits and Condy's crystals. (*Pinky.*)
(d) Methylated spirits, water and cayenne pepper.
(e) Methylated spirits and ammonia. (*White lady.*)
(f) Methylated spirits, ginger ale and benzine.
(g) Methylated spirits and cheap wine (half and half), tablespoon bootpolish, raisins, a little sugar and water; tobacco if desired to make extra "tasty" and quick acting. (*Bidgee.*)

Addicts of these noxious drinks are known as *meths, methos, metho artists* and *pinkeyes*. As a form of beverage, methylated spirits is called *jumpabout, musical nook* and *dancing girl*.

Banyan rum, noted above, was probably named after Banyan creek, which runs through Tully, north Queensland. Less lethal, but hardly less peculiar so far as its ingredients are concerned is another Queensland beverage called the *Diamantina cocktail;* it is compounded of a pint of condensed milk, a pint of Bundaberg rum and a well-beaten emu egg. This is not to be confused with the *Puckapunyal cocktail*, a drink allegedly compounded of metal polish, gin, vinegar and wine (named after Puckapunyal military camp) or the *Normanton cocktail*, a gin and two blankets! While on the subject of Queensland, a slight genuflection can be made in the direction of the *Queensland mystery*, a drink of gin in milk, the *Burketown mosquito net*, a state of drunkenness which renders a sleeper indifferent to mosquito bites, and the *Paroo sandwich*, a drink of beer and wine.

Rum is known variously as *blackfellow's delight, cocky's joy* and *whip*. Gin is sometimes called *parson's wife* – derived from the name of a manufacturer, Vickers ("vicar's"), and gin, an Aboriginal female. Whence doubtless the use of *bush girlfriend* for a gin. A *sputnik* (recorded in 1959) is a mixture of vodka, whisky and soft drink; *ruptured rooster* is a mixture of cherry brandy, advocaat and soda; *western wobbly* is a mixture of advocaat, Scotch whisky, gin, bitters and soda or ginger ale.

Strong drink is known variously as *jollop, fixing, tiger's milk, panther's p**s, shellshock, snakejuice* and *stagger-juice*.

Illicit whisky, as made in stills in bush areas, is known as *mountain dew,*

This is a variation of the standard English use of the term for genuine Scotch whisky. It is also used in America.

Southerly buster is a name given to a mixed drink in which whisky features; a *nor'-wester* is a stiff drink of brandy; a *barmaid's blush* or *maiden's blush* is described as either a drink of port and lemonade or a drink of rum and raspberry. Among shearers, the name *Brindabella* is given to "a half-pannikin slug of rum followed by a bottle of beer."

Some minor dispute exists whether *John Collins*, a drink of gin, soda-water, sugar, lemon and ice, is originally American or Australian. The first printed use of the expression was, according to the "Oxford Dictionary", in the "Australasian" of February 24, 1865. H. L. Mencken claims it as definitely American.

A *Scotch naked* is a Scotch whisky with nothing added. *Water with a coat on* is ice in whisky.

A stiff drink of spirits of whatever kind is a *rosner* or *rozner* or *rosiner* or *roziner*. This has been extended to denote any person or thing of excellence.

One of the first glossaries of Australian drinking slang was collected by F. Fowler in 1859 (published in "Southern Lights and Shadows") and although a good deal of it has long since become obsolete it is worth recalling. Here is his list:

> *Catherine Hayes*, claret, sugar and nutmeg.
> *Lola Montez*, rum, ginger, lemon and hot water.
> *Madame Bishop*, port, sugar and nutmeg. (*Bishop* was in English use for a warm drink of wine, with sugar and orange or lemon juice.)
> *constitutional*, gin and bitters.
> *maiden*, peppermint or cloves.
> *sensation*, a half-glass of sherry.
> *smash*, brandy, ice and water.
> *spider*, brandy and lemonade. (Later used for a drink of ice-cream and lemonade; often *Gunn's Gully spider*.)
> *Band of Hope*, lemon syrup.
> *stone fence*, ginger beer and brandy. (An 1850 definition was given as ale and ginger beer.)

The Misses Hayes and Montez and Madame Bishop were stage personalities who visited Australia in gold-digging days.

Nobbler for a small drink of beer, spirits or wine also came into prominence in those times, being first recorded in 1852. A nobbler was defined under National Security Regulations as one-fifth of a gill, or one ounce, but it is not defined in the Weights and Measures Act. The word acquired verbal forms *to nobblerize* (1864) and *nobblerizing* (1868). Morris suggests that it is derived from "that which nobbles or gets hold of you".

Some more old terms which have become defunct are *colonial*, *colonial tangle*, *jerrawicke*, *she-oak*[6] and *squirt* for beer. According to legend, beer

---

[6] D. M. Gane, "New South Wales and Victoria" (1886), said that a *she-oak net* was "a life preserving net which Victorian authorities have thought it wise to have slung under the gangways of every ship which is moored to the Melbourne wharves". The association is, of

originally made with artesian water at Sale, Gippsland, was called *artesian*, but it is doubtful whether such beer would have been fit to drink.

Additional terms for beer include *sheep wash, stringybark,*[7] *shearer's joy, ketchup* and *catch up, lube* and *shypoo.* The last is a Western Australian word, which also appears in *shypoo joint*, a hotel. It has developed in eastern States to *shypook*, a sly-grog shop, and in North Queensland to *shaboo shop*, a hotel.

To fetch beer from a hotel is *to run the rabbit*, the word *rabbit* sometimes being used to describe a bottle of beer. In the Northern Territory a bottle of beer is called *a black shirt*.

Since Australian drinkers are often at considerable pains to distinguish between *new beer* and *old beer*, it can be pointed out that the former is beer made in European style with bottom fermentation and is lighter and sweeter than *old beer. Old beer* is English-style top fermentation beer.

Whether new or old, a beer (also a wine) that meets with the drinker's approval is a *good drop* or *not a bad drop*.

If there is a moderate sort of unanimity on such matters, there is an extraordinary lack of unanimity between the States over popular names given to various measures of beer. In Melbourne, for example, the smallest measure (4 oz.) is called a *pixie* or *small beer;* in Brisbane, a *small beer* is 5 oz. and is called a *five*, a *pony* or a *lady's waist* (the last two are almost obsolete); in Sydney a 5 oz. measure is called a *pony*, a *glass* and a *lady's waist* (the last is almost obsolete); in Perth the 5 oz. measure is also a *glass*, but in Adelaide it is a *butcher*. On the other hand a *glass* in Brisbane is 8 oz., which in Perth is a *middy*, but the Sydney *middy* is 10 oz. In Brisbane and Sydney, 7 oz. measures are *sevens*, but in Perth clubs the nearest measures (6 oz.) are *bobbies*. I hesitate to go on, if only in an effort to preserve what little sanity I have left. Names given to other measures in the various States are *schooner,*[8] *cruiser, pot* and *handle*.

At various times we have used several other popular terms to denote measures of beer: *tidal wave, war cry, sleever,*[9] *long sleever, long sleeved 'un, deep sinker, gelding* and *spinnaker*. A correspondent recalls the use of *silo* for a pint of beer among wheat lumpers at Barellan, N.S.W.

An extremely old word associated with Sydney was *Bishop Barker* used for a large glass of beer. The "Bulletin" of January 9, 1892, defined it as the largest drink of beer obtainable, and derived it from the tallness of Primate Barker who was consecrated to the Sydney See in 1854.

Here, now, is a group of expressions used to describe various forms of (mainly masculine) conduct involved in drinking bouts: *get a drink across one's chest* or *stop one*, to have a drink; *quickie*, a rapidly-consumed drink; *coupla*, two or more drinks; *drop of the doings* (or *needle*), a drink; *whack down*

---

course, with the beer. There is some reason to suspect that a mutilation of *she-oak* may have given us *shickered*, drunk. The New Zealand use of *titoki* for a shandygaff has probably been affected by the Australian *she-oak*. Both the *she-oak* and *titoki* are trees.

[7] Also applied to bad whisky in the 1880s, a writer of the period giving the recipe as "fusil oil and turpentine".

[8] This was originally U.S. slang.

[9] From English dialect wherein it signified a drink of about three-quarters of a pint of beer.

the grog, grog on, lay (or *get*) *into it,* to drink heavily; *one for the bitumen* (or *gutter*), a final drink, "one for the road"; *to spit chips,* to feel in urgent need of a drink; *leg-opener,* an alcoholic drink, or a series of them, given by a man to a female companion to induce sexual submissiveness; *be in the chair,* to be the person who pays for the next round of drinks (the pertinent question is often *Who's in the chair?*); *to sneeze, to carry the mail* and *to stand one's hand,* to stand treat; such suggestions as *kick the tin, hit the can, hit the deck* and *hit your sky* (from *skyrocket,* a rhyme on pocket) to the person who is due to buy drinks, and such crisp pieces of advice to the prospective buyer as *your belt! your bowl! your bounce! your blow! your dip! your dive! your drop! your hook! your shake! your shout! your shy! your strike!* and *your throw!*

The verb *to shout* first came into use in gold rush days. It was apparently derived from shouting for attention at a bar. Within a short time it had developed into a noun, the original *shout* being a drink that was purchased for another person. In the past century we have put the term to many uses that are not associated with the original drinking sense. For instance, we can *shout* a friend to the pictures, or *shout* him a packet of cigarettes, and in both cases we can do so without expecting anything in return. *Shouter, shoutee* and *shouting* are natural derivatives.

We have many versions of the shout, such as the *American shout, Yankee shout* (we also call it a *Yank* or *Yankee*), *a Scotch shout, Chinaman's shout* and *Dutch shout,* the last, of course, being an Australian version of the English *Dutch treat.* The cant phrase, *going to shout?* used as a greeting, can also be noted. A *captain* is a man who is lavish in shouting for others, a *scratch drinker* is one who drinks only occasionally, and a *dry hash* (now obsolete) or *Jimmy Woodser* is a man who declines to shout and prefers to indulge in what the Australians regard as an objectionable habit – *drinking with the flies.* We will return to *Jimmy Woodser* later.

Australians have a fair selection of terms to describe drinking and drinking bouts, such as *session, rort, beer-up, booze-up, break-out, drunk-up, grog-up, jamberoo, jollo, perisher, shivoo, shivaroo, to go on the scoot* (or *on the squiff, stun* or *a tank*), *to tip the little finger, to swamp* (to spend money on liquor) and *to bash the turps.*

Drunks in general are known in Australian parlance as *beer swipers, booze artists, booze hounds, booze kings, boozicians, boozingtons, caterpillars, leanaways, slurks, tids, swippingtons, jobs, lolly legs, shicks* and *shickers.* To these, of course, should be added some of the wine-drinking terms noted earlier: *wine-dots, plonk-dots,* etc.

A man who is drunk is said to be *blithered, blue, on his ear, plonked up, grogged up, rotten, molo, molly, stinko, full as a goog* (or *egg, bull's bum, fart, boot, tick* or *State school*), *half-rinsed, half-cut, snockered, inked, inkypoo, mastok, out to it, paralytic,*[10] *pinko, shick, shickered, stung, shot full of holes, drunk as a bastard, drunk as Chloe,*[11] *drunk as an owl* or *fowl, unable to scratch himself,*

---

[10] In English slang from 1910, says Partridge. Recorded in Australia in 1890.

[11] The origin is obscure. Perhaps simply by rhyme from the English *drunk as Floey.* The painting of Chloe in Young and Jackson's Hotel, Melbourne, may have helped to preserve the Australian expression, but had nothing to do with originating it.

in the grip of the grape and *drunk as a piss ant.*

Some localized samples: *M.B.* or *to suffer from M.B.* (the initials represent Melbourne Bitter) and *gone to Gowings* (Gowing Bros. Ltd. is the name of a Sydney firm). All mean drunk.

Dingbats for delirium tremens is also Australian.

When Morris's "Austral English" came under review, the "Bulletin" of December 18, 1897, noted that while the author had provided the note, "In Australia, the word *inn* is now rare, the word *hotel* has supplanted it", he had included no mention of the *pub*, which, said the "Bulletin", "is practically the only bush term in current use". The fact that *pub* is in wide Australian use does not, however, make it indigenous; it was originally English. But we have obviously taken it to heart since the forms *rubby*, *rubbity* and *rubberdy*, a hotel, have all come from *pub*, via the rhyme *rub-a-dub-dub*. Towards the end of last century, public houses also served as a loose measure of a settlement's size, e.g. *ten-pub town, eighteen-pub town* and so on.

One of the most important institutions of early outback days was the *bush shanty*, often a tumbledown hut where liquor was sold illegally. It owed a good deal of its early prosperity to gold rush days, and from it was derived the verb *to shanty*, to drink habitually at a public house. *Shanty-keeper* is recorded in 1875.

Sly-grog, for liquor sold illegally, is also Australian, as are its derivatives *sly-grog (shop), sly-groggery, sly-grog seller* and *sly-grogger*. Carboni Raffaello refers several times in "The Eureka Stockade" (1885) to *sly-grog sellers* and *sly-grog tents*.

Two more expressive terms for outback drinking dens were *poison shop* and *lambing down shop. To lamb down* meant to spend money lavishly on drink or to encourage such lavish spending, the latter being a practice in which some shanty-keepers (they were also called *lambers down*) frequently indulged. Before railways were built and when towns were difficult to reach, many a bushman went to a bush pub with a cheque that represented a year's wages or a bag of gold that had taken months to collect. He would hand this across the bar and tell the publican to inform him when it was finished. He would then be blind drunk for several days – or weeks – after which the publican would tell him that his cheque or gold was exhausted and turn him out. The man was said to have been *lambed down* by the publican if he had been treated unfairly.

The last act of *knocking down* a cheque was what Boldrewood described in "The Crooked Stick" (1895) as "a rather old-fashioned bush pleasantry", *to jump one's horse over the bar*. This was done when the drinker, after exhausting his cheque, mortgaged or sold his horse to the publican. When this ritual had been observed the only thing left to do was for the bushman *to take water* – to leave the hotel penniless.

A *blind tiger* (note the use of *tiger's milk* for strong drink, recorded earlier) is a bush store which sells liquor without a licence.

To tie up a dog or *to chain up a pup* are other phrases of wide rural use. They mean "to obtain drinks on credit". As a result, an unpaid score is called *a mad dog* or it is said that *the dogs are barking*.

Here is portion of an advertisement inserted in the Bathurst "National Advocate" in 1937 by a licensee who was leaving his hotel:

> He particularly requests that all dogs tied up at the hotel be released. This reservation specially applies to Kelpies, Alsatians and other large breeds.

The reference was solely to drinking debts. We have seen previously that to *dob in* means to betray (someone); there is a special use of *dob down* to mean putting the cost of drinks "on the slate".

A hotel where fights are common is called a *blood house;* a hotel (especially in Victoria and South Australia) where drinking conditions are poor is a *swillery*. When a hotel (or club) is raided by police for permitting after-hours drinking or gambling, it is said to *go off*. (A man can be said to *go off* when he marries.) To close a hotel is to *put the lid on it*.

Worth noting is the fact that most Australian hotels have what are called *lazarettes*. These are places from which drinks are served to the waiters or waitresses who attend lounge customers. Here is a good example of what can occur to a word when it is plucked out of one environment and twisted to serve the demands of another environment. According to the "Oxford Dictionary", the name *lazaretto* was given originally about 1711 to "a space between decks, in some merchant vessels, used as a storeroom". Apparently we purloined the word (and changed its spelling) from old sailing ships.

Hotel and club stewards or bar tenders have an argot of their own: *one up*, *lily* or *lily of Laguna* (rhyming slang) for schooner; *one down*, a middy; *two bobs worth*, half beer, half stout; *splash*, lemonade, as in *beer with a splash; green*, green ginger, as in *beer and green; ras*, raspberry, as in *beer and ras; sarse*, sarsaparilla, as in *beer and sarse; giggle juice* and *stingo*, wine (the last adapted from English slang *stingo*, strong ale or beer); *a king-sized tray of the widow-maker*, a large tray of drinks; *a mother-in-law*, a drink of stout and bitters.

Brief records can be made of *breakdown*, a small measure of spirits, *alleviator*, any drink of liquor, *a friendly pannikin*, a drink with a companion. These are now virtually obsolete. So is the wartime invention, *Lady Blamey*, for an improvised drinking vessel made from a beer bottle with the neck cut off, named after the wife of Field Marshal Sir Thomas Blamey.

Jimmy Woodser is an interesting Australianism about which there has been a good deal of guesswork and little conclusive evidence. There was not, for instance, a man named Jimmy Woods who became renowned for his lone drinking habits.[12] But there was, according to a record of about 1882,[13] an old Sydney expression *Johnny Warder* used for "an idle drunkard

---

[12] This in spite of the fact that in the "Bulletin" of May 7, 1892, there appears a poem by B. H. Boake entitled "Jimmy Wood" and at the end there is a footnote: "A man who drinks by himself is said to *take a Jimmy Woodser*."

[13] "The Detectives' Handbook" (anon.).

who hangs about pub corners looking for a drink (called after a publican named John Ward who formerly kept a low house in Sydney noted for that species)".

This may explain why we sometimes have the alternative form, *Johnny Woodser*. (Probably related to this is the expression *Johnny Warby*, which Ernestine Hill has recorded in the Northern Territory for a tall tale.)

In the "Bulletin" of August 9, 1902, a staff writer offered the following note to explain the term:

> One yarn is that Jimmy Woods used to always drink by himself; another that a man wanting to drink by himself asked an imaginary Jimmy Woods to come and drink with him.

These are more in the nature of stories concocted after the event than genuine explanations. It is a little sad to have to record that the expression *Jimmy Woodser* is now almost obsolete; many of today's young drinkers have never heard the name.

A *Jimmy Woodser* was not only a lone drinker, but also a drink consumed by such a person. We even extended the expression into figurative uses. Thus, in his book of poems "Nine Miles from Gundagai", Jack Moses calls rain that fails to fall during drought a *Jimmy Woodser* and at another place he calls an early morning plunge in the ocean a *Jimmy Woodser*.

A synonym Australia has forgotten is *Jack Smithers*, which was used, especially in outback Queensland, during the 1890s for a lone drinker. The origin is obscure. *To go Ballarat* was another expression with the same meaning current seventy years ago. In the "Bulletin" of July 2, 1892, a writer noted:

> A *Jimmy Woodser* may mean a solitary drink (or a solitary drinker) in some places, a *Jack Smithers* in others, but in the western district of Victoria if a man takes a drink by himself, he is said *to go Ballarat*.

Just as the *shout* is an institution in this part of the world so are the *bob in*, *two bob in*, *chuck in*, *whip round*, *Tambaroora muster* and a few other variations on the theme, all of which concern the creation of a jack-pot, usually with the object of buying drinks. The *Tambaroora* – taken from the name of an eastern township – dates from the early 1880s. The idea behind these expressions, as behind the *Yankee shout* and others listed earlier, is that everyone pays for himself. However, the *Tambaroora* meant a little more than this. In far-off days when beer was only about sixpence a mug, a number of men drinking together used to put in a shilling each, write their names on slips of paper and drop them in a hat, and the man whose name was on the first slip drawn shouted and pocketed the remainder.

Bar games which also have as their object the creation of a jack-pot – although they allow the winner to pocket a surplus – are *up-and-down*, *selling a horse*, *Yankee grab* and the *Hokitika swindle*, the last of which hails from New Zealand. An old game played in bush pubs was *selling the crow*, and was generally at the expense of a newcomer to a drinking school. The name of a bird was written on a sheet of paper for each drinker as he put in his money – in this case less than the cost of a drink. This paper was then cut into strips, but other strips, each bearing the word "crow", were substituted and put in the hat. The newcomer was given first choice, naturally "bought the crow" and had to shout.

Indigenous toasts are: *here's looking up your kilts! here's lead in your pencil! down the gully!* and *here's to 'ee!* (the last taken from an advertising slogan used by the makers of Toohey's beer, Sydney).

As we get near the end of this Section, here are a few general expressions in our drinking vocabulary: *gigglestick*, a stick or spoon used to stir a mixed alcoholic drink; *hip disease*, the practice of carrying a flask of liquor in one's hip pocket; *alcoholic constipation*, an inveterate taste for liquor, inability to "pass" a hotel; *three or four point drinker*, a man "who calls for a 6d. gin with bitters, limejuice and soda" (an expression recorded in 1938, but long since dead); and *here it is!* or *it!* an effectively simple sign, of obvious import to the initiated, to be seen in many Australian bars.

A rare little book entitled "A Commentary on the Influence which the Use of Tobacco Exerts on the Human Constitution", published in Sydney in 1853, speaks with some displeasure of "the insane rage for smoking, so epidemic in this colony". One would suspect from the book's evidence and from other testimonies over the years that Australia would have accumulated a rather extensive vocabulary of smoking slang. Instead of which, due apparently to "insaner rages" in other parts of the world, we have remarkably little to offer.

Our indigenous contributions are: *T.M.* or *African*, a tailor-made cigarette; *twirlie*, *curler* and *quirlie*, a cigarette, either made by hand or machine (*to twist a twirlie* or *twist a burn* means to roll a cigarette); *O.P.*, a borrowed cigarette, i.e. cigarettes from "other people", whence *give up O.P.s*, to give up smoking entirely, not merely to cease borrowing cigarettes; *Robinson Crusoe brand*, a cigarette or cigar butt, i.e. a butt which has been "cast away"; *dufer*, a cigarette which is borrowed, but not smoked, i.e. it will "do for after"; *one for Ron*, a cigarette borrowed for smoking "later on"; *bumper*, a cigarette butt; *bumper shooter*, a person who picks up cigarette ends and *butt stooper*, used similarly; *tissue* (mainly used in Tasmania), a cigarette paper.

2. RACES AND BETTING

THE AUSTRALIAN'S INTEREST in the vagaries of chance, which at the time of writing induces him to invest some $1,800,000,000 a year on gambling, has led him for much more than a century to focus a good deal of attention on horses. It is only to be expected that an extensive horse-racing vocabulary should have developed as a measure of his enthusiasm.

The Cup, run in Melbourne on the first Tuesday of each November, provided that Tuesday does not fall on the first of the month, in which case the next Tuesday is the date chosen, is an annual fanaticism upon which a national daily once saw fit to comment:

> The unique quality of the Melbourne Cup is its national significance. No other event in Australian life so perfectly sums us up – our love of the outdoors, our love of sport, our capacity for enjoying ourselves whole-heartedly and healthily. Technically the Cup is run over a few flat furlongs near Melbourne. Actually it is run across the heart of the Australian people.

Since 1861, nothing (certainly nothing as trivial as wars and economic crises) has prevented the running of the Melbourne Cup. Probably in no other section of the globe is a nation brought to such a unanimous stand-still for its annual four or five minutes. The Cup's grip on Australian imagination is doubtless one of the reasons why we have earlier uses of *book* and *bookie* for a bookmaker than England. *Book* was in Australian use in 1881 – it is from the English slang *book*, the bets taken or the betting book in which they are noted. *Bookie* is to be found in 1884, a year earlier than the "Oxford Dictionary's" first textual record.

Bagswingers, *bookie boys* or *bookie bhoys* and *tommies* are synonyms popular in sporting journals; *ikey* and *ikey Mo* were used similarly during the closing decades of last century.

Fraudulent bookmakers of one kind and another are known as *balancers*, *besters*, *crushers*, *snipers*, *knockers*, *guy-a-whack bookmakers*, *johnnycake bookmakers*, *blackmarketeers* and *bootleg bookmakers* (the last four are virtually obsolete). Here is a quotation from the Sydney "Telegraph" of December 29, 1941, showing that there are other varieties of the species:

> There are *medical* bookmakers, *egg* bookmakers and *nothing under* book-makers. You've all heard their answers when you go up to price a horse.
> The *medical* bookmaker says, "You'll get better."
> The *egg* man says, "I've laid that."
> The *nothing under* bookmaker is the one who won't accept a bet of less than 10/–.

Until the early 1960s, an essential term in the Australian's racing vocabulary was *S.P.* or starting price business, which gave us a number of expressions, such as *S.P. book*, *S.P. joint*, *S.P. betting*. Wartime inventions for off-course transactions included *bootleg betting, betting on the black* and *black market betting*. The specific reason for the extensive eclipse of *S.P.* was the legal introduction of *T.A.B.* (Totalisator Agency Board) shops in various States – Victoria and Western Australia in 1961, Queensland in 1962, New South Wales in 1964.

The adjective *cronk* is another Australian word which has lost a good deal of ground in recent years, although it is not so long since it was used widely to denote anything unsatisfactory. In the early 1890s it was mainly applied to dishonest racing. A horse run to defraud the public was said to be *cronk*. From these applications the word became synonymous with "ill, worthless, out of order", used with equally good effect about persons, animals or objects. Before the close of last century it was also being applied to stolen goods.

Stephens and O'Brien say that the term:

> . . . came into common use during the prizefighting and boxing boom of '89, '90 and '91. Its first use was to describe a boxer who let himself be beaten either wilfully or through lack of training. Its use was extended and a *readied-up* fight – i.e. one of which the result was prearranged – was *cronk*. Its meaning has further widened to mean anything unfair or dishonest; swindling in either sport or business.

To *shunt* a horse is to start it in a race with no intention of letting it win, so that its handicap will be reduced for a future event; to *strike* a horse is to feed it immediately before running; and to *stiffen*[14] a horse, to prevent its doing its best – these are various *cronk* racing practices. A *shunted* horse is called a *waiter*, and a horse set to lose a race is said to be *in the bag*. A ring-in is called a *possum*.

The earlier use of *stumer*, for a bankrupt or defaulter, appears to have been current in the Australian racing or gambling world of the 1890s. It was later applied to any failure. *To come a stumer* meant to crash financially, but one could also be *in a stumer* when one was anxious or worried. English dialect probably had something to do with the origins of these terms: *stomber*, to confuse or confound, and *stummer*, to stumble, may be related. The Australian *stew*, a fight or race the result of which has been arranged, may also have some link with *stumer*.

The *crusher* has already been mentioned. A *crush bet* is a method of betting whereby a backer ensures himself against loss. For instance, if he takes $14 to $2 about a horse and then lays $8 to $2 he will have $6 to nothing. *Crush betting* or *crushing* was declared illegal in Victoria in 1939. *To bet around*, *to bet back* and *to bet off* mean the same as to crush. A *boss crusher* is the organiser of a crush-betting group. A *balancer* is a bookmaker who pays out only the original stake or part of the winnings.

The *all-up bet* and its derivative *all-upper*, a person who backs horses in this fashion, also seem to be originally Australian. To bet *all-up* is to place the winnings and original stake from one race as a bet on a subsequent race, or to place cumulative winnings and stakes on a series of races.

After World War II, the racing enthusiast was introduced to the *quinella* (*bet*). This appears to have been imported from the U.S. and taken originally from betting in Miami on the game jai-alai. Jai-alai is a Mexican version of the Basque game pelota, which also has a form called *quiniela*.

Here is a fairly comprehensive list of expressions favoured by racing and betting men:

> *bad dog*, a betting debt. (The hotel use of *dog*, a drinking bet, was noted in the earlier Section.)
>
> *battler*, a small-time bettor who attempts to live on what he can earn by following horses. (This term is in general use.)

---

[14] English slang uses the adjective *stiff* (it commonly appears as *stiff 'un*) for a horse set to lose a race. In Australia we use the adjective *stiff* to mean penniless, unlucky.

bet like the Watsons, to bet large sums of money (commemorating some noted big bettors named Watson).

bet on the blue (or *Mary Lou* or *nod*), to bet on credit, i.e. without lodging actual money.

bet on the coat, to lodge a dummy bet with a bookmaker in order to induce genuine bettors to invest their money.

big dish, a major betting coup.

big lick, go for the, to seek to make a "killing" on a race.

bit of braille, a racing tip.

blow out, (of gambling odds) to increase in length.

boilover, a win by a long-priced entrant in a horse or greyhound race; a series of such wins at a race meeting.

bomb, dope given to a racehorse. Also *to bomb* (a horse).

brass, to cheat or defraud.

bring back to the field, to prevent a horse wandering or lagging; whence, figuratively, "to cut someone down to size", to discomfort a pretentious person.

come round on the paint, said of a horse on the inside at the turn.

curbstone jockey, a racing tipster.

dagger, a jockey's bag carrier and general helper.

dead bird, a certainty to win a race. (*Dead cert* was originally English.) *to make a dead bird* (of something) means to make sure of it.

don, a speedy horse. (This virtually obsolete word was probably taken from the name of the cricketer Don Bradman.)

down the course, (of a horse) to finish a race unplaced.

drum, to give a tip or official information about a potential winner. (This term has become absorbed in popular slang.) Also, a certainty. Whence, *run a drum,* to perform and win as tipped; *not to get a drum,* to fail badly.

drummer, a racing tipster.

each-way, a bet placed on a horse either for a win or a place.

emu, a race-course lounger who picks up discarded betting and tote tickets in the hope of finding one which has not been cashed. See use of *emu-bobbing* in war slang.

enter calculations, (of a horse) to join the leaders in the field during a race.

fill up, to fix or nobble (a horse).

flute, a whip carried by a jockey.

fork, a jockey.

get beat by an eyelash (or *eyebrow*), said of a horse which is narrowly beaten for a place.

get lost, (of a horse) to finish a race unplaced.

get tossed, to be beaten, to lose one's money on a race.

goer, a horse that is being ridden honestly with the intention of winning; *one-goer affair,* a race in which only one horse is being ridden to win.

go for the doctor, (of a horse) to gallop at great speed in hopes of a win; whence, in other activities, to adopt firm, decisive measures to ensure success, to bet everything possible on a horse in the expectation of making big money.

go off, when a racehorse, trotter or greyhound is "fixed" to win a race or wins unexpectedly it is said to *go off.*

go up, (of a trotter or pacer) to break regular gait.

greenie, a green-coloured pill of dope given to a greyhound.

gutter, the area in front of a totalisator.

hang up, to cease tic-tacing. See *phone, use the*, etc.

head, a well-known racing or betting man.

heads are turned for home, said when the field enters the straight to the finishing post during a race.

hickey hockey, a jockey. (Rhyming slang.)

home and hosed, successfully completed. Presumably said originally of a successful racehorse; later, a figurative expression which records any successful activity.

hook up a horse, to prevent a horse from winning, especially the "pulling" of a horse by a jockey.

hoop, a jockey.

jinker, a trotting or pacing gig.

killing, a major betting coup.

knock on, take the, (of a bookmaker) to welsh. Such a bookmaker is a *knocker*. A synonym for *take the knock* is *take the olly*, which is extracted from the rhyme *hollyhock*. A horse of great likely success is sometimes called a *knock-taker*, i.e. it is so good that bookmakers will *take the knock*.

lift home, (said of a jockey) to ride a horse to win.

London to a brick, a fictitious wager on what is regarded as a certainty.

longshot, a horse or greyhound priced at big odds.

mass of condition, (of a horse) good condition for racing.

mazuma, money, especially money used for betting.

mocker on, put the, to bring bad luck to (someone).

monty, a sure winner.

mudlark, a horse that performs well on a wet track.

no biscuits left in the tin, (of a horse) to lack reserves of staying power.

no-hoper, a horse that is regarded as having no prospects of success.

nothing on its feet, (of a horse) either shoeless or wearing only light racing plates.

outs, losses, especially in the phrase *run of outs*, a sequence of failures.

pea, a horse that is being ridden to win, especially when there is doubt about the genuineness of other runners.

phone, use the (or *go for the*), to tic-tac or convey by hand signals betting odds or instructions.

pigskin artist, a jockey.

poke through on the rails, (of a horse) to come through the field on the inside during a race.

reef off, (said of bookmakers) to take (money) away from a bettor.

rod in pickle, a horse that is being held for what is regarded as a certain win.

roughie, a horse at long odds.

rub out, to debar a horse, owner, trainer or jockey.

run like a cow (or *a hairy goat*), to perform badly.

run off the course, (of a horse) to run wide during a race. See *down the course*.

run up a lane, (of a horse) to finish a race unplaced.

salute the judge, (of a winning horse) to pass the finishing post.

sharp shooter, a man who mingles with a crowd round a bookmaker's stand, holds out his hand and demands a ticket for a non-existent bet. Whence *sharp shooting*.

skinner, a betting coup, especially *skinner for the books*, which occurs when a favourite loses.

skull, the length of a head, e.g. get *beat by a skull*.

snack, a sure winner. Whence, *snackeroo* and *snackerooroo*.

Snake Gully course, a racecourse in a small country town.

soda, a sure winner.

soup-plate track, a racecourse of meagre size.

speeler, a speedy horse.

spider, a trotting or pacing gig.

spit in the bag and stand up, (of a penniless bookmaker) to seek bets from the public without resources to pay those bets if they succeed.

stand at the peg, (of a horse) to be left behind at the starting barrier in a race.

sting, dope given to a racehorse, especially in the form of a hypodermic injection. *to sting* or *give a sting to* (a horse), to dope it.

stipe, a stipendiary steward.

sure cop, a sure winner.

tipslinger, a racing tipster. *to tipsling, tipslinging*.

toey, (of a horse) restive or unsettled. (This term is also in general use.)

tommy, a bookmaker's ledger.

trot, a sequence of betting successes (*a good trot*) or failures (*a bad trot*).

undertaker's job, a horse that is not being run to win; i.e. a horse that is running "dead".

urger, a racing tipster.

way, a double (in betting). *favourite way*, the most favoured double.

willie, a supply of betting money.

without a mintie, said of a penniless would-be bettor.

Many of these expressions are obviously clichés, but quite a few have enough colour to merit a second look. Here are a few more: Probably at some time on an Australian racecourse you will hear of a horse that wins easily *with its dentures bared to the breeze* and of a horse *so hot you could boil a billy of frankfurts on it*, which usually means that it is being blatantly prevented from winning; if it runs wide at the turn into the straight our cliché expert declares that *it ran so wide it knocked a pie out of a man's hand in the leger;* if the jockey rode a poorly-judged race the expert says the *hoop went to sleep;* if all a gambler's bets fail he says he *can't take a trick;* if a horse eats all the feed in its food box the expert notes that it *didn't leave an oat*, and he applies this metaphor to himself when he says he has *run out of oats*, meaning that he is penniless. Naturally enough, he is unlikely to resist the temptation to say that a horse *sports silk* when it is mounted by a jockey, or that it *looks through a bridle* when a bridle is put on it; these examples, however, are not Australian originals, but have come from England.

More worthy of record is the expression *get under someone's neck*, which is in general use and apparently has horsey antecedents. A person who beats, outwits or anticipates the moves of another is said to *get under his neck;* it means to get in front of him. From racing have also come: *first under the wire*, said of the winner of any contest; *to take a swab*, to make an inquiry into any development (the suggestion being that it is a "fix") – often as a humorous exclamation *take a swab!*; *call for the bridle*, said of someone who is silly or "a bit short" (normally a jockey weighs in with all riding gear except the bridle, but if he is a few ounces short of the correct weight he can call for the bridle to be added to the scales); *weight's right!* everything is in order; *couldn't lay it with a board*, meaning that the outcome is a foregone conclusion on which no one would bet (the *board* mentioned here is a bookmaker's board).

A couple of Australian inventions are worth special attention. The first was the automatic *totalisator* or *tote* (also called a *machine*), invented by George (later Sir George) Julius, of Sydney, and now used on race-courses all over the world. Julius operated the first fully mechanical tote at Auckland, New Zealand, in 1913. Earlier, in the 1860s, the French had developed a Pari-Mutuel system, but this was only partly mechanical. The second invention was almost equally important: this was the *magic eye*, a photo-mechanism perfected by Athol Shmith and B. A. Pearl, of Melbourne, in 1945, and of great value in distinguishing winners of races where the contests are close.

Also meriting a note, but for less commendable reasons, was the *phantom broadcast*. This term was coined about 1938 by a race-commentator named H. Solomons, who, from a Melbourne radio station, gave his idea of how the day's races would be run *before* they took place. In 1939 he was responsible for an extension of the term, for in collusion with several others (unknown) he conspired to broadcast a running commentary on a race *after* it had been completed, thus allowing some profitable transactions to be made with bookmakers. This was also called a *mandrake broadcast* (from the name of a cartoon strip character, Mandrake the Magician). Both terms have now become obsolete.

In many Australian towns, greyhound races are held on circular or oval courses. In Victoria, such circular or oval courses are commonly called *circles*, and from it have been derived many terms such as *circle event*, *circle champion* and *circler*, i.e. a greyhound that runs on such a course.

3. TWO-UP

TWO-UP or *swy* (from the German *zwei*, two) has been called "Australia's national game". It has also been described as "the fairest game on earth". In the hands of certain operators, however, it can be numbered among the most dishonest of all games and no country would wish to claim it as a national possession. Indeed, it is apparently so dishonest at times that one of my informants has insisted that I should not mention his name in case he is on the receiving end of a bullet.

The origin of the game has been traced to China and to English provincial sport. It is scarcely necessary, however, to go much further back in history than our own early days. In an article on the evils of gambling, we find the "Sydney Gazette" of April 15, 1804, recommending "the dispersion of the Little Chuck-farthing mob that generally assembles at one of the wharves in the course of the afternoon". In his "Flash Vocabulary", compiled at Newcastle, N.S.W., in 1812, Vaux refers to the expression *fly the mags*, meaning "to gamble by tossing up halfpence" and uses *gray* for "a halfpenny or any other coin having two heads or tails".

If you saunter down to the docks in almost any Australian port today you will find the lineal descendants of chuck-farthing days indulging in a practically identical game played (out of sight of the police) with pennies. These are mainly casual schools formed when men find the time; the orthodox school, run on organised lines and under strict control, is called an *alley*. Several of these *alleys* operate in Sydney and Melbourne, and there is at least one in Kalgoorlie, W.A.

Probably the best-publicised two-up school in Australia today is *Tommos* or *Thommos*, of Sydney. The "Australian Encyclopaedia" says that it was founded by J. Thomas, but advice I have received suggests that several members of the Thomas family were involved and that the school has been operating for 50 years or more. Much of its reputation – and its endurance – apparently rests on the fact that the game played at Tommos is scrupulously honest and rigidly supervised. Tommos operates in five or six places each week, moving round to avoid police interference as far as possible. Its clientèle reputedly includes doctors, barristers, actors, civil servants, big-time punters and members of the sporting fraternity. A patron comments: "They are raided regularly, about every six weeks, but nobody of note is there when raids occur. About 20 or 30 nondescripts are always playing when police raids are made. They are taken off, their bail paid and duly forfeited next morning. In nearly all cases, fictitious names are used. They collect a couple of quid each from the management for their trouble."

The *alley* is often disguised by a gymnasium or athletic club which provides an excuse for men to congregate, this mask being known as a *square-off*. Many other schools operate in well-protected bush retreats on the fringes of our cities and towns. These are *outside games* and, since their aim is long-term operation, they are usually well organised.

Main figures in the orthodox two-up world are the *ringie*, the ring-keeper (large games may have two *ringies* in action); the *spinner*, who tosses the coins; the *centre*, who holds bets made by the *spinner;* the *alley clerk*, who arranges bets for a player, especially if the latter is inexperienced; the *headie* and the *tailie*, a backer of heads or of tails. Unseen, and serving a most useful purpose as far as the alley is concerned is the *cockatoo*, *cocky*, *nit-keeper* or *long stopper*, who is keeping guard against the approach of police. There are also some minor figures in the alley: the *sleeper-catcher*, a person who picks up bets that have been left on the floor too long (this is regarded as a legitimate perquisite, the *sleeper* being a bet or winnings not picked up by a tardy backer); one or more sturdy men whose task is to keep order if necessary (they are under the direction of the *ringie*); *alley loafers*, moneyless players who are never allowed a seat round a ring; and, of course, the *virgin* or *mug*, as any non-professional player of the game is known among the experts.

"*You've got to protect the mugs!*" is an old two-up saying usually observed in organised schools, since the casual *two-upper* (another Australian term) brings a great deal of money to the game. All the same, the big bettor is the school's mainstay, and he is given special care. For instance, at such a game as Tommos when a man has a large win and wishes to leave, a taxi is called and he is shepherded to it by one of the school's tough employees and no one else is allowed to leave for at least another ten minutes.

Depending on the size of the school, the actual *ring* is twelve to fifteen feet in diameter. The central part of it where the *spinner* stands is called the *centre* or *guts*, and is controlled by the *centreman* or *spinner's stakeholder*, who does not move from his position unless to walk a few yards to collect a stake.

A basic rule is that the money bet by the spinner must be *set* or covered by players before any side-bets are made; hence, the ring-keeper's routine demands, "*Set the centre first!*" and "*No bets on the side till the centre's set!*" If the bettors now begin to edge forward as the spin is near, the ringie has other verbal routines: "*Keep the ring clear!*" "*Ring out!*" "*Make a ring of it!*" and "*Give the spinner a fair go!*" At times, he will go round, pushing the players out in order to make a complete circle.

All two-up games of any significance use only one type of penny – those minted in the reign of Edward VII. Presumably this is not only because the "head" is clearly stamped, but because such coins appear to be somewhat heavier than later pennies. The "head" is polished carefully, while the "tail" is left unpolished, so that the sides are clearly distinguishable. The Edward VII mintings are probably the reason why one not only *heads them*, *skulls them* or *nuts them*, but *neds them*. If a spinner throws two "tails" he is said to *mick them* or throw *two micks*. If he tosses one "head" and one "tail" he *ones them*; it is also called *two ones*. The "tail" of some pennies is sometimes called a *cross*, mainly in cases where, to make identification especially easy, a black cross is painted on the "tail".

The centre has now been set and bets made on the side between various players, and all is ready for the spin. Up to now the two pennies have been lying on the floor, tails up. The ringie picks up these coins and places them, again tail uppermost, on what is known as the *bat*, *kip*, *stick* or *kylie*, a thin and light piece of (preferably hardwood) board, such as cedar, but wood from a cigar box is often chosen, measuring about $3\frac{1}{2}$ in. x $1\frac{1}{2}$ in. x $\frac{1}{4}$ in. which the spinner holds in one hand. The bat often becomes smooth from handling.

The *ringie* now calls "*Come in, spinner!*" or "*Fair go, spinner!*" or "*Up and do 'em!*" and the spinner makes his toss. This toss is generally required to be at least eight or ten feet high. Many schools have a *heading wire* or *heading bar* (it can even be a smoothed tree branch at an alfresco school) which marks the minimum height. The ringie calls "*Bar toss!*" if the minimum height is not reached or if the spin is not otherwise acceptable, such as when a coin falls outside the ring.

When the pennies fall, the *ringie* identifies them as heads or tails or *ones* (although bettors will have already seen this themselves), then turns them tail up once again in the guts while the next bets are made, the centre being set first. The same acts and verbal formulas are followed for the next spin. When the spinner wishes to hand in the bat – perhaps, because as the result of a *good trot*, he has difficulty in getting set and is holding the game up – the ringie announces, *"He's picked it!"* which means that the spinner wants to hand over to someone else. The ringie decides who will be the next spinner, although his choice generally rotates round the ring.

If, before retiring, the spinner has tossed a *trot* (sequence) of heads, the *ringie* (or *ringies*) approaches the head-backers and demands what is known as a *boxer*. This is usually twenty per cent of winning bets, paid towards the cost of running the school and paying its employees. When a spinner retires, he also pays a *boxer*, and if his trot has been good he may *sling* (tip) the *centreman* (stakeholder) something for his pains. On the other hand, if a trot of tails has been thrown by the retiring spinner, the ringie will confine his attention to tail-backers to secure his boxer.

Everything seems to be so well regulated in the game that it would be well-nigh impossible for any form of dishonesty to thrive. But let us see what happens when *hard heads* (as two-up crooks are called) take over – as they do on Anzac Day, at country race meetings and shows and at other snide *outside games*.

Let us begin with the *kip, bat*, etc. Up to twenty or thirty years ago, hard heads often used a kip which had been slotted or grooved so that a double-headed penny (a *nob* or *jack*) or a double-tailed penny (a *gray*) could be inserted. These slotted kips (known as *lannets*) were usually devices of great carpentering skill, and were apparently most effective in early days. When the coins were tossed in the air, the spinner *palmed* (or *sarmed*) one of the pennies, and, with a deft twist of the lannet, allowed the *jack* (or the *gray*, as the case may be) to spin into the air.

Here are a few words from an old-timer: "For long-drawn-out sessions of gambling, a big shearing shed just cut out took some beating. Two-up all day, hazards all night by the light of slush lamps, two-up again from daylight till dark and so on for three days and nights until at the end most of the cash, as well as horses, sulkies, buggies, fur rugs, etc., were in the hands of a few *hard heads*. These men frequently came along a day or so before the cut-out to look for a pen vacated by shearers who had left in order to attend a roll-call at another station about to start shearing."

An expert tells me: "When the spin was made with a slotted bat, if you were watching you would see the spinner's index finger move away from the bat and at the same time his thumb would hold one of the pennies in place. The *jack* (or it might be the *gray*, if he was a tail-spinner) would leave the slot at the same time as the other penny went up, and anyone would think it was a perfect spin. While everyone is watching the coins in the air (the ringie can help this by saying admiringly "A good high toss!"), the spinner turns the bat over and the penny he hasn't tossed is now under the bat. When the tossed coins come down, the spinner walks over, picks them up, *sarms* the nob into the slot, then throws the coins on the ground. The ringie turns them up to show their tails, and the spinner waits to get set for the next spin."

Lannets fell out of use for various reasons, one being the multiplicity of kips needed in a game, the fact that even *bunnies* (victims) might wake up to the difference, and because if the police found a man in possession of such a weapon it would lead to an immediate conviction.

Hard heads have devised other ways of operating: (1) *floating*, (2) *dishing*, (3) *sarming*.

The simplest of these operations is floating. A coin that fails to spin when tossed is called a *floater* or *butterfly*. It does a *flutter spin* and is said to *flutter*, *float* or *gig*. Actually, it is by no means easy to float coins so that all observers are deceived by their rocking movements in the air, but practice has made some hard heads so perfect that only expert players would pick a dishonest toss of this type. It is to be noted that such a toss is often made without a bat and is called *spinning off the hand*. However, it cannot be done with a high toss.

A coin is *dished* when its centre is gently tapped to make it slightly concave – if the tail side is tapped, it will come heads when tossed, if the head side is tapped it will come tails. Dished coins can also be spun off the hand. Such dishing is not noticeable unless carefully looked into, and gives hard heads opportunities to make quick profits.

The most generally used method is *sarming* with a *nob* or *gray*, but without a *lannet*. In this, an ordinary bat is used. When the toss is made, the spinner clamps his thumb on the coin nearer to him and allows whatever double-sided coin he has in his palm to join the other coin on the bat in a toss. The spinner then turns the bat over smartly so that the retained coin is unseen. I recorded earlier that, in a legitimate game, the ringkeeper picks up the coins. In a dishonest game, the spinner always picks up the coins since he has to *sarm* the nob or gray after each spin. This should be the first cause for suspicion. The only time the ringkeeper in this sort of game touches the coins is when one of the victims has been given a turn as spinner, and the ringie is only too anxious to turn them over to suggest that everything is above board. Another clue to the suspicious player should be that, during a dishonest game, no *boxer* is called for; this is because the only significant side-betting done involves members of the mob. Perhaps the most important piece of advice that can be given is that participants in outside games should watch the spinner's hands and not the coins! And be alerted by the ringie's persistent demand for *a big ring*. And be even more alert when he shouts reprovingly, "Who threw that penny into the ring?" – ten to one, three pennies were tossed because the spinner lost control of the coin he should have retained.

What is the method of betting in a game run by *hard heads*? To quote an informant: "There are generally five or six in the mob. I imagine before they start operations they have a meeting some place and the head bloke would give each fifty or sixty pounds for their betting (they would not have any other money on them, so there would not be any lashing in the final split). One of the reasons they need the money is to make a show of a good roll. Usually the jack spinner puts two pounds in the centre and in a short while, thanks to the mob, he gets set for it, then for four pounds, then for eight (third spin). Next it starts to get a bit hard to get set, and one of the rams steps in and says 'I'll have a couple of quid'. The mugs gain confidence and the balance is soon set. The ringie (he's one of the mob) calls out 'No bets on the side till the centre's set'. Then the rest of the mob get to work and have good pickings on the side. That's when their rolls come in, to make a good showing. Up she goes, two heads again. It's now thirty-two pounds. Some of the saps *come in on the grouter*, but it's getting harder to get set. One of the rams bets five pounds, another puts in five single notes and after a while he'll go over to the ring-keeper and say 'Here you are, I'll have another fiver'. With these come-ons, the rest is soon set. Up bob the heads again. The spinner makes a great show of giving the keeper three or four quid – a sort of boxer which makes sure nobody thinks anything is crooked. Then the next spinner takes over. He would get at least twenty quid out of his spin; in some cases, much more if there's a bunny chasing his dough. Side bets would get the mob plenty. Sometimes they get between themselves on the side to give the impression that everything is above board. One might even back the tail, but only against his mate. While someone not in the mob is having a spin, they work the money back to each other for further betting (of course, it's done quietly), which keeps the money in circulation (but only amongst themselves). At the end of the day, they must meet somewhere, pool their dough and split evenly. It's anybody's guess what the chop is, but the amount could be staggering – hundreds of pounds. It would need to be, because of the risks they take."

A comment on dishonest two-up from another source: "I remember one spinner who used to take odds about tossing two heads right off. He'd put a quid in the guts and wait for it to be set. Then he'd make a dinkum spin and if the coins came down heads, the ringie (all ringies worked in with the nob spinners) would immediately turn the pennies over in the ring to show their tails. Next spin, the spinner would have two quid on himself to throw heads and this time he used the jack. It was a pretty good lurk."

Rams and their conduct: "A good *ram*, if you could call any ram good, plays a big part in crook swy. He pretends to have no knowledge of anyone and he plays the clown a lot. Keeping the losers in good spirits, I suppose. You'd be surprised, when the spin is made, how often he is right near the coins when they fall, keeping inquisitive players away from them. Anzac Day in 1965 fell on a Sunday, and there were games as usual in Hyde Park with Diggers being taken for hundreds of quid. One school had four nob spinners, ringie, stakeholder and ram. One of the best of the spinners was a bloke over 70. No one suspected him. The ram would say, 'Give the old boy a fair go; he's nearly too old to spin them!' and 'Hurry up and set the old cove, or he'll be late for church!' He kept up this kind of chatter. Then I heard him say to one of the mob, 'The *pigs* are in!' By that he meant that he'd placed a couple of outsiders and they knew what was up."

A note on the *gray* (a double-tailed penny): "The gray is not used very much. Its main use is if the nob spinner in a dishonest game has been set several times and it's hard to get any more mug money. One of the spinner's mates sets the whole amount and he substitutes a gray so that he can spin out quickly and let someone else take over."

Now for a few general expressions used in two-up:

angels, up among the, said of a high toss.

big dish, a large sum of money won by a lucky spinner.

Burra again! an exclamation used when a player loses and bets against everything in the ring in an effort to recoup losses.

cocked, said of a coin that does not fall flat.

come in, to spin the coins. Ex the common expression *come in, spinner!* addressed to the spinner before a toss is made.

cop-out man, a man in a crooked game of two-up who, according to plan, wins all the money.

coupla, two heads.

covered, said of all side bets when they have been set.

dasher, a daring gambler.

do 'em, to toss heads.

don't rush the kip! take it easy!

dook 'em, (of a spinner) to toss heads three times in succession. Also, *do a dook*.

get tossed, to lose all one's money in a two-up game.

go off, (of a two-up school) to be raided by police. (A hotel or club also *goes off* when it is raided for gambling or after-hours trading.)

greasy pig, as for *grouter* (q.v.), especially in such a statement as "Here's a chance for a *greasy pig*".

ground money, to place bets.

grouter, a bet laid on tails after a long run of heads or vice versa. Whence, *grouter bet* and *come in on the grouter;* the latter implies the likelihood of an advantage on the law of averages.

headie, a man who regularly backs heads.

head 'em, to play two-up. Two-up players arrested by police are usually charged in these days with *heading them*. Versions are *head'n' 'em* and *headin' 'em*.

labouring, said of a nob spinner who has to make several tosses before the honest penny shows a head.

lairs, hangers on in a two-up game.

lick, have a, to spin a nob.

motzer, a big gambling win.

nick 'em, to lose one's money in two-up.

nob them, to toss heads.

pass the bat, to die.

pluck, (of a spinner) to withdraw some of his winnings from betting.

put a knife through money, to split money up among members of a dishonest gang of two-up players.

reign, the period during which any one man acts as spinner.

slip, a small sum of money which a ring-keeper gives to a client who has gone broke to ensure that he will have his fare home. Whence, *slip money*. (This donation was apparently once regarded as a magnanimous gesture on the part of the ring-keeper, but now it has become a traditional right.)

spin out, to die.

spit a kip, (of a dishonest spinner) to spit on a kip or lick a kip with the aim of making a penny stick.

tailie, a man who regularly backs tails.

take the knock, to default in payment.

tarmac, an asphalt floor used in some two-up rings, which ensures that coins will bounce when they fall.

tosser (or *tossie*), a spinner.

two-down, a name sometimes given to two-up.

two ones, a head and a tail when coins fall after being tossed. No bets are permitted that such a fall will occur; the betting is solely on two heads or two tails.

two outs, two tails.

For people interested in studying two-up jargon, I doubt whether it would be possible to recommend anything better than Lawson Glassop's novel, "Lucky Palmer". Many of the terms listed in this Section are to be found in Glassop's book. He also uses the simile *heads on 'em like boils*, which is applied to the heads of two-up coins when a long run of heads occurs, the inference being that the obverse sides of the coins are so big that tails have no chance against them. I have noted a similar example, *heads on 'em like mice*, elsewhere in this book.

This is not quite all. A few games are played with three pennies, which means that a result is obtainable with every toss, but this is not popular. However, *three-up* has a long history in Australia. "The Detectives' Handbook", published about 1880, describes it as "a low gambling game by tossing up three pennies or other coins and crying to them" – which makes it at least 85 years old.

A game is also played with three threepences which are shaken in a leather dice box, about six inches high and two inches in diameter. It is sometimes called *treys in the pot*. This game is also marred with dishonest practices – namely the use of a *nob* (or *pig*), a double-headed threepence, or a *gray*, a double-tailed threepence. It is largely played in the bush; its main characteristic seems to be the rapidity with which money bet on the throws can change hands.

4. CRICKET, FOOTBALL, SWIMMING, SURFING

THE ASHES is a cricketing term we share with England, but the margin in England's favour is not great. The expression, which is used to describe a periodical series of Test matches between England and Australia, originated in a mock obituary notice in the London "Sporting Times" of September 2, 1882, in which it was announced that the dead body of English cricket would be cremated and the ashes taken to Australia. It was quickly adopted in this country. In the "Bulletin" of December 9, 1882, for instance, reference is made to "the revered ashes of English cricket which had been laid on the shelf in England by the Australian Eleven". The "Australian Sportsman" of August 13, 1884, also spoke of "revered Ashes".

However, between the dates of the comments by the "Bulletin" and the "Australian Sportsman", *The Ashes* had ceased to be purely mythical. Real ashes came into being when some Melbourne women burnt a stump used in the third game in the 1882-3 series and presented them in an urn to the Hon. Ivo Bligh, who led an English team to Australia. Later, "ashes" became a figurative symbol again – in cricket contests between Australia and other nations and, by transference, in football contests (especially Rugby League) between Australia and Britain.

Rather in the way that *The Cup* has come in Australia to denote the Melbourne Cup horse race, so *The Shield* always denotes the Sheffield Shield – an interstate cricketing trophy first contested in 1892-3. An *outrighter* is an outright win in the annual Sheffield Shield series.

Googly or *bosey* denotes a ball which breaks from the off, although bowled apparently as a leg break. The latter is derived from the name of B. J. T. Bosanquet, a member of the English Eleven which toured Australia in 1903-4.

In "How We Recovered the Ashes" (1904), P. F. Warner wrote:

> Bosanquet can bowl as badly as anyone in the world; but when he gets a length, those slow *googlies*, as the Australian players call them, are apt to paralyse the greatest players.

Bodyline and *bodyline bowling* are also notable Australianisms. They were used originally to describe the fast leg-theory bowling used by Larwood and Voce during the English cricket tour of Australia in 1932-3. One of the first uses was in the Sydney "Sun" of December 28, 1932. For a time the versions *body bowling* and *body bowlers* were used, but these were eclipsed by the *bodyline controversy* which stirred all cricketing sections of the world.

Several Australian cricketers have left their marks on our slang, notably D. G. (later Sir Donald) Bradman and F. R. Spofforth. The former was known in his heyday as *The Don*, *Braddles* or *Don*, and the adjective *Bradmanesque* was often used. Spofforth, one of cricket's greatest bowlers, was called *The Demon*.

Because so many international cricket contests are played these days, it is difficult to identify the origin of some terms in the game, but these appear to be Australian originals: *lolly*, an easy catch; *sticky*, a damp wicket; *chuck*, to throw a ball when bowling, whence *chucker* and *chucking*; *two-eyed*, (of a batsman's stance) fully facing a bowler; *Chinaman*, an off-break bowled to a right-handed batsman; *dig*, a batsman' sinnings, whence *chuck a dig*, throw a wicket away.

Our use of *good wicket* for a satisfactory or profitable undertaking appears to be indigenous and is certainly derived from the cricket field; so also with *cruel a scheme* (or *plan* or *idea*), spoil or frustrate a scheme, etc., which is an adaptation of the English *cruel the pitch*. The women's game of vigoro, which combines elements of cricket and baseball, is sometimes called *cricko* in Australia.

In the football world our chief contribution seems to have been the brand of rugby known as *Australian Rules* (sometimes *Rules* alone), *Aussie rules* or *the Australian game*. It was founded (in Melbourne) in 1858 and the bulk of its rules were formulated in 1866. Victoria has always been its headquarters, although it is played extensively in other States, especially in Western Australia, South Australia and Tasmania. It has many similarities to Gaelic football.

In these States, *footie* (*go to the footie, see the footie, bet on the footie*, etc.) has only one meaning to most people. It denotes Australian Rules football. And, because of its popularity, *bounce the ball* (which is the way play begins) means to begin any enterprise. That use dates back at least fifty years. Standard contributions to our language from this code are *behind* (colloquially called a *pointer*), "a point scored when the ball is kicked behind the goal-line, within a specified distance on either side of the goal", and a specific sense of "six points" for *goal*.

The Melbourne "Sun" of July 17, 1965, listed (among many others) these samples of the clichés which have developed round Australian Rules: *a major*, a goal; *through the middle, through the high-diddle-diddle* (a rhyme on the former), *through the big fellows*, a goal; *raise both flags* and *notch full points*, score a goal; *backmen*, backs; *time on*, an extension of playing time; *ball hungry*, (of a player) eager; *short of a gallop*, (of a player or a team) out of training; *to shirtfront* and *to iron out*, (of a player) to strike an official; *an Academy Award job*, overacting by a player to receive a free kick.

Just as New Zealand rugby representatives came to be known as *All Blacks* (from the colour of the guernsey worn), *Fernleaves* and *Kiwis*, so Australian representatives of the two rugby codes are called *Kangaroos* (Rugby League) and *Wallabies* (Rugby Union). However, it can be noted that in 1927-8 a Rugby Union team from New South Wales toured Britain and France and were known as *Waratahs*. League has much the same status in N.S.W. and Queensland as Australian Rules has in the South.

A name that survives from the rugged past of League is *Battle of Brisbane* – the second Test of the 1932 series against England, which Australia won 15-6.

While on the subject of popular names, here are some worth recording from Melbourne and Sydney, all denoting various teams (they are occasionally used to describe cricket, hockey and other teams):

MELBOURNE

Bloodstained angels or *niggers*, Essendon.
Blues, Carlton. Also *Bluebirds*.
Bombers, Essendon.
Bulldogs, Footscray.
Cats, Geelong.
Demons, Melbourne.
Dogs, Footscray.
Dons, Essendon.
Gorillas, Fitzroy.
Hawks, Hawthorn.
Jerusalem, St. Kilda.
Kangas, North Melbourne.
Lake Angels, South Melbourne.

Lions, Fitzroy.
Magpies, Collingwood.
Maroons, Fitzroy.
Mayblooms, Hawthorn.
Pivots, Geelong.
Red Legs or *Red Demons*, Melbourne.
Saints, St. Kilda.
Same Olds, Essendon.
Seasiders, St. Kilda.
Shinboners, North Melbourne.
Swans, South Melbourne.
Tigers, Richmond.
Tricolours, Footscray.

SYDNEY

Balmaniacs, Balmain.
Bluebags, Newtown.
Canaries, Balmain.
Cantabs, Canterbury.
Coasters, Corrimal.
Dragons, St. George.
Dragonslayers, St. George.
Harboursiders, North Shore.
Hyphenates, Canterbury-Bankstown.
Highlanders, Gordon.
Magpies, Western Suburbs.
Mains, Balmain.
Newts, Newtown.

Rabbit-ohs, South Sydney.
Saints, St. George.
Seasiders, East Sydney.
Shoremen, North Shore.
Stovemakers, Metters.
Stovies, Metters.
Tigers, Balmain.
Townies, Newtown.
Tricolours, Eastern Suburbs.
Uni, University.
Villagers, Manly.
Waves, Waverley.
Wicks, Randwick.

This type of nickname is to be found in practically every centre where sport is played. Sporting journals have had considerable influence on the perpetuation – and origination – of many of these expressions.

The only other football terms that seem to be indigenous are *blinder*, a dazzling game by a player, the verb *to rabbit*, to collar or trip a player when he is running with the ball, *tackle on suspicion* (a version of the police "arrest on suspicion"), to tackle a player who is not in possession of the ball, but is deemed likely to receive it, and *pig*, a football forward.

Although Australia has played soccer since 1880, it is only since the end of World War II that it has become popular. So far as its impact on the Australian language is concerned, the main point to be noted is that it has never (as in Britain) been called Association Football; the word *soccer* apparently originated at Harrow School and was a slang term in Britain for many years.

Since Australia's first swimming championship took place (in Sydney) in 1846, Australian swimmers have made a fair mark in the sport through-out the world. One of our most notable contributions has been a stroke known as the *Australian crawl*. This was pioneered in 1901 or slightly before by a Solomon islander, Alick Wickham, who was houseboy to a Sydney doctor. Legend says that Wickham was swimming at Bronte baths when a local official commented, "Look at that boy *crawling* over the water". Wickham swam with his face submerged, taking breaths at long intervals, with his legs threshing up and down (in contract to the previously-popular trudgeon stroke, which had a frog-like kicking action), and with his arms moving rapidly. When Australian swimmers took the *crawl* overseas, they scored many successes.

Our swimming vocabulary began to take shape considerably before this. One of the first indigenous terms was *dip*, for a swim or bathe (1880), which has sheep-dipping antecedents. Costumes worn by swimmers became known as *bathers*, *togs* or *a cossie*. The *one-piece bathing suit* was mainly pioneered by an Australian, Annette Kellerman, who was our first woman swimmer to achieve world note.

Some minor offerings: *iceberg*, a person (usually a male) who swims regularly in winter-time; *sharkbait* or *sharkbaiter*, a swimmer who risks attack from sharks by swimming a long distance from shore on an open beach; *belly-buster*, *belly-flop* and *belly-flopper*, an ungainly dive; *honeypot* and *gin's flop*, a way of jumping into water with the arms round the knees; *to crocodile*, to swim with another person's hands on one's shoulders.

More important than these for sea-bathers, the countless thousands who swim or *surf* off Australia's beaches (this is an indigenous use of the term and quite distinct from *surf-riding*, which we will come to later), is that *surfing* is essentially an amateur pastime. But first a small quotation from the "Australian Encyclopaedia": "Prior to 1900, one 'bathed in the open sea'. By 1905 the verb 'to surf' was in common use. Half a century later it could reasonably be claimed that after a summer's week-end a million people might say 'I surfed'." Thus, waters off sea-beaches can be flat calm, yet people can *surf* in them. And, if any such people get into difficulties while swimming, they can quite well be saved from drowning by a *surf-lifesaver* known as a *beltman*, who operates as part of a team using a *surf-reel* (handled by a *reelman*), a *surf-line* (handled by a *lineman* or *linesmen;* note that the plural is not *linemen*).

In short, the Australian *surf* is by no means covered by the "Oxford Dictionary's" definition: "The mass or line of white foamy water caused by the sea breaking upon a shore or a rock". All the same, since most Australian sea-bathers prefer an *active surf* or a *good surf*, the "Oxford" definition is generally applicable. *Surf beaches*, that is, beaches open to the ocean where a good surf is breaking, and a large number of associated terms, have come into use: *surf club*, *surf boat*, *surf race* and *surf flags* among them. *Surf boat* was recorded in England more than seventy years ago, but there it meant any type of boat used for passing through surf. In Australia, the surf boat is a special type of boat; the first was built by Walter Biddell and launched at Bronte Beach in 1906. The lifesaver who mans the steering oar in a surf boat is the *sweep*. Such boats are manned by members of *surf lifesaving clubs* (there are more than 220 such clubs in

Australia); a *surf race* is a race in which such members participate; apart
from providing *surf patrols* or *patrolling a beach*, they select the area where
swimming is safest (i.e. free from current or undertows) and mark it with
surf flags. If a dangerous surf begins to break, a patrol is empowered to
close a beach. *Patrolmen* mount guard on *shark towers*, and warn swimmers
of danger by sounding a *shark bell* or *shark siren* (such occasions are often
called *shark scares*). Apart from club races, *lifesavers* stage what is known
as a *march past*, a ceremonial march, and perform what is called *R. and R.*
The last expression stands for rescue and resuscitation, and often appears
in such forms as *R. and R. team* and *R. and R. title*. A special swimming
costume worn by lifesavers is a *speedo;* a *drag* or *tow* is an undertow of the
sea off a surfing beach. The constant summer danger of attacks on swimmers by sharks has been responsible for the *shark fence*, a fence of heavy
wire, enclosing some small swimming beaches, the development of a
number of terms, all referring to the activities of trawlers which net under
contract off the main beaches, e.g. *shark meshing*, and *shark patrol plane*, an
aircraft which patrols some beaches in order to "spot" sharks.

Space should be made here for *sting* and *get stung*, which have special
significance on our beaches. They refer mainly to burning rashes on the
human skin caused by contact with the tentacles of a *bluebottle* or Portuguese man-of-war, which grow to more than 50 ft. in length. Treatment
for such a *sting* is to rub the skin with dry or wet sand – preferably dry.

As we will see in a minute, *surfing* denotes a good deal more than
swimming in surf. To the dedicated surfer, it has meant for several
generations the mastery of waves so that the surfer is carried for long
distances towards the shore. This is called *shooting the breakers*. The practice
was introduced to Australia between 1880 and 1890, at Manly, N.S.W.,
by a South Sea islander, Tommy Tanna, and the form he used was *body
shooting*. The *body shooter* does not use external aids in *catching a wave*.

In 1915, a major development occurred when Hawaian Duke
Kahanamoku demonstrated the art of riding a *surfboard* at Freshwater,
N.S.W., on a board of sugar pine, 9 ft. long and weighing 65 lb. Although
the first surfboards were heavy, a popular craze ensued. By 1925, we had
virtually abandoned solid boards and substituted faster, hollow surfboards.
With improvements, these remained in use here until 1957, when a
dramatic change occurred.

Among terms which came into use before 1957 were:

> *backbreaker*, as for *dumper*.
> *back shoot*, a wave that drives a surfboat or surfer backwards towards
> the shore. A surfboat sent backwards in this way is said to *get a back shoot*.
> *beacher*, a wave which carries a surfer to the beach.
> *boomer*, a surfing wave of outstanding excellence.
> *broaching*, swinging a surfboard around quickly to gain control against
> a *dumper*.
> *come in*, (of a surfer) to travel shorewards on a wave.
> *corkscrew*, to bodyshoot on one's back.
> *crack a wave*, to find a suitable wave for surfing. Also *catch a wave*.

down the mine, said in reference to a surfboat or surfer caught by a *dumper* (q.v.).

dumper, a wave that breaks with unexpected violence some distance from the shore. *crack a dumper*, to suffer buffeting from a wave that breaks unexpectedly; *dump*, said of such a wave; *get dumped*, said of a surfer.

green, the required colour of a good surfing wave. Whence, *greenie*, such a wave.

howler, a swift-travelling green wave that will bring an accomplished surfer to the shore.

mocking bird, anyone who gets in the way of a surfer when *coming in* on a wave. (Apparently, an alternative for *galah*, a fool.)

scrape up, to rescue a surfer who has been sent *down the mine* (q.v.).

screamer, an unusually big or fast wave.

shoot, to surf. Also noun, a suitable wave for surfing.

ski, see *surf ski*.

surfoplane, a small, inflatable rubber "surfboard". One who rides on such a surfboard is a *rubbery* or *rubbery boy*.

surf ski, an elongated boat-like surfboard. *double ski*, a surf ski that can support two persons.

The date 1957, mentioned before, was the year in which a vast change began to come over the sport of surfing in Australia. It was marked by the introduction of the *Malibu board*, which was much lighter than any other surfboard used here. The Malibu was made of polyurethene foam sheathed with fibre glass. About the same time slightly heavier boards of balsa were introduced.

Exhibitionistic adolescents were entranced. They took over the sport of surfboard riding almost entirely, and after 1960 we were inundated with scores of new terms. I am well aware that many of these terms were not Australian originals (doubtless some came from the U.S.), but adequate references are not yet available for checking. Here is a selection:

angling, said of the course taken when a surfboard rider travels parallel with a wave and across it, but at an angle to the beach.

backhand (or *backside*) *turn*, a turn made by a surfrider when he has his back to a wave as he angles across it. See *forehand turn*.

banana, the amount of turn-up in a surfboard.

beachie, a keen surfboard rider.

big gun, a surfboard about 10 ft. long and weighing more than 40 lb. for use in a big surf. Also, an expert rider.

big-gun board, a *hot-dog* surfboard of balsa used by an expert rider. The Malibu board is about 9 ft. long; the midget (Zip) board, 5 ft. or 6 ft.

bingle, a dent or fracture in a surfboard.

bleeding paper, the porous substance placed inside the mould when a surfboard is being made.

bodgies, gristly lumps on a surfboard rider's knees.

bunny, a surfrider who rarely enters the water.

cut-back, a rapid turn by a surfboard rider across the face of a wave.

cut down, to travel on a surfboard along the face of a large wave.

down the wall, to travel on a surfboard along the face of a large wave.

flick-off, the action of pulling a surfboard back from a wave before it breaks.

forehand turn, a turn made by a surfrider when he faces a wave as he angles across it.

forward squat, the action of squatting on the nose of a surfboard with hands stretched out in front.

go for lunch, (of a surfrider) to lose one's surfboard in a *wipeout*.

goofy, see *natural*.

gremmie, a beach frequenter who avoids the water or is inexperienced as a surfrider. Short for *gremlin*.

gymp, a surfrider who rarely enters the water.

head dip, (of a surfboard rider) to bend low and dip one's head in a wave while travelling at high speed.

hanging five, the action of riding on the nose of a surfboard with five toes curled over the front.

hanging ten, as for *hanging five*, with ten toes.

highway surfer, a youth who travels roads along the beaches in search of good surfing conditions, but remains an onlooker.

hot dogging, turning quickly back and forth across the face of a wave. *hot dog board*, a surfboard used for this practice; *hot-dogger*, a surfie who rides a surfboard in this way.

hump, a good surfing wave.

kick, the amount of turn-up in a surfboard.

kook, a surfrider who rarely enters the water.

lair it up, to behave exhibitionistically on a surfboard.

lunch, the loss of a surfboard in a *wipeout*. See *go for lunch*.

natural, a surfboard rider who stands with his left foot forward. A *goofy* rider stands with his right foot forward.

pick-up, said of a surfboard when the rider's paddling speed equals that of the wave for the *take-off*.

pigboard, a surfboard wide at the stern and tapered to a point.

pod, the stern end of a *hot dog* surfboard.

rails, the sides of a surfboard.

rubbished, said of a surfboard rider who is tipped violently off a wave.

sandie, a keen surfboard rider. Also *beachie*.

sausage board, a surfboard straight for most of its length and rounded at both ends.

shoulder, the steep, unbroken, ridable section of a wave.

skeg, a fin at the back and underneath a surfboard.

skin foam, the outer layer of plastic foam on a surfboard.

soup, the wash of a wave after it breaks.

stall, said of a surfboard when it almost stops at the bottom of a wave because of the weight at the back.

stoked, excited.

surfari, a convoy of surfriders, looking for a beach where good surfing conditions pertain.

surfie, a keen surfboard rider. (See *beachie*, *sandie*.)

take-off, the beginning of a surfboard ride.

take the gas, (of a surfrider) to get caught in the curl of a wave.

teardrop, a surfboard wide at the stern and tapered to a point.

tight, said of water made rough and hard to ride by rips and cross-currents.

toes over, see *hanging five* and *hanging ten*.

trail foot, a surfrider's back foot.

tube, the space where a wave curls and breaks; a good surfing wave that is about to break.

tunnel, as for *tube*.

wakesurfing, a form of long-distance body surfing (i.e. without a surf-board) in the wake thrown up by the propeller of a power boat.

walk the plank, to move up and down on a surfboard to perform various stunts while cutting down a wave.

wall, the face of a wave.

whip 'em up, Hughie! An invocation to God to provide good surf. (A variation on *send her down, Hughie!* noted earlier.)

wipeout, the sudden cessation of a surfboard ride when the wave traps and dumps the rider.

woodie, a wooden-panelled station waggon in which surfriders often travel to good surfing beaches.

Here is a brief sample of how some of these expressions can be put together (from "The Australian" of December 3, 1964):

> "I dunno, it's hard to describe. When you're driving hard and fast down the wall, with the soup curling behind yer, or doing this backside turn on a big one about to tube, it's just this feeling. Yer know, it leaves yer feeling stoked."

I will have more to say about *surfies* and their contemporaries in Chapter XIII, when we look into the social activities of our young.

5. OTHER SPORTS AND PASTIMES

BECAUSE OF their manifold interests in sporting activities, Australians have left linguistic marks in many such areas. Since we ended the last Section on a sea theme, let us continue it here, with yachting, sailing and fishing of various kinds. First, yachting and sailing.

Equipment: *peak-header*, a peak-head spinnaker; *kicker*, a jib; *ballooner*, a balloon jib; *lung* or *lunger*, a cylinder of a yacht's motor, e.g. *one-lung(er)*, *two-lung(er)*.

General: *lift*, a breeze; *hot-water boat*, a motor-boat.

Best-known long-distance yachting contest in Australia is the *Sydney-Hobart Yacht Race*, first held in 1945.

Several types of sailing boat are Australian inventions, notably the *eighteen-footer*, the *sixteen-footer*, the *Sabot* and the *V.S.* or *Vaucluse Senior*, both 15 ft., the *M.J.* or *Manly Junior*, 14 ft., and the *V.J.* or *Vaucluse Junior*, 11 ft. 6 in. The 12 ft. *Moth* is a local variation of an overseas invention.

A *swinger* is a member of the crew of a large sailing boat carried as live ballast. By distributing their weight (*pudding* or *pudden*) where ordered, swingers help to keep a boat upright when hard on the wind. Sometimes a rank of crew members is required to sit on another; they are then said to be *double-banked*.

Fishermen have produced a considerable vocabulary: *weed*, a fish that frequents seaweed; *green prawn*, an uncooked prawn, often used for bait; *berley*, ground bait; *Ned Kelly*, a fishing rod with a wire trace and an unbarbed hook; *boomerang*, a small fish that is thrown back into the water; *baitbobber*, a fisherman who uses a rod or who fishes with a cork on his line, whence *bobbie*, such a fisherman; *breamer*, one who fishes for bream (the pronunciation *brim* is Australian); *hit*, to hook a fish; *skull-drag*, to fish from a drifting boat; *reef*, (of a fish) to seek the shelter of a reef, or (of a current) to carry a fishing line towards a reef; *moonlight*, to catch or seek to catch certain fish by moonlight; *dark moon*, *dark* or *darkie*, moonless conditions which are ideal for netting prawns; *rock hopper*, one who fishes from coastal rocks; *beachie*, a beach fisherman; *spearo*, an underwater spear fisherman; *down under*, beneath the sea's surface, frequented by spear fishermen. (See Chapter XIV for some popular fish names.)

Australian fishermen commonly use *baited* with a meaning directly opposed to that of Standard English. In Standard English a fisherman baits a hook before throwing it in the water. In Australia, the fish *baits* a line by removing the bait from the hook. It is more common to hear a fisherman say his line is *baited* when, in fact, there is no bait on the hook than for him to use the expression when he has just put bait on the hook.

From skiing: Since skiing was a sport in Australia before it was in Austria or Switzerland, we have made a few contributions. A *snow pole* is one of a number of poles erected about two chains apart along tracks on the high plains of north-east Victoria as guides. It is called a *stake* in Tasmanian mountains; a *pole line*, a line of such snow poles, is called a *stake line* in Tasmania.

From boxing: *kiss the cross*, to be knocked out; *catcuff*, a light blow; *fork-hander*, *mauldy* and *mollydooker*, a left-handed boxer (taken from old English *mauley* and *dook* or *duke*, the fist or hand); *to sky the rag*, to admit defeat or throw in the towel.

The simile *thin as a witch's tit* is used in bowling to describe a bowl that is given insufficient green bias to get close to the "jack".

Motor cycle speedway (*dirt track*) racing originated in Australia – in 1925 at Maitland, N.S.W. – whence *cinder shifter* and *cinder shifting*. Another Australian original is *bushwalking*, a sport concerned with tramping and camping in bush-covered areas, with its associated terms *bushwalk* and *bushwalker*. *Scrub pushing* and *scrub shoving* denote the activity of walking through thick undergrowth. *Hoy!* is a name given sometimes to *house*, *housie* or *housie-housie*; called "bingo" in Britain. Less known, but certainly Australian in origin is *sphairee* (pronounced SPY-ree or spy-REE); this is a game which contains elements of orthodox tennis, table tennis and paddle tennis, and is played on a court measuring 20 ft. by 9 ft. The originator (in 1962) of sphairee was F. A. Beck, of the N.S.W. Education Department.

Although men have probably been climbing cliffs and similar obstacles for thousands of years, the terms *cliff hopper* and *cliff hopping* seem to be Australian. The *cliff rescue* is certainly ours; the world's first *Cliff Rescue Squad* was formed as a unit of the N.S.W. Police Force in 1942.

To bog, to shovel blue metal into an ore truck, is no more than a "possible"; an annual *bogging* championship is held at Kalgoorlie, W.A. *Woolshed hop*, a dance in outback style, is ours; so is (or was) *Phar Lap gallop*, an expression once given to the foxtrot.

Our card-playing vocabulary is extensive, but contains many imported terms. Indigenous items include: *bunch of grapes*, the club suit in a pack of cards; *butcher*, a king; *burr cutter*, the jack of diamonds; *gerbera* and *lubra*, rhyming slang versions of Yarborough, in bridge; *pianola*, a hand that plays itself; *onedleton* (pronounced "wundleton"), as a variant of singleton; *blackfellow's game*, euchre; *brumby*, a poor hand of cards about which a player attempts to bluff.

When, in the game of bridge, a player is dealt a hand containing no cards of one particular suit, that suit is called a *blouse suit* or *green suit*. This may be derived from the old solo whist use of *ace (queen*, etc.) *blouse*, which indicates that it is the only card of that suit in the hand.

To go for the doctor in a card game is to adopt firm, decisive measures to ensure success. For example, in bridge, it would involve playing the ace and king of trumps instead of trying to finesse a card of lower value.

Nock and Kirby (the name of a Sydney firm) is an extremely old term used to describe a hand which could be thrown in without any *post mortem* when a distraction occurred. According to one of my more senior correspondents, the name arose this way: "Ships about to sail from Sydney were frequently delayed by the non-arrival of ship's stores from providores and ships' chandlers. Nock and Kirby were among the worst offenders. Ship's officers, to pass the time while waiting for the stores to turn up, would play a game of cards on the understanding that as soon as N. and K's lorry arrived, the hands would be thrown in." Today, the expression is used to denote a game of show or whisky poker played at the end of an exacting game such as bridge, for relaxation and a rapid gamble.

An Australian expression noted by Lentzner in 1891 was *sick*, meaning without trumps. He said:

> In playing nap, if the player's trumps are exhausted he will say *sick*, and if he has a hand full of trumps and challenges the board to see if anyone has any left, he will ask "All sick?"

Kiss the dealer! is a cant phrase spoken when the ace, two, three and four-pipped cards of a suit fall on the table in the playing of a trick.

The card game known as *boxer* appears to be Australian, at least in name. Here is a description of the game as given by Magistrate Oram in Sydney Central Court in December, 1943: "Two players only, known as the banker and punter, hold cards that all the other players wager on with the banker and among themselves as to the value of those two hands. Police describe it, in effect, as a game of *two-up* played with cards." The name *boxer* is doubtless derived from the use of the word for a percentage of a spinner's winnings paid to a ringkeeper.

General card terms worth note include: *workingman's solo*, a solo whist call that is almost impossible to beat; *get shot on a hand*, to be beaten by a better hand; *lead from the duckhouse*, to lead from the bottom of a suit; *take*, *lurkman*, *rorter* or *mechanic*, a person who cheats at cards, especially a professional card sharp (Americans use *mechanic* for a dishonest player at faro); *pitch a game for a gay*, to stage a crooked game in order to mulct a victim; *front man* or *psyche man*, a member of a team of sharpers whose job is to lure victims to the card table; *one out man*, a lone player, especially a card sharp who eschews working with accomplices; *to milk* and *to build*, to stack cards, whence *milking* and *building; tugging*, dealing cards from the bottom of a pack; *clouting*, the palming of cards in a dishonest game; *ring in*, a stacked pack of cards. Incidentally, we generally prefer to use "pack" rather than "deck"; both are originally English, but the latter is now mainly American.

Cant phrases used either as intended statements of fact or with the aim of bluffing other card players include: *things is crook in Muswellbrook* and *things is weak in Werris Creek*. (A large number of such internal rhymes is examined in Chapter XVIII.) A Ballarat correspondent reports that another picturesque phrase is to the effect that a player will *give a gold pig to the Bourketown hospital* if his hand fails.

Dice games are played in Australia, but by no means to the extent that Americans play them. However, we seem to have tossed up an interesting expression in *stuffed rat*, which describes a crooked dice that has been loaded to make it perform the required antics. *To make a blue with a rat* is to allow it to hit the side of the table or some other object, thereby interfering with the natural processes of gravitation, since a *stuffed rat* will always act to schedule unless it hits an obstruction. We also use *percentage dice* and *dispatches* (the American version is *dispatchers*) for crooked dice.

From the game of dominoes come: *down*, a turn to open a game of dominoes by putting the first piece on the table; *go in*, a sequence of reverses that obliges a player to take into his hand a large number of dominoes from the central pool; *make it a count*, a phrase commonly used when a player is in a position to cut off both ends of a domino string.

6. CLOTHES

ALTHOUGH CLOTHES and dressing are not usually classed among the Australian male's pastimes and pleasures – the Australian female looks on the matter somewhat differently and, as pointed out in Chapter VI, the larrikin and his successors have had some odd ideas about dress – this is as good a place as any to run over the small sartorial vocabulary we possess. This vocabulary is mainly notable for the large number of terms devoted to masculine headgear (many of them now obsolete), principal among which are the Australian equivalents of what the Englishman calls a *bowler* and the American a *derby*.

Here are our contributions: *boxer, bocker, bun, plug hat, hard hat, hard hitter, egg-boiler, hop harry* and *peadodger*.

The strong Australian sunshine is probably responsible in the long run for the fact that we can almost interpret our history in terms of hats of one kind and another. First on the list was the *cabbage-tree hat*. In 1799, D. Collins made a diary entry in his "Account of New South Wales" in which he referred to a hat worn by Flinders "made of white filaments of the cabbage-tree". This type of headgear bulked largely in our early days and those who wore such hats were called *cabbageites* and *cabbage-tree mobs*. Even an exclamation *my cabbage-tree!* was in popular use.

Belltopper, a silk top hat (1853), was another Australianism. So, in a special way, was *billycock* (1865). The latter was originally English, but the Australian *billycock* differed from the English in being made of hard instead of soft felt and in having a turned-up brim. *Billy* was an Australian abbreviation.

Then there was the *nan-nan*, a straw hat once favoured by the larrikins; the *nail-can*, a type of top hat; the *digger's delight*, a large felt hat, probably somewhat similar in size to the outback hat now worn by *broad-brimmers;* the *decker, fell-off-a-bus* and *roofer*, terms for hats in general; and, as the Australian equivalent of the U.S. ten-gallon hat, the *Cunnamulla cartwheel* and *lunatic hat*.

Cady was once often used in Australia, but it hails originally from English dialect; the only distinctly new use it has been given in this part of the world is for a straw hat in New Zealand.

The *jumper* was, long ago, given an Australian form distinct from the use of that term in Standard English. The original Australian *jumper* was a type of blouse or smock worn by men during gold-digging days (the first record was in 1852), but C. R. Read, in "What I Heard, Saw and Did" (1853), refers to "a *jumper* of lamb's wool plaid in various shades", thus showing that it was probably the original version of our modern jumper. However, this new sense took a considerable time to develop, and as late as 1858 a writer refers to a blue flannel shirt as a jumper. *You can stick it up your jumper!* (or *guernsey!*) is an old Australian expression, meaning more or less "You know what to do with it!"

This type of garment was probably identical with what was known (from 1877 to 1900) as a *Crimean shirt*. Boldrewood refers to such a shirt in his "Ups and Downs" (1878) as having "black and scarlet in alternate bars". In the "Australasian Printers' Keepsake" (1858) we find it "a flaring red".

Bell-bottomed trousers, once favoured by larrikins, have already been referred to; so has *bluey* for a type of smock apparently once worn by Tasmanian convicts, and the *Tasmanian bluey*.

For the rest, it is necessary to note only *barebum* and *bumshaver*, for a short coat or dinner-jacket; *dungas*, dungarees; *cords*, corduroy trousers; *tweeds* or *ramies*, trousers in general, and *underdaks* and *underchunders*, underpants.

Leggings worn by outback travellers and workers are known as *flood marks, snake charmers, dog stiffeners* or *dog poisoners*. Wrinkled leggings are called *concertinas. Larstins, lastings, laughing sides* or *springsides* were old names for elastic-sided boots. Heavy boots were called *road party boots*.

Of particular interest is the word *bowyang*. This describes a strap or string tied below the knee of a worker's trousers to keep the leg-ends off the ground or to prevent the cloth dragging on the knee. First used in Australia about 1900, the word came from the provincial English *yanks* or *bow-yankees*, which were leather or other leggings worn by agricultural labourers, reaching from below the knee to the top of the boots.

Since the end of World War II, a new generation of Australians has grown up which takes clothes a good deal more seriously than was either possible or deemed suitable in the past. In Chapter XIII, we will have occasion to examine the crucial difference between *gear* and *gear gear*, and suchlike terms used by our young sartorial perfectionists today.

In the past twenty years, we have taken to wearing *jeans*, mainly due to U.S. example, although this is an extremely old English term. An important difference is that whereas American *jeans* are tight-fitting they are generally loose in Australia.

To nugget, to clean one's boots or shoes, is one of the few trade-names that have graduated to the status of a colloquialism in the antipodes. Nugget is a well-known make of boot-polish.

Modesties for baby's pilchers; *aeroplanes*, a bow tie; *storm-stick*, an umbrella; and *headlights* or (borrowed from English) *giglamps*, spectacles, are a few general terms in this country. Our expressions *gig*, a person who stares inquisitively, and *to gig (at)*, to stare (at), were probably derived from the last.

CHAPTER XII

People and Places

1. GENERAL NICKNAMES

IF SLANG IS COLOURFUL it is also utilitarian. A good deal of it is so utilitarian that we may even hesitate to call it slang for the simple reason that it puts into succinct and exact form some concept that might otherwise have to be approached in a roundabout fashion. What better descriptions have we for a person living in the Northern Territory than *Territorian* and *Topender?* What, apart from that laboured hybrid *New South Welshman* and that orthographical monstrosity *Sydneian*, have we to replace *Sydneysider?* How much easier it is to say *Westralian* than *Western Australian*, to say *inlander* instead of "a person living in remote inland areas", to describe the great "scrub" of northern Victoria as *the Mallee* instead of "the districts where *Eucalyptus dumosa* is found in profusion".

Even the simple word *Australian* is a product of our national growth; so, too, is *Commonwealth*, although it involves us in endless battles with the parallel use of "British Commonwealth". Just as the original *New Zealanders* were the Aborigines of that country, so the original *Australians* were our own Aborigines, whom anthropologists now distinguish as the *old people*. Not for some generations after the European's arrival did the native-born white acquire the name *Australian*. He was a *colonial* or a *currency lad*, but he certainly had no desire to be called a *native* of this country when such description would confuse him with a blackfellow. It was a different matter after the Aborigines had been *dispersed* – as the euphemism went – and after arrivals of fresh immigrants had put the numerical superiority of the European beyond doubt. Then he was not ashamed to be called an Australian native; he would be less maudlinly sentimental over *Home*,[1] *the old country*, *the old dart* or *the old land* as Britain was known; he would talk less of being *out here;* he would no longer interpret life in terms of the "Times" and the "Tatler"; he would begin to develop his own sports and customs and ways of speaking, and he would become as firmly rooted in this country as were the Aborigines before Europeans usurped their birthright. These are evolutionary inevitabilities.

If there are still some Australians who try to look at their country and their fellows through European eyes, these pretences do not erase the

---

[1] F. Adams in "The Australians" (1892) wrote: "Ten years ago England was spoken of as the Old Country or Home. Now it is 'home' or more sarcastically "'ome'. The inverted commas make all the difference and the dropped 'h' contains a class of contempt."

fact that they are Australians, but only disguise it a little. As these people become numerically fewer so will the pretences die. (I have left this paragraph as it appeared in the original edition of this book in 1945, but the issue is unlikely to be resolved speedily due to Australia's vast intake of migrants since the end of World War II. Many of these migrants have been English and they have revived the words *Home* and *the old country*.)

We can perceive our growth towards nationalism in the many expressions we have developed to describe those who are Australians and those who are not:

For the Englishman: *pommy, pom, pom wog, jimmy, homey, chum, chummy, choom* and *black hat*.[2]

For the Australian: *cornstalk, cornstalker, gumsucker, Aussie, dinkum* (or *dinkydi*) *Aussie, Aussielander, kangaroo, wallaby* and *billjim*.[3]

For the Aboriginal: *Abo, black, blackfellow, black skin, binghi, bing, boang, boong, darkie, murky, dark cloud* and *myall*.

For the Chinese: *chink,*[4] *chinkie, chow, chow-chow, paddy,*[5] *pat, pong, dingbat,*[6] *canary, dink, john, johnny* and *john chinaman*.

For the Italian: *sky, eyeto, steak, ding* and *dingbat*.

For post-World War II migrants in general: *Balt, New Australian, Naussie, wog*[7] (*wog wog* to distinguish Europeans from an English migrant, *pom wog*, and an American migrant, *yank wog*).

For the Jewish refugee from Europe: *reff* (sometimes slightingly *reff-raff*), *reffo, refujew* and *Jew chum* (a pun on *new chum*).[8]

For New Zealanders: *Enzedders, pig islanders, kiwis, shaky islanders, quaky islanders, Maorilanders,*[9] *fernleaves*.

Several of the terms given above need special attention – perhaps none of them more than *pommy*. There has been a popular theory that *pommy* came from *jimmygrant* (1845), as a rhyme on "immigrant", which was shortened to *jimmy*, the word then being merged by rhyme into *pomegranate* (it is suggested that the rosy-cheeked English may have given some association with the ruddy fruit) and subsequently clipped back to *pommy*. Further clipping to *pom* has also taken place; hence *Pomland*, England; *pommified*, influenced by English traditions and manners. Although claimed by some people to be a long-established word in Australia, *pommy* is not recorded by Stephens and O'Brien (1910), who

---

[2] *Ex* the headgear once worn by *new chums* on arrival. Now obsolete.

[3] Presumably *ex* the popularity of these two Christian names in Australia. Obsolete.

[4] Reference to these terms was made in Chapter I, showing that they were used originally in Australia.

[5] An old use illuminated by J. Inglis, "Our Australian Cousins" (1879): "Their [i.e. the Chinese] usually placid temper . . . seems to be ruffled when the boys take to calling them Irishmen. What there is between *pat* and *john* which calls forth such manifestations . . . I know not, but a Chinaman here is mortally insulted when you call him *paddy*."

[6] Perhaps derived by rhyme on *pat* or by association between *mad as a Chinaman* and *mad as a dingbat*.

[7] Detailed attention to Australia's long association with the word *wog* was given in Chapter VIII.

[8] All these terms are virtually obsolete.

[9] This was probably an original Bulletinism, although the use of *Maoriland* for New Zealand was current before the "Bulletin" was published.

were keen observers, although they noted *jimmy* and *jimmygrant*. This raises a problem, because it has also been suggested that *pommy* comes from the initials *P.O.M.E.* (Prisoner of Mother England), used in reference to a convict. These initials were allegedly carved on several cell walls at Port Arthur, Tasmania, and in 1945 the Clerk of the House of Assembly in Adelaide, Mr F. L. Parker, reported noting P.O.M.E. beside the names of convicts in some old N.S.W. immigration records.

The many nicknames for Chinese were in common use in the second half of last century and stemmed mainly from the fact that thousands of Chinese were drawn to Australia by gold discoveries. The peak number of Chinese in Australia was some 50,000 in 1888. The main imprint they have left with us is an inflexible legal fiction called the *White Australia Policy*. This so-called Policy, which is designed to exclude Asians and other coloured migrants, is not enunciated in either the Constitution or any immigration act.

Within Australia we have been active in devising labels for people from our various States. Thus:

For Western Australians: *gropers, sandgropers, groperlanders,*[10] *straighthairs*[11] and *Westralians.*

For South Australians: *croweaters, magpies* and *wheatlanders.*

For Queenslanders: *bananalanders, banana men, banana eaters, kanakalanders*[12] and *sugarlanders.*

For Victorians: *Yarrasiders,*[13] *cabbage gardeners, cabbage patchers* and *cabbage landers.*

For people in the Northern Territory: *Territorians* and *topenders.*[14] White residents of the Mandated Territory of New Guinea are also known as *Territorians.*

For Tasmanians: *Van Diemenese, Vandemonians,*[15] *Derveners, Derwent ducks,*[16] *mountain devils, mutton-birds, mutton-bird eaters,*[17] *barracouters,*[18] *raspberrylanders, apple islanders, Taswegians, Tassies* and *Tassylanders.*

For people in New South Wales: *Sydneysiders, walers* and *Ma-staters.*

---

[10] These terms are commentaries on the sand and desert of much of Western Australia. There is a Perth journal called "The Groper".

[11] Applied originally to Western Australian convicts.

[12] Used during the closing decades of last century when many Pacific island natives (Kanakas) were imported to work the Queensland plantations.

[13] Victoria, originally a portion of N.S.W., was not created a separate State until 1851. Up to that time, distinctions were made between those who lived on the Melbourne *side* of the colony and those on the Sydney *side*. Thus, in "Robbery Under Arms", Boldrewood alludes to "our side of the country" [i.e. the Sydney side] and again to "Melbourne . . . we all liked that side of the country". Although modern usage has tended to limit the use of *Sydneysider* to describe a resident or native of Sydney, its correct use is to describe any person in N.S.W. When the Murray River became part of the boundary between Victoria and N.S.W. the south side of the river was the *Yarraside* and the north side was the *Sydneyside*.

[14] The upper reaches of the Murray River were once called the *Top End* and people therefrom were *topenders*.

[15] Old terms derived from the original use of Van Diemen's Land for Tasmania.

[16] More old terms, referring to the Derwent River. (The use of *Sydney ducks* for prospectors from Sydney who went to the Californian goldfields was noted earlier.) Hobart convicts were once called *Derwenters*.

[17] Strictly speaking, used to describe people living in northern Tasmania.

[18] An old nickname for residents of Hobart.

In 1894 a writer in the "Bulletin" asked "Why not *Eastralia*, *Norstralia*, *Soustralia*, *Westralia* and *Centralia?*" These names sounded far-fetched in those times, but three of them are now well established, the best known, of course, being *Westralia*. It is easy to use, for the simple reason that it denotes an entire State. *Eastralia*, however, denotes the three States on the eastern seaboard and is not specific enough for general use. *Centralia* is also vague; it was once suggested as the name for what is now called South Australia and, between 1926 and 1931, when the Northern Territory was divided into North Australia and Central Australia, it was attached to a defined area. Today, it is taken to denote the remote inland section of Australia also known as the *Centre*, *Heart*, *Dead Heart*, *Never Never* and *Red Centre*.

Mainlander is used by Tasmanians – also by people on Norfolk Island – to describe a person living on the continent of Australia. *T'othersider* is current in Tasmania for anyone living on the continent, but specifically for a Victorian, by Victorians for a Tasmanian (i.e. on the other side of Bass Strait), by Western Australians for a person living in the eastern States (i.e. on the other side of the continent) and vice versa, and by New Zealanders for an Australian (i.e. on the other side of the Tasman).

Popular names for various Australian states are:

Western Australia: *Westralia*, *Groperland*.

South Australia: *the Wheat State*.

Queensland: *Bananaland*, *Kanakaland* (now obsolete) and *Nigger State* (now obsolete).

Victoria: *the Cabbage Patch* or *Cabbage Garden*.

Northern Territory: *Land of the White Ant*, *the Top End*.

Tasmania: *Tassie*, *Tassyland* or *Tassieland*, *Raspberryland*, *the Apple Isle* or *Apple Island*, *the Speck*, *the Flyspeck*, *the Isle of Sleep* and the now obsolete *Vandemonia*.[19]

New South Wales: *New South*, *the Ma State* or *Ma*.

The use of abbreviated forms is also popular, especially *W.A.*, *Vic.* and *N.S.* or *N.S.W.* By the same token we use *A.C.T.* or *F.C.T.*, although the latter is now rare, to denote the Australian or Federal Capital Territory where Canberra is situated, *N.I.* for Norfolk Island, *T.I.* for Thursday Island and *N.G.* for New Guinea. In recent years, the native peoples of New Guinea have become known as *New Guineans*.

It is worth a special note here that, mainly from 1964, Australia's Aborigines were granted the courtesy of a capital letter. Thus also for Aboriginal, both as a noun and an adjective.

Australia[20] as a whole is known variously as *Aussie*, *Aussieland*, *Kangarooland* and *the Land of the Wattle*.

Here are a few fanciful names bestowed on some of our capital cities:

---

[19] *Vandemonianism* was once used to describe violent or ruffianly behaviour and *vandemonian* was the corresponding adjective.

[20] Commonly abbreviated to *Aust.* with Australasia designated by *A/asia*.

Perth: *the Swan City.*

Adelaide: *City of the Churches, Holy City, Church City,*[21] *Farinaceous City* (or *Village*).[22]

Brisbane: *Banana City, Brissie.*

Melbourne: *City of the Cabbage Garden, Chess-board City, City of Dreadful (K)nights, the Big Smoke.*[23]

Botany Bay seems to have been used incorrectly almost from the outset. In the first place it was used wrongly to denote the convict settlement in Sydney Cove. Then it was used for the colony of New South Wales as a whole. R. M. Martin ("History of Australasia") wrote in 1836: "Many persons long used to the term Botany Bay believe that the colony is founded on the shores of this extensive inlet"; in 1845 D. MacKenzie ("Ten Years in Australia)" alludes to "Sydney, the capital of Botany Bay" and six years later we find S. Mossman ("Gold Regions of Australia") referring to Sydney as "this Botany Bay town".

Nor was this the full extent of the catachresis. Botany Bay was even used as a synonym for Australia as a whole, as shown by T. P. Macqueen ("Australia as She Is and as She May Be") in 1840, who says: "The term Botany Bay is used to represent a country co-equal in extent with all Europe united." Most of this misapplication was due to ignorance and misunderstanding in Britain, for as H. Melville pointed out in 1851 in his "Australia and Prison Discipline": "Twenty-five years back New Holland,[24] New South Wales and Van Diemen's Land were all better known in Europe under the one general expressive term of Botany Bay." It is, nevertheless, extraordinary to find a writer on Australian life[25] declaring, as late as 1863, that "Botany Bay, near Sydney, was the great depot for our convicts from 1788 to 1840". This serves to show that the fault was not altogether with people abroad. This contention is supported by the existence of such expressions as *Botany Bay aristocracy, Botany Bay coat of arms,*[26] *Botany Bay felons* and *Botany Bay swells.* I referred earlier to the long-maintained use in England of *Botany Bay wool* and *Botany Bay tops.*

Newcastle, N.S.W., is often called *the Coal City,* and as the early convict settlement there was originally called the *Coal River* settlement, it has a historic background.

Geelong, Victoria, which W. Kelly said in "Life in Victoria", vol. 1 (1859, was "the point on which the fortunes of the colony culminate and revolve", was once known as the *Pivot City* and its residents styled themselves *Pivotonians.* Geelong sporting representatives are still called by that name in the Melbourne Press. Incidentally, Kelly records that various

---

[21] From the large number of churches in Adelaide.

[22] Obsolete. *Ex* the large wheat-production of S.A.

[23] These last two nicknames are shared with Sydney.

[24] The name originally given to Australia by Dutch explorers.

[25] C. B. Gibson, "Life Among Convicts" (1863).

[26] According to an 1845 writer this signified "a pair of artificially black eyes". Another writer in 1854 said it denoted "broken noses and black eyes".

slang terms and phrases invented by Geelong residents were dubbed *Geelongese* in the Melbourne Press during the 1850s. This is the earliest known reference to anything like a local dialect in Australia.

2. REMEMBERED PLACES AND EVENTS

MANY PLACES on the Australian map have won memorials in our speech, some for trivial reasons, others because they have marked special events. Some of these have already been noted – *back o' Bourke, Murrumbidgee waler, Normanton cocktail, Wagga rug, Barcoo challenge, hang on the Condamine*, etc. – but there are others more important.

For instance, how many readers could tell the difference between *Darwin rate* and *Port Augusta rate?* These are names given to two basic wages, the former covering areas north of the 20th parallel of South Latitude, the latter covering areas south of that parallel, within the western and eastern boundaries of the Northern Territory and South Australia.

And how many could etch in details about the *Battle of Rothbury?* Or the *Tipperary Riots?* Or say where the *Ruined City* is? Or the *Burning Mountain?* Or, being aware that there is a Mullengah station at Gulargambone, N.S.W., care to hazard how we came by the phrase *beef to the ankles like a Mullingar heifer*, used to describe a girl or woman with thick ankles?

Let us start from the beginning. The *Battle of Rothbury* was a serious clash between coalminers and police at Rothbury, N.S.W., on December 16, 1929; during this "battle" one miner was killed by a bullet, nine wounded by bullets and more than forty others seriously injured; ten police were injured by stones and pieces of wood. The *Tipperary Riots* were a series of brawls between Irish and non-Irish miners on the Alma goldfield, near Maryborough, Victoria, in 1855. The *Ruined City* is the *Ruined City of Arnhem Land*, an unusual expanse of sandstone near the Phelp River, Northern Territory, about 300 air miles east of Darwin, which has been described as "one of the wonders of the world". The *Burning Mountain* is Mt Wingen, N.S.W., where a coal seam has been burning (about 500 ft. below the surface) for several thousand years. As for *beef to the ankles like a Mullingar heifer*, there is every likelihood that this is not an Australian simile at all; that it was imported from Ireland, where there is a place called Mullingar in Westmeath; that Mullengah, the name of a station at Gulargambone, is (according to the owner, Mr W. G. Giblin) "not an Aboriginal word, but probably a corruption of the Irish word"; and that it was purely a coincidence that the phrase was first reported to me from the Warren area, since later research revealed its use elsewhere.

Cobar was formerly used to denote a penny – there are copper mines at Cobar, New South Wales – and *Cobar shower* denotes a duststorm. *Darling shower, Wilcannia shower, Wimmera shower, Bourke shower, Bogan shower* and *Bedourie shower* are employed similarly. I. L. Idriess uses the last to describe a red duststorm and adds: "Here [i.e. at Bedourie, Queensland] so they say, the crows fly backwards to keep the dust out of their eyes." This well-worn bush joke was originally publicized by the poet W. T. Goodge. In his "Hits, Skits and Jingles" (1899) he refers to the *Oozlum Bird* which "always flies tail-first to keep the dust out of its eyes".

References have already been made to some of the expressions which follow, e.g. these rough outback gates: *Mallee gate, Mullengudgery gate* and *Bogan gate*. Actually, Bogan Gate (with a capital G) is a place-name.

Ballarat (until 1964, the official spelling was Ballaarat) stars in the descriptive phrase *looking like a Ballarat jewshop*, meaning in confusion or in a turmoil. An old-timer tells me that a large well-built man from Ballarat was formerly called a *Big Balla* in contrast to a weedy type who would be known as a *rat*. A still older term was *Ballarat lantern*, a candle set in a bottle neck.

In addition to *Barcoo challenge*, the Barcoo River and district in Queensland gave us *Barcoo buster*, and the *Barcoo rot, vomit* or *spew*. *Belyando spew* was named after a river in western Queensland. Also from Queensland came *Cunnamulla gun* (or *shearer*), a shearer given to boasting when drunk, *Cunnamulla cartwheel*, a large hat, *Paroo dog*, a tin rattle used to hold travelling sheep, *Burdekin duck*, sliced beef fried in batter, *Gympie hammer* and *Gympie work*, from gold-seeking days, *Brindabella*, a drink of rum and beer, *Moreton Bay*, a trickster's victim or *gay*, and (during World War II) *Brisbane Line*.

From Western Australia: *Albany doctor* and *Fremantle doctor*, refreshing sea-breezes that blow after a hot day, *Coolgardie safe*, a type of outback food safe, and the sentence *till it rains in Marble Bar*, which is virtually equivalent to "never".

Various types of *country* are recorded: *Gulf country*, country in the Gulf of Carpentaria region, *Channel country*, an area of about ten million acres in south-west Queensland, north-east South Australia and north-west N.S.W., *Corner country*, land near Haddon Corner, where the borders of Queensland, South Australia and N.S.W. meet.

And there is a host of Australian *the's*, only some of which are topographical, e.g. *the Tennant*, Tennant Creek, N.T., *the Bar*, Marble Bar, W.A., *the Mallee*, a large expanse of low-rainfall country in north-western Victoria, *the Brigalow*, a large area in central Queensland covered by *Acacia harpophylla*, *the Bight*, the Great Australian Bight, *the Dead Heart*, which soil experts apply, not to the central area of Australia, but to the much drier country round Lake Eyre, S.A.

When the first edition of this book was written Alice Springs, N.T., was commonly referred to as *the Alice*. In the past few years the "the" has been largely dropped.

A few other "the's" worth noting: *The Gabba*, Brisbane Cricket Ground at Woolloongabba, *the Old Bus*, the aeroplane Southern Cross flown by (Sir) Charles Kingsford Smith, *the Wet*, the rainy season in Australia's far north, from December to March, *the Dry*, the dry season in our far north from April to November; *the black stump*, the outward limit of mythical distance, as in *the best this side of the black stump*, *the Trans*, the express train that links Western Australia with South Australia (and other noted trains, *the Ghan, the Southern Aurora*, etc.), *the Lump*, a 10-ton boat (first ferry in Australia) launched at Sydney Cove in October, 1789.

A fairly comprehensive collection of *black days* deserves note: *black Monday*, October 15, 1945, so-called by planters in New Guinea and Papua, when all native labour contracts were cancelled by order of the Australian Government; *black Wednesday*, January 9, 1878, a day on which wholesale dismissals of Victorian civil servants took place; *black Thursday*, February 6, 1851, a day of disastrous bushfires in Victoria and of intense heat in Western Australia; *black Friday*, January 13, 1919, another day of serious bushfires in Victoria when seventy-one lives were lost; *black Saturday*, December 10, 1938, a day of serious bushfires in N.S.W.; *black Sunday*, February 6, 1938, when some 300 bathers at Bondi Beach, Sydney, were swept out to sea by huge waves and five died. The *Black War*, designed to exterminate all Tasmanian Aborigines, lasted from about 1828 to 1831; it included the so-called *Black Line* (2,000 men) which operated for seven weeks and caught one native woman and a native boy.

A few other items of historical note: *Rum Rebellion*, January 26, 1808; *Sydney Views*, gummed postage stamps sold in N.S.W. in 1850; *atmotic ship*, an elongated balloon to be powered with a steam engine invented by Dr William Bland in Sydney in 1851; *bunyip aristocracy*, name given to an abortive suggestion by W. C. Wentworth in 1853 that a colonial peerage should be created; *free, compulsory and secular*, an education system first introduced in Victoria in 1872.

Mahogany Ship was a name given to the wreck of an ancient vessel (sixteenth century) believed to be a galleon and possibly of Portuguese or Dutch origin, found in 1836 on the coast of Victoria near the western end of Bass Strait.

3. NOTABLE FIGURES

IN THE COURSE OF THIS BOOK references have been made to various real and fictitious figures who have won niches in our slang, such as John Furphy, Major Brumby, Lola Montez, D. G. Bradman, Ned Kelly, Roy Cazaly, Buckley, Jimmy Woodser and Jack Smithers. The life of many of the expressions derived from these names has usually been short, but some of them promise to retain national currency, such as *furphy*, a rumour, *Buckley's chance*, no chance at all, and *game as Ned Kelly*, extremely courageous.

Here is a list of expressions commemorating various people and fictitious characters who, at different periods of our history, won themselves notability or notoriety in Australia:

> *Barnardo of Australia, the Dr*, William Mark Forster (1846-1921), of Melbourne.

Berry blight, "A reaction against the selfish and inconsiderate policy of the squatters when they were in power." Commemorating G. Berry, Victorian premier in the 1870s, who sought to break up large estates.

Billarney (or *Bilarni*), the author, poet, bush cook and raconteur, Bill Harney, of North Queensland and the Northern Territory.

Blind Freddy, an unknown person, who is named in such phrases as "Blind Freddy could see it" and "even Blind Freddy wouldn't miss it", which are intended to indicate that a statement, view or deduction is so obvious that it cannot be ignored. Legend has it that there was a blind hawker in Sydney in the 1920s, named Freddy, whose blindness did not prevent his moving freely about the central city area.

Braddon blot (or *the Blot*), political catchphrases which arose out of a Commonwealth constitutional enactment, introduced by Sir Edward Braddon, dealing with the distribution of customs and excise revenue.

Breaker, the, Harry Harbord Morant (1865-1902), balladist, drover, horseman; court-martialled and executed in the Boer War.

brits up, to have the, to be alarmed. From "to have the wind up" and "have the sh*ts", by rhyming slang on the name of a former lightweight boxing champion of the world, Jimmy Britt, who was on vaudeville tour in Australia during World War I. *To have the jimmies* is an extension.

Brumby, Major James, a horse-breeder, who was reputedly responsible for giving us the term *brumby* for a wild horse.

Buckley's chance, one chance in a million or no chance at all. Especially used in the phrases *haven't (a) Buckley's* or *haven't Buckley's chance*. Perhaps commemorating a convict named Buckley who escaped to the bush from the Port Phillip convict settlement in 1803 and lived with the Aborigines for thirty-two years. An argument against this theory is that the expression did not become current until about 1898. More probably, it comes from a pun on the name of the Melbourne firm Buckley and Nunn (founded in 1851 in a lean-to on its present site in Bourke Street by Crumpton Nunn and Mars Buckley; it was taken over by Phillip Nunn in 1853), which would explain the currency of the Australian phrase, "There are just two chances, *Buckley's and none*" meaning that there are no chances at all.

Bully Hayes, ship thief, blackbirder, gun-runner and rogue, was William Henry Hayes (1829-77). He was born and died in the U.S., but spent many years in Australian waters after 1857.

Carruthers curl, a lofty, overswept wave of the hair, favoured by boys; commemorating Australia's first official world boxing champion, the bantamweight Jimmy Carruthers.

Castieau's Hotel, an old name for Melbourne Jail, commemorating an early governor, J. B. Castieau.

Carrington tooth powder, flour. Possibly referring to Baron Carrington, Governor of New South Wales from 1885 to 1890. (Bush slang recorded up to 1897.)

Cazaly! up there, a cry of encouragement. Commemorating a noted Victorian footballer named Roy Cazaly (1893-1963). The cry originated in 1921 and was used as the battle cry of Australia's Ninth Division troops in North Africa during World War II.

Charlie Dunn, give someone a, to run a person out (especially of a two-up school) for cheating.

Charlie Forrester, an oil stove. Shearers' slang of the 1890s "distorted from Charnwood Forrest – the kind of stove once used".

Chinese Morrison, name given to George Ernest Morrison (1862-1920), born at Geelong, Victoria, who was a journalist in China for the London "Times" and was later a political adviser to the Chinese Government.

Chloe, drunk as, extremely drunk. This is a negative entry, for its main point is that the phrase has been only vestigially influenced by the full-length painting of a naked girl called Chloe in a Melbourne bar; its origin was probably an imitation of the English slang phrase *drunk as Floey*, used similarly.

Christopher Wren of Australia, the, a name given to Edmund Thomas Blacket (1817-83), architect.

Clancy of the Overflow, a character in a ballad by A. B.("Banjo") Paterson, who was allegedly Thomas Michael Macnamara; claims have also been made for Thomas Gerald Clancy, Owen Cummins, Jim Spencer, Lachi Cockran and "Hellfire" Jack Clarke.

Cobb, a coach. Commemorating the firm of Cobb and Co., a business started in Victoria in 1853 by Freeman Cobb, J. M. Peck, J. Swanton and J. Lamber.

Dad and Dave, notable figures in the hierarchy of Australian popular literature and humour. They appeared first in A. H. Davis's "On Our Selection" (1899) and were later used for many years in a radio serial entitled "Dad and Dave".

Dear Auntie or *Dear Bill*, phrases from World War I signifying utter weariness or disgust. According to W. H. Downing, "It implied the well-known text of a fictitious soldier's letter: 'Dear Auntie (or Dear Bill), This ain't no ordinary war. It's a bloody b——, and if you want to see your little Johnny again, get right down on your knees and pray like hell.' "

Demon, the, the Australian bowler, Frederick Robert Spofforth (1853-1926).

dinnyhayser, a heavy blow, a haymaker; anything extreme in action or notably good. Commemorating the pugilist Dinny Hayes.

Don, the, the noted Australian cricketer, (Sir) Donald Bradman, born at Cootamundra, N.S.W., in 1908.

Donald of China, commemorating William Henry Donald (1857-1946), born at Lithgow, N.S.W., who became a journalist and adviser to the Chinese Government.

Firm, the, the theatrical firm of J. C. Williamson, Ltd., founded in 1882.

Fisher's ghost, reputedly the ghost of Frederick Fisher, an ex-convict murdered at Campbelltown, N.S.W., on June 17, 1826.

Flying Pieman, the, a notable Australian pedestrian, William Francis King (1807-74), who started a freak race vogue in 1848. In one effort he carried a 100-pound carriage pole in a race against the Brisbane-Ipswich coach; he finished the journey of twenty miles an hour ahead of the horses.

Flynn of the Inland, the Rev. John Flynn (1880-1951). Among his many services to the outback was the *Flying Doctor Service*, formed in 1928, and its attendant pedal radio transceiver (invented by Alfred H. Traeger), which has now been replaced by a battery-operated transceiver. These led in turn to our unique *Schools of the Air;* the first was established at Alice Springs in 1950. Flynn's concept of a *mantle of safety* for the inland has been of vast importance.

furphy, a rumour or report of doubtful authenticity. From the name of John Furphy, who established a foundry at Shepparton, Victoria, in 1874.

Geelong Galloper, the noted mile runner, John Landy.

George and Peter, the given names of two Sydney blackmarketers who earned brief notoriety about 1950. *get it from George* meant to secure an object illegally.

Golden Girl, Australia's (or *the*), the runner Betty Cuthbert, who won three gold medals at the Melbourne Olympic Games in 1956 over sprint distances, and the 400 metres at Tokyo in 1964.

Grace Darling, the Australian, Grace Bussell (1860-1935) of Western Australia, heroine of a shipwreck south of Perth in 1876.

Granny Smith, a type of apple originally cultivated by Maria Ann Smith at Eastwood, N.S.W., in the 1860s.

Greatest Liar on Earth, the, the self-chosen title of Henri Grien, who styled himself Louis de Rougemont. From the 1890s.

Griffo, the pugilist Albert Griffiths (1871-1927), probably born at Bendigo, Victoria. *fight like Griffo*, to fight with great skill and ruthlessness.

Gundy, no good to, no good at all. The Gundy in question is not known, but it is worth noting that there is a place called Gundy near Scone, N.S.W.

Happy as Larry, extremely happy. Possibly but not certainly commemorating the noted Australian pugilist Larry Foley (1847-1917).

Hargrave box kite, a type of kite invented in the early 1890s by Lawrence Hargrave, Australian pioneer in aviation.

Hellen Keller of Australia, the, Matilda Ann Aston (1874-1947) of Victoria, a blind teacher and writer.

Hungry Tyson, nickname bestowed on the squatter James Tyson (1819-98), who "became during his lifetime one of the bush traditions of eastern Australia". Whence, *Tyson*, used to denote beef in bush slang; *mean as Hungry Tyson*, extremely mean. The title *hungry* was not applied to Tyson alone, but to many outback station owners, large and small, whose main interest was in wresting profits from their lands irrespective of the results of their activities – erosion, creation of dust bowls, diminution of artesian supplies, etc. *hungry-gutted*, mean, miserly.

Jacky Howe, a short-sleeved shirt still favoured by many shearers. John Howe (1855-1922) was a champion shearer of the 1890s. His tally of 321 Merinos turned off the blades in eight hours, made at Alice Downs, Queensland, in 1892, still stands as a world record.

Jersey, a red-headed person. Commemorating the red-haired Earl of Jersey, N.S.W. Governor, 1891-3.

Jimmy Woodser, a lone drinker or a lone drink. See Chapter XI. I have a letter from a Victorian resident who says that a *Jimmy Woods*, a heavy drinker with a hare lip, lived at the end of last century at Yarpturk, near Warrnambool, Victoria.

jo-jo, nickname for a bearded man. "So called from a hairy-faced Russian 'dog-man' exhibited in Melbourne about 1880, who was advertised by that name," says Morris.

Kelly, game as Ned, extremely courageous. Commemorating the bushranger, Edward Kelly (1855-80). Also used: *Kelly gang, Kelly country, Kelly methods*, extortionate methods of business, *Ned Kelly*, a drink of coffee, thick cream and overproof Queensland rum, *and they hanged Ned Kelly!* phrase said when someone extorts more than a just sum for a purchase or investment.

Kerr, Andy, a Sydney bookmaker in the late 1920s, whose willingness to bet on almost anything gave rise to the statements, "Even Andy Kerr wouldn't back that", "Andy Kerr wouldn't take that one", etc.

Kidman's joy or *Kidman's blood mixture,* treacle or golden syrup. Commemorating Sir Sidney Kidman (1857-1935), pastoralist.

King of the Road, the, George Sorlie (1885-1948), popular producer of drama, musical comedy and pantomime in country districts.

Lamington, a Homburg hat, as worn by Baron Lamington, Queensland Governor, 1896-1901.

Lasseter's reef, a valuable reef of gold allegedly found by Lewis Harold ("Harry") Lasseter near the border of Central Australia and Western Australia; experts now agree that it was a hoax.

La Stupenda, appreciative nickname (earned overseas) of Joan Sutherland, of Sydney, noted soprano.

Let 'er go, Gallagher! Full speed ahead! This exclamation commemorates Tom Gallagher, a Cobb and Co. coachman. However, a similar expression was used in the U.S. Middle West about 1880-90.

Lithgow Flash, name given to a noted Australian woman sprinter, Marjorie Jackson, of Lithgow, N.S.W., in the early 1950s.

Little Digger, the, name given to Australian politician William Morris Hughes (1864-1952).

Lone Eagle, the, name given to aviator Bert Hinkler (1892-1933) of Bundaberg, Queensland.

Man from Snowy River, the, the man in the well-known ballad by A. B. Paterson has been variously identified as Jim Troy and Jack Riley.

Man in the Boxer Hat, the, an anonymous heavy backer who made some big "killings" on Australian racecourses during the 1930s. (A *boxer* is a bowler hat.)

Man outside Hoyts, the, name given to Charlie Fredericksen, of Melbourne, who reputedly began *fielding* outside various theatres owned by Hoyts in that city in 1908; used especially as a source of rumours.

Man They Could Not Hang, the, name given to Joseph Samuels, of Sydney, who thrice survived attempts to hang him in September, 1803. He was reprieved.

Meldrumites, followers of a theory of art propounded by David Max Meldrum, of Melbourne; also known as the *Meldrum School.*

Mrs Freer Weed, nickname given to a weed known as Paterson's Curse (*Echium vulgare*). Derived from the part played by a Federal Minister named Paterson, in October, 1936, in banning from Australia an oversea visitor, Mrs G. Freer, who was eventually allowed to enter the country in July, 1937.

Mules operation, an operation performed on a sheep to prevent *fly-strike.* Two folds of skin under the thighs are removed. This checks the extent of urine wetting which attracts flies. The operation was first suggested in 1931 by J. H. W. Mules, grazier of Woodside, South Australia.

mullenizing, the clearing of scrub-covered land with a roller pushed by horses. Named after an Irish settler near Adelaide named Mullens.

Nunawading Messiah, Andrew Fisher, of Nunawading, Victoria, who declared himself the Messiah. His sect of a hundred followers was polygamous and he took three sisters as his wives (June 21, 1871).

Oakes' oath, an unreliable affirmation of honesty. An extremely old expression, as shown by G. H. Haydon, in "The Australian Emigrant" (1854), wherein a person says he will "chance it, like Major Oakes did". Who this Major Oakes was remains obscure. In the "Bulletin" of September 28, 1901, a writer says that the expression "I'll chance it, as Oakes did his oath", "refers to one Oakes, a Parramatta celebrity, who, tradition tells, was prosecuting a man for cattle-stealing. Evidence showed that the prisoner had a pair of horns in his possession and Oakes was asked if he could swear that the horns belonged to any beast of his. He hesitated for a space, then suddenly burst out, 'Well, I'll chance it! Yes!'."

Old Master, the, the comedian Harry Van der Sluice (1892-1954), also known as Roy Rene and *Mo*.

Oppy, nickname of Hubert Opperman, Australia's most famous road cyclist (in the 1920s and 1930s), later a Federal Cabinet Minister.

Oscar, money, cash. From a rhyme on the surname of John Stanger Heiss Oscar Asche (1871-1936), born at Geelong, Victoria, noted actor.

Our Glad, nickname of Australian singer and musical comedy star Gladys Moncrieff, born at Bundaberg, Queensland, in 1893.

Owen gun, a gun invented by Evelyn Ernest Owen (1914-49) of Wollongong, N.S.W., and used widely by the Australian Army in World War II.

Patriotic Six, members of the Tasmanian Legislative Council who supported a proposal in 1845 to inquire into governmental costs of the convict system and who later resigned.

Petrov, do a, to seek political asylum in Australia. Commemorating a Russian Embassy official named Petrov, who sought political asylum in Australia in April, 1954.

Prince of Australia, the, self-chosen title of John Piper (1773-1851), who arrived in Australia in 1792.

River Murray spaniel, the, nickname of George Bain Johnston (1829-82), pioneer steamer captain on the Murray and related rivers, because of his many rescues of people in danger of drowning in the Murray.

Sing 'em muck, a "famous saying" alleged to have been uttered by Dame Nellie Melba, 1861-1931, the noted Australian singer.

Smithy, nickname of (Sir) Charles Kingsford Smith (1897-1935), noted aviator. His reference to his plane as *the old bus* was widely known. Also remembered is *Coffee royale*, name given to a camp on the Glenelg River estuary, Western Australia, where Kingsford Smith and three companions were forced down by fuel shortage in March, 1929. Two searchers died.

Tichborne impostor, description of Arthur Orton (1834-98) a Wagga Wagga butcher. He claimed to be the son of Lady Tichborne and also a baronet, and for a time succeeded in his fraud.

Torrens title (or *system*), terms applied to a legal system which simplifies and speeds up the transfer of land. Devised by (Sir) Robert Torrens (1814-84) and first used in South Australia in 1858.

Trickett, a long drink of beer. Commemorating Edward Trickett, Australian professional champion sculler in 1875 and world champion from 1876 to 1880.

Watsons, bet like the, to wager heavily. There were apparently two Watson brothers, but legend disagrees when they operated – it varies from the 1880s to "about 1910". They are alleged to have been born at Bendigo,

Victoria, and also to have been Sydney hotel-keepers and outback N.S.W. shearers.

Whitely King, "a billy fashioned from a fruit tin, so-named from the secretary of the Pastoralists' Union who, during the shearing troubles, sent out bands of non-unionists furnished with these impromptu utensils." – "Bulletin", February 1, 1902.

Wild White Man, the, a convict named William Buckley who lived with Aborigines for thirty-two years, from 1803 to 1835. He is commemorated in the title of a book by J. Bonwick (1856). The "Australian Encyclopaedia" has a section devoted to *Wild White Men*, as a generic title for "*white blackfellows*".

4. GIVEN NAMES

ALTHOUGH GREAT FLUCTUATIONS are to be found in the lower echelons of name-giving in Australia (especially in names given to female babies) there is also a good deal of uniformity. Admittedly, it is difficult to find a good basis of comparison, but we are fortunate to have a brief list of the most popular names given to children in 1856 (published in the "Sydney Morning Herald" of December 10, 1955). For the purpose of illustration, I will also give the comparable Australia-wide list published in the original edition of this book in 1945 and the results of a similar Australia-wide survey in 1965:

BOYS

1856	1945	1965
John	John	John
William	Robert	James
James	David	Andrew
Charles	James	David
Edward	Peter	Peter
George	Ian	Michael
Henry	William	Timothy

GIRLS

1856	1945	1965
Mary	Ann(e)	Ann(e)
Elizabeth	Margaret	Jane
Sarah	Elizabeth	Elizabeth
Catherine	Mary	Louise
Emma	Patricia	Margaret
Ellen	Kay(e)	Mary
Margaret	Lorraine	Michelle

The first thing evident is that, over the passage of more than a century in Australia, John has been the name most commonly given to male babies. The only other name to be found in all lists is James, and that is also well to the top.

While Ann or Anne has remained the most popular name for girls in the past twenty years, it was not listed in 1856. However, three names are found in all lists – Mary, Elizabeth and Margaret.

During the course of my 1965 survey, I noted that one unfortunate male baby had been burdened with the name of Tumbarumbah. This is a N.S.W. place-name (the official spelling is without the final "h"), and since no alternative name was given to the victim one trembles for what is in store for him at school. Generally speaking, however, such oddities are rare, and when colourful outlets are chosen they are mainly confined to hyphenates like Connie-Marle, Jayne-Louise, Jo-Anne and Lee-Anne, and a few rare names like Debra, Elicia, Nardle and Lissa, all for girls. Matters seem to have been less agreeable back in 1856. Some samples: for boys, Too Long, Xray, Alfred The Great, Manly Beach; for girls, Wordy, North Australia, Queachy, Maybe.

Australians are only slowly being persuaded to adopt or invent indigenous given names for their children (one doubts whether Tumbarumbah is a good example). In both Australia and New Zealand girls appear to be more favoured as subjects for experiment than boys, due probably to the fact that many native words end in a vowel. Here are some native names in current use, which give an indication of increasing popularity: GIRLS: *Jarrah* (the tree), *Brewa* (from the town named Brewarrina), *Kylie* (a boomerang), *Coreen* ("the last of the hills", a place-name in N.S.W.), *Eena* (Aboriginal for "good little girl"), *Myee* (Aboriginal for "little girl"), *Bindi* (from a place-name). BOYS: *Kanga* (an abbreviation of kangaroo), *Wilga* (a flowering tree). *Sydney*, especially with the "y" spelling, is popular as a boy's name. Here are some Maori names given to girls in New Zealand: *Huia* (a bird), *Tui* (a bird), *Ngaio* (a tree), *Rata* (a tree), *Kara* (a Maori pidgin version of the word "colour").

Through the influence of the bushranger Ned Kelly any male possessing the name Kelly is invariably nicknamed *Ned*. In the same way a Paterson or Patterson earns the nickname *Banjo* from the popular Australian poet, A. B. Paterson, who styled himself *The Banjo*. An Allen is often nicknamed *Barney* from a once-noted bookmaker, Barney Allen, a Baker is called *Snowy*, a Smith is called *Gunboat*, a Hall is called *Ben*, all in memory of others.

Other popular Australian nicknames are *Blue* and *Bluey*, for a red-haired person, *Chiller*, for Charles, and a large number of hypocoristic forms which employ the -o suffix, such as *Jimmo*, *Tommo*, *Billo*, *Johnno*, *Sallo*, *Daiso*, *Freddo*, *Betto*.

In the early 1950s, a Federal law was passed curbing haphazard changes of name by New Australians. Until then, many refugees, displaced persons and migrants from Continental Europe had been unhindered in their efforts to merge with the dinky-di Australian environment by modifying the spelling of their names or shucking them altogether. Thus, Neuss became Noyce, Hirschmann became Hirshman, Kraushaar became Crawshaw; alternatively, Kruger became Ryan, Molnar became Milton, Schnittlinger became Shelton. There were even more heroic efforts: Nazzareno Vincent Antonio Xuareb became the unpretentious Morrie Wilson; Ioanis Nicholas Ganacopoulos became John Jones; Constantino Coumpis became Con Coombes; Panagiotis Panagakis became Peter Pangas; Anastasious Diamandarus became Richard Diamond; Savas Nicolave became Sam Nicholls.

5. PLACE-NAMES

ONE OF THE REGRETTABLE FEATURES of Australian place-names is their lack of originality and imagination. Many of them read like a catalogue of London suburbs, English provincial towns and U.S. cast-offs. They represent a smear of dullness wiped across the Australian map.

We have used Aboriginal names fairly freely, but we could have afforded to sacrifice many importations in order to use more of those melodious native words.

Where our early settlers managed to impose a glimpse or two of originality, their heirs often seem to have made deliberate attempts to cut out all deviations from dullness. Whither have gone such poetic contributions as Hunchy Mama Creek, Venus Jump Up and Gentleman's Glasshouses (Queensland), Broken Cart and Murdering Swamp (New South Wales), Maggoty Gully, Bust-my-Gall and Break-my-Neck (Tasmania)? Why, on the other hand, are we inflicted with names like those noted by J. Foster Fraser in "Australia" (1912):

> When in Australia I started collecting curious names. In New South Wales alone I found thirty Dead Horse Flats, twenty-seven Tin-Pot Gullies, 130 Sandy Creeks . . . ninety Sugar Loaf Hills.

About 10,000 names of Australian localities are listed in the "Commonwealth Census Bulletin" of 1961, which confines its attention to localities with twenty dwellings or more, or with populations over 49. As a result, some 5,000 small localities are ignored. Of those noted, about one third are Aboriginal or derived from Aboriginal names. Although considerable, this percentage by no means compares with the position in New Zealand where more than 57 per cent of the principal place-names are Maori.

Many Australian Aboriginal names admittedly present confusing problems of pronunciation. People from overseas find difficulty in coping with words like Wagingoberambi, Collarenebri, Dadinulup, Gringegalonga, Mundabullangana, Naringaningalook and Nunjikompita. Even repetitive names like Wagga Wagga, Mogil Mogil, Kurri Kurri, Bong Bong, if not difficult to pronounce, are strange-sounding to foreign ears.

The majority of them, however, display greater imagination, virility and forcefulness on the part of our natives than on that of the Europeans who have named so many of our towns, rivers and other geographical sundries.

Many Aboriginal names are not only beautiful to the ear – when pronounced in their unmutilated, unanglicized versions – but are splendid in their imagery.

W. W. Thorpe, ethnologist of the Australian Museum, Sydney, compiled an excellent "List of New South Wales Aboriginal Place-names and Their Meanings" and, in the third edition issued in 1940, gave some 730 examples. The booklet was later revised and enlarged by Frederick D. McCarthy. Here are a few colourful extracts that speak for themselves:

> *Balagorang*, feeding ground of the kangaroo.
> *Gowrie*, down of the eaglehawk.
> *Beebari*, place of a large brown snake.
> *Wollumbi*, meeting of the waters.
> *Myuna*, clear water.
> *Keelbubban*, the sound of rippling water.
> *Marangaroo*, little blue flowers.

Wrote Mundy in "Our Antipodes" (1852):

> Some of the native names of places are grandly sonorous and poly-syllabic; it is well when they are retained by the English possessors of the lands, instead of substituting vulgar and unmeaning European titles.

Numerous Australian poetasters have been tempted to put together "poems" composed mainly of these native words. In 1824 J. D. Lang gave us:

> I like the native names, as Parramatta,
>   And Illawarra, and Wolloomooloo,
> Nandowra, Woogarora, Bulkomatta,
>   Tomah, Toongabbie, Mittagong, Meroo;
> Buckobble, Cumleroy, and Coolangatta,
>   The Warragumby, Bargo, Burradoo;
> Cookbundoon, Carrabaiga, Wingecarribee,
>   The Wollondilly, Yurumbon, Bungarribee.

In contrast to these, how meaningless sound such filchings from abroad as Cardiff, St Ives (twice), Liverpool, Torquay, Toronto, Texas, Virginia (twice), Jericho (twice) and Jerusalem, especially when we realize that many of these names are attached to places that are little more than trifling settlements. "It is very confusing", wrote Keith Kennedy, President of the N.S.W. Anthropological Society, 1933-4, in a foreword to "Australian Aboriginal Place-names", by James Tyrrell, in 1933 "to use names belonging to other parts of the world which have no significance here, and it is absurd to name places after people of no special note or distinction."

Fortunately, there is a small tincture of imagination in a few examples, such as Blowhard, Wail and Big Pat's Creek (Victoria), Baking Board,

Rise and Shine, and Goodnight (Queensland), Snuggery and O.B. Flat (South Australia), Wishbone and Youanmi (Western Australia), Broke, Come-by-Chance and Nevertire (N.S.W.).

Although at first sight it might be thought that place-names are remote from the general course of the Australian language, there are several reasons why this Section has been pursued at some length. In the first place it stresses the large number of Aboriginal words in constant use and in the second place it shows that a few Australianisms have acquired niches on the map. Some of the more interesting of these are: Billabong, Bunyip, Jumbuk, Smoko, Woolshed, Nuggety (Victoria); Bushranger's Creek, Combo, Jamberoo, Little Billabong, Willi Willi (New South Wales); Woolshed Creek, Boomerang, New Chum (Queensland); Woolshed Flat, Yacka (South Australia); Kronkup, Waddy Flat (Western Australia).

In general usage Jumbuk is spelt *jumbuck*, Willi Willi is rendered *willy willy*, and Yacka is *yakka* or *yacker*. Kronkup seems to be an authentic Western Australian native name, but the Australian uses of *cronk*, spurious, worthless, ill, and *cronk up*, to become or render worthless, etc., immediately suggest themselves. A *combo* is a white man who cohabits with an Aboriginal girl or woman. *Waddy* is an Aboriginal pidgin corruption of "wood", used originally for a wooden club or stick, and first recorded in print in the "Sydney Gazette" of September 2, 1804.

These are minor items among our thousands of place-names, but they provide some evidence that, even in spite of ourselves, we have managed to preserve a few traces of originality. Of course, by contrast we can look to our dreary array of repetitions and almost forget there is such a thing as imagination. Sandy Creek appears eighteen times in the "Census Bulletin" of 1933; Spring Creek, fourteen times; Deep Creek, twelve times; Red Hill, seven times, together with Redhill twice and Redhills once; Reedy Creek, eight times; Back Creek, seven times; and Paradise, five times (there are also three Arcadias and two Gardens of Eden).

Hypocorisms or familiarizations are persistent features of Australian slang. We find them in many popular clippings of place-names, although the bulk of these clippings are mainly local in use. For instance, Bathurst (N.S.W.) people regularly shorten the name of their town in writing to *Bx*, which would be unintelligible to most Australians.

In the "Bulletin" of April 14, 1900, a writer noted the following place-name shortenings from Queensland: *Luck* for Lucknow; *Riddle* for Llanrheidol; *Buck* for Toolebux; *Dot* for Carrandotta; *Bull* for Boulia; and *Dan*, Urandangie.

There are countless other examples, such as *Oodna*, for Oodnadatta; *Coota*, for Cootamundra; *Mullum*, for Mullumbimby; *Wang*, for Wallerawang; *Parra*, for Parramatta; *Berra*, for Canberra; *Willy*, for Williamstown; *Rocky*, for Rockhampton; *Brissie*, for Brisbane, and our "the" series noted earlier. There are also interpolated forms such as *Dim-damn-boola* for Dimboola, and *Warrack-bloody-nabeal* for Warracknabeal. But many of these are localized in use or rarely heard outside the boundary of their home State.

As I have already said, one of the reasons why Aboriginal names have not been greatly favoured by white Australians is that ignorant new-comers had difficulty in pronouncing them. Grave conflicts over the pronunciation of place-names, especially those with Aboriginal ante-cedents, led the Australian Broadcasting Commission to undertake a monumental work of attempting to standardize these pronunciations. To overcome local complaints about mutilation of place-names in radio announcements, the A.B.C. appointed a committee, under the chairman-ship of Emeritus Professor E. R. Holme, to prepare an authoritative guide to the way the more difficult names should be said.

This report pointed out that a major problem with Aboriginal names is to know where to put the most important stress. Thus, Byabarra is, according to the A.B.C. Pronunciation Advisory Committee, pronounced with the stress on the penultimate syllable, By-aBARa. But Byaburra, which has a "u" instead of an "a" in the third syllable, is pronounced By-AB-ara. Cowan takes the stress on the final syllable, but Cowongs takes it on the first.

Goondiwindi is pronounced Gun-da-WINdy. Many people might imagine that Goondoobluie would also take its accent on the penultimate syllable. But they would be wrong. The correct version, according to the A.B.C., which has consulted local opinion in this and other matters, is Gun-DA-bluey. This defiance of logical analogy is a reason why migrants to Australia have great difficulty with our nomenclature. Whereas Mundarlo is pronounced Mun-DAH-lo, the pronunciation of Mundaroo is MUN-da-roo. Youngareen takes the accent on the final syllable, but Youngerrina is pronounced Young-ERRina.

The A.B.C. list repays careful scrutiny in other directions. For example, of Collarenebri – the stress is on the third syllable – it is noted that the name is always pronounced with a "d", even if it is not spelt as Collarendebri.

Geurie is shown to be pronounced as GEAR-ee, Gwabegar is WOBby-gah, Echuca is Ee-CHOO-ka, Sobroan is Sa-BRON, and Dumaresq is Da-MERrick.

Same spellings, different pronunciations: Argyle, W.A., is pronounced AH-gyle, Argyle, N.S.W., is ah-GYLE; Collie, W.A., is COLL-ee, Collie, N.S.W., is COLL-eye; Eschol, Qld, is ESH-ol, Eschol, N.S.W., is ESH-col; Eungella, Qld, is YOUNG-gella, Eungella, N.S.W., is yoon-GHELLa; Gin Gin, Qld, is JIN-jin, Gin Gin (Bridge), N.S.W., is GHIN-GHIN; Glencoe, Qld, is GLEN-ko, Glencoe, N.S.W., is glen-KO; Tyalgum, Qld, is tie-AL-gum, Tyalgum, N.S.W., is TAL-gum.

Similarities: We have three places called Derby – in Western Australia, Tasmania and Victoria. All are pronounced DERby (but note, in the next paragraph, the official verdict on Jervis Bay). We have a Bream Creek in Tasmania and a Bream Beach in N.S.W. In each case, the first word is pronounced BRIM.

Official choices: Mackay, Qld, is ma-KYE (*not* ma-KAY); Jervis Bay, A.C.T., is JAR-vis (*not* JER-vis) Bay; Wollongong, N.S.W., is WOOL-en-gong (*not* WOLL-on-gong); Bondi, N.S.W., is BONDYE with equal stress on each syllable.

There are many other peculiarities. Thus, Rouchel is pronounced ROO-kal, Scheyville is SKY-vill, Foveaux is Fa-VO, Laheys Creek is LAZE Creek. Boonoo Boonoo is pronounced Bunna-baNOO, Mungie Bundie becomes Mucker-BUN-dye, Ghinni Ghinni becomes GHINnee-ghin-NEE. Cobrabald, the name of a mount, is spelt with a "d" at the end, but, according to the A.B.C. list, is pronounced KAW-bra-ball. Pindari looks straightforward, but becomes Pin-da-ROY. Many other Aboriginal words ending in "i", such as Beni, Congi, Crocki, Duri, Mehi, Tomki and Uki, are pronounced with the final syllable sounding like "eye", but there are exceptions. Moonbi is pronounced MOON-bee.

Sometimes a syllable disappears, as in Benandarah, pronounced Ba-NAN-dra, and Canowindra, pronounced Ca-NOWN-dra. Sometimes a new syllable appears from nowhere, as in Booroorban (Ba-ROO-a-ban) and Bourbah (BOO-a-bah). In other Aboriginal names the stress moves around so much that it is impossible to formulate simple rules. Almost every word has to be mastered individually. Here are examples:

> *Stress on first syllable:* Barnato, Banara, Berembed, Canberra, Talbragar.
> *Stress on second syllable:* Allgomera, Ballandry, Barywigil (Bah-YOO-gal), Beabula (Bee-AB-you-la), Eremeran (Er-RIM-a-ran), Genanagie, Gerogery, Jackadgery.
> *Stress on third syllable:* Adaminaby, Balladoran, Currawabbity, Girilambone, Merrimerriwa.
> *Stress on fourth syllable:* Barraganyatti, Belingerambil, Condonbolonga, Murrycumumualah (Murree-cum-OOM-you-ala), Wattamondara.

The longest place-names in Australia are Aboriginal: Lake Cadibarra-wirracanna, S.A., and Lake Mirranpongapongunna, Simpson Desert.

When, in an outburst of patriotic fervour after World War I, we expunged from our map nearly 100 "German" place-names, officialdom remained bogged down in an unimaginative rut. It passed up a golden opportunity to enliven the map with original inventions or to take advantage of the store of Aboriginal words offering. Less than 30 per cent of the new names were Aboriginal. Here are a few of the other changes:[27]

> *New South Wales:* Germanton to Holbrook, German's Hill to Lidster, German Creek to Empire Vale.
> *Victoria:* Germantown to Grovedale, Hochkirch to Tarrinton, Mt Bismarck to Mt Kitchener.
> *Queensland:* Bergen to Murra Murra, Bergenside to Neuve, Bismarck to Maclagan, Engelsburg to Kalbar, Gehrkevale to Mount Mort, Gramzow to Carbrook, Hapsburg to Kowli, Hessenburg to Ingoldsby, Kirchheim to

---

[27] Commonwealth Year Book, vol. xix, 1926, section on changes of German place and district names.

Haigslea, Murden to Frenchton, Roessler to Applethorpe, Stegeht to Woongoolba, Teutelberg to Willa, Fahley to Kilbirnie.

South Australia: Bartsch's Creek to Yedlakoo Creek, Hundred of Basedow to Hundred of French, Cape Bauer to Cape Wondoma, Berlin Rock to Panpandie Rock, Bethanien to Bethany, Bismarck to Weeroopa, Blumberg to Birdwood, Blumenthal to Lakkari, Buchfelde to Loos, Carlsruhe to Kunden, Ferdinand Creek to Ernaballa Creek, Gebhardt's Hills to Polygon Ridge, Germantown Hill to Vimy Ridge, Kaiserstuhl to Mt Kitchener.

Western Australia: Mueller Park to Kitchener Park.

Tasmania: Bismarck to Collins Vale.

By far the greatest number of changes were made in South Australia, where people of German stock had done much pioneering. As Australia grows older this melancholy example of xenophobia will not be regarded as one of this country's proudest achievements.

CHAPTER XIII

The Young

1. FASHIONS AND GAMES

THE WORLD OF CHILDREN is refreshingly simple. Their likes and dislikes are clear-cut, their enthusiasms whole-hearted, their aversions decided. Within these limitations, which are not darkened by adult complexes other than perhaps by envy of the expert and a remarkable ability to injest food, they are lusty practitioners of slang.

Their story, so far as it affects the Australian language, is relatively short, but it has an atmosphere of positiveness about it that is at once delightful and vigorous.

It is impossible, of course, to be arbitrary in saying where child slang begins and where it ends. Many adult terms are used by them, just as many of the terms favoured by children have found their way into popular speech. Most of the expressions for notable or excellent things – such as *curl, curl-the-mo, dazzler, dinker, boomer, caster, bottler, whopcacker, rube, snodger, snodging, grouse, bosker-ann, peb, pebbly, sniddy* (some of which have been noted before) – are used mainly by young people although they frequently find their way into print.

There is, for instance, an old chant favoured by children, *Give a thing, take a thing, is a blackfellow's plaything!* addressed to a child who wants the return of something he has given away. On December 15, 1939, it found its way into the New South Wales Workers' Compensation Court on the lips of Judge Perdriau who rendered it, "Give a thing and take a thing, is a bad man's plaything!" So we cannot lay down too stringent laws about the scope of child speech or impose too many limitations upon it.

This would be difficult in any case, because child slang is subject to an infinite variety of fashions and quirks; it comes and goes unpredictably like marbles and tops; faulty hearing causes many mutilations, imagination is liable to step in and produce a word that will be immediately forgotten. Thus a child who cannot recall the word "oars" concocts *wavers* to fill the breach, calls a traymobile a *dinner pram*, a bookshelf a *book shelter*, and, having misheard the word "windmill", calls it a *windwheel*, because the concepts of wind and wheel are known, and that of mill is unknown. In similar fashion the child misinterprets speech because of the contest between known and unknown concepts, and will ask "Why will a man *bite* a dog?" when its parent produces the hackneyed nonsense about "going to see a man about a dog".

In this way a good deal of purely domestic parlance arises, often confined to single families and rarely graduating to the status of general nursery slang. This type of speech is obviously outside our ambit.

Of slightly more significance is the formula. Many such linguistic enigmas creep into the talk of children – the sort of thing we saw earlier when we looked at the many South Australian uses of *dickon*. Even the simple word *good* can acquire meanings varying from passable to excellent: "How are you?" – "Good!" "How's school?" – "Good!" "How are you getting on in class?" — "Good!" "How's your family?" – "Good!" When all such replies are made in the same disinterested tone of voice, one suspects that the youngster is merely being patient with the adult questioner. Indeed, one sometimes feels that they convey about the same measure of information as *have an apple!* which a child says in answer to something he (or she) does not hear properly.

Many parents find it hard to believe, but children are much less interested in their constant interference than in their known presence in the background. Remove that presence and the child feels deeply distressed. What the child needs is someone to turn to in times of crisis, and not at other times. There are other matters demanding the child's attention.

When cicadas are shouting in the summer trees, who but an expert or a child could identify them? There are many types to identify: *yellow monday, green monday, yellow tuesday, black friday, black prince, black diamond, chocolate soldier, bladder, lamplighter, red eye, washerwoman, cherry nose, whisky drinker, double drummer, Union Jack, floury baker, tom thumb, peter peter, green grocer* and *squeaker.* (I put the *yellow monday* first, because it was from misinterpretation of an Aboriginal's name, *Yellowmundee* or *Yalamundy*, who was met by Watkin Tench in 1791 near Parramatta, that this and other weekday names came.) The pursuit of these insects has led doctors to give the name *cicada fractures* to broken limbs sustained by youngsters at *cicada-time*.

Doctors also have an annual rash of burns and other injuries from what is known as *cracker night*. This is an occasion – either the night of Commonwealth Day (formerly Empire Day), May 24 each year, or of Guy Fawkes Day, November 5 each year – when fireworks are let off; it varies from one part of Australia to another, but is largely confined to the former date in the eastern States.

State preferences also vary in terms for giving a second person a lift on a bicycle built for one. The oldest version seems to be *double-banking* (used generally throughout Australia), but *donkeying* is currently preferred in South Australia, *double-donking* in Victoria, *double-dinking* in Western Australia and *doubling* in N.S.W. A *dink* or a *donk* is such a ride ("Speedway dink for duchess" was a heading in the Melbourne "Herald" of April 22, 1949, and " 'Double-dink' elopement" was used in the Sydney "Daily Mirror" of January 23, 1946).

Double-banking has several applications far removed from children. First, to quote the anonymous author of "Reminiscences of Early Australian Life" (1893): " . . . it behoved us to economize our labour, and to make shifts and contrive in every way to keep our flocks and herds at as little cost as possible, as by increasing and doubling the numbers in our flocks of sheep, and making one man do the work that was formerly alloted to two – double-banking them, as it was then termed." Second, in "The Man from Oodnadatta" (1933), R. B. Plowman alludes to *double-banking* on a camel. Third, I have a letter from an anthropologist in Western Australia, dated 1959, which says in part: "In Western Australia, *double-bank* has quite an interesting history. I first heard it used in the Murchison region as a term of derision, in regard to Aborigines belonging to the south-west. They mean by it that a native from the south-west is untrustworthy, because he'll double-bank a person – that is, in a fight, he'll call on his relatives to help him against one person and thereby outnumber him. But that's not where the story ends. What is most interesting to me is the term's earlier history, which I found in an annual report of the Chief Protector of Aborigines, somewhere around 1919. In the south-west of W.A. there were a number of ration depots for natives and up to 1919 they used to give out rations on different days of the week. Some smart natives got the habit of *double-banking*. They used to travel from one ration centre to another during the week and thereby received double rations. To put a stop to this *double-banking*, the Chief Protector made Monday the rationing day throughout the South."

Since children are basically conservative in their habits, they tend to cling to old terms rather than invent new ones. In some cases, they overwork a word to an extraordinary degree. *Doubler* is a good example. For instance, a *doubler* may indicate two children on one swing, or two swings fixed together, or two children sliding down a slippery-dip, or four children on a seesaw (two at each end) or two children riding on one scooter or bicycle, and so on.

A game like marbles provides us with great variety. Marbles of one kind and another are known to Australian children as *bottlies, bottle-ohs, botts, bodgies, cornies, cornelians, connies, connie agates, chows, dakes, doblars, conks, commos, commonos, stinkies, stonkers, stonkies, stonks, scotchies, dibs, mibs, peewees, clays, glassies, tollies, pinkies, steelies, steelos, immas* and *smokies*. Since marbles are played in many sections of the world (and by adults), it is difficult to say where indigenous influence begins and ends. The same observation applies to such games as *any-every, big ring, little ring, follow on, eyesie, eyedrop* and *nosedrop;* and to technical terms like *knuckling in, die shot* and *tom bowler.*

An article on child marble players in the Sydney "Daily Telegraph" of March 18, 1950, p. 14, recorded a number of undefined exclamations including: *no dubs! dubs over! no clears! kicks my way! no kicks! knocks my way!* and *no knocks!* all of which are apparently intelligible among youthful marble fans. There was also some truck with the equally-baffling terms *firsters, seconders, thirders, poison, straights, topper, spinning out* and *holey.* The *fat* is a ring in which marbles are played; a *funnick* is a shot in which the hand encroaches inside the ring; *moz* is an expression used when the rules of the particular game allow a line to be drawn across an opponent's path to distract him (we have a colloquial use of *moz* and *mozzle*, to interrupt or hinder; *to put the moz – or mock – on someone* is to inconvenience or put a hoodoo on a person); *pinking* denotes a preliminary selection among players to decide the order of play; *poison* is the fourth hole in the game of *three holes*.

In "Saturdee" (1933), Norman Lindsay uses numerous examples of marbles slang not given above, notably *milky*, *Frenchy* and *slatey*, and refers to other children's games such as *egg-cap*, *duckstone*, *stag knife* and *nick-nocking*.

He calls a catapult a *shot-ging*. Other popular terms to describe this essential weapon of all healthy boys before the onset of ray-guns and similar modern products from the U.S., are *ging*, *gog-eye*, *dinger*, *shong*, *wong* and *shanghai*, the last being the oldest and best-known of the group. The term *shanghai* was first used in Australia about 1860; from it come the colloquial uses of *within a shanghai shot*, *to shanghai a stone*, *to get shanghaied from a horse*. About the time *shanghai* first got a hearing, Australian children were playing at *bobbies and bushies*, the former denoting the police and the latter bushrangers.

One of the cheapest of all juvenile games is stone-throwing. Depending on local preferences, a stone is a *goolie*, *quailer*, *gibber*, *yonnie*, *ronnie*, *brick*, *brinny*, *cundy* or *boondie*. The last, sometimes spelt *bundy*, is especially common in Western Australia. To throw is to *lob*, *bish*, *biff* or *peg* (this comes from English dialect).

In his "Timely Tips to New Australians" (1926), Jice Doone refers to *I-ackee*, "a children's game, resembling out-of-doors hide-and-seek in which the word is used as a cry". Another popular exclamation is *baldy!* which is the equivalent of the English *fain I!* or *fainits!* implying a formula of refusal. It probably comes from the English dialectal *barley*, "an exclamation frequently used by children in their games when they wish to obtain a short exemption from the laws of the amusement in which they are occupied". A correspondent informs me that *barley!* is also used by some Australian children, but is regarded as "rather sissy". However, the plural *barleys!* is commonly used in South Australia in a chasing game called *touchey*. An Australian child is more likely to call out *bar!* or *bars!* or spell out the word *b-a-r!* thereby gaining respite or protection from pursuit or attack by another in what is known as a game of *chasings*. If the pursuer does not agree with this arbitrary invocation of unwritten rules granting protection he cries *broken bars!* or *bars over!* and the chase is on again.

As already pointed out, much child slang is subject to fashions; in addition a good deal of it is localized. A chant such as the following – recorded in the "Bulletin" of March 12, 1898 – would obviously be limited to use among children living in or near the Sydney areas mentioned:

> Johnny and Jane and Jack and Lou,
> Butler's Stairs through Woolloomooloo,
> Woolloomooloo and 'cross the Domain,
> Round the Block and home again.
>> Heigh ho! tipsy toe
>> Give us a kiss and away we go!

It is worth recording, if only because I heard a debased version of it recited by two skipping girls in Paddington as late as 1957.

Here is a girls' counting and eliminating chant also recorded in Sydney: "Inty-minty, pumpa-tinty, tan, toon, tassa."

And here is a girls' marching song:

Gin gang gooly wooly wooly wooly,
Watchit,
Gin gan goo, gin gan goo.
(Repeat all.)
Aila, aila shaila, aila shaila, shaila oo-OO.
(Repeat.)
Sully-wully shully-wully, shully-wully shully-wully,
Oompa, oompa, oompa, oompa.

(One group of the singers then chants "Oompa oompa" while the others repeat the whole thing. This goes on indefinitely during marches, parts being taken over in turn by each group.)

2. SCHOOL SLANG

PRACTICALLY EVERY SCHOOL possesses some peculiarities of child parlance, although these are not easy for the adult to collect. I offer, as an example of Australian inventiveness, the following list of expressions used by children in a well-known Victorian school – a list which was compiled by a teacher after many months of patient listening:

bid, a maid or waitress. Hence, *king of the bids*, the head waitress.

blear, to go about in a state of unawareness, "it carries with it a sense of psychological as well as physical unawareness". Thus: "There was Snooty *blearing* along", "He *bleared* into the hall and forgot to say grace."

brinnies, stones. Thus: "We got six for throwing *brinnies* on the grid shed [i.e. bicycle shed]."

cemetery, the sanitary wing. Thus: "I left my sweater in the *cemetery*."

date! used when a person makes an inaccurate or stupid statement which is proved wrong, or when a ruse doesn't come off. Thus: "*Date!* Brown, your number is up!"

dirty big, an expletive similar to bloody or blooming. Thus: "He's a *dirty big* slacker", "I got a *dirty big* cut on my leg."

fanny,[1] a nurse or house matron. Thus: "We've got a new *fanny* this term."

fish, to catch a fish, anger; to be the subject of another's ire. Thus: *To be in a fish*, to be in a temper; "I'll *catch a fish* if I don't finish my prep."

fug-up, a stodgy person, one who prefers a "fuggy" atmosphere to playing out-of-doors.

ice-drill, physical exercises when conducted in shorts only. Thus: "Who's having us for *ice-drill?*"

jack, an expert, a notable person. Thus: "He's a real *jack* at music." "Smith is one of the *jacks* of the school."

---

[1] In English military slang during World War I, *fanny* was used for a member of the First Aid Nursing Yeomanry.

jackish, noteworthy, distinctive. Thus: "Bolter played a *jackish* innings"; "That's a *jackish* bit of carving."

K.O.J., enthusiastic, over-earnest, short for "keen on the job". Thus: "He's much too *K.O.J.* for me."

mum, a mollycoddle, effeminate boy. Thus: "You poor *mum*, why didn't you come for a swim this morning?"

poon up, to dress up, especially with considerable care. Thus: "Jim is all *pooned up* to go out."

pop out! wake up! come out of your coma! Thus: "*Pop out*, we won the boat race two years ago!"

ronnies,[2] stones. Thus: "We rocked Kelly's roof, and did the *ronnies* rattle!"

serves their rights! a solecism for "serves them right". Thus: "Well, *serves their rights* if they get caught, going without leave."

slacks, an aperient. Thus: "Matron made me take *slacks* this morning."

surl, used as a noun and verb, derived from "surly". Thus: "He was in a terrible *surl*", in a rage; "And did he *surl* at us! I'll say!"

tarze, a notable, especially a physically strong person. From "Tarzan". Thus: "He's a *tarze*, that fellow."

tarzy, tarzanish, descriptive of a strong person or work that requires strength to complete. Thus: "He's a pretty *tarzy* chap"; "That's a *tarzanish* (or *tarzy*) job by the look of it."

tit around, to fuss unnecessarily, to be busy about nothing, to interfere. Thus: "There he goes, *titting around* with his bits and pieces."

twirgle, one's turn. Thus: "I haven't had a *twirgle* at the lathe yet"; "Here, give me a *twirgle*, you've had one for long enough."

twit, a term of contempt. Thus: "You poor *twit!*" Whence a verb, *to twit about*, a synonym for *tit around*, q.v.

yegg, an objectionable fellow (from the U.S. *yegg*, a burglar). Thus: "Oh, he's a *yegg*, mucking about all the time."

Here is a somewhat similar list from Adelaide, compiled not by a teacher, but by an adult who is looking back over the years to his schooldays:

auntie, an effeminate.

ay!-pricots and peaches! a trick greeting.

baby's yellow, a baby's excretion, used as a term of contempt.

basic, not up to standard, terrible. "A basic meal", a poor meal.

bath-plug, euphemism for "bastard".

blood nose, a bleeding nose; a blow in a fight which causes a bleeding nose.

bommo, extremely good. (Ex *bomb on*, used similarly.)

bug, a schoolboy, always used contemptuously in "day-bug" and "boarder-bug".

charge, proceed quickly or cheekily – "charge up to the master", "charge down the road". (Almost standard English.)

college lout, a college boy (these colleges were all run by religious organizations) as seen by a State High School boy.

come-bun, a cream bun.

connie, a tram conductor.

cowslip, cowdung, especially when wet.

---

[2] Probably from English dialect *roundy*, a lump of coal, and old English cant *rouny*, a potato.

C.T.J., (1) a narrow, stiff collar, "a sort of badge we imagined was worn by all wowsers, it meant Come-to-Jesus"; (2) a two-stroke motor-bike.

curley comeback, anything that is returned. (Probably from the use of *boomerang* as a verb.)

dickon, yes, no, maybe. (The author notes: "I remember that we used this word so that it could mean almost anything in the way of emphasis.")

dodger, a steam-engine travelling backwards.

donkey, a ride on a bicycle given to another by a cyclist.

dook, a hat.

doorstep, a sandwich cut across only once. (Doubtless ex the wider use of *doorstep* for any thick slice of bread or cake.)

dub, a lavatory.

feather the nest, grow pubic hair.

fly-cake, a cake with currants in it.

French forgets! Excuse me for forgetting!

goog, lay your, to become angry.

goozie, a gob of phlegm.

grimmett, a bowler hat. (A schoolboy's tribute to the noted Australian cricket bowler, C. V. Grimmett.)

hoof, to deliver, surrender, as in *hoof it over!*

hunker, a piece of cake (from *hunk of*).

jiffo, a moment. (An extension of the English slang *jiff* used similarly.)

newie, anything new.

noorie, the nipple of a breast. (This is independent of the Australian use of *nork* for a female breast.)

oldie, anything old; an adult.

paper-o, a newspaper seller or a boy who delivers newspapers.

pasho, a boy who chases girls.

pluck, a stone. See *quailer*.

poppy show, the sight of a girl's bloomers. (This is virtually standard English.)

quailer, a stone. (The author says: "As I understand it, one shies a *quailer*, but chucks a *pluck*.")

queenie, a cry-baby or timid boy, not necessarily effeminate. (The author says: "State school boys often referred to college boys as *queens* or *queenies*, and there was no suggestion that they were effeminate.")

ranji, sexually excited. (The author notes: "I suppose that the original use was *randy*, but it somehow got mixed up with a make of broom called *Ranji* and the popular name of an Indian cricketer.")

reach me, part of a couple of set phrases: *reach me down a watermelon* for a tall girl, and *reach me up a watermelon* for a short girl.

sarftey, this afternoon. (Not *sarvo* or *sarfto*, which are general uses.)

squiz, a look, as in "Have a squiz".

stick, a crude sort of hockey, played with any sticks that are available and with a gum-nut for a ball.

stug, a greedy person. (Backslang for *guts*.)

taddie, a tadpole.

tart-shop, a girls' school.

tooroo, goodbye.

us, often used for "me" as in "Give us a game". (From English dialect.)

warty-tongue, a liar. (The author says: "It came from a belief that to tell lies led to having warts on the tongue.")

whacko the diddle-oh! exclamation of pleasure.

whizz, (1) to steal; (2) to move quickly; (3) to go immediately.

your tin! after you! As in *your tin on the butter; your tin on the tennis court.* This is a mutilation of *your ten,* meaning "after you with the cricket bat", and arose in a S.A. school where, at recreation time, each pupil could have only ten hits at cricket at any one time.

Finally, here is a list of words rounded up from schoolchildren in Sydney. As with the earlier lists, it is important to note that many of the terms given are not localized, although they are perhaps used more regularly in the places where they were recorded than elsewhere:

backaracker, a firework.

bangotcher, a Wild West film (from "Bang! Got you" an allusion to gun-play in these cinema and TV epics).

biffs, corporal punishment.

boof, a simpleton or fool. Also, *boofhead.*

bull, a welfare probation officer.

bungdung, a firework. Also *bunger.*

by jingies! an exclamation of amazement. Also, *by jinks!*

cacks! an exclamation of disgust.

chew, food in general.

chewie, chewing gum. *do your chewie,* become angry (a synonym for *do your block*).

chuttie, chewing gum. (From this word, the child has produced a serviceable verb *to chut;* when chewing-gum is of an inferior quality, a child says: "It won't *chut* properly".)

conky, worthless, objectionable.

dag, a person who is unenterprising, without courage. (Quite distinct from the old use of *dag* for a "hard case" or "character").

dippy, a comic paper.

dosh, money.

eccer, homework. (From "exercise".)

erks! an exclamation of disgust.

fifty-one-a-r, a liar; the "fifty-one" being a reading of the letters *LI* as Roman numerals.

fourbles, quadruple.

get tonked, to receive corporal punishment.

golly or *golly gum,* chewing gum.

hangava, an intensive used by children. Also *hangashun* and *hellishun.*

honkus (or *oncus*), angry, annoyed, wrong.

hook one's bait, to go, leave.

hooray! goodbye. Also, *hooroo!*

hooya! a jeer. (Probably a corruption of "Who are you!")

jamboroo, a celebration. (A version of *jamboree.*)

knee-drill, a form of punishment in which children are made to kneel in certain denominational schools. (*Knee-drill,* kneeling for prayers, is in English slang.)

L7, "a square"; apparently derived from the fact that L and the figure 7 when in conjunction make a rough square.

L

lacky, elastic, an elastic band.

lazo, elastic.

lolly, a sweet. *ice-lolly* or *ice-block*, a small block of coloured and sweet-tasting ice on a stick.

mangle, a bicycle.

mizzle off, to depart.

mudguts (or *muddiguts*), an obese person, especially a fat man.

nong, a simpleton or fool; also *nong-nong* and *ning-nong*.

peanut row (or *gallery* or *alley*), the front rows in a cinema.

plakka (or *placker*), plasticine.

pong (or *ponk*), an offensive smell.

pot, to inform on; *to pot someone* or *to put someone's pot on*.

roar up, to reprimand. Whence, *get roared up*.

scag, a short tear in cloth.

scrunch, food in general.

shelf, the "dress circle" or second gallery in a cinema.

sniddy, (1) sleep; (2) extremely good.

spaze, a dull or "corny" (U.S.) joke. The form *spaz* (probably extracted from "spastic") means silly or stupid.

tribles, treble.

whacker (or *wacker*), a simpleton or fool.

your lip's bleeding! you're using big words!

A few slang expressions used in the mid-1950s at a Sydney girls' school: *it's snowing down south*, said to a girl whose petticoat is showing beneath the hemline of her skirt; *mercy buttercups!* a corruption of the French *merci beaucoup; squashed fly biscuits*, biscuits with currants in them; *pasho*, a heavy "necking" session, usually at a party.

Some fifteen years ago, the visitor from abroad who heard Australia's young hopefuls using such phrases as *greasy mug, you little trimmer, cop this (young Harry), cheeky possum, galah, suck it and see, the dirty mug* and *grouse sort* might have well imagined that our juveniles were somewhat ahead of other countries in the use of vernacular expressions, but most of them were acquired or at least firmly imprinted on their minds through the medium of Australian radio. More precisely, they were tokens of youthful admiration for the Australian comedian "Mo", who used them in his radio sessions and whose repetitive use of such phrases as *very tasty very succulent, I wouldn't say that* and *how true, how very true* gained him many child imitators. But "Mo" is now dead and there are probably few who recall the subtleties of his radio sessions. In cases where such expressions survive, it is usually among older members of the community.

Among nursery expressions which have acquired a fairly stabilized currency in this country are *googy-egg* for an egg; *to see Mrs Murray*, to urinate or defecate; *big fire* and *little fire*, which describe defecation and urination respectively; and the catchphrase, *up to pussy's bow and dolly's wax*, to denote a surfeit, especially of food.

3. TEENAGERS

ONE OF THE MINOR FEATURES of life in Australia after World War II was the commercial discovery that our adolescents represented a valuable market. Many organisations such as radio and TV stations, the Press and department stores began competing hungrily for shares in that market. Indeed, for a period after the mid-1950s, the young seemed to take over (we have already looked into some part of *surfie* language) and general Australian slang was seriously swamped by teenage neologisms. But we soon learned an important feature of juvenile enthusiasms: they are subject to so many transitory fashions and change so rapidly that what seems essential at any one time can quite well be forgotten a month later. A type of dance, a type of popular song, a type of dress, a type of jargon – all can be displaced almost overnight.

Many of those fashions have come to us from the United States. Here is an instructive newspaper comment in 1950, summing up the position in Kings Cross at that time:

Outside a milk bar there I met Harry, 19, Joe, 20, Stewart, 16, and Cali (short for California), 18. They all had American-style haircuts and American-type clothes varying from jeans and check shirt, on Stewart, to Chicago-drape suits on Cali and Harry. Cali, Joe and Harry said they were seamen; Stewart said he worked in a factory. Joe said he was from Perth, Stewart and Harry said Sydney was their home, and Cali said he was English. With the exception of Cali, their accents and their idioms were American; the mannerisms of all of them – the way they looked, held cigarettes, and spoke – reminded me of the acting in films I had seen recently.

While Al Jolson trumpeted nasally from a juke box "I Only Have Eyes for You" they chewed gum, drank orange juice and quite frankly discussed their reasons for adopting American vogues. Cali wore a tie with a drawing of two be-boppers dancing, and above the drawing, the words "Relaxed Square. Beat to the Socks." He said with some satisfaction that Kings Cross was becoming "more solid – like Piccadilly". And to illustrate his point about Piccadilly he produced a newspaper showing London photographs of Negroes with keyboard grins "getting hep" with white girls on the dance floor.

Harry, whose American accent was most pronounced, said he and the others wore American clothes and hair styles because they were modern. He said that every Sunday night about 200 "guys" in American clothes and haircuts went to an Oxford Street club and danced to hot music. "The dames like the guys this way", said Harry. "Most of the parents just let it go until a roast comes up; then they get a bit hot on it."

Tall, fair-haired Joe, who wore pegtop pants with shirt outside, and moccasins, and who seemed psychologically upset, said: "Paris for women, America for men." Harry talked on about sharp haircuts and clothes, Cali said again that Kings Cross was becoming modern. Joe got up to speak to a young blonde, and Stewart held a cigarette like Alan Ladd. The party broke up. Said Harry: "See you guy."

In slight extenuation of this scene, it can be added that Sydney has always been more susceptible to American influences than any other Australian village. The terms *Woolloomooloo Yank*, *Pyrmont Yank* and *George Street Yank*, used to describe Australians trying to pass themselves off as Americans, have been current in Sydney for many years. I have heard the expression *Fitzroy Yank* in Melbourne and doubtless there are adequate reasons for it, but the American influence seems to be less marked there than in Sydney (although I must record that, on a visit to the Victorian capital in 1950, I observed that a *drug store* – actually a chemist's shop without the American etceteras – had appeared in Collins Street.)

However, as is customary with the ideas and slang we filch from overseas, they are almost always subject to local conditioning. In 1950, just when Australia's teenagers seemed ready to transfer their allegiance to America, we became aware of the *bodgie* and *widgie* or *weegie*. In due course, these were recognisable as the modern *larrikin* and his girl, but for some time we were not too sure about their origins. Then we became aware that the word *bodgie* was not American, but was derived from an earlier underworld and Army use of *bodger* for something faked, worthless or shoddy. For example, a faked receipt or false name to dodge the Tax Department is a *bodger;* so is a shoddy piece of material sold by a door-to-door hawker. The application of *bodgies* to certain Australian adolescents was certainly coloured by a suggestion that they were "fake Americans", in that they "aped" many American sartorial, tonsorial and linguistic habits. The origin of *widgie* or *weegie* is obscure. Shortenings were *bodge* and *widge*.

In the early 1950s, *Mr Bodger* was used to denote anyone confusing an issue or becoming notable for his inefficiency. The development of the word took a step further with the following newspaper report:

> An office in town has a mail file marked *bodgies*. It's for letters that don't seem to come under any of the regular classifications. The misfits, in other words.

During the 1950s, *bodgie* was adapted as an adjective, e.g. *bodgie boy*, *bodgie club*, *bodgie cult*. *Bodgiedom* and *weegiedom* also developed.

The *bodgie* remained with us through most of the 1950s, but then a remarkable change occurred due, oddly enough, to the development of the plastic surfboard and its arrival in Australia in 1957. Thereafter, the *bodgie* became the *rocker* and the adolescent surfboard rider became the *surfie*. They were given other names, of course; the *rocker* (originally from the U.S. *rock*, influenced by England) became the *jackeroo* (Australian) and the *ho-dad* or *gremlin* (both U.S.); for a time in Melbourne, *jazzer* was used instead of *surfie*, while in Sydney the *surfie* became the *beachie* and other terms given in Chapter XI. The special point about them was that *rockers* and *surfies* (*jazzers*) regarded each other as enemies, and numerous brawls between them occurred, rather similar to the "battles" between *rockers* and *mods* in Britain and of our early *larrikin pushes*. At the time of writing, *bodgie* is creeping back into use again.

It is worth noting that one of the many manifestations of adolescent disorientation in English-speaking countries since the end of World War II has concerned male hairstyles. Apart from the brief appearance in the 1920s of the *nana cut,* long at the sides and very short at the back – which gave us *lose one's nana* as an equivalent of *lose* (or *do) one's block,* become angry – Australian males, even clothes-conscious larrikins, had not paid great attention to their hair. After 1945 there was an increasing tendency among Australian juveniles to imitate American styles of hair-wearing. The cult of allowing the hair to grow to considerable length gave rise to the common term *Cornel Wilder;* apparently the film actor Cornel Wilde was credited with having inspired this hirsute eccentricity. Other hair styles borrowed from America and recorded in the Australian Press were the *G.I. cut,* very short, *Kramer cut,* low at back and sides with bristles on top, *crew cut,* short all over, *Hollywood cut,* long hair at the sides brushed back close to the head, *dove-tail,* long with a peak at the back of the neck, and *layer cut,* low at back, cleanly cut on top. Then, due mainly to English influence, many of our male teenagers began to grow their hair very long, so that it was difficult at times to distinguish one sex from the other. A minor aberration was the bleaching of the hair by youths who wished to disguise themselves as *surfies.*

Due to lack of modern references, it is difficult to arbitrate on the various influences of U.S., English and Australian slang in teenage jargon. I offer the following list rather as a cross-section of this jargon than as a confident report on indigenous efforts:

bail up, to corner; to call to account. (A revival of old bushranging slang.)

big spit, vomit.

blow, to copulate.

bog, to talk about something of which one knows little; *bog-artist,* such a talker.

boots, shoes.

burn off, to race in a car or on a motor-cycle. *give* (someone) *a burn,* to race.

cazo, casually dressed. *cazo turn,* an informal party.

chest warmer, a necktie more than one inch wide.

con, to find a satisfactory partner. (This term is not easy to explain. Each member of a pair privately claims to have *conned* the other, either for a casual meeting or for a long-standing relationship. In so far as it means to examine, to study, it is virtually standard English.)

conchie, one who is a little over-conscientious. Also adjective.

crash, an excretion. *go for a crash.*

crash on, to "neck".

crook sort of, unpleasant, unattractive. "A crook sort of bat" – an unattractive girl; "a crook sort of crumb" – an unpleasant fellow. (This use of *sort* is standard English.)

daks, trousers. (From a trade name.)

dazzy, excellent; a general term of approval.

drag at the lights, a race at traffic lights to see who will be first away when the lights turn from red to green (*drag* is U.S.).

drop one's gear, (of a female) to undress.

fag, to smoke. *fag-artist*, one who smokes.

fang, to remove the top from a bottle of beer with the teeth – "We'll fang a couple of bottles"; to shout someone down, to humiliate someone by abuse.

fanger, one who humiliates another person by abuse or by shouting him down.

fantastic, extremely good.

gear, female dress.

gear gear, particularly attractive female dress.

greaser, a sycophant, a "crawler".

grouse gear, as for *gear gear*.

hambone, a strip-tease act by a male.

heavy, the beloved partner in a long-term relationship. As adj., it denotes approval or admiration.

herbs, power in a car. *plenty of herbs*, a great deal of power in a car's engine.

king, excellent, first-rate.

lair it up, to behave flashily or ostentatiously.

massive, extremely good.

mob, a group (but not necessarily a large group).

oldie, an adult; anyone over the age of about 25.

pneumatic, excellent, first-rate.

porsh, an expression of minor contempt.

poser, one who dresses obviously well, drives a sports car, etc. In so far as this means *poseur* it is orthodox, but one who dresses obviously badly is also a *poser*, so there is apparently some distinction to be made.

rabble, to have a good time; to misbehave. Whence, *rabbler*, one who enjoys himself, especially by misbehaving.

roll, to capsize (a car).

rubbish, to reject, throw away.

sack, a female, a girl friend.

shaggin' waggon, a car which a male uses for the purpose of picking up a female companion.

shinbone, nakedness. (See *hambone*.)

skate board, a small, fast board for "surfing" on roads or footpaths.

slag, to spit.

snow, to steal.

thrash, (of a car or other vehicle) to drive at great speed.

tube, a can of beer.

turn, a party.

tweeds, trousers.

weird, a person behaving in an unorthodox fashion, i.e. "unorthodox" to a teenager.

wheels, shoes.

zot, a crash, a thunderbolt; an exclamation of surprise.

zotty, excellent.

CHAPTER XIV

Fauna and Flora

1. CONFLICTS AND CATACHRESIS

ONE OF THE WEAKNESSES of Morris's "Austral English" was his overloading of that dictionary with botanical and zoological material. This could possibly have fallen into its right place if Morris had also devoted greater attention to Australian colloquial speech and so given a more balanced picture of the Australian lingual scene. As the "Bulletin" wrote in its critique:

> The dictionary is mixed. Names of plants and animals run in alphabetical order with the Australian *words* which the dictionary professes to connote and explain. There are often whole pages of botanical references and descriptions borrowed from Maiden or Von Mueller or others. Without these and similar lists of fishes, birds and so on, the dictionary would have been a much less imposing volume. Yet it is not clear why botany and philology should be confused. But since it was decided to include lists of animals and plants, with their vernacular names – and these lists, in a popular pan-Australasian form, were certainly much needed – why were not plants and animals listed separately from words included for linguistic and national reasons? It seems as if almost everything in clarity and convenience was to be gained, and hardly anything lost, by such separate classification.

The Melbourne "Argus" wrote:

> If we were disposed to quarrel with any portion of the contents of the dictionary it would be with the inclusion of some of the scientific terms for species, which are not Austral English, because they are not English anywhere, but merely serve as the private labels of scientists.

These comments raise some points that should be stressed, not only because Morris's listings of flora and fauna are now out-of-date, but because his approach to the problem of the Australasian language was faulty.

If it were worth while to include all indigenous scientific terminology the dictionary would obviously, by sheer weight of natural objects unique to this part of the world, become largely encyclopaedic. This is all very well in the case of the "Oxford Dictionary", where the whole scope of the English language is taken into account. But Australia has made only limited contributions to the English language – limited, that is, to thousands, not tens of thousands. Common and scientific names of flora and fauna are accordingly in greater proportion to the Australian language than they are to English. Morris found it simple to take scientific terminology from the works of various authorities on Australian flora and fauna; he did not find it so easy – or he felt disinclined – to make a personal study of Australian colloquial speech.

To a certain extent Morris recognized this weakness. Commenting on the inclusion of scientific words in his dictionary he said: "It is quite true that these can hardly be described as Australasian English."

A dictionary of Australian flora and fauna, complete with scientific terms, is certainly needed. But this work should be kept apart from Australian colloquialisms and slang. The great bulk of our colloquial speech is not yet standardized, whereas scientific terms tend to become fixed immediately. To mix them is to present a hotchpotch of material that is as unsatisfying to the person who desires a purely scientific reference as to the person who desires a reference to our common speech.

G. P. Marsh sums up the American position on flora and fauna in his "Lectures on the English Language" (1860):

> The native names for all these objects were hard to pronounce, harder still to remember, and the colonists, therefore, took the simple and obvious method of applying to the native products of America the names of the European plants and animals which most resembled them . . . Though the American and the transatlantic objects designated by these names in many instances belong to the same genus, and are only distinguished by features which escape all eyes but those of the scientific naturalist, in perhaps none are they specifically identical, while, not unfrequently, the application of the European name is founded on very slight resemblances.

The same story is to be told about Australia. Aboriginal names were ignored, imported terms were falsely applied – e.g. *alligator* instead of crocodile, *badger* for the bandicoot or wombat, *iguana* for the varan, *locust* for cicada, *mimosa* for acacia – and vast numbers of varying species were wrongly grouped together because of careless observation.

Here is an editorial comment on the problem by the "Bulletin" of January 3, 1907:

> When the early settlers undertook the task of naming Australian birds and animals, why on earth couldn't they have adopted more of the aboriginal names? . . . In how many cases has a real or fancied resemblance to something with which they were acquainted given rise to names nearly always misleading, often ridiculous! Surely *koala* is better than the absurd "native bear" and *kookaburra* than that verbal monstrosity "laughing jackass".[1] . . . Then, again, we call the piping crow-shrike a *magpie*, which it is not: what's wrong with the native name *karoo?* Why must we borrow the name *opossum* from a perfectly distinct American animal and apply it to what the aboriginals called the *kooragai?* We all know that an *emu* is not an ostrich, yet emu is but a slight corruption of the Portuguese name of the ostrich; why not use the aboriginal *marriang?* Finally, to refer to the

---

[1] Commenting on the term *laughing jackass*, "The Lone Hand" (November 2, 1908) said: "Familiarity has blunted our perception of the atrocity of this combination, but compare it with such an equally applicable invention as 'grinning tom-cat' or 'smiling billy-goat' and see the result!" However, see Section 3 of this chapter.

huge lizard . . . why can't he have a name of his own? He is called an *iguana* or a *go-anner*[2] when he is no more an iguana than an emu is an ostrich. Scientists call him a varan, South Australian blacks a *kojurrie*. Either name is more suitable than iguana.

Other aspects of the problem were discussed by a writer in "The Lone Hand", who commented on the "wholesale and promiscuous borrowing of old names" for our flora and fauna:

Turning to Australian flora, we find ourselves in a veritable maze of tangled nomenclature. In the first place, the two most important genera of our forest trees bear vernacular names which are not really distinctive at all. Any tree whose branches are suitable for "wattling" or weaving that rough wickerwork which has for so many generations been used in rural England for fence- and hut-building, might lay claim to the name of *wattle-tree*, while *gum-tree* merely connotes an abundance of exuded sap, which in the eucalypti is not really gum in the ordinary sense of the word, but kino. But when we come to separate species, the popular terminology is simply bewildering. To the ordinary man in the street, the common distinctions of red, white and blue *gum*, etc., may seem clear enough, but when he learns that the name "blue gum" is applied to at least eight species of eucalyptus, "red" to ten, and "white" to fifteen, and that, further, in most cases each species has several different vernacular names, he will begin to realise the state of confusion which really exists. Nor is this confusion confined to popular nomenclature. Mr Maiden gives a list of eight or nine different botanical synonyms for the *Eucalyptus amygdalina*, a tree which is variously known in different places as peppermint, mountain ash, giant gum, white gum, stringybark, manna gum and messmate. Even allowing a distinctively Australian character to have been acquired by the names *gum* and *wattle*, it must be admitted that such recklessly imported terms as ash, apple, beech, box, cedar, oak, maple, sassafras, teak and hickory, applied in most cases without reference to any botanical relationships, cannot fail to be misleading. Certainly, a small aboriginal element has been retained in our marvellous system of forest nomenclature, but even here exact definition is sometimes wanting – *mulga* and *brigalow* being applied to several different acacias, while *mallee* is not rigidly confined to any one species of eucalyptus.

In fine, it may be said that our popular zoological nomenclature has suffered both by the spontaneity of its growth and the conservatism of its originators. The early settler seemed determined alike to ignore the aboriginal name and to avoid any tax on his inventive faculties, and so went on tacking English, American and Asiatic names on to bird, beast, fish and tree. The result is that his descendant of today believes that in the black and white crow-shrike he sees a genuine *magpie*, that our phalanger is the original *possum up a gumtree*, and even that the root of a purple-flowered vine, which brightens the hillsides and gullies in the spring season, has medicinal qualities, because it has annexed the name of *sarsparilla*.

---

[2] Since the true iguana is not found in Australia, the term *goanna* has now been adopted as an independent name for the Australian varan. In various forms the word *goanna* has been in Australian use for more than a century. Here are some examples: guanoes (1802), guana (1830), guaners (1858), goanna (1891), gohanna (1896). The abbreviation *go* is also common.

Here, then, is a fairly accurate summary (accurate, at least, in terms of when it was written) of what has happened to our flora and fauna. We find it a field full of anomalies, inexactitudes and confusions. The sooner we have an authoritative dictionary of Australian flora and fauna, which will include the hundreds of terms which Morris omitted and which will give some guidance to the public on the use of indigenous instead of imported expressions, the better it will be.

2. STANDARDIZATION

ALTHOUGH MANY EXPERTS have tackled aspects of Australian flora and fauna, we have not as yet proceeded far in the matter of tidying up nomenclature. It is, perhaps, symptomatic of the overall position that for some years the most authoritative booklet on Australian fishes was offered to the public wrapped round a popular brand of hand-soap.[3]

One of the most confusing aspects of Australian botany and zoology is the great variety of names attached to some species. It was left to the Standards Association of Australia to standardize the names of a thousand or so of Australia's leading commercial trees.[4] In 1947, the names of some forty species of commercially-important fishes were standardized by an interstate conference.[5] The names of some commercially-important plants were standardized in 1942.[6] Such examples have helped scientific progress greatly in recent years, but it will be a long time before our flora and fauna are fully explored. In any case, efforts to standardize various groups of names have not been as successful to date as they deserve to be. For example, in 1947, R. H. Anderson issued a new edition of his book, "The Trees of New South Wales" (originally published in 1932). This was seven years after the Standards Association had published its list of standardized names for Australia's most important timber trees. Anderson ignored this list with a result that old confusions were perpetuated at popular expense. A less glaring example occurred in the 1948 re-issue of Thistle Y. Harris's book, "Wild Flowers of Australia". A number of the vernacular and botanical names the author gives are at variance with the standardized plant names issued by the C.S.I.R.O. in 1942.

Quite apart from such examples, there is a good deal of conflict between popular names accepted for various species. For instance, is a *mountain devil* a lizard or a plant? It is both. In a similar way, *beardie* is a name given to a fish, the *Australian ling*, and to the *jew lizard; peter peter* is applied to both a bird and a cicada; *four o'clock* is a name given to a plant as well as to a bird, i.e. the *noisy friar-bird; paddymelon* is applied to both a wallaby and a plant; and *currawong* is a name variously attached

[3] "Solvol Fish Book", by Gilbert P. Whitley; illustrated by Mary E. Soady (1950).
[4] "Australian Standard Nomenclature of Australian Timbers", issued by the Standards Association of Australia (1940).
[5] Supplement to "Fisheries Newsletter", vol. 6, No. 3, June, 1947.
[6] Commonwealth Scientific and Industrial Research Organisation bulletin, No. 156, "Standardized Plant Names" (1942).

to two trees and six birds. There are also innumerable cases in which vernacular names differ from State to State, or in which the States apply the same names to different species. In short, it is obvious that Australian scientists would do a great service to the public if they could eliminate such confusions as part of a formulated plan.

To make the point clear, let us consider such an example as the minor fodder plant which bears the botanical name of *Anthyllis vulnerarea*. Its vernacular names include *kidney vetch, common kidney vetch, wound wort, wound clover, sand clover, yellow sand trefoil* and *lady's fingers*. Consider also the tree now officially known as the *alpine ash (Eucalyptus gigantea)*; a few years ago it was also known as *red ash* and *woollybutt* in Victoria, *gumtop stringybark* and *whitetop stringybark* in Tasmania, and *Australian oak, Tasmanian oak* and *Victorian oak* in New South Wales and elsewhere. Consider, too, the fish now known as *mulloway (Sciaena antarctica)*; before the inter-state fisheries conference in 1947 it was known under at least seven different names – *jewfish* or *dewfish* in Queensland, *jewfish* or *silver fish* in New South Wales, *kingfish* in Victoria, *mulloway* or *butterfish* in South Australia, and *river kingfish* in Western Australia. Victorians formerly gave the name *kingfish* to the *mulloway*. People in New South Wales and Queensland also had a kingfish, but it was another species altogether (*Regificola grandis*). To add to the confusion, Victorians called this latter fish a *yellow-tail*. So did people in South Australia. On the other hand, Tasmanians took a proprietary attitude to the Regificola and called it the *Tasmanian yellowtail*. Western Australians called it a *yellowtail kingfish*. This type of conflict was most confusing for anyone who travelled interstate, but it was even more of a headache for people in the fish business. The fisheries conference's decision to fix the name *yellowtail kingfish* for the Regificola is clearly a step in the direction of weeding out confusion. Of course, a mere paper decision on nomenclature offers no guarantee that popular conflicts will be eliminated. The term *jewfish*, as used in Queensland and New South Wales and officially displaced by *mulloway*, seems almost as common today as ever it was. The fact that it has bred such familiar forms as *jew* and *jewie* indicates that the battle for the official acceptance of *mulloway* may be protracted.

The success of any movement for standardization depends on the support given by authorities. After all, if the authorities do not conform to the rules they have formulated they can scarcely persuade the public to do it for them. On this matter, the Victorian Aboriginal word *luderick* was selected as the Australian standard name for the fish *Girella tricus-pidata*. This decision was made at the interstate meeting in 1947 over which G. P. Whitley, icthyologist of the Australian Museum, Sydney, presided. Yet in Whitley's "Solvol Fish Book", published three years later, the spelling was changed to *ludrick*. If the public is baffled by such scientific goings-on who can blame it?

Even in the matter of replacing the pretentious spelling *schnapper* with *snapper*, unanimity does not seem to have been reached. Even as late as November 7, 1947, the Melbourne "Age" reported:

The Fisheries and Game department has applied for an amendment of the Fisheries Act to change the spelling of "schnapper" to "snapper". The new inspector of Fisheries and Game (Mr A. D. Butcher) said yesterday Victoria was the only State in Australia which spelt snapper as schnapper.

My own observation is that even today most of the other States are in two minds on the matter – if menus in restaurants and notices in fish shops are any guide.

When such basic questions as these are resolved, it may be possible to look forward to the day when the unskilled observer will be able to place some reliance on scientific edicts.

3. POPULAR NAMES FOR FAUNA

THE MULTIPLICATION of popular names adds a further burden. In some cases, the mind reels when one contemplates the abundance of samples available. For instance, the grey-crowned babbler is also known as the *apostle-bird, barker, cat-bird, cackler, codlin-moth-eater, chatterer, dog-bird, happy family, happy jack, hopper, jumper, parson-bird, pine-bird, twelves apostles* and *yahoo*.

The white-fronted chat is also called the *ballyhead, banded tintac, bumps, clipper, dotterel, gar, jenny wren, moonbird, nun, ringlet, ringneck* and *tang*.

The brown flycatcher is called *jacky winter, peter-peter, postboy, post sitter* and *spinks*.

Some of these are, fairly obviously, direct alternatives for the common name, but others are of the vernacular type that comes within the scope of this book.

Perhaps the point will be better understood if we take the kookaburra as an example and note the many names by which it is known in familiar speech. The common appellation *laughing jackass* dates from 1798 or earlier (as noted previously this *jackass* is probably a mutilation of the French *jacasse*, a magpie, a name which seems to have been bestowed on the kookaburra by early French observers round these coasts; the verb *jacasser* means to chatter, to cackle) and, as will be seen in the following list, many of our popular nicknames for the bird are variants of this: *jack, jacko, jacky, jackass, laughing jack, laughing john, laughing johnny, laughing johnass, john, johnny, clock bird, bushman's clock, shepherd's clock, cocky's clock, alarm bird, breakfast bird, kooka, ha ha pigeon* and *woop woop pigeon*.[7]

Here is a list of some of the more colourful nicknames for Australian birds; the list is by no means complete, but it is as least representative:

Australian nightingale, willie wagtail.	*bubbly mary*, wompoo pigeon.
baldy, white-headed pigeon.	*chickoowee*, white-plumed honey-eater.
black-and-white duck, a magpie.	eater.
bleater, Australian snipe.	*chickup*, yellow-faced honey-eater.
brain fever, pallid cuckoo.	*cranky fan*, grey fantail.

---

[7] Applied to the swamp pheasant in North Queensland. In "Bird Wonders of Australia" (1956 edition), A. H. Chisholm lists forty-five Aboriginal names for the kookaburra.

dishlick, restless flycatcher.
flying coachman, regent honey-eater.
four o'clock, noisy friar-bird.
go-away, white-browed babbler.
goolie or *goulie*, galah.
greeny, white-plumed honey-eater.
grinder, restless flycatcher.
kelly, a crow.
knobby nose, noisy friar-bird.
leatherhead, noisy friar-bird.
mad fan, grey fantail.
micky, noisy miner.
monk, noisy friar-bird.
mourner, grey shrike-thrush.
pick-it-up, diamond-bird.
pimlico, noisy friar-bird.
pluff, grey shrike-thrush.
poor soldier, noisy friar-bird.

razor grinder, restless flycatcher.
ring coachman, rufous whistler.
scissors grinder, restless flycatcher.
shepherd's companion, willie wagtail.
smoker, regent parrot.
snapper, grey fantail.
spiney, spinebill.
squatter, bronze-wing pigeon.
squeaker, noisy miner.
stinker, blue-winged shoveller.
stop-where-you-are, friar-bird.
tobacco box, friar-bird.
twenty-eight, yellow-collared
   parrakeet.
what's o'clock, wattle-bird.
whisky, yellow-tufted honey-eater.
yellow bob, southern yellow robin.
yelper, red-necked avocet.

A bird-name which is often mistaken for an Aboriginal word is *rosella*, for the parrot *Platycercus eximius*. The word was corrupted from *Rosehill*, a district near Sydney where the bird was first observed. For a while, it was apparently called a *Rosehiller*, and this led to its transformation.

The main linguistic traces left by the emu (apart from the word's corruption from the Portuguese *ema*) are *emu oil*, at one time regarded as useful for treating rheumatism, rubbing on saddle leather, curing "the sprains and bruises of horses and cattle" and oiling guns, and what was known as *the Emu War*, a so-called "war" in Western Australia in 1932, which failed utterly in its purpose to destroy the birds.

In the "Australian Museum Magazine" for June 15, 1952, Gilbert Whitley offered extremely interesting data on vernacular terms, in a paper entitled "The Common Names of Fishes". Among names derived from the Aborigines he lists *callop, congolli, mia mia, morwhong, tallegalane, teraglin, tupong, turrum, wirrah* and *wollomai*. Possibly corrupted from Aboriginal words are *mado, maray, cowanyoung, bullrout* and *fortescue*. Many other native names, he says, lie embalmed in published vocabularies or have died out unrecorded. Among White Australian names given to fish, he lists: *balmainer*, a type of perch so-named because it carries the colours of the Balmain (N.S.W.) rugby football team, *barber, butchers, fiddler ray, flake* (used to denote fillets of shark), *government bream, gummy, hardy-head, herring-cale, humbug* (called after the black and white striped confectionery which it resembles), *jollytail, jumping joey, maori* (from the cheek-markings which resemble tattoos), *mouth almighty, nikkie long cod, palmer, poddy mullet, policeman, roughy, snotgall travella, spine-foot, stranger, sweep, sweetlips* and *whaler shark. Barraconda* is probably a portmanteau word derived from barracouta and anaconda; it is sometimes applied to the snaky-looking king barracouta (*Rexea*).

Popular fish-names peculiar to Australia, quite a few of which have been noted earlier in this book, include: *brim*, for bream; *couta*, for barracouta; *cotton-fish* and *tit-fish*, for trepang; *nipper*, a prawn (it may be noted that raw prawns are referred to as *green prawns*, probably because a cooked prawn is always pink or red); *jellyblubber*, an "egg case" of water-clear jelly, not to be confused with the true jellyfish; *cunjie*, a cunjevoi, used for bait; *beakie*, a garfish; *bluebottle*, a Portuguese man-of-war; *pig-faced lady*, a boar fish; *puddingball*, corrupted by the law of Hobson-Jobson from the Aboriginal *puddinba*; *nigger*, a blackfish; and *yabbie*, a small freshwater crayfish, which has given us a verb *to yabbie*, and a verbal noun *yabbying*, used especially among children. Although often used loosely, the term *yabbie* is applied to any one of several freshwater crayfish, especially the small species of Cherax.

The *Queensland lungfish*, which is also a freshwater fish (some observers call it a primitive amphibian), bears the scientific name, *Neoceratodus forsteri*. It is one of the few members of our fauna that has had a railway station named after it – Ceratodus, in south Queensland. For those who are interested in such oddities, it can be noted that the insect Cactoblastis (popularly called *cacto*), which was introduced into Australia from South America to destroy the prickly pear, is the only insect in the world to have had a public memorial erected to it – the Cactoblastis Memorial Hall at Boonarga, Queensland.

Both *witchety grub* and *triantelope* deserve special attention. The former is Aboriginal in origin, and is applied to a large white grub widely esteemed for food by Aborigines. It feeds on the roots of some shrubs or burrows into stems. These grubs were apparently first noted about 1891 in Central Australia, feeding on the roots of witchety bushes, two varieties of Acacia. The "Australian Encyclopaedia" says that the grubs can be eaten raw or cooked in warm ashes: "When cooked they taste like pork rind; when raw they suggest scalded cream or butter." The *triantelope* is a large and hairy (and virtually harmless) huntsman spider, and the word is an Australian corruption of "tarantula"; the term appears to have been in use since 1835 or earlier.

Many popular Australian expressions have been derived from that unique creature, the kangaroo. Best known of these are *roo*, *kanga*, *boomer*, *joey*, *old man* and *paddymelon*.

Boomer, descriptive of a fully-grown kangaroo, has been current since 1830 or earlier. It is probably derived from Tasmanian Aboriginal, although Morris suggests that it may hail from the verb *to boom*, to rush with violence. We have put the word to numerous colloquial uses, notably to describe anything especially large or significant. A writer of 1856 refers, for instance, to "a *boomer* of a flea". A particularly ambitious lie is also called a *boomer*, and we currently use it to describe anything excellent.

A somewhat similar destiny has met the original use of *old man* to denote a large fully-grown kangaroo. (A rare version, *old woman*, for an adult female kangaroo, is recorded in 1861.) Anything especially large or notable can earn the attributive use of *old man*, as, for instance, "an *old man* allotment" (1845) and "an *old man* southerly", a heavy southerly gale. In a roundabout fashion (old man – daddy), it may also have given us *daddy of them all* for the best or most notable person in a group.

Joey, a baby kangaroo, has also been given extensive popular meanings. The young of other marsupials – possums, ͏ ...as, wombats and even Tasmanian devils – are called *joeys*, and from this the meaning has been extended to apply to young children. A woman who is pregnant is said to *carry a joey*. In the same way as *boomer* has come to describe a notable lie, *joey* is used to denote a minor lie or evasion.

Whiptail, a small kangaroo, *flier* and *brush flier*, a swift kangaroo, *blue flier*, the female of the forester or red kangaroo, *pretty face*, a small kangaroo, *soldier*, a fully-grown animal, and *brusher*, a small wallaby, can also be noted.

According to Morris, *paddymelon*, a small wallaby, has been derived by the law of Hobson-Jobson from the Aboriginal *petagorang*, but the evidence is by no means conclusive. However, *paddymalla* is recorded in 1826, and *paddymelon stick*, a stick used by Aborigines for killing wallabies, in 1851. The name is often abbreviated to *melon*, this making its appearance in the derivative *melon hole*, a shallow hole in open country, dangerous to horsemen, which the wallaby is alleged to make.

The *koala* – at various times in our history maligned by the names *monkey* and *bear* – is one of our best-known animals. It is often referred to affectionately as *teddy bear* and *Billy Bluegum. Bunyip Bluegum* is the name given to the koala hero in Norman Lindsay's "Magic Pudding" (1918).

Various Australian lizards are known in popular speech as the *bloodsucker, bluey, barker, land mullet, mallee trout, railway lizard* and *stumptail*. Our only colloquial names for snakes seem to be *boody* and the rhyming slang *Joe Blake*.

A camel is an *oont* (a term borrowed from Hindustani) or a *humpy;* a crocodile is a *gator, crocky* or *scaly;* a flying-fox is a *hairy devil;* a dingo is called ironically a *shepherd's friend;* and *longlegs* is a nickname given to the hare.

So far as popular naming goes, our main attention in the insect world has been focused on cicadas (given detailed attention in Chapter XIII) and ants. For ants some of our oldest names are *old soldier* (1840), *light horseman* (1844), *colonial bulldog* (1852), *soldier* (1854) and *bulldog* (1878). We also have the following names for ants of various types: *bully, elevator, incher, inchman* (Morris says this was an old Tasmanian use), *greeny, red incher, bulljoe, black incher* and *blue incher*.

For anyone wishing to acquire some knowledge of Australian entomology it would be difficult to recommend a more readable book than Keith C. McKeown's "Insect Wonders of Australia" (1944) and, for more studious inquirers, his "Australian Insects" (1945). Here are some of the many Australian terms he uses in the former book: *piedish beetle, lerp-scales, mulga apple, blackboy, skipjack, negrohead, goanna, ringbarker, double drummer, green monday, yellow monday, fiddler, squeaker, floury miller, toe biter, cuckoo spit*. These represent something less than a handful of many thousands of vernacular expressions linked directly with Australia's flora and fauna. Of general linguistic interest are these terms used by McKeown: *buggy*, meaning bug-like; *scalded plains*, desert plains of the Australian interior; *to overwinter*, to spend the winter months (in a certain place); and *witchery hook*, an instrument used for removing witchety grubs from their refuges in shrubs.

Here are some other vernacular terms in frequent use: *toe biter*, a water scorpion belonging to the family *Nepidae; blue fanny*, a species of butterfly common from Cape York to mid-N.S.W. (*Papilio sarpedon choredon*); *pinky* or *bilby*, the long-eared burrowing marsupial known as the *western rabbit bandicoot* (*Thalacomys sagitta*), from which is derived the expression *bilby hole*, a depression occurring especially in the Nullarbor Plains area, allegedly caused by these marsupials; *negrohead*, a rounded nest built high in the branches of a tree by certain termites, connected with the earth by a narrow, clay gallery; *ringbarker, Murphy's ringbarker* and *Lowrie's flying gang*, applied either individually or collectively to a stick and leaf insect *Podacanthus wilkinsoni; mariner*, a bronze-coloured shell of any one of several marine snails belonging to the genus Cantharidus (possibly derived from the Aboriginal *merrina*, a shell necklace); *plat*, a platypus; *platypusary*, a reserve in which platypuses are protected;[8] *platypusiana*, stories and records relating to the platypus;[9] *eucalyptusy*, possessing characteristics of eucalyptus;[10] and *Anti-Ant Week*, a (proposed) regular period each year devoted to the extinction of ants.[11]

As these examples suggest, there is a good deal of interest to be found in examining the vernacular names which litter our zoological landscape. Consider such items as *jewel*, a name given to certain attractive butterflies of the genus *Miletus; jumping joey*, a fish; *jollytail*, another species of fish; *mudeye*, a nymph dragonfly; *woolly bear*, a larva of either the tiger moth or tussock moth, so-named from its hairiness which causes a skin irritation if touched; *madame X*, a species of shark; and *silver Y*, a type of moth. Consider again the many different species that have been awarded the name *kangaroo* as part of their recognized title, e.g. *kangaroo apple, kangaroo bird, kangaroo dog, kangaroo fish, kangaroo grass, kangaroo mouse, kangaroo paw, kangaroo tails, kangaroo thorn*.

4. POPULAR NAMES FOR FLORA

MANY VERNACULAR NAMES given to Australian flora are worth particular note. For example, today we commonly use the word *wattle*

---

[8] "A.M." (magazine), Sydney, November 1949, p. 51. Spelt *platypusery* in "Women's Weekly", Sydney, March 10, 1951, p. 17.

[9] "Bulletin", Sydney, January 24, 1945, p. 2/3.

[10] "I often walk past there on purpose to sniff the lovely eucalyptusy scent." – H. C. Brewster, "King's Cross Calling" (1944).

[11] "This would include an Anti-Ant Week twice a year." – "Sunday Telegraph", Sydney, February 19, 1950, p. 12/6.

for any of this country's 500-odd species of plants, shrubs and trees that have the generic name *Acacia*. As noted elsewhere, early colonists of this country used the word *wattle* to denote a long, willowy cane cut from a tree to make what were known as *wattle-and-daub huts*. But the tree from which the first wattles were cut was not an acacia at all; they came from a tree which has the botanical name *Callicoma serratifolia*. The early settlers called this tree the *black wattle;* it was common around Sydney Cove and was the origin of the name Black Wattle Bay. This Callicoma is still known as *black wattle* and also as *wild quince*. Hardly less worthy of attention because of its peculiar linguistic history is the so-called *Melbourne boronia (Boronia megastigma)*. It is not, as its name would suggest, a native of Melbourne or even of Victoria. It hails from Western Australia, but is cultivated in Melbourne for distribution to other eastern States. The name probably represents a southern attempt to answer the challenge offered by the *Sydney boronia (Boronia ledifolia var. triphylla)*.

More worthy of attention than the wattle is the *eucalypt* – any of about 500 recognized species of the genus *Eucalyptus*. Multitudes of these trees now grow overseas, but all came originally from Australian seed; the readiness of the rest of the world to forget this fact is typified by the fatuous definition in the "Concise Oxford Dictionary" 1964: "Kinds of plants including Australian gum tree". *Gumtree* is one of those misnomers inflicted on us in our earliest days (in this case the culprit was Governor Phillip, in a despatch in May, 1788). Eucalypts do not exude gum, but an astringent, tannic kino. Derivatives include *gumleaves, gumtips, gum blossoms, gumnuts* and an assortment of expressions ranging from *gumleaf band* to *up a gumtree*. Derivatives of eucalypt include *eucalyptoid, eucalyptean, eucalyptol* (a chemical term as well as a trade name) and *eucalyptus oil*.

Although the *brigalow (Acacia harpophylla)* had been sufficiently well-known over the generations to be called *the national scrub*, it was not until 1962 that a large-scale clearance scheme in central Queensland and parts of the Darling Downs drew public attention to what was variously called *brigalow country, brigalow lands, brigalow soils, brigalow leases, brigalow regions* or just *the brigalow*. Much earlier, the *mallee* of Victoria and South Australia had passed through a similar linguistic history – how much earlier is shown by the fact that in 1883 the Mallee Pastoral Leases Act in Victoria officially recognised *mallee country*. Long before 1960, however, brigalow scrub had acquired an unpleasant reputation as the source of a kind of dermatitis known as *brigalow itch*. After the brigalow, we learnt of the *wallum*, an Aboriginal name given to the tall shrub *Banksia aemula*, and had the derivatives served up to us again; for the *wallum lands*, which stretch in a 2,000,000 acre belt of discontinuous sandy lowland along the coast of Queensland from Brisbane to Gladstone, are among our waste areas.

Among popular names for various trees noted by Morris were *Jemmy Donnelly, Jimmy Low* and *Roger Gough* (all of them used apparently with little reason), *axebreaker* and *leatherjacket*. He also records *Major Groce* and *Major Grocer* as names for a fruit of the geebung tribe, and points out that *jil-a-crow-berry* is an English corruption of the Aboriginal name for a species of grass.

An important point stressed by Morris is that the versions *ti-tree* and *ti-tri* are quite wrong for *tea-tree*. This mistake is made continually in print in this country even now and should be weeded out along with other popular lapses.

Additional items noted by Morris include: *bull's wool*, the fibrous inner portion of the bark of the stringybark tree; *traveller's grass* and *settler's twine*, a fibre plant; *settler's matches*, long pendulous strips of bark that hang from eucalypts, used as kindling for fires; *melitose*, an isomeric sugar; *lerp*, an Aboriginal word meaning sweet, applied to a kind of manna secreted by an insect, which has given its name to the chemical substance *lerpamillum* derived from it; *dumplings*, the apple-berry, fruit of an Australian shrub; *job's tears*, seeds of *Coix lachryma*, used for necklace-making by natives in the far north; *mulga apple*, a gall formed on the mulga-tree; and *palberry*, the Native Currant, a corruption of the Aboriginal *palbri*.

In addition to *lerp manna*, a note should also be made of *Australian manna*, which is a white manna-like substance exuded from the leaves and branches of several eucalypts (especially *Eucalyptus viminalis* and *E. rubida*) in dry summer weather.

Some minor colloquialisms worth inclusion are *blackfellow's bread*, sclerotia of *Polyporus mylittae*, rounded lumps varying in size from a pin's head to a human head, often found near decaying stumps or roots of eucalypts; *lady's fingers*,[12] a variety of table grape grown in South Australia; *biddybid*, *biddy-biddy* or *bidgee-widgee*, a herbaceous burr *Acaena anserinifolia*; *cheese*, a compressed, ruddy and ornamental capsule of the medium-sized tree *Phyllanthus ferdinandi*, known variously as *white beech* and *pencil cedar*; *mallee root*, the butt of one of the small-growing eucalypts, which are known as *mallees* – used for fuel; *geebung*, a partly-edible fruit of any one of several species of *Persoonia*, a genus of shrubs or small trees (a corruption of the Aboriginal *jibbong*); *quandong*, an Aboriginal word for the fruit of several trees which bear the same name; *lignum*, a popular version of polygonum; *prickly moses*,[13] a corruption or elaboration of mimosa; *bang alley*, a version of the Aboriginal bangalay; *never greens*, a semi-humorous description of our eucalypts, the pun being on the word "evergreens".

Opportunity should be taken here to note that the following are State floral emblems: N.S.W., the waratah; Victoria, the pink common heath; Queensland, the Cooktown orchid; Western Australia, the kangaroo paw; South Australia, Sturt's desert pea; Tasmania, the southern blue gum; Northern Territory, Sturt's desert rose.

---

[12] *Lady's finger* was used more than a century ago to describe a hardy type of potato in Australia ("Voice from the Bush", 1839: W. Curry and Company, Dublin) and towards the 1900s was applied also to a short, thin banana in Queensland slang. The term is also used in Natal, South Africa, for a "small, delicately-flavoured banana".

[13] This is the accepted common name of *Acacia juniperina*.

5. IDIOMATIC APPLICATIONS

DURING AN EARLIER EXAMINATION of bush idiom (Chapter IV) it was pointed out that numerous metaphors had been evolved around some of our birds and animals, such as *miserable as a bandicoot, mad as a gumtree full of galahs, stone the crows!, game as a piss ant, silly as a curlew* and *flat out like a lizard drinking.*

Our flora and fauna have been put to use in an even simpler form than this, in an effective but economically descriptive fashion, by applying certain words to human beings. Thus we employ (or have employed) words like *geebung, stringybark, bunyip,*[14] *galah* and *dingo* in a derogatory or contemptuous sense. In 1852 G. C. Mundy, in "Our Antipodes", noted that *bunyip* "became and remains a Sydney synonym for impostor, pretender, humbug and the like". Earlier R. Howitt ("Australia", 1845) used *morepork* to describe a simpleton or dull-witted person. Tom Collins also applied the term to a person in "Such Is Life". Today, *morepork* has faded from use, but two other bird-names, *galah* and *drongo*, have taken over. Australian soldiers who served in New Guinea during World War II introduced us to *nong*, which is used in pidgin English and means (I have been told) "pregnant monkey", and we have extended it to *nong-nong*, *ning-nong* and even *nong-nong-nong*, all of which are applied derogatively.

Another old term was *bandicoot*, used to express disfavour when applied to a person. Thus J. I. Hunt wrote in 1889 (in "Hunt's Book of Bonanzas") of "this ole pumpkin-headed *bandicoot* ov a pos'man". Attention has already been drawn to a large number of similes in which the bandicoot features – *bandy as a bandicoot, barmey as a bandicoot*, etc.

Largely because of close association with a great deal of Australian fauna and flora, many figurative expressions of this type originated among people who lived in the bush or outback. For example, *cockatoo*, which later became the highly-useful *cocky*, was used to describe a farmer; *bronzewing* (a pigeon found in large numbers in the bush) came to denote a member of the proletariat, in contrast to *silvertail*, a member of the upper crust; *ringneck* (a bird) was used to describe a jackeroo, because new chums recently arrived from England retained their white collars for a time and bore a fancied resemblance to the ring-neck parakeet.

A talkative woman was called a *budgie* or *budgerigar;* an impudent or daring person, especially a child, was called a *cheeky possum;* a person who betrayed an undertaking was said to *dingo on* that undertaking.

Blue tongue (from the lizard of that name) and *crocodile* are both used outback for rouseabouts; and *joey* (the young of a marsupial) also denotes a handyman, although the more customary expression is *wood-and-water joey.*

---

[14] The *bunyip* is a fabulous Aboriginal animal supposed to haunt swampy areas and lake regions in parts of Australia. Serious attempts to establish its existence have failed. It varies in size and shape according to the imagination of its describers.

But this was by no means all. City people, many of whom had limited experience of Australia's fauna and flora, put some of these terms to their own uses: *to white ant*, to undermine a workers' organization, and its associated *white-anting; cockatoo*, a person who keeps guard while some illegal activity, such as two-up, is in progress; *koala*, a diplomatic car which cannot be booked for traffic violation and is therefore "protected"; *kangaroo a car*, to drive with many stops and starts due to inexperience as a driver; *mallee root*, a prostitute (by rhyme).

Another outback original is *rosella* (a bird) which, in former times, served to denote a European working stripped to the waist, doubtless because he became badly sunburnt and an analogy could be perceived between him and the Crimson Rosella. Australian soldiers describe high-ranking officers as *rosellas* because of the red tabs worn on their lapels and their red capbands.

The terms *cocky* and *budgie* mentioned above are examples of a large group of hypocoristic or pseudo-hypocoristic names given to various items of Australian flora and fauna. As we will see in Chapter XVII, there is a prevalence of *-y* and *-ie* suffixes in Australian speech, among them *muddy*, a mudcrab, *muffy*, a frilled necked lizard, *rocky*, a rock wallaby. To these can be added (with a reservation to be noted later): *bandy bandy*, a small, venomous snake; *beardie*, a fish or a lizard; *bobby*, the stump tail lizard; *bully*, a small fish; *greenie*, a bird of the honeyeater tribe; *gruie*, a tree; *hairy nanny*, an alternate name for the daddy longlegs; *kelpie*, an Australian breed of sheep-dog; *lillypilly*, a shrub or small tree; *nealie*, another shrub or small tree; *perentie*, the largest of Australia's goannas; *roughy*, a fish; *sandy*, another fish; *stripey*, still another fish; *whisky*, a bird; *witchety*, an edible grub; *yabby*, a freshwater crayfish.

The reservation is, of course, that quite a number of these words are Aboriginal, e.g. *yabby*, *nealie*, but I have grouped them with obvious hypocorisms because there is some possibility that the prevalence of native words with an *-i* suffix (anglicized into *-ie*, *-y* and *-ee*) has encouraged the adoption of "feminine" words in Australian English. To give an assurance that the native examples listed above have not by any means exhausted the available supply, here are some more: *barramundi* or *burramundi*, a fish; *cumbungi*, a plant; *wallaby*, a marsupial; and *cadagi*, *cudgerie*, *gidgee*, *karri*, *mallee*, *marri* and *sallee*, all names of trees.

CHAPTER XV

Aborigines and Pidgin English

1. NATIVE CONTRIBUTIONS

FOR A COUNTRY as traditionally concerned as Australia is in fair-going mateship, the treatment we have meted out to our Aborigines has been inexplicable as well as shocking. When the first colonists settled here, it is estimated that there were some 300,000 Aboriginal fullbloods in Australia; today there are only about 40,000 fullbloods and another 31,000 caste Aborigines. The rest have been *dispersed* – i.e. slaughtered in vast numbers, poisoned, driven away from tribal lands – so that land-hungry whitemen have been able to extend their properties and boost bank balances. Their women have been debauched – by whitemen. Diseases, introduced to this country by whitemen, have spread among them. Until most recent times, alcohol of the vilest kind has been peddled to them – by whitemen. Most of those not forced into reserves (which white politicians pilfer at the least sign that they are not worthless) have been driven into slums on the fringes of outback towns (*down on the marsh*, as they say in the Kimberleys); the few who dwell in our larger cities are usually obliged by circumstances to congregate in urban slums. In many parts of Australia, the Aboriginal doing a job that could be performed by a whiteman earns less than would be paid to a whiteman. As for education, only a few have managed to escape the shackles of ignorance forced on them – by whitemen.

How on earth is it possible to reconcile mateship and fair-gos with such treatment? It is time we took a look at the matter. To begin with, the Australian *fair go* is not quite what it implies. It is not given to everyone. Interestingly enough, the colour of a person's skin has nothing to do with it. Whether he is black or yellow is beside the point. If he acts and speaks as one who is willing to stand up for himself whatever the consequences, he is not only entitled to a fair go, but he could quite conceivably be a mate, and the Australian (non-Aboriginal, of course) is willing to treat him as an equal. Even Poms and Yanks can make the grade. On the other hand, should he fail to stand up for himself, he could never be a mate and, *ipso facto*, he is unworthy of equality and a fair go.

That is what happened to the Aboriginal. His culture betrayed him. There was such a vast difference between white thinking and Aboriginal thinking that, after a brief flirtation with the idea of the Noble Savage and seeing the quite distressing efforts that the Aborigines made (under the whiteman's tutelage) in imitating white conduct, our Pilgrim Fathers saw no merit in them and treated them accordingly. Almost everything conspired to this end. Their lack of concern with personal possessions, their nomadic life, their strange customs, their readiness to tell whitemen what they wanted to hear, were at the far end of the newcomers' social spectrum and there was virtually no point at which their interests met.

The whiteman therefore took their tribal lands with the best of good consciences, regarded their protests as impertinences justifying assorted cruelties and massacres, and drove them away. Since these people were just about the most unequal you could imagine, they had no claim to fair-gos. There was never any question in the whiteman's mind that he should try to assimilate aspects of Aboriginal culture or even that he should meet the Aboriginal halfway. On the contrary, the Aboriginal was required to assimilate to him and out of the essential goodness of his heart he would grant the Aboriginal the status of a third-class citizen. Perhaps the Aborigines should congratulate themselves that they have exterminated easily and that, as a result, there are not many of them remaining today to suffer the humiliations that remain with them after generations of maltreatment and indifference.

The lack of authoritative information on Australian Aboriginal dialects is symptomatic of this indifference. In 1788, about 500 different Aboriginal languages are estimated to have been in use. Due to appalling carelessness and neglect, the majority have been lost. Although in recent years some valuable contributions have been made by researchers – many of them have been published in the scientific journal "Oceania" – no matter what efforts anthropologists and linguists may now make, they will be unable to fill gaps in our knowledge.[1]

Although Australian Aboriginal dialects are sources from which we have drawn much of our idiom, there are few subjects upon which the public is more generally misinformed. This is not entirely the public's fault. In the first place, a malignant fate, in the shape of slovenly observers, has helped to perpetuate the allegation that our Aborigines are the least intelligent humans in the world. This allegation has a good deal to do with the admitted fact that the Aborigines are probably the most archaic or most primitive people extant, an unfortunate and quite unwarranted contempt having arisen through a confusion between the time-concept and the intelligence-concept of the word "primitive".

---

[1] The following remarks by Joah H. Sugden, a student of Aboriginal placenames, ("Sydney Morning Herald", June 7, 1949, p. 2) are relevant:

"My work is concerned with sifting records made by other people, rather than with original field-work. One cannot help feeling amazed and a little appalled at the lack of information available on the meaning of Aboriginal placenames. Hundreds of names, which have been used by white men since the earliest days, cannot be translated with any degree of confidence. There are serious disputes over the meaning and spelling of others. Today, it is too late in many areas to attempt to solve these problems. Aborigines have vanished from Tasmania and almost gone from Victoria. In another generation there will probably be no more full-blooded Aborigines in New South Wales. Our chances of clearing up problems of nomenclature are rapidly vanishing, yet neither the State [of N.S.W.] nor the Federal Government seems interested. Although anthropologists have made excellent studies of some Aboriginal dialects, there is no such thing as a collective Aboriginal dictionary for Australia, let alone a comprehensive dictionary of reference to native placenames. That it is possible to say this more than 160 years after whitemen first settled in Australia, is a bitter commentary on our indifference both to Aboriginal culture and to our own."

In the second place, although our academics have (as should, of course, be expected) taken only a belated interest in the Aborigines, enough honest field-work has not yet been done to make more than a minor dent in the subject. As a result, we have no means in our possession of obtaining anything like a complete picture of the Aboriginal even in what one might expect to be the accessible subject of his language.[2]

If the average Australian knows so little about native dialects, it is scarcely likely that he will be able to appreciate how extensive has been the impression they have left on his modern language. *Kookaburra, billabong, bombora, corroboree, gunyah, lubra, boomerang, nulla nulla* – he may have these fixed in his mind as Aboriginal, but ask him about *billy, jumbuck, never never, yabber, waddy, willy willy, jackeroo, humpy, go bung, rosella, dillybag, within cooee* and he will probably be quite unable to pick accurately the words with authentic Aboriginal origins and those which we have imported from overseas.

In 1964, the Australian Language Research Centre at Sydney University published its third Occasional Paper on "The Currency of Aboriginal Words in Australian English". Of its total listing of about 200 Aboriginal words, "some of them now obsolete", three-quarters were native names for flora and fauna. Since the compiler, W. S. Ramson, claimed that another thirty were pidgin, we are left with about twenty more or less authentic Aboriginal words in general use, among them *bunyip, coolamon, didgeridoo, gibber, gin, humpy, kurdaitcha* and *woomera*. Can this finding be true? Let us have a look at the facts.

2. PIDGIN ENGLISH IN AUSTRALIA

IN MY "NEW ZEALAND SLANG" I pointed out that the Maori language was almost certainly modified by its reduction to English writing – by the fact that it was forced into certain alphabetical moulds. Something even more drastic occurred to Australian Aboriginal dialects.

In September, 1796, D. Collins, commenting on the type of speech current between whites and natives, wrote (subsequently published in

---

[2] The most extensive work of its kind is probably "The Australian Aboriginal Dictionary", by W. Bishop (1929), which is in MS. form in the Mitchell Library, Sydney. This contains many thousands of terms, but is rather a catalogue than a dictionary. No effort is made to indicate the dialects or districts to which the words belong. "Work in Progress" at the Mitchell is an MS. by Herbert Ardlaw Lawrance called "Australian Aboriginal Words", which was received in 1953. A "Vocabulary of Aboriginal Words and Names" was published in 1916 by James J. Baylis, but contains some patent inaccuracies. Another work – again incomplete and misleading – in MS. form is a "Vocabulary of New South Wales Aboriginal Dialects" compiled by members of the staff of the Mitchell Library, Sydney (1908). Apart from the fact that it deals only with N.S.W., that much of its material came from black-trackers who moved from district to district and that, as a consequence, the dialects are mixed, the work has the added deficiency that it was never completed. About 1200 examples were listed in "Australian Aboriginal Native Words", by Sidney J. Endacott (1924: republished 1944) and some 550 "euphonious words" from N.S.W. dialects were listed in the 1943 edition of "New South Wales Aboriginal Place Names" by Frederick D. McCarthy; this collection was later expanded considerably.

"Account of New South Wales") "Nothing but a barbarous mixture of English with the Port Jackson dialect is spoken by either party". (He gives such examples as *caw-be* for coffee, and *Midger Plindar* for Mr Flinders.) This "barbarous mixture" was pidgin English. Not the original pidgin of China, but the original of what is now known throughout the Pacific as beach-la-mar. It probably flourished in Australia and New Zealand long before it became established in the small Pacific islands which are its home today. It was the original lingua franca between Europeans and Australian Aborigines and, because the Aborigines were quicker to learn the white-man's imbecilities than the whiteman was to learn the native dialects, their own language became tainted with pidgin.

L. E. Threlkeld, author of "An Australian Grammar" (1834), declared:

It is necessary to notice certain barbarisms[3] which have crept into use, introduced by sailors, stockmen and others who have paid no attention to the aboriginal tongue, in the use of which both blacks and whites labour under the mistaken idea that each one is conversing in the other's language. The following list contains the most common in use in these parts:

boojery, good.	*jerrund*, fear.
bail, no.	*kangaroo*, an animal.
boge, to bathe.	*carbon*, large.
bimble, earth.	*mije*, little.
boomiring, a weapon.	*mogo*, axe.
budgel, sickness.	*murry*, many.
cudgel, tobacco.	*pickaninney*, child.
gammon, falsehood.	*piyaller*, to speak.
gibber, a stone.	*tuggerrer*, cold.
gummy, a spear.	*wikky*, bread.
goonyer, a hut.	*waddy*, a cudgel.
hillimung, a shield.	*wommerrer*, a weapon.
jin, a wife.	*strike-a-light*, to make known.

Even a cursory examination serves to show that, while many of these "barbarisms" represented no more than importations from other dialects, some of them could not by any stretch of imagination be given a place in authentic Aboriginal language. *Gammon, pickaninney, waddy* and *strike-a-light* are obvious examples.

Although Threlkeld was incorrect in dismissing all the words listed above as non-Aboriginal, the point he makes is important. The mixing of Aboriginal dialects – that is, the migration of terms from one district to another – through the agency of the European has probably been so great that it can now never be accurately assessed.

Here is what J. D. Lang wrote in "Cooksland" (1847):

Words quite as unintelligible to the natives as the corresponding words in vernacular language of the white man would have been, were learned by the natives, and are now commonly used by them in conversing with

---

[3] Morris comments: "A barbarism means with Mr Threlkeld little more than 'not belonging to the Hunter district'."

Europeans. Thus *corrobory*, the Sydney word for a general assembly of natives, is now commonly used in that sense at Moreton Bay; but the original word there is *yanerville*. *Cabon*, great, *narang*, little, *boodgeree*, good, *myall*, wild native, etc., are all words of this description, supposed by the natives to be English words, and by Europeans to be aboriginal words of the language of that district.

A similar point had been made a little earlier by C. Hodgkinson who, in his "Australia" (1845), spoke of

> . . . the jargon which the stockmen and sawyers suppose to be the language of the natives, whilst they suppose it to be ours, and which is the ordinary medium of communication between the squatters and the tame black-fellows.

The European influence therefore had two clearcut effects: (a) the introduction of pidgin as a lingua franca between black and white, and (b) the spreading of Aboriginal terms of limited original use in one district to other, and often remote, districts. These effects are so closely allied that they are more or less the manifestation of a single motif – the inevitable degeneration of all native languages with which the European comes in contact.

Two of the most competent reviews of Aboriginal influence on Australian speech yet written were those of A. Meston, in 1896, and of Ernest Favenc, in 1904. Here are some of Favenc's comments:

> The pidgin talk which is considered so essential for carrying on conversation with a blackfellow is mostly of very old origin. Of late years few words appear to have been added to its delirious jumble of the English and Australian languages; and most of it is derived from New South Wales and Victoria. Or it might be better said from New South Wales only, as, when most of it originated, Victoria was not. As the whites pushed on and on amongst new tribes, nothing was taken from the local dialects to add to the general pidgin stock, but the original was carried along, mostly by the black boys who accompanied the whites.
>
> Take the beautiful word *myall*, for example, which the blacks have added to our language, and which is now used all over the continent to signify wild or untamed. This was the name of a Bogan tribe distinguished even amongst the aboriginals for ferocity and aloofness. Sturt first came into contact with them and noticed that they did not object to being called myalls whilst other tribes repudiated the name.
>
> *Cooler*, angry, comes from the Lower Darling, as does *murri*, very.
>
> The Darling blacks, who fought Mitchell so determinedly, were said by the others to be *murri-cooler*.
>
> *Mickie*, quick, another Riverina word, is often made a compound with *murri*, only the pronunciation is altered to *merry;* and *merry mickie*, very quick or look sharp, is the result.
>
> *Bong*, dead, is very old Brisbane River dialect. *Yowi*, yes, *bal*, no, *yan*, go, *mundooie*, leg or foot, *carbon*, very much, *cobbra*, head, *bingee*, belly, etc., belong to New South Wales of the old, old days.
>
> It is true that a few words have been adopted from other tribes, but as a rule they are used only locally, not generally, like the old pidgin which has become Australian now.

For instance, there is *Binghi*, a name applied to a mainland blackfellow at Thursday Island.

Taking it all and through, the Murray and Darling and their tributaries have been the birthplace of most of the pidgin in common use.

An even more thorough examination of Aboriginal material was made by Meston, who concerned himself mainly with establishing the origins of certain native terms in our speech. Here are some of his more important observations:

The first blacks with whom the whites associated were those of Sydney and Botany Bay, followed by those of the Hawkesbury, Hunter and Twofold Bay. To the dialects of those places we naturally turn for the earliest aboriginal words in use among the white men.

The most interesting vocabulary in my possession is one taken down from the lips of Bennelong, one of the two Sydney blacks, who went to England with Governor Phillip in 1792. Attached to this is another taken from a George's River black named Walwarra, in 1803, by Thomas Jarret Ives, who lived with the blacks and spoke their language.

Both vocabularies were printed at the "Sydney Gazette" office in 1809. In the Botany dialect I find the first record of the word *myall*, the name given to a stranger. The Botany district gave the word *kobbera* for head. At Sydney it was *cabboora*. It gave us *mundowie*, the word for leg, though widely used for the foot by the whites. From Botany came the words *wombat*, *wommera*, *yarraman*, *wonga-wonga*, *gunya*, *waddy*, *wollaba* (wallaby), *wallaroo*, *heelamin*, *budjerie*, *corobberie*, *baal* and *curriejung*.

Yarraman was *yeeramahn*, from yeera, the teeth, and mahn, long – literally "long teeth", a name for the horse.

The negative was *beeal* (baal) and the affirmative *yooeen*. From Botany came the once-familiar words, *paialla*, to tell, *durellie*, to fight, *coolahra*, angry, *jerran*, frightened and *goori*, fat.

From Botany comes the word *boomerang*. Walwarra called it "boom-ering" and "bummering". The Botany tribe called the native bear *coolah*, the same as one of the bear-names at Moreton Bay.

All these words were scattered by the pioneer timber-getters, settlers or squatters from Sydney to the Gulf of Carpentaria.

Here is another illustration of the sort of modifying influences that whitemen can impose.[4]

All the aboriginal children at the Finniss Springs Mission Station in South Australia speak with a Scottish accent, especially the elder ones who have been on the station all their lives. This is stated in a report received in Sydney yesterday from the New South Wales Flying Doctor, Dr. J. G. Woods, who recently flew to the station, where nearly 100 aboriginal children are being cared for and educated. "The Scottish accent," says Dr. Woods, "is picked up from Mr. Warren, on whose property the mission is located. It is rather comical to hear a jet-black lassie putting over something which sounds like Harry Lauder's patter. One expects her to break into a song and dance at any tick of the clock."

---

[4] "Sydney Morning Herald", December 28, 1945.

The squalid activities of missions, *plus* a long history of public indifference, *plus* assorted anthropological dishonesties, have stolen Aboriginal dignity almost entirely. On the last point, at a science congress in Adelaide in 1947, anthropologist T.G.H. Strehlow attacked the "old school" of scientists who considered the Australian Aborigines a degenerating remnant of Stone Age savagery. He cited Spencer and Gillen, who studied Central Australian natives around the turn of the century, as typical upholders of this view. Fortunately, some of our modern anthropologists have tackled the subject with greater knowledge and sympathy, but they can never replace hundreds of dialects which have been lost forever nor, except by a sort of academic vote, give us a reliable guide as to how surviving words should be spelt. Ramson's spellings for the Australian Language Research Centre are frequently at variance with spellings given in quotations above, and who is to say what is right?

In this matter, Australia compares most unfavourably with New Zealand where the Maori dictionaries of Tregear and Williams, compiled and published last century, have been of enduring value. When, in November, 1949, an Australian woman sent a native musical instrument called a *didjeridu* to Professor Albert Einstein in America, the newspapers were naturally interested. But they had no standard reference work to refer to in order to arrive at a unanimous spelling. Versions included *didjeridu, didjerido, didgiridoo* and *didgeree-du.* Examples of this nature occur with great frequency. What, for instance, should be the spelling of the Aboriginal name given to a rocky reef near the foot of a cliff – *bombora* or *bomboora*? The newspapers cannot agree. Ramson's selections are *didgeridoo* and *bombora.*

The trouble with hit-and-miss methods of arriving at a standard spelling is that they are more likely to be shaped in accordance with white prejudices than with the original pronunciation. This process is continuing with ever-greater effect as Australia's white population grows and her native population diminishes.

Other influences also operate. This comment by a researcher provides some rather extreme illustrations of what is taking place:[5]

> It is not uncommon to find that in private a peculiar jargon compounded of Gumbaingar and English is spoken, especially among those having a good knowledge of both tongues. For example, the following have been heard at various times: "*wana :silly-unba:* all your life" (don't be absolutely silly all your life), "where's Jack – Oh, he's gon *splitimbeigu wa:gei*" (Where's Jack – Oh, he's gone to split some fire-wood), "Where's that *mi :nja?*" (Where's that what's-its-name?).

Here is a mixture of Aboriginal and English words recorded in a song from south-west Queensland:[6]

---

[5] W. E. Smythe, "Elementary Grammar of the Gumbaingar Language" (North Coast, N.S.W.), published in Oceania, vol. xix, no. 2, December, 1948, p. 130.

[6] "Aborigines Make Music" by Jeremy Beckett, published in Quadrant, vol. 2, no. 4, 1958, p. 37.

Wandiwadiwa (where are you going?) boy?
Good mornin' boy,
Come an' have a nobbler.
Pale brandy, dark brandy
I wandee juramu (I want rum).

How long before someone tells us that *nobbler, wandee* and *juramu* are Aboriginal words?

Here is another example from the same source:

He borrowed a sub and headed straight for the pub,
That boy he ain't no mug,
And very soon he had all us coon
In the mallee cutting a rug.

A *sub* is an advance on wages, *coon* is from the U.S. as a derogatory term for a Negro, *mallee* is here applied to any sort of bush, and *cut a rug*, which U.S. Negroes use to mean jazz, has been converted by our Aborigines to mean "to let off steam, to cut a dash, to get riproaring drunk".

If this sort of thing has been happening since 1788, and there is a good deal of evidence to suggest that it has, we can hardly have much confidence in the list Ramson has compiled which gives *waddy* among authentic Aboriginal words, when it is a pidgin corruption of "wood", *brumby*, a wild horse, as pidgin when it comes directly from the name of an English horse-breeder, and *jumbuck*, a sheep, as pidgin when it is, in fact, an Aboriginal word.

For this reason, it will be necessary to give the subject much more discriminating attention than offered by Ramson. Since we have been examining pidgin here, let us continue with that theme.

While most Australians are probably not inclined to consider pidgin of significance, the fact remains that this lingual bastardization, which was introduced in its original forms by our oecists, is current throughout the northern portions of Australia, from Western Australia to Queensland,[7] and in nearly all places where whites come in contact with native workers. Not only is it deep-rooted in terms of our history, but it was confirmed by the importation of Pacific Islanders during the *blackbirding* days last century to work Queensland plantations, by the admission of Torres Strait islanders to the mainland, and by the strong Australian link with Papua (since 1906) and New Guinea over which we received a mandate in 1921 and have been administering under a Trusteeship Agreement with the United Nations since 1946.

Cursory examination shows that there are wide differences between the pidgin used in New Guinea (to which attention will be given in Section 4) and New Zealand and the pidgin of Australia. So far as New Zealand is concerned, this is due largely to earnest efforts made by the New Zealand Government to educate Maoris in the use of English. Many of

---

[7] On November 7, 1891, the Melbourne "Argus" referred scornfully to "that ridiculous pigeon English which the whites have used . . . throughout Queensland . . . as their medium of communication with the blacks."

the Maoris speak English infinitely better than their white compatriots. But on this side of the Tasman the Government rarely spares a thought for improving Aboriginal education.

If, in order to retain a white concept when speaking his native language, the Maori corrupts missionary to *mihinare*, pipe to *paipa*, regulation to *rekureihana*, or even such a word as torpedoed to *topitongia*, we should not be surprised if we find the Australian Aboriginal doing exactly the same thing. Here are examples from Kimberley tribes, collected by Ernest Worms:[8]

> *mele mele* or *mele mel*, a letter or book, from the English word "mail".
> *bulemano* or *buleman*, a bull, ox, cow or calf, from the word "bull".
> *dyilaman* or *dyileman*, a gun, from "kill a man".
> *dyarge*, a turkey.
> *dyorab*, a strap.
> *dima*, steamer.
> *madyer* or *madyeri*, matches.
> *dyad*, shirt.
> *dyawody* or *dyawodyo*, trousers.
> *dauody*, pouch.
> *baib* or *baibo*, pipe.
> *Breb*, Fred.
> *naib*, knife.
> *waidbel*, *wadbel*, *walybalo*, *walybela*, whitefellow.
> *bamba*, by and by.
> *bagede*, bucket.
> *bolanggar*, *balanggad*, *bolangged*, blanket.
> *bod*, *bodo*, boot(s).

Probably the best review of Australian pidgin yet compiled is the work of Edgar Sheappard Sayer, whose "Pidgin English" was published in 1939. Sayer lived for some years in tropical Australia, and became intimately acquainted with the pidgin used there. His dictionary of Australian pidgin words is still the most outstanding of its kind.

Here are some of the words he lists: *talkum*, *fixem*, *catchum*, *gibbit*, *walkabout*, *ticky-ticky water* (oil), *Big Name* (God), *paper-talk* or *paper-yabber* (a letter), *eatum wind cart* (a car: an expression derived almost certainly from the Malayan pidgin *wind wagon*, a car), *big fella hawk*, *big fella cockatoo* or *firebird longa sky* (an aeroplane), *kid* (£1, ex the slang "quid"), *halfem kid* (10s.) and *taybit* (3d., ex the slang "traybit").

Sayer gives a number of Australian pidgin translations, among which is Psalm 23. Here is part of it:

Big Name watchem sheepysheep: watchem blackfella. No more belly cry fella hab.	The Lord is my shepherd; I shall not want. He maketh me to lie down in green pastures: He leadeth me beside the still waters.
Big Name makum camp alonga grass, takum blackfella walkabout longa, no frightem no more hurry watta.	

---

[8] "Studies in Australian Linguistics", Oceanic Monographs, No. 3.

| Big Boss longa sky makum inside glad: takem walkabout longa too much good fella . . . | He restoreth my soul: He leadeth me in the paths of righteousness for His name's sake . . . |

Sayer notes that "the aborigines use the slang in use in Australia when they are much in contact with whitemen", and he gives some examples: *tinned dog*, for canned meats – *me no likkit tinyd dogy; swig*, for drink – *gibbit swig beer boss?*; chasing the skirts – *chasem lubra*.

Much of this might seem trivial and outside the scope of this book were it not for the fact that numerous Australian pidgin words are finding their way into white Australian speech.

Wha'nim, for instance, is a clipped form of *what name?* which serves as a general utility question mark, meaning why? how? what do you mean? what's it all about? and so on. White residents of the north frequently employ it in jocular speech between themselves, just as they say *no more*, meaning "no", and *youi*, meaning "yes". In the same way they use the expressions *walkabout, piccaninny daylight, finger-talk, footwalk, dillybag, sugarbag, honeybag, mary* and *lollywater. Walkabout*, especially in the verbal form *to go walkabout*, is known throughout Australia and has bred many similar terms: *talkabout, singabout, flyabout, hopabout, dreamabout, eatabout, scootabout, surfabout, swimabout*, etc. Also generally accepted into Australian speech are *dillybag* for any carrier bag, *lollywater*, for a highly sweetened soft drink, *honeybag* for honey and *mary* as a generic name for woman. For generations they have been slowly working their way into popular speech.

Mary is an almost inevitable nickname for an Aboriginal female, in the same way that a native male is often labelled *Billy* (especially *King Billy*) or *Jacky* (*sit up like Jacky*). In pidgin English it is indispensable. J. L. Nicholas recorded it in New Zealand pidgin use in 1815. Mrs R. C. Praed, in "Australian Life" (1885), even ventured to refer to white women as *white mairies*.

Equally useful in Australian pidgin is *piccaninny*, a child, sometimes abbreviated to *pic*.[9] It is a West Indian Negro term (from Spanish *pequena*) imported to Australasia by early adventurers. Morris declares: "After a while English people thought the word was aboriginal Australian, while the aborigines thought it was correct English". It is now in wide use, often by whites, and almost everyone recognises *piccaninny daylight* as denoting the light before dawn.

Another pidgin term of special importance is *old man*. As I have already pointed out, the Aborigines make considerable distinction between *old man*, meaning lusty, strong, outsized, and *old man old man*, which means old

A report in the "Sydney Morning Herald" of November 19, 1963, p. 6, said that the words *boy, piccaninny* or *pic* and *lubra* to denote Aborigines had been banned to Northern Territory welfare workers. Whereas the first three proscriptions were understandable, the fourth was not, for *lubra* is an authentic Aboriginal word reputedly from Tasmania. The fact is, however, that (as we will see in the next Section) whitemen in far northern Australia have created a situation in which *lubra* is often used derogatively.

and therefore probably none of these things. An *old man* is a tribal leader; he knows where water is to be found, the places for the best hunting, where to camp, he is a repository of tribal wisdom. He is not an ancient, any more than an *old man southerly*, *old man kangaroo* (or dingo, boar, snapper, etc.), *old man mountain* and so on is a minor example of its type. In fact, the reverse is almost always true. (In passing, it can be noted that Jean Devanny makes an odd reference in one of her books to an *old lady wallaby!*)

Ernestine Hill gave an interesting round-up of pidgin terms in her book, "The Territory" (1951). Here are some of them:

> *all about*, everyone; everywhere.
> *behind*, after, in time. "Behind you tell me, I tell Paddy."
> *belong(a)*, appertaining to.
> *cheeky*, dangerous, poisonous. "Cheeky blacks", "cheeky snake", "cheeky yam".
> *finish*, to die.
> *longa*, belonging to, near, about, with.
> *mobs*, numbers, quantities, volumes – plenty.
> *muckety*, rifle, an old-time musket.
> *paper-yabber*, the written word.
> *proper*, very much so.
> *which-way?* where or why.

Many English words have been taken by the Aboriginal (or perhaps it would be better to say they have been palmed off on the blacks by the whites) and, after being modified in meaning by the natives, have come back to us with fresh applications. *Whitefellow* and *blackfellow* are examples of this Aboriginal influence on our speech, *fellow* – and its versions *fella*, *feller* or *pfella* – being a persistent intrusive in all beach-la-mar. Thus the Aboriginal uses *cheekyfellow* to describe something that is dangerous or injurious, *sulkyfellow*, angry, to be feared, *bigfellow*, something especially large, *whitefellow devil*, electricity.

Mob is another example. Through Aboriginal use of the word we now employ it to describe any number or quantity. Thus we can have *mobs of water*, *mobs of money*, *mobs of time*, *mobs of jackasses* (of cattle, kangaroos, persons, etc.). We have even developed a slang phrase, *to mob in with someone*, to live with a person.

Yabber, to talk, is closely allied to the English *jabber* and may even have been shaped by it. In "The Eureka Stockade", Carboni Raffaello twice uses the form *yabber-yabber* and we have seen its extension to *paper-yabber* for the written word. *Big smoke* was used by the Aborigines to denote a town long before it was colloquial. As already noted, *waddy* is a corruption of the word "wood"[10] and is now applied to any stick or rough club. We have also made a verb out of it: *to waddy* means to beat with a waddy or stick.

---

[10] A Queensland old-timer recalls how an Aboriginal used to call at his Maryborough home and offer to *yacker waddy* (work wood), meaning to chop firewood.

In short, there are several meeting points between the speech of whitemen and Aborigines in Australia. In the next Section we will find some more, although of a different kind.

3. DREAMING AND REALITY

SOME BASIC POINTS should be made at the outset of this Section.

First, Aboriginal is a singular noun and denotes an Australian native. Thus, too, with sundry combinations, caste-Aboriginal, part-Aboriginal, etc.

Second, Aboriginal is the adjective, as in such examples as Aboriginal myth, Aboriginal ritual.

Third, Aborigines is the plural noun. Thus, one speaks of one Aboriginal, two or more Aborigines.

Fourth, all uses of Aboriginal and Aborigines are capitalised. This includes the abbreviations Abo, singular noun and adjective, and Abos, plural noun, although the sooner such abbreviations are purged from our speech the better.

Since in the course of this Section we will be examining many of the words taken from the Aborigines and absorbed into standard use, other standard or near-standard words used to describe Aboriginal activities, and a large collection of popular slang, we can begin with the first. Due to the disordered nature of early orthography,[11] it is now too late to tell whether any given spelling of a native word is right or wrong; our choice is largely shaped by authoritative practice, but there is no guarantee that any "authority" is correct.

billabong, a backwater or elongated water-hole in the bed of a stream which flows only after heavy rain. From Aboriginal billa, water, and bong, dead, i.e. dead water. The former has given us billy (hence billycan, billypot); the latter survives in the slang go bung, to fail, to become worthless.

binjey, the stomach or belly. Sundry Aboriginal spellings have been recorded, among them binjee, bindi and binge-gung. In his "Account of New South Wales", D. Collins gives the forms ben-de and bin-niee.

binghi (pronounced bing-eye), an Aboriginal. This word, meaning brother, was reputedly used originally on Thursday Island; it was in colloquial use in Australia by 1892. In New Guinea pidgin beangi is used to describe a native from the Bouang area, Morobe District, as in bouang itself, which was possibly the original source of boong.

bogey, a bathe, especially in a river or freshwater pool. It was first recorded in 1834. (Various adaptations, such as bogeyhole, a swimming hole, bogeyhouse, a bathroom, and bogeying, bathing, are now almost obsolete.)

bombora, a hidden rock-reef which, in calm weather, causes the sea to lift, but not to break; in rough weather, it produces a dangerous stretch of

---

11 "Most of the earlier grammars adopted a system based upon Italian vowel-sounds and English consonantal-sounds; but in later works, and in a great majority of the vocabularies words are spelled in all sorts of ways, without any indication of the sounds attached to the letters." – S. H. Ray "Australian Encyclopaedia" (1925-7 edition).

broken water. From Aboriginal *bumbora*, a current off Dobroyde Head, Port Jackson.

boomerang, an Aboriginal throwing weapon of several types, only one of which has the property of returning to the thrower. The first known spelling (in 1834) was *boomiring*. (Given the status of a verb by whites, meaning to return.)

bunyip, a water-dwelling monster of Aboriginal legend, reputedly first seen by a whiteman (Hamilton Hume) in Lake Bathurst in 1821. The Australian fur seal or seal bear is supposed to have been the origin of the bunyip myth.

cooee, an Aboriginal word meaning "come here", often used as a penetrating cry in bush or outback areas; first recorded in 1790. (However, one of my outback correspondents writes: "I have never heard anyone lost in the bush or stockmen who want to keep in touch when mustering call *cooee*. They usually yell whatever they can yell loudest, such as *ya-hee-ohooooo!*") This word has been accepted into general Australian use: *to cooee*, to utter the word as a call; *cooeeing*, calling the word; *within cooee*, within calling distance and, figuratively, near to.

coolamon, a piece of wood hollowed to hold food or water.

corroboree, one of several types of dance mainly divided into sacred and non-sacred. John Hunter, Deputy Governor, gave the spelling *carribberie* in 1793. (Later adapted by whites to mean any celebration, especially a dance.)

didgeridu, a drone pipe made from bamboo or a hollow sapling, up to 15 feet long. Also spelt *didgeridoo*.

gibber (pronounced with a hard "g"), an Aboriginal word meaning stone, applied particularly to fragments of quartzite and silicaceous iron-stone that have been rounded and worn smooth by action of wind and water. Used attributively in *gibber plains*, *gibber country*. Sturt's Stony Desert is largely covered with *gibbers*.

gin, an Aboriginal woman. D. Collins gave the spelling *din* in 1798.

gunyah, a roughly built shelter, made of boughs and bark. Collins gave the spelling *go-nie* in 1798.

humpy, as for *gunyah*. The first convict settlement at Redcliffe in Moreton Bay, Queensland, was called *Humpybong*, believed to mean "dead settlement" or "shelter for the dead". See the use of *bong* in *billabong*.

lubra, a young Aboriginal woman. This word is one of the few relics of Tasmania's Aborigines.

mia mia, as for *gunyah*.

min min, a "ghost light" believed to be derived from a spontaneous combination of methane and other gases given off by a bore in outback areas.

myall, wild. Applied often as a noun, denoting a "wild" Aboriginal. Ernestine Hill reports the use, in the Northern Territory, of *myall express*, "natives to show a traveller the way, or to help".

nulla nulla, a club.

tjuringa, a wooden or stone object sacred to the Aborigines; its shape varies from round to oval, it is flat or slightly convex on both sides, and circular or other decorations are added.

warrigal, an Aboriginal word originally applied to the dingo, but subsequently applied by whitemen to anything wild.

M

weet weet, an Aboriginal toy, consisting of a small knob of wood attached to a flexible twig up to 30 inches long.

wurley, as for *gunyah.*

yandy, to winnow. Whence *yandying.*

Hundreds of Aboriginal words are preserved in the vernacular names of Australian flora and fauna. A few examples:

FISH: *barramundi, bidyan (ruffe), mado, maray, mulloway, nannygai, tabbigaw, teraglin, wobbegong.*

TREES: *belah, boobialla, booyong, boree, brigalow, burrawang, cadagi, cooba, coogera, coolah, coolibah, coondoo, cudgerie, eumung, geebung, gidgee, jarrah, karri, kurrajong, mallee, marri, motherumbah, mugga, mulga, nealie, sallee, yapunyah, yarran, yertchuk.*

PLANTS: *bindieye, calombo, cumbungi, cunjevoi, waratah, wonga wonga* (vine).

BIRDS: *brolga, budgerigar, bulla bulla, currawong, galah, kookaburra.*

ANIMALS: *bilby, euro, kangaroo, koala, paddymelon, perentie, wallaby, wallaroo, wombat.*

ETC.: *cobra* (marine worm), *joey* (the young of the kangaroo or other marsupial), *taipan* (snake), *woma* (snake).

Directly linked with several of the words listed earlier are: *cooee bird,* a small bird also called *koel (Eudynamys orientalis); gibber bird,* a bird also known as the *desert chat (Ashbyia lovensis);* and *myall,* a name given to several species of Acacia.

A variety of other sources have made linguistic curtsies in the direction of our Aborigines: a Tasmanian correspondent tells me that *mia mia* is used there to denote a duck shooting blind; in 1962, the annual Boy Scout jamboree was called a *corroboree,* and not long before a Sydney department store was advertising "a *Corroboree* of Bargains"; in 1955, Melbourne began an annual festival called a *Moomba,* allegedly meaning "Let's get together and have fun" or "Let's have fun" or "Let's celebrate"; a little earlier, the Aboriginal names *Monak, Adina* and *Moona* were awarded to three new varieties of potato bred in N.S.W.; and at our weapons establishment at Woomera, South Australia (a *woomera* is a spear-throwing stick), the *Jindivik* pilotless target aircraft, the *Malkara* anti-tank missile and the *Ikara* anti-submarine weapon system were blessed with Aboriginal names.

Since both words provide a good deal of trouble for the uninitiated, it should be pointed out that neither *rosella* nor *Nullarbor* (the Plain) is Aboriginal. As already mentioned, the former is a corruption of Rose Hill (near Sydney); the latter is a portmanteau word for the Latin *nulla* and *arbor,* meaning "no tree".

Let us now look over some of the formal terms developed by whitemen to illuminate various aspects of Aboriginal life.

blackfellow, an Aboriginal, a term in use since 1823 or earlier. I have referred to this before, but a couple of derivatives deserve special attention: *blackfellows' bread,* sclerotia of *Polyporus mylittae,* "stores of reserve material intended to provide against the strain of fructification" – these sclerotia, rounded lumps varying in size from a pin's head to a human head, are often found near decaying stumps or roots of eucalyptus; *blackfellows' buttons*, another name for *Australites* or *emu stones*, which are small smooth lumps of black glass, presumably meteorites, found in Victoria, South Australia and Western Australia. Also called *tektites*, *obsidianites* and *obsidian buttons*.

black tracker, an Aboriginal used by police to track down a criminal or any other person sought in rough outback country. The earliest known reference to the use of Aborigines for this purpose is 1825.

bone, to direct a ceremonial "death curse" at a person. Also, *point* (or *sing* or *spit* or *cry*) *a bone*. From an Aboriginal ceremony, in which a small, sharpened bone is pointed at the victim by ill-wishers and curses are spoken. In "The Little Black Princess" (1905), Mrs Aeneas Gunn uses the related expressions *singing magic, pointing death-bones, bone-pointing, to be sung, death-bone* and *the bone* (a synecdoche for the evil magic supposedly consequent on the pointing of a bone).

bullroarer, a slab of wood (or stone) pierced at one end by a hole through which a string is passed. It is whirled round and round, making a noise supposed by Aboriginal women and children to be the voice of a great spirit. The bullroarer is used especially in initiation ceremonies. However, it is known to primitive tribes in other countries and, almost certainly, was not originally an Australian term. Also called a *roarer*.

cry, to make a pretence of crying at someone's departure. See H. G. Lamond's "Brindle Royalist" (1956): "They 'cried' him" . . . "They're crying you away . . ." Also *to cry a bone*. See *bone*.

cyclons, a name given to 'cylindroconical stones" inscribed by the Aborigines. Term coined about 1942.

dillybag, a bag made of grasses or of fur twisted into cord. From the Aboriginal word *dhilla*, for such a carrying appliance, to which the English word "bag" has been tautologically added.[12]

dreaming, an Aboriginal totemic site; a place which a totemic ancestor inhabits; a totem, e.g. *emu dreaming*. Extended to *dreaming places* in the "Australian", February 15, 1965, p. 8.

dreamtime, the Aboriginal concept of creation, "in the beginning". Extended to the whiteman's early days in Australia (as in the "Australian", December 5, 1964, p. 11: "All that was some other time, the dream time, when a man could walk into a settlement with a swag on his back and start a town.") Extended again in "A Gulf Burial" (1948) by Brian Vrepont: "Here was his long dreamed place, primitively intimate, pregnant of the aboriginal dream-god."

firesticks, sticks used by Aborigines in making fire.

flesh, matrilineal inheritance. "The matrilineal totem, the word for which means *flesh*, symbolized the inheritance of common *flesh* through the line of mothers" ("Australian Encyclopaedia", 1958, vol. 1, p. 17).

letter stick, a piece of wood bearing certain cuts or marks. The *stick* is generally from 3 inches to 1 foot long and mainly serves as the Aboriginal carrier's passport in hostile country, although the formalized symbols

---

[12] Extended in white use to any bag in which goods are carried. Note also the following use (from "Sydney Morning Herald", May 16, 1953, p. 5): "Mrs. Eunice Woolcott Forbes said in the Bankruptcy Court yesterday that her bank account was a 'joint dilly bag' for the transactions of her bankrupt husband . . ."

marked on it are believed to have some "meaning" in an extremely loose sense.

message stick, as for *letter stick*.
point a bone, see *bone*.
property, an Aboriginal's totem.
songsticks, hardwood sticks which are beaten together to keep tune for an Aboriginal corroboree.

And now for a collection of slang words invented by whitemen to refer to the Aborigines, which are more remarkable for what they tell us about white behaviour in faraway places than for any new light they throw on the Aborigines. A large number of them are concentrated on one subject and we don't have to dig deep among them to find the running sore of a white obsession, which has probably done as much as anything to blight white and black relations. But before we plunge into this unsavoury pool, let us pause to look at some statistics. Of an estimated total of about 71,000 Aborigines remaining in Australia today, some 45 per cent are caste-Aborigines. This has come about primarily because of white fanaticism in tampering with *black velvet* (not an original Australian term probably), as Aboriginal girls and women as sexual objects are called.

Combo and *wamba* or *womba* are never heard in the south-eastern States. They are used to denote a whiteman who lives with a native woman. *To go combo* and *comboing* are heard frequently in all northern parts of Australia from Queensland to Western Australia. Hence, such terms as *Normanton cocktail*, "a gin and two blankets", *my bush girlfriend*, gin as a drink (reported from Queensland), *going on a gin spree*, *gin catcher*, a brightly coloured towel or piece of cloth, *gin shepherding* (or *prospecting*), *gin jockey*, *gin burglary*, the stealing of Aboriginal women for sexual purposes.

On the last expression, here is a quotation from the "Australian" (February 5, 1965, p.10): "In Hall's Creek (W.A.) gin burglary is the local hobby. What chance could she have, however advanced, in an area where the station ringers (stockmen) divide girls into three classes – *albinos*, white, *creamies*, half-castes, and *studs*, black – and treat them accordingly?"

These definitions are not quite correct. The *creamie* or *chocolate creamie* is more likely to be a quarter-caste Aboriginal girl than a half-caste. The half-caste is a *halfie* or *yeller-feller*. Moreover, the implication that the *stud* is virtually rejected is wrong. In many parts of the far north, *studs* are eagerly sought by white males. *The Stud Book* is a Northern Territory name for a Register of Wards – a list of some 15,000 Aborigines.

No doubt it was as the result of these sexual activities by whitemen, and its accompanying reaction formation (which spreads contempt over a source of sexual pleasure), that the word *lubra* was banned to Northern Territory welfare officers in 1963.

An old equivalent of *combo* is *myrnonger*, but it seems to be obsolete now. Ernestine Hill lists *the Lochinvar* as an "old-time term for catching lubras to work cattle, etc.," the accent I presume being on the "etc." A European living with Aborigines is called a *white blackfellow*, and *to go black* is to adopt native ways of life.

Having stolen the Aboriginal's lands and seduced his women, the white pioneer has rounded off his unspeakable conduct by pouring scorn on Aborigines in general, in such terms as *abo* (without a capital A, of course), *boong* (from New Guinea), *binghi* (from Thursday Island), *nigger*, *buck nigger*, *nig*, *boy*, *darkey* and *coon* (all mainly from the U.S.), *bing* (short for *binghi*), *black*, *blacky*, *black skin*, *blackboy*, *blackfellow* or *blackfeller*, *murky*, *dark cloud*, *unbleached Australian*, *swatser*, *kipper* and *whistlecock*. *Kipper* is an old expression for a "hobbledehoy black" and *whistlecock* describes an Aboriginal male who has undergone a crude operation to his penis – "subincision of the urethra . . . to increase the amount of mucous membrane which becomes stimulated during coitus". A half-caste boy is called a *piebald pony*.

Such occasional uses as *black brother* (influenced by *binghi*, meaning brother), *coloured people* and the anthropologist's term *old people* are welcome reliefs in a dismal picture. In a small way, it is a consolation to know that the Aborigines have struck back by using the word *wonk* to denote a white with much the same contempt as whites use with *boong*, etc.

Pindan is the Aboriginal name for desert country inland out of Broome, W.A.; thus whitemen call the Kimberley natives *pindan blacks*. A *pedong* (a distortion of the Aboriginal *bidungu*, which is a directional word for north-east) is a desert native in W.A. A *munjong* (from the W.A. goldfields area) is a derogatory expression for any unsophisticated bush-Aboriginal – "He's a proper *munjong*!" *Myall*, applied to a fierce Aboriginal, was originally taken from the eastern States; it came to mean "wild" and gradually spread throughout the country; in "Keep Him My Country", Mary Durack says it is "usually applied disparagingly" in the far north.

A few minor terms have been taken from the Aborigines: *pink-hi*, holiday, "on *pink-hi* in the south"; *tow-ri*, one's own country; *whirlie*, a whirlwind of sand, possibly extracted from *willy willy; nulla nulla sticks*, women's fighting sticks; *boko*, blind, used especially of a wall-eyed horse; *kweeai* or *queeai*, an Aboriginal woman who helps to muster cattle; *never never*, the remote inland, possibly from Aboriginal *nievah vah* (a suggestion first made by F. de B. Cooper in "Wild Adventures in Australia", 1857): *yindi*, the sun; *mendic*, ill; *yakka* or *yacker*, work (first recorded in the Brisbane area, in 1838); *cookan-jerra*, N.T. cattleman's term for a sheepman.

Aboriginal sources are also evident in these expressions: *mission shy*, used of Aborigines who avoid contact with mission stations; *three* (or *six*) *dog night*, a cold night, allegedly referring to an Aboriginal use of dogs at night to keep themselves warm; *get charged up*, to become drunk, also *to charge up*, to drink; *blackfellow's game*, the card game of euchre; *blackfellow's gift*, a gift made in expectation of something in return.

I cannot close this Section on our Aborigines without reference to a native named Yagan (sometimes called *the Wallace of the West*) who led several notable forays against whitemen in the Perth area in the early 1830s. In due course, he was shot and his head was cut off. To quote from the "Australian Encyclopaedia" (1958): "The head was subsequently exhibited in Sydney and London, and a strip of cicatriced skin from Yagan's back, made into a belt, was for some years a curio owned by a doctor in Perth."

This story on its own gives a fair summary of white attitudes towards our Aboriginal people.

4. PIDGIN ENGLISH IN NEW GUINEA

AUSTRALIAN ATTITUDES towards native races were certainly not improved by a trade in *blackbirds* on her east coast between 1847 and 1904.[13] The so-called *blackbirds* were Kanakas from nearby Pacific islands. The first of them (140 from Tanna, New Hebrides) were brought to Australia in 1847 by Ben Boyd to work on Boyd's sheep stations. The next imports were 67 island natives to work on a cotton plantation near Brisbane in 1863. Beginning in 1864, thousands of Kanakas were imported for forced work on Queensland sugar plantations. Most of these were kidnapped and brutally treated; probably thousands were murdered. A person or ship engaged in transporting such slave labour was known as a *blackbirder*. The trade, which involved imports of at least 57,000 Kanakas, was known as *blackbirding*, with extension to *blackbird catching* and *blackbird hunting*. A *blackbird* was also called *Tommy Tanna*.

One of the consequences of this trade was that Australia, which had already had wide experience of pidgin English in relations with her own Aborigines, found a new source of pidgin influence. Here is an opinion on the matter by William Churchill in his "Beach-la-Mar"[14] (1911):

> Of certain elements of low, cant, vulgar English [in Pacific pidgin] the sailors may have been the carriers. But another source is to be included. It was not all of blackbirding to get the kanaka aboard the schooner of the labour trade; his term of hard labour was to be served in the Queensland plantations. Here he had the opportunity to enrich his vocabulary with words which characterise Austral English. It is to this opportunity, which one might scarcely venture upon saying the moiling exile enjoyed, that we must ascribe in the greater measure the inclusion of such terms as *tumble down* and *blackfellow*, of *flash* and *trash*, of *hook it* and *clear out*, of *hump* and *wire in*, of *gammon* and *bloody*.

Earlier trading contacts with the Maoris in New Zealand and with neighbouring Pacific islands, and later contacts with the natives of Papua and New Guinea have made Australia the most pidgin-conscious English-speaking nation on earth.

The influence has by no means been one way. In 1884, Germany

---

[13] The original *blackbirds* were natives kidnapped from the west coast of Africa and sold as slaves in America and the West Indies. Wentworth and Flexner, "Dictionary of American Slang" (1960), list *blackbirder* as "a Negro slave merchant; one who financed or sailed ships operating in the Negro slave trade".

[14] "L'expression 'bichelamar' est consacrée par un usage déjà ancien et si répandu dans les archipels français de la Mélanésie, que nous le conservons," notes M. Leenhardt in his "Vocabulaire et Grammaire de la Langue Houaïlou" (1935).

annexed New Britain and the northern section of New Guinea (Britain already controlled the Papuan section). One of Germany's earliest discoveries was that pidgin English had anticipated them and served not only as a trading language between the natives and visiting ships, but between the multiplicity of native tribes, who spoke mutually unintelligible dialects. Hence, this comment by Baron von Hesse-Wartegg:

> At the present time it is still possible to eradicate pidgin English. However, if another century passes, this will have to be recognised as impossible, due to the growing population which will by then have become utterly used to it, and in another fifty years the German Reich will here possess a protectorate in which the Mission population will speak only English. This would surely be sad and shameful for the world-position and esteem of Germany.

Although Germany controlled large areas of New Guinea, her efforts to weed out pidgin English were almost entirely unsuccessful. The main relics of her struggle are *ananas*, a pineapple (which the natives could well have got from another trading source, anyway), *bund*, often rendered *bung*, a market, meeting or gathering, *mark*, which the natives still use to describe a silver coin, especially a shilling, the spelling *haus*, *puss-puss*, love or fornication (from the German dialectal *Pussi*, a kiss) and *rauss*, to shift, to move, go away – from *heraus*. Such pretences as spelling *braun* for brown, *doktor* for doctor, *nord* for north, *tausend* for thousand and *handert* (it should be *hundert*) for hundred – as used in books printed by the Alexishafen Catholic Mission – are little more than self-deception.

Germany's experiences could well be drawn to the attention of the United Nations and others, who have repeatedly called for an end to the "debasing" influences of pidgin. Australia's official view is also that pidgin should be replaced at the earliest possible date by orthodox English, but she finds herself in an unenviable squeeze. In the first place, the only *lingua franca* between most of the 300 tribes (covering about 1,500,000 natives in an area of some 180,000 square miles) is pidgin. Second, it is the only common tongue available for the teaching of orthodox English. It is therefore self-perpetuating.

The postwar use of pidgin in radio broadcasts, in the publication of several news sheets, in contacts between Patrol Officers and natives, in mission activities, have widened its area of stabilised application. When the House of Assembly was established in 1964, pidgin was given the status of one of three languages used officially in proceedings (the others are English and Motu). Practice has shown that it is the most used of the languages.

In short, we are now faced with the likelihood that pidgin will become *the* language of New Guinea, and that although the official aim is to make the natives literate in orthodox English only a few of them will be other than bilingual (trilingual, if we count their native dialects).

Where many commentators err is in thinking of pidgin as static baby-talk, practically immune to growth. This is quite wrong. At the turn of the century, even a generation ago, its rate of growth was slow, and the general vocabulary was limited to about 700 words. But the influences of trade and competition for souls among missions forced its expansion. By 1942, when the Japanese brought war to New Guinea and its associated islands, the vocabulary was probably more than 1,300 words. Among these were some extraordinary items (I quote from "The Book of Pidgin English" by John J. Murphy, 1943), *akanggelo*, archangel, *ekistrimunksoo*, the last Sacrament, *imperno*, hell, *komunio*, Holy Communion, *vinivel*, Lent, etc., which had obviously come from the missions; *ensini*, an engineer or mechanic, *giris kaskas*, sulphur ointment, ointment for the treatment of sores, *hausdiring*, a hotel, *lam bensin*, a primus lamp, *masta kot*, a lawyer, *motaka*, a car, *wanwing*, monoplane, etc., which were consequences of the entry into native life of new concepts. In the past twenty-odd years, many new factors have invaded native life and pidgin has grown accordingly. It will continue to do so. As a result, a generation hence pidgin will have a vocabulary of at least 2,000 – 3,000 words, and because of its great flexibility these words will give access to the meanings of 5,000 – 10,000 orthodox English words. This is the level of the average English-speaker's vocabulary.

From a statistical viewpoint it can be noted that the greatest weight of usage is imposed on the first 2,000 most-used words; another 2,000 or so are called on extensively; thereafter, other words are used with decreasing frequency. It is estimated that a few English speakers may have vocabularies of 25,000 words or more, but most of these words are used only rarely and are mainly "recognition" words, i.e. they are recognised and understood when they occur in print.

It is often thought that pidgin is so simple in construction that we can learn nothing from it. This again is wrong. Let us spare a moment to consider what can be done with the word *tumara*, tomorrow. We use four words to say "the day after tomorrow"; pidgin uses one, *haptumara*. We use five words to say "the second day after tomorrow"; pidgin uses two, *haptumara moa*. We use five words to say "the third day after tomorrow"; pidgin uses three, *haptumara moa yet*. We use five words to say "a thing of no consequence"; pidgin uses two, *samting nating*. A tin opener is *optin;* a Roman Catholic is *popi*.

In brief, pidgin is both complex and precise. The sooner the rest of the world gets used to the idea that it is here to stay, that it is not a pseudo-language of bondage, but a language which grew out of bondage into freedom, and that it puts its users not only in contact with each other but in contact with the outside world, the better. Beyond these considerations is the simple fact that its native users want it and there is not the slightest hope (in spite of U.N. wishes and edicts of the Australian Administration) that they will surrender it.

I have no doubt that in due course, the pidgin or beach-la-mar of New Guinea will be accepted as one of the world's languages.

Since Australia has had a good deal to do with the content and shape of that language, it is worth closer attention.

As William Churchill has pointed out, numerous terms current in

Australian speech – although not necessarily originally Australian – made their way from this country into beach-la-mar. *To sool, plant, spell, go bush, bush kanaka, bugger up, capstan* (as a generic name for tobacco), *cranky, goddam, backside, walkabout, dead finish* – these are some of the many words in Pacific pidgin that owe their currency largely to Australian influence. A sound reason for this is given by Churchill:

> The sailors who made up the crews of these legalised slavers [black-birders] were recruited from the slums of the seaports of Australia, particularly the havens of Queensland from Moreton Bay to Cooktown. [The jargon spoken by these men] is not a difficult tongue to acquire [by the Kanaka]: three years in the barracks of a plantation were the equivalent of a university course.

We can assess a little of the vulgar English taint in pidgin – and know that it will err where possible on the side of conservatism – when we examine such a publication as the "Word Buk" issued by the Roman Catholic Mission at Alexishafen before World War II. Here are some of the expressions listed in the mission vocabulary: *bagarap*, to be useless, out of order, broken, from *bugger up* – e.g. *leg belong me i bagarap*, I've hurt my leg; *baksaid*, the rear of, back, behind; *bel*, stomach, used to denote pregnancy – e.g. *Meri i got bel; kam*, the female genital; *pispis*, the act of urination. These expressions may be objectionable to the linguistically squeamish, but pidgin has done something to them which it is almost impossible for the English to do; it has fumigated them and rid them of the taint of prurient, furtive minds.

Evidence of the important linguistic status that pidgin has now attained can be seen in the development of such formalised sayings as:

(a) *Iu noken shutem nos belong mi* (You no can shoot him nose belong me), meaning "Don't try to lead me by the nose".

(b) *Em I stap along nek* (Him he stop along neck), meaning "This is something for your ears only, keep it to yourself".

(c) *Suppose man tok alataim, em i man along gaimin* (Suppose a man talks all the time, he is a man of lies), meaning "A man who talks a lot is usually a liar".

The last example was recorded among the Mawa people near the Waria river, and is really in the nature of a proverb. It is scarcely necessary to point out that proverbs do not emerge in language until it has gained a great consistency of use.

However, at this stage another factor enters the picture and I regard this as entirely objectionable. For the best part of a century, New Guinea pidgin was almost exclusively an oral language. No effort was made to reduce it to printed form. Then, in the course of competing for souls, sundry missions conceived the idea of printing religious propaganda for distribution among natives, and used printed primers in mission schools to educate natives to the level of reading the propaganda. Without making the slightest effort to standardize their orthography, missions pursued independent courses. The results are best illustrated by some examples. Here is the Lord's Prayer as rendered by the Alexishafen Catholic Mission,[15] the Vunapope Catholic Mission[16] and the Rabaul Methodist Mission:[17]

Alexishafen. Fader bilong mifelo, yu stop long heven – Ol i santuim nem bilong yu – Kingdom bilong yu i kam – Ol i hirim tok bilong yu long graund olsem long heven. Tude givim mifelo kaikai bilong de – Forgivim rong bilong mifelo – olsem mifelo forgivim rong – ol i mekim long mifelo. Yu no bringim mifelo long traiim – tekewe samting no gud long mifelo. Amen.

Vunapope. Papa bolong mipela i stap antap – naim bolong ju i tambu – lotu bolong ju i kam – mipela daun olosem ol antap i harim tok bolong ju-ju bringim kaikai tede bolong mipela – ju larim mipela i olosem mipela i larim ol, ol i mekim nogut mipela – ju no bringim mipela klostu long rot i nogut – ju lusim ol samting nogut i raus long mipela. Amen.

Rabaul. Papa bilog mi fela, iu stop an top alog peles bilog iu, i qud mi fela sigsig out tru alog nem bilog iu; i moa beta ol a fasin bilog iu i stop oltuqeta peles. I qud mi fela mekim tru ol a lo bilog iu, ol a sem oltuqeta man i savi mekim alog peles bilog iu. I qud iu givim mi fela kaikai inafim mi fela alog tude. I qud iu no mekim koros alog mi fela alog ol a fasin no qud mi fela mekim, ol a sem mi fela no qat koros alog ol a man i savi korosim mi fela. Iu no bringim mi fela alog ol a samtig no qud; i moa beta iu luk outim mi fela so mi fela no ken mekim ol a fasin no qud. Bikos ol a lo, na oltuqeta strog, na oltuqeta samtig i qud i bilog iu, na i no ken finis. Amen.

The Ten Commandments in three conflicting versions:

Alexishafen
1. Mi Master, God bilong yu,yu no ken mekim masalai end ol tambaran.
2. Yu no ken kolim nating nem bilong God.
3. Yu mast santuim sande.
4. Yu mast mekim gud long papamama bilong yu.
5. Yu no ken kilim man.
6. Yu no ken brukim fashin bilong marit.
7. Yu no ken stilim samting.
8. Yu no ken lai.
9. Yu no ken duim meri bilong enaderfelo man.
10. Yu no ken laik stilim samting.

Vunapope
1. Ju lotu long Deo vampela tasol.
2. Ju no kolim nating naim bolong Deo Masta bolong ju.
3. Long sande ju lotu na ju tambu long vok.
4. Ju hamamas long papa na mama bolong ju.
5. Ju no mekim dai vanpela man.
6. Ju no pilai nogut.
7. Ju no sitil.
8. Ju no gijaman.
9. Ju no laikim meri bolong narapela man.
10. Ju no laikim ologeta samting bolong narapela man.

---

[15] "Buk bilong beten end singsing bilong ol katolik" (1937).
[16] "Buk-Raring na singsing" (1934).
[17] "A Pidgin Him Buk" (1941).

Rabaul

1. Mi leova Qod bilog iu, iu no hirm nada fela Qod, bikos mi dasol i Qod.
2. (An unintelligible jumble of 87 words.)
3. Iu no kolim natig nem bilog leova Qod bilog iu, bikos leova i no laikim wan fela sapos i kolim natig nem bilog im.
4. (117 words.)
5. Iu marimari alog papa bilog iu na mam a bilog iu, ol sem iu kan kesim log fela laif alog peles leova Qod bilog iu i givim iu.
6. Iu no kan kilim wan fela.
7. Iu no kan mekim trobel alog meri.
8. Iu no kan stil.
9. Iu no kan qaman alog wan fela.
10. (44 words.)

It will be obvious from above quotations that the Rabaul mission's efforts are notable mainly for their prolixity and ridiculous phonetic system.

In essence, this meant that pidgin was broken up into dialects in several areas *before* it had become a language. This was by no means all, however.

Early in 1943 a handbook of words and phrases in pidgin was issued by the Army to men on active service in South-west Pacific Islands. Here are two examples:

You-fella you stand fast. You no can walkabout. Suppose you-fella you walkabout me killim you long musket – Don't move or I'll shoot.

You-fella you lookim barid all Japan i sit down long im long fight? – Is there barbed wire in front of the Jap trenches?

Here is a leaflet written in pidgin and dropped by Allied planes to friendly natives in New Guinea during World War II:

OL LULUAI, TULTUL NA MAN BILOG GUVMAN
Yumi sitron nau

Ol dei ol dei balus bilog yumi raunim olgeda Nugini bilog bom im sip, sutim lanis bakarap im somtig bilog Japan.

Yu mas lukaut im masta bilog balus sipos ol i kam daon long bus na nabis bilog yu.

Hait im gut, gifim gut pela kaikai, gut pela haus wok im bet, sipos lek bilog ol i nogut.

Birig im long Kiap, sipos onpela i stap klostu. Olgeda i got Pas bilog Guvman. Yumus halip im ol.

GUVMAN I TOK

Here is a translation:

TO ALL VILLAGE HEADMEN AND GOVERNMENT BOYS
We are strong now

Every day our [Allied] planes fly all around New Guinea, bombing ships, shooting up launches and damaging other things belonging to the Japanese.

You must keep a lookout for any [Allied] airman if he comes down in the bush or on beaches near where you live.

Hide him well, give him good food, and make him a comfortable bed if he cannot walk.

Take him to the District Officer if there is one near. All our airmen have Government passes. You must help them.

GOVERNMENT ORDER

A comparison between these samples of printed pidgin and the efforts of the missions shows that here are more pidgin dialects – semi-phonetic monstrosities which must make New Guinea natives shake their heads in despair at the inconsistencies of whitemen.

At the end of World War II, various news sheets in pidgin were published in the New Guinea area – the "Rabaul News" at Rabaul, the "Lae Garamut" at Lae (a *garamut* is a large drum made from a hollowed-out tree trunk used for conveying "bush" messages), the "Wewak News" at Wewak, the "Lagasai" at Kavieng and the "Buka News" at Buka. The oldest of these pidgin newspapers was apparently the "Rabaul News", which was set up just after the war. The responsibility of collecting most of the news and coping with publication was later taken over by Mr Waiau Ahnon, who tried an informative experiment. The results gave a good indication of what linguistic theoreticians will encounter when, and if, efforts are later made to replace pidgin with orthodox English. He tried putting more orthodox English words into his newspaper to replace cumbersome pidgin expressions. The result was that the natives were seriously confused, and the experiment had to be abandoned.

If the quotations I have given are examined carefully, it will be seene that there is little consistency in their spelling. I, therefore, have two suggestions to make:

(1) That the pidgin or beach-la-mar of New Guinea should be officially accepted as the language of the area.

(2) That some official organisation should be established forthwith to standardize both the spelling and pronunciation of that language, with powers to ensure that its decisions are observed.[18]

5. SECRET LANGUAGES IN NEW GUINEA

THE REPORTED DEVELOPMENT of a number of secret languages in New Guinea is probably of more interest to philologians than to the general

---

[18] Among minor matters, this organisation could be charged with defending us against such a fatuous neologism as *indigene*, pronounced "indigeny", as an imagined parallel to *aborigine*, pronounced "aboriginy", and meaning "native". In the first place, an Australian native is an *Aboriginal* (with *Aborigines* as the plural). Second, the French word *indigène* means "native" and is so used in New Caledonia; the final "e" is not pronounced. This linguistic perversion presumably arose in response to a demand in March, 1956, by the Australian Minister for Territories for elimination of the word "native" in official correspondence as likely to cause offence. At that stage, the native people of Papua were called *Papuans* and the natives of other parts of New Guinea were becoming known as *New Guineans* or *Newguineans*. Some general term was sought. Certainly, *indigene* pronounced *indigeny* isn't it! Since the above was written, the use of *indigenous adults*, *indigenous children*, *indigenous males*, etc., has been reported from Papua.

reader. These so-called secret languages are of two types – those which operate through the medium of the native tongue and those developed with the spread of pidgin English. Since we have been looking into pidgin in the previous Section, it may be worth pursuing the theme further here, if only to give additional evidence that pidgin has acquired most of the aspects of a formalised language.

The examples to be quoted are taken from extensive material compiled by Fr. Albert Aufinger, S.V.D., and published in "South Pacific", journal of the Australian School of Pacific Administration.[19] His pidgin examples fall into two main groups – a form which closely parallels what is called "back slang" in English, and a variety of high-flown allegory combining most of the features of euphemism and euphuism.

Back slang, which is closely related to gibberish and such-like secret jargons, has had a long history in English. "The Detectives' Handbook", an Australian publication of some eighty-five years ago, lists a selection of terms that presumably had at least a fleeting currency among the criminal classes in Australia towards the end of last century. Examples include: *dab*, bad; *delo nammow*, old woman; *delog*, gold; *eno*, one; *kool*, to look; *ogging ot tokram*, going to market; *occabot*, tobacco.

There is little originality in this. Such slang provides a communicatory medium for initiated persons which will be unintelligible to others. It is a not uncommon ruse whereby a speaker seeks to exploit a sense of power over his fellows and to reduce the authority of seniors.

It is, therefore, well within the order of linguistic expectations that New Guinea natives should be reported as using the following: "*Alapui kow, atsam i mak!*" This is a back version – or what is known as "tok-bek bilong pidgin" – of the words "*Iupala wok, masta i kam!*" which can be rendered more understandable in the form "Youfellow work, master he come!" and which is intended to serve as a warning signal at the approach of "the master".

Another example of the same thing: "*Asit i kotkot aromut tagon lukus*". This is a back version of the words "*Tisa i toktok tumora nogat sukul*", meaning "Teacher he talk (say), tomorrow no got school" or, more explicitly, "The teacher says there will be no class tomorrow".

Aufinger remarks:

> Without practice it is not easy to follow a conversation in Pidgin if same is fluently spoken backwards. It is far more difficult to understand natives when they are speaking their vernacular in reverse, which is as often used for that purpose as is Pidgin. The fact that natives do not only speak but also write their mother tongue backwards is shown by the following fragment of a letter which a boy from Manam Island was sending to his friend. It reads as follows: "*Ugangaur aub idula asam aniog ab anikang*,

---

[19] Published originally, and in somewhat shorter form, in "Anthropos", vol. xxviii-xl, 1942-5. Aufinger's observations were made on several small islands near Madang, and at Astrolabe Bay and on the Rai Coast. He reports that "Dr. Georg Hoeltker was able to establish, as a result of his 1936-39 New Guinea Expedition, the existence of secret languages among a number of communities between Madang and the mouth of the Sepik".

aelak ol aneang." Reading each word backwards we find: "*Ruagnagu* (my friend) *bua* (betelnut) *aludi* (some) *masa* (by and by) *goina ba ngakina* (send to me) *kalea ngaena lo* (during this month)" – "My friend, send me some betelnut some time this month".

Aufinger expresses the view that the practice of speaking pidgin or native words backwards developed only as a result of contact between natives and Europeans, and followed the introduction of writing to natives. In short, he believes until the natives learned how to write they did not realise that words could be reversed. The evolutionary steps involved in this view would be: (a) incorporation of pidgin words into native speech; (b) experience of writing these words; (c) discovery that a word can be written backwards; (d) verbalisation of the word that has been written backwards. Aufinger's comment that this is "one of the unintended results of education" perhaps tends to overlook what seems to me a much more interesting point – the fact that pidgin has become such a well-established language that it has independently developed attributes found in many other well-established languages.

The allegorical use of pidgin as a means of conveying secret messages is apparently common in some parts of New Guinea. Aufinger lists many examples. He says:

> One of the most amazing specimens of "picturesque speech" in Pidgin was the report or narrative of a hard fight between three natives, which cost one of them a lot of blood. The whole conversation was to all appearance nothing but an instruction about the best way of chewing betelnut, and it ran somewhat similar to this: *Mi stop long bush, nau mi laik kaikai bilinut. Mi lukautim wanfelo, mi faindim, mi faitim, faitim, faitim, mi kaikaim tasol i no swit long mi, na spet bilong mi i no red. Mi lukautim kambang wantaim daka. Mi kaikai wantaim bilinut, nau bilinut i swit long mi, na spet i red elgeder, i kamdaun plenti tumas.*" In English translation: "While I was in the bush, I wanted to chew a betelnut. I searched for one and found it. I kept beating it [in the betel-mortar], finally I started to chew it, but it was not sweet to my taste and my saliva did not turn red. I then searched for lime and betel-pepper. When I chewed all these together it became very sweet to me and red saliva was flowing down abundantly."

In contrast with the peaceful appearance of this story the actual meaning was:

> I wanted to have a fight with a certain man in the bush. I found him there and we had a long fight between the two of us, but it was not to my satisfaction. So I called for two of my friends and when they joined in the brawl my enemy was beaten to my satisfaction and he lost a lot of blood.

Unless we know that the red saliva produced by the chewing of betelnut, lime and betel-pepper is a prevalent metaphor for blood, few of us would detect the underlying figurative sense of the story.

An example of this kind – others could be offered without difficulty – reinforces our suspicion that pidgin has acquired some highly-sophisticated characteristics.

Secret, at least to the extent that the whiteman has great difficulty in understanding them and their origin has been inadequately explored, are a large number of *cargo cults*, which have been reported in Micronesian and Melanesian areas since the end of World War I. These cults have many forms and names, but they tend to fall into a set pattern. The natives of various parts of West New Guinea (now Irian), East New Guinea (including Papua), the Solomons and the New Hebrides, have a fairly constant legend that whitemen who came to their country or islands are really their ancestors in disguise. The natives cease all work when they hear that whitemen are coming and prepare feasts of welcome. They build platforms and load them with gifts of food. At a certain time each day they sit in ceremonial dress at tables decorated in European style, with flowers in bottles. The leaders order their followers to abandon traditional native ritual and to destroy all objects associated with it. This mode of conduct was originally called *Vailala madness*, because it was apparently first recorded on the Vailala River in Papua in 1919. A form of it occurred later in the Solomons and was known as *Marching* (or *Masinga*) *Rule*, which some people believe to be associated with the word "Marxian". It had a recrudescence in New Guinea after World War II and came to be known among the natives as *Cargo*. Behind these cults was the belief that whitemen would bring the natives large supplies of European goods and that, although these goods were native property, they were being withheld from them by the whites. According to native propaganda, the whites will soon be driven out and the cargo will be entirely at the disposal of the natives. The *John Frum* or *jonfroom* movement of Tanna, in the New Hebrides, the *Prophet* (Milne Bay), the *German Wislin* (on Saibai, Torres Strait), *Naked Cult* (Espiritu Santu), *Johnson Cult* (Kavieng), *Golden Egg Cult* (Galum, New Britain), *Dog Movement*, *Kekesi Movement*, *Samson Movement* and *Wireless House Movement* are a few of the others.

6. NEW CALEDONIA

AUSTRALIAN INFLUENCE on New Caledonian speech has been surprisingly wide. This French colony, 700 miles east of Queensland, provides an interesting example of how Australianisms have gone out into the world on their own account. Although France took formal possession of the island in 1853 and has been exploiting its mineral wealth ever since, Australians know little about this near-neighbour.

Australian lingual influence on the island is perceivable for about a century, originally in the introduction of pidgin English or beach-la-mar and later in the incorporation of numerous Australianisms into French contexts. One fact the early French colonists of the island found hard to stomach was that the natives showed a deep-rooted objection to talking or learning French – much as New Guinea natives resisted the abandonment of pidgin English when the area was controlled by Germany.

Here is a comment by Jules Patouillet, from his "Trois ans en Nouvelle-Calédonie" (Paris, 1872), which speaks for itself:

> Aussi la plupart des colons préfèrent ils, dans leurs rapports personnels avec les noirs, employer un jargon compris dans presque toute l'étendue de la côte; c'est une imitation du sabir africain, mélange d'anglais, de français et de canaque, qui s'appelle le biche-la-mare.

Charles Lemire, author of "La Colonisation française de Nouvelle-Calédonie" (1878), puts the facts fairly clearly:

> Les Anglais ont été les premiers qui aient fait le commerce avec les indigènes sur la côte de la Calédonie et aux Loyalty, et sont restés colons ou négociants dans le pays. Les Canaques engagés comme travailleurs viennent de l'archipel des Nouvelles-Hebrides, . . . où l'on parle anglais. Mais cet anglais, comme le pigeon-english de l'Inde est tout-à-fait fantaisiste. On l'appelle ici le bichelamar, c'est-à-dire la langue du commerce de la biche de mer.[20]

So it is that we find the natives themselves helping to spread pidgin English into a French colony, producing an inevitable mixture of influences that is by no means easy to sort out.

The position in New Caledonia has been complicated by the fact that the country's tribal languages are, as in New Guinea, more or less mutually unintelligible. Julien Berner wrote in 1898:

> On compte en general une vingtaine de dialects employés par les indigènes de la Nouvelle-Calédonie . . . Les premiers Européens établis dans le pays ont été frappés de cette confusion qui resemble un peu à celle de la Tour de Babel.

And Lemire wrote in 1878:

> Quant à la langue canaque, elle diffère entre chaque tribu, au point que les indigènes ne se comprennent pas toujours entre eux.

In the midst of such confusion, pidgin English apparently served as a lingua franca, not only assisting Europeans to trade with the natives, but helping communication between the tribes.

Here is what Mme H. Thiercelin writes in her "Aventures d'une Parisienne à la Nouvelle-Calédonie" (Paris, 1872):

> C'est triste, et pourtant c'est bien vrai – non seulement ici (en Néo-Calédonie), mais à Taïti, aux Pomotu, aux Marquises, partout enfin où flotte notre pavillon – les indigènes ne parlent que leur langue maternelle et un patois anglais . . .
>
> Ils ne savent du français qu'un mot qu'ils répètent, quand ils veulent nous designer. Pour eux, nous sommes des *oui oui*, et tout ce qui nous appartient s'appelle comme nous *oui oui*. Cette expression ridicule témoigne de nos moyens d'action sur les peuples auxquels nous nous imposons, et du soin que nous prenons de nous les assimiler.

---

[20] Among peculiarly New Caledonian terms listed by Lemire are: *farawa*, bread (from flour); *fao*, wire (from *fer*); *popinée*, woman; *pull-away*, to go, depart; *schindo*, to speak; *tomaok*, tomahawk; *louki*, to see (from *look*).

Wiwi (or *oui oui*), designating a Frenchman, was current in New Zealand at the beginning of last century. It is still to be heard among the natives of New Caledonia and neighbouring French islands in the form of *manawiwi* (perhaps it would be better recognized if written *man-of-oui oui*), a somewhat strange conjunction of English and French that occurs also in *menzoreille*, as a Frenchman from France is called in New Caledonia. There are several theories concerning the origin of *menzoreille* (*men-z-oreille*), the most logical of which is that in the big Kanaka revolt of 1878 French soldiers collected rewards for each native head they brought in. Because complete heads were cumbersome, they lopped off the ears (*les oreilles*) and collected their rewards on presentation of these trophies.

The regret of Mme Thiercelin that the native seemed to know more English than French is reflected by Lemire:

> On est tout étonné en débarquant à Nouméa, colonie française, d'entendre parler plutôt anglais que français. Dans les stations agricoles, une barrière s'appelle *fence*, un enclos *paddock*, un garçon de ferme *stockman*, etc.

The use of these and many kindred terms, such as *muster, mob, bucker,* a buckjumping horse, *cowboy* (pronounced coo-boy), and *shop*, a restaurant or milk bar, prevails in New Caledonia today, to such an extent that it would be as impossible to root them out of the *Niaouli's*[21] everyday language as it would be to rob an Australian of many of them.

In "Chez les Canaques de la Nouvelle-Calédonie" (1898), A. Vermast makes liberal use of terms such as *stockmen, store, station, run* and *paddoc (sic)*, remarking of the last two terms, "nous avons emprunté ces deux mots à l'Australie".

In a more modern book, "Dans la Brousse calédonienne" (Paris, 1928), M. le Goupils treats us to "les cris des *stockmans*, les claquements des longs *stockwhips* . . ." Elsewhere in the book he refers to "nos bœufs de travail qu'on amène au *stockyard*", to "une jolie mare ombragée de notre *creek*", and to "les *runs* des *stations* d'élevage calédoniennes" – all of which emphasize an unexpectedly strong Australian influence on New Caledonian speech. This influence should not, of course, be exaggerated, especially today when, theoretically at least, every Kanaka child on the island receives some education in French.

M. le Goupils also gives us the mixed expression, "*Sale blackfellow!*" (dirty blackfellow), which again reveals the Australian influence.

One of the earliest New Caledonian borrowings of Australian idiom was the use of *la brousse* for the country in general outside the capital, Noumea. Our bushmen are the New Caledonian *broussards*. Our expression *to go bush* has its counterpart in Niaouli pidgin, *aller la brousse*.

---

[21] *Niaouli* is the name of a tree (*Melaleuca vividiflora*) that grows as profusely throughout the islands as the gumtree grows in Australia, and has come to be regarded as a national symbol, in the same way as Australians chose the wattle and New Zealanders a fern leaf as national symbols. The New Caledonians call their country *le pays des niaoulis*.

7. NORFOLK ISLAND PATOIS

VALUABLE RESEARCH on the development of the Norfolk Island dialect
(it is really a form of pidgin or beach-la-mar) was done some years ago
by A.R.L. Wiltshire, of Melbourne. This dialect originated when the
"Bounty" mutineers took a number of natives from Tahiti to Pitcairn – a
lingua franca of native and English speech which gradually developed
into a well-defined dialectal form. Dr. H. L. Shapiro, Associate Curator of
the American Museum of Natural History, says:

> Pitcairn dialect today consists of mispronounced English and Tahitian
> words, with a spattering of coined words, the whole employed in a degen-
> erate English syntax.

Pitcairnese is well established on Norfolk Island where, in 1936, there
were about 600 descendants of the original "Bounty" mutineers and their
native wives. Also on Norfolk Island are several hundred Mainlanders,
settlers and visitors from Australia and New Zealand. A census in 1961
showed that Norfolk Island then had 844 permanent residents.
Wiltshire declares:[22]

> The Norfolk *Islanders* all speak good ordinary English in an easy
> deliberate tone, but among themselves use a jargon they call *Norfolk*,
> which to an outsider is unintelligible. Some of the words have a Tahitian
> origin and some others are distorted English.

The reason for the transfer of the Pitcairn dialect was that, because of
overcrowding on Pitcairn, in 1856 all the inhabitants were shifted to
Norfolk Island. Some, becoming homesick, returned to Pitcairn in 1858 or
soon after, since when the two communities have been almost entirely
independent.

Authorities state that the dialects of these two communities remain
practically identical, but there are certain differences that are bound to
increase in course of time, especially on Norfolk Island which is in closer
contact with the mainland than Pitcairn.

The following list of *Norfolk* words was compiled by H. Holland, of
Portland, New South Wales, during a three years' stay on the island,[23]
(a few words from other sources are added in brackets):

> *an'near*, that's true; I think so.
> (*boney-boney*, thin.)
> *boo-oo* (*boo-who*), lump.
> *bout-yer-gwan?* where are you going?
> (*buss up*, broken up.)
> (*car fetch*, can't be done.)

---

[22] In a paper on "The Local Dialects of Norfolk and Pitcairn Islands", published in the
"Journal of the Royal Australian Historical Society", vol. xxv, part iv, p. 331.
[23] Published in "The A.B.C. Weekly", Sydney, June 22, 1946, p. 22.

car-mosser-do, cannot do; will not do at all.

car-what's-it, I don't know what it is.

cut-a-throat, sooner have my throat cut (contempt).

car-wah, I don't know.

dar-da-way (or *weay*), that's right.

daffy, like that (when shown the way to do a thing).

dat-way, that way; this way.

done, stop it.

donner-wah-wh-har, don't put on airs.

eat'it, said to a person staring at you.

e'we, small, undersized.

eat' a home' nan' we, said to a number of staring people.

e' yaller, trying to be older than you are.

eyes' a' stig, you like him (or her).

fus, first.

fut? what?

futto, I feel exhausted or faint.

(*gimie*, give me.)

gurret, angry; very angry.

gurrey, lather, sweat.

ho-yah, said when something surprising happens.

huppa, bad, inefficient.

he-way, throw away.

hooey-hooey, food you would not eat (dirty, mucky).

heppy, can't be bothered, unwilling.

ille' ille', rough sea.

inkerdus, not me; not likely; no.

ise-a-balful, I have had enough to eat.

ise-a-snell, I have not had enough to eat.

ise-a-hilly, I don't feel inclined to work; tired, lazy.

ise-a-sly, I will not do what you ask; certainly not.

kar-bout, I don't know where.

lar-put, overdressed.

(*lebby*, let it be.)

lou-fee, out of sorts, unwell.

libby, leave it alone, let it be.

mahone, pretending sickness (looking for sympathy).

maiolo, to break.

(*mekase*, hurry, make haste.)

mittie-mittie, cuddle.

mono-mono, very good, sweet.

morga, thin person.

naysey, bad-tempered person; cross.

naysey-fo-hut, jealous.

nar-we, swim or bath.

ponto, rubbish; person of no account.

poffa, break off.

pay-hoo, old before time; as for *e' yaller*.

rumma, torch fishing; catching crabs at night.

semithway, peculiar.

(*shep*, ship.)

supa-fay, all broken up.
stay-wal-out, keep quiet; stay where you are.
sorlen, finished; no more left.
stolly, a lie.
sullen, people (English).
ty-ty, not liked; without charm.
tar-phlee, tie together.
uckland, people (island).
umma-oola, untidy in dress.
(*ways?* where is it?)
what-away-you? how are you?
yourl-yer, used when speaking to a number of people.
youse-a-stiddy, you are a deep (secretive) one.

Since about half the population of Norfolk Island is represented by settlers and visitors from Australia and New Zealand, many common Australianisms are used or understood on the island. A point to be noted is that these Australianisms have made almost no impression on the Norfolk dialect.

CHAPTER XVI

Local Jargon

1. PROVINCIALISMS

THE DEVELOPMENT of localized expressions within the wider framework of a dialect involves two main forms of stratification – horizontal and vertical. In Chapter X, Section 3, some attention was paid to horizontal stratification in an examination of craft jargon. Here, we will look into the vertical stratification encountered in localized slang, and this will be seen to have many forms. It varies from terms which apply to large areas, such as *the north-west season*, an official name for the rainy season or *Wet* in the entire north of Australia, to *scurb*, which is a pejorative used by about a hundred people at Rocky Gully, W.A., *The Nut*, for Circular Head at Stanley, Tasmania, and that engaging but somewhat impolite cry of Melbourne University engineering students at football matches, *Argus-Tuft-Argus-Tuft!* Indeed, there is probably no place or group of people in Australia without some small stake in language, whether it i no more than the name of a local festival (such as the *Boab Festival* of Derby, northern W.A., and the *Jacaranda Festival* of Grafton, N.S.W.) or Albury's once-famed *Pyjama Girl*, or Mt. Isa's *medley* (the end, the finish), or Kalgoorlie's *Golden Mile*, Sydney's *Dirty Half-Mile* and *Hungry Mile*, and Perth's *Mad Mile*.

The essential point about most of these expressions is that they are used to denote special things, which have been recorded in the first place only in special communities. Later, because of publicising agents they may have achieved much wider use.

But there are many things that are more or less common possessions throughout Australia. We have looked at some of these earlier in this book; for example, Melbourne calls its smallest beer measure (4 oz.) a *pixie*; Brisbane (5 oz.) a *five*, Sydney (5 oz.) a *pony*, Perth (5 oz.) a *glass*, Adelaide (5 oz.) a *butcher*. Even big eggs have special names in the various States: Extra Large in Victoria, Large in Queensland and South Australia, Grade IA in Western Australia, 2 oz. in Tasmania, 24 oz. in N.S.W. (i.e. for a dozen). Many such geographical distinctions could be listed. For example, in New Guinea and Papua an ear complaint suffered by swimmers is known as *coral ear;* in towns along north Queensland's coast the complaint, or something similar to it, is called *mangrove ear;* to swimmers in the Domain baths, Sydney, it is known as *Woolloomooloo ear* or *Loo ear;* round about Darwin it is called *tropical ear;* and a step or two across the northern seas it is called *Singapore ear*. A type of gastric complaint common in the early 1950s was given the name *Canberra wog* in the Federal Capital, but almost certainly had other names elsewhere. *Pucka throat*, a severe form of throat infection suffered in World War II by soldiers at Puckapunyal Camp, Victoria, is a comparable example. On the other hand, at almost every tourist stopping place in Australia you will hear tourists called *grasshoppers* or *locusts* – "they eat everything in sight".

Since far more space than is available here could be spent in examining such variations, I will content myself with some representative samples from each State:

NEW SOUTH WALES

after darks, term used by Sydney sailing men for paddles (not oars); it was usually after dark when a boat was paddled home because of lack of wind.

Auburn Street farmers, nickname used by Goulburn farmers for residents of that town's financial street (in Sydney, a businessman with minor farming interests is called a *Pitt Street farmer*).

Badge Show Day, a day at Broken Hill on which financial membership of unions is checked.

brown bomber, a parking policeman. (This originated in Sydney in 1946 and has been borrowed by other cities.)

bucket, an ice-cream carton.

Café de Fairfax, an obsolete but remembered name given to a pie and coffee stall which stood nightly outside the "Sydney Morning Herald" office in O'Connell Street. The Fairfax family owns the "Herald", which has now moved to another part of the city.

Callan Park cheroot, a "cigarette" about 12 inches long and 1 inch in diameter made of Government-issue tobacco wrapped in newspaper. Callan Park is a psychiatric hospital.

Carillon City, Bathurst.

Club, the or *Sydney's Open Air Club*, a company of men who met nightly on the footpath opposite Kings Cross Theatre, Sydney. There was no membership fee and no elected officers.

cove streeter, a gust of north-east wind encountered off Cove Street ferry wharf, Balmain, by racing skiffs of the Birchgrove Sailing Club.

Cross, the, Kings Cross, formerly (1897-1905) called Queen's Cross.

dahlia and *tulip*, Albury measures of beer.

Dom, the, the Sydney Domain.

Douche-can Alley, a nickname formerly attached to Kings Cross Road.

Gap, go over the, to commit suicide.

George Gerrard, a lie (reported from Tamworth).

Hills, the, Surry Hills (note that the spelling is different from Melbourne's Surrey Hills and that *The Hill* is Broken Hill).

Hungry Mile, the, a name given to Sussex Street, Sydney, in depression days and still surviving.

Hyde Park bushman, a person who knows little or nothing about the bush or outback.

jacka, Grafton Beer. Also called *jac(k)aranda juice*.

Lane Cove varnish, a mixture of coal tar and kerosene used as a preservative on the bottoms of old boats on the Parramatta and Lane Cove rivers.

Loo, the, Woolloomooloo. (But *The La* is La Perouse.)

Mantique, a long-term (forty years or more) resident of Manly.

Mossie, a resident of Mosman.

mot, to subject new students to an initiation ceremony. (Used at Hawkesbury Agricultural College.)

murk, the, the Sydney sewer outfall at Ben Buckler.

North Shore neurosis, a form of psychological disturbance reputedly suffered by many housewives in isolated areas of the North Shore.

Operation Park, Bondi Esplanade Park, a favourite spot for invalids.

Oxometrical Society, a pseudo-organisation at Sydney University dedicated to the study and measurement of *bull.* Hence, *Oxometry* and *Oxometrist.*

Pick-up Corner, the corner of George and Park Streets opposite the Town Hall.

Pitt Street farmers, see *Auburn Street farmers.*

post, a deferred university examination (called a *supp,* short for "supplementary examination" at Melbourne University).

Poverty Point, originally the corner of King and Castlereagh Streets; later, the corner of Park and Pitt Streets.

Pub, the, the Hotel Australia.

Robbery (or *Robbo*) *Park,* Rosebery Park racecourse.

Rooty Hill, this name (from a township near Sydney) was attached for a period in the 1930s and 1940s to Kings Cross.

Royal, the, the Royal Sydney Show. This term is mainly used by residents in the country. Sydney people generally call it *the Show.*

Scale 'em Corner, a George Street corner, near Central Station, where appointments were (are?) made when intended to be broken.

Scotchman's Hill, Bradley's Head, Sydney harbour, where sailing races could be watched free of charge. (See Victoria's *Scotchman's Hill.*)

Shore, the, the suburbs north of Sydney Harbour Bridge.

sixty-miler, a collier on the run between Newcastle and Sydney.

slave market, the verandah of the Bells Hotel, Woolloomooloo, where packers and storemen were hired for work at Brown's Wharf opposite.

slurb, a suburban sprawl (architectural use).

snowie, a skier (specifically one who skis on the Snowy Mountains).

Stormtrooper Alley, the Victoria Street end of Kings Cross Road.

Sydney rock, a Sydney rock oyster.

ticket, put in one's, to die; to be dismissed from a job. A Balmain expression which originated at Mort's Dock, where employees beginning work each day took a numbered brass disc (the ticket) from a hook in the timekeeper's office.

to, attention should be drawn to some special uses of this preposition at Broken Hill, e.g. "Where'd you get it *to?*" – "Where did you get it from?"; "Where's Tom *to,* Harry?" – "Where has Tom gone, Harry?"; "Where ya *to?*" (A taxi driver's use) – "Where do you wish to go, to what address?"

up King Street, bankrupt, penniless. (Most of Sydney's law courts are in that area.)

Village, the, Manly or Double Bay.

VICTORIA

Argus-Tuft-Argus-Tuft! cry of Melbourne University engineering students at football.

Ballarat lantern, a candle set in the neck of a bottle.

Chaddy, a large shopping centre at Chadstone, Vic.

Chancery Lane, part of Little Collins Street, Melbourne, between Queen and William Streets, where many barristers and solicitors have their offices.

Coathanger, the Sydney Harbour Bridge. (Also used in S.A. and probably other States.)

Collins Street twist, a cigar or cigarette butt picked up in a Melbourne street for subsequent smoking.

crystal highway, nickname given to the Sale-Bairnsdale stretch of the Princes Highway because of many car windscreens broken thereon.

dixie, an ice-cream carton.

duck in, enter quickly. "Dozens of shops round Melbourne have signs, usually illustrated with a sketch of a duck, saying 'Duck in here for shoe repairs', etc."

Farm, the, Monash University, Melbourne.

Footscray Alps, a mythical place. (Footscray is extremely flat).

keep yow, to maintain guard while some illegal activity is afoot. (The N.S.W. equivalent is *keep nit*.)

Li'l Bluk Street, Little Bourke Street, Melbourne, where many Chinese live and work.

Little Lon, Little Lonsdale Street, Melbourne.

Little Muddy, the Yarra River. Used affectionately in Melbourne, but derogatively in N.S.W.

Lydiard street farmer, a dweller in Ballarat who takes only a remote interest in life on the land.

Mount Mistake, a hump-backed bridge built on Geelong Road, near Footscray football ground. (Used in the 1920s.)

nature strip, a strip of lawn beside the footpath outside Melbourne homes in "garden suburbs".

nongapoose, a fool. (Apparently a local equivalent of *nong*).

Pivotonian, a resident of Geelong (sometimes called The Pivot).

Puckapunyal cocktail, a drink consisting of metal polish, gin, wine and vinegar allegedly made at Puckapunyal Army Camp.

Puppydog Corner, the corner of Collins and Swanston Streets, Melbourne.

quanger, a quince. (Reported from Gippsland.)

Rickety Kate, name given to one of several *toast-rack* types of tram, open at both ends, that used to run on the St. Kilda-Brighton line.

Scotchman's Hill, a hill overlooking Flemington racecourse.

Shop, the, the University of Melbourne.

spaggie, an Italian. (Ex spaghetti.)

swanie's (or *swanee's*) *pony*, so long! goodbye! (Ex the name of a successful pony named See You Later, owned by a Melbourne man, Swan.)

Sydney turn, a form of traffic turn (originating in England, but first borrowed in Australia by Sydney) in which a car making a right-hand turn at an intersection pulls in towards the turn, instead of to the outside.

Tait cars, sliding-door railway carriages used on Melbourne suburban services. (Commemorating Sir James Tait, 1864-1940, Victorian Railways Commissioner.)

trammy's cut, a style of hair-cut. (Reported from Ballarat.)

yarra, a fool or simpleton. Also, *yarra bend*, "equivalent to the English word Bedlam" (Morris). The latter is fading from use and is being displaced by *Kew* and *Mont Park*.

QUEENSLAND

bêche, a trepang. (Ex bêche-de-mer.)

Bedourie, a dust and wind storm. (Originally *Bedourie shower*.)

Bully, the "Townsville Bulletin". (Originally applied to the Sydney "Bulletin".)

burry, an Aboriginal.

by hang! an exclamation.

canary, a policeman. (Probably ex the light colour of uniforms worn in the tropical north.)

Cape, the, Cape York Peninsula.

creek, any winding course through coral.

Creek, the, Albion Park racecourse, Brisbane.

curry onion, a resident of Cloncurry.

evening, any time after midday. (This use makes the word "afternoon" redundant; it has spread to parts of N.S.W.)

fit for Woogaroo, silly or stupid. (An old phrase, referring to a mental hospital on Woogaroo Creek, near Goodna.)

Gabba, the, Woolloongabba cricket ground, Brisbane.

Great Australian Bight, the end of Queen Street, Brisbane.

Gulf, the, the Gulf of Carpentaria or the country near it. Also, *Gulf country*.

hengibber, an egg. (Ex the use of *gibber* for stone.) Also called a *chicken-rock* or *roostercrooby*.

house blocks, long piles or foundations upon which houses in tropical areas are built. Also called *stumps*.

hula bula, a term of contempt, especially used in the form *hula bula bastard*.

Ipswich, a grey flannel shirt.

jump-up, a stretch of outback road "which ascends in the manner of a staircase" with a broken surface and soft patches (1953).

manilaman, any native of Indonesia or Malaysia.

medley, the, the end, the finish. Reported from Mt Isa and Toowoomba. (Probably ex *the medley*, which is played at the end of many country dances.)

ox, an Italian.

peanut grower, a resident of Cooktown.

pineapple, the head.

ranch, a plantation cookhouse.

red country, high-level country on Cape York Peninsula characterised by hard-surfaced red soil and red coastal (bauxite) cliffs.

shady, a dark-skinned person.

slop, a policeman. (A rhyme on *cop*.)

sod all, nothing.

spiggoty, an Italian. (Apparently ex "spikka da English").

sport, a coral outcrop, usually of an isolated and minor nature in contrast to the *niggerhead*, a prominent outcrop. See *stag*.

stag, a coral outcrop.

stake (or *steak*), an Italian. (Ex steaka-da-oyst, alleged pronunciation by an Italian restaurant owner of "steak and oysters".)

stop 'em! block 'em! let 'em go! an old cry used by western Queensland stockmen, now often used humorously.

stump caps, protective caps of galvanised iron placed over house blocks to prevent attacks from white ants.

stumps, see *house blocks*.

Telly, the Brisbane "Telegraph" (and so for every other "Telegraph" newspaper published in Australia).

toast rack, an old type of tram used in Brisbane (originally from Sydney, but Sydney now has no trams).

togs, a swimming costume.

trochus shelling, diving for or trading in trochus shells.

tropical frog, any person of French extraction living in the far north.

wad, a school of fish.

wallaby day, a day when country people go to town, often Saturday.

wet desert, sandy country at the tip of Cape York Peninsula, which becomes a bog in the wet season.

white Australians, white workers on sugar plantations. (Probably ex the fact that when mature sugar cane is burnt off, the cutters soon become so begrimed that they could be mistaken for Aborigines.)

wongi, a talk or conversation.

yes-please, a customer's order for everything on a menu at one time.

SOUTH AUSTRALIA

Afghanistan, the east side of the township of Maree. An old term drawn from the presence of Afghan camel drivers; formerly called *Ghans*. There is a memorial to them in the train running from Adelaide to Alice Springs, which is called *The Ghan*.

biscuit factory, a, a men's lavatory. (From the name of an Adelaide biscuit maker called Menz.)

bitzer, a child's "car" made of a box on wheels. Called a *trolley* in W.A. and some other States.

black rabbit, the juvenile practice known as nick-nocking, i.e. knocking at doors and then running away.

blocker, an owner of a vineyard. (This use for the occupier of a block of land has occurred in many parts of Australia.)

cue (or *cuey*), a cucumber.

dingdong! an exclamation of disbelief. See *pull the bell!*

high-top loaf, a crusty loaf of bread.

hock-and-lemon straight, this use of *straight* means without ice.

illy illy oller! a children's game in which this expression is used as a cry.

jack of, tired of, fed up with. (This expression has been absorbed into general use.)

Joe Blitz, have the, to be afraid. (Equivalent of the N.S.W. *have the Jimmy Britts, have the Britts up*, which are nearer the proper name; however, I have a S.A. report that their expression was built round the name of an old-time Adelaide dentist.)

john shop, a police station. (The use in the eastern States is usually *cop-shop*.)

long John, a confection of ice cream, flavouring, cream and nuts, with a cherry on top, served in a glass tumbler that holds about a half-pint.

more front than Foy and Gibson's, said of a person who is extremely daring in his or her demands, or of a girl with large breasts. For the latter, compare with the Victorian use of *Lewis and Whitties*.

oaf, derogatory term for a member of an Old Adelaide Family.

parkland, a public garden or reserve. (Also used in Victoria).

prosh day, the Procession Day festivities held by Adelaide University students.

pull the bell! an exclamation of disbelief. Also, *dingdong!*

Rundle Street Caruso, a poor singer. (An Adelaide expression from depression days.)

slime, a drink of soda and lime. (Reported from Whyalla.)

snickle, a girl.

sook, a timid or dim-witted person. Also, *sooky*.

southoss, South Australia(n).

Tizer, the "Adelaide Advertiser" newspaper.

whacko! an exclamation of approval current in the 1920s, also reported in Victoria. Whence, *whacko-the-diddley-oh!* (*Whacko!* went into general Australian use in World War II and the second expression became *whacko-the-diddle-oh!*)

willy willy whip, a juvenile expression denoting the action of hanging on to the rear of a cart or wagon. Also, *a willy willy whip behind* (1888).

wurley, usually employed in place of *willy willy*. Also, *whirley* or *wirley*. See the special use given to *willy willy*.

yacker, to travel rapidly, and associated terms such as *yacker along* and *fairly yackering*.

yard of fritz, a tall man.

ya ya, a German. (The use of *oui oui* for a Frenchman was noted in Chapter XV.)

yo-yo, a cheque which "bounces".

WESTERN AUSTRALIA

alive to, alert. This almost standard English term as used in W.A. is equivalent to the use of *awake to* and of *awake up* in the eastern States.

boondie, a stone.

Fremantle, a note on pronunciation: Whereas Western Australians say FREEmantle, they change the stress in South FreMANtle.

gilgie, do a, to withdraw from an undertaking, to "back out". (Ex the popular name of a small freshwater crayfish.)

Golden Mile, the, part of Kalgoorlie – one of the world's richest auriferous reefs.

groupy, any one of a group of people who have migrated to W.A. from Britain to work on farms.

jumping jack, an old type of tram used at Kalgoorlie.

Kal, Kalgoorlie.

Kimberley mutton, roast goat.

Mad Mile, the, the Perth-Fremantle road, running through Claremont, a favoured track for speedsters.

morning piece, a schoolchildren's term for food eaten at the morning break.

nor'-westers, people living in the Kimberleys.

on, for more than a century Australians have used this preposition in special ways. For example, a gold-seeker was never *at* a goldfield, but always *on* it. In the Kimberleys and the Northern Territory today one does not take up rice-farming, cattle-raising, crocodile-shooting, etc.; one *goes out on the rice, on the cattle, on the crocs*, etc.

over the range, in the outback.

scurb, a general pejorative of limited use – reported from Rocky Gully where, in 1965, it was current among about 100 settlers.

shag, anything regarded as shoddy or worthless.

shag's roost, any place such as a hotel where men idle away their time.

snarley Charley, a bad mood or fit of temper. "He's in a *snarley Charley* today."

taddying, window-shopping, or looking over merchandise in shops without buying.

Totterdell coat, a backless coat with detachable sleeves invented by a Lord Mayor of Perth, Ald. Totterdell, in an effort to induce W.A. men to dress more sanely in summertime.

tweet, to steal.

virgin's parlour, the ladies lounge at the local hotel at Esperance.

wheelbarrow, any word not understood. "What's that *wheelbarrow*?"

Woop Woop and *Snake Gully*, as fictitious names for a remote outback settlement, the home of the most rustic of rustics, are also worth noting. *Out in the mallee* means much the same thing, but it is mainly localized in South Australia and Victoria.

A common possession of Melbourne and Sydney is (or was) *the Block*. During the 1860s, when Australia was beginning to acquire some hint of fashionable life in her main cities, certain popular promenades in Melbourne and Sydney became known as *the Block*. The term was applied originally in Melbourne to the section of Collins Street between Elizabeth and Swanston Streets. This use still prevails. In Sydney, *the Block* was "that portion of the city bounded by King, George, Hunter and Pitt Streets". Derivatives were *to do the Block*, to saunter or parade in the fashionable part of the city, and *blockists*, people who indulged in this pursuit. In old journals we find such references as "Saturday Block time", the fashionable hour for promenading (1896), "doing the block in Hereford Street" (1902), and a note on a tailor who "dressed the Block for many years" (1892).

It would probably be a mistake not to make some mention of the traditional competitiveness between Melbourne and Sydney. This has erupted in several phrases that bid fair to remain permanently in the language. The Sydneysider boasts – not without reason – of *Our Harbour* and *Our Bridge*,[1] but beyond the borders of New South Wales these expressions are mainly used ironically, together with the term *coathanger* for the bridge, and as a riposte the Sydneysider refers to Melbourne's river

---

[1] Before the noted cricketer, D. G. Bradman, moved to Adelaide in the early 1930s it was a stock joke for Sydneysiders to say that they were "*Three Hours*" ahead of Melbourne. These were *Our Harbour*, *Our Bridge* and *Our Bradman*.

as the *stinking Yarra, the only river in the world which runs upside down* and *Little Muddy* and alludes to the city as *Smellburn*. As seen by outsiders, Sunday in Melbourne and Adelaide (and other places in the Wowser Belt) is described as "The day when life doesn't just stand still; it drops dead".

2. CLIMATE AND TRAINS

AMONG FACTORS which produce localized expressions is the climate. In a country as large as Australia, where prolonged droughts (the worst was in 1902) and tragic floods (the greatest toll of life was at Gundagai, N.S.W., in 1852, when 89 people died) occur, and where the temperature ranges between –8°F. and 127.5°F., it is natural that many climatic expressions should have invaded our language.

One of the oldest terms in this group is *brickfielder* (noted earlier), which originally described a heavy, cold, southerly gale bringing dirt and dust to the Sydney settlement from nearby brickfields. Partridge also lists the form *brickduster*, which, he says, was current before 1880, but textual evidence is lacking to prove his statement.

The *southerly buster* or, as refined people once preferred to call it, the *burster*, is a heavy southerly gale experienced along the east coast of Australia and in New Zealand. Especially heavy gales of this type are often called *old man southerlies* or *old man busters*.

The *black north-easter* or *blackie* of the east coast, the *cockeye bob* or *cockeyed bob* of north-western W.A., and the *willy willy* or *willy* are also climatic features of Australia.

It is often erroneously suggested that *willy willy*, which describes a wild storm of cyclonic type, usually one that moves spirally, is of Aboriginal origin, but it almost certainly hails from abroad. For instance, E. S. Hill, "Official Visit to Lord Howe Island" (1870), says that "miniature whirl-winds, termed *wollies* by the inhabitants, sweep from the deep gullies to the sea". Partridge lists *willywaws* for "squalls in the Straits of Magellan . . . also light variable winds elsewhere" and he suggests that it may be derived from *whirly-whirly*. In Alaska, cyclonic winds are called *willywaws;* W. S. Walker makes frequent reference to *willie-was* in New Zealand in "Zealandia's Guerdon" (1902). *Willy willy*, which has been current in Australia since the early 1890s, may possibly have acquired this form either through Aboriginal pidgin or by imitation of repetitive Aboriginal names. It is worth noting that *willy willy* is rarely used in S.A., its place being taken by *wirley* or *whirley* – which offers some support for the likeli-hood that the term was imported. Waterspouts on our east coast are sometimes called *aquatic willy-willies*.

Cockeye bob is reputed to come from Aboriginal *kack-ay*, to take care. By a process of meiosis, such cyclones are commonly called *blows*.

The Dry and *the Wet*, which describe the dry and monsoon seasons of the year respectively in Australian tropical regions, appear to be indigenous. *The Dry* is also used colloquially to denote desert areas inland. Thus, in the "Bulletin" of January 21, 1909, a writer speaks of "a seventy-five mile *dry*", meaning a stage of a journey across desert seventy-five miles wide.

As I have noted earlier, outback dust storms are known variously as *Bedourie showers*, *Bourke showers*, *Cobar showers*, etc. The only one of these place-names to stand alone in general use is *Bedourie* (which is in Queensland), with no necessity for *shower* to be added.

In W.A. the terms *Fremantle doctor* and *Albany doctor* are applied to cool sea winds which blow after extremely hot days. In the Gulf of Carpentaria the *morning glory* does much the same thing early in the day; it is applied to a strong wind that blows in the Gulf and on neighbouring coasts.

The inland has given us a useful word in *storm* to describe an area of fresh grass that has grown following a rain shower. Stock is often travelled *from storm to storm* across inland wastes or is said *to storm along*.

Banker for a flooded river running banks high is also an Australian term. Such a river is said *to run a banker*. In "Back to Bool Bool" (1931) "Brent of Bin Bin" writes of *creek-banking rain*.

Bogaduck weather for heavy rain and *to fine up*, (of weather) to become fine, are other Australianisms.

Train travellers have also made useful contributions to provincial speech. Thus the train running between Darwin and Birdum has come to be known to history as *Leaping Lena*. Officially known as *The Sentinel*, this train has been the subject of attention from many authors, including Mrs Aeneas Gunn, Ernestine Hill and Xavier Herbert, largely because of the friendly and rough-and-ready way it has been run. Soldiers who found themselves in the Northern Territory in World War II called the train the *Spirit of Protest* – a nickname founded on Victoria's *Spirit of Progress*, the express train formerly running between Melbourne and Albury, which was replaced in 1962 by a Sydney-Melbourne train called the *Southern Aurora* or *Roarer*.

Another well-known train is *The Fish*, an express running between Sydney and the Blue Mountains. *The Silver City Comet* runs between Sydney and Broken Hill. *The Ghost* runs between Sydney and Campbelltown; it won its name because thirsty Sydney folk who could not get beer locally formerly slipped off to Campbelltown where they became *bona fide* "travellers" in the eyes of the law. South Australia also has a *Ghost Train*, which runs from Adelaide to Peterborough, arriving at its destination on Sunday morning.

The Overland runs between Melbourne and Adelaide. *The Trans-continental*, better known simply as *the Trans*, runs between Port Pirie and Kalgoorlie. *The Tea and Sugar* is a train running between Port Augusta and Kalgoorlie, which delivers supplies to fettlers on the transcontinental line across the Nullarbor.

In Queensland, *The Sunlander*, also called *The Sunshine Express*, runs between Brisbane and Cairns, and *The Inlander* runs from Townsville to

Mt. Isa. Several slow trains running on branch lines in Queensland are called *The Sweeper* – an expression that has been officially recognised by the Queensland Railways Department – in contrast to express or mail trains. As one who seems to have spent more than his fair share of time travelling in the square-wheeled cattle-trucks that are passed off as railway carriages in various parts of the Commonwealth, I feel that some special mention should be given to a so-called train known as *The Midnight Horror*, which runs (as the euphemism goes) between Townsville and Cairns. Like *Leaping Lena*, this train is operated as only the outback can operate a train – with stops to boil a billy or call on a friend or snatch a drink or two at a wayside pub. I have no doubt that many other Midnight Horrors or their equivalents are to be found on other outback lines.

Since the above was written, I have been informed that the train between Townsville and Mt. Isa is also called *The Horror*. There are probably adequate reasons.

Fettlers on W.A. railways use what is known as a *kalamazoo*, a three-wheeled hand-operated flatcar, equivalent to the *trike* of some other States (this use is almost standard English); in S.A., the *trike* used is driven by a motor and can carry three or four men with repair gear. A *quad* is a four-wheeled rail motor. The following usages have been reported from Adelaide: *bull* (originally *Barwell's bull*), a rail car; *bluebird*, a country diesel rail car; *dodger*, a steam train with its engine reversed. An old and uncomfortable railway carriage is not uncommonly called a *dog-box*.

3. ALPHABETICISMS

SINCE COUNTLESS alphabeticisms – such as F.N.D., Flinders Naval Depot (Melbourne), T. L.,Townsville lucerne (north Queensland), D.J.s, David Jones' department stores (Sydney) – are localized in use, I will content myself with drawing attention to samples of national importance. Here is a fairly representative selection:

A.B.C., Australian Broadcasting Commission.
A.C.T., Australian Capital Territory. (Its alternative, *F.C.T.*, Federal Capital Territory, was eliminated in the early 1940s.)
A.C.T.U., Australian Council of Trade Unions.
A.I.M., Australian Inland Mission.
A.J.C., Australian Jockey Club.
A.L.P., Australian Labor Party.
A.N.Z.U.S., a security treaty between Australia, New Zealand and the United States of America.
B.H.P., the Broken Hill Proprietary Co.
C.P., Country Party.
C.S.I.R.O., Commonwealth Scientific and Industrial Research Organisation. (Perhaps worth minor recognition since it was one of the oldest digital computers in the world, was *C.S.I.R.A.C.*, designed by *C.S.I.R.O.* engineers in the early 1950s and retired in 1964.)

D.L.P., Democratic Labour Party.
L.-C.P., the Liberal Party-Country Party coalition.
L.P., Liberal Party.
N.G., New Guinea.
N.S.W., New South Wales.
N.T., Northern Territory.
O.T., Overland Telegraph (from Adelaide to Darwin).
P.P., Pastures Protection. Mainly used in country, especially in *P.P. Board*.
Q., Queensland.
S.A., South Australia.
S.E.A.T.O., South-East Asia Treaty Organisation.
T., Tasmania.
T.I., Thursday Island.
V., Victoria. More usually *Vic.*
V.D.L., Van Diemen's Land (obsolete).
W.A., Western Australia.

The alphabeticisms *A.I.F.*, *R.A.N.* and *R.A.A.F.*, together with some other Service letter-combinations, were given in Chapter VIII.

One of the best-known of all alphabeticisms to which Australia has helped give birth is *A.N.Z.A.C.* This has now become so deep-rooted in our language in the form *Anzac* that we are liable to forget it was originally invented to describe the Australian and New Zealand Army Corps. *Ausac* was suggested in 1943 as a term that could be used to describe the Australian and U.S. forces fighting side by side in New Guinea – Australia-U.S. Army Corps – but it achieved little popularity.

Of more colloquial type are *S.P.*, for starting price betting, now being rapidly edged out of use by *T.A.B.*, Totalisator Agency Board; *M.L.*, an abbreviation for Maoriland, otherwise New Zealand; *G.G.*, a Governor General; *G.P.S.*, Great Public School (in N.S.W.) which is rendered *P.S.* in Victoria; and quite a few combinations from well below the salt, *A. over T.*, head over heels (or Arse Over Tit), *B.S.*, bullsh, *D.O.M.*, Dirty Old Man and *P.O.Q.*, go away (from Piss Off Quickly).

Perhaps one should note that at this stage of our cultural Odyssey we use *T.V.* to denote television rather than the English *telly*, although the latter has been gaining ground in recent years.

4. POLITICS

ALTHOUGH AUSTRALIA is blessed with seven Parliaments, the fact that the most recent of these is the Commonwealth Parliament (which met in Melbourne from 1901 to 1927 and thereafter transferred to Canberra) has meant that a good deal of our political jargon has been localized in the States.

The *Braddon blot* and the *Berry blight*, mentioned in Chapter XII, are examples. Others include *Old Hat*, a supporter of Sir James McCulloch (Victoria) in the 1860s and 1870s; *bunyip aristocracy* or *bunyip peerage*, nicknames derived from an abortive attempt made in 1853 to create a colonial "nobility"; *abolitionists*, the section of the Australian public who, between 1820 and 1867, fought for the cessation of convict transportation to Australia – they were also known as *anti-transportationists*, while people in favour of continued importation of convicts were called *transportationists;* and *New Australia*, a name that commemorates the earnest, but unhappy effort of William Lane (first user of the term *White Australia*, in 1888) and his associates to found a social order based on brotherhood.

Members of a body known as the New Australia Co-operative Settlement Association (founded in 1892) left Sydney in July, 1893, for Paraguay, where *New Australia* was founded. Dissension and disillusion reaped heavy toll on the enterprise and although a breakaway movement (the *Cosmans*) continued on communal lines for more than a decade the colony disintegrated after 1905. Supporters of the movement were known as *New Australians*. These *New Australians* were, of course, quite distinct from the immigrants called *New Australians* who came to this country after World War II, although in order to keep the record straight it should be pointed out that the latter application was used as far back as 1926 in a book by "Jice Doone" (pen-name of Vance Marshall), "Timely Tips to New Australians".

Early this century the terms *yes-no*, *yes-no'er* and *yes-noism* had a vogue. A *yes-no* was a person who favoured in some measure both sides of a political question even though they were generally diametrically opposed.

One of the earliest Australian political terms to survive is *stonewall*, applied to parliamentary obstruction, which came into use in the 1870s. Derivatives include *to stonewall*, *stonewalling* and *stonewaller*. The *iron hand*, signifying the closure or *gag*, was popular in former days especially in Victorian politics.

Although limited in number, some extremely important linguistic developments followed the creation of a national parliament. While the words *Commonwealth* and *Federal* were both originally standard English, they ceased to be standard English once they came to be used as synonyms for *Australia* or *Australian*. For instance, we speak of the *Commonwealth Parliament*, the *Commonwealth Government*, *Federal Cabinet*, *Federal policy* and so on, in each case using these words as equivalent to *Australian*. When an Australian speaks of *the Commonwealth*, he usually does not mean the Commonwealth of Nations or the British Commonwealth; he means the *Commonwealth of Australia* as it was proclaimed in 1900 and established in the following year when the six colonies (now known as States) and the Northern Territory were federated. It is of some linguistic interest to examine the wording of The Commonwealth of Australia Constitution Act of July 9, 1900. It states, in part:

> "The Commonwealth" shall mean the Commonwealth of Australia as established under this Act.
> "The States" shall mean such of the colonies of New South Wales, New Zealand, Queensland, Tasmania, Victoria, Western Australia and South Australia, including the northern territory of South Australia, as for the time being are parts of the Commonwealth, and such colonies or

territories as may be admitted into or established by the Commonwealth as States; and each of such parts of the Commonwealth shall be called "a state". "Original States" shall mean such States as are parts of the Commonwealth at its establishment.

The explicit definition given to the expression *original State* indicates that it is worthy of a place here. The subsequent development of the terms *inter-State* and *intra-State* as applying specifically to the States of the Commonwealth can also be noted. Even such a term as *Eastern States* merits attention. It is generally applied to Queensland, New South Wales and Victoria. But in terms of geographical fact, Tasmania is also an Eastern State and, since South Australia has sometimes shown a tendency to throw in her lot with the East, South Australia is sometimes included in references to the *Eastern States*.

Another orthodox English term with a special Australian connotation is *Federation*. This can be used either to refer to the linking of the Australian colonies into the Commonwealth, or the date on which such linking took place – January 1, 1901. The commonly-heard phrase *since Federation* is a way of saying "since Australia became a Commonwealth", and it has a special significance for the Australian.

The growth of Federal power during and after World War II was accompanied by the development of several interesting expressions, among them *Brisbane Line, The Movement, Grouper, anti-Grouper, Faceless Men, unity ticket* and *donkey vote*.

Let us look at these in sequence. In the early stages of World War II when invasion by Japan seemed likely, plans were allegedly made for Australia to defend a line extending from Brisbane to Adelaide or from Brisbane to Perth. Details have never been made public and, indeed, there have been official denials that the *Brisbane Line* ever existed. However, in a recent issue of the "Current Affairs Bulletin" (vol. 34, no. 6, August 3, 1964) the following comment appears: "Among the most concrete reminders of the infamous 'Line' are the fortifications keeling over into the week-end holiday surf-beach sands of Bribie Island . . ." Whether the *Line* existed or not, the term has acquired adjectival uses in *Brisbane Line strategy, Brisbane Line thinking*, etc.

While on the theme of lines, attention should be drawn to what is known as the *leper line* in Western Australia. Under W.A. law, an Act prevents Aborigines from crossing the 20th parallel of latitude from north to south; this is not a manifestation of colour prejudice, but a boundary designed to check the spread of leprosy from the north.

The Movement is the political wing of Catholic Action and originated in Victoria due largely to the efforts of B. A. Santamaria (hence its alternative name *Santamaria Movement*). It began operating actively in Federal politics in 1949 and achieved wide, if not always favourable, receptions in the States. Derivatives include *anti-Movement, pro-Movement* and adjectival uses. Directly linked with *The Movement* are what are known as *groups* and *groupers*. *Groups*, also called *industrial groups*, were formed in 1945 by the A.L.P. to combat Communism in trade unions; they were later disbanded on the ground that they had become instruments for infiltration by Catholic Action. Those who advocate re-formation of the groups or support their use in fighting Communism are called *groupers*. In the mid-1960s the term was used by left-wingers to denote those who still operated within the Labor Party under right wing influences. Derivatives include *non-Groupers, pro-Groupers, anti-Groupers, anti-Grouperism* and various adjectival uses. *Gripper* is a retaliatory term used by groupers and others to denote persons, usually Masons, allegedly having anti-Catholic prejudices.

Faceless Men are thirty-six upper-echelon members of the Australian Labor Party who decide the basic aspects of A.L.P. policy. They are not Members of Parliament. The expression is mainly used derogatively by Labor opponents.

The term *unity ticket* was coined by Communists and A.L.P. left-wingers to denote a how-to-vote card on which the names of Communists and A.L.P. men are linked in union elections.

Donkey vote denotes the collective vote of electors who vote straight down a *ticket* (i.e. the printed list of candidates standing for an election) irrespective of parties or the merits of candidates. Such a voter is called a *donkey voter*.

The terms *cheer-chaser* and *caveman* achieved some political prominence in the early 1940s. *Cheer-chaser* was first used on November 29, 1942, to describe a Federal Minister who was alleged to have been currying favour with the rank and file. *To chase cheers*, to curry favour with the mob, and *cheer-chasing* developed rapidly. *Cave*, a revival of English political slang with a new application in Australia, was first used on April 3, 1943, to describe a National Service group that broke away from the United Australia Party (now defunct, and replaced by the Liberal Party). The term has biblical origin; it refers to the cave of Adullam in I Samuel, xxii, i. English political use applied it to "the secession of a small body of politicians from their party on some special question; also, the malcontent party so seceding". The U.A.P. minority did not, however, split from the main body on a "special question", but on the broad basis of policy. *Caveman*, describing a member of the group, was used in print on April 18, 1943.

Now, an assortment of other political or semi-political terms: *spill*, a resignation of all Cabinet members at one time and the formation of a new Ministry; *State-righter*, a person who supports State Government powers against encroachments by the Federal Government; *new-Stater*, a person who supports the creation of a new State or new States in Australia; *snipe*, a political election poster, the size of which is limited to 10 in. by 6 in.; *Dorothy Dix* or *Dorothy Dixer*, a question asked in Parliament for the set purpose of allowing a propagandic reply by a Minister; *all nighter*, a sitting of Parliament that continues until the following day, usually in an effort to dispose of urgent business; *steamroller*, pressure on a recalcitrant party member to make him vote for or otherwise support party policy; *drop the bucket*, to deliver a speech against an opponent which virtually destroys him politically, at least for the time being; *the numbers*, the numerical strength of a group backing a particular move in a political party – two "famous sayings", mainly within the Labor Party, are: "You don't fight if you haven't got the numbers" and "I like to have logic on my side, but I'd rather have the numbers."

The following catchcries and slogans peculiar to Australia are also worth note: *Advance Australia!*[2] *The Australians are One!*[3] *Australia First! Fill up Our Empty Spaces! Keep Australia White! Wake Up Australia! Above All for Australia! Australia for Australians!*[4] *Trust in the People!*[5] and *Unlock the Lands!*

Since July, 1946, Australian radio listeners have been provided – by the Australian Broadcasting Commission – with the opportunity of hearing Federal Parliament. Not infrequently, listeners have heard the Speaker call Members to order for using certain expressions. These expressions are called "unparliamentary".

All Parliaments appear to have been obliged to place verbal curbs on their Members. In July, 1936, the then-Speaker of the New Zealand House of Representatives (the Hon. W. A. Barnard) tabled a list of words and phrases that had been declared "unparliamentary" in that House between 1912 and 1935. The list cited more than 500 examples, including:

> A blasted lot of Shylocks; blow-fly minded; a heart the size of a peanut, but of a harder substance; the thick skull of a Minister of the Crown; a giggling monkey; a disgrace to the Scottish race; look in the mirror and see a donkey; the face of the honourable member reminds me of a great cheese, out of which a yokel has taken a great bite.

Among single words ruled out of order in the New Zealand House of Representatives were: Ananias, ass, arch-Tory, Barabbas, anti-God, autocratic bully, cad, common brute, coward, scabs, political chameleon.

In "Australia Speaks" I listed some 500 words and phrases "representative of those which have been considered unparliamentary in the Federal House". The Clerk of the House (Mr. A. G. Turner) tells me that the recording of such unparliamentary expressions ceased at the end of the 1926–28 session. He adds: "This was done as it was found the list was of little value in a parliamentary sense because the question of whether a word or a phrase is unparliamentary depends on the context or sense in which it was used, on the mood of the House and on the way in which it was viewed by particular occupants of the Chair".

Among words and phrases which have earned the Speaker's displeasure in the House of Representatives are these samples on the theme of truth:

---

[2] Originally, a favourite motto of public men and writers in the 1850s.

[3] Watchword of the Tasmanian abolitionists about 1850.

[4] Adopted as a motto by the now-defunct "National Advocate", Bathurst, N.S.W. The slogan *Victoria for Victorians*, recorded by a writer of 1883, provides a commentary on the old rivalry between Melbourne and Sydney.

[5] An old cry which called for confidence in, not fear of, the colonists who were descendants of convicts.

Dishonest, bloody lie, bogus attitude, bunkum, cant and hypocrisy, canting humbug, hypocritical farce, deliberate mis-statement, damnable lies, duplicity, fabrication, falsehood, insinuations of untruth, insincerity, liar, lie, mendacious, prevarication, subterfuges, truth cannot (must not) be spoken in this House, you cannot tell the truth, deliberately keeping back the truth, try to be truthful, untruth.

Unparliamentary nouns applied to a Member: assassin, blackguard, bounder, brute, bully, cad, coward, creature, cur, fool, jackanapes, ignoramus, imbecile, impostor, informer, insect, Judas, liar, mountebank, nuisance, pimp, pimple, puppet, rat, renegade, reprobate, scab, scarecrow, scoundrel, slanderer, sneak, snob, thug, traitor, trickster.

Unparliamentary descriptive expressions applied to a Member: bally porcupine, blood-drinker, chattering jackass, insignificant pup, insulting brute, long-haired emotional ass, miserable body-snatcher, sanctified political larrikin, sewer rat.

Since pidgin English is one of the three official languages (and the most popular) of the New Guinea House of Assembly, I look forward with keen anticipation to the proscribed contributions we can expect in due course from that House.

CHAPTER XVII

Special Forms of Slang

1. RHYMING SLANG

RHYMING SLANG has had brief vogues in Australia and its greatest currency has, oddly enough, coincided with wars. At the time this book is being written, in the mid-1960s, we are coming to the end of the World War II phase.

Sydney "Truth" of January 7, 1900, noted that "Cockney slang is quickly displacing the old push lingo in Sydney" and gave the following example of the imported material:

> I 'ad a brown I'm afloat, a green Jacky Lancashire in me left 'andsky and tan daisy roots. When I meets the cheese and kisses and pratted off down the frog and toad, I tell you I was a bit orl right.

A writer in the "Bulletin" of January 18, 1902, gives the following example:

Me mother's away, as I was swiftly-flowing up the field of wheat in the bread-and-jam, a heavenly plan with a big charming mottle of O-my-dear sticking out of his sky-rocket fancy-sashed the girl-abductor on his bundle-of-socks with it cos he wouldn't let him have a virgin-bride for nothing.	The other day as I was going up the street in a tram a man with a big bottle of beer sticking out of his pocket bashed the conductor over the head (i.e. think-box) with it (i.e. the bottle) because he wouldn't let him have a ride for nothing.

An interesting footnote is supplied by the "Bulletin" to this effort. It is a comment that rhyming slang was "twenty years old at least" in Australia, which would take us back to the 1880s. Its hold must have been small, however, for in "The Detectives' Handbook" of *circa* 1882, no mention is made of rhyming slang, although a glossary of back slang is given. Crowe vouches that as late as 1895 it had secured small hold.[1]

However, in 1898, a writer points out:

> The Cockney rhyming slang is popular in Australia and the lion comiques and lydies of the variety stage are helping to make the hold stronger.

The following examples were added to show the type of rhymes used: *Arty Rolla*, a collar; *mince pies*, eyes; *cheese and kisses*, the missus; *Charlie Prescott*, waistcoat; *Joe Morgan*, street organ; *pot and pan*, old man; *tiddley-wink*, a drink; *lamb's fry*, tie; *lump o' lead*, bread; *plates o' meat*, feet.

---

[1] In the "Australian Magazine" of November 1, 1908, J. H. Garth noted that rhyming slang "broke out a couple of years ago".

358

These examples, or the greater percentage of them, anyway, are not Australian. The expressions current about the Boer War period and during World War I were also largely imported, out-of-date Cockneyisms. As noted above, rhyming slang had a vogue in World War II, but an influence delaying its demise has been the large postwar intake of English migrants.

Australians are inclined to resist its use if only for the fact that it is a dull, unimaginative type of slang, and has little of the sharp, business-like nature of other Australianisms about it. What authentic rhyming slang there is in this part of the world, will usually be found in a disguised form.

Thus a Sydneysider uses *Hawkesbury Rivers* for shivers, but cuts it back to *Hawkesburies*. A hotel becomes known in rhyming slang as a *rub-a-dub-dub* – by rhyme on "pub" – and is quickly chopped back to *rubberdy*, *rubbity* and *rubby*. Through a rhyme on "cash", money comes to be known as *Oscar Asche*, and then becomes *Oscar*.

In the same way a disguise is dropped over many indigenous expressions that were originally rhyming slang. *Knock-me* denotes a billy, from the rhyme *knock-me-silly; poddy* is two-and-six, from *poddy calf*, as a rhyme on *half*-a-caser, and *fiddley* denotes £1, from *fiddley-did*, a rhyme on "quid" (such expressions as these are, of course, obsolescent due to Australia's adoption of decimal currency); *maggies* denotes women's drawers, by clipping from "Maggie Moores"; *Robertson* means profit, by extraction from the name of the Melbourne firm of *Robertson and Moffat;*[2] *do a Botany*, to run away, from a rhyme on "Botany Bay"; *Steele Rudds*, potatoes, from a rhyme on "spuds"; *Roy Sleuce*, a deuce in cards, from a combination of *Roy* Rene and Harry Van der *Sluice*, which were respectively the stage and proper names of the Australian comedian nicknamed "Mo"; *don't be auntie!* meaning don't be silly! has travelled even further – it has come by transference from the English rhyming slang *don't be Uncle Willie; dead spotted ling*, is a tautological way of saying *dead ring*, meaning exactly similar; *post-and-rail*, a lie (by rhyme on "fairytale"); *Victor Trumper*, a cigarette butt (by rhyme on the Australianism *bumper*).

A few examples are more complex than this. Listen to some deft words by a *floor flogger* (a drink steward) in a Sydney club, who has taken his order to the bar: "Three lilies new, Paterson Laing old, a oncer, rogans the kembla". Translated, this means "three schooners of new beer, two schooners of old beer, £1 given to buy them, give me the change in shillings". This translation is achieved by knowing that a schooner of beer is referred to in rhyming slang as a *lily of Laguna* and is then cut to *lily;* a deuce, i.e. two, is formed on the name of a Sydney firm *Paterson, Laing and Bruce*, which is then cut to *Paterson Laing* (sometimes to *Paterson* alone); a *oncer* is £1, although this, of course, is not rhyming slang; *rogan* is a shilling, extracted from the English rhyming slang *rogue and villain*, and

---

[2] A former Melbourne firm commemorated in rhyming slang is Lewis and Whitty, used in the form *Lewis and Whitties* to denote women's breasts (by rhyme on "titties"). The link between the Melbourne firm Buckley and Nunn and the expression *Buckley's chance* has already been mentioned.

Kembla means change, extracted from Kembla Grange, the racecourse at Wollongong, N.S.W.

Another good example is *Melbourne* with the meaning of "back". This is how it works out: *Melbourne* is short for Melbourne Grammar, the school; Melbourne Grammar is a rhyme on *hammer,* which is extracted from *hammer and tack,* which is a rhyme for back. In certain cases, the term was taken a step further to mean sixpence, i.e. a *zack.* So what you have here is a series of rhymes.

Unfortunately, a great deal of rhyming slang fails to reach these levels. In the round-up of rhyming terms given below, only a few of the items are worthy of attention; many of them were recorded during World War II in Gavin Long's list of war slang, to which tribute was paid in Chapter VIII (once more, it should be said that many of the currency terms are now obsolescent):

Andy Mac, zack.
Andy McGuire, fire.
Angus Murray, curry. Ex name of a murderer. (Melbourne use.)
Anna Louise, cheese.
applesauce, horse.
aras, bottles of beer. (Usually in plural only; ex *Aristotle* as rhyme on bottle.)
armour float, overcoat.
babbling brook, cook. More often *babbler.* (This is an English military use.)
bag of fruit, suit.
barmaid's blush, a flush (in poker).
barrel of fat, hat.
bat and ball, wall.
Betty Grable, table.
Bill Lang, slang. Ex name of a pugilist.
blood blister, sister.
boots and sox, pox.
bowl of fat, hat.
brave and bold, cold.
breeze, it's a, it is easy.
brown joe, to understand. Rhyme on "know".
bullock horn, to pawn.
butcher's (hook), crook (i.e. unwell).
captain, a child, a "kid". Ex Captain Kidd.
Captain Cook, a look.
carburettor, letter.
cats and mice, dice.
cattle tick, a Catholic.
Charlie or *Charley,* (1) a girl, (2) a lesbian. See next.
Charlie Wheeler, a girl. Rhyme on *sheila.* See *two-wheeler.*
Charlie Chase, race, e.g. *not in the Charlie Chase.*
chock and log, (1) a dog; (2) a dingo, i.e. the Australian wild dog.
chunka or *chunker,* a boss. Ex *chunk of beef,* a rhyme on "chief".
citronella, quinella (racing bet).
Clark Gable, cable.
coca-cola, a bowler (in cricket).

Coff's Harbour, barber.

comic (cuts), guts. *"Comics"* if abbreviation is made.

cow's hoof, a male homosexual. Ex rhyme on *poof(ter).*

cricket bats, "tatts", i.e. teeth.

cry and laugh, scarf.

cuff link, drink (n.).

curry and rice, price.

Dad and Dave, shave.

Dad and Mum, rum.

dark felt, belt. Ex name of a Melbourne Cup winner.

Dave Prince, a quince. Ex name of a Melbourne bookmaker. Note the use of *pear and quince* for prince.

Dawn Fraser, razor. Ex name of swimmer.

deacon skinner, dinner.

dead horse, sauce.

dead wowsers, trousers.

deaf and dumb, (1) inside information (rhyme on *drum*), (2) rum.

Dicky Lee, (1) tea, (2) a pee = piss.

digger's nest, chest.

ding-a-ling, king.

dip and duck it, bucket.

Doctor Beven, seven (Melbourne use).

dog's dinner, skinner (i.e. of bets). Also spinner (in two-up).

dot, a regular drinker of wine. Ex *wine-dot,* itself a rhyme on or perversion of *Wyandotte,* the domestic fowl. See also *plonk-dot.*

down and up, cup.

dribs and drabs, body lice. Rhyme on *crabs.*

ducks and drakes, shakes (as occur in D.Ts).

ducks and geese, police.

duck's neck, cheque.

east and west, vest.

eat 'em alive, five.

eau de Cologne, a (tele)phone.

egg flip, tip (in racing).

eighteenpence, a fence. (In English rhyming slang it means "common-sense".)

fairy bower, a shower. (Sydney placename.)

Farmer Giles, haemorrhoids. Rhyme on "piles".

fiddles and flutes, boots.

fiddley (did), a quid.

Flemington races, braces.

Fred Astaire, a chair.

froth and bubble, double (in betting).

gerbera, a Yarborough (in bridge).

giddy goat, a totalisator. Rhyme on *tote.*

ginger beer, ear.

goanna, piano.

Gordon and Gotch, a watch. Ex name of an Australian firm.

greasy, a policeman, a detective. Ex *greasy mop,* a rhyme on *cop.*

greengages, wages.

Gregory Peck, neck.

gumtree, knee.

Gypsie Lee, tea.

half a neddy, ten shillings. A rhyme on *reddie*.

hammer and tack, (1) back, (2) sack, (3) sixpence (i.e. a *zack*), (4) track.

hanky panky, silly, eccentric. Rhyme on "cranky".

Hawkesbury Rivers, shivers. (Mainly localized to N.S.W.)

Henry Berry, to *jerry*, understand. Ex name of Henry Berry & Co. Ltd., an Australian firm.

hi-diddle-diddle, (1) middle, (2) urination (rhyme on *piddle*).

highland fling, string.

hit and miss, urination. Rhyme on *piss*.

Horace Tottle, bottle. Ex *Aristotle*.

horse and dray, threepence. Rhyme on *tray*.

horse's hoof, a male homosexual. Ex rhyme on *poof(ter)*. See *cow's hoof*.

hot potato, later.

Huckleberry Finn, gin.

I'll be back, sixpence (i.e. a *zack*).

iron tank, Yank. See *ship's tank*.

Ivy's last, past.

Jack and Jill, (1) a fool (rhyme on *dill*), (2) hill.

Jack Benny, penny.

Jack Scratch, match.

Jill and Jack, sixpence (i.e. a *zack*).

Jim Gerald, the (Melbourne) "Herald". Ex name of entertainer.

Joan of Arcs, sharks. Almost always in plural.

Joe Blake, a snake.

Joe Rees, fleas.

Joe Marks, sharks. Almost always in plural.

John Dillon, a shilling. See *rogan*.

John (hop), a policeman. Rhyme on *cop*.

Kembla, change (money). Ex Kembla Grange, racecourse at Wollongong, N.S.W.

kerb and gutter, butter.

keys and locks, socks.

King of Spain, (1) rain, (2) train.

knock me silly, a billy(can).

Lane Cove, stove. (Sydney use.)

lily, a schooner of beer. Ex Lily of Laguna.

lolly, urination. Ex *lolly* = sweet, hence *sweet pea* (the flower), hence *pee* = piss.

loop-the-loop, (1) soup, (2) jockey, i.e. a *hoop*.

lost and found, (1) sound, (2) £1.

lubra, a Yarborough (in bridge).

macaroni, pony (£25). cf. English slang use for an actual pony. Also *macker*.

Marie La Var, car. Ex name of a musical comedy star.

Mark Foy, boy. Ex name of Sydney firm.

Martin Place, face (Sydney use.)

Mickey Finn, £5. Ex rhyme on *spin*.

Mickey Mouse, louse. English rhyming slang has it for a house.

mild and meek, impudence. Rhyme on *cheek*.

Molly Maguire, fire.

Moriarty, party.

Mort's Dock, penis. Rhyme on *cock*. (Localized to Sydney.)

Mother and daughter, water, cf. *squatter's daughter*.

Mother Goose, a florin. Rhyme on *deuce*.

Mother Machree, tea.

Mum and Dad, mad.

nannygoat, a totalisator. Ex rhyme on *tote*.

nappertandy, a shandy.

Ned Kelly, belly.

Nellie Bly (or *Bligh*), (1) a fly, (2) alert ("fly"), (3) eye, (4) tie, (5) "fly" of trousers.

Nelson, urination, a "piddle". Ex name Nelson Riddle.

never better, a letter.

Noah's Ark, (1) a spoilsport or *nark*, (2) a shark.

ocean liner, mate. Ex rhyme on English slang *china* (*plate*).

Oliver Twist, wrist. English rhyming slang has it for "fist".

one another, brother. English has rhyming slang *one and t'other* for brother.

Onkaparinga, finger. (Placename in Victoria.)

Oscar (*Asche*), cash.

over there, hair.

ozone, a (tele)phone.

passing by, a florin. Ex rhyme on *swy*, two.

Paterson (*Laing*), (1) two, (2) a florin, ex name of Sydney firm Paterson, Laing and Bruce = deuce. (Sydney only.)

Pat Malone, on one's own, alone. Also *Pat Maloney*.

pay me rent, tent.

pear and quince, prince.

penny brown, town.

pickled pork, walk. English rhyming slang has it for "talk".

pig's arse, glass.

pill, a foolish or insignificant person. Rhyme on *dill*.

pitch and toss, boss.

plonkdot, see *wine-dot*.

plum pood, good.

Port Melbourne pier, an ear. (Melbourne use.)

red hots, trotting races. Rhyme on *trots*.

Ricketty Dick, (1) a stick, (2) penis, i.e. *prick*.

roaring horsetails, the Aurora Australis.

roaring rain, train.

rogan, a shilling. Ex English rhyming slang *rogue and villain*, shilling.

rolling deep, sleep.

roses red, bed.

Roy Sluice, a florin. Ex name as rhyme on *deuce*.

ruby moon, a spoon.

sealing wax, tax.

Sexton Blakes, shakes. English usage has it for "cakes".

shake and shiver, river.

ship's tank, Yank. Ex R.A.N. use of *tank* for hammock.

silly galoot, (1) sexual intercourse (rhyme on *root*), (2) boots, when in plural.

slippery dip, (1) hip, (2) lip.

Smellburn, Melbourne.

snakes, urination. Ex *snake's hiss*, rhyme on *piss*.

soft as silk, milk.

sons of guns, gums.

squatter's daughter, water.

steak and kidney, Sydney (the place or name of person).

steam tug, a pug (pugilist). English rhyming slang has it for a (bed) bug.

Steve Hart, a fart.

stop thief, beef.

strangle, mother. Ex *strangle and smother*, used as a rhyme on "mother".

St Vitus' dance, pants.

submarine, (1) queen, (2) a male homosexual. Rhyme on *queen* or *quean*, so-used.

Swanee Rivers, shivers, cf. *Hawkesbury Rivers*.

Sydney Harbour, barber, cf. *Coff's Harbour*.

teddy bear, a flashily-dressed young man. Rhyme on *lair*.

teller of tales, nails.

terrace of houses, trousers.

these and those, (1) toes, (2) nose.

thick and thin, (1) gin, (2) skin.

this and that, (1) bat, (2) hat.

tiger, a swim. Ex Tiger Tim. Whence, *tiger in the bols*, a swim without clothes, *bols* being abbreviated from *bollicky*.

tin lids, "kids", children.

tintack, sixpence, i.e. *zack*.

to and from, a Briton. Rhyme on *Pom*.

toe, take it on the, to go (this is a marginal case and perhaps should not be included here).

Tom and Sam, jam.

tomato sauces, horses, i.e. horse races.

twist and twirl, girl.

two-wheeler, girl. Rhyme on *sheila*.

Uncle Ned, bread. English rhyming slang has it for bed and head.

Val Quirk, shirt. (Melbourne use.) Ex name of once-noted boxing referee.

Warwick Farm, arm. Whence, *woofy* (or *whiffy*) *under the Warwicks*, said of a perspiration smell in the armpits. (Localized to N.S.W.)

wasp and bee, tea.

weight for age, page.

willy wag, a swag. Ex *Willie Wagtail*, the Australian bird.

wine-dot, a habitual drinker of (cheap) wine. Ex rhyme on *Wyandotte*, the domestic fowl. By transference, *plonk-dot*.

It is worth noting that in America an odd myth has developed about Australia's use of rhyming slang. A section of the U.S. underworld uses a good deal of rhyming slang and, for some reason unexplained, this is described as "Australian" in the United States.

Dr David W. Maurer, the leading authority on U.S. underworld argots, sent me a list of 352 rhyming slang examples which are classed as "Australian" in America. "This list", he wrote, "has been thoroughly checked by criminals from various parts of the country and, while it is not complete, it is representative of criminal usage." He added that this rhyming slang "is largely an institutional or semi-institutional argot, since it is mostly used in prisons. It is obscure and little known outside the underworld."

An analysis of Maurer's list showed that less than 3 per cent of the terms were definitely Australian; 49 per cent were original Americanisms; 48 per cent had been imported from England; 88 per cent had never been recorded in Australia.

A large proportion of the American borrowings from Cockney are extremely old, many of them being recorded in "The Vulgar Tongue" (1857), by "Ducange Anglicus", and in J. C. Hotten's "Slang Dictionary" (1859).

Although small, the Australian element in the list was highly interesting. The nine definite examples are: *Captain Cook*, a look; *cockie's clip*, a dip (a pickpocket); *Cobar shower*, a flower; *Hawkesbury Rivers*, shivers, *Kennedy rot*, a sot (a drunkard); *mad mick*, a pick; *Pat Malone*, alone; *mallee root*, a prostitute; *Sydney Harbour*, a barber. While *cockie's clip*; *Cobar shower* and *Kennedy rot* are certainly Australian, they are not used in this country in the rhyming senses listed by Maurer, which reduces the strict Australian element in this U.S. argot still more.

Several other terms in the list seem to have an indirect link with Australia. For instance, *Botany Bay*, "in the hay", i.e. asleep; *New South*, mouth (this is a common abbreviation for N.S.W.); *cabbage hat*, a rat, i.e. informer; *cabbage-tree*, to flee; *Jack Shay*, to slay (used in Australia for a tin quart-pot); and, perhaps most significant of all, *Kelly Ned*, the head, which seems to be an inverted tribute to the memory of Australia's Ned Kelly.

Only thirty-eight of the 352 terms given by Maurer had been recorded in Australia, and of these twenty-three are Australian borrowings from England also found in America.

It will probably remain one of the most baffling of philological problems how these terms got into American underworld argot with the senses allotted to them.

A special form of rhyming slang has developed in Australia in the past generation – doubtless because of U.S. precedent. These are the sound-duplications observable in *yeller-feller* (or *yellow-fellow*), a caste Aboriginal; *cobber-dobber*, one who betrays a friend, ex *cobber* (friend) and *to dob in* (to inform on); *cop-shop*, a police station; *walkie-chalkie*, a parking policeman; *grouse-mouse*, an attractive girl; *gas-lass*, an attractive and sexually willing female partner, which sometimes becomes *gassie-lassie* (both ultimately influenced by *gas-lash*, a highly satisfactory sexual experience); *drack-sack*, an unattractive girl (although, by inversion, it is sometimes used to indicate the opposite); *cock-shock*, the shock experienced by an unsophisticated girl at introduction to the facts of life.

The term *Fuzzy-wuzzy*, originally for any New Guinean, acquired special use during World War II; *Fuzzy-wuzzy angels* was used to denote the many natives who did splendid work for the Australian medical service. However, *Fuzzy-wuzzy* had been used long before in Africa, as a nickname, the Oxford Dictionary tells us, for "the Soudanese warrior, from his method of dressing his hair".

During the depression in the early 1930s, and probably based as much on grim experience as on spontaneous invention (those were days when verbal imagination provided a great deal of cheap entertainment), another form of rhyming slang was born in Australia. This consisted of internal rhymes on place-names, most of which were crisp comments. For example:

> *There ain't no work in Bourke.*
> *No lucre at Echuca.*
> *Damnall at Blackall.*
> *Things are crook at Tallarook (or Muswellbrook).*
> *Got a feed at the Tweed.*
> *No feedin' at Eden.*
> *Everything's wrong at Wollongong.*
> *Might find a berth in Perth.*
> *In jail at Innisfail.*
> *Got the arse at Bulli Pass.*

Depending on the speaker's experiences and imagination, this sort of rhyme could cover a considerable part of the Australian map. Interestingly enough, although such expressions had declined in use (and accuracy) by the mid-1930s, some were revived in World War II. Thus, the Tobruk Rats had something new to add to the expression *Things are crook at Tallarook (or Muswellbrook)*; their version was *Things are crook in old Tobruk*. And Australian soldiers in New Guinea, probably remembering *Things are drack at Toorak (or Coolac)* used the version, *Things are drack at Wewak*.

Only a few of these expressions remain – and where they do remain, their history is forgotten. The only comparable modern expression I have heard used is *Bung it in, Gunga Din!* addressed by a building labourer or manual worker to someone pouring concrete or tipping "fill" from a truck.

2. FAMILIARITY

ONE OF THE most constant features of Australian slang is its relentless familiarity. Not only is the tendency old in terms of our brief history, but in many respects it marks a dividing line which newcomers find extremely difficult to cross. There may be several reasons for this – first, perhaps, because these linguistic familiarities seem too trivial for serious attention to be given them, second, because they are difficult to work out and imitate. However, this Section will show that they reach into many corners of Australian life and are collectively far from trivial.

Let us begin with the *-o* suffix. Although this did not attain wide currency until after World War I (possibly as the result of Digger experience in France, where the *-o* suffix has a good deal of use among the lower echelons of society), we do not have to dig deeply into our yesterdays to find its existence here. The abbreviation *Abo* is extremely old. The *smoko* (*h*), a morning or afternoon break from work, is a recognised period of relaxation in woolsheds; it is now applied to any brief period of rest during work. The cry *sheepo!* also hailed originally from the woolshed; later, the form *sheepo* denoted a shepherd or anyone who raises sheep. In the days of cabbies, a *robbo* denoted a horse-drawn vehicle. The terms *goodo* and *righto* are mainly Australian in use and date back several generations; in its original form, *righto* largely served as a form of agreement or acceptance, but later it came to mean "That's enough!" and even "Stop it immediately!" Such permutations largely depend on the stress given to the word.

The *-o* suffix is often tacked on to abbreviated place-names, as in *Darlo*, Darlinghurst; *Flemo*, Flemington; *Kenso*, Kensington; *Kisso*, Kissing Point Road, Sydney; *Paddo*, Paddington; *Robbo Park*, Rosebery Park. It appears in popular names for various religions – *Bappo*, *Congo*, *Metho*, *Presbo*, *Salvo*, etc. It erupts in many given names such as *Billo*, *Daiso*, *Jacko*, *Jim(m)o*, *John(n)o*, *Maiso*, *Sallo* and *Tommo* (Australia's best-known two-up school is called *Tommo's*). It has appeared in such lines of business as *rabbito*, a rabbit seller (it is obsolete in this sense, but a rabbit-skinner is still called a *rabbito*), *bottle-o*, a bottle collector (that excellent term for a nonentity, *bottle-o's rouseabout*, should be remembered), and *The Journos* (a Sydney name for its Journalists' Club).

The following list is representative, but it does not claim to be complete since new confections ending in *-o* are continually emerging:

afto, afternoon. See *arvo*.

arvo, afternoon. Especially in the form *sarvo*, this afternoon.

Bappo, a Baptist.

beauto! a variant of *beaut!* as a term of approval.

beddo, bed.

bombo, cheap wine. Whence, *atombombo*, cheap wine of a lethal nature.

bottle-o, a bottle collector.

botto, a bottle.

bronzo, the anus. Ex *bronze*, used similarly.

bullo, nonsense, empty talk.

cacko, very drunk. (Reported from Victoria.)

cacto, the prickly-pear killing insect, cactoblastis.

Cappo, a Capstan cigarette.

cazo, a war casualty; anyone who has been injured in an accident. As adjective, casual, especially in reference to dress.

chromo, a prostitute.

cobbo, a friend or companion. Ex *cobber*, used similarly.

confo, conference.

Commo, a Communist.

commono, a clay marble.

compo, worker's compensation. Especially in the form *on the compo*, in receipt of worker's compensation.

Congo, a Congregationalist.

demo, a demonstration, especially a demonstration in the form of a public protest.

evo, evening.

galvo, galvanised iron.

garbo, (1) a garbage collector. Also called a *Greta*, ex the name Greta Garbo. (2) a garbage tin.

gastro, the illness known as gastro-enteritis.

go, a goanna.

gyvo or *guivo*, humbug, empty talk. Ex *guiver*, used similarly.

homo, a male homosexual.

ice-o, an iceman.

immigranto, the broken English often spoken by a non-British migrant to Australia in his early days here. (A combination of *immigrant* and *Esperanto*.)

Indo, Indonesia(n). This word was mainly used by Australia's "yellow Press", beginning in 1958, to fit headings. After a flirtation with it, the Melbourne "Sun-Pictorial" converted it to *Indon*.

info, information.

jacko, a kookaburra. Ex *jackass*.

jello, jealous.

jollo, a party or spree.

journo, a journalist.

kero, kerosene.

lavo, a lavatory.

lezo, a lesbian.

mando, a mandarin.

metho, a methylated spirits drinker, or methylated spirits.

Metho, a Methodist.

migro, a migrant (more specifically an immigrant).

milko, a milkman.

muso, a (professional) musician.

myxo, the rabbit-killing disease, myxomatosis.

Nasho, (1) National Service Training, *to do one's Nasho*, *to be Nashoed*. (2) A National Service trainee.

nebo, a habitual drunkard. Ex "inebriate".

oppo, an opportunity, especially in the expression *You've had your oppo!*

pendo, an appendix; appendicitis.

pinko, drunk.

plonko, a habitual drinker of cheap wine. See *plonk-dot* and *wine-dot* under Rhyming Slang.

polio, a sufferer from poliomyelitis.

prego, pregnant.

Presbo, a Presbyterian.

preso, the president of an organisation.

Protto, a Protestant.

rabbito, a rabbit seller or skinner.

rabbo, a rabbit.

Rasho, a member of the Rationalists' Society. (Reported from Melbourne.)

reffo, a refugee (i.e. a Jewish migrant from German-held territory before World War II).

recco, reconnaissance.

receppo, a reception.

reo, a (Service) reinforcement.

revo, revolution. Especially used in the phrase *come the revo*.

Salvo, a member of the Salvation Army.

sango (pronounced sang-o), a sandwich. Also *sando*.

sanno, a sanitary labourer or inspector.

scrappo, a fight. Ex *scrap*.

secko, a person suffering a sexual aberration.

smoko, a period of rest during work, usually for a cup of tea and a smoke.

sonno, an extension of "son" used as a form of address.

spello, a rest or break in work. Ex *spell*, used similarly.

susso, unemployment sustenance payment; a recipient of such payment. *on the susso*, in receipt of such payment.

sypho, syphilis.

thingo, thingumebob, whatsisname.

topo, a topographical map.

whacko! an exclamation of approval. Extended to *whacko the diddle-o!* and then to *whacko the did!*

wine-o, a habitual drinker of cheap wine. See *plonko*.

Homoeoteleutic forms ending in *-ie*, *-y*, *-ssie* and *-zzie* are numerous. "The Fact Digest" (U.S.) of August, 1937, reported: "Most natives of Australia have acquired the odd habit of adding *ie* to many of their words. For example, in the Antipodes many articles are described as *goodie*, *baddie* and *swellie*". The implication here, of course, is that we had only recently begun making hypocorisms of certain words, whereas in fact the process dates from our early days.

While he was doing time at Newcastle, in 1812, J. H. Vaux listed *woollie* for a sheep, and we have an 1825 record of *larky boys*, possibly an adumbration of *larrikin*. Many comparable expressions followed. For example, followers of John Wroe (1782–1863), founder of the Christian Israelites, were known particularly in Melbourne round the middle of last century as *beardies*, due to their long beards (later, they were also called *barber starvers*), and we have already seen how such expressions as *waddy*, *humpy*, *billy*, *cocky* and *Pommy* came into use. A Chinaman was called a *Chinky*, a Corriedale sheep a *Corrie*, a swagman's bundle of possession a *bluey*, and so on.

However, once more it was not until after World War I that what had been a minor feature of Australian slang became strongly marked. The following list is representative, but by no means complete:

anotherie, another drink, serving, helping, etc.

arsie (or *arsey*), lucky.

bandy, a bandicoot.

beachie, a beach fisherman.

berley, ground bait used by fishermen.

bickie, a biscuit.

blowie, a blowfly.

bluey, (1) a swagman's roll of possessions, (2) a blue blanket, (3) a special type of overcoat, (4) a lorikeet, (5) a red-haired or sandy-haired dog, (6) *Bluey*, nickname for a red-haired person.

brickie, a bricklayer.

budgie, a budgerigar, the small Australian parrot.

bushie, one who lives in the bush or outback.

chalkie, a schoolteacher.

charlie, a girl or woman.

chippy, a girl.

chewie, chewing gum. Whence, *do one's chewie*, to become angry or irritated. *Hope you have chewie on your boot!* used to express a wish that a football player kicking for goal misses because there is chewing gum on his boot.

chutty, chewing gum.

clippie, a person who checks and punches tickets at railway stations.

connie, a tram conductor.

crockie, (1) someone who is ill or a *crock*, (2) a crocodile.

crookie, (1) some act or report which is suspected of being dishonest, (2) a person who is ill, i.e. *crook*.

crownie, a bus inspector.

cunjie, cunjevoi, used as bait by fishermen.

dachsie, a dachshund.

darkie, (1) moonless conditions ideal for catching prawns, (2) a night shift.

diddie, a lavatory.

dustie, a garbage collector or "dustman".

fastie, (1) a cunning ruse, sharp practice; whence, *put over* (or *across*) a *fastie*, (2) a fast bowler in cricket.

flattie, a flat-bottomed boat.

footie, (1) football, especially the Australian Rules code, (2) a footpath.

glad(d)ies, gladiolas. Often cut to *glads*.

gooly, a gob of phlegm.

greenie, a lorikeet.

gummy, a type of shark.

hoddie, a hod-carrier or one who carries bricks.

hookie, a hook-worm inspector.

hottie, (1) a tall story, (2) a "hot" story, (3) an example of sharp business practice.

icky, sickly, unpleasant.

jelly, gelignite.

jewie, (1) a jewfish, any of three species of Australian fish, (2) a jew lizard.

Jindie, a Jindyworobak, a member of an Australian nationalistic literary group.

kingie, a kingfish.

kookie, a kookaburra.

lairy, (1) flashily dressed, (2) said of a *lair*.

larrie, a larrikin or street lout.

lavvy, a lavatory.

leatherie, a leather-jacket, a type of fish.

lesbie, a lesbian.
lippie, lipstick.
littlie, a young (hence, little) child.
lokie, a locust.
lollie or *lolly*, a sweetmeat. Ex English *lollipop*.
maggie, a magpie.
marjie, marihuana.
milkie, a milkman.
mouthie, a garrulous person.
muddy, a mud crab.
muffy, a frill-necked lizard.
mushy, a mushroom.
mutty or *mutt-eye*, a green cob of maize.
nanny, a nannygai, a type of fish.
newie, a new idea.
newsie, a seller of newspapers.
nuddy, naked. *in the nuddy*, undressed.
octy, an octopus.
pidgie, a pigeon.
pinkie, a rabbit-bandicoot.
plonkie, an addict of cheap wine or *plonk*.
pokie, a poker machine.
postie, a postman.
prawnie, a person who catches and/or sells prawns.
prem(m)ie, a premature baby.
queany (or *queeny*), an effeminate male or *quean* (or *queen*). As an adjective, referring to such a person.
queerie, (1) an eccentric person, (2) a male homosexual or *queer*.
quickie, a fast bowler in cricket.
ringie, a two-up ringkeeper.
rocky, a rock wallaby.
roughie, a shrewd or cunning ruse. Whence, *put over* (or *across*) *a roughie*.
schoolie, a school teacher.
scratchy, not much good.
scribbly, a scribblygum.
shangie, a child's catapult or *shanghai*.
shrewdie, (1) a shrewd or quick-witted person, (2) a shrewd ruse.
sickie, a day away from work because of a real or pretended illness.
simpy, a simpleton or stupid person.
slowie, (1) a slow bowler in cricket, (2) a person who moves and/or thinks slowly.
snaky, irritable, angry.
snarlie, a grim, depressed outlook; a hatred of everyone and everything. *have a snarlie on*, to be in such a frame of mind.
snowie, a skier.
sonky, silly, stupid and (of a male) effeminate.
souvy, to steal or *souvenir*.
spridgy, a sparrow. Also *sproggy*, *spudgy*.
stickie, (1) an inquisitive person, a *stickybeak*; also verb, to be inquisitive, (2) a humid day.
stringy, a stringybark tree.

stuffie, a baby crocodile, about 18 inches long, stuffed for sale. (Reported from N.T.)

swiftie, a cunning ruse, sharp practice. Whence, *work* (or *put over* or *put across*) *a swiftie*.

tallie, a tall story; a story that is hard to believe.

toughie, (1) a criminal, a "tough", (2) a difficult problem.

tram(m)ie, a tram driver or conductor.

trannie, a transistor radio.

truckie, a truck driver.

umpy, an umpire.

wobbie, a wobbegong, any one of several species of Australian ground shark.

woollie, a sheep. (First recorded in Australia in 1812.)

yachtie (pronounced "yottie"), a yachtsman.

To these can be added several terms which are usually employed in the plural, e.g. *blackies*, Aboriginal girls in an outback convent, *jackies*, Aborigines in general (both these terms are used by W. E. Harney in his "Taboo", 1943, along with *bushies*, people who live in the outback or bush); and *Woolies*, a Woolworths Store (used by H. C. Brewster in his "King's Cross Calling", 1944).

Many Australian placenames have been the subject of hypocoristic attention, but little purpose would be served by listing them in detail. Here are a few, to serve as illustrations: *Brissie*, Brisbane; *Bundy*, Bundaberg; *Freshy*, Freshwater (N.S.W.); *Newy*, Newcastle; *Woolly*, Wollongong.

An excellent example of abbreviation combined with both the *-ie* and *-o* suffixes occurs in the Sydney newsboy's cry, *Pape! Papie! Papo!*

The inclusion of *Brissie*, Brisbane, in the last collection of names serves to draw attention to a special form of hypocorism in Australia. The Australian speaker seems rarely able to resist the temptation to tamper with the form of words containing *s* or *z* sounds. Perhaps the key to this is the word *Australia* itself. In order to convert this into an endearment, the first syllable is treated as though it is *Aus* and *-sie* is added. However, although the spelling is *Aussie*, it is never pronounced accordingly, but always as *Ozzie*. This conflict remains fairly constant throughout the terms listed below, and has been complicated by accepted spellings in the Press and books. Thus, although *Brissie* is the common spelling of the hypocorism for Brisbane it is always pronounced as though the spelling were *Brizzie*. By the same token, although *possie* is the usual spelling for the mutilated form of "position", it is always pronounced as *pozzie*. In short, many of these words have to be learnt individually.

Aussie, Australia(n). Whence *Aussieland*, *dinkum* (or *dinky-di*) *Aussie*.

brassie, a brassière.

Brissie, Brisbane.

bussie, a bus driver or conductor.

Chrissie, Christmas. Whence, *Chrissie prezzie*, a Christmas present.

chryssie, a chrysanthemum.

cozzie, a swimming costume.

Glassie, the Glaciarium ice rink, Sydney, closed in 1955.

goozie, a gooseberry.
gussie, an effeminate male.
Kozzie, Mt Kosciusko.
lizzie, a lizard.
mozzie, a mosquito.
possie, a position.
prezzie, a present.
prossie, a prostitute.
squizzie, a look or examination.
Tazzie, Tasmania(n).
thissie or thattie, this one or that one, as an enquiry.
tizzie, a spasm of annoyance or confusion, *in a tizzie*.
tossie, the spinner in a game of two-up.
trezzie (or *trizzie*), a threepence.

These suffixes are reflected in the following hypocoristic forms of given names: *Crissie*, Christopher, Christobel; *Bazzie*, Basil; *Flossie*, Florence; *Dezzie*, Desmond; *Ozzie*, Oswald; *Nessie*, Nesta.

Worth brief notes are *bitzie*, that which is made of bits and pieces, or an adjective descriptive of the nature of such a thing, and *boysie*, a nickname for a boy.

Indirectly related to words with the *-ie* or *-y* suffix is another group ending in *-ee*. One example of Antipodean origin that has had an exceedingly long history in this country is *escapee*, used to denote a person who escapes from jail or some other place of confinement. It has been current for some eighty years and is reputed to have been inherited through the French influence of New Caledonia. It was originally applied, at all events, to convicts escaping from that Pacific Island, and was apparently formed on the French word *échappé*, on the basis of such terms as *absentee* and *refugee*. More recent examples that have found their way into print in Australia are: *murderee*, the victim of a murderer; *insultee*, a person who will react to an insult; *standee*, a person who stands while travelling in a bus; *quizee*, a person who participates in a quiz; *touchee*, a person who is exploited by another's cupidity, derived from the use of *touch* for an act of borrowing; *ballotee*, a person who takes part in a ballot (this is an illogical example, unless we class as a *balloter* the person arranging the ballot, and for this person the expressions *balloteer* and *ballotist* are already in standard English); *puttee-out*, a person who has been put out or rejected; *massagee*, a person who is massaged or given treatment by a masseur; *interviewee*, a person who is interviewed; *hypnotee*, a person who submits to hypnotism; *bashee*, a person who is being *earbashed* – I suppose it could also denote someone who suffers an actual bashing.

It is of passing etymological interest to note that the Melbourne "Herald" has abandoned "-ee" endings. Thus it renders *employee* as *employe*, which is slightly confusing to the unprepared reader, who may have forgotten or never known that this was the original form (1834) in English – *employé* for a male worker, *employée* for a female worker. However, *employee* (without any accent) was in use for either sex in 1854.

Another group of terms meriting attention possesses the suffix *-up*. It is common in English for *up* to be added in a verbal sense, thus *mess up, rust up, knock up*, and even for certain nounal forms to emerge; but this latter development has been more strongly fostered in colloquial speech in Australia than anywhere overseas. Thus we have a *box-up*, a confusion or muddle (originally of sheep mixed together); *bush-up*, a case in which a person is lost, especially in the bush; *booze-up, beer-up* and *drunk-up*, a drinking party; *eat-up*, a meal; *frig-up* or *muck-up*, a confusion, a row or argument; *quean-up, lair-up* and *mocker-up*, a dressing-up; *bunk-up*, an assistance or helping hand, especially in mounting a horse or in succeeding in life; *rough-up, smack-up* and *stoush-up*, a fight; *ready-up*, a case in which illegal methods are used to influence the outcome of a decision or action; *roll-up*, an attendance at a meeting; *slug-up*, the equivalent of the U.S. frame-up; *wake-up*, a person who is alert.

The verbal Australian uses of *roll up*, to attend a meeting (from 1861 or earlier), *bail up* and *stick up* can be added.

3. SHORTENING

AN ESSENTIAL FEATURE of linguistic development is that it always moves in the direction of word-shortening. Resistance against this in the United States of America, seen in the preference for *apartment* rather than *flat*, *elevator* rather than *lift*, *spigot* or *faucet* rather than *tap*, *automobile* rather than *car*, *locomotive* rather than *engine*, *saloon* rather than *pub*, etc., may partly account for the linguistic stupor in which Americans find themselves today. In Australia, the shorter word is generally chosen in popular use when an alternative is available – even if, in the process, we part with a well-established Australian term. Thus we have seen the currency of *sheila*, a girl, diminished by the English slang *bird; lout* or *hoodlum* is displacing *larrikin;* we are showing a strong tendency to prefer *campus* to *university grounds;* we are more likely to ask for our steak *rare* than *underdone;* *airplane* is displacing *aeroplane;* the *U.S. peanut* has so far edged out the English *monkey nut* or *ground nut* that we hardly know what the latter terms mean.

This tendency goes back a long way. In a note to the word *super*, for a station or police superintendent, the "Modern Dictionary" (1912: Macmillan and Company) declared: "Colonial slang is given to such-like abbreviations". *Super* is also a common abbreviation of super-phosphate.

In this way we find *dile* clipped out of crocodile; *go* and *hanna* from goanna; *tri* from triantelope, the spider; *kanga* and *roo* from kangaroo; *mu* from emu; *lew* from curlew; *pine* from porcupine. We have taken *Tatt's*[3] from Tattersall's; *uni* from university; *Vic.* from Victoria; *New South* from New South Wales; *sesquis* which was used to denote Australia's sesqui-

---

[3] *To take a ticket in Tatt's* means to buy a ticket in Tattersall's sweepstakes, Victoria. *Safe as Tatt's* is synonymous with perfect safety. (It can be added that the *Casket* is the popular name by which the Golden Casket Lottery, Queensland, is known.)

centenary celebrations; *upta* from *up to putty; dofer*, a cigarette butt, from "do for afterwards"; *House of Reps* from the House of Representatives; *perc* from percolator; *dig* from dignity; *para* from paratrooper; *la* and *lala* from lavatory; *delink* from delinquent; *bung* from bungalow, and so on in their scores.

When Child Endowment was introduced in Australia in 1941 it quickly produced the expressions *dows* and *duds, dows* signifying those children for whom parents received en*dow*ment allowances, and *duds* those for whom parents received nothing.

It can be seen that the Australian is not particular where he clips words – the beginning, middle or end. He even clips what has already been clipped. Thus "this afternoon" becomes *this after*, then *this afto* or *this arvo* or *sarvo* and finally *sarve*; Communist becomes *commo* and then *com;* in receipt of unemployment sustenance becomes *on the susso* and then *on the suss.* It is to be expected, therefore, that the Australian will not be shy in cutting down even those expressions which he has invented himself, such as *pom* as a clipped version of *pommy; hop* from *johnhop; ding* from *dingbat; stick* from *stickybeak.*

Melbourne University students use the word *caf* for their cafetaria (it has more of a reputation as a centre for conversation than for eating); they call their "buffetaria" *the buf;* they refer to practical class work as *prac.*

Such abbreviations are fairly general in all languages, but there is a special feature in Australian speech on which comment must be made. We have seen some part of this in the previous Section in such an example as *Chrissie prezzie* for a Christmas present. This can be looked on as (1) baby talk or (2) woman's talk, but in terms of fact it extends far beyond this. True, one can feel fairly sure that a woman will be heard saying, "*Dins* will be ready in a *min*" (i.e. dinner will be ready in a minute), but it is not impossible that you will hear (as I have heard) a man referring to his main meal of the day as *din-din*, that he will say *ta* for thanks and *ta-ta* for good-bye. Since, if you listen closely, it is more than likely that you will hear the same man using such expressions as *kern oath!, bullsh, cowsh, frogsh, filmsh, shouse* and *touse*, it is difficult to regard such terms as other than manifestations of our lasting discontent with leaving words as they are.

4. BACK SLANG AND GIBBERISH

ALTHOUGH "The Detectives' Handbook" of the early 1880s included a short glossary of back slang – apparently with the object of showing that it had some currency in this country at the time – remarkably little of this type of argot is known in Australia. Here are a few examples from "The Detectives' Handbook" to show what is meant by back slang; *dab*, bad; *delo nammow*, old woman; *delog*, gold; *helbat*, table; *nair*, rain; *occabot*, tobacco; *wedge*, Jew; *yad*, day. All these are English importations.

The nearest we can approach to argot of this type is to be found in transpositions of syllables in a number of cases, among which are the following: *eilasha*, a girl, by transposition from *sheila; eeler-spee*, from *spieler* (*eeler-whack* is also used, being more current in the form *whack the illy*, to act as a *spieler*); and *aster-bar*, from bastard. As I noted earlier, this sort of word-mutilation has a minor use among members of the Australian underworld. It is mainly notable for the use of the suffix *-ar*, as distinct from the U.S. use of *-ay* endings. For example, where American crooks would say *ixnay* for *nix*, as a warning or to denote "nothing", their Australian counterparts say *ixnar*. This form of gibberish is known in the Australian underworld as *pig Latin* (or *igpar atinlar* if it is applied to that term). In English slang something similar is called *bog Latin, dog Latin, garden Latin* or *kitchen Latin*. Here are examples provided by one of my underworld contacts: *on the apstrar*, on the strap (penniless), *ucklebar*, buckle (arrest), *ugmar*, mug (victim), *opcar*, cop (see), *oppercar*, copper (policeman), *on the oetar*, on the toe (to run), *illywar*, willy (wallet), *eetswar*, sweet (easily), *ollrar of appar*, roll of pap (banknotes), *itsplar*, split (a division of spoils). I refer the reader to Chapter VII for detailed references to these underworld uses. A few general examples: *ogar*, go, *entwar*, went, *eftlar*, left, *ealstar*, steal, *ationstar*, station, *opstar*, stop, *eetstrar*, street, *eethrar*, three, *unkdrar*, drunk, *ornercar*, corner. Any words which begin with a vowel or the letter *h* cannot be changed in *pig Latin*.

Children are often expert in this type of secret language. This form of slang, or, as it was once called in Queensland, *lotus language*, had some popularity among larrikin pushes round the turn of the century.

Useful examples were given by a writer in the "Bulletin" of May 25, 1901. As can be seen below these are of varying types:

Itsynay, oysbay, erethay omecay ethay eachertay; uspay emthay incesquay intha ourya ocketspay.

Gerriger worriger. Gerriger ariger biriger origer liriger lariger.

Givesy mevesy thavesy bumpvesyervesy whevesy youvesy arevesy dovesy wivesy wesy.

Nitsy, boys, here comes the teacher; put them quinces in your pocket.

Get work. Get a bit of light labour.

Give me that bumper when you are done with it.

The same writer noted the following special alphabet used by the larrikin pushes: A, Bub, Cung, Dud, E, Fuf, Gug, Huh, I, Juh, Kuk, Lul, Mum, Nun, O, Pup, Quh, Rus, Sus, Tut, U, Vuv, Wuh, X (pronounced Ux), Yuh, Zuz. He said that a means adopted by the larrikins to talk without being understood by the uninitiated was to spell out words with this alphabet. Thus, "what" would be rendered *Wuh Huh A Tut*, and so on.

Here is an example of what was once called *lotus language*, dating from 1901:

Carpum rarpound harpeyarpere Tarpom. Tharpat arpold blopoke barpit marpee jarpust narpow arpand arpime gopoarping tarpoo garpive harpim arpay barpump.

Come round here Tom. That old bloke bit me just now and I'm going to give him a bump.

This form of language is better known as gibberish or ziph in English and as *le javanais* or *la langue de Java* in French.

In his excellent study of French argots, "Le Langage Parisien", Sainéan points out that gibberish was popular among Metz children in the seventeenth and eighteenth centuries.

In Hungary a form of gibberish known as *Madárnyelv* or bird language is current among children. This is formed by the intrusion of a consonant – mainly the letter *v* – and a vowel after each syllable of the words being spoken. Nonsense-language in which words are given the sound of real words, but are really quite meaningless, is known in Hungary as *Halandzsa*.

Germany has a form of gibberish closely allied to the English. Grose says that in English-speaking countries gibberish is "a disguised language formed by inserting any consonant between each syllable". If the letter chosen is *g* it is called "the *g* gibberish", if *f* "the *f* gibberish" and so on.

As we have seen in the above Australian examples, there is also gibberish in which syllables like *arp* or *vesy* are intruded. In German-speaking countries a gibberish where, say, the letter *b* is inserted after all syllables is known as *B Sprache*. Thus, *ich habe gestern Anna gesehen* becomes *ibich hababebe gebestebern Abannaba gebesebeheben*. The *b* is interchangeable with other consonants. Another form of German gibberish is found in the changing of vowels in a sentence so that all become identical. Thus *Ei da sitzt' ne Flieg' and der Wand* becomes *I di sitzt' ni Flig' in dir Wind*.

An excellent example of highly confused gibberish as used in Australia was recorded by a writer in the "Bulletin" of January 18, 1902, and ran as follows:

Dojaynarithinsorear Borillyjayrul-litaysithinorin, Poritinkayruatayreeter K. dayrithintjayrusint knayrittysay-fithinorow moritchjayritchchorutch a-tithinjopithinkaybout Austrorittyjori-thinapletralian slorithinkojithinayrang, joridgayrudgchayrithinoring boritty-saykittyory thoritinayrithince soritin-chaysithinjorimpitayrample horittykos-itty jorugoritgsjaysayrot orithinsaychi-thinoroff horithinsaydithinoris chayrit-tyjokittsayrest iritinkaybittinorin B 4/5/01.

Dear Bulletin, Peter K [the nom-de-plume of a correspond-ent] doesn't know much about Australian slang, judging by the sample he got off his chest in B 4/5/01.
[This comment refers to the ex-ample given earlier beginning: Carpum rarpound . . .]

Although he did not give examples to prove his point, Crowe stated in 1895 that back slang was "much used by street sellers and some larrikins as the channel of conveying their ideas". From the material available it seems likely that Crowe was misled by the Australian use of transpositions and gibberish.

The gibberish expression *milfist the balfastards!* was reported to have been in use among Australian airmen in Lae Valley, New Guinea, early in 1944. It signified a faulty manoeuvre or a miss. The origin was a gibberish story which reputedly ran:

Jumping into a trulfuck I went out with my gulfang to shoot dulfucks. After a while I saw some dulfucks. I lifted my gulfang, which went balfang! balfang! balfang! Alas, milfist the balfastards!

Jumping into a truck I went out with my gun to shoot ducks. After a while I saw some ducks. I lifted my gun, which went bang! bang! bang! Alas, missed the bastards!

A correspondent reports that "oppen-gloppen" gibberish was current among students at Hornsby Girls High School, N.S.W., in the mid-1950s. This gibberish is formed by placing the syllable "op" before every pronounced vowel in a word. Thus *Opi hopave opa bopook* means "I have a book", and *Yopou opare mopad* means "You are mad". This gibberish becomes extremely complicated with multi-syllabic words, such as "circumstances", which is rendered c(*op*)irc(*op*)umst(*op*)anc(*op*)es and pronounced "sopperkoppumstoppansoppes".

CHAPTER XVIII

New Words

1. PORTMANTEAU WORDS

TO THIS STAGE, we have been particularly interested in slang words and phrases which have erupted more or less spontaneously in Australian speech. We will have observed that most of them have been pushed up out of the proletarian bog, some to wither almost immediately on exposure to the air, some to change their meanings vastly over the years, just a few to become respectable. And we will have become conscious of the fact that not many colloquial expressions have been consciously contrived and imposed from above.

This brief chapter will be mainly concerned with examining various linguistic contrivances. The first of them is the portmanteau word. Now, in essence, a portmanteau word represents the manipulation of language in such a way that a single word will serve to combine two otherwise alienated concepts. Examples: *disarmistice, impropaganda, tavernacular, insinuendo, riffrafferty rules, surburbanity, alcoholiday.* Quite a number of confections of this kind have won themselves an enduring place in the English language. Lewis Carroll, for instance, invented *chortle*, presumably a marriage of "chuckle" and "snort", and *squawk*, possibly from "squeak" and "squall". *Dumbfound* was a marriage of "dumb" and "confound", *luncheon* allegedly came from "lunch" and the older word "nuncheon", meaning a light refreshment, *electrolier* came from electric and chandelier, *travelogue*, from "travel" and "monologue", *cablegram* from "cable" and "telegram", and *gerrymander* from "Gerry" and "salamander". Most of these have become part of our standard speech and we would feel at a loss if we were robbed of them.

Expressions such as these are usually given their original shapes by authors, journalists and others supposedly blessed with high levels of intelligence and whimsical senses of humour. Oddly enough, one of Australia's first (and longest enduring) efforts in this field was *squattocracy*, a combination of "squatter" and "aristocracy" or "autocracy", which came into use before 1846 to denote big land-owners or *squatters* in general. This portmanteau word seems to have taken shape without help from journalists. The same can be said of *triantelope*, popular name for the huntsman spider, which is a corruption of "tarantula" with "antelope" quite absurdly involved; it also dates back to 1846. The combination of *jimmy*, a migrant from Britain, and "immigrant" gave us *jimmigrant*, and although the last term has become obsolete there is some likelihood that it provoked the rhyming slang *pomegranate* and that this led to *pommy* and ultimately to *pom* as a nickname for an Englishman. These examples are enough to suggest that a portmanteau word should not be ignored because of its novelty; the possibility of enduring life, which haunts all slang, may suddenly emerge, and what at one stage seems too trivial to bear thinking about may last for generations. With these thoughts in mind, I offer the following list of portmanteau words culled from various Australian sources:

Aboriginality, a brief story on an Aboriginal or bush subject. *Aboriginalities* was a feature in the old "Bulletin", first introduced in 1888. *Aboriginaliar* and *Aboliar* were developments.

Abostralian, an Australian Aboriginal.

aggranoy and *aggrovoke*, combinations of "annoy", "aggravate" and "provoke".

barbecorgy, excessive eating and drinking (an "orgy") at a "barbecue".

bedroominess, comments on bedroom conduct (in novels).

bookmobile, a van used for transporting library books. (This is now a standard use.)

bossaroo, a combination of "boss" and "kangaroo", or, if spelt *bosseroo*, a combination of "boss" and "jackeroo".

bustitution, the substitution of buses for tram transport.

coalopolis, Newcastle, N.S.W. – a "metropolis" where there are large coal deposits.

comic strippery, having reference to comic strips.

complexasperation, impatience with psychiatry, especially with what psychiatrists know as complexes.

factuality, realism – a combination of "fact" and "actuality". (It could, of course, be regarded as a straightforward extension of "factual".)

horsecaster, a radio "broadcaster" who reports on horse-races. See *racetator*.

imbuggerance, indifference strengthened by allusion to the phrase *don't care a bugger*.

jackeranding, a combination of *jackerooing* and *jacaranda*.

junglyrics, songs or lyrics written in the jungle.

juntocracy, a combination of "junta" and "autocracy".

kangaberger, minced kangaroo meat fried like a hamburger.

kangarooster, suggested name for offspring of Australian-U.S. marriages.

liftophonist, a lift driver, influenced by "telephonist".

lusterette, an attractive or "luscious" theatre usherette.

magniflorious, excellent – a combination of "magnificent" and "glorious".

merinoceros, a fantasied combination of the characteristics of a merino sheep and a rhinoceros.

musicolumn, a newspaper feature devoted to comments on music.

piecartist, a man who sells pies from a cart or movable stall.

presstitute, a woman journalist.

pulperising, the marketing of pulp magazines.

racetator, a radio reporter who gives "commentaries" on "races". See *horsecaster*.

riffrafferty rules, a rough-and-tumble contest in which no rules are observed.

Santaclaustrophobia, an alleged ailment suffered by people at Christmas time.

Sovietiquette, social customs and manners in Russia.

squatteroo, a combination of "squatter" and "jackeroo".

stamineer, to strengthen (of motor trucks) – a combination of "engineer" and "stamina".

thievocracy, the world of thieves.

tomboystrous, descriptive of the activities of high-spirited girls.

war bookery, the writing of war books.

2. NEOLOGISMS

HE WOULD be an extremely brave man who would predict in Australia that what seems to be a nonce-word, i.e. a word coined for one occasion, may not in fact prove to be a neologism destined for protracted use and that it will not, under a different guise, find a permanent place in our vocabulary. Such terms as *squattocracy* and *triantelope,* at which we cast brief looks in the previous Section, probably had minimal futures when they were invented, yet the former remained current for at least eighty years and the latter is still with us after at least 120 years of use.

Here is an assortment of neologisms culled from the pages of Australian writers: *hardupness,* a state of penury, *bungfoodled,* deceived, *jackerooesses,* female jackeroos (Henry Lawson); *hit the white,* to succeed, *alcoholizers,* drunkards, *to scratch,* to travel fast (Rolf Boldrewood); *snorky,* disagreeable, *shurried,* hastened, *spine-pringling,* electrifying (Norman Lindsay); *burstatiously, parvanimity, supertoploftical,* the intended meanings are not clear (Miles Franklin); *squdgy,* soft, swampy, *weirdities,* oddities, *skinship,* the relationship of one Aboriginal to another – in some respects, this is an orthodox term (Ernestine Hill); *degibber,* to remove stones from something, *bananaologist,* an expert on bananas (S. W. Keough); *buttonedupness,* a person's silence (Henry Handel Richardson); *grasshoppery,* pertaining to grasshoppers (K. S. Prichard); *disant,* to remove ants from one's person (Charles Shaw); *ramshackles,* poorly-constructed buildings (Gavin Casey); *backyarder,* a person who makes things in the backyard of his home (N. Coulihan); *gun-hunted,* hunted with a gun (Carl Warburton).

Although many of the words in the following list seem to have little to recommend them, we should not be too hasty in our judgment. My own view is that we shall hear more of some of them again.

Aboism, (of art) characterised by Aboriginal motifs.

anti-cobberism, contrary to the Australian concept of the value of *cobbers,* friends or mates.

bargainised, (of goods in a shop) to be sold as bargains.

bargainophobia, dislike of bargain sales in department stores.

Bradmania, dislike of the former Australian cricketer, Sir Donald Bradman.

bushery, as for next.

bushwhackery, the writing of stories, novels and poems about the Australian bush or outback.

Caucussed, (of a Labor Party representative) to be called before the Labor Caucus to answer questions.

chophouse, a Chinese restaurant.

cumberband, a cummerbund. (Probably more a Hobson-Jobson distortion than a neologism.)

defongerate, to rebuff, to send away. (Twice used in "The Battling Prophet" by A. W. Upfield, 1956, and probably to be classed more as slang than a neologism.)

depommification, (of a person) induced to surrender English (*Pommy*) characteristics. (This occurs in the title of a 1963 book, "The Dinkumization and Depommification of an Artful English Immigrant", by Bernard Hesling.)

deprotected, removed from price protection given by wartime regulations.

dinkumed, (of a person) converted into a genuine Australian – *dinkum Aussie*.

dinkumization, (of a person) given genuine (*dinkum*) Australian characteristics. See *depommification*.

farmerette, a female farmer.

forelady, a woman who supervises workers in a factory. (Female equivalent of "foreman", although by implication the latter should be "foregentleman".)

guested, (of a person) acting as a guest in a radio or TV session.

gumleavesy, redolent of gumtree leaves. (This was descriptive of a book.)

gusting, (of wind) blowing in gusts.

heatburst, a heatwave.

hosting, (of a person) acting as a host.

I'm-all-right-Jackness, an attitude of indifference to the wishes and welfare of others.

litterbug, (1) someone in favour of the new Roman Catholic liturgy with its increased use of English, (2) a student in literature in the English Department of Sydney University.

lurkmanship, (of commercial firms) a contest marked by the use of ruses or *lurks*.

moding, a reduction in intensity – a "moderating".

mothed, consumed or partly consumed by moths.

outbackery, as for *bushwhackery*.

out-lurked, (of a firm) out-done by an opponent in exploitation of a commercial ruse or *lurk*.

outshopped, (of a firm) to produce from its assembly line or workshop.

phrop, a name given to "a *phrase* that means the exact *opp*osite to what it seems to mean".

politicalize, to give political colouring to.

pommified, coloured by English (*Pommy*) characteristics. Also *pomminess*. See *depommification*.

post-mortemisation, the holding of inquiries into causes.

pure merinodom, the "socially elect" in Australia.

queuer, a person who joins a queue.

rendezvoused, to have met by arrangement. Also *rendezvou'd*.

scrumpter, a word that can mean anything the user wishes it to mean. Also *scrump*.

sequenced, put in proper order of sequence.

snorking, (of a submarine) to travel underwater with its snorkel raised to draw in fresh air.

teenicide, the suicidal activities of teenagers (in car driving).

townette, a village or small town.

trialled, to be tested or given a trial.

trombistic, (of music) suitable for playing on a trombone.

upheavalists, men who work on road construction.

verse, to oppose. Whence, *versed*, said of an opponent. Ex "versus".

whackfest, a game notable for its powerful hitting of a ball. (This use of the German *Fest* for "festival" is common in the U.S.)

wholesaling, (goods on sale) at wholesale prices.

yakker, a conversation. A mistake for the Australian *yabber* influenced by U.S. *yak*, which occasionally means to talk, to gossip.

younging, becoming younger.

A few other neologisms are also worth noting. *Atokism* is a brand of political faith espoused by a trifling group of adherents in Sydney. In brief, the object of *atokism* is to abolish all interests and rents. It was originated by Louis Phillips. Primary hate of *atokists* is the *tokocracy*, "interest mongers who derive huge profits from war".

Consider also what L. G. DeGaris, of Geelong, Victoria, has been doing to language over the years. Mr DeGaris has some strong views on the subject of economics and has gone so far in developing what he calls a "credit crusade" that he has had to concoct a number of original terms in order to keep pace with his ideas. At the top of his list is the word *wice*, defined as "the standard unit of labour for the standard week's work of 40 hours, giving the standard output of 80 grains of gold". Mr DeGaris explains that the word *wice* is an Anglo-Saxon term meaning "week", and that it can also stand for "*W*eekly *I*ndividual *C*laim for *E*nergy *E*xpended". It has been given attributive as well as nounal uses, e.g. *wice currency*, and it has several associated expressions: *basenwice*, "a unit of currency issued for the basic-week's work", a basic wage issued to each person each week; *standanwice*, "a unit of price to provide the standard of living in exchange for the week's work" or "the unit of output in products available in exchange for the basenwice"; and *freowice*, "the unit or profit from which leisure is claimed" or "the unit of surplus output of products, for interest, pensions and incentives to efficiency". To these terms, Mr DeGaris adds *consumet*, "that which has been consumed", *debtocracy, debtarchy, debtarchs, mensiversary* (a "monthly" version of anniversary), *ruripolis*, a garden city in the country, *ruriculture, rusurb* (a suburb of a ruripolis), *facturban*, (a factory town), *orbipolis* (a "world city"), *archipolis*, (a "Federal city"), *centripolis* (a "State city"), *nerp*, a daily routine (which Mr DeGaris says he took from "*New Routine Plan*"), *nerping*, "unexpected changes in routine", *eco-semantics*, "vocabulary in economics", *societal*, "an attitude of society" and *pseudoxy*, "false opinion". These expressions Mr DeGaris uses in carrying on his fight for a new economic deal for us all and in exposing the fallacies of such doctrines as Douglas Credit.

3. -ORIUMS, -OLOGISTS, ETC.

SINCE THE END of World War II, Australia has been heavily burdened by -*oriums* and -*ologists* of various kinds. The idea behind them is quite legitimate – for instance, "emporium" and "biologists" are impeccably standard uses – but even the most tolerant observer is likely to reel away from some of the recent offerings. Like most philological lunacies of such type, they stemmed from the U.S. We have doubtless added some splendours of our own, but these and associated endings are too new for an adequate reference to their countries of origin to have been compiled. However, whereas a *lubritorium* is part of a garage where a motor vehicle is greased and provided with oil, we can certainly claim *lubratorium* (reported from Kiama, N.S.W.) as our own, although there are reasons to suspect that this spelling eccentricity was accidental. It serves to remind me that there is a service station called The Gunyah at Mt. Colah where the amenities are labelled *Jackies* and *Jeddas*.

Here is a round-up of terms reported from various parts of Australia:

alterologist, a tailor's shop.
barbertorium, a barber's shop.
birdmobile, a poultry truck.
botologist, a bottle-collector.
bullologist, an expert judge of bulls.
calfeteria, an automatic gadget for feeding calves.
cargo-ologist, a waterside worker.
chemitel, a chemist's shop (formed on *motel*).
clothing architects, a dry-cleaning firm.
debtorium, a debt-collecting agency.
dentologist, a panelbeater.
discologist, a radio station employee who has the duty of changing records – a *disc jockey*.
dollologist, a collector of dolls.
eatel, a restaurant (formed on *motel*.)
farmorama, a roadside stall selling fresh eggs, honey, etc.
fish and chipscatessen, a fish and chip shop.
fishatorium, a fish shop.
fishorium, a fish shop.
flatel, a motel.
fruitician, a fruiterer.
fruitologist, a fruiterer.
groceteria, a grocer's shop.
grocetarium, a grocer's shop.
hygiene assistant, a night-soil carter.
infanteen, a shop selling clothes and other goods for babies.
infantorium, shop specialising in the sale of clothes and other goods for children.
mindery, a crèche at a church.
mixatorium, a delicatessen.

mixologist, a person who mixes cocktails.

plantorium, a shop specialising in the sale of plants, seeds and other garden equipment.

potatorium, a roadside stall selling potatoes.

preventorium, an institution established for the "prevention" of disease in children.

ragologist, a person who collects rags.

restorium, a restroom for elderly adults.

rubbishologist, a garbage collector.

salamorium, part of a shop where salamis are sold.

shaveologist, a barber.

stockist, a shop which sells spare parts for motor vehicles.

suitorium, a tailor's shop.

toolorium, part of a hardware shop where tools are sold. (It includes a saw bar!)

towbartorium, a firm that fits towbars to motor vehicles.

transportologist, a carrier of furniture and other heavy goods.

tuckertorium, a delicatessen.

tyrorium, special department at a garage for the sale of tyres.

vitaminizery, a stall selling fruit and vegetable juices.

wreckologist, a car-wrecking firm.

4. TRADE NAMES

ALTHOUGH TRADE MARKS have been registered in Australia for less than a century, one trade name dates back to pioneering days. I have mentioned it earlier – *Botany* as an (always erroneous) tag for wool grown in Australia, e.g. *Botany wool, Botany tops, Botany yarn.* Until fairly recent times these terms were applied particularly to fine merino.

Among Australian words commemorated in trade marks for various goods are *Kangaroo, Rosella, Kookaburra, Koala, Wallaby, Boomerang, Digger* and *Aussie.* Registered names for frozen rabbits exported from this country have included *Kangaroo, Emu* and *Eureka!*

Here is a number of trade names for Australian wines registered by a Melbourne firm: *Sheralia, Sautalia, Champalia, Burgalia, Poralia, Claralia, Muskalia, Chabalia, Hokalia* and *Tokalia.* Those who know the qualities not so long ago of some Australian wines and spirits will be interested to note that one man has registered the word *Ammo* for such beverages. *Ausky,* for an Australian whisky, is another indigenous invention.

A distinctively Australian name given to a tweed made at Geelong is *Mallee.* In imitation of the peaty tang given to a genuine Harris tweed, this cloth has been impregnated with an "elusive 'polished saddle leather' aroma." The firm declares:

> Pass the impregnated tweeds in the streets and you'll miss the aroma; hang them in the wardrobe and they'll transport you to that mist-laden fern gully of your memories.

o

I have already had occasion to refer to the *Tasmanian bluey* (or *Tasmanian blue*).

A trade name that has acquired an enduring place in the Australian vocabulary is *Qantas*. This is formed from the initials of the Queensland and Northern Territory Aerial Services (registered November, 1920), which is the oldest airline in the English-speaking world. The *Drover* is an all-metal, three-engined monoplane designed by de Havilland primarily for use in the Australian outback. The *Transavia Airtruk*, a freight plane designed by Luigi Pellarini for Australian agricultural use, is built at Seven Hills, N.S.W.

The C.S.I.R.O. has been responsible for *Siroset*, permanent pleating of woollen cloth, *Sironize*, shrink-proofing of wool, which is used to identify washable non-iron woollen fabrics, and *Sirotherm*, a process for desalting seawater.

CHAPTER XIX

Standard Australianisms

THE MAKING OF A LINGUISTIC COMMUNITY

WHAT IS THE PROCESS whereby neologisms are converted into standard terms? There is no easy answer. Age alone will not do it. Nor respectability. Nor durability. Nor narrow precision of meaning. Nor official blessing. On the other hand, any one of these factors (or others) may be enough.

We have a special advantage in Australia at being able to look at this matter over a relatively short period of time. Here we are, fewer than 180 years from our beginnings. We have seen enough of the tremendous fertility of material available to know quite well that some of it is a good deal more acceptable than the rest – that many Australian words are more generally useful than others – that some terms seem so irrevocably orthodox in this community that we could not sacrifice them without feeling robbed of essential words, no matter what people in other countries may think.

If admission to the pages of such an august work as the "Shorter Oxford English Dictionary" is to be our guide, we are going to hit some snags straight away. In this work we find, among other words, *bluey*, *boundary-rider*, *buck-jump*, *cooee*, *googly*, *hatter*, *jackeroo*, *shanghai*, *stockrider*, *sundowner*, and *willy willy;* but we also find the long-obsolete *cornstalk* and the slang *roll up* (an attendance at a meeting) and *to tomahawk* (gash) *a sheep;* we discover *burster*, but not *southerly buster*, *roustabout*, but not *rouseabout*, and there is no trace of *digger* (soldier), *jumbuck* (a sheep) and *brumby* (wild horse) among hundreds of our long-established terms. In short, the "Oxford's" choices offer us little help.

Since the matter of what is standard and what is not is open to so much misinterpretation, I doubt if we can ignore this opinion from the noted Danish philologian, Otto Jespersen (in "Mankind, Nation and Individual", 1946):

> . . . We are perhaps getting to the heart of the question when we observe that there is something which speaker and hearer have in common, and that this common element really makes many things easy for both of them. This is the linguistic norm which they have both accepted from without, from the community, from society, from the nation . . . They talk and understand one another in virtue of both belonging to the same linguistic community.

That, of course, does not answer our original question entirely, but it takes us a long way. It implies that a standard Australianism is a word which is essential to our linguistic community, and is thereby part of a current (although localized) "norm". Further, it implies that the word must be "accepted", if not by the linguistic community as a whole, at least by a significant part of it. Since we are well aware that linguistic fashions change, either because the influences which once gave certain words currency have ceased to operate or simply because fresher (and briefer) substitutes have been found, we know that standards are not fixed and immutable, but as dynamic as the people who use those words.

As I pointed out in the original edition of this book, the less imagery a word contains and the more utilitarian it sounds, the greater the likelihood that it will attain the status of standard. In short, the measure of orthodoxy is often a measure of dullness.

If we now link this last point with Jespersen's view, we arrive at the conclusion that the "norm" of orthodoxy required by a linguistic community in order to render a word standard is usefulness free from "colour", which may lead to a hearer's misunderstanding the purport of a speaker. Thus one can see no likelihood of standard status for *jumpabout*, as applied to methylated spirits as a drink, *snore weed*, jail issue tobacco, *colour proud*, descriptive of the pride a sunbaker shows in his or her sunburn, and *kangaroo hop* or *kangaroo droop*, applied to a peculiar pose once favoured by women as the result of wearing the straight-front corset. By contrast, the utilitarian nature of *bushfire*, *stockyard*, *billabong*, *woolshed* and *Anzus Treaty* make them automatic candidates for approved status.

Yet, even this does not give the full picture. Perhaps we could begin with no better illustration than the word *Australia* itself. The earliest known printed use of the word was in 1612 in a version of de Quiros' "Memorial" which gave it as the equivalent of *Austrialia* as a reference to the New Hebrides. The New Hebrides were found by de Quiros in 1606 and he named it *Austrialia del Espiritu Santo* as a tribute to Philip III of Spain, who was a Prince of the House of Austria. (By an astonishing chance, when our sole representative at the first modern Olympic Games at Athens in 1896, E. H. Flack, won the 800 metres and 1,500 metres running events, an Austrian flag was raised for his victory ceremonies!) The first known visit of Europeans to Australia was made in 1606 by the Dutch vessel Duyfken – to the western part of what is now Cape York Peninsula – and later discoveries by Dutch navigators led to the western area of Australia becoming known as *New Holland* (or Hollandia Nova or Compagnis Nieu Nederland). A good deal before this – indeed, long before European discoveries of the country had been made – it had been given the name *Terra Australis*, meaning "Land of the South". In due course, to distinguish between the discoveries of Spain and Holland, the name Terra Australis was given to the eastern section and New Holland was accepted for the west. This was more or less the situation in 1692 when an author (believed to have been Gabriel de Foigny), writing under the pen-name of Jacques Sadeur, published in Paris an imaginative novel titled "Les Aventures de Jacques Sadeur dans la Découverte et le Voiage de la Terre Australe, contenant les Coûtumes et les Moeurs des Australiens". In the following year, a translation was published in London. For the first time, this translation gave us the word *Australia* as applied to the Great South Land (not to the New Hebrides), *Australian* as an adjective and *Australians* as the native inhabitants of this country.

Samples: "This is all that I can have a certain knowledge of as to that side of *Australia* . . ."; "I knew not afterwards what to resolve upon, nor what would become of me, nor durst I look an *Australian* in the face"; " . . . the signal he [Sadeur] gave of a prodigious Bravery and Courage, before the eyes of the *Australians* . . ."; "I have here therefore set down the best account of the *Australian Territories* that I could get . . ."

An earlier version of Sadeur's book, "La Terre Australe Connue . . ." was published in 1676 and suppressed. So far as we are concerned here, it was notable for the use of the French form, *l'Australie*.

It has for long been a fiction that Matthew Flinders invented the word *Australia*. This is as erroneous as the absurd conviction that he was the first man to circumnavigate Australia. For these flourishes, he was at least partly to blame himself. In the introduction to his book, "A Voyage to Terra Australis" (1814), Flinders wrote: "I have . . . ventured upon the readoption of the *original Terra Australis*, and of this term I shall hereafter make use, when speaking of New Holland (sc. the West) and New South Wales, in a collective sense, and when using it in the most extensive signification, the adjacent isles, including that of Van Diemen, must be understood to be comprehended." To this he added a footnote: "Had I permitted myself any innovation upon the original term, it would have been to convert it to *Australia*; as being more agreeable to the ear, and an assimilation to the names of the other great portions of the earth". Flinders hoped to call his book "A Voyage to Australia", changed it at the bidding of Sir Joseph Banks to "A Voyage to Terra Australis" and almost had to change it again to "A Voyage to New Holland". (See my biography of Flinders, "My Own Destroyer", 1962).

The crucial point is that Flinders did not invent the word *Australia*; it had been used well over a century earlier. Second, in the early days of colonisation the eastern section of this country was known as New South Wales and the west as New Holland. Only after Governor Macquarie began, in 1817, to use the word *Australia* in official correspondence did it come to be generally accepted.

So right at the outset of our inquiry into standard usage, we find that we have to step warily. A rather similar problem occurs with the State we now know as *Tasmania*. From its first settlement in 1803 to the beginning of 1856, it was officially called *Van Diemen's Land*. However, the name Tasmania was obviously in considerable popular use long before 1856. For example, Launceston's first newspaper, issued originally on January 5, 1825, was called the "Tasmanian and Port Dalrymple Advertiser", and on August 19, 1825, the title of the "Hobart Town Gazette and Van Diemen's Land Advertiser" was changed to the "Colonial Times and Tasmanian Advertiser". But the precise stage at which the words *Tasmania* and *Tasmanian* crept into use cannot be fixed.

A different type of problem arose with the word *squatter*. As I observed earlier, Australia's original *squatters* were rogues and blackguards; not until after the middle of last century did the meaning of the word soften to denote a large landowner mainly concerned with raising sheep and selling wool – and acquiring the respectability of a large bank balance.

Obviously, respectability has a great deal to do with the development of standard usage and this partly depends on official acceptance. But our attention is drawn to the fact that in all of these cases, *Australia*, *Tasmania* and *squatter*, the words were used colloquially before official approval was given. Now, this is an important feature of a large part of language: the movement is usually (but not always) upward from the lower levels of use. Official approval often lags considerably behind the demands of a linguistic community.

Let us take another look at *Australia* and see the large number of derivatives it has spawned. *Australian*, as a noun and an adjective of course, *Australianism*, *Australasia*, *Australiana*, *un-Australian*, *pan-Australian*, *pro-Australian*, *Anglo-Australian*, *Austral English*, *Australia Day*, *White Australia Policy*, and some other combinations *Australian Church*, *Australian terrier*, *Australian Rules football* – these are certainly worth being accepted as standard. But what of *Australianize*, *Australianization*, *Australophobia*, *Australophilia*, *Australienne* (with *Westralienne* as a parallel W.A. use), *Australianity*, *Australianness*, *Australianship*, *Australienese* or *Australese*? We would probably be extremely diffident about some of these. In that case, what about *Australian ballot* (a name originally given to the *ballot box*, which was invented in Victoria and South Australia in 1856), *Australian crawl* (the swimming stroke), *First Australians* (a name given to the Australian Aborigines), *New Australia*[1] (William Lane's ill-fated project in South America), *New Australian* (a migrant to Australia)? We can feel our judgment varying from one expression to the other, but we do not doubt that all these words, even Lane's *New Australia*, are more or less identified with the country as a whole and that this identification reaches back a long way.

If this is so, the reader will suffer some shock when he realizes that there was a strong move in the late 1880s to equate the name *Australia* with the colony of *New South Wales* (which by then, of course, had had the areas of Victoria and Queensland lopped off it). This move was so strong, indeed, that a *Colony of Australia Bill* was introduced in the N.S.W. Legislative Assembly in 1887. The first reading of this bill was moved

---

[1] In 1965, after a special visit to Paraguay to seek survivors and descendants of the New Australia undertaking, in the course of writing a book about that project, Mr Gavin Souter told me that he had heard one of the original New Australians refer to *a creation of cats*, meaning a long time (which may well have been an old Australianism) and another use the term *tucker* and recall the "*Speewa* where we let the sun boil the plum duff". At this stage it is, of course, impossible to assess the linguistic influence of these New Australians on South America, but some Australian has obviously had something to do with "*Tanques Australianos Piletas de Natacion*" galvanised-iron swimming pools, advertised in the Buenos Aires newspaper "La Prensa" on February 3, 1956. An illustration suggests that large "Australian tanks" are about sixty feet in diameter and six feet high. From Mexico I have received an advertisement for *zapatos dingo*, "dingo shoes".

by Sir Henry Parkes on November 23, 1887, and followed a motion by Sir Alfred Stephen, Representative of the Government in the Legislative Council, on July 12, 1887, that "in view of the entrance by the colony in January next on its second centenary, it is desirable to mark the event by a change in its present uncouth and inapt name, substituting for it the word Australia, or some other appropriate appellation, as Parliament may determine". The first reading motion was carried by 59 votes to 18, but thereafter the bill hung fire and eventually lapsed.

The point of this is that Australia is as yet too young in the development of her language for this question of standard and non-standard to be carried too far. To attempt to make an issue of the matter would be like criticizing the appearance of a house while the bricks and building materials are still on the ground. In another fifty or one hundred years the issue will be clearcut; time will have accomplished what utilitarianism may not. Expressions we now consider trifling slang will be bedded deep in Australian speech; words which we might now call standard will have been rejected and forgotten. The years behind us are so few and the years ahead of us so many, that we would be foolish to usurp the judgment that properly belongs to our successors.

At the same time, the matter cannot be entirely neglected if only because many lexicographers at home and abroad are imposing verdicts. It is, of course, far too vast an undertaking to run through our survey of Australianisms in this book and nominate all the "probables" and "possibles"; so I will content myself with a few examples:

Great Australian Basin, the largest artesian basin in the world, covering about 657,000 square miles, most of it in Queensland, but extending into N.S.W., South Australia and the Northern Territory; *Channel Country*, an area of about ten million acres in south-west Queensland, north-east South Australia and north-west N.S.W.; *Q fever*, an acute infectious disease caused by the ricketsial organism, *Coxiella burneti*, first studied in 1935; *Murray Valley encephalitis*, a form of virus encephalitis, believed to be mosquito-borne, reported in the Goulburn and Murray river valleys in 1951; *oecists*, the first pioneers in N.S.W. (use dating from 1963), from a Greek word denoting the founder of an ancient Greek colony; *mimi art*, a form of Aboriginal art found by the Mountford expedition to Arnhem Land in 1949-50 (according to Oenpelli natives, the art was the work of *mimi*, a fairylike people with long, thin bodies who are capable of vanishing into the cracks of rocks, and is quite distinct from what anthropologists call *X-ray art*, which shows some part of the internal anatomy of animals, fish, etc.); *Sydney View*, often abbreviated to *View*, a postage stamp issued in 1850, the central feature of which is a copy of the reverse side of the first Great Seal of New South Wales, showing three convicts being freed from their chains; *Tasmanite*, a mineral, which is a compound of carbon, hydrogen, oxygen and sulphur, found in small reddish-brown scales in shale; *Goodletite*, the matrix in which rubies are found, called after William Goodlet; *bluestone*, a dark, building stone; *singing stick*, a branch or stick on which a toothed-billed bower-bird sits above its so-called *circus ring* to make its varied calls; *basic wage*, the standard wage for unskilled labour (in most of its essential details this wage is unique to Australia); *Harvester judgment*, this 1907 case was the first in which the basic wage was applied; *muster*, a census in Australia's early days – until 1828; *bowser*, a petrol pump, from the name of S. F. Bowser and Co., Sydney, which marketed Bowser petrol and oil storage systems in 1916; *weekender*, a cottage or shack at some beach or bush resort where week-ends and holidays are spent (hence, the use of such expressions as *weekend block, weekend lease, weekend cottage*); *sleepout*, a portion of a verandah, usually partly exposed to the air, used for sleeping; *dogman*, a man who gives directional signals to a crane-driver in the course of building operations (he frequently rides on the goods lifted by the crane); *bopple nut*, a seed of the *Macademia tetraphylla* or *M. ternifolia* (a corruption of *Bauple* mountain, near the Mary River, Queensland); *Day of Remembrance*, November 11 each year, and *Anzac Day*, April 25 each year[2]; *Schools of Arts*, institutions (originally called Mechanics' Institutes) founded in many centres last century to provide facilities for working people to study and attend educational lectures; and such self-explanatory *bush* derivations as *Bush Book Club, Bush Church Aid Society* and *bush nursing*.

However, even here we are faced with conflict. Sometimes our news-papers print such words within quotation marks. *Weekender, old identity* and *bulldust* are examples. On the other hand I have many records of Australian words which we would deem far more colloquial appearing in news-papers without quotation marks: *crack hardy, wowsery, drongos, undressing a sheep, yabbying, Kelly methods, trammie, dillybags of, killer* (the final straw), *up her singlet* (in hand), *get a guernsey* (succeed or be selected, from football), *Buckley's* (no chance at all). Clearly, newspaper quotation marks cannot be relied on.

Even legal processes involving Australian words do not necessarily raise them to an "approved" level. For many generations a form of noise-making which consists of the banging of tins, metal trays and other objects capable of producing a racket has been known in Australia as *tin-kettling* or *tin-canning*. It is commonly incited by weddings and other festive occasions. Here is an Australian legal edict dated 1896 on the subject of *tin-kettling*:

> Persons indulging in the practice of "tin-kettling" may be convicted under s. 7 of the Police Offences Act 1891 (Vic.) of behaving in an insulting manner, although they desisted upon being requested by a constable.[3]

Here is a legal comment on the word "stoush":

> Proceedings were taken before a Court of Petty Sessions by the complainant against the defendant upon a complaint which, as amended,

---

[2] Several other "days" are officially observed in Australia – *Australia Day* (formerly called *Anniversary Day* and *Foundation Day*), *Labour Day* or *Eight Hour Day, Commemoration Day, State Foundation Day* and *Wattle Day*. We also have an *Aboriginal Sunday*.

[3] R. v. Garrett (1896) 2 A.L.R. (C.N.) 321 (Vic. Sup. Ct., Hood, J.).

stated that the defendant made use of abusive and threatening language –
viz. "I will stouch [sic] you in the mouth. You think you are going to run
Clifton. You are a nice gentleman, trying to take people down." – whereby
a breach of the peace might have been occasioned. No evidence was given
to prove that the defendant used the words with the intention of provoking
a breach of the peace, and, in fact, no breach of the peace was occasioned.
The justices convicted and fined the defendant. Held that the complaint
disclosed no offence under s. 6 of the Vagrancy Act 1851 (N.S.W.).[4]

Stoush has been in Australian use since the end of last century, but is
now virtually obsolete. It usually denoted a fight or a brawl, but in the
above example is used verbally to mean "to hit" or "to punch".

Such obviously plebeian words aside, there are enough "approved"
Australianisms in use to make another book – or a dictionary. I have no
doubt that such a publication will appear in due course, for it has long
been evident that, among the thousands of new words and phrases either
developed indigenously or borrowed from abroad and adapted to special
purposes in this country, there is an ever-growing total essential to our
linguistic community. Many of these are free from the taint of earthiness
which apparently has to be eroded away from a colloquialism before it is
accepted as a "norm". There are many marginal cases. *Australorp*, for
instance, the name given to a highly popular Australian breed of Orpington fowl, which has been in use since the turn of the century; *bulldust*
for thick, fine dust found in sections of the outback (but also a slang term
used as an equivalent for *bullsh*); *tips*, toe-plates for shoes or boots (once an
English word, but now almost unknown in Britain); *gumtips*, new growths
of young eucalypts often esteemed as house decorations; *gumleaf band*, a
group of Aboriginal players who can wrest music from blowing on
eucalypt leaves; *chips*, kindling for lighting fires; and *old identity*, an old
and sometimes distinguished member of a community (which has been
in use for more than a century). So far as the Australian linguistic community is concerned, these terms have already become standard. There
are hundreds of words of this type.

Obviously we will have to be our own arbiters. We alone are in a
position to decide on the value of the words we use.

---

[4] R. v. Justices of Clifton; Ex parte McGovern (1903) Q.S.R. 177 (Q. Sup. Ct. F.C.).

CHAPTER XX

Oversea Influences

1. ENGLISH DIALECTS

THE ENGLISH LANGUAGE has been sorely buffeted by the philological winds of the South Seas. William Churchill had no illusions on the matter in his "Beach-la-Mar". He wrote:

> The fact remains that the common speech of the Commonwealth of Australia represents the most brutal maltreatment which has even been inflicted upon the language that is the mother tongue of the great English nations.

The survey offered by this book would hardly encourage much dispute on the point. Indeed, I would go further. In terms of population and length of history, Australia has made more alterations to the English language than America. When we compare U.S. and Australian slang today we are liable to feel overwhelmed by the sheer bulk of American inventions, but we must remember that America has had twice as much history as Australia, that her population is almost twenty times greater and that she sits nearer European and English influences than we do.

In spite of these things we have more than held our own in the development of new language, and struck off on a course of our own from which there is no turning back.

Consider, for example, how close we ran the English in the use of *kodak*, to take a photograph, and of *slanguage*. The former was recorded in England in 1891; Australia was using it in 1895. The latter appeared in England in 1892; it was widely current in Australia five years later.

On the other hand consider the following words, all of which we might suspect of being English, but which were first recorded in Australia:[1]

	Australian Date	English Date
bike (bicycle), a velocipede	1869	1890
billet, a position, job	1854	1870
buster, a heavy fall	1854	1860
caser, a "dollar", worth about 5s.	1849	1859
chance it, to take a chance	1835	1933
chance the ducks, to take a chance	1858	1873
chain gang, a convict gang working in chains	1840	1858
Down Under, used to describe New Zealand and Australia	1900	1908

---

[1] I have culled these early Australian records from old books and commentaries on Australia. The "Oxford Dictionary" has been used mainly for English dates of use.

	Australian Date	English Date
ganging, work as a gang	1849	1865
go to the country, to go to jail	1882	1927
josher (*josser*), an old depraved person	1882	1892
paralytic, drunk	1890	1910
solitary, a sentence of solitary imprisonment	1847	1852
sugar, money	1862	1877
to talk through one's neck, to talk nonsense	1891	1904
yum yum, an expression of approval or enjoyment	1883	1904

It is a principle of lexicography accepted by the "Oxford Dictionary" that textual quotations are sufficient evidence upon which to base the original currency of a word. The expressions above are only a few of those which, upon this basis, can be accepted as of Australian origin.

A similar position arises when we compare Australian English with Craigie's "Dictionary of American English". Here are a few of the many examples in which words listed by Craigie as American are found to have earlier textual records in this country:

	Australian Date	U.S. Date
Australian (adj.), pertaining to Australia	1814	1856
boomer (n.), something notable, impressive	1860	1887
bullpuncher	1872	1874
brush (n.), forest-covered country; bushland	1799	1881
buck (v.), of a horse	1848	1864
buckjumper (n.), a horse that bucks	1848	1878
bush (n.), forest-covered land	1803	1827
bushranger	1805	1830
Chink, a Chinaman	1879	1901
coast (*about*) (v.), to wander, walk about aimlessly	1878	1889
dray (n.), a wheeled waggon	1833	1836
jumper, a man's blouse or smock-like shirt	1852	1853
stockman	1803	1866
stockyard	1802	1867

Many times throughout this book the origin of common Australian-isms has been traced to English dialect. In some cases, almost entirely through Australian influence, dialectal words have gone back into English colloquial speech. *Larrikin* and the verb *to barrack* are outstanding instances of this.

In English dialect *fossick* meant to ferret out; we applied it to gold-seeking. In Suffolk dialect *to cob* meant to take a liking to, to "cotton" to someone. It was almost certainly the origin of our *cobber*. *Fair dinkum* meant fair play in provincial dialect; we hardly modified the term at all to make it one of our best-known colloquialisms for a long period, although it has seriously declined in Australian use since the 1940s.

It is more than likely that *wowser* was developed either from the dialectal *wissere*, a teacher, or from *wow*, a complaint, silly talk, which is related to *wawin'* and *wowin'*, crying or wailing, in English dialect. Perhaps the dialectal use of *wasser*, for anything extreme of its kind, is also involved. At any rate, it is to be doubted whether *wowser* was as much an indigenous Australianism as has been claimed.

Boof, a clumsy or stupid fellow, has given us *boofhead*, a numbskull or simpleton. *Smoodge* comes from the English *smudge* or *smoush*. *Bowyangs*[2] is derived from the old dialectal *bow-yankees*. *Skerrick*, "a small amount", has been converted to a negative form, *without a skerrick*, often meaning penniless.

Stoush is from the English *stashie*, an uproar; *skite* from Scottish *bletherskite* which, in America, became *blatherskite*; *bang*, an intensive, as in *whole bang lot*, from the Scottish *jimbang*; *bisom*, a recalcitrant child, from the Scottish *besom*; *jinker* from the Scottish *janker*; *jonnick* from the provincial *jannock*; *whinge* from Scottish and provincial dialects; *kelly*, a crow, from the Cumberland *kelp*; *snickle*, a girl, probably from *snicket*; *fummy*, a cat, from *fomard*; *smarmy*, falsely-polite, smooth-tongued, from *smawm*, to smear; *vack*, an old woman, from *vecke*; *sool* from the dialectal *sowl*; *poddy* from the provincial use of *poddy* meaning round and stout in the belly; *to peg*, to throw; *to smoke*, to discover; *skillion*, an outhouse or lean-to; *dow*, a pigeon; *to ding*, to throw away – from English dialectal terms used similarly.

In an article on "Australianisms and Their Origin" in "The Lone Hand" of November 2, 1908, a writer asserted: "Many of the words most intimately associated with bush-life have been transplanted from the vocabularies of English provincial dialects".

This process of absorption has now gone a long way past purely bush terms and is a reminder that the English of England has a vast traditional influence in Australia. Whereas, as we have seen in this book, such a traditional attachment has not (as in New Zealand) acted as a brake on our word-making enthusiasms, we generally turn to English guidance on officially-recommended spellings and the pronunciation of individual words even if we borrow – and mutilate – many Americanisms.

In "Life and Progress in Australia" (1897), M. Davitt remarked that Australian slang was derived from that of England with idioms of colonial growth and some American terms thrown in. He could possibly have phrased his view more aptly if he had said that Australian slang was mainly an indigenous growth with numerous English terms and fewer Americanisms thrown in. In terms of percentages today the Australian uses, by preference, at least 60 per cent of his own slang, about 25 per cent English and not more than 15 per cent American. In some groups in this country the percentage is as high as 70 per cent Australian.

We must reject as inaccurate Partridge's (1933) estimate in "Slang Today and Yesterday" that the percentages may be given as 40 per cent native, 35 per cent Cockney and 25 per cent American, although even these figures are sufficient to show that we are not – as many Australians

---

[2] The Australian use of *towyangs* was recorded in 1898.

suspect – overwhelmed by Americanisms. During the past twenty-odd years, the large wartime "invasion" of this country by U.S. Servicemen and (after 1956) the influence of U.S. television programmes has left some linguistic scars, especially in the eastern States, but we are far from being swamped by importations from America.

Indeed, this absorption of overseas slang is to our benefit if (and this to my mind is the crucial point) the new word is shorter than what we have been using. This tendency towards brevity has been a feature of Australian slang for many generations and I can see no sign of any change.

I have pointed out that as soon as expressions are removed from their original surroundings and applied in new surroundings their meanings tend to change. This is what has happened in hundreds of cases of imported terms, as, for instance, in some of the dialectal expressions just mentioned. We can see how their applications have been broadened, how they have taken on new shades of meaning, how their sounds have been modified.

There are, of course, many oversea terms which we have accepted without apparent modification. But sometimes we find that these words acquire greater currency in Australia – are used among more varied classes of people and more continually – than they had in the country of their origin. *Bloke* and *cove* are cases in point.[3]

Many expressions applied to specific things do not lend themselves easily to modification – for example, *bob*, a shilling, *guts*, a greedy person, *ponk*, a stink, *kick*, a pocket, *gob*, the mouth. These are out of English slang and we have absorbed them as naturally as we have the great bulk of standard English. Not all of it, of course, since the environmental influences, the tasks and the enthusiasms of the Australian are often far removed from those which the Briton knows. It would be impossible to make anything like a full study of the Australian's manifold incorporations from abroad, but here is a selection culled from the first three letters of Eric Partridge's monumental "Dictionary of Slang and Unconventional English" (1938), all of which are widely-used in Australia: *come across, the actual* (money), *all of a dither, the altogether* (the nude), *to ante up, to argue the toss, back-chat, back and fill, to save one's bacon, balmy, barge into, batty* (mad), *beak* (a magistrate), *not worth a bean, better half* (wife), *big wig, bilge* (nonsense), *binge* (a drinking bout), *bird* (a girl), *bit of all right, black maria, bobby-dazzler, bold as brass, boneshaker* (a bicycle), *bosh, brass* (money), *browned off, bugger about, do a bunk, busking, butt in, to cadge, call it a day, on the cards, to carpet* (reprimand), *in the cart, like a cat on hot bricks, to chance it, on the cheap, cheek* (impudence), *chew the rag, choosey* (fastidious), *classy, clink* (prison), *clobber, clodhopper, to collar* (seize), *off colour, come clean, conk out, copycat, crackpot* and *crikey!* These are all English originals and, although widely current in Australia, they should be distinguished from the body of authentic Australianisms.

It was natural for such absorption to take place if only because a large

---

[3] Wrote "The Brazier" (trench journal of the 16th Canadian Scottish Battalion) during World War I: "What curious expressions these Australians have. Fancy calling a man a *bloke* or a *cove* instead of saying *gink*, as a *guy* naturally would!"

proportion of migrants to this country from our earliest days came from England and had used Cockney and provincial slang extensively before they set sail. The convicts brought it, the adventurers brought it, people who came to the South Seas to start life over again brought it. If we scan the pages of "The Detectives' Handbook" (*circa* 1882) and the dictionaries of Lentzner and Crowe, the amount of purely Cockney or provincial English material in them will be obvious.

If it might be feared by some observers that these influences are ceasing to operate, let it not be forgotten that, since the end of World War II, hundreds of thousands of English migrants have come to Australia and they, too, have brought the dialects of their own beginnings.

2. AMERICAN INFLUENCES

IF, IN SPITE of the many people who have come to this country from Britain, we have been able to create and preserve a vast vocabulary of our own, we need have no fear that we shall not be able to survive the tide of Americanisms. Environment and geography are primary factors that keep our Australian English individual.

As H. W. Dinning observed in "The Australian Scene" (1939) "to use American slang – that very lively and expressive medium – is not to become Americanized . . . We all use that argot . . . England uses American slang and England is in no danger of Americanization".

Let us remember this point. The extent to which a country absorbs the language of another country is not governed by lexicographers or academicians – or juveniles. The instinct of the people as a whole governs it. They accept what they like, they reject completely words which have no useful application or which do not appeal to them, they modify others. We have used and survived English slang. We will do and are doing the same with American slang.

In "The Australian at Home" (1891), Edward Kinglake wrote:

> It is surprising that the Australian has not more resemblance to the American. There is a decided analogy between the conditions under which a great part of the two nations live, and yet it is only in very slight and trivial points that we notice them to be like each other.

We can go further than this. Two of the best-known Americanisms we have adopted are *bushwhacker* and *squatter*. Yet we have changed their meaning and application entirely. They are no less Australianisms today than are hundreds of other imported terms to which we have given new senses.

Here is a list of words which the Sydney "Telegraph" of July 14, 1936, attempted to palm off on the public as Americanisms current in Australia: *Beefy*, biff, bluff, boss, *break away*, *to chew the rag*, to chip in, *to fade away*, *to get it in the neck*, *to back and fill*, to turn or be turned down, *fake*, *creek*, *push* (a crowd), hitched (married), tough (luck), *for keeps, going strong, also ran, bookie, cove,* dago, *duds, groggy, king pin, monniker, pal,* a peach, *rattled, togs* and *yap.*

The words in italics are either originally English or originally Australian as reference to Partridge's "Slang Dictionary" will show. It is nonsense of this nature that has made the Australian lose confidence in himself.

It is refreshing, therefore, to come across a statement such as the following, which appeared in the Melbourne "Age" of September 9, 1942:

> The all-in [Australian] imitators of Americanisms are still in a minority, despite the enormous influence of "the movies". We have "said a mouthful" when we say that the average Australian, like the average Englishman, does not necessarily adopt every "cute and slick new word".

It was not until Australians found themselves hosts to tens of thousands of U.S. troops and airmen in 1942 and later that they began to realize how vast was the gulf between speech in this country and America. A good many of the vaunted stories of Australia's Americanization vanished into thin air when, to the amusement of our visitors, Australians found that the U.S. slang they had adopted was mainly of an antique brand, that a good deal of it had been discarded long ago by Americans and that it was often misapplied by Australians.

Similarity rather than identity of influences has often misled the Australian into a belief that he is becoming something not much better than an occupant of one of America's colonies. Eighty years ago Frank Cowan[4] wrote of "the Yankee-land beneath the Southern Cross" in a Walt Whitmanish saga of our merits and demerits; but we should not wilfully misinterpret his words. To be *like* the United States is not to *be* the United States, nor does it necessarily imply that we are no more than a carbon copy of the States whatever our political masters do.

Geographically our economic and cultural kinship lies with America rather than with England. We can resist it, just as New Zealand has struggled to resist a cultural kinship with Australia, but the weight of cold fact cannot be wilfully ignored out of existence.

Somewhat illogically, the Australian tends to give way to despair when he hears Americanisms used in Australian speech. "America gives us most of the slang we do not get from England", wrote Brian Penton.[5] "Much of the slang called Australian is really imported from the United States", complained the Sydney "Telegraph" in 1936. "The American element in our slang is growing fast and outstripping the original Cockney element," lamented the "Sydney Morning Herald" in the same year.

While such assertions are made glibly enough, no adequate evidence has ever been adduced to show that they are true.

Let us look back a little to a comment by I. L. Bird in her "Australia Felix: Impressions of Victoria" (1877):

---

[4] "Australia: A Charcoal Sketch" (1886).
[5] "Think – Or Be Damned" (1941).

There is a tendency to adopt words which are rather American than English in their use. Thus a coach is a *stage;* a pair of horses, a *span* or *team;* a light trap of any kind, a *buggy;* light impedimenta, *swag;* a waggon, a *dray;* a mounted policeman, a *trooper.*

At first sight we might accept this assertion as true, but in terms of fact only one of the expressions listed is American – *span*, for a pair of horses.

Although the earlier "Age" comment is undoubtedly right in its reference to the "average Australian", the "Age" could have said the opposite about the "average teenager". As a result of the propagandic brainwashing of American films, comics, television programmes and other communicatory media, our juveniles have become highly susceptible to U.S. linguistic influences. That their enthusiasms are not to be taken seriously, since they change with almost every wind that blows, I do not doubt for a moment, but the casual observer can easily be misled into feeling that youthful word-prejudices are likely to obliterate the Australian language entirely. When I was mortising together "Australia Speaks" (1953), I recorded such teenage uses as *smooth*, pretty, attractive; *mighty smooth* or *royal smooth*, extremely attractive; *sharp*, good-looking (applied to a young man); *keen*, a synonym for *sharp*; *royal keen*, exceedingly attractive; *clueless*, old-fashioned; *mighty*, superfine in every respect; *the end*, an expression of maximum disapproval. Few of these remain in use. I suspect that, in another ten years or so, most of the teenage expressions listed in Chapter XIII will also be forgotten.

Juveniles are not entirely alone in their wish to mimic Americanisms. We do not have to look far to find (at least in N.S.W. and southern Queensland) a considerable overburden of American Snack Bars, Wyoming Basements, Bootlegger Punch, Yankee Lemonade, Hollywood Sundae, Alabama Avenue, Connecticut Avenue, Illinois Road, Pasadena Street and Hollywood and Kentucky Picnic Grounds, and a comprehensive selection of -oriums and -ologists (as given in Chapter XVIII). No doubt we are indebted to Australians for many of these, but we should not forget that, at the time of writing, some 30,000 Americans have migrated to Australia since the end of World War II and have probably brought contributions of their own.

However, even in Australia's eastern States all is not lost. H. W. Horwill's "An Anglo-American Interpreter" (1939) shows many points of difference between U.S. and English word-preferences. Similar word-preferences prevail in Australia. Most Australians probably haven't the slightest idea what Americans mean when they speak of a *dry goods store.* It is a *draper's shop.* Or that what Americans call *notions* are *fancy goods* or that a *carom* is a *cannon* (in billiards). Here is a brief list of similar differences between America and Australia:

American	Australian
alumni	old boys
aluminum	aluminium
apartment	flat
attorney	lawyer

American	Australian
absorbent cotton	cotton wool
billion	thousand millions
bulletin board	notice board
bureau of information	inquiry office
candy	lollies
cigar store	tobacconist's
city hall	town hall
crackers	biscuits
centennial	centenary
drug store	chemist's
elevator	lift
fall	autumn
faucet	tap
fraternal order	friendly society
freight elevator	hoist
gasoline (gas)	petrol
hundredweight	100 lb.
janitor	caretaker
local taxes	rates
locomotive	engine
mailman	postman
prison guard	warder
realtor	estate agent
schoolmarm	schoolmistress
scrubwoman	char
sidewalk	footpath
stockholder	shareholder
spider	frying pan
spigot	tap
ton	2,000 lb.
washroom, restroom	lavatory
witness stand	witness box

Such differences as these should not be allowed to give the impression that we have not quite eagerly absorbed many Americanisms. But a rather interesting point emerges and this is best illustrated by a practical example. Twenty years ago, when I wrote the original edition of this book, I listed the following Americanisms as having wide currency in Australia: scram, boloney, nerts, to gyp, blind tiger, poppycock, jane, lowdown, lay off, okay, pushover, says you, snappy piece of work, so's your old man, attaboy, cinch, crack down on, slick, to bellyache, corny, crackerjack, to high hat, jive, oh yeah, scanties, you ain't seen nothing yet, eyewash, bleachers, to sell a pup, dodger (a handbill), coke (from Coca-Cola), claypan, pash, to ballyhoo, and how, gone coon, suicide blonde, zoot suit, brash, stooge.

I hardly need to ask the question: How many of these survive in Australian use today? So when we confess to the more recent filching of such U.S. originals as *breakthrough, crash programme, escalation* (of a war), *gimmick, image, 64-dollar question, talk off the top of one's head, in orbit, blastoff, goof, gas* and *dig* (understand), we should not necessarily expect them to endure for long. While the Australian has a considerable flair for borrowing linguistic innovations of this type, he grows tired of them rapidly.

Here are notes on observed differences between modes of speech in Australia and America supplied to me by an American, Hugh Morrison, in the course of a two-year stay in the Commonwealth after World War II:

bitumen, we never use the term to mean a substance used to pave streets and footpaths; we call that asphalt. We have two main kinds of coal in America, which we call bituminous and anthracite; when an American first hears Australians say bitumen, he is apt to think they mean a kind of coal.

black, with the meaning blacklisted or just plain taboo, this is unknown in America. In the labour union sense of the word, we would say simply that the union had ruled against working in such-and-such a place or that it was on strike, etc.

block, meaning a piece of land; unknown in America, unless it is a city block.

buck party, unknown in America; we call it a stag party.

canteen, its application to a case of cutlery is unknown in America.

cheese paring, meaning stingy or mean, this is unknown in America.

clothes pegs, we call them clothes pins.

cubby house, unknown in America, although we sometimes call a small room a cubby hole.

cuddling, we call it necking, etc.

docket, we speak of a restaurant *check* or a laundry *ticket*, etc.

dummy, unknown in America; we call it a baby's pacifier.

feeder, meaning a baby's bib; unknown in America.

freight, never used to mean postage in America, and never applied to anything sent by parcel post.

gas-bagging, we call a talkative person a *gasbag* in America, but we have no verbal form of the term.

good on you, we say good *for* you, not *on*.

go to the pack, meaning to go to pieces; unknown in America.

haberdasher, in America, a haberdasher sells things for men only; in Australia, he sells goods for use of both sexes. Near where I live [Sydney] is a shop that does dressmaking and advertises haberdashery which, they tell me, is for women only.

jitney, Australians use the word to denote carrying more than one client or group of clients in a taxi; we apply it only to a bus.

keep nit, unknown in America; we say keep watch, guard, etc.

lane, Australians use it to mean what we would call an alley; it is used to denote a country road shaded by trees in America.

left off, in its application in Australia to second-hand clothing we do not know the term; we speak of cast-off clothing.

meat safe, unknown in America; we wouldn't call it a safe unless it was supposed to be burglar-proof or fire-proof.

mince steak, we call it mincemeat, chopped meat, hamburger steak, etc.

poker machine, we say slot machine.

pop, unknown in America with the meaning "to pawn"; we say *hock* or *soak*.

port, meaning a suitcase; unknown in America.

rafferty rules, meaning no rules at all; unknown in America.

ready, applied to a boxing or other contest, the result of which has been arranged beforehand; we say that the fight, etc., was framed or was a frame-up.

rock melon, unknown in America; we call it a cantaloupe.

safebreaker, unknown in America; we call such a person a safecracker, cracksman, etc.

savage, Australians say, "the dog savaged the man", bit him; but this verb is not used in America.

shaggy dog story, this term, although not the type of story, is unknown in America.

shaker, meaning a surprise; unknown in America.

stop, an American will say that he is stopping at a hotel or at a friend's house for a weekend, but that is practically the only time he will use the word "stop" to mean stay. No Yank ever says that he "stopped" in bed, etc.

sugar basin, we say sugar bowl; we would not apply the term "basin" to anything less than a foot in diameter, e.g. wash basin.

tomahawk, we use this word to mean only the weapon used by the Indians in the past, not for any hatchet.

totalisator, called pari mutel in America.

warn off, to ban from a sport; unknown in America.

welter, meaning a habit, specially in the form *make a welter of;* unknown in America.

These comments should serve as a guarantee that Australia is well able to preserve her linguistic identity, even though at the same time she shows every readiness to accept useful and colourful contributions from America.

There is also a question of spelling. If we spell harbour and favour without a *u*, programme without the final *me*, socks as sox, and even slip in an occasional thru instead of through, these do not imply that our language is going into a decline. Rather the reverse. It is going back on itself.

Take this matter of the *-or* suffix instead of *-our*. It is widely used in Australian newspapers and journals. It is universal in America, yet it is highly unlikely that we inherited it from America, for the simple reason that it has been current in Australia since the early 1850s when the two continents were scarcely known to each other. The Melbourne "Age" has used it from the outset of publication in 1854.[6]

A greater cause for complaint than the appearance of *-or* in our newspapers instead of *-our* is the fact that uniformity is lacking and that *-our* still battles along in competition with *-or* to the confusion of the Australian public. There is no reason in the world, apart from ignorance and prejudice, why uniformity should not be obtained in Australia, either in favour of *-or* or *-our*. Both are old English uses well vindicated by time. But to allow both forms to compete with each other in Australian

---

[6] The Editor of the "Age" wrote to me: "I should hesitate to ascribe this to American influence, not only because the continents were barely known to one another at that date, but also because the *-or* spelling was commonly used in these words from Middle English onwards."

schools[7], literature and newspapers is something so ridiculous that it would be impossible anywhere except in a young country.

In his "Sketches", written in 1758, Launcelot Temple wrote: "Our reformers in the art of spelling . . . at present . . . write Honor, Favor, Labor". That comment is sufficient proof that this -*or* suffix is not a modern fad imported from the United States. The spelling *program* instead of *programme* is another old English use, dating from the early seventeenth century and used by Scott and Carlyle among others. The "Oxford Dictionary" declares that *sox* is the "commercial spelling of the plural of sock" and quotes H. G. Wells' "Kipps" as offering the first example of it. *Thru* for *through* is an old English use that dates from the fourteenth century; the form *thro* was also widely used from the beginning of the sixteenth century.

Admittedly America has made use of these simpler forms of spelling, but they are not American "inventions". Let us lay phobias of this type away among the prejudices unworthy of us.

3. IMMIGRANTS

MANY IMPORTANT EVENTS occurred in Australian life around 1940, as I pointed out in Chapter X. Among these were our first large-scale acquaintance with Americans (in 1942 and later) and our still larger acquaintance with foreign-born newcomers from the Continent of Europe (which began in 1938, continued until 1940, and resumed again on a vast scale after the end of World War II).

The postwar mass migration of hundreds of thousands of Europeans to Australia has provided one of the most important events in Australian history. Linguistically, this has not as yet (1966) resulted in the emergence of any New Australian term which has acquired general acceptance. It has, however, had an extraordinary effect to which I will come in due course. Since this is linked with several important sociological matters, attention should be drawn to some of these.

First, there was the effect upon the Australian's traditionally isolationist attitude towards the rest of the world – a broadening of tolerance, a reluctant admission, as it were, that if other countries persisted in claiming a right to existence Australia could not do anything about it. Second, there was an accompanying tussle with some of the more infantile aspects of xenophobia. It would be underestimating the position to say that Australians resented the arrival of large numbers of alien migrants

---

[7] The "Sydney Morning Herald" of August 22, 1929, reported: "According to the Director of Education [N.S.W.] the department's attitude on the matter of spelling is generally one of strict observance of English usage although it recognises that certain American [*sic*] forms have established themselves. Hard and fast rules cannot be laid down. It sees little objection, for example, to the adoption of such forms as 'labor' and 'realize', but rejects such as 'program' and 'thru'." To augment the confusion it can be noted that the "Sydney Morning Herald" uses the spellings "labour" and "program" while its morning contemporary the "Daily Telegraph" uses "labor" and "programme".

in this country; their antagonism has been coloured by many unsavoury influences, which emerged in such ethnophaulisms as *D.P.*, *reffo*, *reffujew* and *Balt* (in the early stages) and *Naussie*, *migro*, *wog* and *emigranto* (the broken English spoken by alien migrants; earlier called *Baltese* and *Baltinese*).[8] However, although the anti-stranger attitude common to many Australians has inflicted a good deal of unnecessary unhappiness on some newcomers, the efforts made by Federal authorities in speeding up the assimilation of aliens has done a great deal to relieve social tension. Since conquest of the language problem is a central issue of assimilation, it is worth brief attention here.

Although Australia has had less experience of the growth of alien communities than many other countries – notably America – the Little Germanys formed by early German settlers in South Australia, the Little Italys of northern Queensland, the Little Yugoslavias of Western Australia, and the sundry Chinatowns now surviving mainly in Sydney and Melbourne, are reminders of the problems to be faced. By concentrating a frontal attack on the language problem, the Commonwealth Office of Education did a great deal to remove the likelihood that alien migrants would form similar foreign communities in Australia. It is, of course, too early to say whether these efforts will succeed in the long run, but judging from reports overseas the thoroughness and originality of the Australian programme has more chances of getting good results than techniques adopted by some other countries. By 1949, the Commonwealth Office of Education had arranged language-teaching for intending migrants at its European staging camps, aboard ships on the way to Australia, at reception camps in Australia, by continuation classes for migrants after leaving reception camps to take up work under their contracts with the Australian Government, by correspondence lessons for migrants living in remote districts and by the provision of special radio sessions for migrant listeners.

In 1945, the then-Minister for Immigration, Mr A. A. Calwell, was quoted as saying: "All newcomers, of course, will have to learn to speak Australian." Although this might sound absurd to folk who fail to recognise that Australia has acquired substantial dialectal characteristics of her own, it was an issue with which Federal authorities dealt courageously in their efforts to make assimilation easier. It was not enough to teach migrants English according to some loose estimates of what is orthodox English speech; some acquaintance with the specific form of Australian English was clearly necessary. Hence, the publication of a survey of Australian idiom in one of the Commonwealth Office of Education's migrant bulletins.[9]

---

[8] During the 1950s, the ingenuity of German immigrants provided the first hints of verbal opposition to this sort of thing. In German, the expression *Beutel-ratte* denotes an opossum or "pouched rat". With some stress on the "rat", German migrants transferred its meaning to "kangaroo" with figurative reference to a native-born Australian. By the mid-1960s, this was being anglicised into *boot rat*. I await with considerable philological interest the next development in the *boot rat* v. *wog* contest.

[9] "English . . . A New Language", A Bulletin for Teachers of New Australians in Continuation Classes, vol. 1, no. 2, March, 1950.

The Federal Government also urged (and gained wide official support for) adoption of the expression *New Australian* to denote an immigrant. This, of course, led inevitably to a native-born Australian being called an *Old Australian*, but in the process the Aborigines (sometimes called *the old people* and *First Australians*) experienced another spasm of rejection – and, as could be anticipated, finished a long way back in the race. A minor point is that the expression *Old Australians* must be distinguished from what migrants still call *old comers*, i.e. Europeans who settled in Australia in the years immediately before World War II or who reached these shores during the war. The following commentary speaks for itself:[10]

> Practically all D.P.s and post-war immigrants from Europe hate their own countrymen who settled in Australia before World War II. They call these *old comers* the *Mayflower* migrants and accuse them of indifference, unwillingness to help and standoffishness. Their accusations are unfounded. With a few unpleasant exceptions, Australians of foreign origin go a long way to help any newcomer, especially if he is from the *Mayflower settler's* own country. Many Australians think that this "sticking together" is even overdone. But the D.P.s and the new migrants see only that many *old comers* have houses, cars, businesses, jobs and have made a niche for themselves in Australia.

Students of new terminology will not miss the allusions to *Mayflower migrants* and *Mayflower settlers* – an international tribute to American origins.

One advantage which the European migrant has is that he often knows a great deal about foreign languages – subjects upon which the native-born Australian is notoriously weak. The former's ability to correct the latter in some of his mispronunciations has not been a source of nation-wide gratitude. I recall hearing (in March, 1942) an Australian radio actor, playing the part of Albert in "Victoria Regina", call his royal spouse *Leibchen*, which means a corset or a bodice, when what he meant was the endearment *Liebchen*, sweetheart. In Sydney "Mirror" of June 18, 1942, appeared *Auf Weidershen* when what was intended was *Auf Wiedersehen*. In Sydney "Truth" of June 20, 1943, a social writer perpetrated the ridiculous *femme chauffeur*. Other common perversions of French words are abba*TORZ*, for abbatoirs, and *BROA*sher, for brochure. (There is an Australian firm called *Bon Marché*, but it is inevitably pronounced Bon Marsh. *Gourmet* is widely rendered as *GORmay*; *lingerie* is *LON*jeray; *Courvoissier* (a brandy) is called Kaw*VOSS*ia; Mont de Piete, a name given to several pawnshops (actually from the obsolescent French *Mont-de-Piété*, a pawnbroker's shop) is pronounced Mont de Peet.

On the other hand, every alien migrant will readily admit that the Australians have some baffling turns of speech and the understanding of these, let alone their accurate use, is often far from easy. I have, for instance, heard a migrant referring to "the wild *dinkums* in the Australian bush", when what he meant was *dingos*, and another paying what seemed

---

[10] "Daily Telegraph", Sydney, October 8, 1949, p. 20.

a quite unnecessary tribute to a "*bosker* hat" a man was wearing, when what he meant was a *boxer*, an Australian term for a bowler hat. I also recall that an acquaintance from Austria once referred to an Australian folk-hero named *Ted Nelson*. It emerged that he had meant to allude to Ned Kelly!

Such nonce expressions are often highly important stepping stones in the conquest of language. They also offer interesting possibilities that from among them may emerge some term which will enter general Australian speech – much as these from a Czech friend of mine: *blokess*, a female "bloke"; *dullity*, dullness; *wantingness*, a state of wanting something; *good lookinger*, more goodlooking; *offenced*, affronted or suffering a feeling of being offended; *therer*, in that direction, "to there" or thither.

Adaptations from within a foreign language open still another door. A Hungarian newcomer reports that the English word *quarter*, as used in a quarter of a lb., has been rendered *kóta*, which Hungarians apply to musical notation and has nothing to do with weight. The English sixpence became *six pénz*, the word *pénz* peculiarly enough being the Hungarian word for money. More interesting still is the concocted Hungarian word *rézbab*, actually meaning brass beans, applied to what English-speaking folk call rice bubbles; and the concocted word *gépfruti* applied to grapefruit, composed of the Hungarian word *gép*, which actually means machine, and the pidgin *fruti*, which is a version of the English word "fruit", to which has been attached the typical Hungarian suffix *i*. Another Hungarian effort recorded in Australia is *megtésztázni* intended to denote the meaning "to test or try out". The operative part of this word is *tészta*, which approximates the sound of the English "test", but which actually means cake. The rest of the word consists of *meg*, which is used in Hungarian to indicate completed action, *áz* a suffix transforming a noun into a verb, and *ni* a sign of the infinitive. Another example is *csákózás*, used to denote charcoal, but based only on the flimsy resemblance in sound between the first two syllables of this word and the English word; the *óz* is an orthodox Hungarian form of the third person singular of a verb, and *ás* is the ending for a noun that has been made out of a verb. In a different category is such an example as *sorryvagyok*, which represents a straightforward collision between the Hungarian and English languages. *Vagyok* means "I am" in Hungarian, and the invented word is intended to denote "I am sorry".

A Dutch correspondent predicts that the only word from that language at all likely to reach general use is *smoking* for dinner jacket. He adds: "A dinner jacket is generally called a smoking in the Netherlands, and the Dutch migrant stubbornly sticks to his smoking".

The influence of New Australians in improving the eating habits of this community has been considerable although, to be quite fair, this is by no means new. Due to previous migration from China, Italy, Greece and Germany, we had more than a passing acquaintance with their food, but it was often of peasant quality. Modern migrants have done much to refine this influence, in restaurants, espresso coffee bars and delicatessens, at least in the main cities. One result has been the absorption of many new eating terms into Australian use.

In addition, Old Australians have been increasingly confronted with the existence of foreign tongues – in multiple-language advertisements, in radio sessions, in interpreters made available in various stores and shops.

In the early stages of this disturbance of his traditional insularity, the Australian reacted with vocal displeasure. Until well into the 1950s, acceptance tended to be limited to the observation, "Ar, he's not such a bad poor bastard!" – said after a newcomer had shown his worthiness to be regarded by Australians as one of their own. I recall reading three Australian novels in 1962 ("Down the Golden Mile", by Stuart Gore, "The Cruel Field", by John Naish, and "Gone Fishin' ", by Nino Culotta), each of which made some point of this. One of the migrant characters in "Down the Golden Mile" thinks this about Australians: "They intended above all things to remain Australian, and if you wanted to be accepted you must become one also."

As the tide of immigration continued, it seemed less likely that such an attitude could be maintained. But at this point, the Australian responded in a peculiar fashion which he had learned over the generations. This was a largely automatic reaction, but in order to understand its development it is necessary once again to look at the special quality Australians have given to the idea of mateship. To repeat what has been said before: Basic to the concept of mateship in Australia is the principle that when confronted with unpleasant circumstances, many different men will react separately to those circumstances in much the same way. From the days of the work-hunting nomads to Gallipoli and World War II, we have seen how this concept took shape and was polished by practical experience. We have also seen that it was fundamentally a masculine concept. Not exclusively, of course, but enough for us to recognise that mates are primarily men.

We have also been aware that these "unpleasant circumstances" have taken many forms – hardship and peril, *battling* and *bullocking*, social injustice and distress, almost anything where security is undermined. So when migrants poured into Australia after World War II on a scale the Australians had never experienced before – a million by 1955, two million by 1964 – mates unconsciously began to draw together again as though they were closing their ranks and mounting the barricades in defence of their country without being aware of their conduct. Due to various factors, although it later became apparent that the process had begun a good deal earlier, this did not emerge until early in the 1960s.

There were assorted manifestations – a fairly strong tendency on the proletarian level to use Australian words and phrases which newcomers could not understand (including rhyming slang and expressions with homoeoteleutic endings), revivals of obsolescent Australian terms, what appeared to be an increased highbrow use of Australian slang and a wide retreat into use of exaggerated forms of the Australian accent. At the same time, and it is important to remember this, younger Australians – mainly those born after the end of World War II, who had grown up during the time when the Australian identity seemed to be either confused or lost – showed a marked improvement in the quality of their speech (in the city, anyway), a diminished use of Australian slang and an increased use of (mainly out-of-date) American slang.

The contest can then be seen as basically between newcomers and Australian adults, with Australian juveniles more or less neutral until the the age of twenty and thereafter tending to join their elders. It should not be forgotten that, at the time of writing, two out of every eleven people in this country are migrants who have come here since the end of World War II. Since the migrant intake is continuing, the Big Change about which I wrote in Chapter X has many years to run yet.

CHAPTER XXI

Our Idiom in Literature

1. THE NEWSPRINT TRADITION

NO REVIEW of Australian literature and culture could ignore the part played by the original "Bulletin" (not the weekly journal of that name today) in the development of a distinct national psyche.

The old "Bulletin" was remarkable for something more than mere Australianism. It may be said to have formed a mould into which Australian creative talent was poured. It was a mouthpiece for the lusty desire of Australians at the close of last century to use words no matter for what purpose. Even more than this, it became a home-base for all those multitudinous snippets and trifles that form the true basis of Australiana.

From the outset of its career in 1880, the "Bulletin" was nationalistic in the keenest sense of that word. It began publication, it must be remembered, just a little over a century after the First Fleet arrived. Not until after 1850 did the Australian population exceed half a million. By 1880 the population stood at over 2,231,000. Into thirty years had been packed vast national growth.

Time and time again in this book, I have turned to "Bulletin" quotations for enlightment and example. This is not a matter of accident or caprice. The simple facts are that the material on bush lore, slang and idiom collected by thousands of writers in "Bulletin" pages is irreplaceable. Perhaps never in the history of world journalism has a paper stood nearer to the heart of a country than the "Bulletin"; probably never again will so much of the true nature of a country be caught up in the pages of a single journal.

Of course, the quality of it was varied. A good deal of the "Bulletin" material looks as though it had been carved out of the Australian environment with a bush-hook and not a pen, but good or bad the great bulk of it provides a magnificent glimpse of the Australia so few Australians appreciate. What in a few issues of the journal might appear trivial and unessential nonsense falls into place over the period of half a century like minute parts of an immense jigsaw puzzle.

No other Australian journal – not even Sydney "Truth" which started its career ten years after the old "Bulletin", but died before it – used slang more readily, more accurately, more diversely. No other journal attained such authenticity in its use of our idiom.

E. Morris Miller wrote in "Australian Literature" (1940):

> The Australianism of the "Bulletin" writers, led by J. F. Archibald, was a great effort to break away from its [i.e. England's] restricting effects,

and by this conception they stimulated a new sense of nationalism . . . These writers created concepts from their own environment, so that "local colour" became more and more an accident of expression and ceased to be an end in itself, and they checked the tendency of migrants to transplant concepts typical of England into Australia.

This influence was of immense service to Australian literature. It is impossible to dissociate from the "Bulletin" the names of writers like Henry Lawson, A. B. Paterson, John Farrell, Edward Dyson, W. H. Ogilvie, W. T. Goodge, Joseph Furphy, E. S. Sorenson, Steele Rudd, A. G. Stephens, Louis Stone, V. J. Daley and Randolph Bedford. Without that journal some of these names might still have been great, but many would have remained in obscurity. The "Bulletin" found most of these writers, nurtured them, gave them a voice that they could find nowhere else, made many of them famous.

If there is one factor constant among all these writers it is that they are Australian, not only by an accident of environment, but by literary instinct. It was natural therefore that they and other writers of less note should agree wholeheartedly with the "Bulletin's" enthusiasm for local idiom. Here, for example, is a collection of terms that appeared on the *Red Page* of December 17, 1898, proof that "Bulletin" writers were earnestly helping along the cause:

> *Horse-shoeing*, "abuse, obscenity, profanity"; *a bit off*, something inferior; *offsider*, an associate, assistant; *working dead-horse*,[1] working to pay off a back debt; *dead bird*, a certainty; *waster*, "a timber-getters' phrase for worthless logs or flitches, applied to men and things promiscuously"; *duck-shoving*, petty thieving; *nicking the peter*, stealing from tills in small shops; *get dead wet* and *go to market*, to become angry; *nark, Jonah, Noah's Ark*, an informer; *shiker*, drunk; *stoomey*, broke ("a stoomer or *stumer* is a man without money"); *mozzle*, "luck, derived from wurzschmozzle", whence *good mozzle*, good luck, *kronk mozzle*, bad luck; *to throw deuces*, to get along well, succeed nicely; *throw sevens*, to have bad luck, to do badly; *throwing the seven* and *throwing his hand out*, to die; *skiter* and *fluter*, an incessant talker; *to pass the flute* (or *kip*), "to allow someone else to do a pitch", i.e. to talk, this being from two-up slang; *chyack* or *chi-ike*, to cheek; *sweet, roujig, not too stinkin'*, *ryebuck* and *good iron*, good or excellent, the thing desired; *dead motherless broke*, completely penniless; *as mean as Hungry Tyson*, exceptionally mean; *uni*, university; *rotter*, "an adept at learning anything"; *pat*, a Chinaman; *spieler* and *guy-a-whack*, a dishonest bookmaker or a swindler; *gee*, a crook's confederate who "gees up the mugs"; *bludger* and *man-about-town*, a brothel bully; *battler*, a prostitute; *like a bandicoot on a burnt ridge*, lonely and forlorn; *like a possum up a gumtree*, "to express quickness or leverness in doing anything".

These expressions are distinct from what are known as *Bulletinisms*, that is, coinages either by the "Bulletin" itself or by its correspondents. The latter had little vogue outside the pages of that journal; the former belong to the general texture of Australian speech.

---

[1] From an earlier English use of *work for a dead horse* or *pull a dead horse*, employed similarly.

Aboriginalities and *aboliar* are examples of *Bulletinisms*. The first was the title given to a "Bulletin" feature on Aboriginal and Australian subjects which first appeared on April 21, 1888. It continued a few years, was dropped and returned again on December 18, 1897, whereafter it was a regular feature. *Aboliars* was the nickname given to correspondents to this feature; the original form was *aboriginaliar* which first appeared in 1900. *Aboliar* came on the scene in 1906. Synonyms used by the "Bulletin" were *abo writers* (1906), *aboites* (1909) and *abologists* (1914). *All abo-shine*, "all moonshine", was another invention that appeared in 1907, and *abo-lying* was used in 1908. These expressions, however, remained usable only within the pages of the journal itself.

In its early days the "Bulletin" gave a strong editorial lead in coining new expressions, many of which lasted some decades before becoming obsolete. For example, *the Foorce*, police in general (in recognition of the Irish element), 1883; *the Harmy*, the Salvation Army, 1883; *Salv'-army*, used similarly, 1914; the *Rum, Shroud, D.T., Evening Slime, Evenoose* and *Granny*[2], nicknames used in the 1880s for various Australian papers; *Cohentingenters*, Australian soldiers who fought in the Boer War (they were properly known as *Contingenters*, the *Cohen* being introduced by the "Bulletin" as a symbol of capitalism that forced the war), 1902-3; *anti-sosh*, anti-socialist, 1906; *secesh*, the secession movement by Western Australia, 1906; *the Ma Land*, England, 1907; *daily-paperese*, language or journalese used in daily papers, 1908; *Dryberra*, nickname given to Canberra, 1914; *Blawsted Kawlinies*, mimicking the English attitude to Australia; *Afrikanderland*, South Africa.

Partridge's statement that this journal coined *Maoriland* for New Zealand is incorrect. It was in use before the "Bulletin" existed. However, the paper was responsible for the abbreviation *M.L.*

It can be seen that the London "Times" was right when it wrote on August 31, 1903:

> It is hard to over-estimate the extent to which this journal modifies the opinions – one might almost say the character – of its readers . . . The "Bulletin" . . . is the nurse and the critic, somtimes severe, but sometimes friendly, of every young Australian who wants to write about things he feels and sees.

Sydney "Truth", originally published in 1890, was a staunch exponent of colloquialism. Though it had a reputation of scurrility, it had considerable influence in popularizing Australianisms. From its earliest days it strove to represent the city in the way the "Bulletin" had represented the bush; it therefore helped considerably to preserve indigenous slang.

---

[2] First applied to the "Sydney Morning Herald" in 1881; later to the Melbourne "Argus". The "Herald" was also referred to colloquially as *The Old Girl, Grandma* and *the Harlot of Hunter Street* (the "Herald" has now shifted from Hunter Street to Broadway) and at one time, long ago, was called *Aunty*. Other paper nicknames worthy of record – they are not Bulletinisms – are *Ananias*, an 1883 name for the Melbourne "Age"; the *Bully, Crimson Wrap* and *Bushman's Bible*, for the "Bulletin"; the *Digger's Bible*, "Smith's Weekly"; *Telly, Telewag* and *Furphygraph*, the Sydney "Telegraph"; the *West*, the "West Australian", Perth; the *Tiser*, the Adelaide "Advertiser".

Here are a few cullings from the paper in its first year of publication, 1890: *boomer, bushie, overlander, yabber, pointing, dead birds, the Block, rouse-about, Griffo, Telewag, double-banking, guy-a-whack, cockie, stonewalling, to poke borax, back-blockers, to cut out, to box up, give someone Bondi, humping bluey, the Crimson Wrap, bluestone, heading 'em, toe-ragger* and *sool on.*

Early "Truth" inventions, which probably owed much to that giant of journalistic invective John Norton, included *lagland,* Australia, *pilly-winky-popp,* nonsense, humbug, *cliquocracy, Holy Joeism, Safrica,* South Africa, *professional flossiedom,* the world of harlots, *Domainiacs,* frequenters of Sydney Domain, and *larrikinesque.*

"Truth" devoted special attention to sporting news and, as a consequence, developed racing jargon considerably. Bookmakers, for instance, were nearly always referred to as *bookie boys, bookie bhoys, bag boys, bag-swingers, tommies* or the *leather-lung brigade;* the starting post was the *peg,* jockeys were *hoops,* an all-up bettor was an *all-upper,* a favourite was a *hot-pot,* a handicapper was *a weight-juggler,* crooked racing men were *rampologists,* starting-price bookmakers were *S.P. merchants,* an outsider was a *no-hoper, no-chancer* or *a bolter,* a place was a *possie,* the close of a race (or the end of a game) was the *death-knock,* to defeat in a contest was to *stoush,* the racing world in general was *turfdom,* race-goers were *punterdom,* bookmakers were *bookiedom,* old-timers were *ziffsters,* a female bettor was a *puntress.*

Here is an example of the mixed metaphors in which "Truth" commonly indulged in its sporting gossip: "His defection was a life-saver for the bookie-boys, but Burberry took a lot of gilt off the gingerbread by coming with a wet sail and winning with his ears pricked." (From "Truth" of February 13, 1944.)

Frequent usages in football news were *Zam-buck,* an ambulance man; (*at*) *lemons,* the interval; *pigs,* football forwards; the *bag of wind* or the *puddin,* a football; *first* or *second stanza,* the first or second half of a game; and *Aussie rules,* Australian Rules football.

And here are a few general slang terms found in "Truth" pages: *motza,* a large sum of money; *curl the mo,* to succeed brilliantly; *curl,* a successful bet; *dinnyhayser,* something outstanding; *get the drum,* to be "tipped off"; *square off,* an apology; *toey, good* or *bad trot, top-off, con-girl, bottling* and, of course, *wowser,* which was mentioned several times in earlier chapters.

2. USE OF IDIOM BY AUSTRALIAN WRITERS

IF J. MacGregor, author of "Fifty Facts about Australasia" (1883), were alive today he would surely not repeat his generalization that "Australasia is the depository in the east of the language of Shakespeare and Milton". Nor would R. E. N. Twopeny, whose "Town Life in Australia" was also published in 1883, be able to tell us that most of our writers "draw their inspiration from English sources".

In short, during the passage of eighty-odd years, much has happened both to our language and to our literature. It is inevitable that these should be intimately woven together, for words and idiom are the bricks with which literature is built. The aptness of their use is largely a measure of the authenticity of a work, of its strength and colour, of the vitality that flows through its pages.

It is scarcely necessary to point out that most of our early literature failed to be recognizably Australian because the poets were singing in accents imitative of Wordsworth and Tennyson and Shelley or because prose writers were clutching desperately to ideas about English classics. They felt outcasts and exiles in a foreign land. They were not accommodated to their environment.[3]

But once they settled down to the feeling that there was something unique about Australia and Australians and set themselves to study their environment a great change came over our literature. Even the most casual observer will note the virility of numerous Australian books published since the early 1930s.

Here is how Norman Bartlett sums up the present day spirit:

> In the best modern Australian literature there is an authentic use of self-examination, a realism inspired by a search for national understanding, a desire for things as they are. And it is written in a racy, easy Australian idiom.[4]

The writers using this "racy, easy Australian idiom", have been mainly novelists, but poets, commentators and journalists can also be included.

Astonishingly enough, this idea that environment and idiom should be allowed to have anything to do with literature is foreign to some of our writers. Generally speaking, they espouse the cause that anyone with a fair vocabulary and a reasonable knowledge of grammatical rules can sit down and create literature provided he chooses the right (i.e. academically approved) exemplars. In a way, of course, this is true, but they will never get close to fictional characters and the background of those characters unless they are deeply conversant with the subtleties of idiom. This is one reason why our literary adolescence has been prolonged by a surfeit of *bushery* and *outbackery*, for that idiom and its background is fairly

---

[3] This expatriate mood has, in fact, survived in certain Australian quarters until recent times. Here, for example, is part of an address given by a former Governor of N.S.W., Lord Wakehurst, before the Australian English Association in 1944: "There has not yet been a long enough hereditary contact with Australian environment for the British Australian to become a native in his own new land. The time has not yet come when the kookaburra and the currawong can altogether be substituted for the thrush and the nightingale, or when the imagery of wattle-time and the woolshed can altogether take the place of the imagery of the English spring with the greenwood and the primrose, or of the English agricultural cycle with its harvest home." To which I replied in "Australian Pronunciation" (1947): "Ask a cow cocky on the northern East Coast what he thinks of the English harvest home and a cane-cutter what he thinks of the English agricultural cycle. Ask a Fitzroy labourer what he thinks of greenwood and primroses, and push your way into a Pitt Street pub to discuss the merits of thrushes and nightingales. Your questionees will regard you as a certifiable ratbag".

[4] Eric Partridge, in "The World of Words" (1938), says: "Such Australian . . . writers as are bitten with the nationalistic bug are almost as independent [in their use of the English language] as the most lawless Americans . . . because they exalt popular speech."

static, while the idiom of our modern cities is not. Yet there was a time, not many generations ago, when the outback represented just as much of a challenge.

In a review of "The Fiction Fields of Australia" in the "Journal of Australasia" (1856) a writer declared:

> The great mass of mankind can only hope to catch glimpses of the glory of "every common sight" when genius holds it up for them in the right light. This genius has not yet done for Australian nature. Most of us have had more than enough of positive Australian dialogue, but we have never read an Australian dialogue artistically reported. We have heard squatter and bullock-driver and digger talk, and we think it would be very uninteresting, no doubt; a verbatim report of the conversation of Brown, Jones and Robinson, in the old world, would be equally uninteresting, but we know by experience that genius can report it so as to be interesting – yet leave it the conversation of Brown, Jones and Robinson still. The first genius that performs similar service in Australia will dissipate our incredulity, as to this matter, for ever.

The writer was over-optimistic in his final mention of "for ever" because Marcus Clarke, Boldrewood, Henry Lawson, Steele Rudd, Sorenson, Louis Stone, Penton, Tennant and Herbert – among many others – have shown the Australian speaking in a way that is Australian, yet many are still unconvinced. The above writer adds:

> We cannot point out how the great untouched Australian quarry is to be rightly worked. Only as we roam about the motley streets, or ride through the silent bush, we have just sense enough to feel that, when the capable eye comes to look upon them, all these rude amorphous materials may be arranged in form of the highest and most artistic beauty.

Remarkable words these, written a little over a century ago. Just as that writer discovered Australia, felt its immensity and variety and strength, sensed its colours and shades, so must every Australian writer discover this country for himself. He can be helped along the pathway to that discovery, but the final revelation is one that only he can uncover.

If you have ever lived a long time in the bush or the remote inland, you will know what a special form this revelation takes. A theophany, psychologists call it. For months or even years, you will feel lost and resentful amid the emptiness and monotony and savage heat, the narrow round of action, the burden of fatigue that never seems to lift, the mental aridity in everything you hear. And then one day, perhaps at dawn or dusk, unheralded by any incident which you could think of as special, all this resentment falls away and you are one with the country. Cabell experiences such a theophany at the end of Brian Penton's "Landtakers" after a lifetime of hatred:

> Cabell looked out at the landscape as a man might look at a lovely mistress when his eyes had miraculously opened after a long illness. He forgot every imperfection and grudge in the sheer joy of gazing. The valley had never seemed so green before. How many times he had stood on this

spot and groaned to himself in an agony of boredom at the monotonous grey of the bush! But it was not monotonous at all. From second to second it changed . . . A weight lifted from his mind that had lain there since the day he landed in Australia . . . "Perhaps I always meant to stay", he thought, and when he dwelt on the idea he seemed to have known all along that things would end so, seemed deliberately to have planned and worked for it . . .

The discovery of the Australian language often comes as a similar surprise. It is one thing to concede that there are some linguistic relics of the past to be noted and another altogether to realise that this idiom of ours is all round us in every corner of Australian life. A common response is to suspect that these words and phrases must be English or American – or both. Whereas, of course, they are not.

If this book has any value at all, apart from a purely philological one, I hope it will serve to give Australian writers some fresh glimpse of the people who are this country and of the individual language they speak. But there is this point to be remembered: words alone do not make literature. There must be some transmuting genius in a writer. He must exercise the greatest care in his choice and use of idiom. To overload a book or story with Australianisms merely for the sake of using them would be almost as fatal as attempting to interpret Footscray in terms of London's West End.

3. LITERARY METAPHOR

IN THE ORIGINAL edition of "The Australian Language", I examined the way our idiom had been used in some forty books. Looking back now, I suspect that this approach was far from effective since it isolated words from contexts, displaying them like butterflies under glass, rather than as living products of our linguistic community. Here, I want to change the focus from words to phrases and from books to the people who use those phrases.

At earlier stages in this survey, I have noted how, originally in the bush and outback, scores of indigenous metaphors took shape out of contacts between people and the unique Australian environment, out of their special tasks and enthusiasms. We have seen, too, how many of these touch a chord of recognition in most Australians even after generations of use.

Now, there are many turns of speech in the English language that offer no real basis of recognisability at all. For example, *brave as a lion*. How brave are lions? Is bravery an inevitable feature of a leonine adjustment to life? Again, *as fit as a fiddle*. What is this fitness that is allegedly characteristic of fiddles? Can we assess it as a perfection of fitness? There is a multitude of such examples: *cool as a cucumber, thick as thieves, large as life* and so on. We call these expressions clichés. Yet it is obvious that at one time they must have seemed vigorous contributions to colourful speech. The mere fact that they have survived for long periods shows that they must have had some appeal.

The distressing point about metaphor, of course, is that it always holds the potentiality of becoming a cliché – for the simple reason that no turn of speech is ever so accurate or comprehensive that it is fully verifiable. Any non-verifiable statement that finds its way into popular speech is sustained by exactly the same influences as sustain the more obvious cliché. But it has this in its favour – its novelty and freshness are more likely to carry intellectual weight than an old cliché, the popular acceptance of which depends on a social conspiracy to avoid seeing whether it has any meaning at all. It is mainly a question of degree. At the same time, it is clear that we can go a long way towards gaining verifiability for our turns of speech if we exploit a known environment.

For example, the phrase *as dry as the Gobi desert* may seem a reasonable statement concerning dryness for people who know something about deserts; it will have particular point for travellers in out-back China. But it seems to me that the Australian would respond more promptly and intelligently to such phrases as *as dry as the Nullarbor* or *as dry as the never never* or *as dry as the dead heart* (or as dry as any of our three main deserts).

This brings us to an important matter – the localization of simile. Here are five examples from writings by well-known Australians, wherein (for no useful reason) external referents are sought:

(a) ". . . as deadly as a black widow spider". Why not *deadly as a funnel web*, since we have no black widow spiders?

(b) "She was going to cut a swathe like a Texas cyclone through my bee-keepers". Why not *like a willy willy* or *like a cockeye bob* or even *like a cyclone* since Australia knows them well, and in any case such Texan phenomena are called tornadoes?

(c) "She's had as many farewells as a trans-Atlantic liner". Why trans-Atlantic and not trans-Pacific liner? Why not just "ocean liner" if it is thought that trans-Pacific liners do not get enough farewells?

(d) "Gusts of wind sprang up. They were spasmodic and powerful. They roamed like wolves across the plain." Why not *dingos* instead of wolves?

(e) A tucker bag with "a neck as long as a giraffe". Why not *a neck as long as an emu* – or a cassowary or a brolga?

Still another Australian novelist refers to the "light arctic blue (eyes)" and "arctic aloofness" of a character. What does the writer gain from projecting his Australian story fleetingly into the northern hemisphere? It is a matter of trivial significance, it is true, but why "arctic" instead of "antarctic"? Is it bluer in the arctic than in the southern polar region, or does one acquire some additional measure of aloofness north of the equator than south of it?

Instances such as these represent a writer's conscious intervention in his construction of metaphor, but here we would suspect that the writer has been careless. His mind has wandered and he has let us down. He has acted as though he did not know that Australia has funnel web

P

spiders but no black widows, dingos but no wolves, emus but no giraffes, etc. He has failed to seize opportunities for freshening up imagery.

It is difficult to fix an approximate time for the beginning of this literary awareness in Australia. One of the earliest efforts was used in "Ralph Rashleigh" (1845), *roasted like a snake in a log*, but it was not until the "Bulletin" got going in 1880 that writers generally gained enough confidence in their environment to lend some polish to many expressions used widely in Australian speech.

In 1926, Cyril Hopkins wrote (in London) a Biographical Notice of the life and work of Marcus Clarke, 1846-81. In the course of this, he quotes a letter by Clarke:

> The Australian calls a herd of cattle *a mob of cattle*, a compact little mare *a little nugget of a mare*, a vicious horse is *a regular nut and no flies*, a man who stands brandy to his friends at an inn *shouts drinks for the crowd*. A betting man *goes his death* upon his favourite horse, a man drinking beer *puts himself outside his malt;* a poor-looking ill-bred horse is a *scrubber;* a man who boasts is a *blower* or *blowhard*. In the Bush, if you invite a stranger to partake of supper, you say, "Hullo, Mate! Come in and *sport your Dover!*" (A *Dover* is a knife.) A man who tells a good story of his own exploits is a *single-handed pitcher*. An Australian drinks *Hyson's Skin* and smokes *Barrett's Twist*. If he carries his knapsack or blankets on his back, he *humps his swag*. If he works lazily, he does the *real Government stroke* (borrowed from convict days this last). If he robs a man, he *sticks him up*. If he spends fifty pounds, he *knocks down fifty notes*. If he takes the nonsense out of a buck-jumper, he *lambs him down with the raw hide;* if his horse bolts, *he makes tracks for Glory*. If the wind blows hard, it is described as *coming it hard from the tombs*. I could go on for hours! All these expressions are quite different from those in use at home.

Many of these words and phrases have been obsolete so long that it is a little difficult to realise that they were once used in Australia. Others survive almost unchanged. Still others have been given new applications. If it could be said that they have any single quality it would be that most of them are fundamentally earthbound. Marcus Clarke was recording what he heard and making no attempt to develop figurative new dimensions. That did not occur until after the "Bulletin" had led the way towards linguistic emancipation, although some of its early efforts were so full of words that we can sense no more than the vague outlines of useful metaphor: *a harvest so poor the sparrows have to kneel down to get at the wheat, he thinks himself the whole team as well as the little dog under the waggon, tough as a buffalo hide left for six months on a bullants' nest, running like a wallaby with the dogs in full pursuit*. But along with these there were some crisply effective phrases: *a tongue as long as a stockwhip, fleeing like bandicoots before a bushfire, cold and dark as a bushman's grave*.

These did a great deal to give the Australian writer enough confidence in his own environment to realise that it could be used for figurative purposes. Progress was slow at first. It tended to be limited to the sort of metaphors I have given in Chapter IV in a round-up of Bush Idiom, which were mainly verbal uses. Then our authors began to flex the muscles of their imaginations. In "Such Is Life" (1903), Tom Collins spoke of eating "the damper of idleness" and of "the gutter of life", which was not a reference to the lowest point of human existence, but to its converse – the successful, gold-bearing *gutter*. In "Coonardoo" (1928), K. S. Prichard wrote of eyes "like namma holes in viscid orbits", of a new moon that was "a slim gilt kylie in the sky" and of clouds that were "dingy and dirty as greasy wool". In "Here's Luck" (1930), L. W. Lower wrote of girls "gazing with bright lizard eyes at our table", of an event that "thrilled and uplifted me like the fangs of a bullant" and reflected, "What are riches to a man who has just been stung by a bullant?" In "Landtakers" (1934), B. Penton wrote of "enough bits of me scattered round the store to feed a hungry dingo" and of teeth "like the relics of a burnt-out scrub".

These were not much more than scattered beginnings. It was not until 1942, when Eve Langley's novel "The Pea Pickers" was published, that we realised what could be done by a determined author: "screaming like wounded *brumbies*", "cigarettes (so large) a *wombat* could have crawled into them", "like flying *aborigines*", (a hill) "covered with grass like the hide of a *kangaroo*", "*boomerang-shaped*" (leaves), "*aboriginal* with shadow (i.e. dark or sombre),"leapt back like a startled *brumby*".

If these, too, seemed a little earthbound because of the restriction of their referents to the Aborigines and our flora and fauna, they at least pointed the way for others and they had much more to recommend them than one of Henry Lawson's rare similes: "the rifles crack like *stockwhips* amongst the gums . . ."

Let us pause a moment to see what other writers have done with much the same referents: as backward and as wasteful as a *black's camp*, a full-throated shout that wouldn't have been out of place at a *corroboree*, as out of place . . . as an automart in an *Aboriginal reserve*, those eccentric *bower birds*, the students of Australiana, the quarry were silent and elusive as the mountain *dingo*, (a man) ribbed like a poor *goanna*, (a man) wedged like a terrified *lizard* deep within a cleft in the rocks, I'd rather raise a litter of *goannas* than kids who talk like radio announcers pretending to be *Pommies*, a *possum dance* of a conversation, (humourlessness that) might even be trusted to silence a *kookaburra*, (clouds) with the colours of a *galah's* wings, no more passion than a peeved *paddymelon*, as interesting as a *billabong* full of dead *goannas*, (a woman) digging like a *bandicoot* in her *dillybag*, sniffed at me as if she was down wind from a dead *dingo*, safe as a *koala* in a reserve, squinting round like a great *goanna*, (a man who) walked like a *butcher bird* on a frosty rail, like a *mallee-hen* guarding its eggs, has been Australian as long as the *gumtrees*, as Australian as the *billabongs*, (a horse) came curving up like a great *boomerang*, I wouldn't lease this hole (an office) to a *witchetty grub*, they would harry him now as a *dingo* chases its game until it reels from fatigue and despair, his mouth was as big as a *pelican's*.

Upon such foundations as these the Australian writer began to build many effective and complex examples using local referents: free as the *willy-willies* that dance a ballet on the treeless plains, (an elderly woman) yapping like a *kelpie* at the laggard heels of less-energetic females, where the river *boomerangs*, big laughing eyes set in sockets deep as a dried-up *waterhole*, a nose so broad and flat that an *emu* could scratch gravel in it, (a dog) barking and spinning in the dust like a berserk *bunyip*, the men stood close together . . . like *sheep* huddling together for warmth, not as much whiz in him as a sick *sheep*, as easy to sieve the sands of the *never never* through a tea-strainer as . . ., (a face) gnarled like the crinkles in a *mulga root*, about as mobile as *mallee roots*, you can't start a business with a pocketful of *willy-willies*, (a nervous man who) shied past it like a *brumby* colt, a mob of *brumbies* in the engine, (a man) small and wiry as a mountain *brumby*, a thirst like a *sunstruck* bone, as much chance as a starved *bullock* twenty miles from a dry *waterhole*, (rackets that) smelt as highly as a long-dead *bullock* in a boggy *waterhole*, as thick as *gibbers* in Sturt's stony desert, (a pugilist) as open as the Nullarbor Plain to a right counter.

Still others have been adapted from observed peculiarities of Australian idiom: (news) amplified through the ecclesiastical *bush telegraph*, Katie bowled her daily *googlies* down, there always seems to be an *outback* beyond, (allusion to) a two-bowser hamlet, you would not expect a ripple from political *dumpers* to reach this quiet backwater, a rat-infested hole – a tin shanty temple of *bashdom*, *Speewa* imaginations – bachelors and liars all, (allusion to a branch of the Public Service) it is difficult to *point the bone* or apply the boot with precision, (a man) who would need assistance no matter *how hardy he cracked*, propagandists who have to *crack hardy* till the *death-knock*, (a book) which bore the same relationship to an orthodox travel narrative as does a Grecian urn to a U.L.V.A. *schooner*, a rude word lashes his nerves like a *stockwhip*, (a person) roaring like a *bombora*, *burley* to attract the curious, some of the sandwich shops in this town make *Ned Kelly* look benevolent, soundtracks palpably designed for radio's *Blind Freddies*.

Such examples as these (and many more could be offered) show the remarkable way in which Australian writers, some of them journalists in the course of their daily toil, have added new dimensions to our idiom. They do not occur by accident or by simple observation; they demand deep awareness and the conscious use of imagination. If they mean more to Australian readers than they will ever mean to readers in the northern hemisphere, at least they displace threadbare clichés and take another step in the development of colourful language.

4. POPULAR METAPHOR

THIS SECTION provides an important glimpse into a basic aspect of most linguistic development. We have seen how writers can add to the subtle complexities of figurative speech, but we are also aware that little of this will ever earn a place in popular use. Popular metaphor is always terser and less imaginative: *aggressive as a bullant, like a shag on a rock, fat as a match, rough as guts*, etc.

Like most slang and colloquialism, similes such as these are given their shape and original use by the anonymous proletariat. Usually it is impossible to fix even an approximate year for their beginning.

True, it must have been sometime in the days of swagmen that some-one noted that their dogs were rarely plump in order to give us *as thin as a swaggie's dog*; it must have been in the time of horse-drawn cabs that *the first cab on the rank* came to mean early in the day; someone must have had a fair acquaintance of goats to note that something rough could be *as rough as goat's knees*; and some early student of Australian sociology must have observed that the passage *from bowyangs to bowyangs* was often three generations.

Yet something else can be involved. In certain instances there comes a time when a phrase, or even an idea, is transmuted into a proverb or adage. Who on earth would have led the way to the conclusions that *opals are bad luck* and *wattle bloom brought indoors will bring bad luck?* Who first said that *crying babies* (e.g. in cinemas) *should be like bushfires – put out?* We can imagine bush origins for such declarations as *all men are lawyers in the bush* and *why keep a dog and bark yourself?* But how did *you don't have to be dead to be stiff*, *when you're on a good thing stick to it* and *first come, first served* get into our language? And why, of the many proverbs in English, did we renovate items like *don't wake it up!* don't mention it, for "let sleeping dogs lie", *don't do something you couldn't eat!* for "don't bite off more than you can chew", *keep the dingos off the front step*, for "keep the wolf away from the door", and *act the Angora*, for "act the goat"? Why, for that matter, does the Briton say "make rings around" while we say *run rings around*, and "good for you" while we say *good on you*, and "very spit of" while we say *dead ring of* and "a face like a sea-boot" while we say *a face like an old boot?*

Since most of these expressions have made their way up from the lowest rungs of the social ladder, where can we hardly expect that the deciding influence will be cool and leisured judgment, we are back again at our old theme of a linguistic community. These idiomatic phrases have become common between Australian speakers and hearers, and there seem to be few reasons – except perhaps a discontent with the stagnant orthodoxies of standard English – why they emerged in the first place and then caught sufficient attention in Australia to settle into verbal formulas. And many of them are little more than formulas. Consider that Australian greeting, *'ow yer goin' mate orright?* This five-word question is said without pauses. A more orthodox rendering would be, "How are you going, mate? All right?" And what outsider could even guess at the meaning of *send her down Hughie this one's a moral in the mud*, also said without pauses? To explain: *send her down, Hughie!* is an invocation (mainly, but not exclusively rural) for rain or a continuance of rain; "this one" refers either to a favoured racehorse or football team which does well in muddy conditions and "a moral" is a certainty.

There is another reason, of course, and this concerns the Australian sense of humour, which I examined in "The Drum" (1959). Essential elements of it include irony, terseness and the conjunction of seemingly incompatible images. Hence such verbal flights as: *if he threw a quid into the air it would come down a summons* (or *a parking ticket*), *not since Christ played fullback for Jerusalem*, *so crook I wouldn't even put my mother-in-law's money on it*, *he's so far behind on his maintenance payments his wife has threatened to repossess him*, *I haven't got enough oscar to put a deposit on a sav* (i.e. saveloy), *I don't think I'll last my shirt out*, *he's got no brains — and he's just as happy without 'em*, *black as the inside of a dog's guts*, *I was behind the door when it* (charm, sex appeal, etc.) *was served out*, *to know one's way* (to a destination) *with one's head in a bag*. I'm not sure that I shouldn't take this opportunity to mention that overworked phrase *you can't miss it!* (which has all the marks of standard English), used at the conclusion of detailed directions for finding a place; if my own experiences are any guide, many users of this phrase in Australia are too optimistic.

Here, now, is a round-up of the better-known Australian metaphors, set out under various headings to provide (I hope) fairly easy reference. They should be studied in conjunction with the bush metaphors listed in Chapter IV.

ACTIVITY:
   buzz around like a blue-arsed (*blow*) *fly*
   get stuck into

AFFIRM:
   swear on a bag of boomerangs (or *on a stack of Bibles*)

AGGRESSIVENESS:
   as aggressive as a bullant
   crack the (*big*) *whip*

ANNOY:
   get on (someone's) *works* (or *tit*)

ANTICIPATE:
   get under (someone's) *neck*
   get (or *have*) *the wood on* (someone)

AVOID TROUBLE:
   keep (or *come in*) *out of the rain*
   take a tumble to (oneself)
   wake in a stride

BALDNESS:
   bald as a bandicoot (or *a stone* or *a billiard ball*)

BECOME ANGRY:
   do one's block
   spit chips
   go crook at (or *crooked on*)
   go lemony at
   get off one's bike

BEHAVE BADLY:
> *to bung* (or *rap* or *stack*) *on an act*

BEST:
> *the daddy of them all* (or *of the lot*)

BETRAY:
> *put* (someone's) *pot on*
> *dob* (someone) *in*

BETTING:
> *you've got to be in it to win*
> *bet on a Sydney or the bush basis* (i.e. to wager money recklessly in an all-in fashion)
> *bet London to a brick* (i.e. to make a sure bet)

BLACKNESS:
> *black as a burnt log*
> *black as the inside of a dog* (or *cow*)

BOAST:
> *blow one's bags about*
> *big note* (oneself)
> *have tickets on* (oneself)
> *think one is Christmas*

BORROW:
> *stick* (or *put*) *the fangs* (or *nips*) *in*
> *chew* (someone's) *ear* (or *lug*)
> *stick it into* (someone)
> *put the bee on* (someone)

BRAVERY:
> *game as Ned Kelly*
> *what it takes*
> *my* (or *his*) *mother never raised a squib*
> (someone with) *blood worth bottling*

CAPSIZED:
> *head over turkey*

CHEAT:
> *go the knuckle* (or *knock*) *on*

CLUMSINESS:
> *like a duck in a ploughed paddock*
> *like someone with a handful of thumbs*

COLDNESS:
> *cold enough to freeze the tail* (or *nose*) *off a brass monkey*
> *cold enough to freeze the balls off a billiard table*

COMPLAIN:
> *whip the cat*

CONFUSE:
make a box of

CONTAGIOUSNESS:
spread like a bushfire

COWARDLY:
put on a dingo act

CRUDITY:
rough as bags (or *goat's knees*)
rough as a pig's breakfast
rough as guts (or *mullet guts*)

DEATH:
dead as a mutton chop
dead as a meat axe

DECEPTIVENESS:
more kid in him than a goat in the family way (or *than a pregnant goat*)
come the raw prawn

DEMAND:
put the acid on
put the hard word on (a woman)

DEPRESSED:
mopey as a wet hen

DERIDE:
sling off at

DIE (v.):
pass in one's marbles
to have had one's chips

DISADVANTAGEOUS:
you don't have to be dead to be stiff

DISLIKE:
have a snout (or *derry*) *on*

DISMISS:
wipe like a dirty nose

DISPUTE (v.):
argue the toss

DO WRONGLY:
pull the wrong rein

DRINK ALONE:
drink with the flies

DRUNKENNESS:
drunk as Chloe
drunk as a bastard (or *fowl* or *piss ant* or *owl*)
full as a goog (or *boot* or *tick*)
on one's ear

DULLNESS:
  dull (or *slow*) *as a month of Sundays*

EXPLOIT AN ADVANTAGE:
  come in on the grouter
  make your alley (or *marble*) *good*

FACIAL CHARACTERISTICS:
  a face like a gumnut
  a face as black as a wet shag
  a face as long as a month of Sundays

FAIR DEALING:
  fair crack of the whip
  fair shake of the dice

FLATNESS:
  flat as a strap (or *as the Nullarbor*)

FOUL PLAY:
  put in the dirt (or *boot*)

HAPPINESS:
  happy as Larry
  to feel like a box of birds

HURRY:
  go for one's quoits
  go flat out
  bust a gut

IMMATURE:
  (*someone*) *picked before he was ripe*
  three pen'orth of God help us
  (*someone who*) *couldn't keep up with his own shadow*

IGNORANCE:
  wouldn't know . . . from a fly's arse

IMPOSE ON:
  put on the crumb act

INCOMPREHENSIBILITY:
  (*marked*) *like a pakapoo ticket*

INCREDULITY:
  you wouldn't read about it!

IN DIFFICULTIES:
  up a wattle (or *gumtree*)
  up the well-known creek
  up to your knees in mud on a pushbike

INSPECT:
  take a screw at

INTERVENE:
  prat one's frame in

IRRITABILITY:
like a bloke with boils on his arse

LEAVE ALONE:
don't wake it up!

LET DOWN:
die on it

LONELINESS:
all alone like a country dunny
like a shag on a rock
on one's pat

MASTER (v.):
get the game by the throat

MEANNESS:
(*to throw money around*) *like a man with no hands*
to have death-adders in one's pocket

MEET ONE'S WATERLOO:
come the proverbial
get one's chips

MIND ONE'S BUSINESS:
mind one's own duckhouse (or *fowlhouse*)
who's robbing this coach?
who's milking this cat?

MISERY:
miserable as a shag on a rock
like a chromo at a christening

NO CHANCE OF SUCCESS:
not nominated and *not in the race*, i.e. has no chance of winning (from
    racing)
not the bolter's, ibid
hasn't (got) Buckley's
(a fighter who) *couldn't fight his way out of a paper bag*
(of a fighter) *he couldn't do it in the time!*

OBSTINACY:
as obstinate as a bulldog ant

OFFENSIVENESS:
smell like Dead Horse gully
honk (or *hoot*) *like a gaggle of geese*

OUT-DO:
run rings around
come all over (someone)

PAST:
the bowyang era

PLACIDITY:
>   (*sit*) *like a koala*

POVERTY:
>   *poor as a bandicoot* (or a *fowl*)
>   *as stiff as a crutch*
>   *so poor he's licking paint off the fence*

PUT ON A BRAVE FACE:
>   *crack hardy*

RARITY:
>   *rare* (or *scarce*) *as hen's teeth*

REMOTENESS:
>   *out near the Black Stump*
>   *the other side of* (or *beyond*) *the Black Stump*
>   *back of Bourke*
>   *out in the never never*

REPROVE (v.):
>   *give the rounds of the kitchen to* (someone)
>   *take a piece out of* (someone)
>   *roar the tripe out of* (someone)

SAFETY:
>   *safe as Tatt's*

SEEK ONE'S SHARE:
>   *get in for your chop*
>   *get your corner*
>   *put a knife through*

SETBACK:
>   *one up against* (someone's) *duckhouse* (or *fowlhouse*)

SHOW PANIC:
>   *go to the pack*
>   *drop one's bundle*
>   *run (a)round like a decapitated chook*

SICKNESS:
>   *poor as wood*
>   *sick as a blackfellow's dog*
>   *to feel as though one will give birth to bullants* (or *a litter of rattlesnakes*)
>   *have* (or *get*) *the wog*

SLOWNESS:
>   *drag the chain*

SPEED:
>   *to run like a blackfellow*
>   *go through like a Bondi* (*tram*)

STEAL:
>   *get down on*

STUPIDITY:
> *silly as a bag* (or *tin* or *hatful*) *of worms*
> *silly as a two bob* (or *halfpenny*) *watch*
> *silly* (or *mad*) *as a cut snake*
> *silly as a wheel*
> *mad as a snake* (or *goanna* or *beetle* or *dingbat*)
> *mad as a gumtree full of galahs*
> *balmy* (*barmey*) *as a bandicoot*
> *as free from sense as a frog from feathers*
> (a man) *without enough brains to give himself a headache*
> *off one's pannikin* (or *tile* or *cadoova* or *top* or *saucer*)

SUCCESS:
> *get on like a bushfire* (or *like the proverbial bushfire*)
> *go through* (something or someone) *like a packet of salts*
> *go like a bomb*
> *come good*
> *curl the mo*
> (in an amorous exploit) *do some good for oneself*
> *get* (or *draw*) *a guernsey*

SURFEIT:
> *more than you could poke* (or *throw*) *a stick at*
> *fed* (*up*) *to the gills*
> *full to the gills*

SURPASS:
> *leave for dead*

TAKE THE BEST:
> *pick the eyes out of*

TEASE:
> *poke borak* (or *mullock* or *dirt*) *at*

THINNESS:
> *thin as a fence rail* (or *a fowl's face*)
> *fat as a match*
> *poor as string*

TOUCHINESS:
> *touchy as a bulldog ant* (or *a taipan* or *a Queensland buffalo* or *a scrub bull*
> *in a bog*)

TOUGHNESS:
> *tough as fencing wire*
> *tough as seasoned mulga*
> *hard* (or *rough*) *as goat's knees*

TROUBLE:
> *in more strife than Ned Kelly*

TROUNCE:
  to do (or *down*) *like a dinner*
  all over (someone) *like a rash*
  flatten like a tack

TRY:
  give it a go
  give it a bash (or *a lash*)
  have a bash (or *a lash*) *at*
  get stuck into
  come at (something)

UNCONSCIOUS:
  like a stunned mullet
  like a half-stunned duck

UNDERSTAND:
  take a free wake-up to
  latch on to

UNPLEASANT:
  on the nose
  on the bugle (or *trumpet*)
  (a person who is) *a nasty piece of work*
  (something that) *would kill a brown dog at ten feet*

UNREASONABLE:
  over the edge (or *fence*)

UNSATISFACTORY:
  no good to gundy
  not worth a bumper (or *cracker* or *crumpet* or *frankfurt* or *razoo* or *sausage* or *tray bit*)
  not worth a cupful of cold water

UNTIDY:
  look (or *be*) *like a dog's breakfast*
  head like a bird's nest – mud outside and muck inside

UNSUCCESSFUL:
  (applied to a racehorse) *couldn't run down a well*
  (racehorses) *running up lanes*
  run like a hairy goat

VERBOSITY:
  all yak and no yakker

VIGOUR:
  fight like a threshing machine
  full of bushfire
  like a willy willy

WARNINGS:
if you can't be good, be careful!
don't do something you couldn't eat!
take it easy!
easy on!
wake up to yourself!
don't wake it up!
watch your step!
watch yourself!
pull your head in!
break it down!

WEAKNESS:
weaker than a sun-burned snowflake

WEALTH:
a roll Jack Rice couldn't jump over
a roll that would choke an anteater (or *choke a bullock* or *choke a donkey*)

WELL-BEING:
any better, I (*he,* etc.) *couldn't stand it*
any better, I'd (*he'd,* etc.) *be dangerous*

WELL DONE:
home and hosed
home on the pig's back

WITHDRAW:
give the game away

CHAPTER XXII

The Australian Accent

1. DISCOVERERS

WHEN I TACKLED this Section in the 1945 edition of "The Australian Language", I began with the observation that more nonsense had been written about the Australian accent than about any other feature of our language. Perhaps partly as a result of my comments, that is no longer true, for much has been done in the past twenty years, notably by academicians, in giving the subject the attention it deserves. This development was certainly not before its time. For the best part of a century we had been afflicted with the drivellings of people who had opinions to air on the subject of Australian speech, either to damn Australians or to defend them – people who told us that we had a twang or a drawl, that we talked through our noses, that we were Cockney or that we weren't Cockney, that we spoke clearly or were slovenly and careless, that we failed to open our mouths enough, that we were lip-lazy and tongue-lazy, that we were not as bad as we were painted.

There was even lack of unanimity on whether we had an accent at all. For example, in "Oceania" (1873), J. A. Froude commented on the purity of Australian speech. "In thought and manners, as in speech and pronunciation, they are pure English and nothing else," he wrote.

If this was so in 1873, how was it that the N.S.W. School Commission of 1854-5 could report: "Little care is apparently taken [in N.S.W. schools at that time] to correct vicious pronunciation . . . this inattention has a tendency to foster an Australian dialect which bids fair to surpass the American in disagreeableness . . ."? Still earlier, Mrs Charles Meredith had written in "Notes and Sketches of New South Wales During a Residence in that Colony from 1838 to 1844" (1844): "A very large proportion of both male and female natives *snuffle* dreadfully; just the same nasal twang as many Americans have. In some cases English parents have come out here with English-born children; these all speak clearly and well, and continue to do so, whilst those born after their parents arrive in the Colony have the detestable snuffle."

By the same token, if Oliné Keese (Caroline Leakey) could comment in "The Broad Arrow, Being Passages from the History of Maida Gwynnham, a Lifer" (1859) on "the freedom from peculiarity in the tone and pronunciation of the natives" – these "natives" were the Hobart-born children of both voluntary and involuntary immigrants – how is it that in the same year R. H. Horne could remark on "the colonial twang in the speech" in his "Australian Facts and Prospects" (1859)?

If G. L. James was correct when he wrote in "Shall I Try Australia?" (1892) that Australian speech was "free from any distinguishing accent or provincialism to a marvellous extent" how on earth could Boldrewood manage to write in "Robbery Under Arms" (1881) that "most of the natives [i.e. native-born Australian whites] have a sort of slow sleepy way of talking"? Or in "A Bride from the Bush" (1890), E. W. Hornung could refer to "a lingo that declined to let the vowels run alone, but trotted them out in ill-matched couples"? Or on January 13, 1894, the "Bulletin" could publish a poem entitled "The Austrylian Songstress" which concluded with the lines:

> 'Twere better if thou never sang
> Than voiced it in Australian twang.

Obviously, and this is confirmed by quotations given in the next Section, some commentators had either been getting around with their ears closed or had limited their experience to special social groups. There was so much disagreement in their observations that the most that could be said was that Australians *seemed* to have developed an individual way of speaking, which had a "twang" or something American about it, but as to its precise nature there was no guide.

The most constant and indeed the oldest linguistic charge levelled against Australians was that they spoke like Cockneys. This charge was first made – by implication only, it should be added – in 1826, when Cunningham reported in his "Two Years in New South Wales" that "The London mode of pronunciation has been duly ingrafted on the colloquial dialect of our currency youths". He also referred to persons from London and its vicinity who had "thus stamped the language of the rising generation with their unenviable peculiarity". Cunningham's reference to "the colloquial dialect of our currency youths" of course raises a point whether some indigenous dialectal peculiarities had not even then become apparent in Sydney, or whether he was alluding only to local slang, which as this book has shown had begun to take shape by that time. In any case, did he mean Cockney when he wrote of "the London mode of pronunciation"? Did he infer that Cockney was the only dialect spoken in the "vicinity" of London? And what did he mean by "unenviable peculiarity"? Since we can answer such questions only by guesswork, restraint is clearly in order.

2. COCKNEY – FOR AND AGAINST

THAT THERE WAS a considerable Cockney taint in early Australian speech we can have no doubt. We have already seen how London slang and cant was delivered to this country by many of the convicts and their caretakers; it would be illogical to expect that the accent of London slums and prisons should have been left behind. Until 1830 Australia's population numbered only 70,000; these people were mainly established in well-defined groups, at Sydney, Hobart, Port Phillip, etc. Imported English accents (what of the Irish?) would therefore tend to be preserved, or to be absorbed by the strongest of these accents, the Cockney.

That tendency was apparently not only preserved but reinforced by new immigrants. For instance, in "Our Antipodes" (1852), G. C. Mundy alludes to "Sydney Cockneys", and in "Gold Regions of Australia", published in the same year, S. Mossman speaks of "the Cockney drawl of hucksters, selling fish and fruit [which] sounds so refreshing on the ear – so thoroughly English".

It is interesting to note that between the time when gold was discovered in Australia in commercial quantities and the late 1880s practically nothing, apart from trivial comments, was written about Australian methods of speech. Those thirty-five years or so had seen the population grow from 500,000 to some 3,000,000, they had seen the establishment of city life and of home life, the growth of families that were not only Australians but the sons and daughters of Australians, and, as we have seen early in this book, the firm establishment of an indigenous idiom. They had been years of vast development during which little except the material had been allowed to intrude: homes to be built, land to be tamed, money to be made. There was little time for reflection.

The end of the 1880s and the 1890s brought the first period of soul-searching in Australia. One of its minor manifestations was a series of semi-phonetic observations by Samuel McBurney, a schoolteacher, in 1887. Many of these observations are of considerable interest, since they show that several strong tendencies in Australian speech today had taken shape at that time. So far as this Section is concerned, McBurney's most pertinent deduction was: "But why there should be a general tendency, as there undoubtedly is in Australia, to a Cockney pronunciation . . . is a mystery still to be explained."

In "The Australian at Home" (1891) Edward Kinglake wrote of some bush children: "They all had the colonial accent which is almost identical with the Cockney twang."

The "Bulletin" went further in a leader headed "Twang" on January 6, 1893:

> Chief Justice Madden has dared to attend a girls' school Speech Day and tell the angels that their speech is disfigured by a "colonial twang". He besought them to pronounce the English vowels as they are intended and to keep their little noses out of the matter as much as possible. Whereupon the [Melbourne] "Argus" started a solemn enquiry into the why and wherefore of twang in this country and came to the conclusion that it is begotten of mental and physical laziness. Ghastly nonsense is lavished upon the subject of "colonial twang". Practically, there is no difference between the dialect of the London loafer, who leans against a wall and spits, and the pronunciation of the southern larrikin, who does ditto. But in this country the nasal loafer is more generally in evidence, his voice is more heard, and his accent infests the land instead of being localised. The early English convicts, mostly from London, brought it with them. Early Australian parents were too busy, and generally too uneducated, to notice that

their offspring had caught the complaint, and said "kike" for "cake" and "gripes" for "grapes". In England the desire to imitate the twang is knocked out of the children at boarding school . . . If the thing is to be eradicated [in Australia] the reformers must start upon State schools at once, for every year brings its thousands of recruits to the twang brigade. At present there is no effort made to raise the standard of State school accent, nor are the masters in general aware that it is a terrible thing to hear the youngsters reading. They read nearly as nasally themselves. The twang is everywhere – in Victoria, at any rate – ringing in one's ears. If it remains on familiar terms with society for a few years longer, it will become the accepted pronunciation of the country and pass as "good form". But whether the "colonial twang" dies out of Australian mouths or grows and strengthens and is improved, on the American system, the fact will remain that it was never at the beginning anything better than the twang of Cockney vulgarity. We imported it, long before rabbits, sparrows, snails and other British nuisances were grafted upon our budding civilisation.

This commentary contains some important points, which will be dealt with subsequently. The most relevant matter to be noted here is that it plumps strongly for the Cockney theory, although the sole example adduced is for the conversion of the diphthong [eɪ] to [aɪ]. This conversion, plus the conversion of the diphthong [aʊ] into a triphthong, has been accepted by many observers as sufficient evidence to prove that our accent is Cockney from first to last. Kinglake (1891), quoted above, flourished these two examples as support for his indictment.[1]

G. L. James wrote in "Shall I Try Australia?" (1892):

As to the English spoken in Australia, I believe it has already been remarked how correct, as a rule, it is, and I think it is free from any distinguishing accent or provincialism to a marvellous extent, while the tone of voice is pleasing and well modulated. In Sydney, however, more particularly the young girls, especially of the lower classes, are apt to affect a twang in pronouncing the letter *a* as if it were *i*, or rather *ai* diphthong.

Here is a reasonable statement. One diphthong does not make a dialect, nor does it convict us of using an imported dialect *in toto*. Nor, for that matter, do several diphthongs – as listed by a writer in the "Bulletin" of March 23, 1901 – since some of our diphthongal developments do not appear to be mirrored in Cockney or to be collectively representative of any dialect but Australian.

As J. Foster Fraser said in "Australia, The Making of a Nation" (1910):

To charge a person with talking like a Cockney has behind it an intention to be supercilious and rude . . . To say that all Australians talk Cockney is just one of those exaggerations which the mass of people have a right to repudiate . . .

---

[1] A writer in the "Bulletin" of September 3, 1892, noted: "Even tolerably well-educated Australians in pronouncing words containing the long *a* vowel (the writer meant [eɪ]) fall into a branch of Cockney twang, as for instance, pronouncing lady as though it were spelt lydy."

Since no observer has yet been able to produce more than a few resemblances between the Australian and the Cockney accents, the allegation that Australians talk like Cockneys must be regarded as one of the popular myths to which we, as a young nation, are susceptible.

Probably the best words ever spoken on behalf of the anti-Cockney theory were by Thomas Wood in "Cobbers" (1934):

> Australians don't [talk Cockney]. People who say they do know nothing of accents and nothing of voices. They judge by vowels and inexpertly then. They disregard intonation, inflexion and quality. Are the Cockney and the Australian voices alike in these? They are not. The first is husky and the second is thin. The first flicks up and down; the second stays level. The first slides its words into groups; the second drawls them, one at a time. You do not find the Cockney stresses in Australia, nor, incidentally, the wit . . . Australian vowels . . . reminded me of vowels I heard in the South Midlands rather than those I had heard in East London; they are the malformations you can make for yourself if you keep your tongue flat and tighten the lips. Ugly? That is a question of taste. But ugly or not, these vowels, like the characteristic intonation that goes with them, show how our tongue has developed in a particular country, and a condemnation based simply on prejudice is not justified.

Hector W. Dinning is another writer who takes up the cudgels on behalf of the anti-Cockney theory. His extensive observations on our accent in "The Australian Scene" (1939) make interesting reading. He was followed by, among others, T. S. Dorsch, in a chapter on the Australian Accent in "Some Australians Take Stock" (1939),[2] and A. G. Mitchell, "The Pronunciation of English in Australia", a pamphlet published in 1940 and later expanded into a book.

In "Australia Limited" (1942), A. J. Marshall wrote:

> The only product besides wool that Australia has anything like a corner in is her inimitable accent and nobody is likely to want to take that off our hands . . . A lot has been written about the Australian accent, but one thing only has been agreed upon. That is, that of all the accents evolved by British-speaking man, it is along with that of the Cockney, by far the most unpleasant . . . Americans and Englishmen say briefly that "Australians talk like Cockneys". A sensitive ear will tell you that there are noteworthy differences . . . There is nothing unnatural about the Australian accent. It is a legitimate, local variation of speech. The trouble is that it is so damnably unpleasant.

By the early 1940s it could be said that the Cockney Theory had reached its wearisome end. Looking back today, it is hard to realise how much disputation occurred and how much paper was consumed in agonising over those disputes. Of course, we still have to look into

---

[2] Dorsch wrote in "Some Australians Take Stock" that "Always, and generally very quickly, there comes a point at which the dissimilarities [between Australian speech and various English dialects, including Cockney] are seen to outweigh the similarities so heavily that further comparison must be dropped."

Professor Marshall's complaint that the Australian accent is "so damnably unpleasant", but that is a matter to which we will come in due course.

3. OUR SPEECH EXAMINED

IN ORDER TO GET the record straight, a couple of points must be stressed at the beginning of this Section and I will make those points as briefly as possible.

First, the detailed phonetic survey I gave in the 1945 edition of this book was, as I then stated, the first thorough examination ever made of the Australian accent.

Second, this survey led to the deduction that there were *three* unmistakeable types of Australian speech. Although some anticipation of what follows is involved, these were defined as follows:

> A_1, the most slovenly form of our speech, characterized by all the typical Australian features we have noted, the closed mouth, the taut lips, the lowered soft palate and the consequent vocalic and consonantal modifications.

> A_2, an improved form of the above, still retaining the features noted, but to a less degree. In short, a type of speech in which some effort is made to resist the mixing or centralization of vowels, and in which nasalization is avoided in consequence of a more opened mouth.

> A_3, a cultivated type of speech, still containing typical Australian elements, but characterized by an attempt to preserve English vowels by opening the mouth and by an absence of nasalization.

At that stage, my main competitor in the field was Dr A. G. Mitchell. His view was that there were *two* types. To quote from a lecture he gave before the Australian English Association in 1940: "There is a broad, popular form spoken by all kinds of people, and an educated, professional form also spoken by all kinds of people." In the first edition of his book, "The Pronunciation of English in Australia" (1946), Dr Mitchell said: "There are two well defined types of speech in Australia, an educated, cultivated, professional speech, and an uncultivated, popular speech." He subsequently referred to these types as Broad Australian and Educated Australian.

Not until nearly twenty years later, when he handed over to Arthur Delbridge and "The Pronunciation of English in Australia" was thoroughly revised to incorporate findings from tape-recordings made by some 9,000 secondary school students, were *three* varieties of Australian English postulated – Broad, General and Cultivated. In the long interval, before Professor Mitchell left the University of Sydney, his phonetics students had been misled as to the nature of Australian speech.

Let us now turn away from such issues and look into the heart of this speech. (If the general reader has no interest in phonetic matters, he could skip this Section and take up the story in Section 4.) For the sake of elucidation it would be well to point out here that vowels are classified according to the part of the tongue that is raised during their formation. When we talk about the front of the tongue we do not mean the tip: we mean the part of the tongue opposite the hard palate. The back of the tongue is that portion opposite the soft palate. Front vowels are formed by raising the front of the tongue towards the hard palate; back vowels are formed by raising the back of the tongue. Mixed or central vowels are produced when the highest part of the tongue is between the front and the back.

VALUES OF PHONETIC SYMBOLS

i as in bead
ɪ as in bit
ɛ as in dead
æ as in man
ɑ as in pa
ɔ as in caught
ɒ as in not
o as sometimes in the first syllable of molest, obey
ʊ as in book
u as in boot
ʌ as in bun
ɜ as in bird
ə as in the first and third vowels of banana
eɪ as in bay
oʊ as in low
aɪ as in my
aʊ as in now
ɔɪ as in boy
ɛɜ as in where
j as in yes
ŋ as in sing
θ as in think
ð as in then
ʃ as in she
ʒ as in measure
tʃ as in church
dʒ as in judge

Figure I should be kept in mind in reading the following comments on Australian vowel uses, especially because these vowels are treated in the order adopted by Daniel Jones in "The Pronunciation of English" (1927). I have used what is known as the "narrow" form of the international phonetic alphabet, whereas Jones uses the "broad" form. In each case in which the symbols differ I have given an explanatory note. Occasional references are made to New Zealand vowel uses as recorded by Arnold Wall in "New Zealand English" (1938). Much of the material which follows was given in the first edition of this book; to it I have added various examples which I gave in "Australian Pronunciation" (1947), together with later comments and references.

POSITION OF TONGUE (Lips)	FRONT	CENTRAL	BACK
HIGH (Close)	i ɪ		u ʊ
MID-HIGH (Half-close)	e		o
MID-LOW (Half-open)		ɛ ɜ ə ʌ	
LOW (Open)		æ ɔ	
		a ɑɒ	

FIGURE I – *A table of vowels as used in Educated Southern English. (Adapted from Daniel Jones, "The Pronunciation of English".)*

(A) VOWELS

To avoid unnecessary confusion I do not include mutilations of one vowel in phonetic renderings of another vowel, unless these are of a compensatory nature. The word *very* [vɛrɪ], for instance, contains modifications of both the [ɛ] and the [ɪ] in Australian speech, but in the discussion of it in Section 4 on [ɛ] the final vowel changes are not added.

1. [i] as in *meet, sea* (rendered [i:] by Jones).
Australians and New Zealanders both prefer to shorten this vowel to [ɛ] in cases in which it is a primary or intermediate vowel. Thus:

economics becomes [ˌɛkɒˈnɒmɪks] rather than [ˌikəˈnɒmɪks]
evolution becomes [ˌɛvoˈluʃən] rather than [ˌivoˈluʃən]
equine becomes [ˈɛkwaɪn] rather than [ˈikwaɪn]
amenities becomes [əˈmɛnɪtiz] rather than [əˈminɪtɪz]
tenet becomes [ˈtɛnɛt] rather than [ˈtinət]

It is important to note that *both* pronunciations are regarded as "correct" by linguistic authorities. Daniel Jones gives both versions in "An English Pronouncing Dictionary". In Australia, the displacement of [i] by [ɛ] in such cases can be regarded as a national habit.
Where this form of shortening does not take place there is a strong tendency to diphthongize the vowel. The English tendency to transform [i] into [ij], as in *sea* [sij], is noted by Jones and occurs also in Australia. It is not so prevalent as the diphthongized version [əɪ], noted by both

Mitchell and Wall, as in *tea* [tɔɪ] and *sweets* [swɔɪts]. Other Australasian corruptions are in the direction of [iə] (sometimes [ɪi]) as in *seen* [sɪən], *been* [bɪən] (noted by an Australian observer in 1901); [eɪi] and [eɪij], as in *mean* [meɪin] or [meɪijn] and *pea* [peɪi] or [peɪij].

Just as the Australian tends to avoid [i] by using the short [ɛ], he also prefers to use the diphthong [aɪ] in certain cases, such as:

crinoline ['krɪnolaɪn] rather than ['krɪnolin]
iodine ['aɪodaɪn] rather than ['aɪodin]

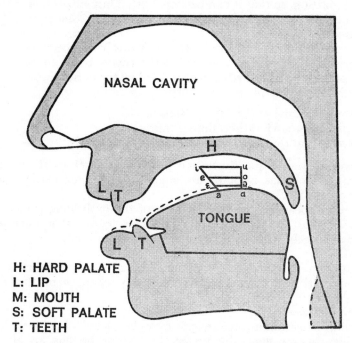

NASAL CAVITY

H

S

L T

TONGUE

L T

H: HARD PALATE
L: LIP
M: MOUTH
S: SOFT PALATE
T: TEETH

FIGURE II – *The dotted line shows in somewhat exaggerated form the approximate position of the speaker's mouth compared with the Educated Southern English speaker's mouth. The diagram drawn on the tongue represents the (formalized) positions reached by the highest points of the Southern English speaker's tongue in sounding the eight cardinal vowels. It will be seen that the closing of the Australian mouth reduces the space, between the tongue and the roof of the mouth, in which the vowels are sounded.*

2. [ɪ] as in *fit, will, beauty* (final vowel). (Rendered [i] by Jones.)

Jones notes a certain Cockney tendency to render this vowel as [ɛ] and to diphthongize it when it is final, as in *twenty* ['twɛnteɪ] instead of ['twɛntɪ]. Wall points out the New Zealand tendency to render final [ɪ] as [i], as in *billy* ['bɪli], *city* ['sɪti], *industry* ['ɪndəstri]. This occurs also in Australia, but a downward pull is exerted by the modification of [i] to [eɪi]. (Jones notes that in Austral English, "[ɪ] is replaced by the corresponding tense vowel, as in *very* ['vɛri]".) In Australia, various pulls can be heard in the direction of [əɪ], [ə], [ɜ] and [ʌ]. This [ʌ] is found in frequent association with the consonant *l*. Thus, *milk* becomes [mʌlk], *shillings* ['ʃʌlʌns], *railway* ['rʌlweɪ], *Phillip* ['fɪlʌp] or ['fʌlʌp]. In some cases, *will* tends to become [wɜl] or [wʌl], *stupid* changes towards ['stjəpʌd] and ['stjʌpʌd], *children* becomes ['tʃɜldrɛn] or ['tʃʌldrɛn]. The pronunciation [ʌt] for *it* was noted in 1901.

As already observed, final [ɪ] tends towards diphthongization – a Cockney perversion; but Australians sometimes take it further into triphthongization, so that it can become [eiɪ]. Thus *billy* becomes ['bɪleiɪ], *nearly* ['nɪrleiɪ] (or, since the *r* is often dropped, ['nileiɪ]), *pity* ['pɪteiɪ] and so on.

The appearance of the pure [ɪ] in Australian speech is somewhat rare, since in both medial and terminal forms it tends to change. The absence of the true [ɪ] is further accentuated by the Australian's preference for the diphthong [aɪ] in certain words, such as:

finance ['faɪnæns] rather than [fɪ'næns]
infinite ['ɪnfaɪnaɪt] rather than ['ɪnfɪnɪt]
vituperate [vaɪ'tjupəreɪt] rather than [vɪ'tjupəreɪt]

However, the unique Australian pronunciation *bream* [brɪm] instead of [brim], which has been in use since the 1890s or earlier, deserves special recognition.[3]

[ɪ] also appears as the first element of the diphthong [ɪɔ] as in *here* [hɪə], *dear* [dɪə] and *interfere* [ɪntə'fɪə]. This tends to become [eɪɜ] in Australian speech, with an occasional variation in [əɪɜ].

3. [e] occurs in standard pronunciation as the first element of the diphthong [eɪ] which has undergone many changes in this country (rendered [ei] by Jones).
Example: *day* [deɪ].
Certain Australian preferences may be noted. For instance, the Australian speaker generally prefers [æ] where he has an alternative pronunciation. Thus *basic* becomes ['bæsɪk] rather than ['beɪsɪk], *matrix* becomes ['mætrɪks] before ['meɪtrɪks], and the Latin borrowings *data*, *status*, *gratis* and *apparatus* are often all rendered with the short [æ] rather than with the diphthong [eɪ].
Rather than use the [ɪ], however, as in the English ['sʌndɪ] for *Sunday*, and so for other days of the week, the Australian prefers to retain the [eɪ] diphthong, although this often becomes [eɪj].
An important modification of [eɪ] is towards [aɪ], although this tends to be absorbed in the triphthongs already mentioned. The gibe that the Australian speaks *Orstrylian*, says "kike" for *cake* and "gripes" for *grapes*, etc., is extremely old and, with rare exceptions, is based on faulty hearing.

---

[3] We have been using the former pronunciation so long that we sometimes spell the word *brim*, e.g. "Sydney Morning Herald", May 24, 1954, p. 8: "Lot of fish in her, too. Cod up to nine pound and brim up to seven."

He is more inclined to use [ʌɪ] or [əɪ] or [əaɪ] than the diphthong [aɪ].

There is also a slight Australian tendency for [ʌ] and [ɜ] to be used in place of the diphthong [eɪ]. Thus *always* becomes ['ɔlwʌz] or ['ɔlwɜz], *Australia* becomes [ɒs'trʌljə] or [ɒs'trəljɑ]. These cases do not occur often, however.

4. [ε] as in *head, red* (rendered [e] by Jones).

As in Cockney this vowel tends to acquire a certain quality of [ɪ] in Australia, but its more general tendency is towards diphthongization. Thus *very* tends to become ['vεərɪ]; *cherry* tends towards ['tʃεərɪ]; *pen* becomes [pεən]. There is also a pull away from the front of the tongue towards the central vowels [ə], [ɜ] and [ʌ] in the cases mentioned, i.e. ['vərɪ], ['vɜrɪ] or ['vʌrɪ]. The Australian use of ['vʌrɪ] was noted in 1901.

The Australian shows some preferences in avoiding [ε] in favour of the diphthong [eɪ], as in *again*, which is rendered [ə'geɪn] rather than [ə'gεn]; *says* which is [seɪz] rather than [sεz]; *ate* which is [eɪt] rather than [εt] – but these are typical spelling pronunciations as well as permissible variations. They are, however, reflected in *get* which often tends to be [geɪt] rather than [gεt] and in *you bet* which sometimes becomes [ju beɪt] rather than [ju bεt]. This was also noted in Australia in 1901. Still earlier, in 1887, it was observed that the vowel [ε] was often lengthened so that *get* was rendered, more or less, as [gεət].

[ε] occurs as the first element in the diphthong [εə], as in *chair, their, there*. The Australian mutations tend towards the simple [ε] or [ɜ] and the diphthongs [εɜ] and [æə]. As a result we find *very* which has already tended to become ['vεərɪ] undergoing a further change towards ['vεɜrɪ] and ['væərɪ].

5. [æ] as in *man, handy*.

The Cockney tendency to modify this to [ε] has been noted in both Australia and New Zealand. Thus *am* [æm] becomes [εm]; *hands* [hændz] becomes [hεndz]; *can* [kæn] becomes [kεn]. It was reported in Australia in 1901.

Certain preferences for [æ] rather than [eɪ] were noted in Section 3. Examples of a reverse process are *azure*, which tends to become ['eɪʒər] rather than ['æʒər] – some Australians render it as a spelling pronunciation [ə'ʒjʊə]; *basalt*, which becomes ['beɪsɔlt] rather than ['bæsɔlt]; *bade*, which becomes [beɪd] rather than [bæd]. The diphthongized version of *basalt* is not correct; nor is the version of *azure* with the stress on the second syllable. The other variations are permissible.

Australians also tend to mutilate [æ] in the direction of the diphthongs [εə] and [əæ]. Thus *man* tends to become [mεən] or [məæn]; *tram* becomes [trεəm] or [trəæm]. The form [əæ] was noted in Australia in 1900. The U.S. variant [æə] occurs occasionally.

A common Australian tendency (recorded as long ago as 1887) is to lengthen the [æ] sound in a word. Thus *cat* [kæt] becomes [kæət] or something indeterminently placed between the two and difficult to render phonetically. A comparable lengthening of [ɛ] is recorded in Section 4.

The Australian preference for [æ] instead of [ɑ] is shown in many examples, e.g. [əd'væns] for *advance*, [tʃæns] for *chance*, which Jones gives as [əd'vɑns] and [tʃɑns] without alternatives. So with the Australian pronunciation of *clasp, dance, disaster, example, France, grant, slander*. So far as English authorities are concerned the [æ] sound is wrong here. Only in a few cases, such as *cenotaph* and *lather*, is [æ] "approved" as an alternative for [ɑ].

6. [a] This vowel occurs as the first element of the diphthong [aɪ].

The modification of this diphthong towards [ɔɪ], which occurs in Cockney, has been alleged in both Australia and New Zealand over the past century or more. Its principal Australasian forms are [ɒɪ] and the triphthongs [əɔɪ] and [əɔi]. The pure [ɔɪ] version rarely occurs in Australasia, the statement that it does being due largely to slovenly observation. It may have been current up to the end of last century, but has since been modified. It appears occasionally in the form [əɔii], the lengthening noted being a somewhat typical feature of Australian speech, especially in [ɛ] and [æ] vowels, as noted above. If the [aɪ] occurs at the end of a word, its approximate mutilation to [ɔɪ] is more likely. Thus the Australian would differentiate between *tripe* [traɪp], often rendered [træip] and [trəɔɪp], and *fly* [flaɪ], which he would tend to mutilate to [fləɔii]. In "A Manual of Good Australian Speech" (1956), P. E. Smythe blames what he calls "our Southern indolence" for the appearance of [ɔɪ] instead of [aɪ].

[aɪ] sometimes forms a triphthong with [ə] as in *fire* [faɪə]. The Australian tendency to lengthen final vowels is shown by his modification of this triphthong to [aɪɜ] or [ɔɪɜ]. Sometimes an intrusive [ə] appears before the triphthong and as a result *higher* becomes ['həaɪɜ] or ['həɔɪɜ].

[a] occurs as the first element of the diphthong [aʊ] as in *now* and *cow*.

The Cockney conversion of this to [æʊ], noted by Jones, also occurs in Australian and New Zealand speech, but it is only one of the variations we use. Wall records the alternative [ɪaʊ] in New Zealand; this was reported in Australia in 1900.

Australians triphthongize it further to [əaʊ], which was noted in 1887, and [ɛaʊ], and have also an even more complicated double-diphthong form (recorded in 1901) in [eɪaʊ].

In such words as *power* ['paʊə], [aʊ] forms a natural triphthong with [ə], and here again the same Australian tendencies appear, transforming the word to ['pɪaʊə], ['pəaʊə] or ['pæʊə], especially when abetted by nasalization. The Australian tendency to lengthen final vowels emerges in the additional modifications ['pɪaʊɜ], ['pəaʊɜ] and ['pæʊɜ].

7. [ɑ] as in *father, bard*.

Australians show a general tendency to avoid the pure [ɑ]. There is, for instance, an increasing preference for the short [æ], especially before nasal consonants, in both Australia and New Zealand. Thus *plant* becomes [plænt] rather than [plɑnt]; *chance* [tʃæns] rather than [tʃɑns]; *cenotaph* ['sɛnotæf] rather than ['sɛnotɑf].

It is in accord with the tendency noted in Section 5 – i.e. the alteration of [æ] to [ɛ] or [ɛə] – that the long [ɑ], which has been altered to [æ], should undergo further changes. Thus *dance*, which is rendered [dɑns] with the long vowel, becomes [dæns] with the short vowel, and then tends to develop into [dɛns] and [dɛəns].

The long [ɑ] rarely remains undiphthongized in Australian common speech. Jones notes a slight English tendency to use [ɑə] when the vowel ends with an *r*, as in *afar* [ə'fɑə]. The Australian often uses the diphthong [ɑə] before any consonant. He also employs, as an alternative, the odd form [ɑæ]. An observer in 1901 also reported the Australian use of [əɑ] as in [ʃəɑnt] for *shan't* and [kəɑnt] for *can't*.

[ɑ] also tends to change in certain cases towards [ʌ] or [ʌə]. Thus *darling* ['dɑlɪŋ] sometimes emerges as ['dʌlɪŋ] or ['dʌəlɪŋ]; *cart* [kɑt] becomes [kʌt] or [kʌət].

In any case there is a strong Australian inclination to avoid the pure [ɑ].

8. [ɒ] as in *tot*, *hot* (rendered [ɔ] by Jones).

Widely used in Australia in preference to the long [ɔ], e.g. *often* ['ɒfən] instead of ['ɔfən], *cross* [krɒs] instead of [krɔs], *salt* [sɒlt] instead of [sɔlt], but also tending to acquire characteristics of the central vowels, especially [ʌ]. Thus *pocket* ['pɒkɪt] tends to become ['pʌkɪt]; *because* becomes [bɪ'kʌz]. A similar tendency is found in the Australasian preference for *hover* ['hʌvə] instead of ['hɒvə] and *hovel* ['hʌvəl] instead of ['hɒvəl], but Jones accepts these alternatives.

Slight diphthongization occurs in the modification of [ɒ] to [əɒ] and [ɒə] (the latter of which was noted in 1900). In any case the tendency is away from the back of the tongue. In a few isolated instances the movement is in the opposite direction from [ɒ] to [ɔ], as used by some Southern English speakers. Ida C. Ward, "The Phonetics of English" (1938), says that "by those who do not use it such a pronunciation is often considered vulgar". Thus *off* [ɒf] occasionally becomes [ɔf], *dog* [dɒg] becomes [dɔg]. Such tendencies were recorded in Australia in 1887, but now seem to be rare.

Australians are often accused (I have an 1887 reference) of inserting an *r* after the vowel. This is also rare.

9. [ɔ] as in *saw*, *soar* (rendered [ɔ:] by Jones).

The English tendency towards diphthongization as in *four* [fɔə] for [fɔ], noted by Jones, has been current in Australia since 1900 or earlier. Another Australian version is [ɔʌ].

The Australian dislike of using this back vowel is underlined by the following (permissible) preferences:

choral ['kɒrəl] rather than ['kɔrəl]
floral ['flɒrəl] rather than ['flɔrəl]
cross [krɒs] rather than [krɔs]
often ['ɒf(tə)n] rather than ['ɔf(tə)n]
fault [fɒlt] rather than [fɔlt]
assault [ə'sɒlt] rather than [ə'sɔlt]

Well-established in Australia, although not officially countenanced in England, is the pronunciation of *auction* as ['ɒkʃən] instead of ['ɔkʃən].

The Australian's marked tendency to push back vowels forward in the mouth was noted in Section 8. We see this especially well in tracing

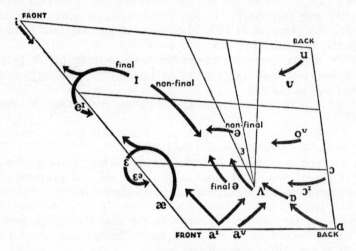

FIGURE III – *The arrows indicate the approximate direction of vowel changes in Australian speech compared with Southern English speech.*

modifications of the vowel in *salt*, from the long [sɔlt] to [sɒlt], and then successively to [sʌlt], [sʌəlt] and [səlt], all of which are current in this country. Among similar examples are *fault* and *somersault*.

The degeneration of *water* ['wɔtə] to ['wɒtə] and *daughter* ['dɔtə] to ['dɒtə] was noted in 1901. The use of *moron* ['mɒrɒn] for ['mɔrɒn] is also current. In the case of *authority* [ɔ'θɒrɪtɪ], we find the tendency towards both [ʌ'θɒrɪtɪ] and [ə'θɒrɪtɪ], which are in keeping with the movement away from the back of the tongue.

[ɔ] is also found as the first element in the diphthong [ɔɪ], as in *boy* [bɔɪ]. The Australian is inclined to triphthongize this, thereby drawing it away from the back of the tongue, by the introduction of an initial [ə] and by a lengthening of the final [ɪ] to [i]. Thus *boy* tends to become either [bəɔɪ] or [bəɔi]. This is in accord with the modifications of the diphthong [aɪ], noted in Section 6, towards the triphthongs [əɔɪ] and [əɔi].

10. [ʌ] as in *but*.

In Australian speech this is generally pure, but it sometimes undergoes changes towards [ə] and [ɜ] and towards the diphthong [əʌ]. The last was noted in 1901. Ida C. Ward, in "Phonetics of English", observes that many people in the north of England and the Midlands have difficulty in pronouncing [ʌ] before *r*, in words like *hurry* ['hʌrɪ]; they use a kind of short [ɜ] vowel in such positions, ['hɜrɪ]. This is a typical Australian feature.

The intrusive [ʌ] has tended to displace [ə] as the general-utility vowel in unstressed syllables.

The displacing of [ə] by [ʌ] is found especially in cases such as *again* [ə'gɛn], which becomes [ʌ'gɛn] or [ʌ'geɪn], *about* [ə'baʊt], which becomes [ʌ'baʊt]; *banana* [bə'nɑnə], which becomes [bʌ'nɑnə].

A movement in the other direction, from [ʌ] to [ɒ], is perceivable in the occasional cases of *dromedary* ['drɒmədərɪ] instead of ['drʌmədərɪ], and *constable* ['kɒnstəbl] instead of ['kʌnstəbl], which are spelling pronunciations anyway, and several other instances where the *ul(t)* spelling occurs: *catapult* ['kætəpɒlt] instead of ['kætəpʌlt], *impulse* ['ɪmpɒls] instead of ['ɪmpʌls], and related samples such as *result, compulsion, ultimate* and *agriculture.* There is nothing peculiarly Australian about this tendency; it is noted by Jones in Southern English. However, the Australian speaker is inclined to take this a step further and convert [ʌ] into a diphthong [ʌʊ], so that this serves as a good example not only of the Australian tendency to centralise vowels, but to raise them.

The influence of the consonant *l* also appears in the conversion of *gulf* [gʌlf] to [gɒlf]. See later comments on consonants.

11. [o], which occurs as the first element of the diphthong [oʊ], as in *know* [noʊ] (rendered [ou] by Jones).

The Cockney conversion of this to [ʌʊ] was noted in Australia by Mitchell in 1940; the additional Cockney version [aʊ] was noted in Australia in 1900 and in New Zealand by Wall.

Australia has, however, produced a number of alternative forms not found in Cockney, such as [ʌə]. In certain unstressed vowels, for instance, it tends towards [ɒ], as in *opaque* [oʊ'peɪk], which becomes [ɒ'peɪk], *November* [noʊ'vɛmbə], which becomes [nɒ'vɛmbə]. The English use of [ə] for [oʊ] in unstressed vowels is noted by Jones; it is common in Australia, as in *swallowing* ['swɒloʊɪŋ], which sometimes becomes ['swɒlərɪŋ]. In final vowels many Australians tend to render it [ɜ] rather than [ə]. Thus *piano* [pɪ'ænoʊ] becomes [pɪ'ænɜ] rather than [pɪ'ænə]; *window* ['wɪndoʊ] becomes ['wɪndɜ] rather than ['wɪndə].

Australians have also developed this diphthong extensively in the direction of triphthongs. In cases where [oʊ] is followed by an *n* the diphthong is often rendered [oʊə]; thus *grown* [groʊn] becomes [groʊən]; *sown* [soʊn] becomes [soʊən]. The form [oʊʌ] often displaces [oʊə] in the above cases.

Other Australian triphthongal versions of [oʊ] include [ʌoʊ] and [əoʊ], both reported in 1900].

12. [u] as in *boot* (rendered [u:] by Jones).

An Australian tendency towards [əu] has been noted, but this is more generally given the form [ɪu], recorded in Australia in 1887 and 1901 and in New Zealand by Wall. Thus *boot* [but] becomes either [bəut] or [bɪut]. A form of compromise is sometimes reached in the use of [зu]. In any case the general Australian tendency is, like the Cockney, away from the back of the tongue.

In words such as *room* and *broom* the [u] fairly regularly becomes [ʊ], as with many English speakers. Thus [rʊm] instead of [rum], [brʊm] instead of [brum]. The [ʊ] often tends to change in the direction of [ə] and [əu]; thus [rəm] or [rəum]. *School* [skul] frequently becomes [skəul] and even [skəul].

Although some lack of phonetic definition is involved, a common change is in the direction of [ɪu] in *truth* and *food*, sometimes also in *school* – a combination of frontalization and raising the vowel in the mouth.

Again revealing the Australian tendency to push back vowels forward in the mouth is the long-established mispronunciation of *maroon* as [mə'roun] instead of [mə'run].

13. [ʊ] as in *book* (rendered [u] by Jones).

The general Australian tendency to bring forward the back vowels is shown by a frequent preference of [ə] for [ʊ]. Thus [bʊk] becomes [bək] and sometimes even [bʌk].

[ʊ] occurs as the first element in the diphthong [ʊə], as in *poor*. Jones says that the form [ʊ] is preferable to [u], which is sometimes used.

Jones notes that Educated Southern English speakers often use [ɔ] in place of the diphthong. Thus *poor* becomes [pɔ]. This use is popular in Australia, but fresh diphthongs – showing once again the tendency to frontalize back vowels – in the form of [ɔə] and [ɔз] are also widely current.

In cases where [j] tends to be included before [ʊə], triphthongization is often observable in Australian speech. Thus *curious* ['kjʊərɪəs] becomes ['kəjʊərɪəs], *fury* ['fjʊərɪ] becomes ['fəjʊərɪ], *cure* [kjʊə] becomes [kəjʊə]. The same triphthong also makes its appearance in *jury* ['dʒʊərɪ], which becomes ['dʒəuərɪ]; *plural* ['plʊərəl], which becomes ['pləuərəl], etc.

14. [з] as in *bird* (rendered [ə:] by Jones).

As noted in Section 10, [ʌ] has tended to displace [ə] as the general-utility vowel in unstressed syllables. However, [ʌ] has a keen competitor in Australian speech in [з]. There is much less distinction between [ə], [ʌ] and [з] in Australasian speech than in any other form of English. Just as it was noted in Section 10 that [ʌ] tended towards the diphthong [əʌ], so [з] tends towards the diphthongs [зз], [зʌ] and [зə], showing how intimate has become the relationship between these vowels. Thus *girl* [gзl] becomes [gзəl] and [gзʌl], and when the ending is slurred in typical Australian fashion it becomes [gзəl].

Just as the Australian tends to lengthen a final [ɪ], as in *billy*, by pushing it forward in the mouth, so he tends to convert a final [ə] into [ɜ] by the same process. Thus *bonzer* tends to be rendered ['bɒnzɜ] rather than ['bɒnzə], and *digger* tends to be ['dɪgɜ] rather than ['dɪgə].

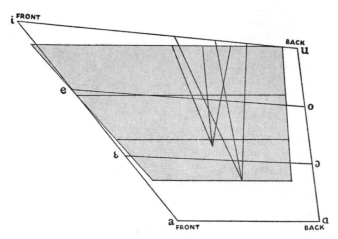

FIGURE IV – *The shaded portion shows the approximate "tongue area" in which Australian vowels are sounded compared with Southern English speech. See Figure V.*

15. [ə] as in the final vowel of *china* and the initial vowel of *about*.

It has already been pointed out that this tends to become [ɜ] when final, and [ʌ] when it is succeeded by a consonant, as in *china* ['tʃaɪnə], which tends towards ['tʃaɪnɜ], and *alight* [ə'laɪt], which becomes [ʌ'laɪt].

This cannot be laid down as a watertight rule, however, for many variations occur. Thus *octopus* ['ɒktəpəs] becomes either ['ɒktɜpəs] or ['ɒktʌpəs]; *monologue* ['mɒnəlɒg] becomes either ['mɒnɜlɒg] or ['mɒnʌlɒg]; *bulletin* ['bulətɪn] becomes either ['bulɜtɪn] or ['bulʌtɪn]; *central* ['sɛntrəl] becomes either ['sɛntrɜl] or ['sɛntrʌl]; *cupboard* ['kʌbəd] becomes ['kʌbɜd] or ['kʌbʌd]; *moment* ['moʊmənt] becomes ['moʊmɜnt] or ['moʊmʌnt].

In the case of *banana* both forms sometimes appear, as in [bʌ'nɑnɜ], which may undergo a reversal by becoming [bɜ'nɑnʌ].

The vital part played by [ə] in the general modification of Australian vowels towards diphthongs, triphthongs and even quadriphthongs has been noted in the detailed comments above. It is evidence of the extraordinarily strong pull in Australian speech towards mixed or central vowels. In every one of the fifteen Sections dealt with the vowel [ə] will be perceived, even though in some cases its influence may be small.

SUMMARY

For the purpose of easy reference, the principal vowel tendencies in Australian speech noted in the above analysis are given below:

i > ij, əɪ, iə, ii, eɪi, eɪij
ɪ > eɪ, eɪi, i, əɪ, ə, ɜ, ʌ
ɪə > eɪɜ, əɪɜ
eɪ > aɪ, eɪj, əɪ, ɜ, ʌ
ɛ > ɛə, ə, ɜ, ʌ, eɪ
ɛə > ɛ, ɜ, ɛɜ, æə
æ > ɛ, ɛə, əæ, æə
aɪ > ɔɪ, æi, əɔi, ɔice, əɔii
aɪə > aɪɜ, ɔɪɜ, əaɪɜ, ɔɔɪɜ
aʊ > æʊ, ɪaʊ, əaʊ, ɛaʊ, eɪaʊ
ɑ > æ, ɑæ, əɑ, ɑə, ʌ, ɛʌ
aʊə > ɪaʊə, əaʊə, æʊɜ, ɪaʊɜ, əaʊɜ, æʊɜ
ɒ > ʌ, əɒ, ɒə
ɔ > ɔə, əʌ, ɒ
ɔɪ > əɔice, əɔi
ʌ > ə, ɜ, əʌ, ɒ
oʊ > ʌʊ, ɑʊ, ʌə, ɒ, ə, ɜ, oʊə, oʊʌ, ʌoʊ, əoʊ
u > əʊ, ɪʊ, ɜʊ, ʊ, ə
ʊ > ə, ʌ
ʊə > ɔ, ɔə, ɔɜ
ɜ > əɜ, əʌ, ɜə
ə > ɜ, ʌ

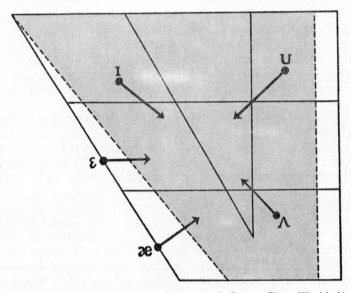

FIGURE V – *Vowel changes in United States speech. Compare Figure IV with this formalized diagram from Ida C. Ward's "The Phonetics of English". She explains the diagram as follows: "Dots represent normal British English vowel positions; arrows, the direction towards the position in which American vowels tend to be pronounced; the dotted lines, roughly the front and back limit of American vowels."*

The lasting deficiency of such a list is that it is largely unintelligible without textual examples. Its merit is that these mutations let us see with reasonable clarity some special features of the Australian accent:

(a) A strong preference for half-close or half-open vowels.
(b) A strong intervention of mixed vowels.
(c) Avoidance of pure back vowels.

In short, there is a marked tendency not only to push vowels forward in the mouth, but also to raise them. At this stage, we are not concerned with different types of Australian speech, although it can be said that these qualities invest *all* Australian speech in greater or less degree.

(B) NASALIZATION

Nasalization is one of the most persistent features of Australian speech, practically every vowel (especially front vowels) tending to acquire nasal characteristics. For considerably more than a century, various observers have noted this tendency. Lloyd James comments on the frequent Australian use in his "Historical Introduction to French Phonetics" (1929).

Nasalization is produced by lowering the soft palate (see Figure II) so that air from the lungs escapes through both mouth and nose.

In my analysis of Australian vowel sounds no mention was made of nasalization, since it would have entailed much reduplication of vowels with a tilde (~) over them, as in [ĩ], [æ̃], etc. It can be accepted as beyond question that many Australians indulge in large-scale nasalization.

This is doubtless brought about by the fact that the Australian does not open his mouth as widely as the Southern Englishman; he has less space to breathe through and this encourages greater breathing through the nose when speaking. Vowel sounds therefore escape more readily into the nasal cavity, because of the lowered soft palate, than in Southern English speech.

(C) CONSONANTS

The main differences between Australian and Educated Southern English speech are vocalic, but the consonants are also worth attention.

English consonants fall into five main groups – the labial, dental, palatal, velar and glottal. Twelve, including the fricative [ɹ], are included in the dental group; six in the labial group. If the Australian has modified his consonants at all, such modifications should be best perceivable in these main groups. And this is found to be the case.

The bi-labial [p], [b], [m] and [w] – sounded, that is, by bringing the lips together – have all undergone certain changes, because the Australian tends to draw his lips back against his teeth more than the Southern Englishman. His lips are often stretched tightly across the teeth and are much less supple in their movements than English lips. The oft-mentioned but inaccurate description "lip-laziness", of which Australians are accused, is largely based on this *spreading*. Although, of necessity, he uses his lips to enunciate the bi-labial consonants [p], [b], [m] and [w], it is with a more forward part of his lips than that used by the Southern English speaker (see Figure VI).

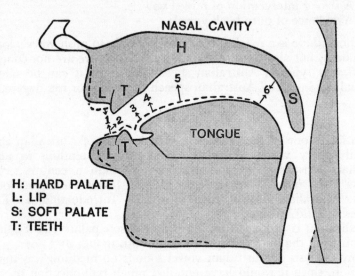

FIGURE VI – *Diagram showing places of formation of all except glottal consonants in the Southern English speaker's mouth, compared with the more closed mouth and the spread lips of the Australian (indicated in slightly exaggerated form by the dotted lines). The consonants indicated are: 1, bi-labial; 2, labio-dental; 3, dental; 4, alveolar (which are often identified with dental consonants); 5, palatal; 6, velar.*

The labio-dental [f] and [v] – formed between the bottom lip and the top front teeth – are affected similarly.

Because the Australian does not open his mouth as widely as the Southern English speaker, the dental and post-dental consonants, [n], [l], [r], [θ], [ð], [s], [z] and [ɹ] – which are sounded between the tip of the tongue and the top teeth – tend to become markedly alveolar. That is, they all tend, more than in English speech, to be sounded between the tip of the tongue and the gums. This tendency is particularly evident in the fricatives [θ], [ð], [s], [z] and [ɹ]. The nasal [n], the lateral [l] and the rolled [r] are also formed slightly further back in the Australian mouth than in the English. The dental plosives [t] and [d] are rarely modified.

Wall notes that [l] tends to be dull and to become inaudible. This can be noted especially in the combinations *alt*, *ult*, *uls*, *ault* and in such pronunciations as *only* ['oʊni], *although* [ɔ'ðoʊ] and *all right* [ɔ'raɪt].

The consonant [ʒ] and the affricates [dʒ] and [tʃ] are often palatalized. Incidentally, the special Australian pronunciation *spinach* ['spɪnɪtʃ] instead of ['spɪnɪdʒ] should be noted.

The palatal [j] seems to have undergone no noticeable change, but the velar [k] and [g] tend to move forward slightly in the mouth, not only because the Australian is generally inclined to open his mouth less than the Southern Englishman, but because he often lowers the soft palate in sounding his vowels. The velar [ŋ] also seems to be slightly displaced for a similar reason.

The glottal [h] tends to be lost in Australian speech because of the lowering of the soft palate, which allows it to pass into the nasal cavity instead of into the mouth. The glottal plosive [ʔ] (as found in the Cockney and Scottish rendering of [bɒ ʔl] for [bɒtl], i.e. *bottle*) is practically unknown in Australia – in fact, I have heard it clearly only twice in more than 30 years from Australian speakers.

(D) STRESS, INTONATION

As pointed out in my comments on New Zealand speech in "New Zealand Slang" (1940) there is a tendency in both Australia and New Zealand to use longer word groupings than the English. This is reflected in the slower rhythm of our speech – the quality of monotony that has been observed for generations.

In "New Zealand English", Professor Wall writes:

> There is a strong tendency to stress the first word or syllable at the expense of those which follow. Examples are *all the same, after all, Guy Fawkes Day* in the pronunciation of which, in standard English, *same, all* and *day* are more fully stressed. This is also noted in single words:'magazine, 'armchair, 'mankind, 'icecream.

A disposition to place emphasis on words like *by, and, but, to, in* is strongly evident and certainly helps to give our speech a quality that lacks music and cadences. The long-observed terminal use of *but* by some Australian speakers (e.g. "I don't like it but") instead of placing it at the beginning of a qualifying statement is a good example of this stressing of minor words. *Well* is sometimes used similarly as in "I'm going down the street well".

The lengthening of many vowel sounds, which was reported on in 1887 and was undoubtedly evident in Australian speech long before then, also adds its own contribution to monotony. Samples are *very* ['veri], *Sunday* ['sʌndeɪ], *cat* [kææt], *get* [gɛɛt], *stop* [stɒɒp], *mud* [mʌʌd]. The lengthening of many unstressed syllables gives them what amounts to a secondary stress. For instance, the lengthening of the final syllable in *very* and the diphthongization of the final syllable in *Sunday*.

Wall reports on the New Zealand development of secondary stress in such simple words as *reeport* ['ri'pɔt] and *beefore* ['bi'fɔ] instead of [rɪ'pɔt] and [bɪ'fɔ]; *eleven* tends to become *eeleven* ['i'lɛvən].

The use of strong vowels in unstressed positions is closely related to what are called spelling pronunciations, and these also reduce the musical quality of speech. Thus *mountains* ['maʊn'teɪnz] instead of ['maʊntɪnz], *forward* ['fɔ'wad] instead of ['fɔwəd], *forehead* ['fɔ'hɛd] instead of ['fɒrɪd],

Melbourne ['mɛl'bɔn] instead of ['mɛlbən], *Brisbane* ['brɪz'beɪn] instead of ['brɪzbən].

To some extent, it is incorrect to call these "spelling pronunciations" without a necessary qualification being made. Often, they seem to come about through a simple process of logic. For example, if the word *occur* is pronounced [ə'kɜ], why should not *occurrence* be rendered as [ə'kɜrəns] rather than as [ə'kʌrəns]? If *coral* is pronounced ['kɒrəl] and *oracle* is pronounced ['ɒrəkl], each with a short *o*, why shouldn't *oral* be pronounced ['ɒrəl], *floral* ['flɒrəl] and *choral* ['kɒrəl], also with a short *o*? But no, English authorities would have us say ['ɔrəl], ['flɔrəl] and ['kɔrəl], with a long *o*. If *shovel* is pronounced ['ʃʌvl] and *shove* [ʃʌv], why shouldn't *hover* be rendered as ['hʌvə] and *hovel* as ['hʌvəl]? But Jones wants us to say ['hɒvə] and ['hɒvəl]. And on the basis of *transfer* [træns'fɜ] why shouldn't one pronounce *transference* as [træns'fɜrəns] instead of ['trænsfərəns]? In any case, since many such pronunciations are in fact quite acceptable alternatives, why shouldn't the Australian use them if he wishes to?

There are obviously two main factors involved in the development of this "monotonous" Australian speech. One is the redistribution of stresses in oft-used words and the consequent modifications of traditionally approved English pronunciation; the other is the redistribution of stresses in phrases and sentences. They are clearly related. In Occasional Paper No. 7 (August, 1965) of the Australian Language Research Centre at Sydney University, J. R. L. Bernard reported an experiment which gave "partial support to the contention that Australian speech is unusually slow and rhythmically even".

Another matter must be considered. One of the reasons why the Australian is charged with speaking in a monotonous fashion with little of the musical cadence that can be heard in some varieties of English (and American) speech, is the fact that such charges are often made by non-Australians or by expatriate Australians. These charges usually overlook a simple point: given the dialectal influences that have been imported to Australia from Britain, it is unlikely that the Australian could have developed any other kind of accent. As many overseas actors and actresses have found out, our accent is virtually inimitable. The Australian is almost the only person in the world who can speak like an Australian.

Except in the most slovenly form of our speech, where carelessness can lead to misunderstanding of meaning, we have nothing to be ashamed of.

4. DEDUCTIONS

THE FIRST CONCLUSION forced upon us after an examination of the vowel sounds of Australian speech is that a large-scale reshuffling has occurred compared with the vowel sounds of Educated Southern English. In Figure III the general directions involved in these alterations are indicated by arrows: we can see the main tendency is away from the back of the tongue, combined with a tendency to raise the low or open vowels.

In Figures II and IV we find what has happened. The Australian's tongue movements are much more restricted than those of the Southern Englishman. His vowels are brought more closely together; they are more liable to influence one another. We find this influence in the extensive corruption of pure vowels into diphthongs and triphthongs. The central or mixed vowels, [ə], [ʌ] and [ɜ], seem to be almost everywhere. This can be only because Australian vowels are in relatively closer relation to each other than in Southern English speech.

It must be remembered – as shown in Figure II – that the tongue has little space in which to move in the creation of vowel sounds. If the vowels are pushed closer together there can be but one result: the vowels will tend to change their "standard" English identity. There can be little doubt, also, as to *why* this has occurred. The reason for the vowel changes indicated in Figures III and IV is that the Australian's tongue is closer to the roof of his mouth than the Southern Englishman's.

The simple conclusion is that most Australians do not open their mouths as widely as the Southern English. As a result the tongue has less space to move in. Vowels are pushed into closer relation to one another. To compensate for this compressing, there is a slight movement forward in the mouth (shown in Figures III and IV).

If we examine Figures II and VI we can appreciate not only what has happened to our vowels, but what has happened to our consonants. The dotted line in Figure II shows the relatively closer relationship between the tongue and the roof of the mouth in Australian speech than in Southern English. In Figure VI we see this combined with a drawing back of the lips against the teeth.

Certain changes in the labial consonants have already been linked with this spreading and tightening of the lips.

It is in accord with the closing of the mouth, which produces distinct Australian vowel sounds, that dental and post-dental consonants should tend to become alveolar.

It is also in accord with the lowering of the soft palate and the consequent nasalization of vowels that they should tend to be sounded further forward in the mouth than pure vowels.

As I have already said, the Australian way of speaking collectively represents something new in world speech: but a good deal of it is inherited. Some of the elements approximate those of Cockney, others are reflected in the English provinces, especially in the north. These were imported tendencies, confirmed and exaggerated or modified by our way of life and our environment. And these tendencies have bred other tendencies.

One of the most astonishing features of the Australian accent is its nationwide distribution. Since this country is almost as large as the United States and has a population a good deal less than Canada's, there would be some excuse for imagining that it would have developed at the outset into regional dialects, at least between the far west and the far east or between the far north and the far south. This vertical development has not occurred. Some observers here have claimed that such distinctions exist, but they have never been satisfactorily demonstrated. Even if there were the beginnings of such distinctions, I suggest that they have been obliterated – perhaps for all time – by the vast intake of migrants since the end of World War II.

On the other hand, three main horizontal developments have occurred in the Australian accent. These are:

A_1. The most slovenly form of our speech, characterized by all (or most) of the vowel features I have noted, by large-scale nasalization, monotony of intonation and lack of clarity.

A_2. An improved and widely-used form of the above, retaining the most dominant vowel characteristics, but tending to preserve more back and low open vowels and to avoid excessive use of mixed vowels. This is less nasal than A_1, has a wider range of intonation and greater clarity.

A_3. A cultivated type of speech, still retaining Australian elements but characterized by a greater consistency than is observable in A_2 in the use of back and low open vowels, in avoidance of intrusive mixed vowels, in avoidance of nasalization, in its "music" and clarity.

I asserted before and I reassert here the view that A_3 must eventually become a norm of Australian speech. However, a special point must be noted. A_3, which is what may be described as Educated Australian English, is spoken by two reasonably well-defined groups – by cultivated Australians who do not resent being Australian and by people who, although native to this country and speaking (unknown to themselves) with many of our dialectal peculiarities, attempt to graft on some of the more exaggerated features of Southern English in the belief that they are thereby passing themselves off as full-blown Educated Southern English speakers.

Dal Stivens has described this latter group as exponents of "P. and O. English". In the first edition of this book I wrote: "I have been content to group these people together, because I am confident that Educated Australian will prevail over P. and O. English, though the struggle may yet be long and arduous." In view of our findings that A_3 should in fact be rendered as A_3a and A_3b it is pertinent to note the comment of Dr Henry Seidel Canby, Professor of English at Yale University, while on a visit to Australia in 1945: "There is no such thing as an 'Average Australian' dialect. I have heard English spoken in Australia with at least four different accents."

It seems possible to me that observers who have postulated the existence of sundry regional dialects in Australia have in fact been comparing one of the types in one part of the country with another of the types in a different part of the country.

The wide distribution of the Australian accent throughout the three million square miles of Australia is anything but a new discovery. It has been remarked on frequently since the beginning of the century and, by implication, much earlier. In 1902, J. H. M. Abbott referred to

"Australia, where all people speak more or less alike", an opinion reflected by Thomas Courtney in 1928 when he remarked:

> Nowhere else on the earth's surface is there an area so large as that covered by Australia in which one may travel from end to end without noticing any difference of language, dialect or even pronunciation.

Valerie Desmond (pen-name of journalist Montague Grover) declared in 1911 that the Australian dialect is "as strongly developed among the educated people as among the peasantry [sic]".

In 1937 Sir Richard Terry, examiner for the Trinity College of Music and Elocution, London, told us that we possessed the great advantage of a uniform speech, that it was not as bad as Australians thought it was, and that, although it was naturally in process of formation, it did not seem to be developing "any very bad faults" – probably as good an answer as any to Professor Marshall's charge that the Australian accent is "so damnably unpleasant".

Several other points have to be made.

In the first place, most Australians tend to regard not only with distaste but with positive distrust all forms of affected speech. This applies particularly to A_1 and A_2 speakers. A_3 speakers, since they shade into practitioners of "P. and O. English", are more tolerant, but since they represent not much more than 10 per cent. of Australians they are in a decided minority. "Pommy", "sissy", "effeminate", "You can't tell whether he's a Pom or a poof" are fairly routine comments.

Second, dialectal variations often occur within a family. As J. F. Fraser noted in 1910, the Australian accent "is not limited to one stratum of society". In 1942 Vance Palmer wrote: " . . . the divisions cut through classes, even through families. One brother will speak well, another badly; a man working at the bench may be worth listening to, while his employer talks like an uncultured boor."

Third, as I reported in the first edition of this book, Australian women are, generally speaking, better exponents of good speech than the men, although, conversely, some of the worst corruptions in Australian speech are heard from women in the A_1 group. Sir Richard Terry, Trinity College examiner, remarked in 1937 that Australian women spoke better than the men because they opened their mouths. A. J. Marshall, "Australia Limited" (1942) writes that "from primary school to the grave" Australian women speak better than the men. These views received interesting confirmation in 1964, as the result of study of tape recordings of 9,000 Leaving Certificate schoolchildren. In the "Sydney Morning Herald" of August 15, 1964, Mr Arthur Delbridge of Sydney University reported that the speaker's sex was of major importance in determining the type of accent used. "Seven boys speak Broad Australian (A_1) to every three girls. In General (A_2) the balance is more even: four boys for every six girls. But only one boy speaks Cultivated Australian (A_3) for every nine girls who do, i.e. a girl is nine times more likely to speak in a Cultivated accent than a boy." A smaller survey conducted by John Gunn among students at Sydney Teachers' College was reported by the "Sunday Telegraph" on July 19, 1964; one of its findings was that there was "little difference in the proportion of broad accents (A_1) between country and city males, but country girls show a marked preference for broad accents".

Fourth, I have the impression that the speech of Australian city children today is less slovenly and marked with A_1 characteristics than it was twenty years ago. This observation also applies to city university students. But there is this qualification: the current tendency is for the proportion of A_2 speakers to increase at a far greater rate than for A_3. This process may continue for some considerable time.

5. STRINE

LONG AFTER ITS ORIGINS have been forgotten, *Strine* will probably be remembered as one of those brief and spectacular storms that sometimes blow across the face of language. The word Strine denoted Australian speech, especially of the A_1 variety, and its main emphasis was on elisions and all forms of telescopic speech mutilations.

Its nature is best understood by the simple example of how it began. Towards the end of 1964, an English female novelist came to Australia to help promote the sales of her latest book. This promotion included the sale of autographed copies. Among would-be purchasers was a woman who, in response to the novelist's inquiry as to her name, said what the novelist interpreted as *Emma Chisit*. This turned out to be not a name but a courteous question, "How much is it?"

A report of the occurrence appeared in the "Sydney Morning Herald" on November 30, 1964, and was followed by other (real or imaginary) examples of Strine, e.g. *Heather hip ride*, head of the hit parade, *I doewna goattha pitchers*, I don't want to go to the pictures, *egg nisher*, air conditioner.

However, it was not long before what began as a fairly accurate series of observations on A_1 word-distortions became an outlet for smart Alec inventions.

Lack of consistency was a major weakness of Strine contributors. Apart from general agreement that the [eɪ] diphthong should be rendered as [aɪ], which is not fully accurate as we have seen in Section 3 of this chapter, most of the other vocalic mutations were ignored. In any case, Strine was not new. During the 1930s, the Australian poet C. J. Dennis wrote these lines, according to the Dennis-expert Mr Alec Chisholm:

> Supposya meetim inna street,
> "Owdoo", sezee, "I oped ide meet
> A chapat adda bobertoo,
> Cozime as dryasdust. Ainchoo?
> Wahsaywe dodgin ovaeer?
> They gotta decent branabeer,"
> Anso, ocorse, we duzzaduck,
> An' I sez "Selth" An' eesez "Sluck".

At the same time some of these elisions are worth recording – *oright* for all right, *goodonyer* for good on you, *owyerdoon?* for how are you doing? *gument* for government, *seketry* for secretary, *yoosan we?* for didn't we? (or "usen't we?").

However, they are not originally or even especially Australian. They are used by juveniles and careless speakers wherever English is current. They merely provide us with examples of linguistic telescoping common on the A_1 level.

The wide interest taken in Strine during its brief life is another matter. I suspect that this was less a joke in which A_2 and A_3 speakers indulged at the expense of A_1 speakers than a joke in which all Old Australians indulged at the expense of New Australians. To many of the latter born in foreign-speaking countries it was completely unintelligible. It is possibly to be linked with other defence-of-the-barricades manifestations on which I have commented elsewhere in this book.

List of Words and Phrases

Course, down the, 237; Snake Gully, 239
Cove, 44; Sydney, 98; — streeter, 342; 397
Cover, — the waterfront, 145; — ed, 246
Cow, not to care if the — calves or breaks her neck, 91; Malley's, 94; fair, 133; poor, 181; to run like a, 238; black as the inside of a, 423
Cowal, 40
Cowanyoung, (fish), 301
Cow Banger, 64
Cowboy, 59; Curtins — s, 183
Cow Conductor, 59
Cowflop, 134
Cow Kicker, 65
Cowsh, 134, 375
Cowslip, 287
Cow Spanker, 64
Cowyard, — Confetti, 134
Cozzie, 372
C.P., 351
Crab, — hole country, 39; draw the — s, 147; to, 147
Crack, to — it, 130; to — on, 139; diamond — ing, 156; to — a lay, 180; — it for a dill!, 204; — it, 212; — down on, — hardy, 218; fair — of the whip, 218; to — a wave, 252; — hardy, 392, 420; no matter how hardy he — ed, 420; to — the big whip, 422; to — hardy, 427
Cracker, 59, 64, 115; not worth a, 219; 220; — Night, 283
Cradle, 67
Cradler, 97
Cradleseat, 208
Cranky fan (bird), 300
Crash, 170, 184; go for a, — on, 293
Crawl, the Australian, 250, 390
Crawler, 29, 152
Crayfish, 152
Cream, — puff, 162; jungle, 177; Yankee, 186
Creamy, (orie), 67, 324; chocolate, 324
Creation, a — of cats, 390
Creek, 21, 40-1; up the well-known, 218; The, 345; — banking rain, 350; up the well-known, 425
Creeked, 105
Crick see Creek
Cricko, 249
Crim, 156

Crime, book, 119
Crimea, a — n shirt, 259
Crimp, 57
Crimson Wrap, The, 412-3
Crinkle, like the — s in a mulga root, 420
Crippen, 81
Crissie, 373
Croc, Crocky, 66, 303
Crockery, 139
Crockie, 370
Crocodile, 66; to, 251, 307
Cronk, 17, 104, 123, 235-6; — up, 278
Crook, go, 127; — ed on, 180; 180, 181; things is — in Muswellbrook, 258; a — sort of, 293; — ie, 370; to go — at (or — ed) on, 422
Crookie, 370
Crople, — on, 139
Croppie, 31
Cross, 60; Kiss the, 127, 256; the, 342
Cross Beasts, 32
Cross Brander, 68
Crossbred, 25
Crow, 26; — 's nest, 49, 72; stone the — s, 86; have a — 's eye, 91; stone the — 's, 95; 173; speed the — s, 180; stone the — s, 203; to cop (or draw) the, 218; selling the 234; — eater, 263; stone the — s, 307
Crown, Maori half-, 116; 117
Crownie, 370
Cruel, to — a scheme, 249
Cruet, silly in the, 170
Cruiser, 229
Crumb Act, put on the, 147, 425
Crumpet, bow the, 145, 148; not worth a, 219
Cruncher, 154
Crush, 63; — er, 235-6, a — bet, a boss — er, — ing, 236
Crusoe, Robinson — brand, 234
Crust, 147; doing the, 153
Crutch, 50, 55; stiff as a, 146; — merchant, 218; as stiff as a, 427
Crutcher, 54
Cry, for — ing out loud!, 204; war, 229; to — a person away, to — a bone, 323
Crystal, — highway, 344
C.S.I.R.A.C., 351
C.S.I.R.O., 351
C.S.R., port, 108

C.T.J., 288
Cubby, — house, 402
Cuckoo, — Scab, 60; — spit, 303
Cuddle-seat, 208
Cuddling, 402
Cuddy, 66
Cudgel, 312
Cudgerie, 322
Cue (or Cuey), 346
Cueing, 64
Cull, 57
Cult, bodgie, 292; cargo — s, Naked, Johnson, Golden Egg, 335
Cumberband, 382
Cumberland Disease, 45
Cumbungi, 322
Cundy, 285
Cunjevoi, 322
Cunjie, 302, 370
Cunnamulla, — cartwheel, 259, 267; — gun or shearer, 267
Cunning, — up on oneself, 153
Cup, The, 235, 248
Cuppa, 86
Curbstone, a — jockey, 237
Curl, big, 211; Carruther's, 269; — the mo, 282, 413; a, 413
Curler, 184, 234
Curlew, silly as a, mournful as a — 's cry, 90; silly as a, 307
Curley, — comeback, 288
Curl-the-Mo, 131-2; 282; 413; 428
Currawong, 298; 322
Currency, 3, 14, 25; rum, 30; lad, lass, belle, female, criminal, sprout, urchin, youth, 26; rum, 116; lad, 119, 126, 261
Curriejung, 314
Curry, give him — or curried hell, 125; — onion, 345
Curse, 106; carry the, 107
Curtin, — s chosen children, 176; — 's cowboys, 183
Cush, all, 123, 131
Custard, 213
Cut, 50; to battle for a —, fine, rough, tight, 52; in, out, 53; second, double, 54; 61; out stock, 63; 72; 101 (mining); — out, 153; — lunch commandos, 176; — the rough stuff, — the kidstakes, 204; half, 230; a back, a — !, down, 253; the burr — ter, 257; — -a-throat, 339; to — out, 413

R

INDEX
Including Bibliography

INDEX

Kennedy, E.B. ("Four Years in Queensland"), 41.
Kennedy, Keith, 277.
Kenyon, A.S., 106.
Keough, S.W., 381.
Kerr, Andy, 272.
Kiama, N.S.W., 384.
Kidman, Sir Sidney, 272.
Kimberleys, Western Australia, 40, 70, 82, 348.
King, Governor, 30.
King, William Francis, 270.
Kinglake, Edward ("The Australian at Home"), 398, 433, 434.
Kings Cross, Sydney, 342, 343.
Kingsford Smith, Sir Charles, 267, 273.
Kingsley, Henry ("Geoffry Hamlyn"), 31, 196.
Kirby, J. ("Old Times in the Bush of Australia"), 67.
Kittle, Samuel ("Concise History of the Colony and Natives of New South Wales"), 23fn.

"Lae Garamut", Lae, New Guinea, 332.
"Lagasai", Kavieng, New Guinea, 332.
Lake, Joshua (compiler of Australian supplement to Webster's "International Dictionary", 1898), 17, 18, 26, 135.
Lake Eyre, South Australia, 267.
Lamber, J., 270.
Lamington, Baron, 272.
Lamond, H.G. ("Brindle Royalist"), 66, 323.
Landowners in rural areas, 34-37; dishonest practices, 36, 37; small farmers, 37, 38.
Landy, John, 271.
Lane, William, 353, 390.
Lang, J.D. ("Cooksland"), 277, 312.
Langley, Eve ("The Pea Pickers"), 68, 82, 419.
Language, comments on, 2, 3.
La Perouse, N.S.W., 343.
Larrikins, 119ff; terms used by, 119-140; features of, 119; "pushes", 119, 124; dress, 120, 125, 258; and underworld, 141.
Lasseter, Lewis Harold, 272.
Latrobe, C.J., 99.
Launceston, Tasmania, 389.

Lawler, Ray ("The Summer of the Seventeenth Doll"), 208.
Law of Hobson-Jobson, 135, 302, 303, 382.
Lawrence, H.A. ("Australian Aboriginal Words", MS in the Mitchell Library), 311 fn.
Lawson, Henry ("While the Billy Boils", "In the Days When the World Was Wide", "Over the Sliprails"), 29fn, 39, 42, 53, 54, 75, 89, 103, 104, 107, 108fn, 135, 381, 411, 415, 419.
Leakey, Caroline, see Oliné Keese.
Leechman, Frank ("The Opal Book"), 102.
Leenhardt, M. ("Vocabulaire et Grammaire de la Langue Houaïlou"), 326.
Legal decisions on Australianisms, 200-202, 392, 393.
Lemire, C. ("La Colonisation francaise de Nouvelle-Calédonie"), 336, 337.
Lentzner, Karl ("Worterbuch der englischen Volkssprache Australiens"), 13, 15, 18, 22, 105, 257, 398.
Leroy, Oliver ("A Dictionary of French Slang"), 133.
"Letters from Victoria Pioneers", 29fn.
Lexicography, dated texts, 4; confusions, 4.
Liberal Party, 352, 355; Liberal Party - Country Party coalition, 352.
Lindsay, Norman ("Magic Pudding", "Saturdee"), 132fn, 285, 303, 381.
Literary uses of idiom and metaphor, 413-420; journalistic influences on, 410-413, 420.
Localized slang, 341-351; localization of simile, 417; New South Wales, 342, 343; Victoria, 344, 345; Queensland, 345, 346; South Australia, 346, 347; Western Australia, 347, 348.
Locke-Elliott, Sumner ("Interval"), 130.
"Lone Hand", Sydney, 8, 13, 296fn, 297, 396.
Long, Gavin, 168, 175, 360.
Lotteries, 117, 118, 374fn.
Lower, L.W. ("Here's Luck"), 419.

MacGregor, J. ("Fifty Facts about Australia"), 413.
Mackaness, George, 197.
Mackay, Kenneth ("Out Back"), 39.
MacKenzie, D. ("Ten Years in Australia"), 265.
Macnamara, Thomas Michael, 270.
Macquarie, Governor, 207, 389.
Macqueen, T.P. ("Australia as She Is and as She May Be"), 265.
McBurney, Samuel, 433.
McCarthy, F.D. ("New South Wales Aboriginal Place Names"), 277, 311 fn.
McCombie, T. ("Australian Sketches"), 99.
McCulloch, Sir James, 352.
McIntosh, Hugh D., 207.
McKeown, Keith C. ("Insect Wonders of Australia", "Australian Insects"), 303, 304.
Madden, Chief Justice, 433.
Maitland, N.S.W., 256.
Mallee lands, 43, 70, 77, 96; Mallee Pastoral Leases Act, 305.
Manly, N.S.W., 252, 343.
Maoris, 315, 316, 317, 326.
Marbles, game of, 284, 285.
Maree, South Australia, 346.
Mark Twain, 39.
Marsh, G.P. ("Lectures on the English Language"), 296.
Marshall, A.J. ("Australia Limited", "Journey among Men" with Russell Drysdale), 82, 435, 436, 455.
Marshall, James Vance ("Timely Tips to New Australians", "Jail from Within", "World of the Living Dead"), 20, 150, 353; see Jice Doone.
Martin, Desmond ("Australia Astride"), 69.
Martin, R.M. ("History of Australasia"), 265.
Maryborough, Victoria, 266.
Masons, 355.
Mateship, 109, 121, 165, 166, 187, 309, 408, 457.
Maurer, D.W., 363, 364.
Melba, Dame Nellie, 273.
Melbourne, Victoria, 100, 106, 203, 210, 235, 344, 348, 349.
"Melbourne as I Saw It", by A Minister, 31.